THE FEUDAL
TRANSFORMATION

900–1200

THE FEUDAL TRANSFORMATION

900–1200

Jean-Pierre Poly

Eric Bournazel

Translated by Caroline Higgitt

EUROPE PAST AND PRESENT SERIES

HM

HOLMES & MEIER

New York   London

Published in the United States of America 1991 by
Holmes & Meier Publishers, Inc.
30 Irving Place
New York, NY 10003

Originally published under the title *La mutation féodale, x^e–xiie siècles,*
copyright © Presses Universitaires de France, 1980.

Book design by Dale Cotton

This book has been printed on acid-free paper.

Library of Congress Cataloging-in-Publication Data

Poly, Jean-Pierre, 1941–
  [Mutation féodale. English]
  The feudal transformation : 900–1200 / Jean-Pierre Poly, Eric
Bournazel; translated by Caroline Higgitt.
    p. cm.
  Translation of: La mutation féodale.
  Includes bibliographical references and index.
  ISBN 0-8419-1167-3 (cloth: acid-free paper).—
  ISBN 0-8419-1168-1 (pbk.: acid-free paper)
  1. France—History—Capetians, 987–1328. 2. Middle Ages—History.
  3. Feudalism—France—History. I. Bournazel, Eric. II. Title.
DC82.P6513 1991
944'.02—dc20   90-42094
                                                  CIP

Manufactured in the United States of America

To Jean-Francois Lemarignier

CONTENTS

MAPS

FIGURE

PREFACE

It is customary to begin a book with acknowledgments, and this is no exception. The medieval historian will have no difficulty in recognizing our extensive borrowings from favorite authors. But the reader with less experience of historiography needs to realize that even a reference work, in order to avoid being a chaotic mosaic, must be arranged according to broad directions of analysis and must give a special importance to certain prior studies. Acknowledgments are due, therefore, and so is recognition.

To Jean-François Lemarignier, who in the past has given us so many tools of analysis that have extended and gone beyond the rigorous and sometimes rather strict historiographic tradition of legal history: exemptions, the rise of ecclesiastical seigneuries, the break-up of the *pagus*, social changes in the royal entourage; these are all major reference points for the understanding of the tenth, eleventh, and twelfth centuries, and they open up a whole new area of research into the origin of the relationships between power and space. It was he who, initially, was to undertake this work on the feudal period for the "Nouvelle Clio" series. Instead he generously offered the task to us, supporting and encouraging us until its completion.

To Jean Schneider, who has over the years "militated" for a proper understanding of a little-known period of French history, the early Middle Ages in the south, laying the foundations for its study in his lectures at the Ecole des Hautes Études to the great profit of those who heard them. The fragility of the bonds of vassalage in the Midi, the specificity of the structures of power and of the seigneury, or the relationship between the lords and the Church—everything here with a bearing on the south comes from his teaching.

To Georges Duby: there are few medievalists today who are not greatly indebted to him and it is hardly necessary to list everything owed to him by the history of the Middle Ages and, *a fortiori*, by the authors of this book.

Let us thus acknowledge the chief of our debts, without however discharging them. An essential contribution to a work of this kind are the fundamental studies that, by tackling problems head on, sometimes resolve outstanding ones. Their authors will find themselves mentioned—and not, we hope, misrepresented—in the pages of this book.

Finally, we must express our gratitude to those who provided the assistance that so often facilitated this work and, especially, to Jacques Lelièvre who was so kind as to subject our entire manuscript to review and criticism.

J.-P. P.
E. B.

ABBREVIATIONS

AB	*Annales de Bourgogne* (Dijon)
Adel	*Adel und Kirche, Gerd Tellenbach zum 65 Geburtstag dargebracht von Freunden und Schülern.* Freiburg/Basel/Vienna, 1968.
AE	*Annales de l'Est* (Nancy)
AESC	*Annales, Economies, Sociétés, Civilisations* (Paris)
AM	*Annales du Midi* (Toulouse)
AN	*Annales de Normandie* (Caen)
A travers	Halphen, L. *A travers l'histoire du Moyen Age.* Paris, 1950.
BEC	*Bibliothèque de l'Ecole des Chartes* (Paris)
BISI	*Bulletino dell'Istituto storico Italiano per il Medio Evo*
Boll.	*Acta sanctorum Bollandistarum* (Brussels, 1643–1658). Paris, 1863–1867.
BPH	*Bulletin philologique et historique* (Paris)
BSAN	*Bulletin de la Société des Antiquaires de Normandie* (Caen)
Carolingians	Ganshof, F. L. *The Carolingians and the Frankish Monarchy.* Translated by J. Sondheimer. Aberdeen, 1971.
CCM	*Cahiers de Civilisation mediévale* (Poitiers)
Cluny	Bernard, A., and Bruel, A. *Recueil des Chartes de l'abbaye de Cluny.* Paris, 1876–1894.
CRAIBL	*Comptes rendus de l'Académie des Inscriptions et Belles-Lettres* (Paris)
Culture	*La culture populaire au Moyen Age* (Fourth Symposium, University of Montreal, 1977). Montreal, 1979.
Etudes	Génicot, L. *Etudes sur les principautés lotharingiennes.* Louvain, 1975.
Europe	*L'Europe aux IXe–XIe siècles; aux origines des Etats nationaux* (International Symposium, Warsaw 1965). Warsaw, 1968.

Famille	*Famille et parenté dans l'Occident médiéval.* Edited by G. Duby and J. LeGoff. Paris, 1977.
Francia	*Francia, Forschungen zur westeuropaïschen Geschichte* (Paris).
GCN	*Gallia Christiana nova.* Paris, 1715–1865.
Hérésies	*Hérésies et sociétés* (Symposium, Royaumont 1962). Paris, 1968.
Hommes	Duby, G. *Hommes et structures du Moyen Age.* Paris, 1973.
HGL	Devic, C., and Vaissette, J. *Histoire générale de Languedoc.* Toulouse, 1875.
Informatique	*Informatique et histoire médiévale* (Symposium CNRS, Rome 1977)
IRMA	*Ius romanum medii aevi*
Jean Bodin	*Recueil de la Société Jean Bodin* (Brussels)
JS	*Journal des Savants* (Paris)
Karl der Grosse	*Karl der Grosse* (Aachen 1965). Vol. 1: *Persönlichkeit und Geschichte.* Dusseldorf, 1967.
Lexicographie	*La lexicographie du latin médiéval et ses rapports avec les recherches actuelles sur la civilisation du Moyen Age* (Symposium CNRS, Rome 1977)
Lot and Fawtier	Lot, F., and Fawtier, R. *Histoire des institutions françaises au Moyen Age.* Paris, 1957–1958.
MA	*Le Moyen Age* (Brussels and Paris)
Mansi	Mansi, J. B. *Sacrorum conciliorum nova et amplissima collectio.* Florence, Venice, 1757–1798.
Mélanges	Bloch, M. *Mélanges historiques.* Paris, 1963.
Mélanges . . . L. Halphen	*Mélanges de l'histoire du Moyen Age dédieés à la mémoire de Louis Halphen.* Paris, 1951.
Mélanges . . . G. Le Bras	*Mélanges et études d'histoire du droit canonique dédieés à Gabriel Le Bras.* Paris, 1965.
Mélanges . . . E. Perroy	*Economies et sociétés au Moyen Age. Mélanges offerts à Edouard Perroy.* Paris, 1973.
Miscellanea . . . J.-F. Niermeyer	*Miscellanea mediaevalia in memoriam Jan-Frederik Niermeyer.* Groningen, 1967.
MGH	*Monumenta Germaniae Historica*
Narbonne	*Narbonne, archéologie et histoire* (Actes du XLVe Congrès de la Fédération historique du Languedoc méditerranéen et du Roussillon). Montpellier, 1973.
Noblesse . . .	*La noblesse au Moyen Age, essais à la mémoire de Robert Boutruche.* Edited by Philippe Contamine. Paris, 1976.

PL	Migne, J. P. *Patrologiae latinae cursus completus* . . . Paris, 1839–1864.
Pour un autre Moyen Age	Le Goff, J. *Pour un autre Moyen Age*. Paris, 1977.
RB	*Revue bénédictine* (Abbey of Mardesous, Belgium)
RBPH	*Revue belge de Philologie et d'Histoire* (Brussels)
Recueil . . .	Lot, F. *Recueil des travaux historiques de Genève*. Paris, 1968, 1970, 1973.
RH	*Revue historique* (Paris)
RHD	*Revue historique de Droit* (Paris)
RHE	*Revue d'Histoire ecclésiastique* (Louvain)
RHEF	*Revue d'Histoire de l'Eglise de France* (Paris)
RHF	Bouquet. *Recueil des Historiens des Gaules et de la France*. Paris, 1738–1833; 1840–1876.
RMAL	*Revue du Moyen Age latin* (Strasbourg)
RN	*Revue du Nord* (Lille)
Settimana . . . *Mendola*	*Atti della . . . settimana internazionale di studio, Mendola* (Milan)
Settimane . . . *Spoleto*	*Settimane di studio del centro italiano di studi sull'alto medioevo* (Spoleto)
Speculum	*Speculum: A Journal of Medieval Studies* (Cambridge, Mass.)
Structures . . . *de l'Aquitaine*	*Les structures sociales de l'Aquitaine, du Languedoc et de l'Espagne au premier âge féodal.* (Symposium CNRS, Toulouse 1968). Paris, 1969.
Structures feodales	*Structures féodales et féodalisme dans l'Occident méditerranéen* (Symposium CNRS, Rome 1978)
Studi . . .	Violante, C. *Studi sulla cristianità medioevale: Societa, Instituzioni, Spiritualità*. Milan, 1972.
TVR	*Tijdschrift voor Rechtsgeschiednis* (Groningen)
ZSS	*Zeitschrift der Savigny-stiftung für Rechtsgeschichte* (Cologne)

THE FEUDAL
TRANSFORMATION

900–1200

—

INTRODUCTION

What is feudalism? When François-Louis Ganshof asked this question in the fifties he identified two types of answer that had become usual among medievalists, at least since Marc Bloch.[1] One was a "narrow" answer, where feudalism referred to that group of institutions related to the fief and to homage that had grown up in Carolingian society, flowered around the year 1000, and then declined without completely disappearing as the power of the monarchy increased. The other was a "broad" answer, where feudalism referred to feudal society as a whole and, as Marc Bloch would say, to a whole made up of interwoven elements of which the fief itself is no longer the most important. This second hypothesis embraced the first, though not without some differences. For one group of historians, inclined to the juridical approach, the institutions of fief and vassalage were central to the period. For others, more concerned with applying new approaches to history, these institutions, although vividly described, had lost their prominence to become merely institutional symptoms of a deeper evolution. In these circumstances, this word "feudalism" that was to have so great a future was, it must be admitted, very ill-chosen, not so much because the political formations of the period, territorial principalities or seigneuries, had not all been fiefs, but above all because a social organization could not correctly be described by its political aspect alone and even less by one of its legal characteristics, the fief, "one form of title among many others."[2] Hence the route to pursue was clearly marked. First, pride of place should be given to the fundamentals of social evolution, to monetary history, to demography, to the history of technology, and above all to the history of all that is most humble and everyday in agrarian society. Second, and equally importantly, the "mental tools" of the men of the period needed to be more closely examined.

While a history in which the ideas and the political schemes of princes took the place of social movement was open to criticism, it would be equally absurd to reduce history to a mechanical process where the only important thing is "the development of the forces of production," elevated to the status of an allegory. Here "idealism" and mechanistic materialism come together in a cult of abstraction that deliberately ignores the complexity of relationships and social tensions. As Georges Duby forcefully reminds us, the attitudes of individuals and groups to their respective conditions, and the behaviour which dictates these attitudes, are not directly determined by the reality of their economic situation, but by the image which they have of it, which is never a true one but which is always disturbed by the effects of a complex interweaving of mental representations. To see social phenomena merely as the product of economic phenomena is to restrict the area of enquiry, greatly to impoverish the argument and to reject a clear perception of certain essential forces.[3]

The conclusion of this warning was very simple: "if social history is to progress . . . it must be directed towards a convergence of a history of material civilization and a history of collective thought." However, although it is probably the only desirable one, such a review of history implies a vast program of research and extremely various areas of investigation. From the archaeology of tools to theology, from "Justinianic Law" to climatology, from ethno-psychology to musicology, from the art of the cathedrals to numismatics . . . few historians are able to follow a path so full of dangers and strewn with pitfalls without flagging. And this is the moment to alert the reader to the limits and reservations of this book, which sets out to be a history of society and yet is, however, far from being such a broad synthesis. It is a compromise between what is desirable and what is possible, between what has already been done—and which often represents to our eyes a good point of departure—and that which—despite or because of all those studies that continually renew our acquaintance with the medieval world—remains in great part still to be done: a *Feudal Society* that would be for our time what Marc Bloch's great work was for an earlier generation.

Thus there are limits, and first those traditional ones of time and space. The beginnings of feudalism are sometimes set at the end of the fifth century, and its end, it is still energetically asserted, does not occur until the French Revolution. Our field of vision is more restricted or perhaps more conventional. It embraces the tenth, eleventh, and twelfth centuries, but is prepared to go back, where necessary, as far as the seventh century. This is basically the period in which feudal institutions established themselves, and far from being one form of title among many others, they dominated all other social relations. As for the limits of space, it is difficult nowadays to restrict a study to the boundaries of the kingdom of France as it then was. Indeed, is it possible to separate a study of the Naumurois or Cambresis from that of Picardy, of Lorraine from that of Champagne, of Catalonia or Provence from that of Septimania? This is all the more important because we are far from being equally well informed about all the regions of the kingdom. Naturally we would wish, when examining for example the themes that develop around the French royalty of the twelfth century, to draw a brief comparison with what is going on elsewhere, in Galicia or Cologne. Nevertheless, this book is essentially a study for feudalism in the area bounded by the Rhine, the Alps, and the Pyrenees.

Feudalism as an institution is the point of departure of this study. But it is impossible to explain institutional, legal, or political relationships without relating them to a broader study of the relationships between social groups, their theories when they are expressed, their ideas when we know them. Naturally, it has never been thought possible to study feudo-vassalic relationships without frequent reference to ecclesiastics and the Church, or without at least some mention of the peasants. But there are many other relationships that need to be looked at: "the new clerks"—respected masters or quarrelsome goliards; women, noble or peasant; dissidents, like the heretics; outsiders—brigands, magicians, lepers, or hermits. Although we often fail through lack of both precise or accessible information and of time, we have tried to make these connections. "Remake, recreate the interplay of all this, the reciprocal action of these different forces into a movement which would become life itself."[4] What a dream for a historian— or a magician! But how many of these voices that we need to call up are indistinct or distorted, how many are still waiting to be properly heard? Such a study necessarily comes up against the very basic problems of the material reproduction of social life, productive forces and the less clear-cut relations of production. We offer no more than a brief look at the problem, to draw attention to some of the chief links between institutions, society, and economy. And yet at the same time we should be adopting the opposite approach from the one we have outlined. That is, starting from a complete description of all that is most material in the life of the early Middle Ages, we need a detailed examination of agricultural land, the physiology of peasant or urban populations, and the study of the techniques of production so as to reveal their implications for society.

"Dark Ages" or unknown ages? We should not underestimate the difficulties of the research and the lacunae in the documentation. Our view of the centuries around the year 1000 is not clear. Between the relative abundance of Carolingian sources—and these for some regions only—and the revival of written sources from the twelfth century, the West, "this land of forests, of tribes, of sorcery, of petty kings hating and betraying one another"[5] still remains in the eleventh century and central to our history if not unknown territory, at least a land where those who venture in are sometimes tempted to bring with them their own dreams or fantasies. The temptation is great to turn away from the laborious erudition of the specialist in order to set up the historical foundations of an "alternative" that has, perhaps, never existed and whose chief merit is simply to demonstrate a theory.

Indeed, it is not easy to avoid the intrusion of the mentality, or even the prejudices, of our own time in a consideration of those of ancient times. The historian of fiscal registers, land surveys, or rents rolls can hope or believe that he is objective when he places individuals on different levels of a scale of wealth, when he describes the accounts of a city or the trading activity of a port. But the historian of ideas—without which social history could not exist—cannot have the same illusions. Lucien Fébvre rightly criticized Robert Pfister for having discussed the matrimonial alliances made by Robert the Pious in the light of the psychology of a bourgeois comedy instead of seeing in it a conflict between aristocratic clans. Being less colorful, and less amusing, than those of a more sensational history, mental anachronisms are all the more dangerous because it is difficult to avoid them. Can we really imagine that a particular layman had the same way of thinking as a modern entrepreneur? Can we forget that the clerics, whose logical reasoning on the subjects of law or theology we so much admire, also believed in werewolves? Because there were merchants, was there also a market economy? Because a certain ritual seems to us absurd, because a certain hypothesis shocks us, should we then reject it as having no interest?

Furthermore, the period shows us the fragility of our own mental categories, of these *summae divisiones* by which our minds are formed and to which they are so accustomed that they seem to be an integral part of the very nature of things. Does banal lordship, a central feature of the eleventh century, come under economics, law, or politics? Or from a point of view that today seems hardly less academic, is it an infrastructure or a superstructure, a relationship of production or an ideological apparatus? Such categories, which help us to focus a particular point of view, to rearrange themes and methods of analysis suited to different disciplines—in other words, to differentiate—are not without their value. The direct origins of this method can be found in the development of scholastic thought in the twelfth century. But in overdifferentiating, we sometimes forget that perceptions and learning, dreams and rituals, emotions and institutions and the view of the world held by those who live them are not so many scattered elements, even if the documents make them seem so today. They were linked by a close cohesion, lived by if not understood by the people of the time who sometimes had their own explanations for it. The yoke and the windmill are inseparable from stories about donkeys and the miller's songs.

In order to avoid bringing too many of our modern interpretations and perspectives to the study of feudal society, it is best to expose them at the outset and, in particular, to ask or remind ourselves what the notion of feudalism means in our mental universe, in our way of thinking. Robert Boutruche had already commented on the extent to which the word was not neutral, on the meaning it has taken on since the official decease at the end of the eighteenth century of the social structure that it was supposed to describe.[6] Today it is noticeable how frequently the word appears in political utterances, even or particularly when the latter are not very erudite. Feudalism, in 1978 as in 1789, is still a threat to France. Of course it has rather changed its appearance, adapting itself to the tastes of the day. A baron who has carved out a fief for himself in the provinces will be the first to denounce, in his harangues to the electors, the threat to the unity of the nation posed by the feudalism of other parties. Thus feudalism comes to mean division, separatism, federalism, or even anarchism. And it is easy to see to what the notion refers, by antithesis, in the rather simplistic manichaeanism of our century: the opposite of feudal division is union through the state. In the dominant political thinking of our day, feudalism appears as something that should not be, and which serves both to bolster up the cult of the state and as a timely reminder of an ever-threatening regression. In fact, the hydra of feudalism lies in wait in the depths of historical ignorance, and the "dark ages" are strongly reminiscent of the shadows of the collective unconscious.

In some ways, the research of the last few decades has not dented this image, which in any case has hardly been concerned with it. Rather, by stressing—and not without reason—the "first feudal age," modern scholarship has been led to insist on the phenomenon of territorial subdivision and political disintegration. Thus the chronological shift in the research has had the effect of obscuring in part an older view, going back to the feudalists of the ancien régime, for whom feudalism was also a social order or, if one prefers, an established disorder.

Notes

1. Ganshof, *La féodalité* [189], p. 11ff.
2. Bloch, *La société* [70], pp. 12, 13, and 208.
3. Duby, *Les sociétés* [476].
4. Michelet, quoted by Duby, *Les sociétés* [476].
5. Duby, *L'an mil* [615], p. 10.
6. Boutruche, *Seigneurie* [98], p. 11ff., and earlier Bloch, *La société* [70], p. 11.

EDITOR'S NOTE: Numbers in brackets refer to bracketed listing in the bibliography.

=

PART
I

WHAT IS KNOWN

Informed historiography can today concede at least this to the commonly accepted view presented by the mass media: before being an order, feudalism was certainly a disorder and a dark confusion. Before new social relationships became established, the feudal crisis destroyed the old ones. This is the point of departure of our study: the phenomenon of the disintegration of public authority that took place for the most part during the tenth century. The second stage is equally well fixed: it is not possible to speak of feudalism without looking again at that old topic, the feudo-vassalic bond, its use and its meaning. At this point it is, of course, necessary to attempt to define the social position of the principal groups and their evolution, insofar as we can see them, in order to examine the concept that some of them had of their own world. Having described the death of the state, it then remains, if we are to follow the pattern of modern thought, to examine its rebirth.

CHAPTER 1

Forms of Power: From Public Peace to the Castral System

888: each kingdom decides to set up a king chosen from within its own borders.

—Regino of Prüm

At Christmas in the year 800, the Frankish host, armed to the teeth, came to Rome to make its king a new emperor of the West. Two centuries later, an abbot or even a mere lord of the manor could say that in his territory he was more powerful than the king. Historians have been very divided on the question of this collapse of the Carolingian Empire: some see it as a dramatic decline of civilization, whereas others, by contrast, underline the superficial character of the structure developed by the great emperor and his counselors.[1] Certainly, when one speaks of the Carolingian state, we should not imagine a modern, policed bureaucracy, a well-regulated administrative machine, or even the relative efficacy of the administration at the very end of the late empire. But it is also an oversimplification to consider the Carolingian Empire as a mere veneer, a glittering decor of antiquities created to satisfy the taste for the past of a palace clique.

To understand the collapse of Carolingian rule and its different stages, we need to recognize two levels of political life, of which contemporaries were very well aware. First there was the empire proper, as perceived from the palace at Aachen—a mosaic of disparate territories, more or less firmly held, more or less well controlled, concentric circles where Frankish influence became increasingly weak

9

as it neared the borders, the marches, beyond which lay barbarism. Then there was what was known by the great majority of the inhabitants of this empire. Even if the wandering of penitents, pilgrims, or merchants or the stories of soldiers who had been to fight in distant places might sometimes widen the horizons of most people, the social framework remained essentially that of their *pagus,* their birthplace. The collapse of the empire in the broadest sense can be found on these two levels, when the influence of the king and his decayed palace barely reached further than the center of the old land of the Franks, around the citadel and hill of Laon. Then those whom the annalists still faithful to the idea of monarchy bitterly call tyrants or petty kings set themselves up to build their own dynasties. These princes now had their own territories. But less than a century later they in turn were to feel their power being eroded and the ground giving way beneath them. Insignificant people, rich landowners, chief men of the cities, or the stewards of the great fortresses, refused to obey and in turn established an almost autonomous power.

The Weakening of Royal Power and the End of Public Institutions

In Charlemagne's vast empire, the independence of the margraves or counts created by the emperor had always been very real and it continued to increase. However, at the end of the ninth century there was a phenomenon of quite another dimension, one that modern historians have had difficulty in establishing and on which they are still working—the birth of the territorial principalities. From this time on, it is agreed, as Dhondt puts it, that "the history of France in the ninth and tenth centuries is not characterised . . . by the replacement of the Carolingian dynasty with that of the Capetians, but by the elimination of centralised monarchy in favour of the territorial princes."[2] Nevertheless, the sources—mostly annals—generally give only a negative and superficial picture of this phenomenon.

Negative: for the palace clerks who describe them, these changes are seen as a serious decadence, and the modern view of the decline of Carolingian rule to some extent always echoes this. Superficial: the accent is placed on accounts of single events listed from the political viewpoint of the upper aristocracy. Boso has himself consecrated king, Rannulf imposes rule on Aquitaine, Bernard Plantevelue (Hairy-sole) collects *pagi* (local districts) to create himself a homogenous territory. . . . From this material controversies arise as to what annalists' words really conceal. From this material also arise the difficulties in establishing a strict chronology. While we cannot seek the exact hour of the birth of feudalism, could it not be possible between the end of the ninth and beginning of the tenth centuries to determine a threshold, a line that could be useful to today's historians while still reproducing a reality that was perceived by the majority of contemporaries? Put another way: how does a governor—*rector, praefectus*—already independent, transform himself in the eyes of all into an autonomous prince or, as the famous expression puts it, into a *roitelet*, "little king." What are the concrete manifestations of this autonomy, and what are its limits? But the greater or lesser autonomy of the princes is only one aspect of the problem, and perhaps not the most important. The Carolingian Empire was based also on local structures that predated it and were also for a time to survive after it. To see when and how these structures, which in war as in peace united free men around the heart of the *pagus*, decayed will be the second aspect of our inquiry.

The Territorial Principalities

The origin of the principalities can be traced to the great decrees made by Charles the Bald to resist the Viking invasions. But we need to go even further back. When the Carolingian king once again sent out the Frankish soldiers for conquest and pillage in order to impose or reestablish everywhere the *regnum francorum*, there already existed in the kingdom of the Franks huge and stable territories, which were also called *regna*—in the south, Gothia, Aquitaine, Provence, Burgundy; in the east, Bavaria, Thuringia, Saxony. The term *regnum* did not at that time imply the presence of a *rex*.[3] These "kingdoms without a king" must still have been extremely flexible social groupings. One only has to think of the extraordinarily frequent references in the sources to *populi*, Burgundians, Alamanni, Aquitainians. What we do not know is what these formulae concealed, whether profound cultural differences or the pride of the noble families of the region.[4] Whatever it was, the existence of such a reality almost always brought with it the presence of administrators who stood in relation to the count as the *regnum* did to the *pagus*.

The terminology that refers in the Carolingian period to those people ranking above the counts probably conceals, despite variations, distinct institutional characteristics. The chief uncertainty is due to the ambiguity of the language used by the scholars of the period. They often vacillate between a literary style, varying somewhat with each author, which is full of classical echoes and implies a complex code of allusions, and a more fixed legal language that borrows the greater part of its vocabulary from the chancery and the vernacular. *Praefectus* is a good example of the first kind of image, a word that could mean a marquis from Friuli, a Frankish nobleman commanding in Bavaria, or the successors of the provincial governors of the south, *rectores*. On the other hand, we have a word like "margrave," practically never used during the reign of Charlemagne, when periphrases such as *custos limitis* were preferred. Still little used in the time of Louis the Pious, it becomes frequent in the chancery vocabulary in the reign of Charles the Bald and in the documents of Hincmar, who was then the royal annalist. Yet at this moment it starts to lose its precise meaning of a "commander of a march (border county)" and is applied simply to someone who holds under his authority several counties. But the majority of authors and the chancery clerks of the kingdom of Germany continue to avoid *marchio*, preferring *dux*. The term refers sometimes to the military leaders who led an army in time of war, sometimes to the ruler, Frankish or indigenous, of a vanquished people—German historiography has devoted many studies to this question of national duchies, and sometimes to the administrator of one of the larger territorial units of the south, Aquitaine, Provence, or Septimania.[5]

The territorial princes were to inherit this vocabulary and take advantage of these uncertainties. At the end of the ninth century, "the insolence of the margraves" was unleashed.[6] In 879, one of them is still dithering when he calls himself: "I, Boso, by the grace of God, that which I am."[7] A few weeks later he dares to make himself king. We find less audacious peers similarly hesitant in their attempts to adjust ancient titles to their new ambitions. The title of duke—and what memories that evoked!—reappears in Aquitaine. In Burgundy, Richard the Justiciar and his sons are turnabout *dux*, *archi-comes*, or *princeps*. Herbert in Champagne is referred to in 968 and 980 as *comes Francorum*, while in Normandy the successors of Rollo seem to favor the title *princeps*.[8]

In the mid–tenth century, the title of *dux* was used with great effect by the Robertians to bolster up the authority that they had extended in the preceding generations over the whole of Neustria—the royal court was to give Hugh the Great the title of *dux francorum*—and perhaps in order to legitimize their attempts to expand into Burgundy and Aquitaine, which, according to Flodoard, Hugh received from the king in 954. Others too tried to distinguish themselves with titles. The count of Toulouse, having for a time called himself duke of Aquitaine, demonstrated his preeminence in the old towns of Septimania by awarding himself the title of *primarchio*.[9]

This phenomenon was to become even more widespread. All through the tenth century, whether on the edges of the *regna*—Comminges, the Maconnais—or in one of the larger areas, still at least nominally under royal authority—Catalonia, Provence—and soon in the very heart of the ancient duchy of the Franks—Anjou, Maine, Blois, Chartres—a second generation of dynasties established in turn by differing routes autonomous powers. Most of them, as we know, were to assume the title of prince, as those who had come before had done.

The use of *princeps* comes in later than one would expect: in Catalonia and Provence only at the end of the tenth century; in Anjou the title appears from 1040–46, but in 1062 Geoffrey Martel uses it in the ambiguous *populi sui princeps et Francorum regis comes*. In the south, at that time a region without a king, this late reference indicates perhaps the strength of survival of royal prestige. In Anjou on the other hand it may be an indication of a prudence prompted by the proximity of the king and the memory of a closer dependence on him.[10]

This raises the problem of those viscounts who commanded the cities and who were to become counts at the end of the tenth century. We know that this was the case with the counts of Blois and Anjou, and also those of Auvergne. The counterproof is provided by those counts of *Francia* who, as Jean-François Lemarignier rightly points out, still put their names to the charters of Robert the Pious with simple formula: *signum talis comitis*. Further north, the six Carolingian counties of Picardy broke up in the tenth century without the subsequent creation of a territorial principality. Quite the reverse: the princes here were first the king of France in person and on the northern borders the count of Flanders; in the middle of the century, Ponthieu was no longer ruled by a count but, as we learn from Hariulf, by *milites regii*. It seems that here the structures that grew up around the great royal abbeys were no strangers to the presence of the king.[11]

Whatever the title taken, contemporaries were quite clear: "he held Aquitaine and Gothia in his own right"—*suo jure*—writes Abbot Odo of Cluny about William of Auvergne; "the power that the kings formerly had here is now held by Count Hugh," asserts the spokesman of the count of Ampurias.[12]

The desire to upgrade a title was not only an indication of increased power. It is also an indication of the gradual adoption of the principle of heredity. The descendants of Eudes passed on without a break the counties of Toulouse and Rouergue, while Rollo was the ancestor of the dukes of Normandy and Baldwin II that of the counts of Flanders. One or two centuries later, clerks—often guardians of the funerary abbeys where the founders were buried—endeavored to perpetuate in writing the glory of these "almost royal" families. Only rarely do they go further back than those limits of the collective memory marked by the end of the ninth or the beginning of the tenth centuries to the historic moment when the fame of the ancestor had established the dynasty, as in the case of Arnulf the Great of whom we read that he had "by succession the hereditary monarchy of Flanders."[13]

It was at the moment when the members of the upper aristocracy ceased to owe their fortune to the temporary favours of a sovereign, holding power and land for life and then revoking it, at the moment when their power rested on a patrimony which was freely transmitted from father to son, then it was that family groups, until then flexible and without a firm structure, became ordered according to the strict rules of lineal descent.[14]

Dynastic genealogies or the pursuit of new titles only represent, however, one aspect of the autonomy of the princes on the threshold of the early feudal period. As Léopold Génicot has stressed, "to be independent meant at the time behaving like a king, or, to be more precise, to have the powers of the king and espouse his mentality."[15]

"The powers of the king" means that part of the prerogative and those public rights that still belonged to the king in the counties. Most importantly, the coinage. It was not so much a question of the profits from the mint, which the king had often given to the churches, as the incomparable prestige conferred by the portrait reproduced a thousand times on the *deniers* that passed through so many hands. At first the mints, which had come under the control of the princes, continued to mint coins with the royal portrait, but following a stylized type, often of Lothar. Then the royal figure disappears from the obverse, replaced by the simple reproduction of the name of the mint. Sometimes the name of the sovereign remains and that of the prince is substituted for the name of the mint. At a later stage, the name of the prince appears in the place of and instead of that of the king.

In Brioude, around 925, the mint was producing coins bearing the name of William of Aquitaine and Auvergne. In the same principality, the Bourges mint went on using for a long time the stylized figure of Lothar, then it produced some anonymous coinage. In Normandy, still in the mid-tenth century, the Rouen mint put out a coinage of Carolingian type, but a penny found outside the kingdom, in Denmark—a Norman trick?—bears the name of William Longsword. From the time of Richard I the ducal coinage became current. In 960–970, on a penny from Champagne, we find † *Hlotarius,* † *Heribertus comes*, while in Narbonne coins were produced in the name of a certain Raymond, probably the count of Toulouse, in 924–40. In Provence the archbishop had his initial struck on the coinage of Arles in 963–85. The time lag in relation to the coinage of Barcelona is interesting; there the name of the count appears around the year 1000. Even more interesting is the situation in imperial Lorraine where the bishops of Metz, Toul, and Verdun added their names to that of the sovereign, the latter's name not disappearing until the mid-eleventh century.[16]

The old system of dividing by three the revenues of tolls and other taxes imposed on the merchants is another witness to the reality of princely autonomy. Several charters of immunity granted by Louis the Pious and Charles the Bald to the southern churches give them a third of the local tolls or the rights attaching to them; the other two-thirds had to go to the count. These charters have proved to be false or interpolated deeds, forged at the end of the ninth century. In 957, one of the beneficiaries, the bishop of Vich, did indeed enjoy those rights that he calls *res regales*. It is clear that the king was no longer entitled to collect any part of the southern tolls.[17]

The royal fiscs, or estates, also attracted the envy of the princes, enriched at the expense of royal power. Concessions were still few in the reign of Charlemagne; they became more frequent with Louis the Pious, though remaining limited to south of the Loire. In the time of Charles the Bald they reached a peak, decreasing after 877 when the king had no more to give away.[18] When in their turn, around 950, the princes wished to alienate these possessions, royal authorization was still apparently indispensable. By the end of the century they could dispose of them freely without it.

In the Mâconnais, the last charter authorizing the count of Mâcon to pass on a property of the *comitatus* was issued in 946; a last fisc was alienated at the request of Count Gilbert. In the mid-tenth century the Carolingians still had control of the fiscs in the Champagne area. As for Catalonia, Bonnassie's studies show that in the tenth century the counts of Barcelona alienated mainly their allods with only three cases of fiscs, in 976, 998, and 999. In 950 the king of Burgundy ceded another fisc in Provence; in 976–78 he was still approving the granting of land by the count. Even in the eleventh century the memory of the king's particular rights over royal fiscs seems not to have been entirely forgotten. Eudes II of Blois, in a famous letter of 1023, acknowledges that he has inherited his *honor* from his ancestors, but through the favor of the king. In 1026 the royal right through which the counts possessed their lands was still evoked in Catalonia; in 1036 Ermengol II of Urgel declared himself owner by virtue of his rights as a count.[19]

Another indication in the negative of the independence of the princes can be found in the charters that can be established to be royal grants of immunity made in favor of the churches. Before 987 the protection of a written document from the king, though less frequent than in the ninth century, is still relatively common. The areas where it is absent are important: the west beyond Tours and Angers and the southwest in Aquitaine and Gascony. Everywhere else there is a greater or lesser degree of royal presence. Curiously—and this is a paradox that we must try to explain—there are even many charters for the southern borders between Narbonne and Barcelona.

After 987, the geographical retreat increases: suddenly in the Midi, where the respect for legitimacy that had continued to uphold the last Carolingians no longer applied to the first Capetians; gradually in other areas, for between 987 and 1031 we still find charters for Burgundy, Touraine, and a few for Normandy. Under Henry I, the map is restricted further to the triangle Tours–Montreuil–Châlons-sur-Marne and still later, under Philip I, to the axis Orleans-Paris-Compiègne.[20]

At the same time as they were deserting the royal court, at the end of the tenth century—and this provides the counterproof—the Catalonian abbots were seeking, with the agreement of their princes, the protection of the papacy. Furthermore, when Robert the Pious undertook a journey around the Midi, whether it was political or religious, not one of the seven great abbeys where he stayed appears to have asked him for a charter.[21]

The Church, a loyal supporter of Carolingian royalty at the end of the ninth century, fell in its turn into the hands of the princes. We know that around the year 1000 the king still had the last word in the nomination of some twenty bishops, grouped chiefly around the metropolitan sees of Rheims and Sens.[22] Elsewhere, however, the investiture of bishops was probably carried out by the princes. This change was in fact late, if we go by the legal sources. In 908 and 947 the *decreta* of election of the bishops of Gerona and Elne still mention the involvement of the king along with that of the prince. The royal charters back up the evidence of the *decreta;* the same bishop of Elne, Riculf, as elsewhere the archbishop of Narbonne or the bishop of Puy (941), is called "*fidelis* of the king." It is only in 990, 1013, and 1017 that the bishops of Cahors, Vich, and Roda are elected without royal agreement being mentioned. In 982 the new bishop of Elne is no longer qualified as *fidelis noster* by the royal chancery.[23]

It is important to take care in distinguishing on each occasion between the *de facto* and the *de jure,* even if at the period with which we are concerned the legal relationship often remained tenuous. The old Carolingian procedure for the election of a bishop was composed of many different stages and hence equally many possibilities for intervention and consequently for influence. In the bishopric of Limoges at the beginning of the eleventh century the investiture of the bishop was a matter for the count of Poitiers, the duke of Aquitaine, but the consecration remained with the metropolitan, the archbishop of Bourges, a friend and appointee of the king. Olivier Guillot has shown in precise detail how in Angers the position of the bishop at the end of the tenth century was even more ambiguous. In a deed of 972 the bishop confirms, at the request of the count, the usage according to which the incumbent of the see should be ordained in the church of Saint-Aubin. The abbey came under the jurisdiction of the count and the ceremony could not take place without his authorization. But in the same document the prelate recalls insistently that this abbey had been founded "on the order of King Childebert" and that it had the status of a royal abbey. If this was the justification for the installation of the bishop in this place, then it means that the choice of prelate was still considered to be a normal royal prerogative. Thus the count in accepting this affirmation accepts the possibility of the king's involvement. It is enough for him to have a legal title that allows him to control procedure.[24]

Once again these formal but nevertheless precise criteria lead us to believe that the independence of the princes probably grew into being later and particularly in a less absolute way than is suggested by the complaints of a few learned clerks, nostalgic for the *City of God.*

But could the independence of the *magnates,* or magnates, be total as long as the monarchy existed? In the time of Hugh Capet, Abbo of Fleury composed with the help of ancient texts the traditional *Mirror of Princes*—a requirement for any informed account of the function of royalty, the *ministerium regis*—and he tackles therein the question of the fealty owed to a king: "Since the function of the king is to regulate the affairs of the kingdom in its entirety, how could he attend to such tasks if the bishops and the magnates of the kingdom are not in agreement with him? How will he exercise his function if the great men of the kingdom do not provide him with help and advice, with the honour and respect which are owing to him?" This is a revealing anxiety about the liberties that the important men of the kingdom were taking with the *servitium regis*. The old Carolingian rhetoric was no longer managing to conceal the feudal reality.[25] Should we for all that see this as an imaginary concern and imagine that these "great men of the kingdom," the territorial princes, now masters in their own lands, no longer had any links with the monarchy? A close study of the royal entourage of the last Carolingians reveals that this is not at all the case.

Let us leave aside the ancient controversies about the nature of the fealty owed to the king. From a formal point of view they appear to be resolved: the *fideles* of the king are his *vassi*, since they pay him homage. They still had to come in person for that—in the France of the year 1000 there was no homage by proxy. At the end of the tenth century, the princes of the Midi, the counts of Toulouse, Roussillon, or Barcelona only communicated with the king through envoys. Unable to qualify them as *fideles*, the royal chancellery had to make do with awkward formulae like *amicus noster, comes nostrae ditionis . . .* or even *princeps* for one of them.[26]

In the reign of Louis IV the majority of princes seem to have been at any given moment *fideles* of the king, even if their homage was often late and insecure. The situation changed in the time of Robert the Pious. Among the counts who came to the court there were first of all those of Francia, the counts of Soissons, Beauvais, Blois, Anjou, the Vermandois and Amiens-Vexin-Valois. But should all these be considered as territorial princes? There were also some magnates, at least on solemn occasions; the duke of Aquitaine, the count of Flanders, and the duke of Normandy.

It was precisely at this time that Dudo of St Quentin, a member of the Norman duke's entourage, was to defend the thesis that the duke only owed to the king a personal homage that would create links of friendship and concord, but which did not entail *servitium*. Here we are faced with the whole problem of the real content of homage and fealty, a matter that is more complex and far-reaching than the question of the autonomy of the territorial princes.[27]

However diminished the numbers present, however relaxed the links, there still existed around the year 1000 with Robert the Pious the appearance of a Carolingian court. Power here or there could change hands, princely titles could reveal a still new glory, but in people's minds the royal *imago* endured. The merchants or peasants who handled the coins, the abbots who laid up the precious charters in their chests, the bishops who drew up the *decreta* continued to respect a king, distant and ineffectual perhaps, but no matter! The mysterious aura that remains when all or almost all of that which makes up his material strength has disappeared—that is royalty. It was a need in the hearts of the men of that time, a need so strong that those who defeated it, the territorial princes, could not efface its image.

Public Institutions

Institutions are not only a creation *ex abrupto* of power, imposed from above. They are also a reflection in the ideas of the leaders of social habits that it is their business to take into account, or indeed to assume. Thus there is nothing surprising about the fact that after the disappearance of Carolingian power, the structures that supported it remained, since they too continued to be upheld by certain constants of the social order. This phenomenon is even more marked in relation to "local" institutions, which regulated the social life of those on whose existence, daily activity, and labor the empire depended.

Beyond the perpetual rivalries of a few important aristocratic families, this canvas of social relationships is often very revealing, even if it is still hard to interpret. Nevertheless, there are two structures that can give us some idea. One is that which gathers together in the main center of a territory men wishing to resolve peacefully their conflicts. The other is that which lines up those same men around the most enduring groups of the Carolingian army. The status of a free man in the society of the time is expressed in this double participation. The survival, or rather permanence, both in the north and south of the assembly of free men has often been emphasized. In the extreme south of the kingdom, in Catalonia, an unusually precise terminology reveals the extraordinary coherence of the political and judicial system in the first years of the eleventh century. There was a public tribunal presided over by the count or viscount along with specialized and professional judges nominated by the count. Then around this group were the *boni homines*, free and wealthy landowners who were not only possible witnesses for the case under examination but also the guarantors, by their presence, of the public character of the tribunal. Court procedures made use of the written act of probate, inquests, evidence given under oath and attorneys or advocates—*adsertor, causidicus, advocatus*. Above all, as instructed in the old capitularies, there was reference to a written body of law. Similar if not such clearly defined structures can be found in the Narbonnaise and Provence.[28] At the other end of the kingdom on the borders of Picardy and Flanders, the terms are different but not the essentials of the institutions. There too then lived men "sufficiently rich in inherited property to prevent them from being subject to anything except public judgement." The counts always presided over the *mallum*, accompanied by *scabini* and the *boni viri*. The same type of tribunal was in existence in the city of Mâcon and in Poitiers with *scabini* in the presence of the free men of the *pagus,* the *pagenses.* Everywhere, as was said of Duke Godfrey ("the Bearded") of Lorraine, "the count presided according to custom in an audience, to dispense the law publicly."[29]

The date and place of these periodic large meetings had long been fixed by custom, making it possible for every man to attend. In Tours, the *mallum* was held on the site of the old Roman tribunal; in Ponthieu, custom insisted that it be held annually at Saint-Riquier. The capitularies that provided for the taking of the vow of fealty speak of "those customary places . . . where the *mallum* must be held." But the same texts show also the dangers threatening the assembly of free men, when they forbid the count to change the place of the sitting, or to increase the number of sessions—all practices that were evidently aimed at excluding the peasants.[30] The results of these manipulations became clear in the tenth century. From the time of Gerald of Aurillac, the *placitum ex condictu* was in practice reserved for the *nobiles viri.*[31] From 950 in the Mâconnais, 990 in Provence, the assessors, like those who participated at the judicial assembly, are given the title of *fideles.* In Béziers or Nîmes at the beginning of the century, among the *boni homines* of one area there were still both *majores* and *nobiliores* along with *mediocres* and *minores.* In Arles, on the other hand, in 965 the *boni homines* are simply the notables of the city. In Catalonia as in Provence, the college of judges got progressively smaller: in the ninth century, eight, ten, or twelve judges sat together at one session; around the year 1000 there were only one or two. Does this indicate less frequent courts? In the first decades of the eleventh century the southern judges disappeared, like the *scabini* of the Mâconnais or, shortly before, those of Poitou. In Saint-Quentin, in Picardy, the composition of the count's tribunal changed, making way for a group of dependents and domestic officials—*vassali, milites, prepositi, senescalcus.*[32]

Above all, the old justice of the counts or the newer courts of the immunists were now facing competition from the emergence of new types of justice, which subdivided the previous areas of jurisdiction, reducing them sometimes to the limits of the city.

Two examples allow us to put a firm date to the weakening of the idea of public justice. In the mountains of the Auvergne at the end of the ninth century, Gerald of Aurillac presided—in his capacity of *vassus regalis* and hence perhaps by royal authority—over the court session to which the free men of the region were to come. Three generations later the abbey of Aurillac, which he had endowed, forged or interpolated a deed in which the bishop of Clermont recognizes the possession of a public assembly. It recalls—in order to cement it more firmly—the wide extent of the abbey's customary jurisdiction. In Saint-Quentin, in 970–76, Count Albert ceded the place where the assemblies and the *mallum* had been held in order to found the monastery of Saint-Prix. The tribunal, now become a feudal court, had moved from the public square to the count's "hall."[33]

The *placita generalia* that had brought together the community of freemen, presided over by the count, the king's representative, became mere seigneurial or abbey courts. The term *placitum generale* continues in use, but in Arras it refers to a particular category of dependants of the abbey—*homines de generali placito*—while in Dijon and Autun it indicates the fair dues.[34]

In Burgundy in the eleventh century the terms *placitum generale* and *placitum vigeriale*, vicarial court, came to be equivalents. This raises the question of the fate of the lower public courts. Georges Duby shows that as late as 1004 in the Mâconnais *vicaria* sessions were being held to resolve minor disputes. But at the same time around certain castles the *vicaria* refers only to taxes levied at particular occasions or under the *bannum*.[35]

The Carolingian military system, as set out in the capitularies between 751 and 840, is well known, at least in general terms.[36] It was an essential structure in a society which each year sent out armies in search of slaves and booty—armies with the additional task of inculcating respect for the empire and its boundaries in the new barbarians who surrounded it. All free men should in principle have taken part in these faraway expeditions. In practice the call to arms was limited geographically, being confined to those contingents nearest to the theater of operations, and socially, calling on only those landowners who had at least three or four manses, or holdings, in addition to their own *curtis*.[37]

The general nature of service, emphasized in the capitularies, should not disguise the basic division in the army in the Carolingian period. On one hand there were the conscripts—*collectae*—a heterogeneous and undisciplined assortment of leather-clad and well-armed landowners alongside peasants carrying their "double-ended sticks."

The bearers of these weapons are generally depicted as ragged beggars brandishing cudgels. The aristocratic disdain of those writing the capitularies has been matched through the centuries by the additional incomprehension of citydwellers. We forget how scarce metal was in the countryside, the need to save such a precious material—a man owning a breastplate would leave it at home—and the peasant tradition of stick fighting. Besides, these men were ordered to bring not their sticks but their bows, which were a more deadly weapon when fighting against cavalry.

On the other hand, there were the bands of professional horsemen—*scarae*—sturdy lads, *vassi*, equipped and trained. These fighting teams are often to be found grouped around the big royal monasteries. At Ferrières in the Gâtinais or Saint-Quentin in the Vermandois the abbots' letters speak frequently of the problems of this service to the king. At Saint-Riquier in Ponthieu, an inventory of taxes mentions that one-hundred-and-twenty of these soldiers lived around the abbey and that the advocate had a list of their names. At Corbie, the abbot Adalard mentions their house and specifies that the abbey provided them with bread of a good quality.[38]

A capitulary of Louis the Pious of 817 issued at the Council of

Aachen, perhaps at the request of St. Benedict of Aniane, gives a list of the abbeys that owed something to the emperor.[39] They are divided into three groups: some owe military service, *militia*, and gifts, others gifts only, while the last group owes only prayers for the well-being of the empire. This list does not include all the abbeys in the kingdom: some are missing from the Midi, and particularly some important ones from the north that were held by powerful magnates. Other sources allow us to add to the list of abbeys maintaining groups of soldiers. The map that emerges is revealing, even given some important lacunae (Saint-Aubin, Angers; Saint-Cybard, Angoulême; Saint-Martial, Limoges; Saint-Maurice d'Agaune; Saint-Victor, Marseilles; the great abbeys of Vienne): all the "military" abbeys are situated to the north of a line Tours-Besançon, except for two that guard the road to Italy through the Jura and the Alps. Conversely, the concentration of abbeys owing only "prayers" in the Midi and particularly in Septimania is striking. There were, however, military contingents connected with abbeys in Aquitaine,[40] but they were probably to be found near the abbeys that are lacking from our list, such as Saint-Martial, Limoges, and Saint-Cybard, Angoulême. The soldiers appointed along with the abbots by Charlemagne in 778 had been chosen from among the Franks, and this was probably something new. The system of abbey contingents, one of the most secure structures of Carolingian power, was a Frankish one that existed little or not at all in the Midi. It shows that the army relied essentially on Frankish soldiers and not on local contingents. The *scarae* of the great churches of the north probably carried as much weight in the military and consequently the social structure of the empire as did the dependents of the magnates.

The system of the abbey contingents was still in existence in 981 in the empire, where the Ottonian dynasty took a firm hold of the reins of power.[41] At the same period in the western kingdom the royal abbeys were being dismantled by the magnates. A letter of Abbo of Fleury of around 997 relates how Fulk of Anjou had destroyed the patrimony of the monastery of Ferrières, giving it to his men. The *villae* of Saint-Riquier were in the hands of soldiers loyal to the Robertians. Saint-Quentin became the residence of the count.[42] The dismemberment of the estates brought with it, in part, the destruction of the military units.

A good example is that of a certain *Patericus*, Patry, who in 895 possessed, wrongly according to the monks, certain possessions of the abbey of Saint-Martin, Tours. He had to provide three light horsemen, three *scuta*, for the service of the lay abbot, at that time Robert, the future king. But *Patericus* had also obtained a benefice from Berengar, count of Le Mans. When questioned by Robert, the advocate of the monastery was able to say how many horsemen *Patericus* was obliged to provide. But it is clear also that this person was from that time onward more concerned with accumulating wealth than serving in the army.[43]

The dispersal of the vassal groups can be detected in the tenth

Map 1. Royal Abbeys and Warrior Contingents West of the Rhine in 817

Omitted: — "Episcopal" abbeys (owing prayers?)
        — A number of large abbeys, probably "military," given in benefice to magnates

century by the fall in the number of military contingents, or at least of those participating in large-scale offensive actions. Hugh the Great—son of the same Robert who was able to demand the service of *Patericus*—still had in 922 two thousand horsemen. After 940 the numbers appear to fall, becoming sometimes quite derisory. In 985 Hugh Capet could only muster six hundred horsemen. Louis IV at the taking of Amiens in 944, Hugh at the siege of Laon in 988 are accompanied only by their *domestici*, the *milites regii*.

This explains the use of Norman pirates to swell the armed forces and it explains more clearly at the end of the tenth century the first mention of mercenaries—*conducticii*. What had happened to the Frankish soldiers? The documents still mention them, but in a different way: they are called *oppidani, castellani, milites castri*, words that underline the area that was now their habitual theater of activity, the castle. In Laon the *oppidani* who repelled the royal horsemen of Hugh Capet can be identified with the bishop's horsemen of which Guibert of Nogent will speak a century later. Organized violent war has become crystallized around the *castrum*.

Such were the fortunes of those for whom war was the principal activity. But what remained in the tenth century of the conscription of free men? In Catalonia there was still mention of "royal service" or "public duty." There is no ambiguity in these words: service is what "is performed by those men living on their own allods in the county"; duty means "the army and the rest of service to the king." And we know that in the first decades of the eleventh century small allodial (nonfeudal) landowners still possessed lance, sword, and warhorse. Of course, as early as the ninth century the military service of ordinary free men was not restricted simply to fighting; labor and supplies, *hostilicium*, were also required. These services were called in Catalonia the "count's tax" or "fiscal tribute" and included the provision of billets *(albergue)* (very commonly in the Midi) and of warhorses, *paravereda*.[44] All these requisitions of goods and services were still carried out by the count, even, as was normal for a public tax, outside his own lands.

This double aspect of soldier and laborer of the peasants' military obligations can be found in other areas: in Anjou and Champagne, in Flanders as in Normandy, and always to the benefit of the count. In Anjou and Poitou in the first half of the eleventh century, the peasants—*villani, rustici*—had first to provide twice a year carting services or laboring for fifteen or seven days (twice seven?), called *bidannum*, defined in the charters as a *genus bannitionis*. Even if they were exempted from this, the count reserved expressly what he calls his *summonitio* to call them to "public war," albeit for only fifteen days—*bellum publicum, expeditio publica*, or *praelium generale pro defensione regni ac principis*. The documents specify that this war would be one happening on the frontiers, *in marcha*, of the county. Military service was to be supported by the count's *fodrum*, which supplied fodder for the cavalry. The same organization existed in Champagne in the first third of the eleventh century, with work *ad opus castelli*, *exercitus*, and the equivalent of the *fodrum*, the *anona equorum*. In Normandy, an act of 1060 speaks of the possibility of a "public call-up by the king or the count" and, in 1081–87, the duke may levy a general call-up "in case of necessity when a war with foreigners is threatening." Associated with this levy is the *brenaticum*, another name here for the *fodrum*. In Flanders, the count dropped the call to arms of his castellans but continued to reserve the right to call up, in case of need, all the men of his land, from whom he also demanded *fodermolt*.[45]

From this geographical approach three distinct zones have emerged. In Catalonia, military service performed by free men is well attested until after the year 1000. In the north, over a wide area, that of the old Frankish territories from Poitou to Flanders, the same service existed throughout the eleventh century. Between these two is a zone where we see only a passive participation by the free men in the form of services and the provision of billets.

It is necessary to make an exception in the Narbonnais for the *aprisiatores*, the Spanish refugees who held in allod the lands that they had cleared and whose military ability earned them the name *hostolenses*. But it was precisely in the tenth century that the regime of *aprisio* disappeared. In 888, the king handed over to the archbishop of Narbonne all those *aprisiatores* who lived in these areas. In 896 a papal bull placed them under the authority of the same archbishop. In 918 the *vicarius* of the count of Toulouse in Carcassonne held in benefice from his lord the rights over the *aprisiatores*, in particular the *cavalcata*. Thus we see their military service being transformed into obligatory duties. The system of *aprisio* thus appears as a short-lived extension into the Midi of institutions and habits of Spanish origin.[46]

How can we explain these geographical disparities? In northern France, threatened by Viking raiders, a tradition of peasant resistance had continued despite the collapse of royal power. This tradition is codified in the capitulary of Meersen in 847, with the general call to arms of the Franks, the *landweri* or *arrière-ban*. In 925 King Raoul was again to use the "levy of the Franks" against the Normans.[47] At the end of the century this practice was generally replaced by the selfish and ineffectual maneuvers of armed bands of aristocrats, with whose interests the levy often conflicted. In 859 the peasants between the Seine and the Loire came together to repel the Vikings, but their contingents were crushed by the princes' cavalry. Again in 884 the villagers formed guilds to resist those who pillaged them.[48]

When peace returned and the great lordships were reestablished, the princes who governed them were able to turn these warlike traditions to their own profit and advantage in the defense of a reduced *patria*. In Catalonia and more generally in Spain, the vigor of the military institutions can be explained by the persistence of a hostile frontier—a theme dear to Spanish historiography. The lack of documentation for southern Aquitaine, Septimania, and Provence—the *cavalcata* did not appear there again until the end of the twelfth century—indicates perhaps another tradition. Military activity in some areas was limited in practice to the *juniores* of the counts and of the *vassi regales*. In these areas the free men were obliged only to provide dues sufficient to allow ease of movement to those restricted groups that carried out policing and governing duties. That these dues were of a public nature, *ad opus publicum*, is still clear at the beginning of the eleventh century.[49]

The persistence in peace as in war of so-called Carolingian institutions in the tenth century most likely conceals other equally ancient social realities. Whatever the taxes or services imposed on them, the peasant neighborhoods were not fundamentally disturbed. Until the mid-tenth century in some places, in others perhaps even until the early eleventh century, the traditional way of life continued.

A time came when the *mallum* was no longer an assembly of free men but the property of the count, of his friends, or of his rivals. Free men in the country, or at least those of them who had managed to avoid servitude or dependence, now lost the main center of their collective social life. A more effective and also more grasping power forced them to bow their heads; a narrower framework restricted them. The castles ceased to be refuges and became threats. The rule of the *bannum*, until then more or less justified by collective necessity, now became a legitimized and daily servitude at the disposal of the lord.

The Creation of Banal Lordship

For a long time now the terms "castle" and "feudalism" have been associated, both in the popular consciousness and in learned theories. We tend to project a contemporary landscape into an "indefinite" past, without making any distinction among the many ruins clinging to hills and crags, between those dating from the end of the Middle Ages and those dating from their beginning.

In the absence of properly documented studies, the beginning of the Middle Ages has been placed in that dark period of the last invasions, in a period of disorder and general upheaval when audacious adventurers covered the land with strongholds to protect a helpless peasantry from the raids of Viking, Hungarian, or Saracen pirates: a romantic picture where the image of the noble hero and a messianic confidence in individual prowess are mingled. But in 1938 a jurist dealt a blow to this theory by shedding doubt on the "spontaneity" of the fortified constructions. Since then, archaeologists have continued to demolish this picture by providing us with the means of accurate dating. The theme of protection, or at least its "generous and beneficient" nature, no longer stands up to the analysis of the most recent historians.[50] "Encastellation"[51] remains a major phenomenon, in the most material sense, but beyond the creation of the castles lies the question of the protection they provided to the country people and at what price.

Castles and Castral Garrisons

There is a tendency today among archaeologists to distinguish three phases in the creation of a network of castles. To these three stages correspond three types of fortification.

Leaving aside the question of the survival of the old city walls of the late empire, the majority of castles up to the Carolingian period consist of rocky plateaus, natural strongholds only roughly adapted, often on the site of old Gallic *oppida*. They evolved in order to protect large populations in times of danger and do not appear to have been inhabited on a regular basis. In the course of the tenth and at the beginning of the eleventh centuries, smaller buildings occasionally begin to appear on the same sites. Their defensive strength was often reinforced by earthworks and a mound, but the area protected was considerably reduced. Finally, in a third stage, less imposing but much more widely spread defensive fortifications were built: small mottes or simply fortified houses.

This pattern varies according to the geography of the area. In Auvergne, Vollore, Thiers, and Château-Marlhac there were in the sixth century rocky plateaus of several dozen hectares where, according to Gregory of Tours, "whole peoples" took shelter—*populi* that recall the Italian *pieve, plebes*. In the eighth century, Bourbon, Chantelle, Escorailles, Turenne, Carlat, and Aurillac are described by the Franks who besieged and captured them as "rocks and caves." In the tenth century, these early *castra* were either rebuilt as small castles, as in Vollore or Thiers, or abandoned for a less steep site nearby, as was the case at Escoraille or Carlat.

These "popular" *castra (Volksburgen)* differ from the residences of the great lords, *curtes* or *villae*, even where the latter are surrounded by palisades, as at Ennezat and at the other counts' seats in Auvergne. And this contrast between castles as refuges and the lordly *curtes* can be found in the documents. In 801, when Lieutaud ceded a *villa* in Rouergue to the abbey of Conques, he adds "the rock where we and our families had the habit of encastelling *(incastellare)* ourselves against the evil pagans." In 890 Beuve of Provence took refuge on the rock of Peire-Impie and his biography relates: "Fortresses were rare in the region and, before this incursion by the pagans, each man staying in his own *villa*, he would live there and be self-sufficient." Toward the middle of the tenth century mottes were constructed in the middle of the old *curtes* of Auvergne. This order of development is not particular to the Midi, being found also in Argonne, though with a time lag, the "small" castles not appearing until the eleventh century.[52]

The cartularies confirm the archaeological evidence, revealing around the year 1000 a signficant increase in the number of castles. In

Auvergne they more than doubled at the beginning of the eleventh century, while (in the charters) the mentions of *castra* replace those of *casae* or *curtes indominicatae* at the end of the tenth century. In Provence, there were a dozen castles in the first half of the tenth century, several dozen a little before 1000, and a good hundred around 1030. North of the Loire, from the end of the ninth century the work of fortification appears at first to have been limited to the restoration of old city walls and the fortifying of the great abbeys as a defense against Viking raids. Not until the second half of the tenth century do we see the building of the majority, some thirty, of the great castles of Picardy; in the west, Hugh Capet built the fortresses of Ponthieu. In Flanders, the first castle of Guines was built around 960. The majority of strongholds in existence before 1050 in the eight *pagi* of the Chartres region were built in the first decade of the eleventh century.[53]

A lot of these castles were built on mounds, consisting often of no more than simple towers of wood. This was the case with the castles of Guines and Ardres. In Champagne, the carts *ad opus castellum* supplied stakes and faggots of sticks. In 1196 in a text from Chartres "the 'custom' for the making or reparing of the fosse" is glossed: "in the vulgar tongue this is called the stake." Archdeacon Gauthier de Thérouanne recalls "the custom among the richest and most noble men of the region . . . of making, by heaping up earth, the highest mound that they could manage; of digging all around a ditch as wide as possible and of a great depth; of fortifying this mound all around its outer edge with a palisade of planks . . . of building in the center a house, or rather a fortress which dominated the whole. . . ."[54] He was describing here the simple mottes of the twelfth century, rather than the more important fortresses.

This growth in the number of castles, as also the increase of smaller fortresses, cannot be related to the need for defense against invaders—the Viking raids north of the Loire ceased around 930 and in the Midi the Saracens of Freinet were wiped out in 972.[55]

Nor do these constructions owe their existence to adventurers. The majority of the castles in Picardy were held by the count or on his behalf. In the Chartres region, half were built by the king, the count, or the viscount, and of the ten others, nine were built by vassals of the king or of the bishop. The first Angevin castles were connected with the count. In these areas the territorial princes prolonged the Carolingian tradition of the Edict of Pitres: in Flanders and Normandy they went so far as to destroy unofficial castles and in Champagne and Anjou they at least demanded the right to authorize them.[56] In the south the situation is less clear: the older of the large fortresses were probably constructed on royal estates, but Peyre-Impie in Provence, Saint-Martin du Larzac in Rouergue, Aurillac in Auvergne, and La Tour-Megon in Poitou, built or converted by powerful allodial landowners in the hearts of their estates, have a less clearly public character.[57]

In the tenth century, there were no longer any castles without garrisons. The same documents that show us the proliferation of old fortresses also tell us of the activities of those who occupied them: *castellani, oppidani, milites,* or *equites castri.* A dozen families, or a little more in the older cities, constituted a class of their own called a "chapter" in a text from Auvergne, a *mesnie* (household) in Catalonia.[58] In charge of the castle and its inmates was a *princeps castri,* a *vicarius castri,* or a *castellanus.*

This head of the garrison may not have been found everywhere and it is only in some regions where he played such an important role that the title of *castellanus* is given to him. In Catalonia he appears as a veritable entrepreneur for his master the lord of the castle, running affairs and often recruiting knights for the castle himself. In Flanders and Laon, the *castellanus* is a representative of the count or the bishop. We see too that the early Flemish texts appear to be reluctant to use this word, too humble or too vague, to designate the count's officer. In other cases, as in Alsace, they speak of a *sculdahis.*[59]

Within the castle, the military tasks were divided very precisely, especially the most onerous duty, guard duty or *estage.* Two systems could be used. In the first, there was a division of time, as in Vendôme at the beginning of the eleventh century, where seven families of *milites castri* worked in relay for a month each, and for two other months the guard was undertaken by the count's *camera,* while the last three months were the responsibility of the people of the surrounding *bourg.*[60]

The usual garrison of the castle was sometimes reinforced in the twelfth century by the knights of the region—*milites patriae*—and even, in case of need, by *fideles,* relations or more distant friends. Georges Duby has shown this to be the case in Brancion, where to the dozen knights of the castle were added on occasion some twenty other *milites.* The same happened in Brabant, the Amiénois, Normandy, and in the west. In Catalonia, the *castla* had to maintain in Mediona five *milites* who made up his suite, *sequum.* In time of war he had to engage twelve more and three times a year he was to present his lord with fifty extra knights.[61]

A second system consisted of dividing the fortified area to be guarded between the different groups of knights. Such was the case for the thirty-one *milites* of the castle at the Arena in Nîmes or the *vassi civitatis* of Arles; the *castellani* of Carcassonne had to perform seven months of *estage* in the tower that had been entrusted to them.[62]

"Customs"

These military structures were not only aimed at ensuring peace in the countryside—they also aided the lord of the castle in extending his *bannum* and making it more profitable. The vocabulary used in the charters to describe the rights exercised by the lord—or those he claimed to exercise—over everything that lived in the shade of his castle is abundant and, making allowances for certain semantic shifts according to region, relatively precise. Firstly there is the *bannum*, the right to give out orders and to levy the fine of sixty sous. In Catalonia, Provence, and Septimania they prefer the term *manament/mandamentum*.[63] Frequently associated with this power is the *destreit/districtus*, the right to apprehend and arrest. These two terms, close in meaning, are sometimes interchangeable in lists; on the other hand, the latter often refers to the rights of justice indicated generally by the words *vicaria*, *placitum*, or more simply *justicia*.[64]

It is necessaary to distinguish between the three terms: *vicaria* meaning the right of justice; *vicaria* meaning the area of jurisdiction of the lord; and *vicarius*. *Vicaria* in the sense of the right of justice is far from universally used. Four areas emerge on the map. First the Ile-de-France, the Chartrain, Touraine, Anjou and Poitou. Here the term is commonly used in this sense. Second, Catalonia, Provence, and Septimania, where it is more or less unknown. It is rare in Berry, Auvergne, and Burgundy, perhaps because these are areas in contact with the aforementioned regions. Lastly, Normandy, Picardy, Flanders, and Champagne, where the term *vicecomitatus* is preferred.[65]

The word *vicaria*, used to refer to the lord's court of justice, does not pose the question of the institutional origins of banal lordship in the same way in all areas. Is the lord the continuation of the count's *vicarius* of the Frankish period as he appears in the capitularies? The first problem is that the lord's *vicaria* is a court of high justice, even though the capitularies forbade the count to delegate to his *vicarius* the hearing of criminal cases. But it is this very prohibition that reveals that the practice was in fact common. Instead of dividing up the cases according to the gravity of the crime, the counts preferred a division according to social class: to them came the notables, to the *vicarius* the peasants. Hence the clearly repressive nature of vicarial justice.

We can presume then that where it exists, the lord's *vicaria* was not a court of lower justice, but that it implied precisely the hearing of the four major crimes that are enumerated in the Carolingian capitularies: homicide or crimes of blood; abduction; arson; theft or larceny. In Saintes, Poitiers, Angers, Tours, and Paris we find that *vicaria* is a term for the "four crimes," the "four charges." In those places where the capitularies were more closely observed, different systems evolved. In Septimania and Catalonia at the end of the ninth century, we find the following list of crimes: homicide; cuckoldom—the southern equivalent of abduction!—and arson. So too in Picardy, where the *bannum* covering the public roads and larceny was dealt with by the count's castellan, while the count and viscount dealt with crimes of blood themselves. The place of theft was unclear; sometimes it was considered a major crime, other times it was sent down to a lower court.[66]

All these systems were able to evolve. In Anjou, in the heart of the "four case" area, the count ceded the public rights to Saint-Aubin and retained only three "customs," homicide, abduction, and arson. The Norman lists, on the other hand, make a distinction between robbery—theft with breaking and entering—which was a matter for the count, and simple theft—*furtum, latrocinium*, which was dealt with by the viscount. But in Auxerre in 1035 simple theft was added to the three other cases, while *infractura* (theft with breaking and entering) was listed between the infringement of the *bannum, taxia*, and physical aggression, *assaltus*. We see here the outline of the distinction between what the Catalan texts of the eleventh century call the great sessions and the lesser sessions, or elsewhere sessions and tribunals—*placitos* and *rexiones*. In the twelfth century the lists became more mixed, expanding to include tolls and hunting crimes. Through a false etymology, the French *voirie* (from *vicaria*) came to mean the policing of the highways, while as a result of the activities of the magnates, the distinction between higher and lower courts became more apparent.[67]

The second difficulty comes from the fact that the *vicaria* in the sense of "jurisdiction" was nothing like as widespread as later on was banal lordship. It is not found in Provence, while in Septimania and no doubt in many other regions it was not a systematic division.[68] It is only in the tenth century that the *vicariae* appear to multiply.[69] We need not suppose that the count created new *vicarii*. We know that traditional assemblies were held on the site of the old public fortresses, the old *oppida*; once the idea of *castrum* and justice were associated in people's minds, it was possible to call the area of jurisdiction of a new castle the *vicaria*. Thus at Antoingt in Auvergne a motte was built in the tenth century on the site of what was still a *villa* in 937; shortly after this date we see reference in the documents to the new *vicaria* of Antoingt. In this region, from the beginning of the eleventh century, *vicaria* and *confinium castri* have become interchangeable.[70] The lords who in the eleventh century exercised the rights of *vicaria* were thus able to assume them without for all that being the descendants of the Carolingian *vicarii* of the count. It was sufficient for them to hold a fortress where the *vicarius* had formerly presided over the customary sitting. The proliferation of *vicariae* in the tenth century thus indicates an increase in the number of castle jurisdictions and no doubt of peasant courts. It does not necessarily imply an increase in the number of the count's *vicarii*, and still less a deliberate policy on the part of the count. In future the lords of the castles were to have in turn their assistants to whom they naturally gave the name of *vicarii* and whom they generally chose from a relatively lowly social position.[71]

The only decisive argument for placing the origins of banal lordship in the Frankish *vicaria* would be to establish the succession in one family of the office of *vicarius* and of the exercise of the lord's *bannum*. This appears to be possible in Poitou. In Catalonia, the *vicarii* certainly became lords, but the continuing use of the old title of *tiufath* is perhaps an indication that here we have a Gothic system "dressed up" in Carolingian garb.[72] It was possible for the founders of the great castellan families to be simple *vicarii*, but it would be dangerous, given the present state of documentation, to generalize from this. The strength and material power of the lords are sufficient to explain how they were able one way or another to grasp the rights needed for the domination of the peasantry, foremost among these being the *vicaria*.

The *vicaria* and the other types of judicial rights also changed over time: the powers changed to taxes, *exactiones*—a sign that the lord and his knights saw public order simply as a way of getting rich. The heaviest tax was introduced along with the *bannum*. It represented the price of the personal security offered by the lords. It was commonly called "tallage"—*taleia, talleata*—or sometimes more euphemistically "collection" or *quista* in the Midi and Mâconnais, "request" or *precatura* or *precaria* in the Liège area and more realistically *tolta*, or in Catalonia *forcias*.[73]

Georges Duby has shown how heavily the tallage bore on the peasants. To his examples can be added others for Poitou and Provence. During the twelfth century the tallage moved from being made an arbitrary to a fixed sum. The protection of the lord is the justification for the tallage, the old right of board and lodging *(gîte et albergue)* a sure way of imposing it. In the hands of the lord this ancient military right becomes a redoubtable weapon: he and his men did not hesitate to install themselves in the villages to eat, pillage, and despoil. The peasants preferred to preempt this, handing over to the castle the rations demanded.[74]

Everything became an excuse to put pressure on the peasants. The public carting duties became obligatory duties on the lord's estate; the transfer of property was taxed; in Catalonia even the meeting of a couple wishing to marry was taxed.[75]

At the end of the eleventh century the first *banalités* begin to appear. It was forbidden to grind one's corn anywhere but in the lord's mill, to cook in any other oven but his, to sell wine just before the new harvest in order that the lord might empty his own barrels, or to open a tavern without his permission. In Catalonia, people might not use any grindstone but the one in the lord's forge or store grain anywhere but in his loft. In Provence, the lord had the monopoly on buying and selling vermillion.[76] Although the system of *banalités* did not apply equally everywhere, it nevertheless indicates the increasingly strong grip of banal lordship on every aspect of peasant life. His concern with income often induced the lord to involve his *milites* in these new profits. In Catalonia the *castla* and his men generally received an aggregate portion. Elsewhere the *milites* shared out the rights accompanying strips of land. In the eleventh century a new kind of official of the lord was to appear, the provost or bailiff, who was to ensure that the profits of the estate came to the lord.[77]

This accounts for the decline and sometimes disappearance of peasant allods. This is clear from a study of the necrology of Notre-Dame in Chartres, dating from around 940 to 1130. From the different hands the lists can be grouped into four periods: from 940 to 1030 80 percent of the donations concern allods; between 1030 and 1060 a dramatic fall brings the figure to 45 percent; from 1060 to 1090 the figure stays at 38 percent; from 1090 to 1130 it drops to 8 percent. André Chédeville, to whom we owe this essential data, shows how these allods, or freehold lands, localized in small villages or hamlets, were probably of a modest size. The only difficulty in interpretation lies in the high percentage for 940 to 1030. This could be explained by a flood of donations already made under the pressure of banal requirements. (Better surely to be answerable to Notre-Dame than to a lord?) According to this hypothesis, the fall in the number of allods would thus have to be placed a little earlier in time. The wealth of documentation in Catalonia enabled Pierre Bonnassie to study the sales of allodial plots. They produce comparable percentages: 80 percent for the period from 990 to 1000; 65 percent from 1000 to 1025; 55 percent from 1025 to 1050; 35 percent from 1050 to 1075; and finally 25 percent from 1075 to 1100. The curve is at its highest point in 990 and, apart from a slight rise around 1030, falls regularly, reaching 10 percent between 1120 and 1130.[78]

It is not hard to imagine the process by which allods, and their holders, fell into the hands of the lords. The new direction taken by the judicial system facilitated confiscations. To deprive the holder of an allod of his possessions, it was sufficient to invite him to prove his right to it, by "for example, plunging his arm in boiling water. If necessary, the unfortunate man could be convicted of some crime, his house and his fields going to pay the fine."[79]

Charles Edmond Perrin shows similar procedures existing in Lorraine, but he believes they were applied to tenants from the beginning of the eleventh century. In the twelfth century, the process bore the significant name of "crossing of inheritance," *crusagium*, because the lord had a cross planted on those tenements taken over by the *bannum*.[80]

In order to avoid a similar fate, many holders of allods anticipated events and gave their allods to the lord, becoming their tenants. In other cases they might sell theirs for a few sous.

The collection of prerogatives and rights exercised by the lord was soon grouped together with its own vocabulary borrowed from the vulgar tongue—the "customs" or, as was said in the Midi at the same period, the *usatges* or *consuetudines* or *usatica*. This vocabulary merits a closer look.

The use of the word meaning public taxes, *exactiones*, is ancient but not very frequent. It is found in the ninth century in some capitularies or conciliar canons, in a royal charter, and in the charter of a viscount of Vienne in 977. It is important to distinguish the interpolations. The word appears in a forgery of Charles the Bold made at Saint-Denis a little before 1008.

From 1005 or 1006, the word "custom" slips into royal deeds and particularly into grants of immunity. It becomes extremely common in the reign of Henry I. At the same period we see in the charters of the duke of Normandy the appearance of the phrase *ab omni consuetudine* in the clause of franchise. Conversely, the old formulas of immunity fall into disuse and are used only to confirm earlier charters.[81]

This intrusion of a vulgar term into the ultraconservative language of the royal chancery dates irrefutably a phenomenon of major importance. Henceforth "the powers derived from the king are no longer based on an express delegation of sovereignty, but on the habit and evidence of the collective memory."[82] The generalization of the word also reveals the patrimonialization of rights: the "customs" can be given, bequeathed, and sold. They are no longer only the expression of a more or less legitimate power, but they constitute the elements of a patrimony and the opportunity for profit.[83] Thus not only do they reinforce the ancient estate of a powerful lord by operating at the expense of its tenants, but above all they prolong that power and enlarge it by applying it, whether they like it or not, to all those small allodial landowners and people on church lands who live in what the lord now deems to be his seigneury. The old public divisions, the *pagus* and *vicariae*, are eclipsed by a new jurisdiction, less clearly defined because it is still expanding—the territory of the castle.

The same words are often used to refer both to the power and to the land over which it is exercised: in the Mâconnais, *bannus* and *salvamentum*; *firmencia* in Auvergne; *mandamentum* in Provence and Septimania; *vicaria castri* and *castellania* in Poitou; *vicaria castri* also in Auvergne; once we even find *civitas*. The majority of these areas of jurisdiction still often correspond to today's districts.[84]

The lord's customs, when he extended them in this way—the texts speak of "tyrannical invasions"—became new customs, which is to say "bad customs," according to an expression that appeared in many places in the first half of the eleventh century.

The "bad customs" appeared in the first decade of the eleventh century in Anjou, Champagne, and the Mâconnais, around 1029 in Poitou, in 1051 in Picardy, perhaps around 1046 in Liège, and around 1060 in Provence. These differences in chronology are perhaps significant. In Auvergne, the term appears exceptionally early, in 994, and then numerous mentions occur at intervals until 1111, with a last isolated appearance in 1151. In the Chartrain it appears between 1080 and 1132. The extension of banal lordship at the expense of the Church's lands was perhaps later here than in the former areas.[85]

The first time that the customs appear in a royal charter, in 1005–06, it is with the qualifying adjective "bad." The expression appears again a little later in the famous charter of 1008 issued to the monastery of Saint-Denis. These references to bad, unjust, or iniquitous customs, still relatively rare in the reign of Robert, become more frequent in the deeds of Henry I, and particularly in those of Philip I. In these the king is often confirming renunciations on behalf of individuals, but sometimes it is he who is abandoning certain "exactions," now thought to be intolerable by those who had to suffer them.[86] Thus a number of customs that could be found in the charters of Robert the Pious were no longer accepted as such in the reign of his successors.

The extension of the clause of exemption from "customs" in the charters drawn up by the king for the churches indicates more than just a decline in the rights of public power. It reveals the moment when the castral system, impelled by its own dynamic, moves beyond its own framework; when the greed of the lords pushes them to attack not only allodial possessions but even the church estates in order to find new areas for their jurisdiction.

It is no accident that one of the earliest mentions of "bad customs" appears in the text of the peace council held in Le Puy in 994. The ecclesiastics are the spokesmen, concerned perhaps for the men of their estates for whom the protection of the saints is not longer sufficient to shield them from the exactions of banal lordship.[87] The misfortunes of the villages on church land are the same as those of the allodial communities. In both cases they were obliged to accept the enforced protection of the powerful.

The Origins of Lordship: Advocacy and Comenda

This protection appears to have developed from existing institutions into distinct structures in the Frankish areas and in the rest of the country: advocacy[88] and *comenda*. We know that the institution of advocates, in the Carolingian meaning of the word, seems to have been linked to the reorganization and strengthening of the immunity as a system of government. Ancient immunity, a continuation of the immunity of the late empire, meant first and foremost the exemption from taxes and public duties. The practical consequence of this was to prevent the representative of the fisc from entering the territory of the immunist or exempted person. From the Merovingian period onward, it would also have implied the concession to the beneficiary of the income of the public taxes and particularly of judicial fines. Does this mean that he, particularly the ecclesiastical immunist, was able to exercise from then on justice and military command over the free men who lived in his territory? In the Carolingian period, this fact seems to be undeniable for the larger Frankish churches, and the setting up, on imperial orders and despite the reservations of the chief ecclesiastics, of an advocate or *vidame* as obligatory representative of the immunist was specifically intended to remedy that which might be upsetting to canon law. In the Midi, on the other hand, the absence of advocacy in the Carolingian sense and the exercise by the count of powers that in the north were devolved to the advocate—as in the case of the administration of justice, even if the fines went nevertheless to the immunist—corresponds with the continuation of a less active tradition of ecclesiastical immunity.[89]

It has been shown that the southern *advocatus* was only a legal representative, *mandatarius,* of the monastery. Thus the abbot of Aniane had chosen two advocates: one who would represent him in minor causes, the other, whom he had presented to the Emperor Louis, a *vassus regalis* who could, if necessary, stand up to a count. But neither of these two men presided over an immunist tribunal or led the free men living on the abbey lands as soldiers in the royal army.[90]

Feudal advocacy began to develop at the time when the large military and judicial immunities of the north were starting to collapse. These had been of considerable importance: the immunity of Corbie at the end of the ninth century covered more than 1,700 square kilometers and the monks received the revenues of the lands in 45 of the 180 villages within this area; at the end of the twelfth century, the abbey had power over only a third of this area. The immunities of Saint-Denis covered the greater part of the Vexin, while Saint-Germain-des-Près was the biggest landowner to the west and south of Paris. It was at their expense, and only thus, that the noble families of the Ile-de-France could hope to establish a banal lordship of any importance.[91]

We see here a double phenomenon. On one hand there is a confusion at the level of the count of the advocacy and public office.[92] The count of Flanders was the advocate of Saint-Amand, the count of Ponthieu that of Saint-Riquier—one could even say that it was the advocate who has become count. The castellans of Béthune, Ancres, and Aubigny were, respectively, the advocates of Saint-Vaast, Corbie, and Marchiennes. If we add the existence of *vidames* for the cathedral churches, there is hardly space in these regions for allodial seigneuries.

On the other hand, the princes could give in fief to special advocates, *subadvocati,* their rights to provide protection and the profits that derived from them. In certain regions such as Flanders these *subadvocati* remained for the most part under the control of the count; elsewhere, as in the Vexin on the land of Saint-Denis, they managed to become independent. But whoever the holder of the advocacy was, the office underlay all important banal lordship by allowing its formation at the expense of the church estates, which were in the majority in these regions.

In places where there was no advocacy, the encroachments of banal lordship on church lands took another form—that of the old contract of *comenda.*

The *comenda* appears very early in the texts. The archives of Cluny, heirs of those of Vézelay, provide a very ancient example: a man named Boso swears to a Count Gerard, probably the famous Girart of Vienne, to aspire to no *comenda* in the *obedientia* of *Polliacum* (Pouilly-sur-Saône?). The archives of Saint-Julien de Brioude have preserved the oath of the important laymen who protected the *obedientiae* of the monastery. Those of Grasse provide the *convenientia de comenda* made in 950 between Sulpice, abbot of Camon in Carassès, and his kinsman Amiel Sulpice. In 994, the Council of Le Puy shows that the magnates of Auvergne generally had at their disposal, in addition to their allods and their benefices, *comendae*.[93]

We shall return later to the southern *comenda*. Let us confine ourselves here to noting the application in one particular area of a contractual form—doubtless older and more widespread—whereby a mandate was given to a certain person to manage the estates of another. These possessions were then confided, *comendata*, to the representative. When the usufruct of the possession was the latter's reward, vulgar law sometimes confused *mandat* (French for "mandate") and *commodat* (French for "ready for use"), *res comendata* and *res commodata*, a confusion or fusion found in certain manuscripts of the Breviary of Alaric and then the *Lex Wisigothorum*.[94] In the period that concerns us, such a contract was not yet confined to relations between churches and laymen; a widow or a landowner too far away from one of his estates might have recourse to it. In this way, by using the disguise of a contract, the powerful were able to superimpose their own authority over the control of the proprietor. And the rich estates of the southern churches were tempting prizes. The lords were thus able to legitimize the hold they had over the ecclesiastical lands neighboring their allods. The peasants evidently took a dim view of this practice because it resulted in their getting two lords instead of one. Having become customary, the contract of *comenda* probably became the *commendise* that was so frequent south of the Loire from Berry to Septimania. Naturally, the owners of allods could also "commend themselves," that is, put themselves under the protection of the lord. A text from Marmoutiers illustrates well the essential role played by the *commendise* in the extension of the lord's customs; "what these customs are, it is unnecessary to relate by listing them, for at their head stands that *commendise* of which we have spoken, and it is from this that all the others have proliferated."[95]

In the eastern zone of the *commendise*, from the Lyons region to Champagne and particularly Burgundy, the texts prefer the term *salvamentum* to indicate the costly protection of the lords. It has been suggested that the use of this term may be related to the rise of the great councils of peace in Burgundy. Lastly, in the north, in Francia and surrounding areas from the Vendômois to the Vermandois through Brie, they used the term *tensement*. This word appears to come from the Latinized Frankish word *tangonare* (to accuse in law, to reprimand), and might give us some idea of the possible role of the *advocatus* in the court of the immunist.[96]

Corresponding to the collapse of the *pagus* is the collapse of the old Frankish immunity, and more generally, of the Church lands. From this time, in the charters granted by the king or the princes to the great abbeys, the privilege that was previously general is now restricted to certain places, and especially to strictly defined territorial limits. These are the areas that it was essential to prise out of the grasp of the thieving castellans.

In Saint-Denis it was the precinct that corresponded to a perfectly demarcated area of some thirty square kilometers beyond the *castellum* that protected the monastery. At Cluny, the "sacred *bannum*" extended for five kilometers around the monastery. Other more humble churches had to content themselves with the thirty paces allowed to them by the assemblies of peace.[97]

Around such an ecclesiastical oasis, a few villages managed more or less to escape from the grasping "protection" of the lords, sometimes at the price of a compromise. This accounts for the many new offices that are difficult to relate to Carolingian advocacy. These ecclesiastical lordships of some three to five villages were all that remained of the vast immunist territories of the past.[98] But within such a restricted area, the abbot made it clear that he alone held the power to command, and to judge, to supervise and to punish. The vocabulary used was to be henceforth that of the "vulgar tongue" that so disgusted the clerks but which was used by their turbulent neighbors, the *milites:* "To speak in the vulgar tongue . . . ; if one can say it thus . . . ; as one says in 'little' Latin . . . ." The banal lordship of the Church—the secular word intrudes into the language of the clerics—succeeded in establishing itself in the face of the *bannum* of the powerful laymen.

The last but not the least consequence of the collapse of the *pagus* was the transfer of all or a part of the powers exercised by the count, *comitatus,* into the hands of certain of the bishops. Earlier historiography tended both to generalize this phenomenon and to give it a very early date. According to this account, episcopal lordship, having become general by the twelfth century, was supposed to go back to the fall of the western empire. It has long been realized that the change had a more recent origin, but when—in the tenth or at the end of the eleventh century? It is necessary to be precise. The formal granting by the king of county rights remains fairly rare, but it dates from the tenth century: there are examples in Rheims in 940, in Langres in 967, and in Le Puy in 924.[99] Here we see the suggestion of a policy imitated from the Ottonians. In the kingdom of Burgundy, the change occurs later: there are charters for Tarentaise in 996, for Sion in 999, for Lausanne in 1011 and for Vienne in 1023.[100] But many bishoprics without royal charters had nevertheless succeeded, before the beginning of the twelfth century, in taking possession of the powers of the counts, in the cities at least. It is undeniable that the bishops had already been holding fiscal lands and supporting military dependents. From 912 the archbishop of Vienne was referring to a "comital" estate of his church; from 1043 the archbishop of Arles, who had held all the fiscs of Arles since the tenth century, was speaking of the county of the holy church of Arles; from 957 the bishop of Vich was in possession of *res regales;* from 941 the bishop and not the count presided over the court of justice in Cambrai.[101] Now, among these churches, many had received charters of immunity or the gift of various public revenues, such as those of the mint or the tolls. In the face of the claims of the counts and lords, there was a natural temptation to interpret these charters very broadly, sometimes even adding interpolations or forging false ones. Whatever the case, it remains that with or without a royal charter, episcopal lordship probably rested on ancient and solid foundations that the Gregorian Reform merely reinforced. A reaction and at the same time an adaptation to the appropriation of the *bannum* by the laity, it was to be in the same way as monastic lordship one of the favorite pieces of royal power on the feudal chessboard.

We might question whether territorial principalities "of the first type" ever really existed. There were undeniably territorial princes, and the groups of ecclesiastics who had placed all their hopes on the idea of a single empire suffered sorely from the independence of the magnates. The decline of the *pagus* and the public institutions is, in our opinion, another matter. One could see it as the inevitable consequence, more or less long-term, of princely autonomy. Having said that, it was also a profound and longlasting attack on a peasant society that had roots deep in the past. The collapse of the *pagus*—as Jean-François Lemarignier has emphasized—was not just a step in an evolution; it was also a profound, and essential, change in social relations, as lived by thousands of free smallholders. Banal, or judicial, lordship was not just a stage in the process of decline of public authority; it was something new.

From the institutional point of view, the old debate between those who saw the *bannum* as having a public origin and those who believed it to be a result of the power deriving from landed wealth appears to be settled.[102] The prerogatives and rights that the charters of the eleventh century show to be in the hands of the lords are those very ones that the capitularies and the records of assemblies had formerly attributed to the king or to those who, whatever their title, shared in his power. The *bannum*, certainly, was changed and redirected; it was not usurped but grasped by those very men—the great landowners—who needed it to reinforce or even preserve their domination over the peasantry. The weakness in the theory of the origin of large estates is not that it "bypasses so casually the chief obstacle—the sudden and general appearance of seigneurial rights in the documents at the beginning of the eleventh century"; it is also that it underestimates the social importance and strength of the peasantry. By seeing "the power of command [as] inherent in the quality of *dominus fundi*," when one considers the landed property "a social body where it is natural that there has always existed . . . a minimum of social discipline, thus at one and the same time principles of command *(bannus)* and principles of obedience," then the customs, beliefs, and rites of countless village communities are reduced to a mere problem of estate management.[103] We can easily imagine what the ambitions were of many of the great landowners. But if one supposes that this ideal had been realized from time immemorial, then the monopolizing of the *bannum*, shortly before the year 1000, loses its *raison d'être*.

The destruction of the *pagus*, the more or less total disappearance of the *mallum*, patrimonialization, the extension and the increase in public dues are the symptoms in our documents of a phenomenon that is often less apparent but more profound: the disappearance or the weakening of the free peasant communities. This is a phenomenon that, furthermore, can be found to be identical outside the "French" boundaries under consideration here. Let us stop here. We now need to go over the same ground again in order to see the changes, both in form and in aim, in those legal relationships—the feudo-vassalic bonds— which were to become so dominant at this stage that they were to enter into political relationships and could even be said to have epitomized them.

Notes

1. Halphen, *Charlemagne* [490], p. 411ff.; Fichtenau, *L'Empire* [480]; Perroy, *Le Monde carolingien* [504], p. 187ff.; Dhondt, *Le haut Moyen Age* [475].
2. Dhondt, *Principautés* [108], p. 231.
3. Werner, *Les principautés périphériques* [520].
4. See chapter 7.
5. Dhondt, *Le titre* [107].
6. This famous expression is from Odo of Cluny, *Vita Geraldi* [34], 1: 32, col. 660.
7. R. Poupardin, *Le royaume de Provence sous les Carolingiens* (Paris, 1901), p. 96.
8. Bur, *La Champagne* [74], p. 113; Boussard, *Les destinées de la Neustrie* [96].
9. Dhondt, *Principautés* [108], p. 224.
10. Bonnassie, *La Catalogne* [72], p. 165; Poly, *La Provence* [87], p. 54; Guillot, *Le comte d'Anjou* [83], p. 356.
11. C. Pfister, *Etudes sur le règne de Robert le Pieux (996–1031)* (Paris, 1885), p. 280; Lemarignier, *Le gouvernement* [455], p. 128; Fossier, *La terre* [79], p. 481ff.
12. Dhondt, *Principautés* [108], p. 173; Notice of assembly of 1019, quoted by Bonnassie, *La Catalogne* [72], p. 165.
13. Quoted in Génicot, *Princes territoriaux* [138].
14. Duby, *La littérature généalogique* [293]. On the study of these genealogies, see pp. 92–93 below.
15. Génicot, *Empereurs* [136].
16. Lafaurie, *Le Trésor du Puy* [147]; Devailly, *Le Berry* [77], p. 228; Dumas, *Le Trésor de Fécamp* [115], p. 48ff.; Bur, *La Champagne* [74], pp. 111 and 114; Castaing-Sicard, *Monnaies . . . en Languedoc* [100]; Poly, *La Provence* [87], p. 233; Bonnassie, *La Catalogne* [72], p. 156; Parisse, *La noblesse* [261], p. 127; Fournial, *Histoire monétaire de l'Occident médiéval* (Paris, 1970), p. 66.
17. Magnou-Nortier, *La société laïque* [86], p. 84; Bonnassie, *La Catalogne* [72], p. 155.
18. Table in Dhondt, *Principautés* [108], p. 270.

19. Duby, *La société [78]*, p. 146; Bur, *La Champagne* [74], p. 321; Bonnassie, *La Catalogne* [72], pp. 145 and 153; Poly, *La Provence* [87], p. 36; Halphen, *La lettre* [194], p. 242.

20. Paraphrase of J-F. Lemarignier, *La France médiévale. Institutions et société* (Paris, 1970), p. 156.

21. Abadal, *Els primers comtes* [90], p. 271ff. and p. 302ff.; they were probably not the only southerners to look to Rome at this period; Helgaud, *Vita Rotberti* [49], 27, p. 125.

22. W. M. Newman, *Le domaine royal sous les premiers Capétiens (987–1180)* (Paris, 1937), p. 216ff.

23. Magnou-Nortier, *La société laïque* [86], p. 330; Lemarignier, *Les fidèles* [199], shows that *fidelis* should be taken in the literal sense of the word.

24. Fontette, *Les évêques de Limoges* [364]; Guillot, *Le comte d'Anjou* [83], pp. 198–99 and n. 12; this analysis is supported by the remarks of Yves Sassier on the bishopric of Auxerre, *Recherches sur le pouvoir comtal en Auxerrois du Xᵉ siècle au début du XIIIᵉ siècle* (thesis, Paris, 1978), pp. 24 and 43. For Meaux see Bur, *La Champagne* [74], p. 185.

25. Abbo of Fleury, *Collectio canonum*, c. 4, *PL*, 139, col. 478, with the commentary in Lemarignier, *Le gouvernement* [455], p. 32. On *consilium et auxilium* in Carolingian vocabulary, see Devisse, *Histoire d'une expression* [106].

26. Lemarignier, *Les fidèles* [199].

27. Lemarignier, *Le gouvernement* [455], p. 50.

28. Bonnassie, *La Catalogne* [72], p. 183; Magnou-Nortier, *La société laïque* [86], p. 273; Poly, *La Provence* [87], p. 43. Pierre Toubert has shown the vitality of this type of structure in Rome, *Le Latium* [89], p. 1209. On those people who could not take part in the judicial courts, see Dhondt, *Le haut Moyen Age* [475], p. 22.

29. 891–900; Ganshof, *La féodalité* [189], p. 39 and *La Flandre* [128], p. 409; Duby, *Recherches sur l'évolution* [112]; Génicot, *Empereurs* [136].

30. Boussard, *L'Origine* [223]; Hariulf, *Chronicon* [48], 4: 189; Perroy, *Le monde carolingien* [504], p. 228.

31. *Vita Geraldi* [34], 1: 11, col. 649.

32. Fossier, *La terre* [79], p. 490.

33. M. Boudet, *Cartulaire du prieuré de Saint-Flour* (Monaco, 1910), no. 1; Fossier, *La terre* [79], p. 488; Lemarignier, *Le gouvernement* [455], p. 181; Bur, *La Champagne* [74], p. 509.

34. Ganshof, *Les homines de generali placito* . . . [126], p. 397; Richard, *Les ducs de Bourgogne* [160], p. 91.

35. Duby, *Recherches sur l'évolution* [112]; on *vicaria* and *vicarii*, cf. pp. 29–31 above.

36. Ganshof, *L'armée* [131].

37. Perroy, *Le monde carolingien* [504], p. 237, shows that the *adjutorium*, which made it possible to mobilize small landowners by calling on the assistance of neighbors, was a palliative used to reinforce the army in the difficult years of 807 and 808. He thinks too that it was a failure. The Carolingian palace may have been inspired by a Visigothic practice, derived in turn from the late empire, cf. the discussion of Ganshof's article in *Settimane . . . di Spoleto* (1967), p. 189. There again it was sometimes the count who decided on the number of those who grouped together to send a man to the army.

38. L. Levillain, *Les statuts d'Adalhard de Corbie*, MA (1900), p. 352.

39. *RHF,* 6: 407.
40. Cf. pp. 51–52 below.
41. Werner, *Heeresorganisation* [170].
42. Guillot, *Le comte d'Anjou* [83], p. 3; Hariulf, *Chronicon* [48], 4, c. 12, p. 205.
43. Boussard, *Services féodaux* [95]. The name *Patericus* evokes Brittany. The "shields" *(scuta)* mentioned here can be compared with the distinction made in 981 between *loricati* and ordinary *clipeati,* Werner, *Heeresorganisation* [170].
44. Bonnassie, *La Catalogne* [72], pp. 158 and 306. By "the rest of royal service" was probably meant the guarding and maintenance of the fortresses. *Publica functio* similarly in Poitou in 989, Garaud, *Les châtelains de Poitou* [81], p. 114; in Provence in 963, Poly, *La Provence* [87], p. 116. The term is usual in Roman formularies, see Toubert, *Le Latium* [89], p. 1067; the horses seized by the lords were still called in 994 *equi publici,* Fournier, *Le peuplement* [80], p. 370.
45. Guillot, *Le comte d'Anjou* [83], p. 379ff. At Saint-Maixent in Poitou, the countess raised the *arrière-ban* in 1023–1026, and the penalty was, as also in Anjou, sixty sous, Garaud, *Les châtelains de Poitou* [81], pp. 114 and 117; Boussard, *Services féodaux* [95], notes the importance of footsoldiers in the Angevin contingents of the eleventh century; Bur, *La Champagne* [74], pp. 367 and 494. Public levies in Normandy, called *publica collecta,* Yver, *Les premières institutions* [175]; Ganshof, *La Flandre* [128], p. 417. In Picardy, levies and provision of fodder, Fossier, *La terre* [79], pp. 495 and 688. For late examples in Burgundy, see Richard, *Les ducs de Bourgogne* [160], p. 138.
46. Dupont, *L'aprision* [119].
47. Boussard, *Services féodaux* [95].
48. Ganshof, *L'armée* [131]; Dhondt, *Le haut Moyen Age* [475], p. 39.
49. The absence of *fodrum* in these areas may also be an ancient tradition. If so it would go back to a capitulary of Charlemagne that exempted Aquitaine, Brühl, *Fodrum* [98], p. 574.
50. Aubenas, *Les châteaux forts* [91]; Bur, *Vestiges d'habitat seigneurial* [99a], distinguishes in Champagne between the great Carolingian fortresses, only sketchily fortified, on rocky spurs, and the eleventh-century castles that reduced the area defended and reinforced it with earthworks and a mound, and lastly the castles or fortified houses built in flat areas and surrounded by water. The same chronology is suggested by Heliot, *Les châteaux forts [143];* on the fortified house, see Richard, *Châteaux* [161]. For quadrangular stone towers of the eleventh century in the west, see Chatelain, *Donjons romans* [101]. On research into medieval castles see *Château-Gaillard. Etudes de castellologie médiévale.* For a general work on castles in medieval France, see Fournier, *Le château* [125].
51. We have borrowed the term from Pierre Toubert's *Le Latium* [89], which uses the Italian historiographical term *incastellamento.*
52. Fournier, *Le peuplement* [80], pp. 330ff. and 373ff.; Desjardin, G., *Cartulaire de l'abbaye de Conques, en Rouergue* (Paris, 1879), no. 1 (Saint-Martin du Larzac); Poly, *La Provence* [87], pp. 76 and 125; Bur, *Vestiges d'habitat seigneurial* [99a]. For Poitou, see Garaud, *Les châtelains de Poitou* [81], p. 16.
53. Fossier, *La terre* [79], pp. 485ff. and 490ff; Chédeville, *Chartres* [76],

p. 268. In Burgundy the new castles date chiefly from the eleventh century, Richard, *Châteaux* [161]; in the Roannais they date from the end of the twelfth century, E. Perroy, "Les Châteaux du Roannais du xı^e au xııı^e siècle," *CCM* (1966): 13.

54. Bur, *La Champagne* [74], p. 367; Chédeville, *Chartres* [76], p. 297; Gauthier, *Vita Johannis episcopi Tervannensis* and the famous description of the castle of Ardres by Lambert, *Historia comitum Ghisensium* [53], c. 127, p. 624; texts quoted and translated in Ch. M. La Roncière, *L'Europe au Moyen Age* (Paris, 1969), t. 2, pp. 152 and 155.

55. Musset, *Les invasions, le second assaut* [502], p. 142; Poly, *La Provence* [87], p. 28.

56. Guillot, *Le comte d'Anjou* [83], p. 281; Aubenas, *Les châteaux forts* [91].

57. *Vita Geraldi* [34], 1: 36 and 39, col. 664 and 665; Garaud, *Les châtelains de Poitou* [81], pp. 16 and 20.

58. 955, *milites* levied in the castles of Auvergne; c. 1102, *totum capitulum militum castri*, Fournier, *Le château* [125], pp. 366 and 368. Bonnassie, *La Catalogne* [72], p. 572, describes the *maisnada* of Mediona.

59. Bonnassie, *La Catalogne* [72], pp. 598 and 603; a similar system in Provence, Poly, *La Provence* [87], p. 152; Ganshof, *La Flandre* [128], p. 399. On Laon, see Bournazel, *Le gouvernement* [418], p. 50. In Anjou things seem to have been rather different; cf. however that of the *oppidanus* of Chaumont, Guillot, *Le comte d'Anjou* [83], p. 331.

60. *De consuetudinibus Burcardi comitis in Vindocino* in Bourel de la Roncière, *Vita Burchardi* [35], p. 33, and the commentary and dating of Lemarignier, *La dislocation* [148], of Boussard, *Services féodaux* [95] and of Guillot, *Le comte d'Anjou* [83], p. 49, n. 231.

61. Duby, *La société* [78], pp. 329 and 161. Lists of guard duties of Picquigny, Fossier, *La terre* [79], p. 671; of Bayeux, Navel, *L'enquête de 1133* [154]; of Logne belonging to the abbey of Stavelot, Ganshof, *Les ministériales* [306], p. 282; Garaud, *Les châtelains de Poitou* [81], pp. 91, 94, 98, and 101 also reveal castle garrisons (notably at Talmont), guard duties of two weeks, and the hiring of extra knights; Chédeville, *Chartres* [76], p. 293, mentions guard duties of two weeks or two months. For Mediona, see Bonnassie, *La Catalogne* [72], p. 572. Such systems did not exclude peasant guard duties and patrols in Anjou, Guillot *Le comte d'Anjou* [83], p. 390, and in Catalonia where they were turned into corvées, Bonnassie, p. 588.

62. Duby, *Les villes du Sud-Est* [531]; Magnou-Nortier, *La société laïque* [86], p. 177; Poly, *La Provence* [87], p. 292; traces of a similar system in Saint-Maixent, Garaud, *Les châtelains de Poitou* [81], p. 98, and in Senlis, Bournazel, *Le gouvernement* [418], p. 48.

63. In Normandy, *bannum id est prohibitio*, with indications of the lower fine of fifteen sous, Yver, *Les premières institutions* [175]; Bonnassie and Poly, *La Provence* [87], in the indexes; Lewis, *The development* [85], p. 310.

64. However, an Angevin text speaks of the *vicaria* of 60 sous, which makes it seem like the *bannum*, Guillot, *Le comte d'Anjou* [83], p. 381.

65. Lot, *La vicaria* [152]; Chédeville, *Chartres* [76], p. 299; Boussard, *Le droit de vicaria* [97]; Garaud, *La construction* [132] and *Les circonscriptions* [133]; Bonnassie, *La Catalogne* [72], do not give any examples; Magnou-Nortier, *La société laïque* [86], p. 184, gives one;

Poly, *La Provence* [87], p. 43, vicarial jurisdiction is almost nonexistent; Devailly, *Le Berry* [77], p. 215; Fournier, *Le peuplement* [80], pp. 451, 536, and 571, for the end of the eleventh century; Duby, *La société* [78], pp. 144 and 257; Richard, *Les ducs de Bourgogne* [160], p. 91; Yver, *Les premières institutions* [175]; Fossier, *La terre* [79], p. 494; Bur, *La Champagne* [74], p. 334. A more general view for the west and north can be found in Koch, *L'origine* [145].

66. Magnou-Nortier, *La société laïque* [86], p. 173; Bonnassie, *La Catalogne* [72], p. 589; Fossier, *La terre* [79], p. 495.
67. Lemarignier, *La dislocation* [148]; Yver, *Les premières institutions* [175]; Bur, *La Champagne* [74], p. 336; Chédeville, *Chartres* [76], p. 301.
68. The use of the word to mean a piece of land is rivaled or replaced by other terms: *centena, ministerium* in Rouergue, *aicis* in Auvergne, the Limousin and Quercy, the Celtic *condita* in the Loire area, *ager* in the Rhone area.
69. Cf. the table in Devailly, *Le Berry* [77], p. 75.
70. Fournier, *Le peuplement* [80], pp. 509 and 389.
71. Bonnassie, *La Catalogne* [72], p. 581; Garaud, *Les châtelains du Poitou* [81], p. 170. On the distinction between provosts [*prévôts*] and "hundred-men" [*voyers*] in the Loire area: Halphen, *Prévôts et voyers* [141], Boussard, *Le gouvernement* [420], pp. 316 and 319, and Guillot, *Le comte d'Anjou* [83], p. 403. In the Midi, *vicarius* in the twelfth century refers to an urban officer, Poly, *La Provence* [87], pp. 50 and 227.
72. Bonnassie, *La Catalogne* [72], p. 173.
73. Duby, *La société* [78], p. 254; Génicot, *Les premières mentions* [135]; Poly, *La Provence* [87], p. 134; Bonnassie, *La Catalogne* [72], p. 590. For a chronology and geography of customs, cf. Duby, *L'économie rurale* [300], p. 452.
74. Garaud, *La construction* [132], p. 134; Chédeville, *Chartres* [76], p. 297; Bur, *La Champagre* [74], p. 371; Poly, *La Provence* [87], p. 134.
75. Bonnassie, *La Catalogne* [72], p. 592.
76. Perrin, *Recherches* [156], p. 664; Bonnassie, *La Catalogne* [72], p. 595; Poly, *La Provence* [87], p. 224.
77. Halphen, *La lettre* [194], p. 222, n. 2, quotes a text that speaks of "farming" rather than the purchase of a position [*achat de charge*]. Examples of the sharing of profits are in Bonnassie, *La Catalogne* [72], p. 600ff.
78. Chédeville, *Chartres* [76], p. 289 (which relates to 153 donations); Bonnassie, *La Catalogne* [72], pp. 578 and 893.
79. Bonnassie, *La Catalogne* [72], p. 577; Poly, *La Provence* [87], pp. 118 and 131.
80. Perrin, *Recherches* [156], p. 667.
81. The word appears around the year 1000 in Anjou, Poitou, and Champagne, Guillot, *Le comte d'Anjou* [83], p. 370; Garaud, *La construction* [132], p. 114; Bur, *La Champagne* [74], p. 365. Around the middle of the century in the Chartrain, Auvergne, Picardy, Berry, Chédeville, *Chartres* [76], p. 294; Fournier, *Le peuplement* [80], p. 111; Fossier, *La terre* [79], p. 563; Devailly, *Le Berry* [77], p. 216; or in the Midi, Magnou-Nortier, *La société laïque* [86], p. 74; Bonnassie, *La Catalogne* [72], p. 589; Poly, *La Provence* [87], p. 123. A general work, Lemarignier, *La dislocation* [148].

82. Duby, *La société* [78], p. 174.
83. The distinction between domainal income and public customs was still made in the early eleventh century, Lemarignier, *La dislocation* [148], p. 294.
84. Duby, *La société* [78], p. 175; Lewis, *The development* [85], p. 310; Garaud, *Les châtelains du Poitou* [81], pp. 22 and 24; Fossier, *La terre* [79], p. 389; Duby, *La carte instrument de recherche* [114].
85. Garaud, *Les châtelains du Poitou* [81], p. 158. The new character of these extensions is perfectly expressed by a pair of synonyms from Poitou of 1029, *malae consuetudines = malae adinventiones*, Sanfaçon, *Défrichements* [88], p. 17; Guillot, *Le comte d'Anjou* [83], p. 371; Bur, *La Champagne* [74], p. 365; Duby, *Recherches* [112]; Garaud, *Les châtelains du Poitou* [81], p. 113; Fossier, *La terre* [79], p. 454; Génicot, *Les premières mentions* [135]; Poly, *La Provence* [87], p. 133; Fournier, *Le peuplement* [80], pp. 370 and 389; Chédeville, *Chartres* [76], p. 294.
86. Lemarignier, *Le gouvernement* [455], tables.
87. On contemporary evidence, see pp. 174–75 below.
88. The work of Senn, *L'institution des avoueries* [164], which delineates on p. 104 the area covered by the institution, has to be complemented with, for Lorraine, Parisse, *La noblesse lorraine* [261], p. 59ff, and, for Champagne, Bur, *La Champagne* [74], p. 343. Advocacy was equally important in Flanders, Ganshof, *La Flandre* [128], pp. 365 and 372; it was nonexistent in Normandy, Yver, *Autour de l'absence d'avouerie* [174]. On the right to provide protection in the Mâcon area that was of different origin, see Duby, *La société* [78], p. 185.
89. Ganshof, *L'immunité* [129].
90. Magnou-Nortier, *La société laïque* [86], p. 589.
91. Fossier, *La terre* [79] p. 497; La Motte Colas, "Les possessions territoriales de l'abbaye de Saint-Germain-des-Prés . . . ," *RHEF* (1957): 49.
92. These conclusions are qualified by Génicot, *Monastères* [137].
93. Mabillon, *AA SS OSB*, saec. 6, pars 1, p. 648; Fournier, *Le peuplement* [80], p. 371; Magnou-Nortier, *La société laïque* [86], pp. 170, 190, 245, 298 and 623ff.; Bonnassie, *La Catalogne* [72], p. 181.
94. *Form. Turon.*, 45 and Marculf, 2: 31, *MGH, Formulae*, p. 159 and p. 95; *Lex Wisig.* 5: 5, quoted in Bonnassie, *La Catalogne* [72], p. 740.
95. Duparc, *La commendise* [117]; *Vita Geraldi* [34], 1: 41, col. 667. Boso's oath to Count Gerard probably signified the renunciation at the time of the foundation of the abbey of a *comenda* previously granted by the latter to the former.
96. Duparc, *Le sauvement* [116]; Bur, *La Champagne* [74], p. 363; Duparc, *Le tensement* [118]; Devailly, *Le Berry* [77], p. 212; traces in the Chartres area where we find the significant synonym *tutela*, Chédeville, *Chartres* [76], p. 299.
97. Lemarignier, *Autour d'un diplôme* [151]; Duby, *La société* [78], pp. 147, 168 and 518.
98. Lemarignier, *De l'immunité* [150].
99. Bur, *La Champagne* [74], p. 178, and a résumé of theses in Sassier, *Pouvoir comtal*, p. 4; Richard, *Les ducs de Bourgogne* [160], p. 56; P. Lauer, *Robert Ier et Raoul de Bourgogne* (Paris, 1910), p. 300.
100. Perret, *Les concessions* [155].

101. Perret, *Les concessions* [155]; Poly, *La Provence* [87], p. 204; Despy, *Serfs* [292].
102. Génicot, *L'économie namuroise* [247], 1: 24, recalls this dichotomy. As recently as 1970 a medievalist as acute as Robert Boutruche could declare:

> It is our opinion that the great domain of the early Middle Ages was the seat of powers resulting from the discipline that the master enforced in his household. Communal life requires an organisation and methods of control ensured by a set of legal rules. It was necessary to keep the peace in the village, regulate it and oversee it. Widespread after 900, these prerogatives had their origins in the wealth or the social quality of the richest and the absence of power from above. . . . They developed within the ancient domains, reached the places where the powerful had no land, took into their clutches the allodialists. . . .

Boutruche, *Seigneurie* [98], 2: 126. Robert Fossier gives a timely reminder in *La terre* [79], p. 518, that "it was the *ban* which was the decisive element for success, but it was only possible to grant or usurp it by reason of the landowning basis on which the master's authority depended." To this extent only the "domainalist" point of view had some basis, but, notwithstanding the attempts Fossier makes to take into account the upheavals caused by the creating of banal lordship, he continues when all is said and done to depend on the idea that communal peasant life had been unable for many years to exist outside the framework of the great estate—an assumption that today is challenged, cf. chapter 8.

103. Cf. the critique of Georges Duby of Léo Verriest's integral domainialism in *Les idées* [113]. Léopold Génicot, in his study of *Les premières mentions de droits bannaux dans la région de Liège* [135], stresses that the new rights

> presupposed lords who were sufficiently free and strong to be able to guarantee or impose on the peasants the protection of their castles and to make them pay dearly for this protection. They presupposed above all an economic expansion which would increase the peasant's ability to contribute. . . . These conditions were certainly met in France around 1050, but it seems unlikely that they were before 1000.

CHAPTER 2

Honorable Dependence

The emperor, your master, does not hold for himself alone the power which comes from his own virtue. He allows his men each free use of his personal power; in this way he shares between them the regions of his kingdom, in the belief that this will make them more faithful and more submissive. This is far from being the case!
—The caliph of Cordoba to John of Gorze

For a long time historians saw feudalism as a tragic stuggle between the dim but enduring memory of the Roman *respublica*—respected ancestor of our own state—and the bond of man to man felt by them to be an inevitable evil. Thus was explained the "inevitable" decline of Charlemagne and his successors. It was a provisional setback neverthe-less: happier times would come when the *respublica* was born again from the ashes and the state, that eternal or almost eternal form, would exist again. Between the passion and the resurrection, there occurred the dark interval of feudal society, when the reaction to the dislocation of public institutions was the emergence of the so-called feudo-vassalic relationship.

This version of events has long since been revised, although it has not ceased, slowly, to be enriched. Research must be directed prin-cipally toward the old texts, with a more careful reading of the hetero-genous medieval Latin, a learned language that was both distant and familiar. It was distant when it was taught in the schools, which were concerned with beautiful style, speaking of real facts only through metaphors. It was familiar when it hastily dressed up a more familiar Romance language. This contrast is not only between north and south, or between the decline or the renaissance of culture. It is also a contrast between social classes, or even between two similar individuals in different situations. Thus it has been necessary and it is still necessary

for historiography to take the reverse of the attitude of a whole generation of historians who tried to reduce these contradictions in levels of
language and word systems by use of forced analogies—a procedure
already found in medieval glossaries and before that in the *interpretatio romana* of Celtic and Germanic societies.

In 1157, legates from Hadrian IV arrived at the court of Frederick
Barbarossa, bearing a pontifical letter. Reminding the emperor of his
coronation, the pope promised him yet more favors—*majora beneficia.*
The imperial chancellor, a crafty jurist, translated *beneficium* by
lehen, fief, backed up by the customary usage of his own notaries.
Hearing it said that their emperor held his crown from the pope, the
German courtiers had to be restrained from attacking the legates.
Moving to the other end of Europe, to Castile, we find the clerks of the
canons of the council of Burgos in 1117 writing: *feudum quod in
Ispania prestimonium vocant.* But sometimes a clause will reveal the
uncertainty of those who used such an improper assimilation: one
chronicler speaks of the *feuda temporalia,* referring to the old concessions *ad tempus* given to reward the fidelity of the Castilian magnates.[1]

The uniting of fief and vassalage, the characteristic structure of
feudalism, was, when the feudal crisis broke out, both ancient and
restricted to relatively small social groups. It is this period of the
formation of the feudo-vassalic bond, before the establishment of the
banal lordships made it more general and widespread, that we shall
now examine.

Fideles and Vassals

In prefeudal society, man was never isolated. Beyond the bonds of
family, free men entered into multiple and complex relationships that
formed a network of social links that were often very strong.
Charlemagne, conscious of his high mission and of worldly realities,
wished to attract and orientate these links to his own person in order
that, through his own glory, the intentions of Providence and the City
of God should be accomplished.

The classic analysis has for many years identified in the period of the
formation of the feudo-vassalic bond two principal elements: a "personal" element, the act of homage, and a "real" element, the fief. This
formulation, clear but oversimple, cannot today entirely satisfy us,
both because of the anachronistic nature of the categories used—
personal-real—and because of the analysis that it implies *a priori,* the
shifting of the center of gravity from the personal element to the "real"
element being supposed to mark the change from a passionate and
almost mystical conception of the bond of vassalage to a more "mate-
rialist" interpretation. Nevertheless, this analysis contains an interesting contrast, and one that we shall take up.

The Origins of Vassalage and Fealty

When the dependent warriors, who were to give domination over the greater part of Western Europe into the hands of a few Austrasian leaders, appeared on the scene, very different juridical traditions were coexistent. *Vassus*, "young boy," the key word of vassalage, an institution that is thought to be, at least in the Carolingian period, typically Frankish, is an old Gallic word, a word from the "vulgar" tongue. Of all the terms used to refer to the "freemen in dependence" of a "suite," the *ingenui in obsequio—bucellarii, soldurii, gasindi* and, for the king, *antrustiones—vassus* was the only term to survive, with what success we know. It had, like the Latin *puer*, three meanings: "One when we call slaves 'boy,' the next when we say 'boy' as opposed to girl, and the third when we mean childhood."[2] *Vassi* appear as humble dependents in the Salic Law from the sixth century and in a Neustrian formulary, that of Marculf. In the seventh century, on the other hand, in Alsace and Swabia the *vassi* maintained by the magnates in their household were probably free men, since they attended the assembly.[3]

In order to become a *vassus* it was necessary to entrust oneself to another, *se commendare*. The term, from classical usage, refers in the second quarter of the eighth century to a precise type of *convenientia*, as defined in the famous formula of Tours.

> He who recommends himself to the power of another. To the magnificent lord [name], I [name] . . . I have neither food nor clothing. I have begged of your pity . . . to deliver me into your protection . . . in such a way that you will succour me and support me with food and clothing in order that I may serve you and be worthy of you and for as long as I live, I must offer you *servitium* and *obsequium* in the manner of a free man. . . . And it is agreed that if one of us two wishes to withdraw from these *convenientiae* he shall pay a certain sum to the other, that this *convenientia* will remain firm (in duplicate).[4]

Thus the deed assimilates a free but poor man with the freed man, *libertus*, who owed his master *obsequium*. And as the text shows clearly, this is a two-way contract: the two parties help one another reciprocally, the obligations on both sides being reinforced by a penalty clause, while a copy of the contract is given to each party as a proof.

That excellent jurist François-Louis Ganshof was temporarily perplexed by this text when he commented on it: not only does it not breathe a word of the *intermixtio manuun* (joining of hands), so characteristic of what was later to be called homage, which could if necessary be explained, but above all it implies that it is through the *convenientia* that the bond is formed. In that case what is the point of the giving of hands? From this he makes this too ingenious interpretation, quite unjustified by anything in the text: "The essential part of the act . . . only creates a secondary obligation, to wit a penalty clause sanctioning the obligations of the parties to the principal legal act which is the recommendation." Having disassociated the "essential part of the act" and the "principal legal act," F. L. Ganshof asks himself how the latter was concluded and hypothesizes a "gesture of the hand" [*Handgebärde*] of which furthermore there is an indication preserved in the formula of the oath of antrustion. And he admits, with much honesty, that "this is possible, probable . . . it is not certain, and wisdom demands that we confess our lack of knowledge." Nevertheless, he concludes: "All that one can assert is that the contract was concluded verbally and in conformity with a ritual: that was the general custom of the time."

What makes the ritual of the giving of hands "probable"? A text of a later date than the Tours formula, the fragment of the *Annales regni Francorum* that relates the submission of the Duke of Bavaria Tassilo to King Pepin, is unambiguous: "Tassilo, duke of Bavaria, came there, commending himself in vassalage with his hands . . . like a vassal to his master." Elizabeth Magnou-Nortier and Michel Rouche have drawn attention to two important texts: the first is the "Malberg" gloss *vassus, id est horogavo*; thus, the need was felt among the Franks of the sixth century to translate *vassus*. This type of synonym, far from establishing the identity of the two institutions, rather allows us to glimpse the differences between them. The second text, a revision of the *Annales regni Francorum*, reinforces this impression of duality when it adds to the description of the vassalage of Tassilo this short but instructive phrase, *more francico*.[5] Thus there was a Frankish way of commending oneself, by the giving of hands, which leads one to suppose that there was at least one other way of doing it, and this could well be *without* the giving of hands.[6] The synonym *vassus id est horogavo* would then be, as with so many others, an approximation that conceals from us the profound divergence on this essential point between two cultures, one, that of the *convenientia*, of the contract, and the other that of the ritual, the giving of hands.

Whether or not ritual or *convenientia* were involved and whatever the habitual content of the obligation created, vassalage and *commendatio* are certainly in origin marks of an unequal exchange, the instruments by which the most desperate of the poor subjected themselves to the power of the powerful.

Now there is the thorny problem of the pledge of loyalty *(fides)* and *fidelitas*. Although the "covenants of *commendatio*" make no mention of it, we cannot exclude the possibility from this period onward of a confirmatory oath; the insistence of a certain number of canonical texts on specifying or limiting the practice of confirming an agreement with an oath leads one to imagine its force and its frequency. In the tenth century, the covenants in the south were very frequently if not always followed by an oath. And if such an act affirms that "faith is not in the hand but in the words and the spirit," should we for that reason see a condemnation of the oath,[7] or, more likely, a reminder of its profound significance, conforming with the line of the canonical texts?

Or could it be a sign of defiance toward practices that were probably too Germanic and still pagan or paganizing?

We can only understand the *fidelitas* of the *vassus* by reference to three other forms of pledge: those created by the *trustis*, the *securitas*, and the *leudesamium*. The *trustis*, a group of warriors in arms bound by an oath, was certainly very ancient among the Franks; there had been local *trustes*, led by a chosen *centenarius*, who pursued thieves. Later texts mention only the *trustis dominica*, the royal "great guard," even though they sometimes indicate that certain men created their *trustis* only to devote it to banditry. At the period when Marculf's formula is able to give us a hint of what it was like, the promise of the royal antrustion, an important personage and quite different from the *vassus*, took place not only with the characteristic gesture of the *immixtio manuum*, with *both* hands, but by an oath in the hand of the king, "that is to say, by touching with one's hand the hand of the king."[8] Thus it is only partly true to consider the *vassi regales* as being identical with the antrustions. Some Carolingian texts seem to invite this by speaking still of the "royal *trustis*"; but the magnates who wished or had to submit themselves to the king were now doing it by "hands in hands," like the *horogavo* and the *vassi more francico*. The *trustis* was an ancient institution of free warriors—the same could not be said of Frankish-style vassalage, at least in the beginning.

The oaths of safety, *securitates*—later called assurances—are no less difficult to interpret. They are found both in Marculf and in the more Romanizing formularies, such as those of Tours or Angers. The Frankish and more generally Germanic pseudosynonym seems to have been *treuwa*, and the word itself implies fidelity, *treue*. People had recourse to these oaths in order to resolve feuds between kinsmen. Thus the *securitates* along with the system of composition formed an essential part of the machinery that controlled social violence.[9] When at the beginning of the eleventh century the count of Poitiers forced two important members of his entourage to call a truce—*treva*—it was said that he "had taken their two right hands"; these right hands were then "put in brief," that is to say, in writing. A few years later we find in the Midi oaths made "to you who hold me by the hand," presumably the right hand.[10] The gesture, or one of the gestures, of the *treuwa* was thus the same as that of the antrustion, with just one difference, albeit an essential one: the antrustion bore arms, those swearing to the truce very probably did not. It remains to assure ourselves that the doublet *securitas-treuwa* was really a synonym from the start; nothing is less sure.

Lastly there is the *leudesamium*, the oath of fealty made by all free men to the king. This tradition already existed in the southern countries, and the frequency of the institution would tempt one to look for its origins in the late Roman period,[11] despite a Frankish synonym. Like Ferdinand Lot, we will reject immediately the false analogy *leudes regis-leudesamium* (the king's people are not precisely the same as the "assembly of people").[12] In Marculf's time, this oath involved the touching of a *res sacra* (holy relic); later ancient custom made it a more negative thing, similar to the truces. Its collective character made the *fidelitas regi-leudesamium* a *conjuratio*. It would be interesting to compare this oath of fealty with other *conjurationes*, which seem by contrast to be well rooted in the Frankish past, and with those "oaths to guilds which are taken reciprocally," proper associations for mutual help, which supplied charity for the soul of a dead man, aid in the case of fire, or support after a shipwreck, or even, in the tradition of the ancient *trustes*, defense and the pursuit of thieves. The oath was sworn and drunk in the name of the king and St. Stephen, and these *Stephan* or *Karlsminne* recall the very ancient *Wodansminne*. But we learn from a capitulary that the oath was not the only way to create these forbidden unions; they could also be "affirmed by the right hands," *firmare per dextras.*[13] In all these cases we see that the oath can exist alongside a ritual with the right hand that is very different from homage, and which it would be better to compare to the *paumée*.

In the texts from before the ninth century, it is probable that two distinct traditions coexisted under the name *fides-fidelitas*. One goes back to the Roman *sponsio*, which had for a long time been confused with a written promise, and which therefore, as can be seen in the opinion of the Church Fathers, places little emphasis on the oath, even if sometimes it had to adapt to it. The other tradition appears to have had its roots in a continuing tradition of clannish leagues and confraternities, still strongly influenced by magic ritual. The promise of vassalage, of warrior tradition, made by homage and perhaps already reinforced by an oath, was probably only common in the entourages of some of the Austrasian or Alaman chiefs. It was from these different traditions that the Carolingian dynasty was to try to construct and extend its own type of vassalage. Royal policy in this area had three different threads: an extension of vassalage, an attempt to limit the use of oaths to those under royal control, and a renewal and reinforcing of the old *leudesamium*.

As the new Frankish monarchy reconquered the lands formerly subject to the Merovingians, it set up garrisons from which the bond of vassalage started to spread. Thus after the disaster of Roncesvalles in 778, Charlemagne and his counsellors carried out what we would call a purge of the leading figures in Aquitaine, counts and abbots, and substituted "many of those other men who are called in the vulgar tongue *vassi*, of Frankish race." When southerners such as the Spanish who had fled to Septimania wanted "to commend themselves" to the counts, they were to do it *more solito . . . apud nostrates homines.* Vassalage "in the Frankish style" was also beginning to spread in the Midi.[14]

Not only did the Carolingians start to introduce far from their ancestral homes a system of domiciling their armed dependents, they also carried vassalage to a social level that until then had been ignorant of it—to the future "imperial aristocracy." The best example is the powerful and proud duke of Bavaria, Tassilo. After his defeat he was ordered by the palace to "commend himself in vassalage," in other words, he should place himself vis-à-vis the king in that humble position of submission of the *vassi*. In 838, we know that the bishops, abbots, counts and *vassi dominici* of Neustria offered the *commendatio* "by the hands" to the king. Even the sons of the king commended themselves to him and he would sometimes remind them that they were his vassals.[15] There multiplied in the kingdom particularly the *vassi dominici* or *vassi regales*. These "Vassals of the Lord" should not be confused with the vassals without domicile, *pauperiores vassi*, who formed the greater part of the king's guard; the former were people who, as the texts of 838 remind us, were members of the *primores* of their province. Already the capitularies of 792–93 on the taking of the oath indicate that they were swearing fealty directly to the *missi*, royal commissioners such as the bishops or the counts—a sign both of their social importance and of their distance from the palace.[16]

To begin with, these *vassi regales* were Franks, endowed by the favor of the prince not with a few acres but with generous estates carved out of the Church's lands, with at least thirty, sometimes fifty, a hundred, or even two hundred manses—as many as the richest counts.[17] These benefices constitute the most obvious part of the fortunes of these men. Quite different, in our opinion, is the situation of a certain number of large allodialists in the south who entered into royal vassalage. Thus the Spaniard John, a powerful *aprisiator* who had set himself up in the Narbonne area with many of his entourage, had agreed to commend himself by hands to Charlemagne and had become a *vassus regalis*. A century later, Gerald of Aurillac, a rich allodialist who also had a large entourage of *milites*, was a royal vassal, as was the redoubtable Ebbes of Déols in Berry or in the Spanish marches Estève and Theodosius. Was it the lure of benefices that caused these southern magnates to become royal vassals, or was it rather the concession by the king of a priceless privilege—that of the right both to judge the men of their cantons and to keep out of their lands the Frankish count and his men?[18]

At the end of the ninth century, four sorts of *vassi* coexisted in the territories of the empire. First, there were the military servants without benefice, then other more fortunate men who were the prosperous owners of four to twelve manses. Both these types were grouped in bodies attached to a bishop, an abbot, a count, or else to a royal vassal. For the writers of the capitularies, all these people are little more honorable than the *vassi* of the sixth century. On the social ladder they are placed between the ordinary free men of the county, *pagenses*, and the peasant tenant farmers, *coloni*. Paul the Deacon, a Lombard who had come into the service of the Franks, judged the submission of the vassal to be little better than that of the *servus*, inspired by the fear of blows, and he says scornfully of the bad monk: "If it is because of the *professio* which he has made that he serves God, then he is [no more than] a vassal."[19] The two other groups, Frankish and southern *vassi regales*, are on the other hand much closer to the upper aristocracy of the empire, with whom they have in common the acceptance of the humble posture of submission that had originated in the entourage of the Austrasian servitors.

The bonds of vassalage in Carolingian times were thus to be found on two quite distinct social levels, that of the big or very big land-owners on the one hand, that of the warrior units on the other. Other-wise, many were probably still oblivious, or wished to be, of vassalage. Then Charlemagne had no option but to turn to a bond that no one could in principle refuse him, the oath of fealty to the king, and attempt to make a daring but dangerous amalgam out of that. In order to give greater importance to the oath to the king, it was first necessary to attack the practice of taking mutual oaths. As a result the popular oaths were harshly condemned, whatever their purposes.

After 779, after the defeat of Roncesvalles that was to lead to the repossession of Aquitaine by Charlemagne, mutual oaths—*ghildes-gildoniae*—were forbidden, even when they supported charitable asso-ciations or were for mutual aid in cases of disaster such as shipwreck or fire. Ten years later this prohibition was reaffirmed for Aquitaine. In 805 the prohibitions were renewed, in 821 against servile organization, in 857 against those who organized *trustes*, in 884 against the bands of villagers "that are vulgarly known as guilds." And was it not the same insistence on a "horizontal" fealty that is dictated a century later in the charter of franchises of Cardona in Catalonia: "If one of you wants to be above the others, let him be treated as a youth . . . if some evil man rises up against you to attack you, rise up, all of you, against him to fight him and to kill him, as you may with the help of God."[20]

From 779 the only vows that were in principle authorized in the empire were those "made to us or else to each lord for our utility and his" and also those "that men owe to one another reciprocally, accord-ing to the law"—in other words, the oath to the king, the oath of the vassal, and the judicial oath.[21] In this way Charlemagne turned the tradition of the oath to his own advantage. Nevertheless, as we can tell from the renewed prohibitions, the habit of collective and reciprocal promises made with a vow continued among those unknown people dismissed rather too hastily in the capitularies as *pauperiores*.

We can understand why the vow of fealty to the king had fallen into disuse at the end of the seventh century: when some of the magnates were to share out the pieces of the *regnum francorum*,[22] neither the duke of the Aquitani, the patricians of Provence and Burgundy, or the palatine mayors wished to administer the venerable *leudesamium* in the name of the Merovingian puppet. As for substituting their names for his, the time had not yet come for that. After his coronation, Pepin did not yet dare administer the oath except to the princes—and there is not agreement even on this fact. In 786, his son Charlemagne only required it from the Thuringian and Franconian aristocrats involved in the Hardrad conspiracy. In these two cases it is not clear which oath was at stake, *securitas* or *leudesamium*? In 787, it was the entire population of Benevento that took the oath to the king, and in 789, that oath was extended to the whole kingdom in the simple and no doubt ancient form: "I promise to my lord the king Charles and to his sons that I am faithful and will be so all the days of my life without fraud or deception."

It is striking to see how this simple formula becomes in the course of time modified and more complicated. In 802 it is specified: "Faithful as an upright man should be to his lord," which is an explicit reference to the situation of the vassal. Why this innovation? The capitularies provide the answer: the introduction of this reference was to oppose a negative view of the fealty due to the king, a view that had apparently been very widespread until then. "Many people have thought until now that fealty to the emperor was only for his life and that it consisted of an obligation not to bring an enemy into his kingdom for hostile purposes, nor to consent to or conceal an infidelity towards him." That is clear: fealty to the king for those who lived in the empire consisted, at least until 802, of respecting the king's person and his property. It was in no way different from the oath of *securitas*, except perhaps in the obligation to reveal aggressions of the same type.[23]

The campaign of explanation that the *missi* were ordered to carry out among the population led in the same direction as the introduction of the clause *sicut homo*. They had to show "how numerous and how big" were the duties arising from this oath. Not only did it contain other negative requirements, like the prohibition against usurping royal lands or benefices, harming churches, widows, or orphans, or cheating the law, but also positive duties such as paying taxes, carrying out imperial orders, and above all answering the call to arms. Those who were unconvinced were reminded of the penalty for perjury, the amputation of the right hand. It remains to be seen whether such a campaign was successful in materially changing people's ways of thinking and behaving.[24]

The introduction of the clause *sicut homo* did not of course make free men into vassals of the king. It was a means of combating the negative character and passive content of the oath of fealty: a free man should not be content merely to respect the king, he must also serve him, like the vassal his lord.[25]

It is significant that the reign of Charles the Bald marked a reversal of the royal policy of bringing the oath of fealty to the king closer to vassalage. The formula was modified once again in 854, the clause *sicut homo domino suo* being changed to *sicut francus homo suo regi*, which is a clear indication of a quite different conception of the oath. This conception can be seen to develop in parallel in the official texts and in the writings of Hincmar, the leader of what some have called the episcopal faction, a sign that of the counsellors of the king, it was the bishops who had the most influence. We know that Hincmar was personally very hostile to the *immixtio manuum* of the bishops.[26] The humble posture of the commended man was always seen as something degrading or at least not very honorable, a clear indication of total submission. And the vocabulary of the great assemblies of the years 843–877, such as Coulaines and Quiersy, evokes the image of a royal government whose mission it was to ensure the reign of law. It is not hard to see why such a conception was favored by the bishops, and one can understand the favorable judgements passed by a number of modern historians on this policy.[27] The underlying power struggle and political situation regarding this question have long been understood.[28] The contractual monarchy of Coulaines was no more nor less than the plan of government of the magnates. For all that, a man who rejected the idea of vassalage for himself did not hesitate to use it to subjugate others. The clause *sicut homo seniori suo* reappears in the oath of the turbulent Hincmar of Laon, after his condemnation. Fulk of Rheims at the end of the century invested his suffragans *more beneficiali*, an indication that he was confusing the promise of obedience and the oath of vassalage. *More beneficiali:* this expression alone is enough to show the degree to which the benefice had become, at the end of the ninth century, an essential element of the bond of vassalage.[29]

Origin and Evolution of the Fief

The history of the idea of the fief is no less varied than those of the acts of homage and fealty. Here too we find ourselves faced with an apparent doublet: *beneficium-fevum*. We will examine this first in the north and then in the Midi.

In the north we find the synonym given in 1036–43 in the Vermandois and in 1087 in a deed from Hainaut: *beneficium quod vulgo dicitur feodum*.[30] But from when does it really date?

Beneficium can be found in the Merovingian formularies, which we know often consist of Roman law in the vulgar tongue, or what remained of it. The term embraces a whole category of contracts: the *precaria*, the loan of a sum of money (without interest?), a gift to a servant, or usufruct allowed to a seller.[31] All the contracts basically involved the same social relationship: the subjection of the *humiliores* to the *potentes*.

Let us imagine a school example: once upon a time there was a powerful man. Some small allodialists lived not far from his *villa*, their farms lying among those of his *coloni*, "poor people," he said when speaking of them. One fine day, or rather one bad month, the allodialists had a poor harvest. The winter had been too cold, the spring too wet, or else perhaps Frankish or other soldiers had passed through. Anyhow, they turned to the lord of the area. First of all the powerful man lent the unfortunate peasants some money or some corn. That was the first "good deed" *(beneficium)*. When the famine or difficulties persisted, they were not able to pay the powerful man back, so they sold him their land. He allowed them the income from the land. That was the second "good deed." And if they died? The powerful man conceded the land to them in *precaria* to their descendants. That was the third "good deed." And if misfortunes should continue? They could become servants of the powerful man and if he was pleased with their service he would crown his fatherly generosity with a last "good deed"—the gift of a plot of land on which to spend their last days. Thus was favor allied to precariousness. For the charity and benevolence of the powerful man are fragile. Let us take the case of the gift, apparently clear-cut, made to the servant. According to Roman law this could quite well be revoked for ingratitude, and one wonders how many servants were judged to be ungrateful by the benefactors to whom they owed everything. What had been given could quite well be taken back.[32]

There remained a fifth "good deed," which Michel Rouche, in the continuation of the studies of Claudio Sanchez-Albornoz,[33] rightly brings to our attention. This was a particular form of benefice, the *beneficium pro stipendio*, or *ad stipendium*, granted by the public power, *potestas publica*, or the state as we would say, to someone who participated in the *functio publica* and who needed to be paid. Here we definitely find the notion of service: like the soldier's wage, which it replaced, the *beneficium pro stipendio* was allowed in advance for a service and lasted as long as the service but no longer.

This was not always clearly understood or accepted by some barbarians. The widow of the ex-mayor of the palace Badegisel refused to return that which had been given to her husband, saying "It was his wage *(milicia)*." Gregory of Tours, who attributes these words to her, clearly saw this as abnormal.[34] But was the evil Frankish widow thinking in terms of *stipendium*? We shall return to this. Suffice it to say that the idea of service, absent in the case of "private" *beneficia*, except in the diffuse form of recognition or of actions that needed to be rewarded, is on the contrary closely linked to the *beneficium pro stipendio*, an exception to common law because it is an act of the public power.

We only have to read Hincmar of Rheims's *Pro Ecclesiae libertatum defensione* to see the similarity in the ideas he has of the benefice and of the old *beneficium pro stipendio*. In his treaty Hincmar tackles the question of the *beneficia de rebus ecclesiasticis*, that is, of the domiciling of knights who made up the ecclesiastical *scarae* of the north, those of the great abbeys or bishoprics such as the *milites remenses*. For Hincmar, the *beneficium de rebus ecclesiasticis* is a *roga*, a wage, the *stipendium* of the *milites* of the *exercitus*. If a man could no longer perform his service, then he should no longer hold his benefice, unless his son could replace him. The archbishop states bluntly: "If you do not raise the calf, you cannot harness the ox to the plough."[35] We know from the correspondance of Lupus of Ferrières how heavy a plough for the men of his abbey was the Carolingian war machine. This clearly functional view has little to do with the famous bond of man to man: the powerful did not attach knights to themselves, but rather nourished soldiers as one would raise cattle. We are in quite another situation from that of the dependants of the Frankish or Alaman aristocracy. The leaders of the powerful northern churches, also heirs of the civilization of the Roman Empire, knew the meaning of *potestas publica*. The *beneficium* of which Hincmar speaks is the public *beneficium*, which cannot be compared with that of the formularies.

Nevertheless, the latter continued to be used by the southern magnates. Thus Gerald of Aurillac "did not lightly give benefices, but rarely took back what he had given." Some others of his powerful neighbors were less fair, and Gerald, always a charitable man, had to intervene on behalf of the *vassi*, objects of his solicitude, whom his biographer places among the ranks of the humble: "He would not allow a lord to take away the benefice of a *vassus* on a sudden impulse; (when that happened) he would mention the affair, and half by prayer and half by authority he would calm the impulse of a hasty anger."[36] Such variations in meaning remind us of the need for prudence: when the texts tell us that the *vassi* of a certain lord, for example the duke of Alsace, received benefices, we cannot be sure whether they received them when still of a age to carry out their functions as warriors, along the lines of *beneficium de rebus ecclesiasticis*, or whether in their old age they received the reward due to a loyal servant. We still do not know whether or not *beneficium* conceals its future equivalent, *feo*.

Fehu, we learn from the lexicographers, was either a valuable movable possession, or livestock. This very ancient term does not appear in the Frankish sources of the Merovingian period, but its use at the same time period in England is much more frequent than might be realized from the traditionally accepted interpretations. It was not just a precious object, but a form of gift, which created bonds of peace. In the Carolingian period, the Franks too had an ancient tradition of the giving of a gift of friendship. "*Francisco more veterno . . . equum necnon, ut solet, arma simul,*" writes Ermoldus Nigellus when evoking the horses and arms given by Louis the Pious to the Danish King Harold, which is what in England would have been called a *feoh-gyfte*. Only Harold, unlike the Anglian warriors, kneels down before Louis and places his hands in his;[37] in the early ninth century, in the Frankish court, the *immixtio manuum*, the *horogavo*, usually accompanied the ancient ritual gift.

However, *feo* hardly appears at all in the Frankish texts. The royal chancery appears to have been loath to use the word, and this was also the case with those who drew up charters. Could this be because the idea was one that they found it difficult to assimilate? The only early example of such usage is the one found at the end of a formulary from Sens at the end of the seventh century. It is a rather biting polemic between the bishops of Paris and of Tours, referring particularly to the role played by the latter with regard to his old protector, the mayor of the palace Grimoald, at the time of his fall in 656. The relevant passage of this prolix satire runs:

> He who forgets the man who helped him
> And banishes the memory of his provider
> Tramples right and honor under foot.
> He who forgets the gift of a *feo*
> And the acquirer of his former allod
> Is a filthy pig who spews up his honor.[38]

The word from the vulgar tongue has crept in, with others, through such invectives. But the epigram is aiming at a very precise juridical situation, no doubt one in which Robert of Tours had been in relation to Grimoald: an allodialist who, having been helped by a powerful man, sold his allodial land to him, though retaining the income, which a notary would have called *beneficium*. But the ungrateful "client" "forgot" his fallen protector; more than that, he had assisted in his fall and having become bishop took it upon himself to shut up the protector's wife in one of the city monasteries. What is Robert's adversary insisting upon here? On the contract, the *convenientia?* On *fidelitas?* No, he is insisting only on what he calls a *feo:* if you forget the *feo* that you have received, you are spewing up your honor. It is the *feo* that is binding. What exactly was its role in the relationship of patronage that the Sens epistle envisages?

For an answer we need to look at the texts of the ninth century. At this time, *feo* creeps into the formulary of the deeds of St. Gall and in Burgundy. In the former it means rent in kind, in the latter it means price, in the ancient—and obligatory—clause that mentioned its effective receipt by the seller, "*accepimus in precio solidos tantos*" becoming for example "*accepimus in feos compreciatos valentes solidos tantos.*"[39] *Feo*, then, would be in the full meaning of the word a thing of worth, something "valued or evaluated," and we know that this equivalent of the price—and this synonym of the word price—often consisted of livestock or horses. But it would be a mistake to narrow *feo* down to this meaning alone. The clause *in feos compreciatos* is in fact one particular example of a broader meaning. In the north selling disappeared, while in the Midi an equivalent in goods began to be substituted for the price, generally referred to with the terms *in res preciatas, valens,* and *in valente.*[40] Is the substitution of *feo* for *res* due only to the whim of the scribes? It must be understood that the use was a rare occurrence: out of 117 Burgundian deeds of sale between individuals that are preserved in the archives in Cluny, there are no less than eighty-eight cases of synonyms for price, and out of these *feo* is only used eleven times.[41]

Burgundy was, like Rhaetia, a region of contacts between different cultures, Roman in tradition, but where barbarian influences and settlements, Frankish or Alaman, were very ancient and even in some cantons earlier than the great invasions. Selling found itself confronted by a culture that knew nothing of it. We can understand the difficulty of the scribe who in 866 had to certify the *andalang* made by a Frank of Burgundy. Leaving aside his formulary, he begins bravely: "Notice in place of sale. . . ." Later his less scrupulous fellow scribes introduced the term *andalang* in the formula of sale, but carefully mentioned the *lex salica* of the "seller."[42] The mention of *feo* seems to indicate the same preoccupation; when Garnier, a scribe from Mâcon, replaces the formula that he habitually used, *valente*, with a *feos compreciatos valentes*, it is not just by chance. For a part of the population of these regions, it is not the price that is replaced by an equivalent, following the growing scarcity of coinage, it is the sale itself that has no meaning. We are now dealing with something more like an "exchange gift," where the compensatory present is substituted for the price, in the manner of the Lombard *launegild*. The Sens *feo* had no other meaning. Despite everything, the prestige of the written deed is here such that the scribe is asked to draft a document. He, yielding to the pressure of the contracting parties, clings to his formulary and continues to speak of selling, thereby confusing the gift with the "exchange gift." The assimilation with price on the part of the medieval scribe is a kind of ethnocentrism, while on the part of the historian it is an anachronism. The few Burgundian charters to mention the *feo* thus reveal both the attempts at assimilation that were occurring in an intermediate region, and the survival during the ninth century in the Frankish regions of the original sense of "fief," a meaning that extended a long way beyond the relationship of vassalage. This sheds light on the clause in the Aachen capitulary of 802–803 forbidding the vassal to leave his lord *postquam acceperit valente solido suo*[43]: refusing to use the word *feo*, the chancellery substitutes for it the formula of monetary equivalence. It does not dare to speak of *beneficium*.

Thus the word fief already had a long history when it came to refer to the concession of a piece of land and the piece of land itself. Marc Bloch has suggested a plausible explanation for this evolution: "In the seigniorial households where it was in daily use, it came to be associated exclusively with the idea of remuneration *per se*. . . . What happened if a companion received a piece of land from a chief who had originally maintained him in his household? This in turn was called the vassal's *feus*."[44] But if *beneficium* and *feodum* had become synonymous at the time when the majority of vassals became domiciled, that is to say at the end of the eighth century, then it is strange that the deeds from Picardy, Champagne, Lorraine, and Paris delayed until the end of the eleventh century before using *fevum* in the sense of fief.

Paradoxically, it is the southern texts that are the first to find a place, and a considerable one, for the *terra de feo*. It is unlikely that the Burgundian meaning of *feo* as a pseudosale was known in the Midi. When the scribes have to speak of the equivalent of the price, they use ordinary expressions such as *res compreciates valentes*. But in the first years of the tenth century, a quite different clause appears in the charters of donation *pro anima* to the churches. It forbids the *rector* of the recipient church to alienate the donation: he is not allowed to sell, or to exchange, or to give as a benefice, or to give as a *feo*. Fief and benefice are clearly not the same thing. In the mid-tenth century, the expression *tenere a feú* is found in the charters of the magnates and in the *brevia divisionabiles* of local lords who held these same fiefs. In Catalonia, *feo* takes over from *beneficium*.[45] What does the word *feo* mean? The distinction made in the charters between donations in benefice and donations in fief alerts us to the fact that here, at the end of the Carolingian period, the two are still clearly different. A second clue is provided by the synonym, typical of the southern tenth century, *fevum sive fiscum*. So the feudal concession in the Midi is in origin a fiscal concession.[46] *Feo* becomes frequent in the relationships of public power, that is, during the ninth century, in the vassal entourages of the southern governors: the lands given in fief were first of all fiscal lands, those vast chunks of estates seized from churches that were despoiled more than was usual elsewhere or "confiscated" from local magnates, who, if not rebellious, were at least constantly suspected of treason. The shift in meaning described by Marc Bloch—from fief-gift to fief-land—certainly took place, but in the Midi, and in rather different conditions from those that he imagined.

So it is no surprise to see in Catalonia the *feú* meaning the natural dependency of a fortress, *kastrum cum suo fevo*. Nor to see in the whole of the Midi the expression "priest's fief" used very regularly from the eleventh century onward to mean the land and above all the rights—oblations, burial, baptism, or tithes—related to a rural church; or as a charter put it "all the ecclesiastical honor which belongs to the seigniory of the castle of. . . ."[47]

The southern fief did not remain only this. The introduction of the phrase *nec in feo dare* in the donations *pro anima* in the early tenth century is an indication of this. It was just at this time, as Elizabeth Magnou-Nortier has shown, that the fief becomes linked with the contract of *comenda* by which landowners consigned the management of one of their estates to someone better placed than they were to administer it. The southern abbeys were among the chief users of this type of contract. There are two deeds that illustrate well how this evolution came about.

The first is a note that relates the story of a group of fiscal estates in the Narbonne region that ended up by being absorbed into the episcopal household. The countess of Carcassonne and two of her sons had mortgaged the estates to some Jewish moneylenders for one thousand sous. A man named Gairo paid the debt. In exchange they sold him one of the pieces of land for 300 sous, which is to say that they paid him back three hundred sous in giving it to him, and in order to make up the rest they gave him a *feo* of 200 measures of wheat. We see here the same procedure as that used by buyers in Burgundy who were short of cash. But in the example that concerns us, the countess and her sons did not have the wheat any more than they had the money; so they gave the *bailia* of the remaining estates to Gairo in order to allow him to recover his *feú*, that is, the two hundred measures they owed him.[48] The fief seems here to be first of all an income attached to a piece of land given in guardianship. The moneylenders of Narbonne were probably copying the system by which counts and viscounts had remunerated the stewards of the fiscal castles. Fortunately for us, the more complex character of the operation forced them to split up the component parts. This analysis is confirmed by the Catalan expression *censalis publicus quod vulgo feum dicitur*.[49] The southern *feú* is first of all a way of conceding a revenue, public in origin—and it was to remain so more firmly in Catalonia—which was to become more widespread in landholding relationships at the beginning of the tenth century.

This is clearly shown in another contract of *comenda*, made in 988–1002 between the monks of Conques and Bernard of Najas. Here the *feú* appears to consist of a certain number of manses held in *comenda*, while the others remained in the *communia* of the monks. On the fief, the monks retained half of the rights of *vestitio*, the better to maintain their superiority. By contrast, on the *comenda* all they asked was a small rent of oats and hens from each manse.

Such is the origin of all those small southern *vicarii*, the *vicarioli*, which historians have tried in vain to connect with the Carolingian *vicaria*. The term here signifies merely the delegated nature of the power that they exercised and that they held, as numerous documents make clear, only in guardianship or command.

Why then did the people of the south turn so early to the vulgate pseudosynonym of what they too, in the Carolingian period, called a *beneficium*? Very probably because "benefice" had kept much more markedly than in the north its general sense and was always used to refer to the type of contract *ad tempus*, such as the *precaria-prestaria-prestimonium*,[50] where the usufruct was retained after a sale, or even perhaps the donation pure and simple to a *fidelis*. These were contracts that did not all necessarily imply a reciprocal service, but which did involve, through the *traditio cartae*, the transfer of property. It would be interesting in this context to see whether any investitures of a fief *per festuca* were practiced in the Midi and for how long. There would probably be very few, if any. Later, when the vocabulary of feudalism was introduced into Castile, a southern region that had never known Frankish domination and had no experience of the fief, the *tenencias* of the magnates were called *feuda temporalia*.[51] For a southerner, a concession *in feo* was not limited in time, and in this way it differed from the whole category of "benefices." In fact, it created for the beneficiary a kind of allod.[52] On the other hand, it differed from a donation pure and simple to a *fidelis* in that it very strongly implied a service. Importantly, it was deemed necessary in the early ninth century to remind the Spanish *aprisiatores* of Septimania who received benefices that they owed "the same *obsequium* as that customarily shown by men of this land to their lords for similar benefices." The concession *in feo* is distinguished also by its indivisibility and masculine character, all traits derived from the public nature of the property originally conceded. The southern *feú* is, basically, a *stipendium* that has become hereditary.

The synonyms fief and benefice are almost as misleading in the north. Evidence of this lies in the extraordinary delay of the chanceries in using the word *fevum*. Marc Bloch explained this delay as indicating their purism. We shall see. Could the false doublet *beneficium-feodum* not be concealing the conflict of meaning to which Hincmar had already alluded? How far, indeed, should the refusal of the chanceries to use *beneficium* be seen in the light of their concern to emphasize the temporary nature of the military concessions? To what degree does the late triumph of the vernacular word *feo* imply the definitive character, except in cases of serious misdemeanor, of the acquisition of the property by a family?

The key to understanding the direction taken by the bonds of vassalage among the warrior families of the Frankish lands can perhaps be supplied by an analysis of the ritual of *exfestucatio*, by which in these areas vassals and lords broke the bonds between them. Marc Bloch wrote a masterly article on this subject, where he described the ritual—the throwing or breaking of a piece of straw—determining the territorial limits of the custom and listing its appearance in the texts in the early twelfth century. He remarked also on the similarity, or rather the apparent identity, of this practice with that of the renunciation of land, but then found himself obliged to reject this analysis: "renunciation" meant the renunciation of a piece of land, while *exfestucatio* broke a personal bond, without for all that preventing the vassal from keeping the fief. Hence the idea of seeking the origin of the "repudiation by the straw" in ancient Frankish rituals for the breaking of kinship.[53] Interesting as this is, we would like to put forward another hypothesis, taking up Marc Bloch's analysis at the point where he felt it had collapsed. He had established that *exfestucare* in the texts of the period referred both to the ritual of the breaking of a bond and that of renunciation, which *a priori* leads us to suppose that contemporaries did not, or could no longer, distinguish between the two rituals. It is in this identification of the two that the answer to our problem lies.

In the ritual of renunciation, the throwing of the straw does not strictly speaking represent the renunciation of the land, but rather the ritual destruction of an earlier ritual of investiture, which marked the legitimate passing of the land from one man to another. However it may appear to our modern and juridical eyes, this relationship is not merely a property relationship, it is just as personal as those created by homage or oaths. The word *feodum*, which then meant land given *in feo*, expresses the same idea; the stress is on the gift that creates a bond between two men. Both in the case of the renunciation of land and that of the renunciation of the bond, the *exfestucatio* does not in any way prejudice the fate of the property previously transferred: in one case the party that acquires the land has lawful possession of it, in the other, the vassal, himself in lawful possession, will expect to keep the land. It cancels the bond existing between an old and a new possessor: in the case of renunciation of the bond, that means that it was now impossible for the lord to base any claims on the investiture that he had performed; in the case of the renunciation of the land, it prevents the party who renounces the land from using his former investiture by an original owner as an objection to lawful possession by the other party. In both cases the ritual is the same.

The fact that contemporaries, lords or vassals, demonstrated renunciation in this way shows clearly that the bond of vassalage was in their eyes based essentially not on homage or an oath but on the *feo*, the gift-which-obliges. Among the warriors of the north is it not that most ancient concept of the relationship of man to man, one created by a gift, which triumphs? It is because he had received at least "the value of a sou" in fief that the Carolingian vassal owed something to his lord.[54] Should we conclude from this that homage and fealty, the first foundations of obligation for the Carolingians, had become of only secondary importance? Here we have the central problem of the evolution of the feudo-vassalic bond from the year 1000, and, in a way, that of the failure or the success of "Charlemagne's program" beyond the Carolingian kingdom. For the system that he had tried to develop was to become dominant without him.

No Man without a Lord?

At the end of the tenth century, the fortresses were to become the essential element in social organization.[55] From this time the peasantry, whether they liked it or not, were drawn into their orbit. Around them there began to crystallize proper feudal relationships between all those who, one way or another, were involved in the exercise of seigneurial power. We find evidence of the emergence of these new relationships not only in the increasing number of references in the documents to "feudal" institutions—homage, oaths of fealty, fiefs—but above all in the way in which these terms were used differently, in many cases, from the way that had prevailed in the previous century. And this diffusion and extension of a truly feudal system took place on two levels: that of the petty country notables and that of the local aristocrats, the masters of the fortresses. This distinction helps us to understand the ambiguity of the feudo-vassalic bond at the beginning of the eleventh century.

The Fealty of the Knights

The spread of the feudo-vassalic bond in the upper levels of the peasantry started from the lordly houses, gained ground as the castle garrisons were set up, and reached finally, in the territories of the new castles, down to country squires and local big shots, who were drawn into vassalage to the lords.

The life of Gerald of Aurillac gives us a first reference point. In several passages, his biographer describes the entourage of his hero: the "great number of warriors" who "march with the prince," the *juvenes* who precede the *senior*. These are his "nurselings," whose homage he bestowed at will in favor of other magnates. Kind though he was, Gerald "did not give benefices easily." We have seen how he made up for the scarcity of his benefices by their permanence. The entourage of the saint, like those of his neighbors, the lords of the Auvergne, was thus principally composed of unendowed vassals.[56] In the early years of the tenth century, the armed escorts of the magnates were not normally domiciled by their lord. A century later, a lord's entourage consisted partly of knights whom he had installed around his castle. Thus in Vendôme, the castle at the beginning of the eleventh century was guarded by some dozen *milites*. Each of them was domiciled, performed *commendatio* to the master of the castle, and for this performed a service, the most onerous part of which, guard duty, was fixed by custom. When there was a change of master of the castle, the garrison received a new lord.[57]

These *casamenta* (domiciles) were still in the eleventh century quite modest holdings. In Poitou they were as big as the area that could be worked by two oxen; in Anjou a few dozen acres.[58] Those *milites* who had nothing more than their *casamenta* were called *casati*.

We should compare this system of *casamenta* with that of the *caballerias de feu*, which for Catalonia has been so well described by Pierre Bonnassie. The term appears in 1047 and becomes widespread in the second half of the eleventh century. It describes a relatively small landholding, the area scarcely exceeding that of a manse. The texts specify "that it should be able to support a fully equipped knight." These *caballerias* were carved out of the land belonging to the castle in order to house the garrison, and we see magnates awarding them as they saw fit. This system may also have existed in Provence with the *mansi caballes*; there too the holdings represented the sole possessions of those who occupied them.[59]

It is no coincidence that the clearest and earliest examples of the system of *casamenta* appeared around the major churches—Cambrai, Rheims, Tours, Chartres, Langres, and Montierender in Champagne. The *casati* then formed something like a college; in Limoges the *casati ecclesiae* who participated alongside the *proceres* or *optimates* at the election of the bishop were regarded as the equals of the clerics of the cathedral.[60] We shall return to these knights of the cathedrals later, but for the moment suffice it to say that the system of the *casamenta* was nothing other than the adaptation to the castle of the Carolingian system of ecclesiastical *vassi*.

Not all the lord's vassals were *milites castri*, and the power of the lord of the castle gave rise to many expressions of loyalty from motives of self-interest in the area around his fortress. The small landowners, the village squirarchy, seeking to associate themselves with his power and to enjoy his protection, came to join his *casati*. By kneeling and offering their hands, they too entered into the circle of vassalage.

In Poitou, the *milites* who accompanied Ebbo of Château-Larcher in 969 were for the most part, like their lords, holders of allods. It is possible that they had already been granted by him some of the tithes or other small profits of his lordship. Until c. 1020–30 in the Mâcon region these faithful allodialists rarely received fiefs, but rather gifts of allods. This largesse was granted to them at the end of the service that they had performed for their lord—a last act of charity that often arrived too late. The lord of the castle of Talmont, for example, made a donation to the monks of Sainte-Croix for the soul of one of his knights "because he had served me for a long time and I had given him nothing."[61]

In the second decade of the eleventh century the first *fiefs de reprise* began to appear in the regions of Mâcon and Burgundy. A certain knight of Bresse gave the abbey of Cluny his own property and received it back in benefice along with part of the family allod that he had earlier ceded to the monastery.[62] The *fiefs de reprise* of Septimania reveal a rather different social structure. From the 1060s and until the beginning of the twelfth century, a number of small allodialists, masters of the hilltop villages that clustered around their castles, would take the oath of fealty to some great lord and hold the village from him *de reprise*. These *fiefs de reprise* seem not to have involved any other obligation than that of handing over the castle when asked to do so by the lord.[63] This explains the progressive disappearance of the allods and the multiplication of fiefs, a phenomenon that is however more noticeable in some regions than in others.

Two cartularies from Picardy record, for an area of 250 square kilometers to the south of Hesdin, some three hundred land transactions between 1090 and 1150. Only 55 fiefs and 87 allods are mentioned. It has to be acknowledged that since churches, which wished to acquire lands free of services, are involved, the number of allods is probably greater in this case than in others. But Robert Fossier shows that between 1040 and 1135, allods are still numerous in the inheritances of knights in the region.[64]

The fairly regular transformation of allods into fiefs was not without consequences: the use of the benefice, now increasingly common, was beginning to be combined with other types of concessions of land, like the classic *precaria* or peasant sharecropping; and increasingly the benefice modeled itself on the more precise tenure. The fief was no longer a present from the lord, but part of a family patrimony.

In the first half of the eleventh century, in the Mâcon area, it is clear that many of the benefices are not yet hereditary. In the years 1020–30, we see the grantor insisting on the solemn promise to return the land on the death of the feudatory. The monks of Cluny in 1023 still considered hereditary fiefs unreasonable, but there were cases where they appear to have been forced to allow them. From 1075 onward, inheritance was commonly allowed, but it is significant that the concession of a fief *ad vitam* was retained until the end of the eleventh century and that, conversely, the need was sometimes felt to specify that a fief was hereditary.[65] In Catalonia, inheritance was established in the second half of the eleventh century, although we still find life fiefs, conceded particuarly by the churches, in 1052 and 1079. From information taken from some fifty wills, Pierre Bonnassie has shown that in an inheritance, the sons generally shared the fief, although daughters can also inherit. Sometimes the fiefs are left to several sons and daughters in common. There is no right of primogeniture; the testator can chose the *melior filius* [best son] to whom to leave the fief. At the beginning of the twelfth century, there are even some cases where the beneficiaries are not members of the family. Inheritance of the fief is accompanied from 1053 by a right of transfer, called here not the relief but the *avere*. By contrast, the sale and donation of fiefs are still forbidden except with the agreement of the lord, and deeds of sale do not mention fiefs.[66] In Normandy, the principle of inheritance was established at the end of the eleventh century.

The often-cited example from Anjou of the knight Hamelin of Beaupréau, who was refused a benefice from the count in c. 1028 that had formerly been held by his father and his brother, is not very persuasive, because this man had abandoned his fealty to the count in favor of one of the latter's enemies. The move toward the inheritance of a fief or benefice is, however, clearly shown in a lawsuit brought by the monks of Marmoutiers against the brother of a deceased *ministerialis*. The monks agree to appoint him to his brother's office—*commendare*—so that his descendants cannot reclaim it as a fief—*quasi fevum vel beneficium*. This is hardly classic feudalism.[67]

The move toward patrimonialization is thus a relatively late phenomenon that should be placed no earlier than the second half of the century. From then on it appears as one of the chief characteristics of the transformation of the concept. Gradually, as the fief spreads among the big peasant allodialists, it adjusts itself, as Georges Duby has shown, to the rules of land tenure. The services owed on account of the fief are similarly changed.

Of the sixty knights who performed castle guard for the lord of Picquigny at the end of the twelfth century, twenty-five, the closest to the castle, had to carry out a much more onerous guard duty. These may have been the descendants of the old *casati*. Among the others, less burdened, it is not surprising to find several local notables[68]

In those places where the *casati* often had to perform a uniform type of service, the feudatories had to adjust the amount of the service to the importance of their holdings, for which it represented the rent. And now also it was possible to negotiate over service.

So it was in Burgundy with a certain Henry, who had managed to extort some manses from the abbey of Bèze. This prudent knight had, after many hesitations, agreed to defend the monastery, but he made it clear that "so that I suffer no harm, that I am not obliged to defend it against those who are stronger than I, but only against those to whom I am equal in birth and power or against those who are weaker." This prudence is understandable. As the circle of *milites castri* grew and incorporated the families of the local squires in the surrounding areas, so it became involved in their rivalries. The death of a knight became an event with serious consequences that rocked whole families. At the end of the eleventh century, certain knights of castles were carrying on private battles against their peers.[69]

The result of this spread of the feudo-vassalic bond into the wealthier class of peasant society meant that the magnates of the eleventh century could lead larger armies into battle.

The lord of Amboise, a vassal of Geoffrey Martel, count of Anjou, commanded two hundred horsemen and a thousand foot soldiers. When this same count defeated Theobald of Blois, he took more than seven hundred knights as prisoners. When Hugh of Lusignan took one castle, he took prisoner some forty knights. This same Hugh proudly bore the nickname *chiliarch*, commander of a thousand, probably a mixture of horsemen and foot soldiers. A certain noble "youth," vassal of Bernard "Pelet," lord of Anduze, had sole command of fifty knights.[70]

It would, however, be a mistake to believe that the spread of the fief and of homage was limited to these groups in society in exchange for services in war. Quite the reverse. We see in the southern regions especially from the twelfth century on "an invasion of the relationship between the owners of the land and their peasants by the vocabulary and even the rituals of feudalism."[71] Rented plots were considered as being held in fief; commoners and "serfs" did homage.

The castellans of Catalonia speak in 1045 of the "men of our homage" when referring to the people born on their estates. From 1035, taxable plots of land were called *fevum* and from 1064 a distinction is made—a juridical paradox—between the *alodium fevale* and the *alodium francum*. Common fief, free allod; the homage given by the tenants was very early here, but it can be found all over the Midi from Narbonne to Toulouse and Arles and even in Berry and Champagne.[72]

It was to distinguish them from these common fiefs that some allods, yielding to the general movement toward feudalism in the twelfth century, were called *feudum honoratum* or *feudum francum*. The only service they involved was homage and fealty. From 1152 the need was felt to specify that this type of fief was held "honorably"; in 1164 the first *feudum honoratum* appears and the area of origin of this term seems likely to have been eastern Septimania, from Béziers to Nîmes, where the practice of the repurchase or taking back in fief of small allodial castles had been frequent in the eleventh century. From there the free fief appears to have spread all over the Midi, from the Pyrenees to the north of Lyons.[73]

In all these cases, the word fief, which the practice of the warrior entourages established in the Midi had imposed, is no more than a special synonym for tenure, apart from one important difference: the men who held a fief had probably done homage. From this stems the ambiguity of the word "feudatory" when it appears at the end of the eleventh century. It certainly refers to a man who holds a fief, but it is not clear whether he is a knight, a *ministerialis*, or a peasant.[74] At the end of the eleventh century, the feudo-vassalic bond had made considerable inroads into peasant society, until then largely untouched. At the same time it was becoming general among the local aristocracy and under the aegis of the territorial princes it governed the aristocracy's internal relationships.

The Fealty of the Lords

In the second half of the tenth century, the important men of a *pagus* would normally do homage to the count. In 955 when the new count of Auvergne and duke of Aquitaine, William of Poitiers, came to the court of Ennezat, the magnates of Auvergne—*seniores arvernici*—commended themselves to him. In Normandy, all the great men did homage to the future count when his father presented him to them. In Poitou, Provence, and the Mâconnais the lords of the chief fortresses were all vassals of the count. In Anjou, if we limit ourselves to the comital castles, which are the oldest, it appears that a strong feudal bond attached the occupiers to the count.[75]

The power acquired by the counts over the richest and most powerful of the inhabitants of their counties was based on a triple tradition. The first is vassal fealty and the *commendatio* of the *vassi regales*. At the beginning of the tenth century, the territorial princes had begun to bring the important royal vassals into submission. Shortly before 910, one of these "lords of Auvergne," Gerald of Aurillac, was still refusing to give homage to Count William, but he had sent his nephew and heir to commend himself to the count. Around 920, his peer Ebo of Deols, a vassal of King Raoul, was also a vassal of the same William. A little later, the *vassi dominici* of Provence became vassals of the count.[76] The second tradition is the oath of fealty of the free men, made to the count by the *pagenses*. When the royal vassals had entered into the count's vassalage, the wealthier *pagenses* must have deemed it prudent to join them.[77] Finally, the count had in his own household young men of good family who since the time of the upheavals of the early eighth century could be set up by him on public lands, fiscs, church lands, or confiscated land and could establish a family line. Did the mingling of these three traditions, to the advantage of the count, bring with it the definite submission of those whom he dominated? As with the ancient oath to the king, the promise to the count was obligatory. Of the great lords of the land, none could refuse. In the name of this promise the count demanded service in the army and the ancient duties of the free man.

However, this general entry of the local aristocracy into the fealty of the count—which after all was only the realization of the old Carolingian plan—is not enough to characterize the system that became established at this time. The complex interaction of multiple homages is another fundamental element of it. We find a perfect illustration of this in the *Conventio Hugonis Chiliarchi*.[78]

In the years 1020–25, Poitou, like many other regions of the kingdom, was rent by the rivalries and ambitions of the great castellans. Hugh of Lusignan was one of the most dangerous. First of all, this was because of his wealth: to the great allods on which his grandfather had built the castle of Lusignan were added the protection of the abbey of Saint-Maixent with the lands that provided its income and the great forest that extended toward the city of Poitiers. This forest had formerly belonged to the church of Poitiers and was now in all probability held by the count. Hugh was also powerful by birth. For four generations the Lusignans had handed on the same name without deigning to change it, whatever their alliances, and their already legendary history only distinguished one from the other by mysterious nicknames. After many differences with his lord the count, Hugh had written down in a vulgar but lively Latin a long and doubtless partial account of all his grievances.[79]

The *Conventio Hugonis* allows us to understand the delicate balance that had been reached in Poitou at the beginning of the eleventh century between the great castellans. The system relied on the shared command of the fortresses, and particularly those on the frontiers of the old *pagi*, now come together under the authority of the count of Poitiers, the duke of Aquitaine, on the borders of Poitou, Saintonge, Angoumois, and Limousin. The duke appeared as the most important if not most respected master of all the strongholds, which could not legitimately be held except with his agreement. In these places the old principle of the public character of fortresses could be found, whatever kind of land they were built on, be it allod, fief, or *comenda*.[80] At the same time these fortresses were becoming integrated into the family properties and dominance over them tended as a consequence to follow the rules of the devolution of patrimonies. It is at the point where these two traditions meet that developments were to take place.

The duke's tactics had several aspects. First, he tried to maintain the scattered distribution of the *honores* of each of the magnates. Thus, Hugh of Lusignan held Mouzeuil, in the fiscal area around Fontenay-le-Comte; the lords of Châtellerault, who protected the abbey of Saint-Maixent for the duke, held Sainte-Soline; Aimery of Rancogne held Civray.[81] This way the duke maintained a healthy competition between the lords. The lords of Thouars, because they held Hermenault, had their eyes on Mouzeuil, while Hugh coveted Sainte-Soline, which lay close to his castle; Bernard of La Marche wanted Confolens, while Hugh would have been glad to take Civray from him. This competition could be accentuated by the division of estates: Hugh's father held a quarter of Civray, Hugh himself had, at Vivonne, half the castle, the lord's house, and two parts of the "fiefs of the vassals." In addition, the duke whenever possible introduced, between himself and these lords, counts who were his neighbors or vassals, or bishops, with the same aim of encouraging the splitting up of the magnates' seigneuries. Aimery held Civray from the count of La Marche, while the latter held Gençay from the count of Anjou, from whom also were held Loudun, by the lord of Thouars, and certain possessions in Saintonge, by some lords unknown to us; Hugh held his possessions in Vivonne from the bishop of Poitiers and at Confolens from the count of Angoulême[82]; if he supplanted the lords of Civray and Gençay, he would, like them, have to hold the possessions from the counts of La Marche and of Anjou. But always the count remains lord over all. Thus was ducal peace maintained in Poitou.

The tactics of the lords were of course the opposite from those of the duke, and the *Conventio* details Hugh's desperate efforts to get his hands, by succession, by marriage, by agreement, and if necessary by violence on the fortresses near his castle of Lusignan. Adhemar of Chabannes tells us of the efforts made by Aimery, who originally commanded the fortress of Mussidan in Périgord, to set up a second lordship in the northern Angoumois around the castles of Rancogne, Marival, Civray, Chizé, and Brizambourg; the bishopric of Angoulême, which he had obtained for his son, was his Trojan horse.[83] Each time such an attempt clashed fatally with the conflicting ambitions of the neighboring lords. The duke's web that entrapped them was strongly woven, and he maneuvered unceasingly to upset the lords' attempts at entente.

So it was with the marriage planned between Hugh and the daughter of Raoul of Thouars, at that time on bad terms with the duke, the count of Poitiers. The text reads:

> The count, very angry, came humbly to Hugh and said to him "Do not take the daughter of Raoul for wife, and I will give you anything you ask of me, and you will be my friend above all others, except for my son. . . ." At that time it happened that Joscelin died, he of the castle of Parthenay, and the count said that he would give the honor and the wife of Joscelin to Hugh. [A little later] the count summoned Viscount Raoul and said to him: "The agreement that Hugh has with you, he will not carry out because I forbid

him to, but I and Fulk (of Anjou), we have made an agreement to give him the honor and the wife of Joscelin, and we shall do it for your confusion, because you are not faithful to me." At these words, Raoul, very sad, said to the count: "For the sake of God, I beg you, do not do that." And the count said: "Give me your promise that you will not give him your daughter and for my part I shall see that he has neither the honor nor the daughter of Joscelin." Thus they did, and Hugh had neither one nor the other. [Raoul, leaving the count, came to Hugh and] told him that they were being made fun of . . . and he said to him: "On my faith, I promise you this: promise me not to betray me, give me your word that you will help me against Count William, and I will keep our agreement and I will help you against all men." Hugh refused all this for love of Count William, and Raoul and Hugh separated sadly.

This touching story shows the degree of duplicity that the count's policy could and had to reach. In this system, based entirely on faith, the duke never keeps his word. In order to maintain the balance of divided lands, he can only answer the demands of the lords with promises that he has no intention of keeping. The barons saw things differently: what for us is no more than a series of instructive misfortunes of a covetous lord becomes for Hugh the history of a great love ever betrayed, ever disappointed.

In such a system, two social institutions remain truly stable, the duke and the castle garrisons, the *caballarii castri*. And on the latter the whole structure depended. Care was taken to share out their fiefs among their peers. The destruction of a fortress necessitated their elimination: Geoffrey of Thouars, having burned down Mouzeuil, had the right hands of all the knights of the castle cut off. Most importantly, the *caballarii* are the obligatory guarantors of all the agreements, all the *convenientiae* that in Poitou as in many other regions[84] had become the preponderant form of relationship between the magnates. Hugh of Lusignan thus had as hostages forty of the best knights of Thouars. The castle garrison, in order to save relations and friends, would obey the lord who held them or put pressure on the lord's adversary. This explains why the duke demanded in the name of the fealty that they owed him that the lords entrust to him all the hostages taken in his principality. This way he could check that the proper forms be respected. It was to him, at the end of the day, that the garrison would restore the castle.

In order to strengthen their homage of peace, the magnates were thus obliged to involve the castral garrisons. Their own lord would invite the men of the castle to do homage to another lord. This was the case in Vendôme where Count Renaud was pressed by the Bishop of Chartres, Fulbert, from whom he held the castle, to obtain for him the *commendatio* of the *milites*. Having received it, the bishop in turn asserted his right to demand service. Naturally, it is made clear that this second fealty and new service should come after that which they owed to Renaud. In fact Fulbert was seeking not so much an effective

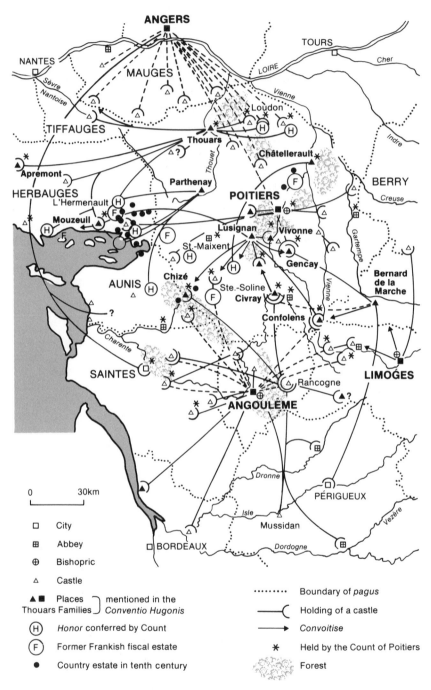

Map 2. Castles in the Principality of the Count of Poitiers, Duke of Aquitaine

(After *Conventio Hugonis* and Adhémar of Chabannes)

Legend:

□ City

⊞ Abbey

⊕ Bishopric

△ Castle

▲ ■ Places mentioned in the Thouars Families / *Conventio Hugonis*

Ⓗ *Honor* conferred by Count

Ⓕ Former Frankish fiscal estate

● Country estate in tenth century

········ Boundary of *pagus*

——(Holding of a castle

——▶ *Convoitise*

✳ Held by the Count of Poitiers

🌫 Forest

and regular service as the recognition of a bond that would allow him to neutralize the possible hostility of the *milites* of Vendôme or to obtain their provisional obedience if he or his men occupied the castle with the agreement of Renaud. In this last case, Fulbert promised to obtain for Renaud an oath of fealty from his own *milites* of Chartres.[85]

In this way, between two groups of warriors and their leaders, a veritable chiasmus of vassalage, a system of crossed alliances was created. At first sight the practice indicates the state of submission in which the *milites castri* found themselves; their lord can even tell them where to give their homage and order them to "make a lord," whom they are no longer allowed to choose. But at the same time the practice shows the importance assumed by the garrisons.

The logical consequence of this structure was an effort to reconcile and order the different types of homage. The simplest and oldest method consisted in giving primacy to the homage that went with the most important benefice. We find examples of this from 895 in Tours and again in 1090–93 in Montpellier.[86] One is a "better man" because one has a "better benefice." Another system was that of introducing into the promise of fealty an exemption clause—*salva fidelitate talis*—which made the promise, whatever its nature, subordinate to another more important promise. Such a clause is used by Fulbert of Chartres from 1007–08 in the letter where he asks Renaud of Vendôme for his fealty, *salva fidelitate regis*, and for that of Renaud's *milites*, *salva fidelitate tua*. In the case in point, the criterion of the best benefice could not be used because there was only one. These attempts to clarify matters became more precise in the 1040s in the Vendôme region with the idea of the liege lord, which established unambiguously who should be the "better" lord. We find liegemen in Flanders in the second half of the eleventh century, in Normandy in 1087, and in Burgundy in 1097.[87] In the south at the same period there is mention in the Catalan charters of the *solidus*, the "solid" man, as opposed now to the simple *fidelis*.

The similarity between liege homage and *solidentia* is clearly shown by the unusual use of *hom lige* in a Catalan document of 1098–1112. At this period the influence of Norman or Burgundian knights is probable.

The *solidus* promised to "defy," which is to say to abandon, the lords whom he had had until then and to take no more lords without the permission of his liege lord. This petty knight or *castlà* was once again entirely in the hands of his lord, and the other homages that he might have given, if they continued at all, had only a very secondary value.[88]

At the end of the eleventh century, from Catalonia to Flanders, the feudal system is fully set up with its own rules all in place. There are good reasons for its complexity. The tangle of feudo-vassalic bonds is not a sign of the decadence of the structure but is its essential condition, extant from the outset. It is indeed from this system that the truly feudal principalities, as opposed to the still-Carolingian type of principality, arose.[89] It took root at the end of the tenth century in a situation of constant warring between the old principalities—wars principally undertaken by the great castellans of the marches.

There was in Limousin a border abbey on the frontier with Quercy, that of Beaulieu. It had been founded by an ancient family whose descendants bore the title of viscount, and who had held Turenne and Comborn, providing the abbey with its secular abbots and its protectors. These viscounts were the vassals of the count of Périgord. On the other side of the Cère river lived their enemies, the lords of Castelnau, vassals of the counts of Toulouse. Around the year 980, the lords of Castelnau with their kinsmen and friends crossed the river, crushed the Turenne faction, and seized the monastery. The two sides decided to leave things as they were and came to this agreement: the count of Toulouse handed over the abbey in fief to the count of Périgord, who handed it over to his vassal the viscount of Turenne, who in turn conceded it to its actual if not its legitimate owner, the lord of Castelnau. The vassal pair of the count of Périgord and the viscount of Comborn lived on by fitting itself in with the opposing vassal pair of the count of Toulouse and the lord of Castelnau.[90] Thus peace was concluded, and the agreement survived until the Gregorian reform.

When we compare the *Conventio Hugonis* and the writings of Adhemar of Chabannes, it is clear that the *convenientiae*, which regulated the fate of the great castles of Poitou, Angoulême, or the Limousin, had their origins in a process that resembles the one described here. Evidence for this can be found in Loudun, which stabilized relations between the count of Angers and the duke of Aquitaine after the wars at the end of the tenth century, or in Civray, which had for a long time been attacked by the count of La Marche and his vassals in Périgord before being subjugated by the duke.[91] In Catalonia the situation was the same: the lords of the frontier, like Gombaud of Bésorra, were the initiators of a movement that the count of Barcelona took over and turned to his own advantage; lacking as yet the power to lean on the allodial communities, he had to look elsewhere for his base.[92] From the border regions the system spread into the heart of the principalities.

It is not surprising that in these conditions the minimum content of homage was now similar to that of the old oaths of security, a promise not to harm. Such a promise was adapted to the new political realities and to the territorial stabilization of the great principalities.

Thus there was to come about, probably at the end of the eleventh century, a veritable custom of "march" homages on the frontiers of duchies and counties. The count of Champagne in this way did homage for Troyes to the duke of Burgundy; the count of Nevers to the same duke for Montbard and Rougement. And even, a borderline case, the duke of Normandy performed "march" homage to the king. The texts are clear: these homages came as a result of the conclusion of peace; they are true homages of peace and concord performed in "the places of ancient custom."[93]

This explains the term used sometimes for the oath of fealty that accompanied homage: *securitas*. It was a *securitas* that Fulbert of Chartres asked Renaud of Vendôme to make to him. It was a *securitas* that—according to Dudo of Saint-Quentin in 1015–26—Louis IV was supposed to have concluded with Richard of Normandy. In 1101 the count of Flanders in an accord with the king of England "assured him by oath of his life and the members attached to his body, and against the captivity of his body to his detriment."[94] In the twelfth century, the *securitas*, in the strict sense of a promise that preceded the oath, became an equivalent for *fidelitas*. As such, it was in common usage in Flanders, and Galbert of Bruges in 1127 distinguishes between *hominium, securitas* and *juramentum* in the homage of the vassals to the count. Far from Bruges, in Arles in Provence at the same period, the archbishop was demanding of the knights of Saint-Chamas "the seigneury of all the castle and the security of fealty with service."[95]

This process, which renders the oath-homage very passive, can be seen with particular clarity in the documents of the Midi. Here the more deeply rooted practice of having a written legal document has meant that quite a few texts of oaths have been preserved—oaths that, if we take the most general meaning of the word, could be called oaths of fealty. These oaths were generally an accompaniment to agreements, also written, which were called *convenientiae*.[96] The tradition of *convenientiae* in the Midi was an old one and probably went back to the usages of vulgar Roman law, but their proliferation in the second half of the eleventh century must be seen in relation to the troubles of the preceding decades. These *convenientiae* were used for many ends: they could carry out the division of an undivided inheritance, arrange an alliance between important men or the protection of a monastery by a lord, hand over a castle to the existing guardian, or specify the service owed by a dependant. In all these cases, the text of the promise by oath hardly varies and basis is always either the clause *fidelis ero* or its equivalent, a promise to respect life, members, and estates. Only after this comes the aid or the service if the *convenientia* specifies them. But in all these cases the term *fidelis* appears linked to the use of the old clause *sicut homo seniori suo*.[97]

Were these oaths always accompanied by an act of homage? Homage was certainly not unknown in the south. The royal vassals, the *aprisiatores* who had entered into fealty to the count, and the Franks who had set up in the area were certainly aware of it. We find frequent references to homage in Catalonia, in texts and in iconography, and more rarely in Septimania and Provence. Can we be sure that the making of an oath of fealty necessarily implied the act of homage? This is the case in Catalonia. Elsewhere it is less certain. Raymond of Saint-Gilles or William of Poitiers, at the end of the eleventh century, considered it normal to take an oath of fealty rather than perform an act of homage.[98] Nevertheless, the interest of the argument should not distract us from some pieces of evidence: it is the role of the oath that the written sources have preserved and in terms that are modeled on the real utterance of the formula, not on a description of homage; in Catalonia the demands that the lords made of their vassals are always based on an oath—*per nomen de sacramento*—and not on homage. In Italy the *libri feudorum* similarly link the investiture of the fief to the oath. It is clear that in the south the heart of the feudo-vassalic relationship is the oath of fealty.[99]

Beyond these formulae, what is really involved is the actual commitment implied, and in many cases this commitment appears to have been very slight. Thus at the same period in the north as in the south through different cultures we can see the same phenomenon of the weakening of the bond of vassalage among the magnates. However, it would not be correct to suppose that we have purely and simply returned, as far as princes and lords are concerned, to the old tradition of the assurances or *securitates* of the eighth century. A number of these homages of peace were attached to a benefice, to a piece of land, or to a castle. If the faith was broken, the benefice, at least in law, was forfeited. The benefice became a pledge of peace.

Two "beneficial" structures coexisted in the feudal world: the holdings of the *casati*, which were grouped around the castle, and the great fiefs of the powerful lords that stretched along the borders. The fealty of the first group consisted of active dependence; that of the second group tended to be reduced to a pact of nonaggression.

The Content of the Bond: A Legal Controversy

Was the bond of vassalage strong or weak at the dawn of the eleventh century? The answer depends on which social group and which region we are talking about. At the time when the power of the masters of the fortresses became firmly established, and when, in order to establish this, they introduced the system of vassalage to the wealthy peasantry, this system took on a different meaning in their own class. The breaking up of the *pagus* was also a physical expression of this uncertainty, of the precariousness of fealty among those who dominated. But we cannot resolve the question of the content of the oath of fealty among the lords and princes merely by describing the structure of the feudo-vassalic bonds. Indeed this content was not fixed once and for all; it was always to be disputed between the opposed ideas of the two sides. An illustration of this controversy is provided by a comparison of the *Conventio Hugonis* and the advice given to the duke on this matter by one of the best jurists of the time. Fulbert of Chartres.[100]

One day, frustrated by his failures, Hugh, lord of Lusignan, "went to the court of the count and demanded justice, but in vain. Then, full of sadness, in the presence of all, Hugh 'defied' the count except for his city and his body." As Olivier Guillot has shown, the text is unambiguous: Hugh is breaking all links of fealty with the count, except for a negative promise, of not harming either the body or the land of the count—in this case the city of Poitiers.[101] When he reduces his promise to his lord to a simple *securitas*, Hugh maintains he no longer holds a fief of him. The count had made this fief the pledge of his agreements with Hugh over the castle of Gençay. With the agreements renounced, the pledge was, according to Hugh, nullified and the benefice had become an allod. Thus for Hugh, no fief meant no fealty other than negative fealty. Despite the previous act of homage, what remained between Hugh and the count when there was no longer a benefice was nothing other than the old passive fealty of free men.

Such was Hugh's point of view: the count of course saw things differently. He had said as much one day to Hugh when he had ordered him to perform homage to the count of La Marche. As Hugh showed reluctance, the count shouted angrily: "You are so dependent on me that if I told you to take a peasant for your lord, you would have to do it," and another time he said: "You are mine to do my will and let everyone know this." The total submission required by William of Aquitaine is the same as that demanded by the duke of Normandy when he gave a count, his vassal, to the king of England "like a horse or an ox."[102]

It was not enough for William to assert his point of view, it was also necessary for him to persuade the court that was to condemn Hugh—a court made up of Hugh's peers. He went to Fulbert of Chartres and asked him what exactly a man who swore fealty was promising. The answer followed the expected lines: the man who swears must not cause harm to his lord; more than that, if he was to deserve his *casamentum* and be worthy of his benefice, the *fidelis* must give his lord both help and counsel. It was a reply worthy of such a wise rhetorician and excellent jurist.

Claude Carozzi has shown that the *libri*, on the authority of which Fulbert based his answer, are two works by Cicero—the *Ad Herennium* and *De Inventione*. The bishop uses both the vocabulary of Cicero— *utilitas, incolumitas, tutum, honestum*—and part of his construction. But where the Roman author spoke of *corpus civitatis*, Fulbert transfers it to the physical body of the lord. "This juggling is not without its consequences. It introduces a social ritual which is essentially concrete into an abstract structure, it changes its sense by introducing terms with moral connotations which were not there before." Fulbert's strength here is to apply the framework of ancient rhetoric to the traditional formulae of the oath of fealty.[103]

Fulbert's reasoning is rigorous. In his continuation of the reasoning of Hincmar of Rhiems, not only does he link service and benefice, but above all with one word—*casamentum*—he puts Hugh of Lusignan and the humble *casatus* of a castle on a par: have not both of them sworn fealty for a fief?[104] But the implicit threat, sufficient against a domiciled vassal, is here doubly derisive: Hugh can maintain that he no longer holds a benefice, and in any case the importance of his allod puts him in a position to be able to prevent a possible confiscation. And Fulbert hastens to add: the *fidelis* must give counsel and help if he wishes to be worthy of his benefice "and keep the fealty which he has sworn." He concludes logically: "If he is caught violating his promises or allowing them to be violated, he is perfidious and perjured." Thus the sanction would not be just the confiscation but above all the punishment for perjury, that same punishment that the capitularies decreed for those who betrayed their oath of royal fealty: the cutting off of a hand.[105] It now remained to soften the blow, and Fulbert does it with great elegance; to the perjury and perfidy of the vassal who fails in his obligations corresponds the bad faith of the lord who has failed in his obligations. A rhetorical balancing, but a false symmetry: bad faith is a sin, perjury a crime. The duke and Hugh were reconciled. In 1095 Hugh's son and successor made a grant to the church "by order and will of the count of Poitou, in the honor of whom are all my goods." The distinction between fief and allod became of secondary importance.[106]

But the same dukes and counts who claimed total fealty from the lords who were their vassals were quite willing to use the latters' arguments when it was a question of their own promises to the king. It was at this level that the idea—and the theory—of the homage of peace began to spread. Its best interpreter was a clerk in the service of the Norman duke, Dudo of Saint-Quentin. Writing the history of the duchy in his own manner, Dudo systematically reinterpreted the relations between the king and the duke. The initial deed, the agreement of Saint-Clair-sur-Epte of 911, by which Charles the Simple entrusted to the Norman leader Rollo the administration of several *pagi*, is nothing other for him than an agreement of peace, concord, or friendship; of course, he says, Rollo performed *commendatio* to the king, but baptism took the place of service, and he received Normandy as an allod, not as a benefice. Thereafter his successors held the duchy from their fathers and not from the king. Similarly, when the chronicler deals with the events that followed the assassination of William Longsword in 943, Louis IV d'Outremer and Hugh the Great had persuaded the lords of Normandy to become their vassals: Dudo introduces into their oaths a clause reserving fealty in favor of the duke, weakening in this way the force of this deed. And returning to the oath that had been taken, as early as 911 according to him, by the king to the duke, he defines it as a *securitas regni, regnum* being here the kingdom of the duke. A little later he indicates that Lothair was supposed to have promised the duke "the faith of an inextricable peace." He concludes from this that the two men are allies, *foederati.*[107]

At the same time as Dudo was writing, a letter that can be attributed to Fulbert of Chartres gives us some valuable evidence about the relationship between the king and the magnates, from the latter's point of view. Around 1023 a dispute had broken out between Robert the Pious and his vassal Eudes, count of Blois. The latter had just inherited the county of Troyes and, secure in these possessions that encircled the Capetian domain to the east and west, he was a serious threat to the power of the king. The quarrel seems to have been sparked off over the *comitatus* of Rheims, which the king wished to see back in the hands of the archbishop of that city. The king decided to proceed with the confiscation of Eudes's fiefs, that is to say of all his *honores*. In his reply to Robert, which he wrote on behalf of Eudes, Fulbert returns to the question that he had dealt with not long before: how does a vassal remain "worthy of his benefice"? He begins by discussing a distinction that had had to be made about the "quality" of the *beneficium*. Robert had indeed invested Eudes in 1021 with the county of Champagne, for which there was no longer any direct heir, and he appears to have considered the confiscation of such a recent benefice as legitimate, and we could say also as acceptable to the other princes. *A contrario*, this means that it was now hardly possible to envisage the confiscation of Eudes's ancestral counties—Tours, Blois, and Chartres—even if they too were held from the king. Fulbert also accepts this distinction, but he tries to show that it is inapplicable in this case; the benefice, he says, does not come from the royal domain "of your fisc"; it is one of those *honores* that are handed down by hereditary right—here through the collateral line—"by the grace of the king." Having thus consolidated his position, Fulbert tackles the problem of the service due. He mentions briefly that counsel and aid had been given and he lays the responsibility for their cessation at the door of Robert, who had withdrawn his favor from Eudes. There remained the hostile acts, which were definitely infringements of the negative obligations of the oath of fealty. Eudes had done them *necessitate coactus*. Fulbert ends his defense with an elegantly disguised threat—"I should prefer to die honored than live without honor," where he is playing on the two meanings of the word *honor*, and with a brief reminder of the duties of the king linked to his office, very much in the tradition of the Carolingian experts on canon law.[108]

The magnates clearly wished to concentrate the argument not on the service due but on the benefice. Where Dudo of Saint-Quentin maintains that there is an allod, Fulbert insists on an inheritance. In either case, service is certainly involved, but only in so far as it is in proportion to "the quality and quantity" of the benefice, or to the idea held of it within the general framework of concord and peace—no concord, no service.

This concept of a proportional fealty, even with regard to the king, can already be found in 989 in a letter in which Gerbert of Aurillac defines his situation vis-à-vis the Emperor Otto III. He recalls that he had taken an oath to the emperor "and to no other man," but today, he says, how can one preserve the necessary fealty, *fides servanda*? He no longer has a benefice *ob fidem retentam vel retinendam*. However, the enemies of the emperor have offered him enormous benefices. For how long will he keep "this kind of friendship"? The implicit conclusion is obvious: without a benefice, Gerbert will no longer serve the emperor, despite his oath of fealty.[109]

This was the period when the princes began to desert the royal court.

Of course, something remained of the majesty of the king. The magnates still gathered in the great solemn assemblies, and when events forced some of them to unite with the king, they felt obliged, not without impatience, to let him command and to "follow his banners."[110]

In the first decades of the eleventh century, homage and the oath of fealty had almost everywhere become closely linked. This is why from now onward legal documents and learned writings give prominence to the *forma fidelitatis*. We are dealing here not so much with a dislike of homage, although that may well have existed, or with a church tradition more favorable to a sworn fealty, as with the possibilities offered by the promise, which was more flexible than the ritual of the giving of hands. With the addition of this or that clause, the formula of fealty can be altered to accommodate different and sometimes even contradictory needs: the freedom of the princes and the lords, or the submission of the knights. From this time onward also we can speak of a feudal society. A paradox of history—at last the Carolingian plan seemed to have been realized: fealty and homage have become the dominant forms of social relationships. But the Carolingian attempt to associate one with the other, extending the obligations of vassalage to reinforce fealty, ultimately failed either to break down the southern tradition of fealty by *convenientia* or to reduce the warriors of the north to the condition of the ancient *horogavo*. In the south, this attempt succeeded merely in imposing a ritual of homage onto the oath, a homage that the magnates were long reluctant to adopt. There the oath always remained the essential element and the homage a mere accessory. But what is decided by a contract can be changed and altered by a contract. From this idea came a singularly adjustable idea of fealty. This raises the question: was it not this conception of fealty that finally won the day in the whole kingdom, particularly in relations between the magnates? And then there is the fief. In the north in the old Frankish territories the term embraced a popular notion that was very deeply rooted, that of the "present that binds" him who receives it. Having passed into vassalage, the fief encounters the Carolingian *beneficium* or *casamentum*, which may well have been a creation of the clerks. From this time on "fief" tends to assume only its popular meaning— that understood by the *vassi* rather than the *domini*—and as such to imply the idea of the permanence of the concession, as opposed to the *casamentum*, which perhaps implied more the will and arbitrary nature of the lord. It was one thing to receive a present that obliged; it was another thing to be provided for like the calf destined for the plough. In the Midi, the *feo* was not an original creation; it was the southern interpretation of the Frankish institution in very different surroundings, where the idea of public authority was still alive and strong. It was not a popular notion but a vulgarized notion. In the north, with the glorious days of the Frankish Empire passed, the pressure of the *vassi* brought it back to its point of origin, or almost.

The Carolingians had attempted to construct a power based on state control in a society not yet ready to receive it. Neither the magnate nor the allodial communities were ready then to accept that a king could be more than a kindly mediator between man and God, the incarnation of a pledge of celestial harmony. To pay him respect was necessary and almost sufficient. But he expected to be served. For that, it was not enough for the scholars of the palace to repeat the old refrains of the *respublica*. Thus there emerged the idea, one of breathtaking realism, of introducing the posture of dependence into the ranks of the aristocracy, of forcing the magnates to show in public, with ritual gestures, a submission that they could thereafter never totally efface, of creating between them and the vassal guards common attitudes and commitments, which were finally to unite them in a single idea of service. An illusion? But a social fiction can also be a reality.

It has often been thought that feudal society in the eleventh century marks the end of Carolingianism. This is true insofar as that time sees the triumph of ideas that we are tempted to call pre-Carolingian. But the multiplication, the reproduction on a kingdomwide scale of the model of the domiciled vassal groups, where the idea of service was vigorously maintained, was preparing the ground in people's minds for the subsequent construction of a hierarchical power.

Notes

1. Ganshof, *Féodalité* [189], p. 147; Grassotti, *La durée* [192], pp. 87 and 94.
2. Dig. 50. 16. 204. On the parallelism between *puer* and *vassus*, see Hollyman, *Le vocabulaire* [194], p. 115; Rouche, *L'Aquitaine* [511], p. 382.
3. *Lex salica*, 15, 9, *Leges alam.*, 36, 3 and 79, 3, texts quoted by Hollyman, *Le vocabulaire* [194], p. 116; Ganshof, *Féodalité* [189], p. 19; Marculf, 1 no. 18, *MGH, Formulae*, p. 55.
4. *MGH, Formulae*, p. 158, text translated and commented on by Ganshof, *Féodalité* [189], p. 21.
5. Magnou-Nortier, *Foi et fidélité* [206]; Rouche, *L'Aquitaine* [511], p. 382 and notes 218 and 241. *Horovago* can be compared with the German *hörig*, servant.
6. In 839, some Aquitainians "commended themselves" to Charles the Bald *more patrio*, Rouche, *L'Aquitaine* [511], p. 386.
7. Ourliac, *La convenientia* [503].
8. Ganshof, *Féodalité* [189], p. 23; Rouche, *L'Aquitaine* [511], p. 382, identifies *antrustions* and *vassi*.
9. Thus in the Angevin *Formulae* 5, 6, 7, 39, 42, 44; in those of Tours, 38; in the formulary of Marculf, 2: 18. The corresponding Germanic term was probably *treuwa*.
10. *Conventio Hugonis* [32], p. 536; Poly, *La Provence* [87], p. 348.
11. Rouche, *L'Aquitaine* [511], p. 381, who puts forward a military origin.
12. We have only the formula by which the king orders the count to have the *pagenses*, in the presence of the *missus*, swear *fidelitas et*

leudesamio in the *loci congrui*, Marculf, 1: 40. On *leute*, cf. the remarks of Lot, *Le serment de fidélité* [185].

13. Ganshof, *Charlemagne et le serment* [186].
14. The Astronomer, *Vita Hludovirci, MGH*, ss. 2: c. 3, p. 608; Dupont, *L'aprision* [119].
15. Ganshof, *Féodalité* [189], pp. 42 and 43.
16. Ganshof, *Charlemagne* [186]. Some of them may have made the oath directly to the king; conversely the *pagenses*, the ordinary freemen of the county, would have made the oath to the count; see pp. 68–69 above.
17. Dumas, "La grande et petite propriété à l'époque carolingienne," *RHD* (1926): 213 and 613.
18. Dupont, *L'aprision* [119]; Schneider, *Aspects de la société* [512]; Devailly, *Le Berry* [77], p. 123; D'Abadal, *Els primers comtes* [90], pp. 254 and 258. Although Gerald was called neither count nor *vicarius*, it is clear that he was the usual judge in the region.
19. Ganshof, *Charlemagne* [186] and *Féodalité* [189], p. 46. Naturally it is all relative; the writer of the capitulary of 792–793 considers that it is an honor for the serfs and the *coloni* of the fisc or the churches to enter into vassalage.
20. Dhondt, *Le haut Moyen Age* [475], p. 39; Coornaert, *Les Ghildes* [182]; Bonnassie, *La Catalogne* [72], p. 315; Doehaerd, *Le haut Moyen Age occidental*, 202; Devailly, *Le Berry* [77], p. 99.
21. Ganshof, *Charlemagne* [186].
22. Werner, *Les principautés périphériques* [520].
23. Ganshof, *Charlemagne* [186].
24. It is not enough here to say that the contemporaries were unable to deal with juridical abstractions, as does O. E. Odegaard, "Carolingian oaths of fidelity," *Speculum* (1941): 284. There is nothing abstract about making an oath or paying a tax.
25. Ferdinand Lot refused to see in the clause a reference to the duties of the vassal, but its introduction in 802, as with its modification in 854, cannot be explained in any other way. On this subject, see Ganshof, *Charlemagne* [186], and Lemarignier, *La France médiévale*, p. 92.
26. Ganshof, *Charlemagne* [186], p. 79; Halphen, *Charlemagne* [490], p. 417; Lot, *Le serment de fidélité* [202].
27. Halphen, *L'idée d'Etat* [489]; Magnou-Nortier, *Foi et fidélité* [206].
28. Dhondt, *Les principautés* [108], p. 20, and Dhondt, *Le haut Moyen Age* [475], p. 78. Did Charles and his counsellors try at this time to seek the support of the *arrière-vassaux* (vassals of vassals)? Cf. Halphen, *Charlemagne* [490], p. 416. This was later the imperial policy in Italy. The treatises on law and justice would have been intended for the *vassi vassorum*.
29. Lot, *Le serment* [185], Imbart de la Tour, *Les élections épiscopales dans l'Eglise de France* (Paris, 1890), p. 202. Again in Orleans in 1008, Fulbert, *Lettres* [38], no. 7. In the province of Arles in the tenth century, Poly, *La Provence* [87], p. 64.
30. Ganshof, *La féodalité* [189], p. 145.
31. Poly, *Le vocabulaire* [210]. On the role of lending with interest, see pp. 258–59 below.
32. On this revocation, see p. 57 above.
33. Rouche, *L'Aquitaine* [511], 2: 387.

34. Gregory of Tours, *Historia francorum* 8: 39, commented on by Rouche, *L'Aquitaine* [511], 2: 387.
35. Hincmar, *Pro Ecclesiae liberatum defensione*, PL, 125, col. 1050.
36. *Vie de Géraud* [34], 1: 12 and 17, col. 651 and 656.
37. Poly, *Le vocabulaire* [210].
38. *MGH, Form. Senon.*, add., p. 224. On the people, Duchesne, *Fastes épiscopaux*, 2: 365 and 468.
39. Bloch, *La société* [70], p. 236.
40. J. F. Lemarignier, "A propos de deux actes sur l'histoire du droit romain," *BEC*, 101 (1940): 157. The different situation in Catalonia, Bonnassie [72], p. 369ff.
41. Between 845 and 950, Poly, *Le vocabulaire* [210].
42. Poly, *Le vocabulaire* [210].
43. *MGH, Capitularia*, 1, no. 77.
44. Bloch, *La société* [70] p. 237 [English trans., p. 166].
45. Poly, *Le vocabulaire* [210].
46. Magnou-Nortier, *Note* [204]; Bonnassie, *La Catalogne* [72], p. 146.
47. Poly, *Le vocabulaire*, [210].
48. Magnou-Nortier, *La société laïque* [86], p. 165.
49. J. M. Font-Rius, "Les modes de détention de châteaux dans la 'vieille Catalogne. . . .'" in *Les structures sociales . . . en Aquitaine*, p. 63.
50. On the changes to *precarium* in the seventh century, see Rouche, *L'Aquitaine* [511], p. 388, which shows that the Franks did not clearly understand, or did not want to understand, the notion. This explains how in the Midi as well it was possible to confuse in the long term the *precarium stipendii causa* and the old, wider category of the *beneficium*, cf. the word used by Hincmar.
51. See p. 47 above.
52. Bonnassie, *La Catalogne* [72] p. 214, where the text speaks of a "curial allod."
53. Bloch, *Les formes* [178]. For a reexamination in depth of this analysis, see Le Goff, *Le rituel* [196].
54. See p. 123 above. For fief still with the sense of gift in *The Song of Roland*, see Boutruche, *Seigneurie* [98], 2: 172.
55. Duby, *Les villes du Sud-Est* [531] and *La diffusion du titre chevaleresque* [236].
56. *Vita Geraldi* [34], 1: 22, 24, 32, col. 656 and 660.
57. Guillot, *Le comte d'Anjou* [83], p. 49 and note 237.
58. Garaud, *Les Châtelains de Poitou* [81], p. 96 [in 1090]; Guillot, *Le comte d'Anjou* [83], p. 368 (in 1077).
59. Bonnassie, *La Catalogne* [72], p. 749ff.; Poly, *La Provence* [87], p. 138.
60. Tours, Guillot, *Le comte d'Anjou* [83], p. 4, note 18 (before 1068); Chédeville, *Chartres* [76], p. 394 (before 1028); Bur, *La Champagne* [74], p. 370 (before 1050); Richard, *Les ducs de Bourgogne* [160], p. 75 (in 1080); Ganshof, *Les ministeriales* [306], pp. 198–202 and 339 (in 1073–77 and 1106). Olivier Guillot (p. 51) is right to ask whether this system might not have been ecclesastical in origin. J. de Font-Reaulx, *Cartulaire de Saint-Etienne* (Limoges, 1922), no. 121.
61. A colorful portrait of Hugh of Nesmy can be found in Garaud, *Les chatelains de Poitou* [81], p. 95, and for Château-Larcher, Ibid., p. 96; Duby, *La société* [78], p. 151; Poly, *La Provence* [87], p. 138.

62. Duby, *Les villes du Sud-Est* [531], p. 151; Richard, *Les ducs de Bourgogne* [160], p. 106.
63. Bonnassie, *La Catalogne* [72], p. 861; Magnou-Nortier, *Fidélité et féodalité* [205]; Poly, *La Provence* [87], p. 151.
64. Fossier, *La terre* [79], p. 550.
65. Duby, *Les villes du Sud-Est* [531], pp. 152 and 155.
66. Bonnassie, *La Catalogne* [72], p. 760ff.; Poly, *La Provence* [87], p. 145.
67. Ganshof, *Féodalité* [189], p. 173; Guillot, *Le comte d'Anjou* [83], p. 298.
68. Fossier, *La terre* [79], pp. 669 and 671.
69. Richard, *Les ducs* [160], p. 74; Garaud, *Les châtelains* [81], p. 101; Duby, *Bouvines* [429], p. 140.
70. Boussard, *Services féodaux* [95]; *Miracles de Sainte-Foy* [29], 1: 12, p. 44.
71. Toubert, *Les structures du Latium* [89], p. 1182.
72. Bonnassie, *La Catalogne* [72], p. 582; Magnou-Nortier, *La société laïque* [86], p. 165; Ourliac, *L'hommage servile* [207]; Poly, *La Provence* [87], p. 164; Devailly, *Le Berry* [77], p. 527; Bur, *La Champagne* [74], p. 398; Hollyman, *Le vocabulaire* [194], p. 46.
73. Richardot, *Francs-fiefs* [213]; Vidal, *Le feudum* [217]; Ganshof, *Féodalité* [189], p. 156.
74. Hollyman, *Le vocabulaire* [194], p. 48; Chédeville, *Chartres* [76], p. 314 (in 1078–94); Magnou-Nortier, *Fidélité et féodalité* [205] (988), sees the *fevales* of the south as the officers of the domain, the "*ministeriales* of the Midi"; this is possible in some cases, but the term is more general: it refers to those who hold [land] in fief, "nobles or non-nobles"; Poly, *La Provence* [87], p. 164 (1067); Duby, *La société* [78], p. 153 (1067).
75. Fournier, *Le peuplement* [80], pp. 222 and 497; Yver, *Les premières institutions* [175]; Garaud, *Les châtelains de Poitou* [81], pp. 30 and 39; Poly, *La Provence* [87], p. 163; Duby, *La société* [78], p. 107; Guillot, *Le comte d'Anjou* [83], pp. 299 and 351.
76. *Vita Geraldi* [34], 1: 32, col. 661; Devailly, *Le Berry* [77], p. 124. Poly, *La Provence* [87], p. 54; Guillot, *Le comte d'Anjou* [83], p. 350, for the Loire area, and Painter, *Castellans* [208], for Poitou, observe the same synonym of *vassi dominici* equals the *vassi* of the count in the first half of the eleventh century; but it did not necessarily refer to people of the same social level.
77. Duby, *La société* [78], pp. 97 and 126. Public oaths in Catalonia, Bonnassie, *La Catalogne* [72], p. 139.
78. *Conventio Hugonis* [32], with comments by Garaud, *Un problème d'histoire,* [190]; Beech, *A Feudal Document* [177], and Boussard, *Services féodaux* [95]. Similar documents are found at the same period in Catalonia, Bonnassie, *La Catalogne* [72], pp. 615 and 638, and in Septimania, *Plainte de Bérenger, HGL,* 5 col. 496.
79. Painter, *Castellans* [208] and *The Lords of Lusignan* [209]; Garaud, *Les châtelains de Poitou* [81], p. 45.
80. In Catalonia, the fortresses are "curial allods," the magnates being forbidden to sell them without the agreement of the count's court. We find the same situation in the north, see Génicot, *Noblesse et principautés* [139], p. 53, for a comment on a remarkable passage in Gislebert of Mons.
81. *Conventio* [32] and Garaud, *Les châtelains de Poitou* [81], p. 44, cf. map.

82. Adhemar of Chabannes, *Chroinicon* [24], 3: 41, p. 163.
83. *Ibid.* 3: 36 and 60, pp. 159 and 185.
84. See p. 75 above. This structure seems to be similar to that found by Georges Duby at Cambrai. See *Les trois ordres* [616], p. 38.
85. Fulbert, *Letters* [38], nos. 9 and 10.
86. Ganshof, "Depuis quand a-t-on pu en France être l'homme de plusieurs seigneurs?" in *Mélanges . . . P. Fournier* (Paris, 1929), p. 261; Magnou-Nortier, *Fidélité et féodalité* [205].
87. Ganshof, *Féodalité* [189], p. 136; Kienast, *Untertaneneid* [195], p. 260, for England.
88. Bonnassie, *La Catalogne* [72], p. 745.
89. Génicot, *Noblesse et principautés* [139], p. 42, note 16.
90. The Turenne family descended from the counts of Quercy, founders of the abbey, M. Deloche, *Cartulaire de l'abbaye de Beaulieu* (Paris, 1859), p. ccxx; they still had it in 940, p. ccxlviii; Hugh of Castelnau had acquired it before 984 *jure belli armisque victricibus*, p. cclii; the Council of Limoges of 1031 describes the final structure, p. cclviii and cclxiii. According to a famous folk tradition in the Limousin, the Castelnau family only owed the Turenne family one egg. Service here was not an important thing.
91. Guillot, *Le comte d'Anjou* [83], p. 7; Adhemar, *Chronicon* [24], 3: 34, p. 156.
92. Bonnassie, *La Catalogne* [72], pp. 625 and 685.
93. Lemarignier, *L'hommage en marche* [197], pp. 113 and 161; Richard, *Les ducs de Bourgogne* [160], p. 24, sees the origin of these homages in the peace assemblies of the eleventh century.
94. Fulbert, *Letters* [38], no. 9; Lemarignier, *L'hommage au marche* [197], p. 86; Ganshof, *Féodalité* [189], p. 115.
95. Ganshof, *Féodalité* [189], p. 163; Poly, *La Provence* [87], p. 167.
96. Gervase of Tilbury had remarked on this, *Otia* [43], p. 368.
97. Bonnassie, *Les conventions féodales* [178a]; Font-Rius, *Les modes de détention*; Magnou-Nortier, *Fidélité et féodalité* [205]; Poly, *La Provence* [87], p. 164.
98. Poly, *La Provence* [87], p. 351; Rouche, *L'Aquitaine* [511], p. 485.
99. Ganshof, *Féodalite* [189], p. 107.
100. Fulbert, *Letters* [38], no. 51.
101. Guillot, *Le comte d'Anjou* [83], p. 17, rather than Garaud and Beech.
102. Ganshof, *Féodalité* [189], p. 101. The portrait of William by Adhemar of Chabannes is well known: "One would have thought he was a king rather than a duke," in *Chronique* [24], 3: 41, p. 163.
103. Carozzi, "Introduction," in Adalbero, *Carmen* [23].
104. A century later, St. Bernard was to act in the same way when he said to the count of Champagne as he invited him to pay homage to the bishop of Langres: "Offer him humbly and with respect the homage which you owe for the estate which you hold," Bur, *La Champagne* [74], p. 397.
105. On *comenda* in the Carolingian period, see Ganshof, *Féodalité* [189], p. 64; on the punishment for perjury, see his *Charlemagne* [186]. It is known that Fulbert had access to collections of capitularies, Fulbert, *Letters* [38], p. 283.
106. *BN, MS. LAT.* 12767, fol. 223.

107. Kienast, *Untertaneneid* [195], p. 61; Lemarignier, *Autour de la royauté* [198]. We are reminded of the form fief-*feudus* where Hollyman, *Le vocabulaire* [194], sees the influence of *fœdus*.
108. Fulbert, *Letters* [38], no. 86; with the comments of Halphen, *La lettre d'Eudes II* [193a]; Lemarignier, *Le gouvernement* [455], p. 61, and Bur, *La Champagne* [74], p. 157. On the policies of Eudes, see Dhondt, *Quelques aspects* [180].
109. Gerbert, *Letters* [42], no. 159.
110. William of Poitiers, *Gesta Willelmi* [47], 1: 29, p. 66. Against this interpretation see Boussard, *Services féodaux* [95], p. 167, who sees here a recovery of royal authority.

CHAPTER

3

Nobles and Knights

No will can destroy what race gives; the lineages of the nobles descend
from the blood of kings.

— Adalbero of Laon

For a long time the social history of feudal times was confined to the
history of the nobility; for a long time, too, the themes that dominated
the subject were those of continuity and, curiously, of Germanness.[1]
The nobility, born of the tribes of the great Germanic forest, endured
unbroken through the ages. Historians did not study a social group and
its evolution, but described, or sometimes dreamed up, a caste, espous-
ing its overriding illusion, that of its continuity, its identity through
the centuries. After that it only remained to make a list of the "factors"
that constituted nobility, that is, a list of the numerous "virtues" of the
social elite: power, fighting prowess, wealth, and purity of blood.

This idea of the biological continuity of nobility clashed first of all
with the research of those who opposed to the primordial nobility,
Uradel, a nobility of service, *Dienstadel*, which was established
around the Frankish monarchy. The king became the source of all
nobility, and one was noble because one was part of his house: the
Dienstadel was also a *Hausadel*. Marc Bloch went further in this
critique of the theories of noble continuity, distinguishing between
Carolingian nobility, a nobility in formation, "*de facto*," in the tenth
and eleventh centuries, and, only from the twelfth century onward,
nobility in the full sense of the word, one legally defined by a hereditary status; in this evolution, chivalry, its rituals and its ideals, were to
play a determining role.[2] Of course, if nobility is defined in terms of an
effective and almost total heredity, the only thing the historian can
study is that nobility—relative in any case—created by the judicial
exclusivity of the social group under consideration. What distinguishes

caste from class is not heredity but the fixing of the group in a legal status, and Marc Bloch was well aware of this.[3] But what is the object of the controversy: the idea that contemporaries had of nobility, or its social reality as a group, as we can see it? Can historical study separate them? If we try to define the concept of nobility *a priori* as a transmissible juridical condition and only then look for its actual existence, we face, whether we like it or not, the problem of a simple piece of evidence: the vocabulary of nobility is found in the texts considerably before its institutionalization.[4]

Let us look again at the existing evidence for feudal aristocracy, trying as far as possible not to simplify the contradictions. The first of these, and the most interesting one because it best expresses the historical movement of this period, is the distinction between nobility and knighthood. They do not both necessarily have the same structure everywhere; we have to distinguish between the structure of the nobility and the concept of it, and to observe who considered himself to be a noble or a knight, who was considered as such, and by whom. To orient ourselves, it is a good idea first to have a look at what nobility means and then to find the meaning of knighthood, in order finally to observe the birth of a common aristocratic model—lineage.

Nobility, a Changing Splendor?

To avoid losing ourselves in the mists of an *Uradel*, grandiose perhaps but hard to discern, let us look at the texts of the tenth and eleventh centuries to see what they tell us about nobility. We shall then see how the term is applied.

What Is Nobility?

We shall start with what it is not. The hagiographies are careful to distinguish in their praises between nobility and a certain number of other values. Nobility is not strictly speaking wealth, even if it is natural that nobles should be rich; neither is it power, even if it is normal that nobles should command—there are serfs who were counts and bishops in the Carolingian period. And the chronicler of Gembloux, recalling the nobility, wealth, and power of the founders of his abbey, affirmed very correctly that "wealth in possessions brings the power of the nobility to the fore." Neither is it the wisdom that is its ornament, nor being a warrior, *militia*. Wealth and power, wisdom and military valor, like generosity or even pride, are all attributes of nobility, but nobility itself is something else. That is our first piece of evidence.[5]

Another piece of evidence for contemporaries is that nobility comes from birth: to be *nobilis* is to be *ortus parentibus nobilibus, ex nobili genere, ex nobili prosapia*. One is born noble, one does not become it.

Noble origins are here rooted in the mystery of birth. For the men of the Middle Ages, as for the men of many other periods and for many other peoples, the material, pseudobiological vehicle of nobility is the blood: one is born noble because of a particular quality of the blood. The formulae return again and again to this: "he was noble by blood," "of a blood made proud by nobility"; *affinitas sanguinis* unites one noble line with another.[6] From this arises the age-old question: Of whom is the child truly born, the woman or the man? Does nobility come from women, *per ventrem*, or from men, *per virgam?*

The texts are rarely clear on this matter, and the controversy is still wide open. In certain cases, nobility was clearly handed down through the female line, in Champagne and perhaps Flanders, but the evidence is late. Other texts have perhaps had too much read into them, such as the application for the *servi* and others who were not free men of the old rule *partus sequitur ventrem:* liberty is first assimilated with nobility and then the procedure follows logically: because nonliberty is transmitted by women, then liberty, its opposite, must have the same origin. Even if it is admitted that liberty is the equivalent of nobility, there is nothing to say that opposites are transmitted in the same way, all the more so here as it is a matter of very different categories. The *partus sequitur ventrem* rule was born in Rome in the time of slavery and can be explained very simply: the master does not always have the means to control the alliances or unions of his female slaves and in most cases he is not worried about it; what does concern him is the offspring that will be the manpower of his lands. It is a very ancient saying that *mater semper certa est,* the father on the contrary not being known with certainty except in "legitimate marriage": *pater is est . . . ,* but there is no legitimate marriage for slaves. By contrast, the *sainteurs* accused in law of being serfs could only insist, as Georges Duby remarks, on the freedom of their ancestors.[7] The transmission of servitude seems *a priori* different from that of nobility. A second indication of the transmission of nobility by women is more interesting; we find it in the quite frequent mention of the mother only in oaths of fealty: "I, so-and-so, son of [female name]." On the other hand, the few very old forms from the tenth century mention both the father and the mother. Even ignoring these few examples, the interpretation of the others is not easy. Does it imply the social preeminence of descent from the mother? One is inclined to think the opposite: a large number of these oaths were taken on matters of land by heirs who held it from their fathers, and the implicit descent through the male line seems to be the very basis of the deed. Perhaps the maker of the oath wished to mention his mother because of the advance of legitimate marriage and the fact that in the eleventh century bastards were not allowed to succeed. According to this hypothesis, the mention of the maternal line would provide no information about the transmission of nobility, but it would tell us something about the reaction against bastards and the division of noble inheritances.[8] As for the mention of nobility through the female line in certain chivalrous genealogies, we shall return to them when looking at that of Lambert of Wattrelos.[9]

The last and most important piece of evidence can be found in the sources. A man is called "very noble," "amongst the most noble," "not least of the nobles," "of equal nobility," or "of petty nobility."[10] Thus nobility has an intensity; its splendor depends on alliances. Sigebert describes in this manner the marriage, a little before 950, of the sister of Guibert, founder of Gembloux: "the sister of the very noble Guibert married Heribrand, eminent among the nobles of Brabant for his family and his riches," and, he adds, by doing this "she is increasing her nobility with another nobility."[11] It is also possible to reduce one's nobility by means of misalliances, or, at least in the eyes of the clerks, by illegitimate alliances. Thus Richer of Rheims, recalling the royal race of the count of Vienne Charles Constantine, bastard of Louis the Blind of the Boso family, adds: "Born, certainly, of royal race, but sullied to the great-great-grandfather's generation by a illegitimate genealogy."[12] This is not overimaginative gossip but an accurate summary of the royal alliances in the genealogy of the Boso family. By the choice of their spouses, then, the nobles were able to increase or maintain the degree of their nobility—a particular application of the same idea of selective breeding that provided their warhorses and their hunting dogs.

And indeed, the sign of nobility of these horses is their individual name, their "own name," as William of Poitiers said. So the name is the external manifestation of blood and nobility. Hence the texts that say that a person is "noble by name."[13]

An example as famous as it is ancient is found in the words of Guntram when he baptized his nephew Chlotar: "May this child grow, may he understand the significance of his name and may he have the same power as formerly had he from whom he received the name." In 870, the deacon Roland made a donation to the Abbey of Vabres, one of the great Frankish foundations of the Midi, "for the soul of my uncle Roland who gave me his name." At the end of the tenth century, Richer said of the Carolingian Arnulf, nominated by Hugh Capet to the archbishopric of Rheims, that he had been "endowed with an honourable dignity, being the only survivor of the royal line, in order that the paternal name should not be forgotten."

It is striking too to see in certain families how the names are transmitted without any change to their two roots or elements. It is a matter then of transmitting unchanged the name of an ancestor whereas the system of the recombination of the elements at each generation implies on the contrary the absence of a genealogical memory. The custom of retaining a single name was probably followed first by the kings and the dukes before being adopted by the nobles.[14]

The selection of names is thus for the nobles paralleled by the selection of alliances; one implies the other. Georges Duby has given us a striking example of this in his study of the transmission of names in noble families in a canton in the Mâcon region during the eleventh century. Forty-seven active male laymen around the year 1000 share thirty-five names; a century later, their hundred and fifty descendants bore thirty-nine names. Duplication of names had become frequent, but not just any names: the five most common names belonged to the families of the count and to the two families holding castles. Of all the names borne by their ancestors, the nobles of the Mâcon region retained a preference for those that recalled "the most exalted roots of their ancestry." The spread, during the tenth century, among the seigneurial families of the middle Loire area of a few great names belonging to famous and powerful Carolingian families of the region a century earlier can be explained in the same way.[15] The ancient ancestry of the noble is a product of his own political aspirations.[16]

However, the noble is not merely the bearer of a famous name, he is also the one who remembers the individuals who bore that name before him. The past for him is no longer a collective legend, but a structure of ancient relationships. And just as his ancestors had chosen their alliances, so his own memory selects what it chooses to recall. The intensity of nobility is also an intensity of memory. To observe this we need to look at those places where this memory was looked after, in the abbeys whose job it was to protect with their prayers the souls of the illustrious dead and sometimes to watch over their tombs. One of the most revealing sources in this context is provided by the "memorial books," which were placed around the altars of the great imperial sanctuaries and bestowed the benefits of prayers to the Divinity on the names written there. The study of these *libri memoriales* sheds much light on the structure of noble kinship in the great families of the imperial aristocracy in the early tenth century. Its essential character is that of giving the same importance to cognatic and agnatic kinship. The Frankish or Swabian noble of the Carolingian period sees kinship above all as a horizontal network of alliances in which the women are as important as the men.[17]

This might explain the difficulties encountered by modern historians trying to establish genealogies going back before the eighth, ninth, or even tenth centuries. Not only is there a scarcity of documentation and an absence of family names, but above all there is a difference in mental attitude that placed more importance on kinship—*consanguinitas*—than on direct descent (filiation). It is interesting to see in a southern chartulary of the tenth century, that of Vabres, the same broad kinship groups whose names are written in the *libri memoriales*.[18]

This particular structure of kinship has been related to the situation of the Carolingian aristocracy: a social class that unites its collective exercise of power under the aegis of the sacred monarchy; families that pass the *honores* from hand to hand and whose degrees of power are measured by their nearness to the throne. The *optimates* become allied in marriage over and over again, just as they forge links with the

Church and with the king. They are forced into this complex game of matrimonial alliances that is a substitute for political maneuvering. The referee in the game, the one who maintains a balance, is the king.[19] In this unceasing quest for "more nobility," the king is recognized as the most noble and as the one with whom an alliance will most enrich the blood. To dispute this, to want to establish one's own house, is to be banished from the imperial aristocracy. It is remarkable that in the Frankish period the only lineage that appears with any clarity is that of the king. But, as the great families began to separate themselves from the monarchy to establish their own power, this picture begins to change.[20]

The first written genealogy that we possess, that of Arnulf of Flanders, composed in Saint-Bertin in 951–959, is characteristic. After the eulogy of the prince, accompanied by funerary prayers, it traces through patrilineal descent the *sancta prosapia domni Arnulfi*. Arriving at Baldwin I, the *ex bassalus* of Charles the Bald, the author mentions his marriage with Judith, the king's daughter. At this point, abandoning Baldwin's paternal ancestors, he unwinds the "genealogy of the most noble emperors and kings of the Franks," which in any case he borrows uncritically from the *scriptoria* of Lotharingia. In the eleventh century, a fragment of the genealogy of the same Arnulf insists on the fact that "he came from the blood of great kings, Elstruda, daughter of Edgar [Alfred], king of England, having borne him to Baldwin." It is to this model of nobility that as late as the beginning of the eleventh century the aged and conservative descendant of an old family of the *Reichsadel*, Adalbero of Laon, is referring when he exclaims: "What one acquires from one's birth, no will can destroy. The titles of the nobles come to them from the blood of the kings from whom they are descended and the true glory of the kings and princes is their noble origin." The connection with the *stirps Karoli* (the stock of Charles) is a theme that reappears later in the genealogies of the counts of Boulogne as well as those of William of Malmesbury, Guy of Basoches—anxious to ensure the alliance between the count of Champagne and the counts of Flanders—and the bishop of Metz, stressing the saintliness of his predecessor Arnulf.[21]

The importance of this model of nobility renders even more remarkable the rather different genealogies of which the written traces seem to be of a later date. These are genealogies in which the founder of the princely line is not related to the royal house, but is an adventurer sprung from nowhere who marries an heiress. Thus, Lambert of Ardres gives as the *auctor* of the Guines family a Danish adventurer, Sifrid, who marries a count's daughter. Lambert of Saint-Omer, tracing the genealogy of the counts of Blois, revives a tradition already known to Richer at the end of the tenth century and goes back to a mysterious Gerlo, at one time described as the son of Ingo, a royal groom who received as wife the widow of the viscount of Blois, and at others described as a Norman leader. Similarly, the Angevin genealogies make

Tertullus the Forester the founder of the house of Anjou. This element of legend should also be compared with the current of the supernatural that deeply influences the whole of the twelfth century.[22]

All this genealogical juggling reveals the fictions used to assert the continuity of the nobility. Contemporaries were well aware of this. Thus we see the author of the *Gesta* of the lords of Amboise aptly recalling Sallust when he says:

At the time of Charles the Bald, *several new men, more endowed with goods and honor than the nobles,* became great and illustrious. *Fixing their eyes on the seekers of military glory* they did not hesitate *to throw themselves into danger and through it to seek fortune.* There were also in those times *men of ancient stock and many ancestors* who could boast of the high deeds of their ancestors, more so than of their own. These men, when they were sent for some important duty, *would take one of the inhabitants to guide them in their office.* When the king ordered them to *change their style of government,* they wanted to *change emperor.* For this reason Charles had only a few members of this nobility with him. It was to the new men that he confided the military duties and the inheritances acquired with much effort and danger. Tertullus was of this kind.[23]

A text with a double meaning, where the claims of the local nobility in the twelfth century can dress themselves up with ancient and imposing memories. But is the legend so far from the truth? The king of the *Gesta,* Charles the Bald, is strangely reminiscent of Richer's Charles the Simple, who chose his counsellors from among people supposedly without nobility "as if the nobles did not exist!"[24] The most recent research, in fact, does not contradict these affirmations; it complements them when it shows the ancestors of the counts of Anjou allying themselves in marriage with the great families of the Carolingian court.[25] Once again we see the essential role played by women. Through them an ancient nobility can be attached to new men without any doubt ever being cast on their pedigree.[26]

Nobility, this mysterious aura, is not then properly speaking a social group. It is first and foremost the justification of the masters of their own hereditary dominance. As such, nobility is a matter of opinion. Nobility, an idea that the dominant class has of itself, is a dominant idea both among those who carry it in their veins and those who support it by their labor, for those who have it as for those who covet it.

Who is Noble?

As a result of these considerations we now have to ask: who is, or is not, noble in the tenth, eleventh, and twelfth centuries? This is a tricky question, since the texts are often contradictory. Recent historiography has been at pains not to simplify in an arbitrary manner these contradictions and to emphasize by contrast the different social levels, and, we would add, the tensions that they express. To know who is noble is first a question of where and when.

In all the large regions of the kingdom, *patriae, regna,* or simple *pagi,* one group is singled out in the texts with expressions like "the first in the land" or "the lords of the land," *principes, proceres, primores, primates, optimates, magnates.* When the document allows them to be identified, these "princes"—in the etymological sense of the word— turn out to be the masters of the major fortresses, the *domini castri:* there is no doubt that these men are called nobles.

In Catalonia there are in the county of Vich-Ausona thirteen great castellans; in Poitou, a dozen; in Provence, about twenty, and in Auvergne, perhaps the same; in the Mâcon area we find six; in Picardy in the eleventh century, six families dominate, and by far, all the others; about a dozen castellans appear in the royal entourage after 1028.[27]

Once again it is Catalonia that provides us with a good example of such a group, the *proceres regionis,* shortly before the year 1000. The families of castellans regularly bear the title of noble; the heads of household are the old *vicarii* or viscounts, all are vassals of the count and this relationship is so strong that we see a scribe coining the title of *procerus (sic) comitalis*—later the *comtors.* They are all united by a tight network of kinship. Some of them marry daughters of the count's family, but the count seeks a wife from outside Catalonia.

Let us remain on what Georges Duby calls the Mediterranean side of Latin Christendom. We see in southern France the same correlation between the *principes, primates, magnates* and those whom the great councils of peace of the eleventh century call the *nobiles provinciales.* In Auvergne, the great castellans are also called nobles, for example the Mercoeur family, the viscount of Clermont, the lord of Escorailles and the lord of Montboissier, the founder of Saint-Michel de la Cluse in Italy. These were all *seniores arvernici* or *principes arvernorum,* whom the texts of the tenth century depict as performing the *commendatio* to the count or as splitting up into opposing factions. The situation is the same in Berry, at least in the south, which looks toward Auvergne more than toward the Loire.[28]

To the west, in Poitou, during the whole of the tenth century the references to assemblies and the formulae of corroboration of charters regularly mention *nobiles viri* or *nobiles personnae* whom they some- times distinguish from the *pauperes.* It is clear that the nobles were an important group in this area. But individual mentions that would allow us to identify the noble are rare; at most we know that Ebbo, lord of Château-Larcher, was in 969 "a not ignoble man, citizen of Poitiers," and that the famous Hugh of Lusignan still bore in 1025 the old title of *vir clarissimus.* We have a similar picture for the Chartres area, where the majority of the *nobiles* appear to be the possessors of castles.[29]

In Normandy the charters of the duchy in the eleventh century reveal around the duke a large group of *principes* or *optimates Nor-*

manniae. The important men indicated by these titles are also called in the same deeds *nobiles.*

However, when we read the studies devoted to Normandy we sometimes get the impression that the heads of the great Norman families were more proud of their claims of Danish origin than of their noble titles. There are only a few individual mentions of *nobiles* in the eleventh century in the collections of *Miracula.*[30]

Leaving Normandy for the old Frankish lands, we see first in Picardy a similar group of *proceres curie, principes patriae.* And the charters seem to identify this group with the count's entourage, which would explain the synonyms *nobiles palatini* and *nobiles optimates sui* (of the count). Among these nobles there are the officers of the count, the viscounts of Abbeville, of Rue, the castellan of Amiens, the advocate of Saint-Valéry and that of Saint-Riquier.[31] Nobles on this high social level are found also in the Namurois. Guibert, the founder of Gembloux, was anything but a petty noble, being in a position to bestow four *villae* in the Namurois, one in Limburg, one near Mainz, seven in the Gâtinais and near Etampes, a *curtis* in Sens, and a mill in Lassois. Similarly, Eilbert of Florennes, when he founded Waulsort, concedes five *villae* and also some allods in Thiérache, some fiefs on the borders of the Laonnais and Vermandois and the land of Ribemont to the southeast of Saint-Quentin; it is no accident that he had sent his son to the household of Raoul of Cambrai. Eilbert was probably descended from a vassal of Louis the Stammerer; Guibert was the nephew of the count of Namur. The Lotharingian nobles are few in number and rich in allods. The upper levels of nobility take root here— and it comes as no surprise—among the *vassi regales* and the *comites mediocres* of the Carolingian era.[32]

And so, from Ghent to Barcelona, from Poitiers to Mâcon, no one is in any doubt: the nobles are first of all the lords, descendants here of royal vassals, there of *vicarii,* and sometimes of the great allodialists to whom the count has delegated the command of the public fortresses. But several texts show that in certain regions it is necessary to share nobility with people of a lesser caliber.

In Flanders and Picardy, the chronicler Hariulf of Saint-Riquier, speaking at the end of the eleventh century of the *vassi* of the abbey in Carolingian times, stresses that they served nobly; and we know that the chapel that was reserved for them was called the chapel of the nobles. A little to the north, the author of the miracles of Saint-Bertin, speaking of those who in the early tenth century had commended themselves to lords because they were not rich enough in allods, embraces both with the one term *nobilitas terrae.*[33] Just as there was at Saint-Riquier a chapel of the nobles, so there was a cemetery of the nobles at Waulsort in the eleventh century. In all these cases the nobles are petty lords who in the Midi would have been called knights. So not far from Gembloux there lived at the end of the eleventh century a knight, *miles,* grandson of a noble, *vir nobilis,* nephew of the abbot and cousin of another *miles* who was to become a monk. This man married the daughter of the mayor of the abbey *(villicus)* and, when he died in battle, his widow married the *villicus* of the bishop of Liège. The brother of this woman was a cleric.[34] Many of these petty nobles did not even have a fortified house and had to take refuge in the church tower. In times of famine they were no longer able to help their *familia* and the monasteries of the region had to come to their assistance. Thus the group of nobles in the Namurois probably contained many petty lords: forty-seven families in the twelfth century shared three hundred and seventy villages or hamlets. All these nobles, rich or poor, had their law, the *lex nobilium*, the old Salic law.[35]

An exceptional document that allows us to see "inside" one of the families of petty nobles is the "genealogy of his ancestors" included by the canon of Cambrai, Lambert of Wattrelos, in the *Annales Cameracenses* written in 1170. Lambert was born in 1108. His paternal grandfather, who was living around 1050, was a *miles casatus* who, having made a happy marriage, had settled down on an estate brought by his wife; later alliances, notably with the house of the lords of Avesnes, further consolidated the nobility of the family. Was it not through his maternal grandmother that nobility came into the blood of those of the line of Lambert? He only uses the terms *nobilis* and *nobilia* about her lineage. Such a family orientation evidently strengthened the position of the maternal uncle, in both the social habits and in the way of thinking of this petty nobility. It did not prevent—in fact quite the opposite—the Lambert family from being organized in a knightly lineage from at least as early as the mid–eleventh century. We see too how the vocabulary used depends on the source under consideration: Lambert often uses the word *miles* to mean a noble kinsman; he is thinking of the old wider sense of "warrior," rather than referring to the category of *milites* used in the charters of his region at that time.[36]

Further south, in Frankish Burgundy, a significant anecdote shows us some similar nobles at a very early date. An abbey serf, Stabilis, claimed that he was free and had even married a noble woman. The abbot of Fleury had him sent for by his provost. The matter came to a judicial duel, and Stabilis, a poor fighter, thought to get out of it by objecting to the champion of the monastery, saying that he was too humbly born. The latter, outraged, exclaimed: "I am free, and indeed of ancient nobility. I shall make it my business to teach you to know the power of St. Benedict in the heart of God."[37] Not far away in the Mâcon area, in the approximately one hundred pieces of land around the abbey of Cluny, there were no less than thirty-four noble families, all in a greater or lesser degree kinsmen of the masters of the castles.[38]

Going down to the Midi, the use of the term *nobilis* by the authors of the charters seems to be somewhat different. In the tenth century the accounts of assemblies in Septimania and Catalonia show that among the *boni homines* who owned land not far from the cities and who were called in to bear witness in law, some were considered *nobiles* or *nobiliores,* and this allodial nobility is reminiscent of the nobles of the Poitou formularies. But a century later when the texts allow us to identify individuals, the circle of *nobiles* seems to be very narrow. In Provence, the few petty nobles that one can pick out are all members of families from Arles, vassals of the archbishop or the count; some of them were, in the twelfth century, to become truly great lords. In Catalonia the nobility is even more restricted and is limited to the group of *proceres.*[39]

Thus the nobility seem to be more or less numerous depending on whether they are in the north, west, or south. Are there similar differences when we relate the quality of nobility to freedom? In the Namur area and in Brabant and Lorraine at least, the answer in the eleventh century seems clear: if they are not one and the same thing, there is at least a strong correlation between nobility and freedom. Naturally these two categories will never coincide exactly, but *liber* or *ingenuus* and *nobilis* are practically interchangeable terms for the writers of deeds. This can be explained if the petty nobles are numerous and if banal lordship has more than elsewhere increased its oppression of the peasantry. As Léopold Génicot points out, the virtues that are elsewhere connected with nobility are attributed, in the Namurois, to liberty; the expression *lex nobilium* here has as a synonym *lex ingenuum.*[40] And the genealogical fragment of the eleventh century that celebrates the royal ancestry of Arnulf of Flanders, calls this noble or royal blood "free," *ingenuus.* At the same period, the Lorrainer Adalbero of Laon merges *nobiles* and *ingenui* to contrast them with *servi* and has nobility deriving from the blood of kings.[41] By contrast, when an important southerner in 813 speaks of "the splendor of liberty"—once again *ingenuitas*—it is in order to grant it to the slaves whom he is freeing in his will and who will continue to live under his patronage—*patrocinium.* Liberty for him is something quite different from nobility.[42]

The coincidence between nobles and freemen can then depend as much on the relatively wide spread of the nobility as on the increasing rarity of free peasants. It does not in any case hide the fact that these are two fundamentally heterogenous categories: a quality of the blood is not a legal status. Servitude can be created by a legal act, nobility cannot—or at least not yet. While we were speaking of petty nobles, a new word appears in the texts: knight, or rather *miles.* Distinct as these categories are, the question of the relationship between noble and knight must be examined.

Chivalry, a Shared Ideal

The word *miles,* an approximate and literary synonym of the less common vulgar Latin *caballarius,* has as rich and various a history as has the word *nobilis.*[43] From late antiquity, when the military condition was not much valued, the word had inherited a sense of humble and sometimes contemptible service. And it is no doubt a concern for humility that prompts clerics to describe the most heroic of their number as *milites Christi* and their asceticism as a service—*militare Deo*. When the first *vassi*, the dependent warriors *in obsequio*, appeared, it was quite natural to use the word *miles* as a synonym for those who objected to the vulgar expression *caballarius*. In this sense, still in the tenth century a writer with an enthusiasm for classical Latinity speaks of the misalliance of Charles of Lorraine saying that he had taken "a wife who was inferior to him, of the military class, *(de ordine militari)*";[44] and, echoing the popular traditions about the origins of the Robertians, he makes them part of the *equester ordo*, borrowing this phrase from Sallust. So we see that the *miles* originally comes from a very different social level than the *nobilitas*, from the *ingenui in obsequio*, the *vassi*, or the *casati*.[45] But two different concepts are involved as well. As the texts from Chartres were still saying in the eleventh century, using, perhaps deliberately, expressions from Paul the Deacon, one becomes a *miles* by *professio*, which is to say by a promise that creates a state of affairs.[46] Here too monastic and military vocabularies appear together. In this sense, *miles* also means *vassus*, a meaning that is sometimes reinforced with a possessive or a genitive: *miles suus, miles alicujus*. At the same time, there was nothing to prevent the word from having its ancient classical meaning, "devoted to the career of arms," particularly in such formulae as *seculari militiae deditus*, once again a monastic expression. However, by the thirteenth century, *miles*, knight, has become a title, and chivalry a virtue balancing that of nobility. Once again, in order to define its evolution we need to distinguish between places and times and between southern or northern France.

We are not concerned here with the fact that a domestic warrior might bear the title of *miles* or its romance equivalent, *caballarius*, but with the moment when more elevated people begin to be referred to by this word. Then knighthood ceases to be a condition, or a profession—there are knights just as there are bakers[47]—and becomes an ideal model, where an ambiguous unity between people at very different social levels with very different origins—the landowning aristocrats, the wealthy allodialists, and mounted servants—is apparently achieved.

Knights, Freemen, and Nobles

Who is called knight, and from what period? Georges Duby recently examined an area running from Catalonia to northern Italy.[48] The word *miles* is rarely found in this area in the first decades of the eleventh century. This is because the scribes prefer *caballarius*, in Catalonia as late as c. 1050, and perhaps also because these first *milites* have neither the desire not the means to make donations to the churches. After 1020–30, on the other hand, the spread of the fief brings the knights greater wealth, but more importantly the magnates begin to call themselves *miles*—except as yet in Catalonia. It is worth mentioning that here it is always the most ambiguous Latin form that is chosen by the scribes: a lord is never called *caballarius*. Moreover, the word *caballarius* was to fall into disuse in the language of the charters. In the years 1040–50, in Cremona, Provence, the Nîmesois, and Le Puy, the *milites* are contrasted in the formulae of corroboration sometimes with *populus* or *rustici* and sometimes with clerics. Identification of the persons involved confirms that *militia* here refers equally to the old *caballarii* and to the most powerful lords. In the Narbonne region and in Catalonia it is only toward 1080 that the opposition *milites-rustici* appears, and the great Catalan nobles appear reluctant to bear the title.[49] Thus in the Midi we find side by side nobles, knights from the cities—sometimes nobles themselves—and knights domiciled in the country. But, as Pierre Bonnassie emphasizes, a psychological rapprochement is not social fusion, and at times the distinction was made, as at the Council of Saint-Gilles in 1042–44, between the great and the lesser knights, *milites majores* and *minores,* or as at Melgueil a little later between the *milites nobiliores* and the others.

The divisions that we find in the documents of northern France are of quite another order. In the representative example of the Namurois, the charters of the twelfth century are at pains to distinguish between *nobiles* and *milites*. Furthermore, when a *miles* is free, it is carefully pointed out. Conversely, the *milites* are very often classed in the *familia* along with the *ministeriales* or are confused with them. There is the same rigorous dichotomy in Brabant, where the first *milites* in noble families only begin to appear, and then only rarely, in the second half of the twelfth century, at a period when the class of *ministeriales* is beginning to become important. In Picardy, after 891, a monk of Saint-Bertin divides soldiers into *nobiliores* and *inferiores*. Later, Hariulf and Lambert of Ardres similarly contrast *proceres* and *milites;* among these *proceres*, the nobles, a certain number of petty lords appear to have neither *bannum* nor office. There are no examples of a noble calling himself a knight, nor is a knight called noble before the end of the twelfth century. The earliest examples date from 1194 and concern Ponthieu. In these regions the *militia*, far from being a company where petty allodialists turned vassal prided themselves on rubbing shoulders with the masters of the castles, served in the twelfth century to designate fairly consistently a clearly individualized group of dependent warriors.[50]

This structure is reminiscent of one found further to the east in the Germanic lands where at the beginning of the twelfth century the monk of Regensburg, *Honorius Augustodunensis*, explains that mankind was divided up after the flood into three social categories, the *liberi*, children of Shem, the *milites*, children of Japhet, and the *servi*, the children of Ham.[51] Similarly the chronicle of the Alsatian monastery of Ebersheim contrasts the *principes* with the *milites* of the *familia* and dates this division back to Julius Caesar's German auxilliaries and the Gallic wars. It is notable that the chronicler indicates that Caesar, before returning to Rome, had made these *principes* "Roman senators," which is to say, nobles, and the simple *milites* "Roman citizens," which is to say free men; for him therefore their presence in the *familia* did not imply a servile condition. The author, writing around 1163, clearly identifies with the *ministeriales*.[52]

The case of Normandy is more difficult to interpret. The collections of *Miracula* give a tripartite division of the *magnates-nobiles-milites* type. The *scriptoria* are reluctant to use *miles* too frequently and the few mentions in the charters appear to refer to people of quite humble rank. Here too the writer is sometimes careful to point out whether or not a *miles* is *liber* or *ingenuus*.[53]

We find in Normandy examples of contradictions in the sources. William of Poitiers, knowledgeable in Roman history, makes a distinction between the upper nobility and "the *milites* of middle nobility and the *milites gregarii*,"[54] but it may be that the use of *miles* for the petty nobles is here a literary device. Similarly, the ducal chancellery once uses *miles* to refer to a magnate, but with the possessive *suus* that makes it the equivalent of vassal. Lucien Musset also stresses the use in the second third of the eleventh century of the more realistic qualification *eques*. Could this not be because there was uncertainty at this period about the meaning to give to the word *miles*?

There remains a vast area from the Ile-de-France to Poitou, including Chartres and Anjou. Despite some careful and thoughtful monographs, it is not easy to draw any conclusions. Let us take the example of the Chartres area. Very early in the cathedral obituaries we find two important people—one "very noble" and the other noble and a viscount of the city. The writer of the obituaries changes between 940 and 1130. These two men died in the tenth century, but can we be sure that these are not titles awarded at a later date? Three other mentions use *miles* for a castellan, the first referring to Amaury of Montfort, appearing in a deed subscribed by the king—one of the king's entourage. The second mention refers to a man originating from Chartres but a castellan in Berry, Humbaud of Vierzon. The last mention, which dates from the end of the eleventh century, is the only one definitely from Chartres. André Chédeville points out that it is from just this time that the *domini* stop calling themselves knight, until 1200.[55]

The lords seem not to have liked the qualification *miles*. The term appears to be reserved for the *milites castri*, particularly those of Chartres whom we know were called nobles in the second half of the eleventh century. André Chédeville has counted the occurrences of the expression *quidam miles talis* in the charters, finding five before 1050, twenty-two between 1050 and 1100, forty-three between 1100 and 1150, and twelve between 1150 and 1200. The formula consisting of the localization *talis miles de tali loco* peaks at a later date: there is one example before 1100, nine between 1100 and 1150, and eighteen between 1150 and 1200. It is only in 1199 that the use of *miles* as a proper title appears: *ego talis miles*. So *miles* refers to a military state that is neither very noble nor very humble. Among the twenty-two dependants with horses of the abbey of Saint-Père of Chartres at the beginning of the twelfth century, only one is called *miles*.

The spread of the word *miles* in the deeds of Chartres indicates without doubt a rise in the social status of the *milites*. This should be seen in relation to the appearance of the same term in the royal charters from 1022–23 and particularly in 1031, a phenomenon that is even more difficult to interpret because it is concerned here with *milites regii*. Some of them are obviously members of the city garrisons, of Paris or Senlis for example, the equivalent of the *milites carnotenses*.[56]

In Poitou, a charter from Saint-Maixent of the tenth century divides the *nobiles* into *superiores* and *inferiores*. Certain *nobiles* seem at the end of the eleventh century to be quite poor. Conversely, free men who are neither nobles nor knights may be rich. We find at times the contrast *principes-nobiles* or the equivalent *proceres-milites*; and at the lower level the opposition *primores castri*, or *nobiles castri*, the knights of the castle, and *populares*. The frequently used formulae *quidam nobilis* and *quidam miles* are interchangeable; the title *ego miles* appears in 1065. From 1070 to 1110 the texts contrast the *ordo militaris* to the *ordo popularis*; the *militia* is a *ministerium* to which the noble can consecrate himself. The formula *talis miles de* is frequent from 1070. But we do not find the great castellans taking the title of *miles*. There are mentions of *milites ignobiles* in the *familia* of the lord of Talmond and in that of the lord of Mortemer at the end of the eleventh century. Some of them at least are dependants. So we do not find in Poitou a perfect correlation between *miles* and *nobilis*. It is possible to be noble, like the *superiores* or the castellans, without being a *miles*, and it is possible to be a *miles*, a dependant, without being noble.[57]

The Mâcon area seems to be a case apart. The title of noble seems to adorn indiscriminately both lords and village squires. From the early years of the eleventh century the great castellans have no hesitation in calling themselves *ego miles*. The evidence here is all the more convincing because we see the word *miles* being introduced into the ancient formulae of legal documents. The expressions *ego miles* and *signum talis militis* first appear in 971; *quidam miles* in 1000; *miles de N*, appearing c. 1050, becomes common after 1075. At the end of the eleventh century, we find the opposition *milites-rustici*. The *ministeriales* are not called *miles*, being still in the twelfth century *vassali*. Soon *miles* almost completely replaces *nobilis*.[58] The juxtaposition of nobility and knighthood here seems both early and total, and knighthood is a quality that even the highest of the nobles were keen to attribute to themselves.

Thus it appears that in the regions of Flanders and the neighboring imperial territories, in Picardy and perhaps in Normandy, *miles*, semi-servile, is clearly the opposite of *nobilis*, which is more or less the equivalent of free. In the south including Provence and Septimania— and in relation to which the Mâcon area would appear to be anticipating later developments—the nobility willingly adopts the title of knight, but it seems less eager than in Mâcon to become related in marriage to families of *milites*. This dislike of mixing the *nobiles* of old stock with *milites* is particularly noticeable in Catalonia. Last there is a third area, from Poitou to Chartres, where *miles* and *nobilis* are one and the same, but only on the level of the petty nobility. How can we explain these disparities?

The Church and Knighthood

The role of the Church appears to be of primary importance. The Christianization of the old practice of the giving of arms to the young warrior has long been emphasized. We know of prayers in England and in Mainz for the blessing of weapons,[59] but it was only very slowly and by an unknown route that Christian ritual invested the ceremony of dubbing: the blessing of weapons is one thing, quite another the fact that the future knight receives them from the hands of a priest. It is only in this case that one can speak of a Christianization of dubbing, because the word "to dub" really means to equip. But the study of known cases of dubbing up to the beginning of the twelfth century shows that princes and petty knights generally received their arms from the hands of a layman. Even in the first half of the twelfth century the *Chansons de Geste* rarely use the term "dub" to refer to the first solemn handing-over of arms and retain its common meaning of "to equip with armor."[60] However, in a pontifical from Rheims of the early eleventh century, we find alongside a benediction for the sword that follows the Mainz pontifical a clear indication that it was the archbishop who gave the arms. Around 1093, the bishop of Cambrai used a "ritual for arming a defender of the great churches, or another knight."[61] The only way of resolving these contradictions is to assume that these liturgies were first applied only to *milites ecclesiae*, these "defenders" of the great churches. "The bishop orders the knights of the church as he orders the clerics of the diocese; he conducts the handing over of the baldric and the sword; then he pronounces the words which are those, adapted, of the royal investiture; lastly he invokes the soldier saints, Maurice, Sebastian and George." The Christianization of the dubbing ceremony takes root here among the city knights, the *casati* of the bishop.[62]

This helps our understanding of a famous text of the bishop of Chartres, John of Salisbury.[63] In Book 6 of his *Policraticus*, John deals with knighthood. Two things, he writes, make a knight, as they make a cleric: the *electio* and the *professio*. The first term according to him means the choice of a knight by a *dux*, a choice that he compares to the choice of the cleric by the bishop. The *professio* is, for the knight, the oath of fealty to his lord, and John insists that without "military oath" no one is allowed to bear arms—*militare*. And in order to justify the duties of the knight to the Church, he argues thus: many knights are not bound to the Church by a solemn oath, but it should be supposed that besides the oath made by some of them to their Church, there is a tacit oath made by all the others. John justifies this idea by the custom of having the handing over of arms performed in a church with the sword being placed in the altar, thus clearly alluding to the old ritual of benediction. From this he concludes that a *legitima professio militiae* has been made in favor of the Church *non verbo sed facto*. The knight who is, he says, illiterate, places his sword on the altar in the same way as the bishops or abbots place there their professions of faith and their promises of obedience. And he concludes "it is only thus that the word *fidelis* is worthy of its true sense." John's text thus inclines us to think that the analogy first made between the *sacramentum fidelitatis* of the knights to the bishop and the *professio* of the clerics has been transferred into the milieu of the knights as a whole by the intermediary of a presence in the church that implied, in many cases, the making of an oath of fealty to the lord. It seems possible that the church of Chartres as much as that of Rheims had a part in the spread of this model. From 1050–60 deeds from Chartres begin to show examples of the expression *professione miles*, meaning the station of knight of Chartres, and there is an increase in the use of the metaphor *seculari militiae deditus*.[64]

This shaping of a model of knighthood through ceremonies where an oath of fealty, the blessing of the sword, and dubbing are intermingled may explain why the petty nobles of the Chartres area, the Ile-de-France, and Poitou no longer hesitated to assume the title of *miles*. The service of God—a true public service according to John of Salisbury—became a more important part of the duties of a knight than service to another man. The last stage in the development of the ritual is reached at the beginning of the thirteenth century when the Cistercian Helinand of Froidmont tells us that "in certain places it is the custom for the knight who is to be consecrated the following day to spend the whole of the previous night in vigil and prayers without being permitted to lie or sit down."[65]

How then should we interpret the precocity and strength of the phenomenon in the Mâcon area where all the nobles, both great and small, are knights? It is difficult to avoid seeing a connection with the presence in the heart of this region of the most powerful and influential abbey of Christendom, whose incessant prayers can assure their beneficiary of salvation in the next world. Two facts need to be taken into account. The count of Mâcon is an advocate of the abbey; it would be interesting to know in which church and over what relics it was customary to offer him the oath of fealty—at Saint-Vincent in Mâcon

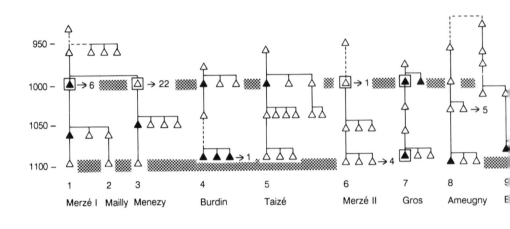

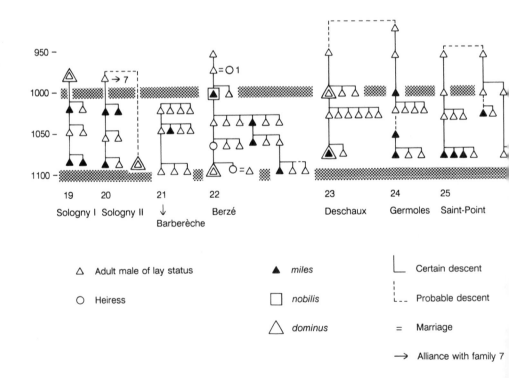

△ Adult male of lay status	▲ *miles*	└ Certain descent
○ Heiress	□ *nobilis*	└--- Probable descent
△ *dominus*		= Marriage
		→ Alliance with family 7

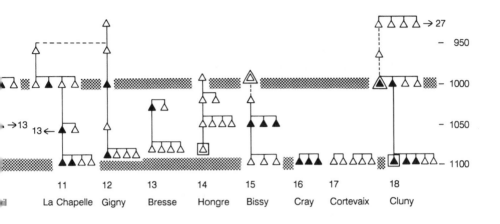

11	12	13	14	15	16	17	18
La Chapelle	Gigny	Bresse	Hongre	Bissy	Cray	Cortevaix	Cluny

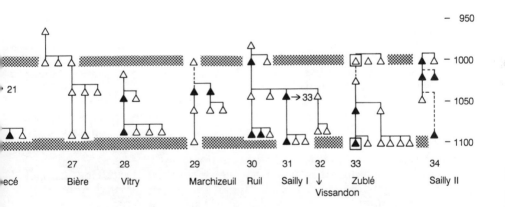

27	28	29	30	31	32	33	34
Bière	Vitry	Marchizeuil	Ruil	Sailly I ↓ Vissandon		Zublé	Sailly II

Figure 1. Lineage, Nobility, and Knighthood in the Mâconnais

(From Duby, *Hommes et structures du Moyen Age*)

or at Cluny? Some castellans performed the act of homage and made the oath to the abbot of Cluny without holding a fief from him. The abbot, when he traveled about, was accompanied by his own *milites*. One thinks of the invectives of Adalbero of Laon against those monks who would not remain in their place: "I am a knight now and, if I remain a monk, it is in another manner. I am not a monk because I serve—*milito*—under the orders of a king. My lord is the king Odilo of Cluny"—these are the words he puts into the mouth of the monk in the *Carmen ad Rodbertum Regem;* and further on he calls the abbot *princeps militiae.*[66]

Could it also have been under the influence of Cluny that knighthood became honorable, in the wake of the peace movement?[67] The texts that resulted from the first wave of this movement, those of the assemblies of 989–94 at Charroux, Limoges, Le Puy, Anse near Lyons, and Narbonne, make no mention of *miles;* the categories of people opposed are masters and subjects—the nobles and magnates on one side and the *pauperes* on the other. The word knight only appears with the second wave, more closely connected with Cluny, of the years 1019–25, and then in its vernacular form of *caballarius* and only in the text of oaths taken by certain magnates and their men. The title does not appear to be particularly honorable and it still has associations with the peasantry: the oath of Vienne speaks of the "villein knight," that of Verdun on the Doubs of a "knight with the plough." The practice of taking oaths of peace spread from these areas to the regions of Beauvais and Soissons, where two bishops, vassals of the king of France, were trying to resist the schemes of Eudes II of Champagne. It was not until 1031 and the relaunching of the movement at Bourges and Limoges through the intermediary of an archbishop who was a member of a family that had been for a long time friendly to Cluny, the Bourbon family, that we see the word *miles* take on a more elevated sense. In the accounts of the sessions of the council of Limoges, which translated the vernacular used into Latin, the magnates are called *principes militiae*, and it is proposed that these *principes* and their *milites* should be dealt with severely. Finally, in the councils of truce and peace of the 1040s, particularly that of Saint-Gilles, the *principes* have themselves become *milites majores.*

It is striking that when the great southern castellans are called *miles*, generally with the addition of a term expressing their nobility or power, *domnus* or *nobilis*, the scribes are either Cluniacs, from Cluny or Lérins, or their friends, the entourage of Raimbaud of Reillane, or that of the lords of Anduze. Similarly it is at around the time when he attends a council of peace in Berry between 1034 and 1044 that Eudes of Deols assumes in a charter the title *miles.*[68]

"Thus we find an expression of both the hierarchical nature of secular society—the *militia* obeys the princes it serves—and its homogeneity—the *militia* is gathered around a common function by the same anathemas, the same codes, the same ethic."[69]

By various routes, knighthood merged with nobility. Once again we can trace two different cultural areas. The first, around Rheims and Chartres where the bishops relied on homogenous groups of city knights grouped around their Mother Church. The other, from Lyons to Narbonne, where an alliance of interests was formed between the most active of the monks, the abbots of Cluny, and some of the great castellan families. A double policy whose immediate results should not be overestimated: many decades were to pass before chivalry overtakes nobility. But from the middle of the eleventh century the uncertain forms where *miles* and *nobilis* combine reveal the inevitable alliance of all those who imposed the *bannum* on others and escaped it themselves.

Lineage, a Common Model?

The assimilation between nobility and knighthood did not take place only on the level of vocabulary. One of the most marked characteristics of the new aristocracy seems to be the diffusion on all levels of a system of direct inheritance. Its aim, whatever the regional variations, is always that of ordering and tightening a family group around its now immutable estates, which are handed on from father to son—patrimony, in the proper sense of the word.

But this subject needs to be approached with caution. The elemental structures of kinship are among the most difficult to discover, even in the thirteenth century when the number of documents is greater and juridically more reliable, allowing patient jurists to glimpse the geography of "customs."[70] This obscurity is all the more annoying because the map of the customary jurisdictions appears to have been determined at just this period, at the very time when new usages born of the social needs of those exercising the *bannum* were beginning to emerge from a legal system that had remained very close to the old legal *codices* of the early Middle Ages.[71]

Certain striking pieces of evidence led Jean-François Lemarignier to date the creation of a "custom" in Normandy from the time of William the Conqueror, while Olivier Guillot places that of Anjou in 1040–54. He shows that the map of "customs" of the west drawn up by Jean Yver corresponds to the period of the political domination of the count of Anjou between 1052 and 1056. Olivier-Martin saw its appearance in the Ile-de-France at the end of the twelfth century. It is in the twelfth century that we find in Flanders and the Namurois references to the law of the free men, also called nobles. For the customs of Barcelona, Pierre Bonnassie suggests two stages: a first attempt in 1060–70 and the final drafting around 1150.[72]

We saw earlier how in the Mâconnais nobility and knighthood became merged very early on. So it is particularly interesting to see the beginning there from before the year 1000 of a crystallization of lineage, at the expense of daughters and younger sons.

The most characteristic manifestation of this development here is the development of the indivisibility of estates under the form of common inheritance by brothers *(frairêche):* before 1000 28 percent of the deeds preserved, 33 percent in 1000–1050, 50 percent in 1050–1100. The percentage of *frairêches* implying consanguinity is respectively 2 percent, 6 percent, 14 percent. A second characteristic is the *laudatio parentum* (consent of relatives): for the same periods, 4 percent, 7.7 percent, 33 percent. (A piece of evidence that fits in with these but is of less significance is that of the validating "marks" of the members of the family: 10 percent, 16 percent, 20 percent.) Last, the claims made by families to recover former family property that had passed to a monastery: in 1000–1050, 1.6 percent, in 1050–1100, 3 percent. In these last percentages the part played by consanguinity is more significant: it rises from 12 percent to 35 percent of the total number of disputes. This tightening up is accompanied by a noticeable tendency to deprive girls of some or all of the inheritance, endowing them with peripheral pieces of land, broken up or disputed, on the eroded edges of the patrimony and strictly controlling their dower. The situation is not the same for the sons, who appear to inherit equal shares but, in practice, this is considerably limited by the frequency of celibacy. Donations from uncles to nephews are frequent. From 1030 there begins to be signs of primogeniture in castellan families. Finally, from 1025 the rights of sole legitimate descent become established.[73]

The wealth of legal documents in Catalonia in the eleventh century reveals the emergence of a similar parallel system. The essential points of family law are here still regulated by Visigothic law, the old *liber judiciorum* that postulated the equality of sons and daughters in the succession *ab intestat,* and that imposed restrictions in their favor on the testator in the provisions made for succession: the bequest should not exceed a fifth of the inheritance. The heirs could not be disinherited except for serious reason and only after a legal decision. But one of the children could be given an advantage by receiving, separately from any division, a third of the succession, *mejora* or *melioratio.* As late as 1011 this system still claimed to apply to nobles as much as to commoners. A close study of the legal documents shows both its astonishing survival and the beginning of its decline. Around the year 1000, donations to the Church often exceeded the Visigothic fifth, reaching a third or even a half of the property. In other cases testators, respecting the form only, twisted the law by burdening the inheritance with rent to the profit of the Church. At the moment of the crisis of feudalism, between 1020 and 1060, family relationships appeared to be seriously under strain and it is as if in reaction to these tensions that the closure of the lineage takes place.[74]

Once again we see the practice of indivision *en frairêche* triumphing. Around the year 1000, this was often provisional; from 1030 it began to spread from the upper layers of society right through to the peasants, and it was not uncommon to see four or five brothers living in one household even if they were married or in holy orders. The same types of disputes over inheritance appear as those found in the Mâcon area; in wills the tendency to leave property to close relatives, a brother, uncle, nephew, or cousin becomes more marked, in contrast to previous usage. This new usage is elaborated through testamentary clauses: one that became common appoints a head of family benefiting from the *melioratio*; one benefits several sons together on the condition that they do not split up the inheritance; one appears in the 1030s revealing both the right of the family to an estate that a member wished to alienate and the succession from brother to brother in Poitou. Endowed daughters succeeded with the obligation that their dowries should revert to the family, but from 988 we see in a deed the beginning of a practice whereby the dowry was equated, whether big or small, with the daughter's share of the inheritance. The very word used to refer to the dowry, *escovare*, means "share" or "lot." From 1002 and 1022 the insistence on legitimate birth is affirmed. More or less the same evolution can be seen in Provence, albeit with a far more scanty documentation.[75]

Let us leave the Midi and turn now to the west. Reasoning by analogy, it seems likely that the equality between heirs that continued into the thirteenth century as the original mark of common inheritances was the original situation and that the noble "customs" were also the work of the eleventh century.

The first example of *parage* in Anjou in the first half of the eleventh century appears to have been organized on the orders of the count; in his family we find an example of this in 1060 and the right of primogeniture is found from 1044 onward among the lords of Ile-Bouchard in Touraine. A deed from Marmoutiers of 1062 specifies that bastards may not succeed. In Poitou succession from brother to brother appears in 1015 among the lords of Thouars; brothers succeed one another and it is only on the death of the last of them that the eldest son of the first brother to die inherits. It is also possible that *parage* existed in Berry among the lords of Vierzon and Déols in the eleventh century.[76]

In Picardy the sources are hard to interpret. The *laudatio parentum*, so characteristic of the move toward direct inheritance, appears to occur later and seems to concern chiefly the nobility.

In the region of Hesdin between 1000 and 1070, out of some thirty donations, nine include the *laudatio* and these are aristocratic donations; the twenty others seem mainly to involve small peasants. Between 1070 and 1120, of eighty-five donations, the *laudatio* only appears in 27 percent of the cases. Here again, the majority are aristocratic.[77]

It seems then that we should regard the new familial customs of the eleventh century as models originating from and introduced and spread by the aristocracy. Traditions of succession and relations of kinship changed during the eleventh century in the direction of a pronounced emphasis on the elements of lineal descent. This contraction appears to occur earlier in the families that possessed *honores*, castles, and the *bannum*. Doubtless political structures and kinship patterns influenced these changes.[78] Agreement on the nature of this influence is still lacking.

Sometimes the "lineal solidarity" of the eleventh century is contrasted with the so-called "individualism" of the tenth century. It might be more correct to say that the solidarity has changed its basis. It seems unlikely that those people who appear in the donations or sales of the tenth century as individuals disposing of their property could have lived outside the solidarity of a social group. Rather the opposite: a deed from Catalonia shows two orphans complaining bitterly of having been abandoned, even though they were surrounded by close relatives and cousins. Similar accounts of assemblies show us the *boni homines* of a canton or the small allodialists of a village banding together. The Catalan franchises in the tenth century and the guilds of the north in the ninth century bear witness to the existence of strong lateral bonds. Among these confederates or neighbors, there were of course many related people. Quite simply, this tenth-century sociability was based on the assembly of free men, and it sank from sight for the most part around 1000 with the establishing of banal lordship. The Catalonian deeds also give evidence of this foundering, and likewise also of the extraordinary tensions that it brought about in the very bosom of the family.[79] The social and juridical forms that developed in the eleventh century had as their specific aim remedying this explosion and reducing these tensions. They attached the family to one territory and to one rule, just as, perhaps, in some regions they attempted to attach the peasants to their tenements. They also gave much greater importance to one member of the family, reducing the others to a condition that was often one of dependency. The younger siblings had often to grow old in their brother's home without marrying: He would have the "house" and they would be part of it—a tyrannical dependency indeed. No one of the people of the household now had the means to lead his own life. As Georges Duby remarks,

> many of the characteristics of the chivalrous mentality—the love of distant adventure, the wanderings in search of pillage and profit, the disagreements which arise so often between the father who will not die and the son who dreams of ruling in his turn over the family group and seeks asylum with rival lords—can be explained by the constraints of the indivisibility of inheritance. On the other hand, it is also a powerful factor of cohesion; it imposes discipline.[80]

One of the natural outlets for the smaller knightly household was a larger and more generous household, that of a magnate. There was a longstanding tradition among the princes of keeping in their household a military escort consisting partly of domestic soldiers and partly of the younger sons of good families who received their education there. We know the men of the household of the archbishop of Arles in 954–963. He acted at that time as count in Lower Provence and had in his entourage some dozen youths, of whom some were a few years later to be heads of great castellan families. To all, or almost all, of them he had given small benefices—some manors, a few pieces of land. Similarly, Guibert of Gembloux had sent his son to Raoul of Cambrai "and he served him with other young nobles, and as a servant, and under arms." The magnates, these elite warriors, and their men of lesser rank taught the young recruits—*tirones*—soldiery—*officium militare*—and especially the art of horsemanship. There was an oft-repeated proverb of the Carolingian period: "He who cannot be a horseman at the age of puberty will never be one . . ."; or again "he who, without riding a horse, has stayed at school until twelve years old is only good to be a priest." The lord provided his *pueri* with clothes, arms, and horses. Thus from one household to the next reciprocal friendships were forged; the young Gerald of Aurillac had been brought up by Bernard, count of Auvergne, and later, having become in turn the lord of a household, he received the son of his old patron among his *nutriti, his juvenes.*[81]

In the entourage of a magnate, young nobles serving their apprenticeship, loyal relatives, and armed domestics mixed. Whatever their rank, they were all his *nutriti;* they had in common a state, a way of life. They were all unmarried, none of them established, they were "youths," bachelors, a turbulent and unstable group. As the growth in population swelled the numbers of younger members in the princely families, the habit grew up of setting up around the young heir a group of friends who had sometimes been dubbed at the same time as he had. In this way there crystallized around the leader who maintained them, providing them with arms and money, a company of young men who under his orders left in search of adventure and its prizes. "A swarm of children reaching adulthood emerged in this way from the great lord's household . . . and escaped towards the adventures of youth." In addition to the sons of the vassals of the father, the *familia* of the heir began to include other elements, clerics, courtesans, and professional jousters. This group of young people formed the audience par excellence for a literature composed above all for use, the literature of the *cantilenas,* songs and mimes, of the minstrels, the legendary stories of ancient exploits and adventurous quests. How could they fail to identify themselves with the bachelors in ragged clothes urged on by William Short-Nose in the *Charroi de Nîmes,* who promised them castles in Spain!

William of Orange was one of the heroes particularly favored by the knights. We know that in the *familia* of the earl of Chester, the chaplain invited to preach on the exemplary life to the knights would choose as the theme of his sermons not only the lives of the warrior saints, George, Maurice, and Eustace, warrior demigods and patron saints, but also that of William who had been a marquis who then took holy orders. The model of the young adventurer who conquers by his prowess the love of a rich heiress and thus establishes himself as a lord is tranferred into the genealogical literature. Was it not said that the Capetian king too was offspring of the "order of knights"?[82]

The dream here becomes confused with reality. At the summons of William of Normandy, younger sons and adventurers from Flanders, Anjou, Maine, and Brittany flocked to the conquest of England. The Norman knights, one after the other, uncles calling on nephews, braved the interdicts of the duke to win southern Italy and establish the principality of Sicily. Those of Burgundy and Champagne, familiar faces on the roads to Santiago, revived in Spain the legend of Charlemagne and consolidated Castile and established the kingdom of Portugal. At the end of the twelfth century, the knights of the Ile-de-France reenacted the exploits of William of Orange at the expense of the southerners, against new infidels whom they burned or slaughtered.[83]

Around the years 1000–1031, the names of Oliver and Roland appeared among those used by the knights. At the same period the name Vivian becomes common. Not surprisingly, this has been attributed to the influence of the *chansons de geste*. True, but there are problems in this. It is generally accepted that the only names that could be used at this period were those of blood or of baptism. How then can we explain the appearance of such an unusual name as Oliver? Could it have been the knightly equivalent of a clerical name, given at the time of baptism with the authorization of the priest to a child promised by his parents if not to the crusade then at least to an ideal type of the Christian knight?[84]

But at the end of the twelfth century the tightening of the structures of kinship are not enough to protect the aristocratic families.

> The little that we know as yet of this evolution leads us to think that around 1175, in the north of France, the heads of the aristocratic families ceased to ensure that only a single son, the eldest, married. Now they began to give wives to the younger sons and set them up as lords of smaller estates, taking for this purpose parts of the patrimony, building satellite houses around the ancestral home. Thus the power to judge and to tax the villeins was divided up. . . . All the gentlemen began to be lords. But the majority held sway only over a village or a parish; the rise of the State and the rise in money were becoming an increasing threat. Conscious of their growing vulnerability, the old families . . . came together, seeking shelter behind the system of chivalrous values.[85]

The "new aristocracy" of the eleventh century is perhaps a social class, but it must be recognized that it is composed of many elements. Its upper level is formed by the old nobility of Carolingian times. We will look later at its origins and structure.[86] The middle levels appear to have taken shape differently in the north than in the south. In the north, the allodialists, long since integrated into the Frankish army and then passed into the service of the lords, managed by a process that was no doubt continuous and relatively early to ally themselves with the old nobility, heads or younger sons of the *Reichsadel,* and lay claim to being of the nobility themselves. From the allodialists, nobility then spread through the ranks of the *casati.* Both groups married the younger daughters of lords, and in their genealogical memory nobility came through the female line, even though their families were to be organized according to direct patriarchal lineal descent.

This may explain the triple meaning of *franc*—noble-free-Frankish— which may have been favored by an older and more widespread concept of the "collective nobility" of the Franks. In the Midi, the situation was very different. Nobility appears to have been jealously guarded at the level of the "provincial princes," that local nobility that had dominated the imperial aristocracy; conversely, the wealthy allodialists seem to have disdained for a long time the bonds of dependence. It was only later and through the intermediary of chivalry that the alliance of nobility and the small landowners really came about. Even then it was never total. This "ideal fusion" that chivalry created between social groups that were very unequal seems to have originated from two distinct centers. The first was Cluny, and this would explain the early and at the same time distinct character of the phenomenon in the Mâconnais; the second, the episcopal military households from Chartres to Rheims. In both centers it is possible to detect the successive waves of the peace movement, first in the south and then taken up by the bishops of the province of Rheims in the 1060s.[87]

The process by which the old nobility, breaking up the allodial communities, attached the important men of the village to itself in order to make them the indispensable accessories of the extension and increase of the *bannum* in its new seigneury was essentially the same everywhere, although the vocabulary varied, although it occurs sometimes earlier and sometimes later, sometimes more and sometimes less successfully. At times the process descended to an even lower level of society: among the knights we find the isolated figures of the impoverished younger sons of large families or the hired man risen from the peasantry or servant classes. The history of the nobility brings us back to that of the peasantry.

Notes

1. The nobility of the late empire was eclipsed by the Germanic *adalungen.* On this question of a double origin of the nobility, see chapter 7 of this book.
2. Génicot, *La noblesse* [248]; Bloch, *La société* [70], p. 395.

3. Medieval historiography has still not resolved such problems, cf. the conference organized by Roland Mousnier in 1966, *Problèmes de stratification sociale* (Paris, 1968), p. 24.
4. Texts that Marc Bloch knew but skillfully dismissed, see *La Société* [70], p. 399.
5. Génicot, *L'économie namuroise* [247], p. 5; Dhondt, *Le haut Moyen Age* [475], p. 31.
6. Duby, *La noblesse* [230]; Richer, *Histoire* [66], 3: 79, 2: 98.
7. Cf. the comments of Georges Duby, *La noblesse* [230].
8. Magnou-Nortier, *Fidélité et féodalité* [205], with the comments of Paul Ourliac, p. 141. Goscelin of Fleury was at first refused in 1012 by the inhabitants of Bourges because he was "the bastard of a prince who was very noble among the Franks," Adhemar, *Chronicon* [24], 3: 39, p. 161. A few years later Eudes of Blois exclaimed: "If one takes account of birth, it is clear thanks to God that I am capable of inheriting," Fulbert, *Letters* [38], no. 86. On illegitimacy, see Chevailler, *Observations* [225], which gives an example of the inability of the bastard to succeed dating from 1062 in Marmoutiers.
9. Cf. p. 96 above.
10. Flori, *Chevaliers* [241].
11. Génicot, *L'économie namuroise* [247], p. 2.
12. Richer, *Histoire* [66], 2: 98, 1: 288.
13. William of Poitiers, *Gesta Willelimi* [47], 1: 40, p. 98. As opposed no doubt to generic names such as Lauret for one of the cart oxen or those of the animals in the fables. *Equi insignes*, individualized by their names in the wills of Catalan noblemen, Bonnassie, *La Catalogne* [72], pp. 292 and 296.
14. Gregory of Tours, *Historia Francorum*, 10: 28, *MGH SS Rer. Merov.*, 1: 440. Charters of Vabres in Rouergue, BN Coll. Doat. fos. 31 and 20; Richer, *Histoire* [66], 4: 28, 2: 188; Karl Ferdinand Werner, *Liens* [279], summarizes the historiography and explains the methodology. The system of combining radicals was still followed by peasant families in the ninth century, see Verdon, *Les sources* [655].
15. Duby, *Lignage* [235]; Boussard, *L'origine des familles* [223]; Werner, *Untersuchungen* [278]. For the same phenomenon of the restriction of the stock of names in Provence, see Poly, *La Provence* [87], p. 52. On the fashions current in the eleventh century, and on the names Roland and Oliver, see below chapter 10.
16. Cf. the study of the matrimonial policies of the nobility of Lorraine in the twelfth and thirteenth centuries, Parisse, *La noblesse lorraine* [261], p. 380.
17. K. Schmid, "Zur Problematik zur Familie, Sippe und Geschlecht, Haus und Dynastie beim mittelalterlichen Adel," *Zeitschrift für die Geschichte des Oberrhein*, 1957. Cf. however the reservations of K. Leyser, "The German aristocracy . . . ," *Past and Present*, 1968, who asks whether "these men who were conscious of being members of a very wide and fluid group when it was a question of perpetuating their memory, were similarly conscious in all the other domains." An admirable example of the work of the school of Gerd Tellenbach is the edition of the *liber memorialis* of the abbey of Remiremont in Lorraine.
18. For reference, see n. 14 above.
19. Tabacco, *La connessione* [269].

20. Duby, *Remarques* [233].
21. Génicot, *Noblesse et principautés* [139]; Bur, *La Champagne* [74], p. 489; Parisse, *La noblesse lorraine* [261], p. 234. Guenée, *La fierté* [443], shows how the genealogists of the twelfth century hesitated between the memory of the Carolingians and the prestige of the Capetian monarchy.
22. Lot, *L'origine* [256]; Halphen, *Le comté d'Anjou* [82], p. 1. On the supernatural, see chapter 10 in this book.
23. *Gesta consulum andegavorun* [31], p. 25; the passages in italics are borrowed from Sallust. On this text, see Boussard, *L'origine des familles* [223].
24. Richer, *Histoire* [66], 1: 15, p. 38.
25. Werner, *Untersuchungen* [278], p. 269.
26. These successive contributions are well described in Parisse, *La noblesse lorraine* [261], p. 212.
27. Bonnassie, *La Catalogne* [72], p. 284; from 1045 they were to be called *comtors* (p. 785); Garaud, *Les châtelains de Poitou* [81]; Poly, *La Provence* [87], p. 94. Information on the Auvergne from Christian Lauranson who is at present working on a study of these families; Duby, *La société* [78], pp. 127 and 141; Fossier, *La terre* [79], p. 542; Lemarignier, *Le gouvernement* [455], p. 68.
28. Duby, *La diffusion* [236]; Poly, *La Provence* [87], p. 137; Devailly, *Le Berry* [77], pp. 177 and 182.
29. Garaud, *Les châtelains de Poitou* [81], pp. 217 and 219; Chédeville, *Chartres* [76], p. 308, which counts only about twenty mentions in one-and-a-half centuries. In the mid-eleventh century the title is borne by a knight of Chartres.
30. Musset, *L'aristocratie normande* [257].
31. Fossier, *La terre* [79], p. 535; and the continuation by L. Génicot, "Une thèse: Campagnards et paysans de Picardie jusqu' au XIIIe siècle," *AESC* (1970): 1475.
32. Génicot, *L'économie namuroise* [247], p. 14. On the great families of Lotharingia, cf. also Baerten, *Les Ansfrid* [220], Bernard, *Les Régnier* [222a]; E. Hlawitschka, *Lotharingen und das Reich an der Schwelle der deutschen Geschichte* (Stuttgart, 1968), and *Die Anfänge des Hauses Habsburg-Lothringen . . .* (Saarbrück, 1969) and Parisse, *La noblesse lorraine* [261], which describe the fortunes of the descendants of Wigeric, Matfrid, and Odelric. For Alsace, see Wilsdorf, *Les Etichonides* [280].
33. Hariulf, *Chronicon* [48], 3: 3, p. 96, and the inventory of rents in the appendix, p. 308, where the chapel of the nobles is contrasted with the chapels of the *populus vulgaris*; Ganshof, *Féodalité* [189], p. 39.
34. Génicot, *L'économie namuroise* [247], pp. 71, 30 and 19.
35. Ibid., p. 45.
36. Duby, *Structures* [232].
37. Andrew of Fleury, *Miracles* [25], 6: 2, quoted in Bur, *La Champagne* [74], p. 344. The text written about 1050 recounts events of the end of the tenth century; the advocate that Stabilis fights is not the advocate of the abbey, but its champion in trial by combat.
38. Duby, *Lignage* [235].
39. Magnou-Nortier, *La société laïque* [86], pp. 271 and 277; Poly, *La Provence* [87], p. 140; Bonnassie, *La Catalogne* [72], p. 284ff.
40. Génicot, *L'économie namuroise* [247], p. 32 and the important

qualifications on p. 47; Bonenfant and Despy, "La noblesse en Brabant aux XIIᵉ et XIIIᵉ siècles," *MA*, 1958, p. 27; Parisse, *La noblesse lorraine* [261], p. 240.

41. Génicot, *Noblesse et principautés* [139]; Adalbero of Laon, *Carmen* [23], vv. 22 and 279.
42. Magnou-Nortier, *La société laïque* [86], p. 215.
43. Duby, *Les origines* [234].
44. Van Winter, *Uxorem* [274].
45. Van Luyn, *Les milites* [273].
46. 1050–1060, "an inhabitant of the city of Chartres, rich in possessions, knight by *professio,* young in age, noble in condition," quoted in Chédeville, *Chartres* [76], p. 309; cf. also Van Luyn, *Les milites* [273], p. 313.
47. Cf. Rather of Verona, quoted pp. 296–97 below.
48. Duby, *La diffusion* [236].
49. Magnou-Nortier, *La société laïque* [86], p. 253; Bonnassie, *La Catalogne* [72], p. 806. A text from Aniane (1114) speaks of *caballarii,* men or women, see Hollyman, *Le vocabulaire féodal* [194], p. 133, so then it is a social condition. Conversely, in 1035–1080 in Rouergue, a wounded knight had to leave the *militia, Miracula Sanctae Fidis* [29], 4: 10, p. 194.
50. Génicot, *L' économie namuroise* [247], pp. 33, 74 and 78; Bonenfant and Despy, *La noblesse en Brabant,* p. 27; Fossier, *La terre* [79], p. 537; Parisse, *La noblesse lorraine* [261], p. 250ff. seems to have shown that in Lorraine the *milites* were far from being confused with the *ministeriales.* Perhaps there is a cultural frontier.
51. Honorius, *De imagine mundi, PL,* 172, col 166, quoted in Duby, *Les origines* [234].
52. *Chronique d'Ebersheim,* p. 432, quoted by Bosl, *Castes* [290]. On this text see also pp. 134–35 below.
53. Musset, *L'aristocratie* [257].
54. William of Poitiers, *Histoire* [47], 2: 33, p. 232.
55. Chédeville, *Chartres* [76], pp. 310, 313, 316. On the deed of Amaury of Montfort: Lemarignier, *Le gouvernement* [455], p. 134.
56. Lemarignier, *Le gouvernement* [455], p. 133; Bournazel, *Le gouvernement* [418], pp. 40 and 70.
57. Garaud, *Les châtelains de Poitou* [81], pp. 217, 220, 223.
58. Duby, *La société* [78], pp. 150 and 191, and *Lignage* [235].
59. Génicot, *La noblesse* [248].
60. Van Luyn, *Les milites* [273]; Flori, *La notion de chevalerie* [239] and *Sémantique* [240].
61. Bloch, *La société* [70], p. 439; Duby, *Les trois ordres* [616], p. 358.
62. The *milites ecclesiae remensis* are well known from the mid-tenth century, Flodoard, *Annales* [36], p. 106; Gerbert, *Letters* [42], no. 137; and Guibert of Nogent, *De vita sua* [46], 1: 11, p. 31, puts side by side the *milites* and the *clerus* of the city. On the *milites* of the church of Cambrai, see pp. 64–65 above.
63. John of Salisbury, *Policraticus* [51], 6: 5, 7, and 10, t. 2: 16, 20, and 24; Georges Duby, *Les trois ordres* [616], p. 359, points out a passage in the same text that shows the omission of certain knights from John's interpretation.

64. Chédeville, *Chartres* [76], pp. 309 and 315. On the household of Fulbert of Chartres, see p. 101 below.
65. Duby, *Les trois ordres* [616], p. 360.
66. Duby, *La société* [78], p. 150; Adalbero of Laon, *Carmen* [23], vv. 113–115. In the twelfth century St. Bernard commented on the knightly entourage of the abbot of Cluny, *Apologia ad Guillelmum*, 11: 27, *PL*, 182, col. 914.
67. Duby, *La diffusion* [236]. On this movement, see chapter 5, below.
68. Poly, *La Provence* [87], p. 191; Devailly, *Le Berry* [77], pp. 145 and 188.
69. Duby, *La diffusion* [236].
70. Yver, *Égalité entre héritiers* [282].
71. Olivier-Martin, *Histoire de la coutume* [259], p. 11, had already said "even among nobles, the institutions of family law were broadly determined by considerations derived from the military interest of the lords." Some of these usages have been studied since long ago. For example the right of the family to an estate that a member wished to alienate, cf. R. Caillemer, "Le retrait lignager," *Studi . . . C. Fadda* vol. 4 (Naples, 1906), p. 13; Falletti [238], Génestal [245], Ourliac [260]; on the exclusion of endowed daughters, see Didier, *Les dispositions* [229], Yver, *Égalité entre héritiers* [282]; the *affrairement*, cf. Aubenas, "Le contrat d'*affrairamentum* dans le droit provençal du Moyen Age," in *RHD* (1933): 478 and *Réflexions* [219]; *parage*, see p. 109 above. In many cases, however, the question of origins remained obscure.
72. Lemarignier, *L'hommage en marche* [197], p. 20; Guillot, *Le comté d'Anjou* [83], p. 373; Olivier-Martin, *Histoire de la coutume* [259], p. 25, and in the Gâtinais from the eleventh century; Bonnassie, *La Catalogne* [72], p. 718; Génicot, n. 35 above.
73. Duby, *Lignage* [235].
74. Bonnassie, *La Catalogne* [72], p. 258; Bastier, *Le testament* [222].
75. Bonnassie, *La Catalogne* [72], p. 547; Poly, *La Provence* [87], p. 157.
76. Legoherel, *Le parage* [255]; older studies by Génestal [244]; Didier, *Le droit des fiefs* [228]; Chevrier, *Les aspects familiaux* [227]; Garaud, *Les châtelains du Poitou* [81], p. 74ff.; Devailly, *Le Berry* [77], p. 194.
77. Fossier, *La terre* [79], p. 552.
78. Duby, *Lignage* [235].
79. Bonnassie, *La Catalogne* [72], p. 545.
80. G. Duby, *Histoire de la civilisation française* (Paris, 1968), 1: 66.
81. Poly, *La Provence* [87], pp. 144 and 162; Génicot, *L' économie namuroise* [247], p. 6; *Vita Geraldi* [34], 1: 32, col. 660; same type of entourage in Catalonia, Bonnassie, *La Catalogne* [72], p. 569, in Normandy, Ganshof, *Féodalité* [189], p. 127. Two versions of the proverb can be found in Bloch, *La société* [70], p. 410, and Riché, *La vie quotidienne* [646], p. 92. On the evolution of this structure in the twelfth century, see chapter 6.
82. Duby, *Les jeunes* [428], *La noblesse* [230]; Boutruche, *Seigneurie et féodalité* [98], 2: 193. The origin *ex equestri ordine* of Robert the Strong is found alongside several other legends about Eudo in Richer, *Histoire* [66], 1: 5, 16; *contra*, Van Winter, *Uxorem* [274], which interprets it as "belonging to the cavalry."
83. Defourneaux, *Les Français* [613], p. 125ff.; Duby, *Histoire de la civilisation*, p. 122.
84. On the *Chansons de Geste* and the pair Oliver-Roland, see chapter 10.

Georges Duby sees the appearance around 1100 in the stock of names borne by the knights of Mâcon the hitherto-unknown names of Girard, Roland, and Oliver, Duby, *Lignage* [235].

85. Duby, *Les trois ordres* [616], p. 355, based particularly on the conclusions of Michel Parisse, *La noblesse*, [261], pp. 272, 302, 325.
86. See chapter 7.
87. See chapter 5.

CHAPTER

4

Serfs or Free Men?

The villeins and the peasants . . .
Held several parliaments.
They spread about this command:
He who is higher, he is the enemy . . .
And several of them made an oath
That they would never agree
To have lord or master
    —*The peasants' revolt in Normandy,*
      in 997, recalled by Wace in 1172

"A man is either a serf or a free man" was the answer given by one of Charlemagne's counselors to the question of a *missus*.[1] However, the formularies, charters, collections of miracles and lives of the saints offer the historian several different words for referring to the dependent peasantry. This multitude of words is at first disconcerting and alarming: how can we be sure that a certain word, used in two different places, refers to the same situation? The language here is evidence of an enormous social tension that confronts the powerful, masters of the land and the weapons of war, with the peasant workers, perhaps too often imagined as being without power or resources. Despite some excellent scholarly studies, the true history of these peasants who formed the vast majority of the population in the Middle Ages has not yet been fully written. By a true history, we mean a history written from the point of view of the peasants themselves and that shows them, not as almost all our texts do, through the eyes of the master and the lord,[2] but as the protagonists in their own history. Here we will limit ourselves to describing as well as possible, through the vocabulary, the variable point of confrontation where the greed of the lord— the inevitable reverse side of the generosity of the noble—meets the

119

resistance of the peasantry. The general tendency has been understood for a long time, even if chronology and geographical forms are sometimes still not quite clear. Starting from a situation in which the legal status of the peasantry in the country areas was relatively heterogenous, the movement is toward a unification of the status of peasant.

Between Freedom and Servitude

As Jan Dhondt said with grim humor, "at the point of departure of any study of the tensions within a population lies a very simple element: how many producers are needed to support a parasite?"[3] This calculation, which contemporaries must have made too, is not however so simple. Of course, it is possible to imagine a floor below which any more pressure on the peasant would be impossible because he then would not even exist at a subsistence level. But in practice, and the slave masters of Rome had discovered this, it is not so easy to convince a man to work for another under these conditions. Everything here is a matter of circumstances. What could be called Dhondt's theorem is thus susceptible to many variations, but all of them hinge on two fundamental possible situations: either the magnates succeed in acquiring by treaty or conquest a sufficient number of slaves to compensate for the physical losses, the escapes, the occasional granting of freedom—and this situation is not without risks—or they "persuade" free men in greater or lesser numbers to work for them. Between these two options a whole series of legal conditions begins to grow up, a collection of compromises, legal relationships that crystallize earlier relationships of power and that can be called into question once more as a result of new pressures.

Servitude

The first situation—the constant supply of "savages" taken into slavery—was one known by the Carolingians, at least in the earlier part of that period, and many pagan Saxons must have experienced it. But this supply certainly dried up fairly quickly.[4] At the end of the ninth century, the brand-new slave became a luxury object. The trading in slaves, drawing on the Slavs through the towns of the Rhine, Verdun, Lyons, Arles, and Narbonne, now looked toward Moslem Spain.

Is it possible to speak of slaves in the Carolingian period, or, to put it in another way, at what point did the old slavery disappear to make way for serfdom? First it is necessary to define precisely what slavery is and what are its limits. It has been said that a slave "is the instrument endowed with speech" of the Roman farmers. To a jurist, a slave would be a thing and not a person with legal rights. The serf on the other hand is a member of a Christian community, subject to certain restrictions of rights and to taxes seen as degrading. Put in these terms the problem is partly insoluble, because slavery is in a way a legal fiction. Even in antiquity, the quality of *instrumentum vocale* was difficult to maintain. Beyond the apparent juridical unity that postulated the definition of the slave, many *de facto* situations existed that Roman law itself, and after it the barbarian laws, were forced to take into account. The slave doing business for his master had inevitably a personality of his own, just as much as did the criminal slave. The royal slaves were always in a different category and the *pueri regales* of the Merovingian kings were, perhaps, just as much the ancestors of the royal vassals as were the antrustions.[5] At the time of Louis the Pious, the so-called *servus* could himself claim his freedom in law. So can we say that this is a serf? But at the same period, Jonas of Orleans tells us that dissatisfied masters punished their *servi* with amputation. Even at the end of the century, Saint Gerald of Aurillac would threaten his disobedient *servi* with mutilation.[6] Are these serfs? The ambiguity is not new; still at the end of the thirteenth century, Beaumanoir was struggling to differentiate between serfs and slaves with the single word *servus*. At the beginning of the thirteenth century, the word "serfs-livestock" is sometimes used, and in the fourteenth century the custom of Burgundy coined the apparently tautologous "serf-serfdom."[7] The ambiguity of the vocabulary conceals both a chronology and a geography of serfdom, but also two diametrically opposed points of view, that of the dependant and that of his master. If a dividing line is to be found, should it not be sought in the arbitrary nature of the punishments inflicted? When the lord brings his *servi* to judgment before the same tribunal as the one-time free men of his estate, then certainly we are no longer dealing with slaves. But are there now any free men?

Whatever one thinks of the situation of the *servi* in the Carolingian period, it cannot be denied that at the end of the eighth century the trading in Saxon slaves, at the same period as Charlemagne's victories, supplied certain lands in the empire with agricultural workers. In the years that followed, this connection between the slave traffic and the large estates is much less clear. The only people to be taken henceforth into slavery here and there would be a few offenders, a few free men compelled by famine, or children abandoned on the church doorstep, in addition to the children of the *servi* themselves.[8] The consequences of such a situation are clear. In the south, *mancipia* or *servi* have practically disappeared by the beginning of the tenth century.

When the count of Toulouse makes an important donation to his foundation of Vabres in 862 he only gives it fourteen servile families, and from them he retains seven children. In 901 Leudoin of Roussillon and his wife sell some allods for the considerable sum of 1,600 sous, but on the lands there live only nine servile families. From 950 we find only small groups of *mancipia*, a few individuals, and always in the entourage of the great lords.[9]

We know that slaves remained more numerous in the north. But from the beginning of the ninth century, the number of free men who held servile manses of the estate of Saint-Germain-des-Prés is a good indication that the quantity of tenant *servi*, already small, was falling, because many of the plots of land formerly created for them were now occupied by *coloni*.

The polyptyque of the abbey lists 1,430 free manses, 25 "half-free" and 191 servile, but at the period it was written there were only 120 servile households against 45 "half-free" *(liti)* and 2,080 *coloni*. The proportion of *servi* seems to be more significant in the middle of the century at Saint-Bertin, where it reaches nearly 50 percent of the tenants. The number of dependent *servi* does not seem very great, even though the stewards of certain churches, men of modest means, sometimes had a few in their service. But the *villa* of Ingolstadt, offered by Louis the Pious to Niederalteich, only had twenty-two *servi* for an area of eighty hectares of arable land. The *curtes* of Santa Giulia of Brescia had eight *servi* for forty-nine hectares in 905–906. There were ten on the estate of Saint-Bertin in Barlinghem for some forty hectares of arable land.[10]

One reason for the shrinking of the servile group is undeniably the freeing of slaves, but it is very difficult if not impossible to ascertain the extent to which this happened. Instances of freed slaves are rare on Church lands. This is no surprise, since the canons forbade the sanctuaries for a long time from freeing their *mancipia*. We find none in the polyptyque of Saint-Victor of Marseilles and we know that their number was less than that of Saint-Germain; it seems likely that they were given in this state to the monastery. The evidence from secular documents gives a rather different picture: certain landholdings bequeathed by the patrician of Provence, Abbo, in the eighth century were cultivated by families of freed slaves, *liberti cum obsequio*.[11] Nearly two centuries later, Gerald of Aurillac freed one hundred of his *mancipia*; he could, his detractors emphasized, have been still more generous.[12]

Among the freed men, there was one particular category whose statute was to become common for many dependants, the *cerocensuales*. These were freed slaves whom the master wished to commit to the upkeep of his tomb, even, one could say, to his personal funerary cult. Each year on a fixed date they had to come and place offerings and candles, not of course on his tomb but in the church near which he was buried; their service was almost entirely limited to this. From the sixth and seventh centuries the majority of these *servi* were placed under the patronage of the funerary church, from which they acquired their name of *cerocensuales* or *luminarii*. In assigning them to this task, however, their master made their situation permanent, thus creating between servitude and liberty a halfway state.[13] Other dependants of the Church, prisoners redeemed by a bishop who had been unable to pay back the costs of their ransom, seem also to have remained in the service of the Church.[14]

Dependence

The *coloni,* on the other hand, were from the start free men who cultivated the tenements of their masters. It was, however, a very compromised form of liberty, as their masters forbade them to leave this land.

Marc Bloch thought that the imperial rescripts that attached the *coloni* to the land had been forgotten in the "great upheavals of the pre–Middle Ages." "No one," he said, "thought of it any more." We shall see. The capitulary of 803–813, whose significance he is rejecting because it is only posing a rule of procedure, nevertheless clearly indicates that a lord can have claims on a *colonus.* Attested practice corresponds to the legal text: one day Gerald of Aurillac was walking with his escort when he met a large group of his *coloni* who, leaving their farms, were going to set up elsewhere. The first instinct of Gerald's followers was to take them back to their holdings *manu militari.* Gerald forbade this, but this was a mark of his great saintliness and was not the usual habit of a lord. At the moment of scarcity of labor, how could the great landowners have allowed the *coloni* the possibility of choosing the best conditions of work? It goes without saying, and the anecdote proves it, that the *coloni's* point of view was the opposite.[15]

It also appears that the *coloni* did not take the free man's oath of fealty to the king, except for those of them who, dependent on the fisc or on a church, had been honored with a benefice or an office in the same way as were certain privileged serfs.

This brings us back to the famous capitulary to the *missi* of 793. Having enumerated the free men of the *pagus—pagenses—*and the different *vassi,* the text adds: "and also the *fiscalini* and even the *coloni* and the church serfs who honourably hold benefices and offices— *ministeria—*or who honourably make up the entourage of their master in vassalage and can have horses and arms." By contrast, the other *coloni* did not take the oath.[16]

A little later, Charles the Bald extended the use of corporal punishment, hitherto applied only to slaves, to *coloni* guilty of various crimes.

We can see in the texts the beginning of a response to the increasing shortage of servile labor—the solution was to consider all tenants as *mancipia,* regardless of their legal status. In 745 we find an example of this annoying linguistic confusion, used by the pope, Zacharias; in 814 we see it in the polyptyque of Saint-Victor in Marseilles, and from the time of Charles the Bald onward it becomes frequent. This is the probable explanation for a polemical text that attributes twenty thousand *mancipia* to Alcuin, the patron of four abbeys including Saint-Martin in Tours, one of the richest abbeys in the kingdom.[17] This figure must be understood as including all the dependants of these monasteries. The same sources that point to this confusion also reveal its limits: the polyptyque of Saint-Victor, which is called "List of the *mancipia* of the church of Marseilles," is careful to distinguish on this list between the different legal situations of the tenants.[18]

Reference has often been made when determining the situation of a *colonus* to the response of a palatine counsellor to a *missus* who asked to whom did the offspring belong in the case of marriage between a female *colonus* and the slave of a master? He was instructed to refer to the rules of devolution of children in cases of marriage between slaves of different masters. The response concludes with the affirmation that there is no other condition than that of serfdom or liberty. It is a difficult text to interpret and has a conclusion that probably does not have the general value that has sometimes been attributed to it. It should be compared with the polyptyque of Saint-Germain, which in several passages indicates that the children of *servi* "are *liti* because they are born of a *colonus*." So the habit had arisen in some public domains of giving the children of these mixed marriages an intermediate status, that of freed men who owed the *litimonium*. The answer to the *missus* shows a reaction against this usage. It affirmed the freedom of the *colonus* and refused to consider the status of the *litus* as other than a transitory condition between serfdom and freedom. It went against the tide.[19]

We must add to these tenants other people who emerged from we know not quite where and were taken into the community, the "guests," *hospites, accolae.*[20]

All these people then are the men of a master and he tends to lump them together in a dependence that becomes increasingly oppressive, bringing them closer together. But they are not entirely defenseless. First, there are the tribunals: the peasants of Antoigné in 828 refused to pay the abbey of Cormery dues that had not been demanded for a long time; the matter was taken to court and the representatives of the monastery only won the case because they were able to produce a polyptyque where these requisitions had earlier been written down. At times the peasants were known to manifest their discontent in violence. The records of a court held in 834 show them all together, *coloni, servi,* and humble free men, invading an estate belonging to the abbey of Nouaillé and causing damage.[21] Others, *coloni* of the fisc, sold the land attached to their manses and then claimed that they no longer owed the dues or the services that burdened them. This implies that these tax dodgers cultivated other lands in order to feed themselves, which they may have bought as allods or that they rented from a neighbor.

We find a similar example in the polyptyque of Saint-Germain, which describes an old allod that had become a tenement in Corbon near Mortagne-en-Perche. A large family, of some twenty people by now *coloni* of Saint-Germain, worked seventeen *bonniers* (perhaps around seventeen hectares or forty-two acres) of ploughed land, with half the produce going to the master, but they had bought four *bonniers* free of a lord and held five others from a lord other than the abbey.[22]

In spite of the lord's claims, the families of dependent peasants conducted on their level their own land policy, now buying, now selling, exchanging elsewhere, and sometimes clearing a few unofficial plots of land at the edge of the master's forest. But the most powerful weapon remained, as in the late empire, flight or desertion of the estate. Flight was easier in the areas where the military presence was small, and flight sometimes became necessary when troubles ravaged the country and famine threatened.

It is no coincidence that around the year 800 several southern documents mention fugitive *mancipia*, calling for thirty years banishment—when they have been found! At the same period, the only polyptyque preserved in the south, that of Saint-Victor of Marseilles, shows that half of the estates of this great church were empty of workers. As for other tenancies, the writer merely notes the name of the former occupants with the laconic remark "to be found." A century later, if the peasants of Gerald of Aurillac left his land, it was because they had, they said, been given away by Gerald as a benefice. And that is without taking into account individual fugitives or those resourceful peasants whom their masters found established elsewhere and greatly enriched.[23]

The capitulary of 803–813, which in the case of disputes ordered *coloni* or slaves of the fisc to return to their places of origin, is also intended to prevent people wandering off and escaping from dependency. However, flight was not always necessary. When famine or invasions emptied the manses of their inhabitants, the survivors could bargain over their services.

In 893 at a *villa* in Prüm in the Ardennes, numerous manses were deserted after the passing through of the Vikings, while certain nearby tenements were crowded with peasant families. At Remiremont, after a Hungarian raid, the abbess agreed to halve the service required from some of the peasants, an act of generosity necessary to the good management of the estate.[24]

For the toughest and most desperate of the peasants there remained finally brigandage, the first step sometimes toward revolt. Here too the *Vita Geraldi* furnishes us with a good example. The brigands of Auvergne sometimes recruited among Gerald's tenants: when the band was caught by the master's *milites*, their eyes were put out. However, one of them had been forced to join the band; learning this, Gerald, always fair, ordered that the man be given a hundred *sous*. The recipient of this tardy generosity nevertheless found it expedient to go and live in the Toulouse area. At the same period bands of outlaws appeared in the Alps, controlling the passes and providing travelers with guides, porters, and a "protection" that it was unwise to refuse.[25]

The Freedom of the "Poor"

But the absolute weapon of the dependants was neither revolt nor flight, it was the existence of significant groups of free peasants outside the tight control of the lords. How else can we explain the fact that runaway serfs managed to masquerade as free men? It must have happened quite frequently. In those domains of Saint-Bertin that enjoyed immunity, there lived free men who owed only two days of duty each year, in other words, probably a public service. In Guines, alongside sixteen tenants and about one hundred dependants, there were forty free men. At Wizernes there were twenty-one free men to eighteen tenants and about a hundred dependants. Large numbers of allodialists could be found also in the Mâcon region. In Varanges, a little hamlet near Cluny, there were at least forty-seven small landowners; in Montpeyta in Catalonia, there were one hundred thirty. Obviously they did not all live in the two villages in question, nevertheless the allodial communities must have been important there. We know of similar groups in Septimania as well as Provence. In addition to their own fields, they held in common certain places and land, *exagum communale* or *terra Francorum.*[26]

Among these allodialists we find very different levels of wealth. In a study of the territory of Montpeyta, Pierre Bonnassie shows that three allodialists are mentioned more than 20 times, 4 between ten and twenty times, 18 from five to ten times, 105 less than five times. It is probable that this last figure included at least in part not the residents of the village, but the inhabitants of neighboring villages who held small plots of land as a result of inheritance or marriage. The same Catalan source shows the relativly comfortable circumstances of some of these free peasants. In Mortagne-en-Perche, the twenty children and grandchildren of Ainhard, before becoming *coloni* of Saint-Germain, were free to cultivate their twenty-five hectares. Near Arles, the children of Ansbert lived in the midst of some twenty other small allodialists with about fifty hectares. In Catalonia, Septimania, Provence, and the Mâcon region they were called *boni laboratores, honesti viri;* from their ranks the country priests were recruited. Gabriella Rossetti has described in great detail the communities of this type in the region around Monza, drawing on the rich archives of Sant' Ambrogio in Milan.[27]

Of course, we should not underestimate the precariousness of the situation of the allodialists, and the Carolingian capitularies paint in somber colors the fate of the small free peasants whom they disparagingly call the *pauperes.* The way they were treated was not new and hardly original; it was the way of the *potentes* of the late empire. As small free producers, the *pauperes* had to perform a certain number of services for the public power. A count or a *vicarius* had only to increase this burden in a bad year for the peasants to be faced with famine before the next good harvest. They would then go and borrow a few measures of corn from the nearest important landowner who would have considerable reserves. He would lend it out at interest, demanding three or four times more than he had lent. When the time came to pay it back, except when there was an exceptionally good harvest, the peasant would have to sell his already mortgaged property. While waiting to be paid, his creditor would put shackles on his legs and keep him bound in this way.[28] Other methods could simplify the operation: the use of a different set of weights and measures for lending and paying back, or wills extorted from the peasants in difficulties by their "benefactors." The victims favored with these stratagems were— noblesse oblige—widows and orphans.[29] This gradual enslavement of the free peasants did not, however, work as well as might be supposed from reading the capitularies and councils. It relied on agreement between the local masters and those who exercised the *bannum*, and the support of the village notables, *boni homines* or *scabini*, who would assess the true price of the land mortgaged when it came to be sold as well as the value of the bequest.[30] In point of fact, there remained in the tenth century a lot of free village communities. What is certain, however, is that the ravages of the Vikings must have compromised their existence and destroyed the structures of their society. Where war passed, servitude followed in its wake.

The victims captured by pirates could be sold in the market of a nearby town. Their families and friends thought only of buying them back and never of freeing them, an indication of the degree to which the selling of men had become accepted, which throws a worrying light on the complicity that the raiders could rely on. This explains the passivity of some of the magnates: the raiders, even without wanting to, could be of considerable use to them.[31]

What the last invasions began, it remained for the banal lords to put into action. Then the *pauperes* would no longer have to deal with cautious stratagems in which force was hidden behind the law, but with outright violence and pillage.

Freedom Is Not What It Was

At the beginning of the ninth century in Thiais and in Villeneuve-Saint-Georges in the Paris region, out of a good hundred heads of family dependent on Saint-Germain-des-Prés, only 10 percent were described as *servi;* three centuries later in these two villages, almost all the population were serfs. Thus, as Marc Bloch has observed, from the ninth to the eleventh century a slow and inexorable revolution was bringing the greater part of the French countryside into serfdom. The decisive period seems to come around the year 1000, taking account of regional differences.[32] At that period there seems to have been operating a process of the leveling out of the many categories of "semi-freedom," often to the detriment of the people involved. This explains why in the twelfth century there was a tendency to be rather too hasty in identifying serf with villein. These two terms need to be looked at more closely.

The Development of Dependency

A report of an assembly in Cambrai, which still has the usual characteristics of a public assembly, shows that as late as 941 the *mallum*, here presided over by the bishop, will not allow one of the bishop's vassals to place in servitude a woman and her six children. They claimed the rights of their birth and the mother produced six peasants who took oaths with her; the tribunal agreed that she owed only the head tax and not service. Thus a distinction is still being made between simple dependants and *servi*.[33] But toward the end of the century things changed. In an area stretching from Burgundy to Flanders, the Church dependants, *mundiliones, cerarii, sanctuarii, tributarii*, who had been hitherto supplied, apparently, by the freeing of the *servi*, saw their numbers swelled by the entry of numerous free men.[34]

At St Peter's, Ghent, the status of the freed slaves placed by their old master under the *mundium* of the monastery was a model in the tenth century for the status of the free men who gave themselves to this abbey; they are called *tributarii* in allusion to the head tax that they paid in return.

What is striking is that it is often women who come with their families into the protection of the Church. These widows and orphans represent the most fragile category of the poor but free that the capitularies tried to protect. As the documents sometimes make clear, the arrival en masse of these people into church protection indicates the many pressures being placed on them by the secular lords. The result was perhaps inevitable but dangerous. Until c. 1030 those who placed themselves under the protection of Saint Bavo of Ghent were careful to specify that they were free. After this date the clause disappears. The book of the *Miracula* of the same abbey confirms in the eleventh century what we saw in the charters. A "noble" woman had been forced to enter into the *familia* of the saint; ashamed of having to pay the head tax, she ordered one of her own serfs to take her place.[35] We are better able to understand why the majority of the charters in the twelfth century identify nobility and freedom. It was indeed overhasty to decide that the *homines ecclesiae*, so numerous in all the towns of the north, were not free men.

If the category of people protected by the Church had greatly increased in the eleventh century, not all the free men had yet joined in. A certain number of them still claimed to owe only public obligations, as in the case of the *homines de generali placito* of Saint-Vaast in Arras.

When between 1023 and 1036 the abbot tried to define their obligations, he mentions first that of coming to the *tria placita generalia*, then he specifies that they do not pay head tax nor anything to the *advocatus*. The abbot calls the property of these men "allods." These *homines* are then the descendants of the free peasants who lived on the exempted estates of the great abbeys of Flanders and Picardy. Of course by 1023–36 their position had changed; they could neither sell or mortgage their allods except with the permission of the abbot who could refuse it. They could not marry a woman from another manor; within the manor of the Church they had to pay dues if they married a dependant; if the woman was free they were not taxed but instead they owed a mortuary payment to the lord. It is not surprising if the lordship of the churches, benefiting here from the precedent of immunity, was able to impose extra obligations on these men. The amazing thing is that they were able to retain as much independence as they did.[36]

In the Ile-de-France and in the Orleans area there were *coloni* who seem to have had to bear the weight of the new servitude. Marc Bloch has given one particularly striking example. The traditional clause of the charters granting immunity—"no public judge shall enter . . . into the possessions of this church . . . to constrain the men of this church both free and serfs"—is now replaced in Lothar's charters for Sainte-Croix in Orleans, Saint-Benoît-sur-Loire, and Notre-Dame in Paris with the formula "the men of this church both free and *coloni*.[37]

In the Chartres area the situation is similar. The ratio of *servi* to *coloni* there was, according to the polyptyque of Saint-Germain, even lower than elsewhere: on the fisc of Villemeux there were 82 *coloni* out of a population of 1,639 people. In the eleventh century, on the other hand, we find no *coloni*. The condition of the tenants must have become more unified, because the monk Paul, recopying a Carolingian polyptyque in around 1078, calls all the tenants *agricolae*, carefully separating them from the *capaticii* who individually owed head tax of four deniers. The unification of the peasants' condition was made around the term *servus*; from this time onward Paul's *agricolae* appear under this name in the charters. Soon even those who had dedicated themselves to a saint and owed the four derniers found themselves obliged to assume the name of serf.

André Chédeville has remarked how in the eleventh century one finds serfs particularly on the manors of counts, of the cathedral chapters, and of the old abbeys. By contrast, the abbeys or chapters created at this time did not have any serfs to speak of. So it appears that it was the dependants of the ninth century who formed the servile group of the eleventh century. He notes also the use made of Roman law, particularly by Ivo of Chartres, to clarify the condition of these *servi*, and he attributes the duration of the servile condition in the region to this influence.

Nevertheless, in the Chartres region in the eleventh century serfs are only found to the east of a line Chartres-Châteaudun, that is to say on the border of the Orleans-Paris area. In the twelfth century they were also called *homines de corpore.*[38]

The lands around the Loire to the south of the Chartrain and the Orléanais need to be looked at separately. In these areas too the true *coloni* had disappeared in the tenth or at the beginning of the eleventh century and the expression "servile *coloni"* is sometimes used to describe the condition of the peasantry. But what makes the lands of the Loire different from other areas was the survival of a mysterious category—the *colliberti.*

The *colliberti* have provoked much controversy and this uncertainty is explained by the fact that here we have a residual category whose status was increasingly difficult to distinguish from that of the *servi* of the eleventh century. The first *colliberti* appear in 973–975, decreasing from the beginning of the twelfth century and finally disappearing after 1163. They were characteristic of Maine, Anjou, Touraine, and Blois, but they were also found in Poitou, Limousin, and Berry.[39]

The etymology of the word indicates clearly its origin: the setting free of groups in a will. The word *collibertus* is used in ancient Italy and particularly in funerary inscriptions placed by freed men on the tombs of their masters. In the eighth century the *colliberti* of Lombardy were still freed men *cum obsequio*, and this type of emancipation was also known at the same period in Provence.[40] However, the *colliberti* of the tenth and eleventh centuries are special in that their condition has become permanent: they can be given, exchanged, and sold. Here again a type of dependant seems to have been created whose condition, at the outset at least, was probably better than that of the *mancipia*. Thus it was that probably under Angevin influence that, when William's counsellors found in England a group called *buri*, who were dependants but not serfs, they called them *colliberti*.

C. Van de Kieft has suggested that the *colliberti* were originally freed men according to Frankish law, because it seems that this law only knew of freeing *cum obsequio*. But Guy Devailly has pointed out that in this case it would be difficult to account for the fact that *colliberti* appeared in the south of the Limousin and not in the old Frankish areas between the Meuse and the Loire. The example of the patrician Abbo shows that freeing *cum obsequio* was not unknown to those who followed Roman law in the south. As for the evidence of the formulae, it is less convincing than one might think: the fact that a formula from Berry carefully attributes to the freed man *melior libertas* by setting aside the *obsequium* seems to indicate that the opposite was a possibility.[41] It would be unwise to base too much on the possible survivals of Visigothic or Burgundian law in areas where there can hardly have been landowners living under these laws in the ninth century even if there once had been. A possible hypothesis is that the descendants of the freed men *cum obsequio* following the Frankish ritual of the *denier* must have been, as Marc Bloch thought, what were to be called *liti*, hence the frequency of the word *litimonium*, and in fact in the preponderantly Frankish regions we find *liti*. The use of the terms *libertus* or *collibertus* can on the other hand be linked with an area of southern culture, as can be seen by the first appearances of the term. Why in this case was it only preserved in the northern fringe of this area? It is worth noting that at the time when the term *collibertus* appears, there were hardly any *servi* left in the south, in Provence, and in Septimania. Thus there cannot have been any more *liberti* either. The persistence of the term in the lands of the Loire on the other hand reminds us that there were still regions where it was possible in the early tenth century to free many *mancipia*. But the very fact that the *colliberti* became a fixed category at the end of the century implies the increasing infrequency of both freeing and of servitude in favor of new forms of dependence. Supporting this hypothesis is the fact that small groups of *colliberti* are found in Italy and in northwest Spain.[42]

By contrast, the apparent disappearance of any intermediate status between freedom and serfdom can be observed in Burgundy. In the ninth century the masters who freed their *servi* made them pay head tax to Saint-Etienne of Dijon on the saint's day. From the tenth century and particularly in the eleventh century, when receiving men subject to an identical charge on the same day, the same church calls them *servi* or *mancipia*. In 1062, the *villa* of Berzé was given to Cluny "with the male and female serfs who lived there . . . whether they be free men or serfs." But here the title of *servus* was to be less longlasting than in the Paris region. After 1105 the word disappears in the Mâcon area while in the twelfth century in the Sénonais servitude and *comenda* are confused.[43]

In the south, we know that the allodialists were still numerous in the tenth century. From the 1050s they were in their turn caught in the net of the banal lordship. The castellans considered them to be their men, giving, selling, or exchanging them with their allods. To consolidate his *bannum*, the lord extended his protection, his bailiwick, in all directions.[44]

One of the foundations, or pretexts, for this protection was comendation. But the origin of the *commendaticii* and their condition are not yet fully understood. In many cases it appears to mean the tenants belonging to a manor that had been given in *comenda*. But it is also thought that there may have been a personal *commendatio* made individually by small allodialists to a powerful lord. However, such examples are rare and late. Similarly we must be cautious before assimilating peasant commendation and "servile" homage. The *commendatio* of the Frankish *vassi* definitely involved homage, but we should not assume that this was the case, at the beginning, for all types of *commendatio*.[45] Nevertheless, peasant, and not necessarily servile, homage is found in the Midi from the mid–eleventh century.

It occurs too in Catalonia, where many peasants do homage to their lord and as a result, just like the liege knights, are called his "stout men." The charters of the early twelfth century give the synonyms *homines solidi–homines proprii.* But the same text seem to show that this homage of a lord's men was required when they received their tenements; among these tenants, it is very probable that there were many former allodialists who had handed over their allods to the lord in order to have them in tenure. Nonetheless, it is quite possible that those of the *manentes* who, at the end of the eleventh century, were still called allodialists had been able to enjoy a less servile condition.[46]

The few descendants of the *servi* of the ninth century gradually became merged with the mass of originally free small peasants who were now confined to a tenement. Perhaps the "given men" of Septimania were also former *servi.* Elizabeth Magnou-Nortier says that these men had no link with a tenement. However, they occur only rarely.[47]

It seems that in the Midi the same evolution took place, though with varying intensity. In Catalonia, banal lordship, perhaps more oppressive, reduced tenants to *pagesia de remensa:* the peasant, tied to his land, owed the lord the *mals usos,* the *exorquia,* and the *intestia* that were the rights over succession, the *cugucia* and the *arsina* that were fines on cuckolds and victims of fire, and the *ferma de spoli* that was a permission for marriage. We recognize the equivalents of the marriage and mortuary payments of the serfs in the north. But here Pierre Bonnassie has shown that the *mals usos* came directly from the banal rights of the lord.[48] Now such an evolution does not seem to have occurred in the rest of the south where the new serfdom was to remain, except in clearly localized cases, something exceptional.

Almost everywhere in the eleventh century, the peasant becomes the "man" of a lord. But this rather vague term could embrace rather different conditions according to place. A map of dependence can be drawn up where, despite different vocabularies and traditions, we find curious similarities. Picardy and Flanders with their large groups of *sainteurs* (dependants of the saint) and the lands around the Loire with their *colliberti* are areas where a dependent condition had appeared that was neither strictly speaking serfdom nor freedom, even in its degraded form within the framework of lordship. In the Ile-de-France, the Chartrain, and Orléanais the distinction was made only between serfs and free men and in the thirteenth century it was serfdom that was to gain the upper hand. In the south, the same duality was to evolve, generally to the advantage of the peasants, except in Catalonia. Even in this last region the term *servus* was avoided: it is true that the Saracens were to bear the brunt of a new slavery and bring about a revival, much against their will, of the expression.

But this kind of map of serfdom risks concealing an essential fact: the terms and their content are far from being fixed in the twelfth century, in fact quite the opposite. The controversies about the true meaning of a tributary, a *collibertus,* or a serf are not as innocent as they seem: they all hinge on one question—are dependants free men or not? This is a problem that still divides today's historians, but it divided much more so, and with reason, the men of the twelfth century. The hesitations in certain texts, or should we say their contradictions, far from being a sign of a lack of precision in legal minds, are the signs of a confusion at the very time when ambiguities of meaning were less possible.

The New Serfdom

It is clear that in the twelfth century in northern France a vast movement was taking place that led to the consolidation of a new serfdom, reduced to the lowest level that the term could denote. A valuable piece of evidence of this is that the *servi* could not be witnesses in law. Recent research shows that in the Ile-de-France in the eleventh century custom had no difficulty in recognizing the serfs' right to give evidence and the right to fight in a trial by combat. The old legal texts that set out the serfs' incapacity were now no longer applied, even if they were remembered. This is perfectly explicable if we accept that these serfs were indeed the descendants of more or less free dependants who had never stopped exercising these rights. At the beginning of the twelfth century the situation had changed. This is confirmed by the fact that from this time on the king was granting charters to the great abbeys to authorize their serfs to give evidence and if necessary to fight against free men or, and this amounts to the same thing, to give them the status of royal serfs.

We have nine authentic charters from between 1106 and 1153, of which seven date from 1006–1118. The tenth is a forgery made in the mid-twelfth century by the monks of Saint-Germain-des-Prés to whom the king had apparently refused to grant what had become a privilege.[49]

Significant also were the legal proceedings that were taking place to clarify the condition of whole groups of dependants. An example of such a case is that between the canons of Sainte-Geneviève and their peasants of Rosny-sous-Bois who claimed that they were not serfs but only *"hospites* and *coloni,"* exempt from head tax and marriage payment. The peasants lost their case, but they continued to appeal against the verdict until 1126.[50]

It has been suggested that Roman law, introduced here by the canonists, was a weapon in the hands of the lords and the masters. André Chédeville has found traces of this in the Chartres area. In the case of the men of Rosny, the abbot of Sainte-Geneviève was none other than the famous decretalist Stephen of Tournai, who had studied in Bologna. All of a sudden his adversaries feel the need to add to the vulgar term *hospites* the word *colonus*, which by this date was a learned reference to Roman law.[51]

Resistance to this movement of enserfment was all the more active because on the great estates groups of rich and active dependants had grown up who were impatient both with their ancient servitude and of the new restrictions. Everybody, estate administrators, domestic officers, knights of the retinue were part of the *familia* of a great lord and were called his *ministeriales*. Among them, those of the great northern abbeys were the most important, whether they were rich town merchants or domestic warriors.

These armed dependants who followed their lords on horseback were already to be found in the Carolingian period on the lands of the royal abbeys.[52] They were called *caballarii* in Saint-Bertin where Folcuin differentiates their benefice from that of the *milites;* they held large manses of some forty hectares worked by *mancipia*, tenements similar to those of the mayors of the abbey.[53] In Prüm and Trier they were, significantly, called *scararii* or *scaremanni*, a name that evokes the prestige that they had gained by mingling with the abbey vassals in the *scara*. Elsewhere they were also called sergeants, *servientes*.[54] In Flanders and Picardy as in Lotharingia, as we have seen, the custom grew up of reserving the word *milites* for this group. Certain of these *ministeriales* had by the beginning of the twelfth century attained a social level that placed them well above the petty nobility. An example is the Erembald family, castellans and counts in the county of Bruges and chancellors of Flanders; related to powerful figures, lords or even peers of Flanders, they had made their fortune in the service of the count. In 1127, a group at court reminded the latter of the supposedly servile origins of the Erembald family and he thought it wise to get rid of this family that had grown a little too important. The Erembalds, determined "to die rather than allow themselves to be reduced to servitude" assassinated the count. It was a desperate act that did little to delay their fall; besieged and captured, they died after terrible torture.[55]

At the same period, accusations of this type were made against certain members of the king of France's household, such as Henry of Lorraine, friend of the powerful family of Garlande, which was soon in disgrace. Similarly, a Burgundian chronicler, recalling the servile condition in the twelfth century of a deceased provost of the viscount, added: "I shall be silent on the name of this man so as to avoid wounding his descendants who bask today in all the brilliance of knighthood."[56]

A text from outside the French kingdom, the chronicle of the monastery of Ebersheim in Alsace, shows the response of the *ministeriales* to those who wished to assimilate them with the serfs, and remarkably it appeals immediately to Roman history. Julius Caesar, it reads, when taking leave of his German auxiliaries after crushing the Gauls, had given to the leaders, *principes*, the title of Roman senator—in other words, nobility—and the title of citizen, or freedom, to the common soldiers, *minores milites*, and he had commended them to the princes, that they might not treat them as slaves or servants, *servi ac famuli*, and that having become their lords and defenders they might use them not for *opus servile* but for *ministeria*. From this time the *milites* became the *ministeriales principum*. And the chronicler carefully distinguishes the *ministeriales* from the other members of the *familia;* there is the *familia ministerialis* "which is also justly called *militaris,*" he says, playing on words, "it is noble and warlike or at least of free condition"; then there is the *familia censualis,* "both glorious in its obedience and satisfied with its rights"; and lastly the *familia servilis,* with no comment.[57] Among the dependants, the small group of those who served in arms tends to be clearly distinguished both from a middle stratum that pays head tax and is probably composed of abbey merchants, the future bourgeoisie, and from a lower category, that of the peasant tenants abandoned to their servile status.

At roughly the same period when the chronicler of Ebersheim was singing the praises of the *familia ministerialis,* an anonymous author in Regensburg commented on the word *collibertus,* insisting on the fact that freed men given to the Church to become part of its *familia* are the co-freed men, *colliberti,* of their masters and have the same freedom as they, since all are the serfs of God and the saints.[58] In the same spirit, the preamble of the forged charter for the serfs of Saint-Germain, returning to the theme of a sermon by St. Augustine, adds a passage from Abelard who wrote in the *Expositio in Hexaemeron:* "God has not placed one man over another, but only above the creatures devoid of sense and reason."[59] In both these documents, by adapting Roman history or drawing on St. Augustine, dependents of the Church or *ministeriales* were affirming their freedom. They responded in this way to those who, like Nithard, Raoul Glaber, or Geoffrey of Vigeois, identified servitude with cowardice and deceit or, like the anonymous writer of a deed from Chartres, with the love of worldy goods. Through the complaints of so many monastic writers, who complained about the perfidy, greed, or insolence of these bad servants, we glimpse the energy of a social class that supported its condition with ill-concealed impatience.[60]

The *ministeriales,* in northern France as in Germany,[61] thus formed in the twelfth century a rich and powerful group, swelled by all those who in the previous century had preferred to seek a security denied them by secular society in the shelter of the churches. In partly alienating their liberty they thought to protect it. But the power of the *ministeriales* poses a problem in the twelfth century. How can these people, whom the nobles and their relatives insist on considering as serfs, enter into the entourage of princes and kings, command in their name, and marry noble daughters? The song of *Girart of Roussillon,* one of the most aristocratic of the *Chansons de Geste,* does not mince words: "How badly is he rewarded, the good warrior who makes of the son of a villein a knight, then his seneschal and then his counsellor."[62] The counterposing in the princely houses of knight and villein becomes the leitmotif of courtly literature. This insistence should not deceive us; quite the opposite. The "villeins" increase in number in the entourage of the master, riding with him in arms or looking after his affairs, ready to do anything to make themselves equals to their disdainful rivals.[63]

Side by side with the ancient nobility, now extended to the lesser families, there appears a new aristocracy, grown up in the entourage of the lords. Forced willy-nilly to respond to the attacks of those who disputed its increasing power, it was to make of service, the very thing for which it was reproached, its glory and its dominant idea.

Serfdom, or if one prefers, the new serfdom of the twelfth century, is thus rather different from the Carolingian *servitus*. In many cases it is less restrictive, since the free origin of those now called serfs had an influence, despite everything, on the custom that fixed their obligations to their lord. This explains why the obligations that increasingly came to be considered as part and parcel of serfdom—the head tax or marriage payments or payments to obtain exemption from mortuary dues—were formerly those of dependants and not of the Carolingian *servi*. On the other hand, the number of those taken over by serfdom is incomparably greater. What it has lost in intensity, it has gained in extensiveness. Despite the similarity, deliberate, of the terms, the *servi* of the twelfth century resemble hardly at all their homonyms, who three centuries earlier were people whom the master forced to work directly for him. Now they were much more often tenants, essentially more dependent than other tenants, from whom the master could, because of this dependence, claim a larger rent.

At the turn of the eleventh century, the establishment of this properly manorial society was not accomplished without upheavals and clashes. The most striking manifestation of this was without any doubt the peasants' revolt in Normandy in 997. There the great estates did not have the strong roots that had developed elsewhere; the establishment of banal lordship, with its "bad customs," its suppression of common rights, the taxes on the mill, the oven, the fish pond, and its hostility toward the small allod, must have been seen as an intolerable innovation. But the uprising was too sudden and too visible not to be mercilessly crushed. A few years later in Catalonia, at the other end of the kingdom, a true reign of terror was necessary to suppress the free peasants. At the end of the century in the Le Mans area and in Picardy, peasants commited arson and stoned the great lords. Gradually, in defiance of the lords and their knights who suppressed with equal inhumanity peasants, villeins, allodialists, and *colliberti*, the answer of the Norman peasants made itself heard: "We are men as they are." As yet the day-to-day form this resistance took is not known to us— sabotaged labor service, poaching in the lord's forest, a furrow gradually extended at each ploughing into the lord's fallow land.[64] A century later, the spread and radicalization of the movement of the "hooded men of Puy" shows the degree to which tension remained between the lords and the peasants. As earlier in Berry in 1038, the peace militias were turning into a thoroughgoing antiseigneurial revolt, which aroused the amazement and indignation of the monastic chroniclers. Reading between the lines of these diatribes, the peasants' objectives emerge clearly: a return "to the origins," to the time of Adam, when there were neither masters nor slaves. The egalitarian and libertarian tendencies shown in the peasant revolts, which will appear again, are thus as ancient as the system that sought to deny them and attempted to base its social order on hierarchy and inequality.[65]

Despite revolt and resistance, new social relationships grew up. The use made by the lords of their banal power as an element of their lordship had first of all a double effect. It drew to the nobility certain peasants—those who could or wanted to bear arms for the nobles and who thus helped the lords increase their power over the rest of the peasantry. It drove the rest of the inhabitants of the countryside into dependence. This analysis should not however lead us to overestimate the depth of the division thus created and the homogeneity of the groups on either side of the *bannum*. On one side of the divide we know that the difference between simple knights and true nobles was felt keenly and sometimes even specified in law. On the other side, among the dependants, some were much more than humble laborers and their way of life brought them near, if not to the nobility, then at least to the knights. Finally, and despite the legal barrier that it had created between men, banal lordship appears above all to have increased and benefited one layer of society, lying in the middle. This middle layer was in principle a servant of the interests of banal lordship, but its increasing weight of numbers was sometimes to bring with it by its own momentum the true birth of feudal relationships. Before examining this phenomenon, we need to look at the idea that contemporaries had of their own society in the midst of the social upheavals of the year 1000.

Notes

1. *MGH*, Capit. 1, no. 58, p. 145.
2. Duby, *Guerriers* [532], p. 45.
3. Dhondt, *Le haut Moyen Age* [475], p. 21. "If the productive class was treated in this way, it was to a certain extent because the military class, at the moment of its most insolent triumph, could not ignore the natural solidarity which linked it to the class whose labor assured its survival: the exploitation of the lords had always to stop before the point where the productive class, reduced to abject poverty, could no longer create wealth or multiply," Olivier-Martin, *La coutume de Paris* [259], p. 9.
4. On the Saxons and others, see Verlinden, *L'esclavage* [321], pp. 668 and 706. The archbishop of Lyons, Agobard, considered the *servi* provided by the slave trade to be pagans, p. 704; the capitulary *de Villis, cap.* 67, in indicating that the *mancipia* were acquired in the royal domains, shows that not all were sold outside the frontiers of Europe, Verlinden, *L'esclavage* [321], pp. 719 and 216.

138 | *The Feudal Transformation*

5. On the Frankish *pueri regales*, the Burgundian *Wittiscalci* and the Visigothic *servi fiscales*, see Verlinden, *L'esclavage* [321], pp. 662, 678, 641, and 81.
6. Ibid., p. 703; *Vita Geraldi* [34], 2: 11, col. 677.
7. Petot, *L'évolution* [313], notices the proximity of the Carolingian serf and the slave; Verlinden, *L'esclavage* [321], p. 741; see also chapter 5 below. We have chosen to opt for what Robert Boutruche has caustically called "a lazy solution, which is to keep the Latin, leaving the reader to work out why," *Seigneurie* [98], 1: 130.
8. Verlinden, *L'esclavage* [321], pp. 697 and 719.
9. Magnou-Nortier, *La société laïque* [86], p. 219; Bonnassie, *La Catalogne* [72], p. 298; Poly, *La Provence* [87], p. 108.
10. M. Bloch, "Comment et pourquoi finit l'esclavage antique," *Mélanges . . .*, p. 268; Génicot, *Sur le domaine* [535]; Duby, *L'économie rurale* [300], p. 101. For figures for the Chartrain, see Chédeville, *Chartres* [76], p. 357.
11. Poly, *La Provence* [87], p. 104.
12. *Vita Geraldi* [34], 3: 4, col. 692; Schneider, *Aspects de la société* [512].
13. Marculf, *MGH, Formulae* II, no. 34, p. 96. Verlinden gives examples of this practice in Paris, Le Mans, Angoulême, and Castile, *L'esclavage* [321], pp. 686, 737 and 121.
14. Verlinden, *L'esclavage* [321], pp. 664 and 668.
15. Bloch, *Les "colliberti"* [284], p. 434; in the same area, Boutruche, *Seigneurie* [98], 1: 137, which quotes however (p. 311) the fragment of the capitulary of 803–813; *Vita Geraldi* [34], 1: 24, col. 656; Schneider, *Aspects de la société* [512].
16. Ganshof, *Charlemagne* [186]. By contrast, Bloch, *Les "colliberti"* [284], p. 435. If a serf was taken with a lance, it was broken over his back, Riché, *La vie quotidienne* [646], p. 133.
17. Bloch, *Les "colliberti"* [284], p. 437, n. 3, references to texts.
18. Bloch, *Liberté et servitude* [285], pp. 333 and 335; Duby, *Guerriers* [532], p. 100; Poly, *La Provence* [87], p. 101.
19. On *liti*, the offspring of a *colonus* mother and a *servus*, see Verlinden, *L'esclavage* [321], p. 738. Marc Bloch, *Les "colliberti"* [284], p. 438, considers this response to be an assimilation of *colonus* with *servus*, but points out that it was probably inspired by a fragment of Gaius, preserved in the *lex romana Wisigothorum*. Boutruche, *Seigneurie* [98], p. 127, thinks that "the imperial agent was avoiding making a direct pronouncement."
20. They seem to have been particularly numerous in Picardy, Fossier, *La terre* [79], pp. 318 and 554.
21. Duby, *L'économie rurale* [300], p. 118; Garaud, *Les châtelains de Poitou* [81], p. 205; Verlinden, *L'esclavage* [321], p. 725, shows a peasant barely escaping, in a *mallum* of the early ninth century, being attached to the fisc of Remiremont.
22. Duby, *L'économie rurale* [300], pp. 93ff. and 307, and *Guerriers* [532], pp. 99 and 111.
23. Poly, *La Provence* [87], p. 101; *Vita Geraldi* [34], 1: 24, col. 656. On runaway and enriched serfs, ibid., 1: 30, col. 660, and the example of Stabilis, p. 93 above.
24. Duby, *L'économie rurale* [300], p. 116; G. Constable, "The *liber*

memorialis of Remiremont," *Speculum* (1972): 261.

25. *Vita Geraldi* [34], 1: 18, col. 654; Poly, *La Provence* [87], p. 27.
26. Génicot, *Sur le domaine* [535]; Duby, *L'économie rurale* [300], p. 125; Magnou-Nortier, *La société laïque* [86], pp. 156, 207, and 284; Poly, *La Provence* [87], p. 87.
27. Bonnassie, *La Catalogne* [72], p. 305; Duby, *L'économie rurale,* [300], p. 307; Poly, *La Provence* [87], p. 104. Cf. also in Bonnassie, *La Catalogne* [72], p. 275, the personal fortune of Volenda, a peasant woman of Reixac in Vallès; for common rights, see Bonnassie, p. 307; Rossetti, *Società* [316].
28. *Vita Geraldi* [34], 1: 17, 24, 28, col. 654, 657, 658, which should be compared with the very numerous references to shackles in the southern *Miracula.*
29. Duby, *L'économie rurale* [300], p. 113. All these mechanisms are described in detail for northern France by Le Jan-Hennebicque, *Pauperes* [309]. Cf. also on the *pauperes* in Carolingian times, Devisse, *"Pauperes" et "Paupertas"* [294]; Mollat, *Les pauvres* [311], p. 45. For the same development in England in the eighth century, see Dufermont, *Les pauvres* [302]. On these manoeuvres and their economic consequences, compare p. 258 below.
30. Bonnassie, *La Catalogne* [72], p. 310.
31. Toubert, *Le Latium* [89], p. 312; Poly, *La Provence* [87], p. 11.
32. Bloch, *Liberté et servitude* [285], p. 330, and *Les "colliberti"* [284], p. 442.
33. Despy, *Serfs* [292].
34. Bloch, *Les "colliberti"* [284], p. 446; Pierre Duparc, *La question des "sainteurs"* [303], which gives a bibliography, opposes vigorously the assimilation of the two different categories of people, the *sainteurs* or *traditi* on the one hand and the *mundiliones, censuales,* or *tributarii* on the other. For Lorraine, see Tellenbach, *Servitus* [318].
35. Bloch, *Liberté et servitude* [285], p. 340, and Huygbaert, *Les femmes* [628].
36. Ganshof, *Les "homines de generali placito"* [126] and brief commentary by Bloch, *Liberté et servitude* [285], pp. 323 and 329.
37. Bloch, *Les "colliberti"* [284], p. 440.
38. Chédeville, *Chartres* [76], pp. 357, 370, 375, and the map p. 367.
39. The work begun by Marc Bloch has been enriched, but not always clarified by the research of Boussard [291] and Devailly [293] and *Le Berry* [77], p. 206ff., Van de Kieft [319], Garaud, *Les châtelains de Poitou* [81], p. 207ff.
40. See p. 122 above.
41. Verlinden, *L'esclavage* [321], pp. 697, 720, 723, and 726.
42. Nevertheless, in 1060–68, a monk of Maillezais, Peter, no longer knows the origin of the *colliberti* who lived around his monastery; he only knows that they are quick-tempered, irreligious, and wild, Bloch, *Les "colliberti"* [284], p. 408. It is no coincidence that in the vernacular French form, *culvert,* the word became an insult, Bloch, *Collibertus* [286].
43. Bloch, *Les "colliberti"* [284], p. 449; Duby, *La société* [78], pp. 112, 128 and 249; Bloch, *Liberté et servitude* [285], p. 341.
44. Bonnassie, *La Catalogne* [72], p. 812ff., p. 824ff.; Poly, *La Provence* [87], p. 131.
45. Thus Pierre Duparc, *La commmendise* [117], speaking of personal

comendation, is forced when describing the southern areas to deal with the contract of *comenda*, of whose "material and territorial spirit" he is aware, and which he puts down to a "difficulty . . . in expressing themselves in legal terms." In fact there is no personal commendation by the peasants. The *commendaticii* are not then "commended" peasants but peasants who live on the manor in *comenda*, and who possibly therefore paid an extra tax, cf. p. 36 above.

46. Bonnassie, *La Catalogne* [72] p. 577.
47. Magnou-Nortier, *La société laïque* [86], p. 225.
48. Bonnassie, *La Catalogne* [72], p. 824.
49. Guillot, *La participation* [307].
50. Bloch, *Le procès* [287].
51. Chédeville, *Chartres* [76], p. 376.
52. U. Berlière, "La *familia* dans les monastères bénédictins du Moyen Age," *Mem. Acad. roy. Belgique* 2 (1931): 1, Ganshof, *Les ministeriales* [306], pp. 35 and 37; Petot, *Observations* [315] and especially Génicot, *L'économie namuroise* [247], pp. 63 and 77.
53. Hollyman, *Le vocabulaire* [194], p. 133; Génicot, *Sur le domaine* [535].
54. Ganshof, *Les ministeriales* [306], particularly for Cambrai, p. 197.
55. Dhondt, *Les solidarités* [295].
56. Bournazel, *Le gouvernement* [418], p. 109; Bloch, *La ministérialité* [288], p. 523; Georges Duby, *La société* [78], p. 300, shows that in the early twelfth century the *ministeriales* of the monks of the Abbey of Cluny lived alongside the petty knights, without however merging with them.
57. On this text, see Bosl, *Castes* [290], and p. 52 above.
58. Bloch, *Les "colliberti"* [284], p. 411. Notice the traces of "French" influence at St. Emmeran, Regensburg: so also with the cult of St. Denis, p. 333 below.
59. Guillot, *La participation* [307].
60. Nithard, *Histoire des fils de Louis le Pieux*, ed. L. Halphen (Paris, 1964), 2: 3, p. 44; a scribe from Chartres in 949, Hollyman, *Le vocabulaire* [194], p. 95; Glaber, in David, *Les laboratores* [352]. On this scorn, see Dhondt, *Le haut Moyen Age* [475], p. 23.
61. Bosl, *Die Reichsministerialität* [289].
62. Bloch, *La ministerialité* [288], p. 522.
63. Duby, *Les trois ordres* [616], pp. 334 and 261, and the analysis of this major contradiction, p. 387ff.
64. Bonnassie, *La Catalogne* [72], p. 615; Fossier, *Les mouvements* [365] and *Remarques* [366].
65. Duby, *Les trois ordres* [616], p. 393. The Norman revolt was known through texts dating from the end of the twelfth century.

CHAPTER

5

Violence and Peace

Men's customs change and so also does the order of things.
—Adalbero of Laon

It is not enough to reconstruct as precisely as possible the state of the groups that make up a society and to elucidate in part its social vocabulary. We need also to ask the question: how did this society see its structure, how did it articulate the different elements of this vocabulary? In this respect no historical moment is so revealing as one in which the speed of social change breaks acquired habits and shakes existing relationships. Then the old ideas shatter and dogma wavers, leaving the way open for doubts and even heresy. Then too little by little another justification for the existing social order appears and is adopted.

How did the men of those times see these upheavals and changes? The immediate answer, as we might expect, is not easy to get. We see the tensions and the conflicts of the tenth, eleventh, and twelfth centuries almost entirely through the eyes of the Church whose job it was in those times to explain the order of the world, if not as it was, then at least as it ought to be. The scholars who attempted to do this, even if they had the viewpoint of their own milieu—that of clerics praying and living in the cloisters that surrounded the larger churches—also introduce into the systems they created some of the ideas of their contemporaries. Naturally their ideas, worked on by formidable social pressures, shifted. Corresponding to the changes in society were upheavals in ways of thinking. This was all the more the case because the Church was to feel very directly the repercussions of the crisis of feudalism. It was the Church's peasants too that the lords protected or held to ransom. It was the Church's chapters and bishops'

141

sees that were invaded by a new generation of younger sons of the nobility. What did these clerics, indistinguishable from their elders who remained on the paternal manors, have in common with the most worthy of their predecessors? "The archbishopric of Rheims would be a nice job, if one didn't have to say mass," the Archbishop Manasses used to joke. He had purchased his see and was chiefly concerned with gathering knights around him, neglecting the clergy. His election had so far turned his head "that he imitated the splendors, as well as the savagery, of foreign monarchies."[1] The archbishops of Rouen and Sens and the bishop of Laon too all behaved in a way that caused talk among the clergy. It even happened that laymen rose directly to an episcopal see, as in the case of Ebles of Roucy in Rheims, and it was only the authority of Fulbert that was able to reassure the conservative bishops.[2] What value had a benediction given by a bishop who carried a lance and kept a wife and concubines? In Septimania and in Provence the situation was very similar.[3] The crisis in society was parallelled by one in the Church. Although it is possible to distinguish between the religious and the social controveries, we cannot separate them.

For doubting contemporaries it was necessary for the best of the scholars and the most rigorous monks to offer one total vision of the harmony of the world. But which one? The theoretical controversy embraced and augmented the conflict between opposing currents.

The Harmony of the World

The theoretical reply to social agitation had been ready for a long time before the preambles of the charters set it out in the early years of the eleventh century: "He who resists this power resists the Order established by God": happy combination of divine providence and social conformism. Similarly, it is no accident that the theme that dominates all the descriptions of the tensions in society is that of the organic unity of all its parts. The image of the social body is not yet a mere metaphor. Society, the house of God, is also a very physical body, with its head, eyes, ears, nostrils, ribs, hands, feet and even its excrement.[4] This body is the body of Christ. To break its unity is to mutilate Christ; to contest the power is to be an acephalous monster, a thing with no head, a madman. As a monk reporting the revolt of the Le Mans insurgents said, with an extraordinary lack of awareness: they even burned the castles and that with no reason.[5]

But now it was no longer enough to quote St. Paul or to revive the old image of the body and its members. Two ideas emerged: first, the vision of a society divided into three orders, an old concept perhaps but now the object of interpretations or even distortions by the clerics. Then another idea developed, which in a mystic unity juxtaposed the peace and truce of God.

The Origins of the Tripartite Society

When the scholars of the tenth and eleventh centuries spoke more or less explicitly of the *ordines tres*—those who pray, *oratores*, those who fight, *pugnatores* or *bellatores*, and those who work or labor, *laboratores*—they were not, or not only, referring to rank, but rather—and the Latin of antiquity provided them with the example—to real social entities.[6] Where did they get this vision of human society? And more importantly, how did the tensions and conflicts to which these scholars were submitted and in which they were involved express themselves through their tendentious or polemic presentations of an original schema?[7]

Not surprisingly, when it appears in the writings of these scholars who were familiar with the episcopal libraries, this ternary scheme comes up against and is merged with the theoretical material that they had used for so long; reflections on hierarchy in St. Augustine, Gregory the Great, or the Pseudo-Dionysius the Areopagite on rank or social functions that were sometimes arranged according to other systems, binary, ternary, or quadripartite.[8]

A mental image that was probably much stronger in people's awareness than the writings of the Fathers of the Church was that of a holy and triple monarchy. Was it not the need to resort to this image, even if it meant making adjustments to it, which prompted the theoreticians of the crisis of feudalism to abandon or to adapt their old models?

This balance of three functions under a pacific and benevolent king can be found in a text from Lorraine, the life of a martyr king, one of the last Merovingians, St. Dagobert. Written a long time after his death, probably at the end of the tenth century, for the *fraternitas* of the monks of Stenay near Verdun at the time when the cult of the king saint, assassinated when out hunting, obscured the memory of the first dedication of this church to St. Remigius (St Remy):

> The priestly order sang hymns to God the All-Powerful at the prescribed times; militant, the priests dedicated themselves to their king with repeated service. The order of farmers cultivated the land with an unalloyed joy, blessing him who had brought peace to their parish and who satisfied their hunger with the abundance of wheat. The young men of the nobility, following ancient custom, besported themselves in due season, hunting with dogs and birds. They did not fail for all that to perform the actions prescribed by the Lord, giving alms to the poor, supporting those in difficulty, aiding widows and orphans, clothing the naked, taking in even beggars without a roof over their heads, visiting the sick and burying the dead. For those who behave like this, the practice of hunting does, it appears, no harm. . . . Let the temporal princes then venerate with fervor the most holy saint and martyr Dagobert, for the Supreme King has made him prince over his people. . . . Let the priesthood honor him in all things; for he was linked

with Him in heaven, Him to whom it is said: "You are a priest in Eternity according to the order of Melchisedech." And also the farmers should show their respect to him by performing the proper services, so that, through his intervention and his great merit, their lands will supply them with a sufficient harvest. Let not even the humble wine grower neglect to show his devotion with all his heart to the saint; he will have his help in his joyful work.[9]

Whatever date is given to the *Vita Dagoberti*, it is clear that the vision put forward here is placed at least in part outside historical time: a happy, playful countryside, peopled with melodious clerics, joyful hunters, and productive peasants. A Cockaigne with a Magician King. Is this not the most ancient expression of the *tres ordines*, an archaic representation of holy monarchy?

The same image, but stripped of its religious context and reduced to its simplest expression, is found as early as 891–901 in a vernacular gloss to the Anglo-Saxon translation of Boethius' *De Consolatione Philosophiae*, made for Alfred the Great: in order to exercise his power with virtue and efficacy the king must have "men to pray, men to fight and men to labor."[10] Despite the language used to convey it, such a concept was not, or not only, Saxon; counsellors from the continent were to be found in the entourage of the king who hoped to revive a Carolingian type of power that would bolster his position. Among these was a monk from Saint-Bertin, sent by Fulk, archbishop of Rheims. So it is interesting to find at the same period a second formulation of the *tres ordines* in this same monastery.

On 18 April 891 the sanctuary had been attacked by the Vikings. The people of the abbey, emerging from the protection of its walls, managed to drive off the looters, returning loaded with glory and booty. The latter was divided into three parts: the first for the Church, the second for the *oratores* and the *pauperes*, and the third divided equally—*aequa lance*—between the *nobiliores* and the *inferiores* who had fought respectively on horseback and on foot. The abbot and his monks had thus taken the lion's share, probably two-thirds, since the Church depended on them and the poor probably only received what was due to them through the intermediary of the *oratores* with whom they are associated in the text. Apparently this division provoked protests from those who, having dared to confront the terrible warriors from the north, imagined that they would receive a more generous reward for their daring and their military achievements. Hence the question that the author of the text, a monk at Saint-Bertin, attempts to answer: "To whom is this victory chiefly owed, the *oratores* or the *bellatores*?" He goes on to describe the walls in sight of which the battle took place, and behind their battlements, the *oratores* praying aloud, mothers with their babies, dishevelled, weeping, tearing their faces with their nails, the cries of the defenseless common people—*imbelle vulgus*; all with their arms stretched out to heaven, with open palms—the early Christian *orantes* position—begging God in his mercy to bring a successful end to the battle.

> If then, just for argument's sake, you would wish to debate which order is responsible for the victory in this affair, let us say, my very dear brothers, yes, let us say, and I would say moreover, let us bear witness and not beat about the bush, it is the *oratores* and the *imbelles* who in the anxiety of the fight . . . besought God to help those who doubted their own strength and steadied the hand of the *pugnantes*. . . . If then the victory is quite rightly attributed to the latter, the *oratores* equally deserve the crown, for untiringly and ceaselessly they serve Christ.[11]

The Saint-Bertin text shows us two things. First, that the warriors were not a homogenous group, since the monk distinguishes between *nobiliores* and *inferiores*. This is in other words the division that must have predominated in this region between the nobles and the *ministeriales-milites*: the *laboratores* are only mentioned in disparaging terms—*pauperes*, *vulgus*, *imbelles*, and are ranked after the *oratores*. The second thing we learn is that the *tres ordines* are not an essentially learned theory, but, because they were implicated in the context of an often bitter debate between the clerics and soldiers, they may well have developed from secular culture.

Rather of Verona, born in Liège and brought up in Lobbes in the first years of the tenth century, uses the theory of the three orders in a very similar way. Here too we are dealing with rather special circumstances. Having with great difficulty become bishop of Verona in 932, Rather tried to reform his church, which had been greatly impoverished by his predecessors, who were more concerned with worldly matters than with the honor of God. He was obsessed by the need to defend the church's patrimony against the grasping hands of powerful men backed by royal favor in the reign of a prince whose greed was notorious. So he used the *tres ordines* with great skill to support the idea of a radical separation of the three portions of land: that which belonged to the priest, that which was held of the king by the *milites regni*, and that of the inhabitants of the *pagus*, each portion being protected by its own particular and distinct sanction, which were, respectively, public sacrilege, lèse-majesty, and the sanction of law. Rather explains that these three portions cannot be combined, and particularly the first two, as the prince does, without going against the order of things. The *tres ordines* are introduced here to militate against the confusion, very frequent at this time, between the fisc and the property of the *episcopatus*.[12]

The superimposed character of the ternary system as presented by Rather is very obvious, since it is used in a work whose aim is that of enumerating the different human conditions by indicating what is suitable for each of them, according to sacred texts. Rather enumerates no less than nineteen social categories. Like the monk of Saint-Bertin, Rather uses a *topos* whose indisputable and well-known character allows him to consolidate the position of his church in the face of the greed of the warriors.

A third text of the same period reinforces this impression. This is the life of Gerald of Aurillac written by Odo of Cluny with the specific aim of edifying powerful men, giving them as an example "a leader of their order."

Odo found himself obliged to reconcile the usual canons of sanctity of the period with the elements of a life that was very worthy, no doubt, but in many ways very profane. The most difficult to deal with was the matter of the blood shed by Gerald when handing out justice or fighting. Odo settles the first problem by affirming that Gerald always managed to avoid condemning anyone to death. As for the soldiering, Odo justifies it by referring to the *ordines:* "and so it has been permitted to a layman, established in the order of fighters—*in ordine pugnatorum posito*—to carry a sword in order to protect the unarmed people . . . and also in order to force by right of war or by legal constraint those whom the Church's censure has been unable to bring to heel."[13]

Here we see stated, besides their duties, the subordination of the *pugnatores* to a Church that, far from confining itself to prayers, means to instruct them in whom to fight. The dedication to Bishop Turpin of Limoges, whom Odo greatly admired precisely because he fought against the wicked, brings us here to the ambiance that anticipates the first Peace of God, at the end of the tenth century.[14]

The last version of the ternary system that we find in the tenth century, that of Abbo of Fleury, is even more obviously distorted than the others. Abbo offers an audacious combination of the old dualist division suitable for men of the Church—clerics and laity—and the tripartite system. He regroups the fighters, *agonistae*, and the cultivators, *agricolae*, into a single order, the *ordo virorum, id est laïci*; conversely, he divides the *oratores* into two distinct orders, that of the clerics and that of the monks, the latter coming last in the list—last, but not least.

This text was written by the abbot in his defense—*Apologeticus*—doubtless following the council of Saint-Denis in 993–994, when the population had sided with the monks against the bishops and had chased the latter from the monastery. We know that the prelates had denounced the monks who collected tithes, saying that they were no better than laymen. Our text is obviously one of the elements in the response of the abbot of Fleury, leader at this time of what has been called the monks' faction.

At the same time as he was hardening his position against the bishops accused by him of allowing laymen to exact tithes, Abbo, perhaps reversing an argument used by his adversaries, also uses the *tres ordines*, but in his own way. By claiming for the monks an *ordo* distinct both from that of the clerics and that of the laity, he avoids the dilemma in which others had tried to trap him: either monks are *oratores*, in which case they are subservient to the bishop—and we know that Abbo's efforts were directed in precisely the opposite direction, toward exemption—or else monks are independent from the bishop, in which case they are laymen and their right to tithes has no basis in canon law—and this was the proposition that Abbo was fighting against at this period, when he chose from the ancient *codices*, kept in his abbey library, texts that he assembled into a veritable campaign collection. The abbot of Fleury thus uses the ternary system to mask and to justify the negation or the reversal of a whole Carolingian tradition. He was also, it would seem, the first to introduce a passage on the hardships of the peasants.[15]

All these texts are in fact closely linked. Alcuin was the abbot of Saint-Martin of Tours, where Odo of Cluny was later to study, and he was in correspondence with the clerics of Canterbury; Alfred the Great, Rheims, and Saint-Bertin were also in close touch. Adalbero of Laon and Gerard of Cambrai, whose attitudes we shall look at later, had studied in Rheims and when Gerard develops this ternary system, he evokes as a basis for his argument, "the decrees of the Holy Fathers." Is this a reference to the Fathers of the Church, or even to the commentaries and glosses absorbed into the text of the great Carolingian schoolmen? There exists a gloss by Haimo of Auxerre on the Apocalypse, which uses three orders, *senatores, milites, agricolae;* the manuscript containing this commentary was found in Laon.[16] So it is not surprising to find the three orders in the cultural area of the Carolingian schools, that is, in the diocese of Rheims, Lorraine, and the great abbeys of the Loire Valley. Furthermore, the formulation of this system with its three pillars and its house of God, is curiously reminiscent of the Carolingian "temple" denier of Louis the Pious.

It is clear at least that the aim of this ternary structure was not in the tenth century a real division of social functions. Many bishops were warriors, while there were still in certain areas of the kingdom peasants capable of fighting. On the other hand, too much should not be made of these possible exceptions. If certain bishops, by inclination or political necessity, were prompted to take up arms, in the eyes of the Church they were irritating exceptions. Even if the peasants were called up to the army, this was probably not sufficient in the eyes of the nobles to make them proper professional soldiers. The peasants were for them menial helpers, of use especially for military laboring jobs.[17] But this is not the main point. In the tenth-century texts, the theory of the *tres ordines* appears at least as much a theory of royal government and a symbolic representation of power as a realistic representation of the body social and its divisions. A mental portrait that "belongs to mythical and not historical time."[18]

Those who pray, those who fight, and those who work are the tools necessary to the king to carry out his task of creating balance and harmony. At the same time as using them, he overtakes and transcends them. King of the *oratores*, he takes part in sacred ceremonies and maintains an ambivalent relationship with this order, being, according to the Bible, king and priest following the order of Melchizedek. King of the *bellatores*, he is, as Adalbero reminds us, the most noble of the nobles, he from whom all nobility proceeds. King of the *laboratores*, the *Libri Carolini* call him: "The great farmer, the good sower and wise cultivator of the harvest." As Jacques le Goff says, the ideological aim of the tripartite system is to express harmony, interdependence, and solidarity between classes and orders. If the balance between the three groups is not respected, the state collapses. The king is the guarantor of this equilibrium and the figure who literally incarnates it without any distinction between temporal and spiritual realms.[19]

To what extent is this structure a branch of very ancient mythical divisions? We have seen that it is often invoked in discussions with laymen, and we can imagine the popular origins of this triple image of a king full of wisdom, surrounded by bishops, of a king who is a fiery knight, riding at the head of the warlike "youth," and of a benevolent king greeted and called on as he passes the peasants assembled on the edges of their fields.

This triple royal *imago* can be found in the legends surrounding St. Denis from the seventh century onward.[20] Denis, the ideal bishop, is accompanied by two companions, Eleutherius, whose name means free, the context showing us that he freed young men, and Rusticus, the meaning of whose name is obvious. Claude Carozzi has put forward one theory: since the fifth century, the Church had insisted above all on the separation of the laity and the ecclesiastics, and with good reason: it was important to establish the independence of two structures that had an unfortunate tendency to become confused, and to affirm the preeminence of the priesthood. The tripartite system, which gives the chief place to the king, is something quite different. This would represent the point of view of the laity and would be something that could quite well adapt to the old popular traditions of the Frankish monarchy. It is this popular origin that could explain the reluctance of the scholars to use it, and it would have taken the troubled times at the end of the ninth century and then again those in the early years of the eleventh century to induce the clerics to "lift a part of the veil which covered the traditional ideas stemming from pagan times."[21] It should be said however that the tripartite division found in German myth resembles very little the three functions of the *ordines*. The example of Denis and his companions shows perhaps that we must look elsewhere for the popular origins of the *tres ordines*.

The system of *ordines* was, we know, considered by the scholars to be very ancient, if not eternal. Gerard of Cambrai said, "It has existed since the origins of mankind." In fact, at the very moment when we first find the system in the texts, it is no longer fulfilling its original function; already the clerics who use it are bending it to fit in with their own needs. Thus as early as the tenth century we see the beginning of the process that was to alter the immobile perfection of the three orders. But Abbo of Fleury, for example, even if he did some violence to the old system, still respected it enough to refer to it, showing what influence it still had over men's minds. Evidence of quite another sort comes to us in the speech made by Gerard of Cambrai at the assemby of Douai, and in Adalbero of Laon's poem to King Robert.[22] Both men are representatives of the old Carolingian Church, isolated and perturbed in the face of the upheavals of the times with peasants who preached, and monks who emerged from the cloister to work for peace—unheard-of transgressions of the principle of the three orders that struck directly at their power as bishops and their pride as nobles. Would "illiterates" spread the word of God in their place? Would monks dictate to the old families of *bellatores* where and when they could fight? Their affirmation of the *tres ordines* is no skillful utilization of an undisputed social structure, but rather an appeal to what was already no more, an outdated response to the new exigencies of the great popular movements.

Corresponding to the social and political identities of the two prelates is an extraordinary similarity of language. They are of course both referring to the provisions of the council of peace of Verdun-sur-le-Doubs of 1021–22 and to its continuation, the assembly of Compiègne of 1023. Georges Duby has shown that Gerard's address to the Douai assembly closely followed that of Compiègne and dated from 1024–25. Adalbero's pamphlet is of the same period or perhaps a little later. His recent editor, Claude Carozzi, has found some striking similarities of vocabulary between these two texts and a third one, the address make by Gerard against heretics at the synod of Arras in 1025. Either one author is borrowing from the other, or else, since they both studied at Rheims, they are both drawing on a common text.[23]

And what do the two bishops say to the innovators whom they are attacking? Gerard explains:

Mankind, since the beginning of time, has been divided in three, those who pray, those who cultivate, those who fight, and each of the three is comforted on either side by the two others. He who, forsaking the world, gives himself to a life of prayer owes it to the warriors that he is able to carry out his holy task in safety, while he owes his bodily nourishment to the farmers. Similarly, the farmers ascend to God through the prayers of the ecclesiastics and are defended by the weapons of the warriors. So also, the warriors are fed by the produce of the fields and benefit from the income therefrom, while the holy prayers of the pious whom they protect will expiate the crimes which they commit in battle; their office does not mean they do wrong if sin is not in their conscience.

Adalbero's version bears even more strongly the mark of its author. After praising the king and painting with an ironic brush the harsh picture of a world "turned to chaos" by the innovators,[24] the bishop sets out his idea of what society should be. He begins with a reference to the celestial Jerusalem and continues logically by praising the priests, "children of the Great Architect." Their task is to give the sacraments and to preach; the whole of mankind has been placed under their commandments by God, even the great lords: "the holy law which separates them from all earthly stain" puts them on a par with a king's sons. This is the first great division of society, separating the clerics, especially the bishops, their priests and their monks, from the laity, even the most noble. After this "holy law" comes "human law," which distinguishes two conditions, the nobles and the serfs. At the head of the former are two men, the king and the emperor—and here Adalbero, who was from Lorraine, betrays his proimperial opinions. Under their command the state, the *respublica*, is secure. After them come those "that no power constrains, as long as they avoid those crimes which the king's sceptre suppresses; these are the warriors—*bellatores*—protectors of the churches; they defend the people, great and small." Then come the serfs, "this oppressed race owns nothing without difficulty." "Who could calculate on the abacus the labours of the serfs, their tasks and their innumerable jobs? To provide all men with wealth and clothing, that is the lot of the serf. No free man can live without the serfs. . . . The lord is nourished by the serf whom he flatters himself he feeds. There is no limit to the tears and the suffering of the serfs."[25] He concludes: "The House of God is thus triple at the same time as we should believe it to be One. Some pray, some fight and others work; these three functions go together and cannot be unjoined: the service rendered by one is the condition of the works of the two others, each in turn assisting the whole."

The characteristics that we have observed elsewhere are here at their most developed. Despite the attempt at realism, this is an abstract system: *bellatores* does not mean all those who fight, but those whom a little further on Adalbero calls the order of the powerful, *ordo potentum*, who accompany the king when he dispenses justice. These people are noble and free; opposite them are only serfs. However, Adalbero is perfectly able to list, as Rather had before him, the sailors, butchers, innkeepers, shepherds, goatherds, swineherds, cooks, launderers, doctors, or knights—*milites*. But all these categories are submerged in an argument in which the serfs are merely a substitute for the old category of *laboratores;* where the *milites* and the monks are only the creatures, one is tempted to say the extensions, of, respectively, the great lords, the only true *bellatores*, and the bishops, the only authentic *oratores*. What is more, the original system that placed in the foreground the idea of harmony through the monarchy is here quite unbalanced in favor of the *oratores*, the whole of mankind being placed under their command. We are a long way from the theory that the orders were instruments of the king, as put forward by King Alfred's counsellors. It is useless to assert that the functions are indivisible—the keystone has disappeared.

In fact, both in Gerard and in Adalbero, the reference to the three orders is probably by now no more than a last-ditch defense. The aged

Ascelin[26] was quite aware of this and mocks himself saying: "When the Loire flows over the countryside of Calabria . . . then you can worry about the approach of your wishes." Under the neat arrangement of the *ordines* we begin to perceive the disarray of its partisans before the new exigencies that it is unable to control. And first and foremost was the phenomenon of the extraordinary Peace of God movement.

Peace and Truce

The movement for the Peace of God had begun at the end of the tenth century in the Midi. The Carolingian monarchy, considered there to be the only legitimate one, had disappeared. The disputes between territorial princes by increasing the general insecurity encouraged a more radical dissociation of public structures. Some southern bishops and princes met together to restore the peace. The first council of peace was held in Charroux in 989, the second in Narbonne in 990. From these two political centers, the movement spread in 994 to the Limousin area, to Auvergne and the kingdom of Burgundy with the councils of Limoges, Le Puy, and Anse. And in the first decade of the eleventh century peace assemblies were still being held at Lalbenque in the diocese of Cahors, Saint-Gilles, and Poitiers.[27] The first edicts of the councils in the tradition of the right of sanctuary forbade the forcing of entry into the precinct—*infringere*—or the plundering of a church. It was reaffirmed that it was sacrilege to strike an unarmed cleric and it was prohibited to carry off the livestock of the farmers or other poor people. The text of the council of Le Puy gives examples of the kind of circumstances in which this "taking of meat" could occur: it might be to feed oneself when journeying or "in order to take some to one's house" or at the time of the building or besieging of a castle. But it makes it clear that the prohibition did not apply to all lords on their own land. Furthermore, it adds three very revealing measures. First, it was forbidden to arrest villeins in order to force them to buy themselves out, except, once again, on one's own land or on a disputed property. It is not hard to recognize here the lord's justice seen from the very practical viewpoint of the *districtus*. Second, it was forbidden to extend the "customs" to the lands of the Church, except when they had been conceded in *precaria* by the bishops or the monks. Last, merchants and their goods were protected. All these measures were presented in the form of a monitory letter sanctioned by anathema. Oaths seem to have been taken, although their terms and range are not fully known.

The idea of peace was not new, and the very traditional vocabulary used shows this. What is new is that the bishops have substituted themselves for the king in the mission to defend the churches and the "poor" free men. This is manifest proof that the public tribunals were no longer working satisfactorily. Truly ecclesiastical sanctions were coming to the assistance of crumbling laws. This whole movement seems suddenly, but temporarily, to have been stopped short.

While in Auvergne and Provence fires were raging, no peace council met. Some great lords, such as Amblard of Nonette, had the houses of the peasants burned down by their knights so frequently that the villagers began to put out their household fires at night to prevent the pillagers from using the burning wood to start new fires.[28] By contrast, in Poitou peace was restored by the duke of Aquitaine, who used it to his own advantage. In 1011–14, he called and presided over a council in Poitiers to "restore peace and justice." All litigation in the *pagi* of the *principes*, here meaning the lords, would be submitted to their jurisdiction or to that of a judge of the *pagus*; with or without the agreement of the parties involved, they would give judgment. If they refused, they would lose the hostages that they had given to the duke at the end of the council; if they were unable to come they would call other important men present at the council, lords or bishops, to pass sentence on the guilty. The Peace of God disappears here in favor of a system that we have already encountered.[29]

The Peace of God movement does not reappear until 1021–22. This time the movement begins in Burgundy.[30] The council of Verdun-sur-le-Doubs included, together with the archbishops of Lyons, Besançon, and their suffragans, two bishops of "France," Béraud of Soissons and Oury, who was soon to replace Thierry, friend of the heretics, as bishop of Orleans.[31] One or two years later in May 1023 the assembly of Compiègne took place; there, in the presence of King Robert, Béraud of Soissons and Guérin of Beauvais swear to and have sworn "the judgement of the bishops of Burgundy." Fulbert of Chartres was absent from this assembly, but we know from one of his letters that he considered it forbidden to travel armed during the Easter period. One of his poems celebrates the joy of the peace in these terms: "Adore Our Father in your simple way, all you poor people . . . from now on the great men who had forgotten the rules of the Laws will learn to recognise and uphold what is right." At Compiègne there were present the ambassadors of the emperor, Gerard of Cambrai and Richard, abbot of Saint-Vanne.[32] A few months later King Robert met Henry II at Ivois. The same year several peace assemblies were held in Provence, these clearly influenced by Cluny.[33] In 1024 the king himself held an assembly in Burgundy, at Héry in the diocese of Auxerre, where the bishop was his kinsman Hugh, count of Chalon-sur-Saône.[34] A similarity of policy between several prelates of Burgundy, some bishops of Francia, and the monarchy thus materialized. This agreement is also well illustrated by the similarity in the formulae of the two oaths taken at that time in Burgundy and in the Ile-de-France.[35]

What did these formulae establish? The immunity of the churches is here explicitly extended to their dependencies—*atria* in Burgundy, *cellaria* in Beauvais and Soissons, or, more generally, to their exempted areas, but with the exception of evildoers who might wish to take refuge there. The protection of unarmed clerics now covers also those who accompany them, but here too there is an exception: they or their property could be seized if wrongdoing had previously been proved in law. The confiscation in this case would be limited to the reparation of the injury and to a fine where that applied. Then it was forbidden to take beasts of burden, then to seize villeins, which included merchants. Here the texts become more precise: along with buying back they mention a *tollere denarios* in which it is easy to recognize the southern tallage, the *tolte*. The formulae specify also that one should not beat the peasants in order to take their goods: from this we see how the tallage came into being. From this point onward the formulae introduce innovations: the protection of horses at pasture, of houses that might not be burned down nor destroyed except if an enemy knight or a thief had taken refuge there or if these houses adjoined a castle, of vines and lastly of mills from which corn could not be taken except on one's own land or if one was in the army or riding abroad. Finally it was forbidden to give assistance or protection to known public thieves or to those who broke the peace. It appears that here there was, after the mention of the status of the guarantors of the oath, the end of a first text. At this point a series of exceptions rather clumsily linked to the sentence that precedes them are introduced into the formulae: "As it is written in this brief I will keep it as long as I live with regard to those who have sworn it and who will keep it to me." The phrase is interrupted in the middle in the Burgundian formula with a huge lacuna and in the Guérin formula by a long interpolation, which returns to the idea of the protection of merchants, villeins, and their livestock by adding pilgrims, noble women traveling without their husbands, widows, nuns, and finally hunters. The two texts then join again to stipulate a block of exceptions that place outside the peace the lands of each lord insofar as they concern him, and those of all when they participate in the building or the siege of a castle in the army of the king or of the bishops—the Burgundian texts add the army of the counts to this. But here too the texts apply a hairsplitting precision: one could take things for the army, but take nothing home, except the shoes that had been put on the horses; nor could one use the pretext of the army to infringe on the exempted areas of the churches. But immediately an exception is added to the exception: the churches could not refuse to offer normal supplies to the army, nor safe-conduct, or even the sale of the necessary foodstuffs. After all these detailed specifications and counterspecifications, the two texts finish with what is probably a true innovation in 1021: "From the beginning of Lent to the end of Easter, I will not attack any unarmed knight, nor will I take from him by force what he bears with him. I will abide by all that which has been said above until the next feast of St. John the Baptist and from then for seven years. May God and his saints help me."

The formulae of 1021–22 and 1023 reveal two things. First, the renewal of the prohibitions of the councils of 994 to the degree that the same phrases are sometimes used, but from this point on these prohibitions are made very specific by the introduction of multiple exceptions that puff up the text and leave an unfortunate impression of bargaining and bad faith. Second, the Burgundian bishops, not satisfied with this legal quibbling, innovate and transform the formulae. The formula from which they take their inspiration was probably a permanent oath; they change it to a provisional oath of seven years,[36] and this limitation confirms our first impression of hard-fought negotiations. All those who are knights—*caballarii*—in the diocese and who carry arms had to take this oath. Those who refused or who broke the oath would be excommunicated.

Oddly, the bishops of Beauvais and Soissons acted differently. Less sensitive to the canonical dislike of bishops' oaths, or perhaps under pressure from their knightly kinsmen, they were the first to take the oath. And the oath of peace is made to the king. Thus we have a perfect explanation for the difference in titles of our two texts, the first being a *convenientia pacis*, the second simply entitled *sacramentum pacis*.

Thus we see clearly the meaning of the Burgundian peace. It was intended not so much to protect the peasantry as a whole as to curb the violence and aggressiveness of the *caballarii*, formerly necessary to the setting up of banal lordship but now a threat. Or putting it another way, to contain the exactions of the lord's henchmen within supportable limits by holding up the threat of the only thing that they still seemed to fear—eternal damnation. But the bishops were only the guarantors of a reciprocal and collective promise between all those who bore arms and used them as they pleased. The twists and turns of the formula and its limited duration show clearly that the weight of excommunication was hardly sufficient to persuade the knights to give up excesses that had by now become habitual. The Burgundian bishops appear here as ambiguous mediators between a peasantry overwhelmed with violence, of which the text itself gives us a terrifying idea, and a grasping knighthood that in many respects was also their support.[37]

But this policy, as we shall see, was far from creating unanimity in the Church. Already the attempt to extend the system carried out through the efforts of Guérin of Beauvais and Béraud of Soissons had turned out to be ill-conceived, because half-hearted. What is the meaning of an oath given by a bishop not to attack a church? What is the meaning of an oath taken to the king for seven years? The peace of 1021, removed from its original context, became difficult to adapt to new circumstances. The biographer of Gerard of Cambrai sees in it "the weakness of the king" and, at the assembly of Douai, Gerard himself rejects "the false peace of the bishops of Francia" in the name of the theory of the three orders. He follows closely the interpretation of Fulbert of Chartres when he imposes on his vassal, the castellan of the city, the following form of oath: "I will keep the fealty promised to you for as long as I shall be yours and hold possessions from you, and I will show you the honour which the *milites* of Lorraine show to their lords and bishops, without taking into account the usages and customs of the *Karlenses*," that is, the knights of Beauvais and Soissons who had sworn the peace.[38] Adalbero of Laon also protested the new royal policy and openly pointed at Odilo as its instigator. Similarly, Dudo, provost of Saint-Quentin in the Vermandois, when commanded to write a work praising the first dukes of Normandy, was careful to insist on the public and ducal character of the peace.[39]

The supporters of the peace were meanwhile scoring some successes. The pope confirmed the peace at Saint-Vaast in Arras as early as 1024. It probably dated from the previous year, having been brought there from Compiègne by the abbot, Leduin, despite the hostility of his bishop, Gerard of Cambrai. In 1030 the peace reached the diocese of Amiens and into Flanders under the impulse of the count.[40] An attempt seems to have been made to introduce it in Normandy in 1041– 42. Encouraged by some seven assemblies of peace, Richard of Saint-Vanne tried to go even further and introduce the truce, but without success. Could it not have been he too who brought the formula of Beauvais to Metz?[41] We see here the important role played by Richard and by his disciples, Leduin of Saint-Vaast and Rouy of Saint-Bertin. If we try to summarize the situation, we can say that the movement of the second peace in the 1020s started from the Burgundy region, and extended naturally into Provence and the areas of the first peace in eastern Aquitaine. But also and most importantly, it gained ground in the north of the kingdom, in Chartres, Beauvais, Soissons, and Arras, and then in Amiens and Flanders, despite the hostility or indifference met with at Laon, Cambrai, Noyon, Saint-Quentin, and probably also in Normandy, Champagne, and the principality of Poitou. We will find these regional differences again after 1041, when the Truce of God starts to develop.

Truce, *treuwa, treuga*, was an old vernacular word of Germanic origin, but as widespread in the south as in the north. The truce was originally an oath—the Latin equivalent would have been *fidelitas*— which halted for a period the feuding, *faida*, between relations. Then, at least from the Carolingian period, the habit had grown up of considering Sunday as a day of obligatory truce, in an extension of the traditional Sunday prohibitions. Still in 1024 in Cambrai and in 1027 at Toulouges in Roussillon, there are reminders that Sunday should be a day of general truce.[42] However, another element emerges at this time in the Burgundian peace: a special protection for the period from Lent to Easter, though without the word truce being mentioned. Already the interdictions of the peace were concerned with not only space but also time. They now tried not only to place some isolated islands outside the general violence, but by inviting the warriors to put down their weapons for a time, they suggested to them an attitude more in keeping with the sanctity of the great liturgical feastdays from which this society drew its cohesion.

Around 1040 these two ideas—that of the Sunday truce, extended to part of the week, and that of the times of peace, which had also multiplied—were to become one. From this point on it was during the three great annual liturgical periods of Christmas, Easter, and Pentecost that great and small knights had to put up their weapons, unless authorized otherwise by the bishops. The Cluniacs put at the disposal of this Truce of God the powerful network of their churches and friends. In the south, Leger of Vienne and Raimbaud of Arles proclaimed the truce in the kingdoms of Burgundy and Provence. In 1041–43 they tried to extend the movement to Lombardy; in 1042–44 at the council of Saint-Gilles they attracted their first Septimanian supporters. In 1043 the archbishop of Narbonne agreed to hold a truce council in his town. The same movement was set up in Catalonia. In the North, Richard of Saint-Vanne, Leduin of Saint-Vaast, and Rouy of Saint-Bertin also militated for the truce, despite obstacles and rebuffs in Normandy and the Cambrai area.[43]

As well as the chronicles and histories that sometimes give us information about the measures of the truce, we also have the formulae that are copies, with a few variations, of two very different models. The first, (A), is southern; we find examples in Vich, Barcelona, Elne, Gerona, and Narbonne. It begins by repeating the measures of the peace of the 1020s, particularly the immunity of thirty steps around the churches, the protection of the *inermes*, clerics or peasants, and the prohibition on the taking away of livestock. To this it adds the truce's own prohibitions: the four days of the week and the longer or shorter festive periods when there was to be no fighting, as well as on a variety of saints' days,[44] The second model for the truce formulae, (B), is by contrast clearly "French," and it is to be found in Avranches, Mont-Saint-Michel, Jumièges, and Fécamp as well as Laon, Thérouanne, and Marchiennes in the diocese of Cambrai.[45] While the southern model takes the form of an oath, the model in Francia takes that of a monitory letter from the bishops to their diocesans. Above all, the text does not refer back at all to the old peace, the word being used here simply as an equivalent of the *Treuga Dei*, and constructed entirely around the idea of truce: "Beloved brothers in the Lord, Greetings in this Peace of God which is popularly called truce." It reads as if the truce, far from being grafted onto the peace and forming a kind of extension to it, had a development of its own in these areas.

Despite some useful attempts to establish it, the general chronology of the movement is still not fully known, making interpretation rather difficult at times. The influence of the Cluniacs, through their followers and supporters in southern Burgundy and Provence, is indisputable from 1041 on, and the encyclical letter from three Provençal bishops and Odilo, which describes the truce in terms that differ little from the southern formula (A), definitely dates from this period. Besides the precedents mentioned above, earlier origins have been put forward: the formula A, or at least the most important part of its measures, is supposed to have been used as early as 1033 by the bishop of Vich, Oliba, the architect of the first council of Toulouges in 1027. The B formula, on the other hand, has been attributed to the activities of Gerard of Cambrai and of Adalbero of Laon and was their answer to the formula of the Burgundian peace of 1021–23.[46]

To a debate that is still unsolved we can add a few contributions. First, for the Catalonian peace: the letter from Oliba to the monks of Ripoll, which relates the decisions taken by him in his diocese of Vich, has as its only fixed point for dating the death of this prelate in 1046. If Oliba's role is accepted, then the date of 1033 is rather suspect, and it would be quite reasonable to imagine that he had acted in concert with Odilo around 1040.[47] The certain dates of the A model in its most extended version and therefore, admittedly, its most recent version, are 1064, 1065, and 1068. For the truce of Laon and Cambrai, it seems that the evidence of the biographer of the Bishop Gerard runs contrary to what we might expect: reporting the murder of a "youth" of the bishop's household, he specifies that the man was "protected by the truce," and that it was Sunday. This, according to the monitory letters of the B type, would be a kind of tautology. It seems therefore that these truces from Cambrai are the old oaths of security between given people and for a limited time and not the Truce of God.

So at what period can we place the B formulae?[48] The chief piece of dated evidence seems to be a letter from Alexander II to the bishop of Soissons, Alard, of 1063–64, of which unfortunately there remains only a torn fragment: "Because you have extended to thirty years the penance for homicide committed during the Truce of God, we do not give our *auctoritas* to your constitution, for we do not find anything of this in the canons. However, in so far as the Truce of God has been set up by wise and religious men in order to maintain the peace among the people, we do not condemn it entirely."[49] A prudent reply, and very much in the manner of the pontifical chancellery! It informs us that in the 1060s the fixing of the punishment for homicide at thirty years in time of truce was considered to be a debatable innovation. In fact the letter from the Provençal bishops in 1041 specified only that the exile, which is to say the pilgrimage, should be far, without saying anything about duration. This conforms, as Alexander remarks, to canonical tradition. Custom, at least from the ninth century, fixed the penitence of a homicide at seven years.[50] "The exile of thirty years" is, then, characteristic of the B formula, which must be the constitution referred to by the pope in his answer to the bishop of Soissons. Other indications seem to support this dating: the formula of Thérouanne was formerly dated at 1062–63; that of Normandy was probably from a little later in 1064.[51] The southern model, (A), may date from 1033 or 1041 in its least expanded version, when the periods of truce at Easter and Pentecost were not yet merged, and from the 1060s in the version where this extension is found. The "French" (B) model must date from the 1060s, as seems to be confirmed in the *Miracles of St Ursmar* in Flanders.[52]

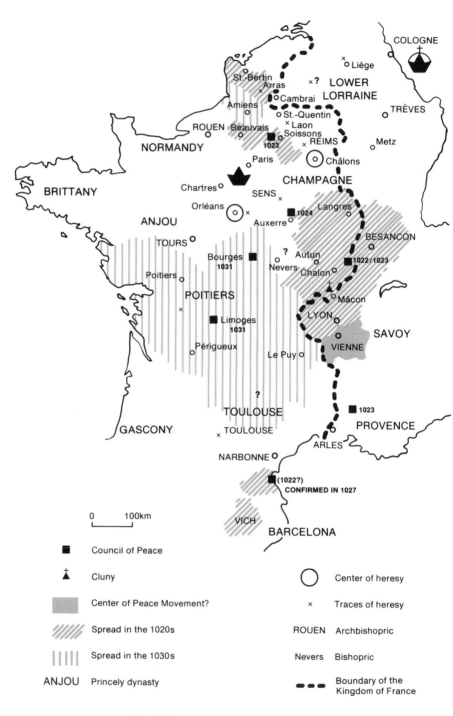

COLOGNE

× ○ Liège

LOWER LORRAINE

×? ○ St.-Bertin
Arras ○
× ○ Cambrai TRÈVES
Amiens ○ ○ St.-Quentin
ROUEN Beauvais × Laon
○ Soissons
○ 1023 × REIMS ○ Metz
NORMANDY ○ Paris
○ Châlons

Chartres ○ CHAMPAGNE

BRITTANY

Orléans ○ × SENS ×
ANJOU Auxerre ○ Langres BESANÇON
■ 1024 ○
TOURS ○ ? Autun ■ 1022/1023
Bourges ■ ○ Nevers Chalon ○ Mâcon
Poitiers ○ 1031 ┼
POITIERS LYON SAVOY
× ○
■ Limoges VIENNE ○
1031
Périgueux Le Puy ○
○
■ 1023
?
TOULOUSE PROVENCE
× TOULOUSE
ARLES ○
NARBONNE ○
■ (1022?)
CONFIRMED IN 1027
VICH
BARCELONA

■ Council of Peace	
┼ Cluny	
(shaded) Center of Peace Movement?	○ Center of heresy
///// Spread in the 1020s	× Traces of heresy
|||| Spread in the 1030s	ROUEN Archbishopric
ANJOU Princely dynasty	Nevers Bishopric
	●●● Boundary of the Kingdom of France

Map 3. Peace of God and Heresy, 1020-1030.

🕆	Cluny
+	Documented truce
■	Truce formula A
□	Truce formula B
?	Possible truce (presence at a council)

ANJOU	Princely dynasty
△	"Comitatus" to the bishop
●━━●	Boundary of the Kingdom of France

0   100km

Map 4. The Truce of God before 1095

From the available documentation, it seems that the truce originated in the south, following on from the movement of peace of the 1020s and still under the influence of Cluny. It was only around 1062 that it spread in its full form into the more northerly regions of the kingdom, to Normandy and Flanders, but also to Soissons, Laon, and Amiens and perhaps even to Rheims and into all the dioceses that came under its jurisdiction. After 1066 the truce reached England and then, in 1081, the diocese of Liège, where it in fact overlaid a much older system, that of the "general synods" of the bishop.[53] Ivo of Chartres commented at the time on the spread of oaths of truce and the variations in the formulae from diocese to diocese. He said that they should be carefully checked in each case in order to determine exactly what promises had been made by the oathtakers.[54]

In the province of Rheims and in Flanders the truce was probably taking the place of usages that were very different from those in the south. The Burgundian formula of 1023 insisted on the protection of the *inermes*, and this was also, it appears, the aim of the Catalan councils. Certain Flemish texts, on the other hand, see in the truce not so much the end of the warring between lords as the eradication of *faidae*, the vendettas that decimated the knightly families.[55]

When the count of Flanders decided to gather together his lords to seal between them a peace alliance so strong "that no mere mortal could set it up for all the gold in the world," he had saints' relics brought to him. The monks of Lobbes in Brabant set out, bearing the reliquary of St. Ursmar on their shoulders. At almost every stage they had to "persuade their enemies to make peace for the love of the saint." At Blarenghem, two knights had quarrled one day and despite the kiss of peace that Hugh, their lord, had forced them to exchange, one of them had treacherously run the other through with his lance and taken refuge in the church. Pledges were taken, a time fixed to decide on the affair, in front of the church. At dawn on the day appointed two armed groups assembled: "The whole forecourt glowed red with shields, the steel of the weapons glittered in the morning sun; the confusion was further increased by the neighing of the horses. Hugh's men were waiting around the church, their swords drawn, thirsty for blood. . . ." The monks of Lobbes intervened, going in procession with the holy relics. Amazed, the knights humbly lowered their eyes and soon all were weeping. Piety had triumphed over anger.

More than five hundred knights had gathered at Liswege when the monks exhibited the relics. "Suddenly, one of them, who had slipped like a thief into the crowd . . . threw himself at the feet of another, face down, his arms spread out like a cross . . . and, calling a hundred times for mercy, asked for his forgiveness. He had in fact killed two knights, brothers of the other man." The offended party, "the famous Robert, young and powerful, who commanded an army of nearly two hundred knights, astonished by this confession, his sadness revived, collapsed back onto the knights surrounding him." All were speechless, some weeping. The suppliant knight was raised to his feet, he threw himself to the ground again. The affair seemed to the monks to be hopeless, but they pleaded with the young lord on behalf of the guilty man. The lord resisted their prayers. But the other remained there, still "crying for mercy, by God and by the saint; then Robert was silent and he too began to weep. He changed colour, now pale, now red, still refusing, in a frenzy, gnashing his teeth." Suddenly, the monks placed the reliquary at his feet. "He staggered—alas!—his face wet with tears, he fell and grovelled in the dust with woe." A deep silence fell, which lasted for three hours, while the knights, standing around the two men on the ground, wept silently, "their moustaches and beards wet with tears."

Woe betide those who resisted the saint. At Nieuwekerke, revenge stirred up the knights against one another. Many refused to bow to the exhortations of the monks. "Then, said the leader Baldwin, let us form a circle around the saint . . . and let those who are not in agreement follow their leader, the devil, and leave our company." As the opponents of the peace left the circle, a black dog passed. Three months later they were involved in a battle—in which they all died.[56]

In this game of appeasement, the reliquary is the most important piece: it is brought, it is moved, it is advanced toward this or that person; the collective fervor is relaxed or increased; at a given moment, the tension snaps and torrents of tears manifest the effusion of refound unity.[57] The saint calms the knights' anger as he cures those possessed by the devil. Here, the saint comes to the very heart of the violence, among the armed warriors. This is the common basis of all the movements of peace, in the north as in the Midi, and more than the practice of oath-taking constitutes their originality: at these impressive gatherings, where, under the triple impulse of the princes, the bishops (natural leaders of the diocese), and the monks (guardians of the sacred relics), the emotional atmosphere conducive to the knights' abandon is created. However, the similarities in the ceremony do not necessarily imply the same result: depending on the region, the accent may be placed on the suppression of violence outside, or sometimes within, the knighthood, on the development of the Cluniac and monastic influence, or on the reinforcement of the penitential justice of the bishops.

Between the system of the imperial or royal churches and the banal lordship, the Cluniacs opened up a middle way. During the crucial decades of the early eleventh century, the bishops of southern France, abandoned by the monarchy in an area where territorial integration was more than usually important, began to rely on monastic sanctity, finding in it the justification for the power that they exercised *de facto* or *de jure*. Then they had at all costs to oppose the unleashing of violence and to respond in this way to the immense need for peace of the peasant masses. By paralyzing the uncontrolled fighting of the knights for two-thirds of the year, the truce brought stability once again to a society briefly rocked by its own dynamism. The truce was also an attempt to put an end to the feudal crisis itself in the first decades of the eleventh century and to justify to some extent the banal lordship as an essential structure of social life. In doing this it restored a social tripartition that seemed to take account, in a way that was both more total and solid, of all human activities. The clergy, encouraged to model itself on the monks, became more clearly separated from the laity. The free peasants, merged in villeinage with the dependants, are categoried as *inermes*. The aristocracy, enlarged by the knights, can now claim the bearing of arms as an exclusive privilege. The reformers, by integrating into the prescriptions of peace and truce, especially from the 1040s, key words naming the new social categories—*cabellarius* and *vilanus*—made them appear more clearly as "the signifiers of a social state." "Knight" came to mean from that time less a situation of dependence than an office, "the duty common to all men of arms to make up for the deficiencies of royalty, to work together, showing solidarity, observing the same prohibitions, for the creating of a new order."[58] "Villein," which also now grouped together hitherto quite distinct categories, merged them together in a common social inferiority. Thus was made manifest in a more firmly legal language the appearance on the scene of a new middle layer in society, that of the wealthy peasants. In the symbolic image established by the Peace of God, the frontier separating *laboratores* and *bellatores* had deep repercussions on the class of the allodialists, offering some of them the honor of the lordly houses and casting off the others into servile dependence. This was the price of peace, at least temporal peace.

In reality, things did not always go this way. Those clerics emerging from the monasteries who ascended to the bishop's throne thanks to the peace movement rapidly found themselves implicated in tasks that had only a distant connection with prayer. In trying to contain the aggression of the knights, the clergy attempted to bring their activities under the ecclesiastical control of the clergy. In order to do this, was there not a moment when certain bishops were tempted to arm those very men who should have stayed unarmed?[59] The old tripartite system founded on royal preeminence was thus in fact completely subverted. From this we can understand why there was hostility to such a pernicious version of the *tres ordines* in the regions where the old Carolingian methods of imposing order were still asserted. But those who believed in these methods were to learn how far the mental images that had upheld this order had been shaken by the feudal crisis. The increasing influence of the popular, evangelical, or heretical movements were a demonstration of this, and they reminded the traditionalist bishops and even the first reformers, carried away in their turn by the movement, that they had too far forgotten the kingdom of God to be able to become the strongest of the pillars of the terrestrial kingdoms.

Controversies in the Church

The apparent success of the movement of peace and truce after more than half a century of effort should not hide the profound divergences that had come to the surface in the Church, and which explain the hostile reactions from the 1020s to the Cluniac initiatives. Nor should we be deceived: the victory of the supporters of the truce was only a partial victory. Even while more and more bishops seemed to be rallying to their side, other critics were emerging, and a new current of reform appeared in the Church that was to push the most determined of its members onto the dangerous paths of the apostolic life.

The Bishops and the Monks

The conflict between those who could be called the "faction of the bishops" and the "faction of the monks" begins at the end of the tenth century with the question of exemption. From 1023 the Cluniac movement exacerbated the problem. It started to be resolved at the end of the eleventh century when the Gregorian reforms brought to the fore the problems posed by lay investiture.

The opposition between the two bodies became apparent for the first time, it seems, at the council of Saint-Basle de Verzy in 991. At this council Arnulf, archbishop of Rheims, was to be tried for treason. Two very different points of view were put forward. The episcopal faction, inspired by Gerbert and presented by the bishop of Orleans, another Arnulf, maintained that the episcopate of the Gauls, meeting in council, had the power to depose the archbishop. This position could be supported by Carolingian tradition, as earlier illustrated by Hincmar of Rheims and revived later by the Ottonian dynasty to whom Gerbert was entirely devoted. The opposing view, on which the defense of the accused archbishop was pinned, that only Rome was able to decide such matters, was put forward by Abbo, abbot of Fleury, a monastery in the diocese of Orleans, a fact that did little to improve relations between the two factions. In setting himself up as the champion of Roman primacy, Abbo of Fleury now appeared to be the leader of the "monks' " faction.

The quarrel was pursued, more fiercely, at the council of Saint-Denis in 993–994. The bishops, including Gerbert of Rheims, who had tried to celebrate a liturgical *statio* in this monastery, were chased out of it in a veritable riot. Both before and after this council, Abbo had gathered together texts supporting exemption that he obtained for his monastery in 997.

Exemption already had a long history when it reappeared at the end of the eleventh century. Its origins seem to be triple: the policy of Gregory the Great with regard to certain Italian monasteries, an "Irish" view of monastic freedom, and lastly the donations of abbeys to the holy see. The first true privilege of exemption was given to the abbey of

Bobbio, which was Italian though founded by Columbanus, and this passed into the formulary of the pontifical chancellery. Privileges were then granted to some English monasteries and to Fulda and Saint-Denis, the centers of the activities of the Anglo-Saxon reformer Winifred-Boniface in Germany and in Gaul. The Carolingians, despite the attempts of Nicholas I, halted the progress of exemption. Then at the end of the ninth and the beginning of the tenth century, the donation of monasteries to St. Peter's in Rome began; such grants do not of course necessarily imply exemption, but, through the expedient of pontifical protection, they were to provide favorable ground for it.[60]

A year after Abbo, Odilo of Cluny also obtained a privilege of exemption. A decade later it was the turn of the Burgundian and Norman monasteries reformed by William of Volpiano. At the same time, the abbot of Saint-Vaast of Arras had a privilege of Stephen II, forged in order to protect himself in a dispute that brought him into conflict with his bishop, the bishop of Cambrai.

But for all that the bishops did not lay down their arms. Arnulf of Orleans had said as much at Saint-Basle: "We teach that the sacred canons promulgated (by the councils) in different places and at different times . . . have an eternal authority. . . . Can a new decretal nullify the canons and decretals of the first popes? . . . What is the point of established laws, if everything is subject to the whim of a single man!" In 993–994, the council of Chelles had logically decided that those decisions of the "Roman pope" that were contrary to those of the fathers should be null and void. In 1008 the bishop of Orleans, still in disagreement with Fleury, tried to enter the monastery by force, and a riot broke out. The bishops held a council, the abbot of Fleury produced his privilege, and some of the prelates tried to rip it out of his hand and burn it; the abbot was excommunicated.[61] Fulbert of Chartres then exhorted him to submit, for it is not possible, he said, to find any canonical text, lex, or type of argument, modus ratiocinationis, to justify his claim to be exempted from the authority of the bishop. "To find such an argument," he says with irony, "you would need to be a new rhetor, descended, or rather fallen, from heaven."[62] Gaucelin had to go to Rome to seek his salvation there.

At the end of the tenth century, the paths of monastic reform started to diverge. Opposed to the Cluniac spirit that animated the greater number of the southern reformers there was another reform, symbolized by the monastery of Gorze and by Gerard of Brogne in Lorraine. Cluny, an abbey right from the start part of the patrimony of St. Peter, was for that reason able to avoid both the founding princes and the jurisdiction of the bishops. In Upper and Lower Lorraine, the Carolingian legacy left on the contrary ample space for the prince's control.

At the beginning of the tenth century, the opposition between these two forms was not great. Thus Odo of Cluny, when he had reformed Fleury, installing Archambaud, had been quite prepared to admit that the monastery would continue to depend on the king. There had been a certain conciliation in the restoration of the old Carolingian monasteries that had fallen into decay, the best example being that of the successive reforms of Gerard of Brogne and Archambaud of Fleury at Saint-Pierre in Rheims. From Rheims the reform had reached the Angevin monasteries, while from Cluny it had spread to Marmoutier. Cluny, Gorze, and Saint-Bénigne in Dijon were at that time veritable reservoirs of sanctity from which the northern princes were able to draw exemplary men, capable of uniting around them true monastic communities.[63]

It was during the abbacy of Odilo that the gulf between Gorze and Cluny opened up. Odilo began to attach the reformed monasteries more firmly to the mother abbey, thus establishing a tight network of Cluniac churches. The priors and abbots of the dependent monasteries were to promise fealty to the abbot of Cluny. From this point two structures were to come into sharp opposition to each other. In the first case, exemption, removing the patrimony of the abbey and the abbot from any control other than that of the distant pope made the head of the community, as Adalbero rightly remarks, into a veritable king to whom the monks paid homage, like *milites*.[64] In the second case, the monastic patrimony was equally free of lay interference, but three elements were required for the creation of an abbot: election by the monks, the approval of the prince, and the benediction of the bishop.

So this controversy was already old when at the council of Anse in 1025 the abbot of Cluny was violently taken to task and the papal privileges that he produced in his defense were deemed worthless. Exacerbating the dispute was the involvement of the Cluniacs and their friends in the movement of peace. The "Burgundian peace" and its continuation the "peace of Francia" encouraged the monks to emerge from their monastic estates and opposed them in a magic struggle, with relics and sacred banners as their weapons, against the great and rapacious castellans. This was the last straw for the bishops hostile to the movement, and it finally worried or caused to hesitate even those prelates who had formerly been supporters of the peace.[65]

Although we have no annals or chronicles, the texts that do survive, often incomplete fragments or scraps, reveal the speed with which events moved in the 1020s, and from this we can deduce the bitterness of the struggle that broke out at this time. In 1021–22 the council of Verdun-sur-le-Doubs was held; in December the friends of Cluny in Francia obtained the condemnation of the heretics of Orleans; the future bishop of the city was in Verdun-sur-le-Doubs, where it was said of him: "Oury, *de facto* honourable priest, soon, it is hoped, venerable bishop."[66] Then in 1022 things went wrong for Cluny. Several influential Burgundian and Provençal castellans attacked the monastery's lands. At the same time, the Angevins devastated the lands of the church in Tours. In April 1023, King Robert was in Rome; and at this date Odilo's envoys obtained from the pope a bull against the "invaders and plunderers" of Cluny's property.[67] In May the king presided over the assembly of Compiègne, where he supported the initiative of Béraud of Soissons and Guérin of Beauvais to extend the measures taken at Verdun-sur-le-Doubs; he also received there the emperor's ambassadors and he met the emperor in August at Ivois. At the beginning of 1024, the king and his friends held the council of Héry in Burgundy and planned a council in Orleans for the end of the year. The same year the council of Douai was held, where the count of Flanders tried to persuade Gerard of Cambrai to accept the peace. In July, Odilo obtained from a new pope a new privilege. In 1025 he had to defend himself at the council of Anse. In March 1027, another journey was made and new papal bulls were issued.[68]

It is against this turbulent background that we must imagine the violent diatribes of Gerard of Cambrai and Adalbero of Laon.[69] Both of them were deeply shocked by the new measures. Gerard, "moved by the newness of these measures," roundly denounced the "false peace" of the bishops of Francia; Adalbero, though "his breast was racked with sobs"—as a royal bishop it was more difficult for him than for Gerard to reject the movement and the summonses to the peace councils—sneered at "the edict of Caesar . . . the precept of the Master"—here Odilo of Cluny—and the new "Crotoniatae" who do violence to the nature of things. However extreme the style, these polemics are interesting also in that they show us, besides the text of the decrees of peace that we examined earlier, how their adversaries understood and interpreted them.

Gerard first: he was doubly opposed to the peace, not only as a matter of principle but also because he did not want his old enemy, the castellan of Cambrai, to escape from having to pay the reparations he owed him. The castellan presented himself, with his protector the count of Flanders, as an apostle of the new peace. Thus we find Gerard presenting a mixture of theoretical and elevated discussion on the subject of the peace, justice, and the reform of the Church, along with a matter-of-fact account of his quarrels with the castellan, in theory his vassal but in fact secretly supported by the count, who was keen to insinuate his own power into the city to the detriment of the authority of the bishop and of the emperor. We can understand why Gerard did not trust these sudden outbursts of piety, the collective fasting, the pacifism aimed at damping down the ardor of his *milites*. In his opinion, a warrior should not allow himself to be disarmed by such attitudes; he has a job to do and his necessary violence is no crime "if sin is not in his conscience." The obligation to "make reparation" is in the Bible—meaning: the castellan must give up his ill-gotten gains. Vengeance—one of the "youths" of the episcopal house had been killed—is normal, and one cannot expect family and friends not to demand it. Fasting on Fridays and Saturdays cannot wash clean all sins and as for getting rid of the penitential justice of the bishop—what a wonderful advantage it would be for his adversaries to escape from the penitence that he has in store for them in exchange for having to undergo a few meatless meals! As for forcing people under threat of excommunication to take the new oath of peace, that is impossible. First, it would be to force those who would take it in these conditions to expose themselves to perjury that could not be imputed to them; second, the old oath of fealty to the lord-bishop is sufficient. It should be renewed and all should observe it. More generally, we sense in Gerard, beyond his immediate preoccupations, a deep mistrust of a movement that claims to reunite all men in the same effusion of purifying faith. Constraint and violence are the consequences of original sin, they cannot be eliminated, and it is up to the bishops, and to him, Gerard, to moderate and direct their manifestations, and not the job of assemblies where the people are seduced by dramatic performances and beautiful words.[70]

But the harshest and certainly the most profound criticism comes from the aging Adalbero of Laon, who sees the movement as pure subversion. This is the world turned upside down, he exclaims, soon we will see the peasants crowned, the warriors wearing cowls and taking a vow of silence, the bishops pushing the plough. As for the monks, they are leaving their monasteries and joining with the *milites*, they form themselves into warlike processions, banners flying at the head, and celebrate "rural councils." If this continues, they will soon be dressing like young knights and wanting a wife and children. And with a vengeful energy, the old scholar ironically sketches a burlesque epic, where the Cluniacs, led by the "prince of the Militia" Odilo, set off for war against the "new saracens," advancing in disorder, ridiculously accoutered and armed, riding grotesque mounts, donkeys, buffaloes, and camels. He constantly returns to one basic accusation: by allowing the monks to escape from the authority of the bishops and lead the faction, the king is destroying the very foundations of his power; "formerly the first of the Franks, you are no more than a serf given the name of king"; the true king is "King Odilo of Cluny," served by his new knights, the monks.[71]

Once the learned rhetoric of this extraordinary text is understood,[72] the tumultuous enthusiasm that made the strength of the great assemblies of peace and of the man who was their chief instigator, the new head of the party of the monks, Odilo of Cluny, becomes apparent. The monks as gallant new knights liberating the country from the Saracen pillagers? The comparison may have been meant as a jibe, but this idea of a crusade of peace would probably not have displeased Odilo. There are brief hints at the popular miracles that stimulated the peasant faith of the massed crowds, letters falling from heaven,[73] allusions to "that law which claims to be so old," to the "song of our first parent"—when Adam delved and Eve span. . . ?—a whole world in tumult forcing its way in the rather pedantic satire of the old pupil of the Rheims schools. Where was the place, for him and his peers, amidst these excited peasant crowds? "I have not learned how to work the land, I have not known battle; a bad state of affairs. What I know is despised, what I do not know is sought after."[74] And the descendant of the old Frankish families of Austrasia rages when he is summoned to councils held in the fields.

Adalbero's complaint was echoed in other quarters. Claude Carozzi has concluded from the appearance of the manuscript that the work was interrupted by the death of Robert or by that of the author himself. For the sake of argument, let us propose another hypothesis. As with all tracts, the poem is both allusive and very precise. If we can identify correctly the points he is scoring in it, things may become clearer. All are agreed that the old bishop's target is the council of Orleans of 1022, to which he was not invited. He also attacks the *procurator regis* whom Claude Carozzi identifies as the count Eudes of Blois-Champagne, who had become count palatine in 1021. This person "asks for what is not his, demands his own property without giving anything in exchange and is still separated from the patrimony of his wife." Should we not see here the events that had given rise to the famous letter from Eudes to King Robert, among which was the business of the castle of Dreux, dowry of Eudes's first wife, Matilda of Normandy, which became a permanent part of the royal domain? The following line is even more specific when it says: "For him, no hope, if those who chase after inheritances do not become kings." This jibe refers to the attempts of Eudes's friends, William of Poitiers and his son, to gain possession of the crown of Italy in September 1024. The remark is both very accurate—it was these events that moved the magnates toward reconciliation with the king—and chronologically very precise—William's plan had collapsed on his return from Italy, as we can see from his correspondence. It is true that this passage could also refer to Eudes's own plans to succeed his uncle, King Rudolph of Burgundy. If we take the text literally, it could refer to both attempts, since he uses a plural; in this case it would be possible to date the document to the end of the year 1024.[75]

Claude Carozzi has commented on the fact that in the collection containing the *Carmen ad Robertum regem* there are other apparently unrelated pieces: a group of charters concerning the restoration of the abbey of Baume in Escuens and a life of the saints Nazarius and Celsus. The latter of course recalls Autun, these being the patronal saints of the cathedral there. The documents concerning Baume could well show a link between Autun and Cluny. Baume was restored by Berno, whose name is mentioned in these deeds. Sometime later, the same Berno was to found Cluny, given by Duke William the Pious to Saint Peter's in Rome. On the death of Berno, the two monastic patrimonies had not been merged; Cluny had gone its own way, while Baume remained under the strict hand of a nephew of the founder.

It appears that in the first half of the eleventh century the rule of the abbey was poorly observed. The question of which authority should reestablish monastic discipline there must have arisen: Cluny, where

Berno had died, or Saint-Martin in Autun from where, as a monk, he had come to undertake his work of restoration?[76] This could shed some light on the destination of the manuscript, all or part of an anti-Cluny collection composed for the bishop of Autun. But when? Before the death of Odilo, which would deprive Adalbero's spiteful remarks of interest; perhaps in relation to the crisis of 1025, since Helmoin of Autun was present at the council of Anse. Thus we can understand Adalbero's intention—not so much that of influencing King Robert as of providing a weapon for Odilo's many enemies. The composition of the manuscript remaining to us appears to indicate a much wider and better organized coalition than might at first be imagined. This would explain also the small number of copies; Cluny's victory condemned the work to failure and obscurity.

At last it seemed that the ideas defended by Cluny were to triumph. New support came even from the ranks of its enemies. We see the astonishing change of heart of Fulbert of Chartres, who from being a sarcastic adversary of exemption becomes in 1021 one of Odilo's admirers, calling him "this archangel among monks." It is easy to imagine what the support of one of the most eminent theologians of the time must have meant to the Cluniacs. Originally from Châlons and similarly a pupil of the Rheims school, Fulbert had been drawn through his training into the faction hostile to the monks. However, shortly before the scandal of 1022, he came to see that such an attitude was out of date and that if one wished to overcome other more serious upheavals, it was necessary to accept both Cluny and the Burgundian peace. We see also the attitude of Bruno of Toul after he became pope: in a papacy of six years he was to grant no less than forty-seven privileges of exemption for the Empire, seventeen for Burgundy and seventy-two for Italy.[77]

Through tenacity, exemption, and the truce, of which the frail abbot of Cluny had appointed himself the untiring champion, at last the very stronghold of the enemy was breached—the old Carolingian lands of the Rheims area and Upper and Lower Lorraine. However, despite appearances, the triumph of Cluniac ideas in the second half of the eleventh century is less clear than might be expected. The truce spread widely in the north, but there it was essentially an extension of the penitential justice of the bishops. Henceforth exemption and truce did not necessarily go hand in hand. Alexander II, who in 1063 at the time of the launch of Leo IX's *Klosterpolitik* sent Peter Damian to sort out the quarrels that had once again arisen between the bishops and the exempt monasteries, showed himself, as we have seen, cautious on the truce of Francia—this must surely have been because it had become an instrument of the bishops. Despite the prestige of the abbey, despite the development of its priories all over Christendom, the heyday of the Cluniac "monarchy" was now over and the bishops were taking over from the monks. The northern bishops eventually rallied to the truce for the same reasons that had originally caused them to reject it. They had rejected a movement that was not under their control and was inspired by the Cluniacs and their friends, that is, the supporters of an exemption that threatened episcopal jurisdiction; they accepted it when they became the leaders of the truce movement with the support of a number of territorial princes, and they used it to consolidate and extend their penitential justice. This explains, among other things, the increase in and fixing of punishments. In the great bishoprics of the north, heirs to the Carolingian tradition, the truce was more likely to adapt itself to ancient structures than to change them.

In a parallel development, in the first half of the eleventh century, we see the scholars of the episcopal schools begin to distinguish between the spiritual and the temporal—something probably not unconnected with the spirit of the Gorze reform. Wazo of Liège thus distinguishes between *fidelitas* and *obedientia*.[78] Before him, in 1008 Fulbert of Chartres, a former pupil of the Rheims school, had outlined the same response to the secularization of the Church. At the time of the disagreement between the bishop of Orleans and the abbot of Fleury, he had made a distinction in the obligations of the abbot between the promise of obedience, owed according to canon law, and the oaths of fealty and "all that which belonged to secular law." From Fulbert the distinction passed to Marmoutier where the abbot was Albert, former dean of the chapter of Chartres. Under his influence there appeared in the lands of the Loire, in Normandy, and in Champagne around 1040–50, a vigorous theory of lay investiture that restrained its tendency toward the temporal. The formulae of the election of the abbots then distinguished between a *potestas exterior* and an *interior cura animarum*, the prince conferring the first with the cross and the bishop the second with the benediction. The ancient rituals were now being interpreted to the letter, each one confined to the now separated domains of either the temporal or the spiritual. This was a fundamental distinction, adopted by Lanfranc, taken up by his pupil Ivo of Chartres and eventually recognized, after the period of Gregorian intransigence, by the Council of Worms in 1122, and it was to be the basis of the relative independance of episcopal power.[79]

The distinction made by the Chartres faction on a theoretical level and which was eventually to rescue the temporal power of the bishops was at this same period being made by contrast on the level of everyday life. Cluny, overtaken by bishops—Gregorian perhaps, but moderates— was overtaken on the other side by those who, while claiming to renounce the world, wanted to return to the origins of the Gospel—the Cistercians,[80] who wished to live only by the work performed in their own house, and particularly the more or less fanatical supporters of a return to a "truly apostolic life."

The Apostolic Life

This second wave of reform, less easy to grasp than the first but which today appears even more far-reaching,[81] began around the 1070s and was based on a double critique, implicit and explicit, of the reform movement that had preceded it and of the wealth and the power of the great Burgundian abbey and those like it.

Implicit in this critique was an enthusiasm for the hermit life and for retreat to the wilderness—now the forest. Clerics left the world and went to set themselves up in some isolated clearing, often very far from their points of departure. They lived there in poverty supporting themselves, a few vegetables, milk, honey, and a small amount of bread providing all their nourishment, basket-making earning them if necessary a few pennies. Disciples came and went, small communities of brothers formed and disbanded.

It cannot be stressed too often how much the life of the worker hermit of the eleventh century resembled the much wider movement that had forced so many peasants, suffering under banal lordship, into new clearances in the big forests. Half-farmers, half-foresters, at first marginal and sometimes disturbing figures, they had begun the clearing that gradually cut into and pierced the vast forested edges of the estates in the year 1000. Unable properly to control these somewhat wild pioneers, the charcoal-burners and rough-looking peasants who were to be found in increasing numbers in the vast solitude of the woods where once his hunters had, not without fear,[82] ventured almost alone, the lord agreed to come to terms with them. His rule was relaxed, with fewer requirements, limited powers, and the granting of franchises. At the same time, the lord tried to prevent them from entering those areas of forest where he, hunter par excellence, was still to pursue monsters, a ritual designed as much to demonstrate his power as to amuse him.

It appears from the documents available that the most well-known itineraries and bases of the preaching hermits form a wide diagonal area going from the forest of Craon to the borders of Brittany and from Maine to the edge of Fürstenberg well to the east of Cologne, passing though the wastes of Perche and the forest of Voix near Laon. In the middle of this area, large blanks: Normandy, the Ile-de-France, and Champagne were hardly suitable for the setting up of hermit communities; travellers passed through but did not stop. At the two extremities, on the other hand, around Le Mans and Lower Lorraine, there were many hermit communities.[83] To the south of the region in question, hermits ventured into the Limousin, Périgord, and Lorraine, though not into Bourges or Besançon.[84] This distribution recalls the areas where heretical ideas spread at the beginning of the twelfth century, and indeed a certain number of these preachers of the apostolic life had to confront such ideas, as in the case of Norbert of Gennep, who had to fight against Tanchelm's heresy in Brabant. The distribution also possibly corresponds with the regions where forest clearing was most extreme and intense.

Thus the movement of hermit-preachers took firm root in northern France in the second half of the eleventh century. But how much did it owe to external influences? Examples have emerged of the presence in these regions of eastern hermits, probably coming from southern Italy.[85] A look at the lives of two famous preachers of this period can give us a good idea of the sixty adventurous years of the hermit movement in the eleventh century.

Born in 1092 in the duchy of Cleves, Norbert of Gennep was at a young age placed by his family in the chapter of Xanten where he had a prebend. He followed the normal path of a secular canon at this time and attended the courts of the archbishop of Cologne and the emperor. Little by little he began to forget his canonical obligations, even nearly breaking his vow of chastity. But in 1115 the grace of God was bestowed on him. At first he tried to persuade his fellow canons at Xanten to lead a more regular life, but this was in vain. He then retired to the seclusion of Fürstenberg, near a hermit named Liudolf. Shortly before 1118 he came out of solitude and began to preach against the wickedness of the times; his activities met with hostility from the council of Fritzlar. In order to continue, Norbert and his followers—including a cleric from Orleans—made the journey to Montpellier to obtain from Pope Gelasius II permission to preach. On the death of Gelasius, Norbert went from Valenciennes to the council of Rheims to have the authorization renewed by Callixtus II. There, certain bishops favorable to him—his friend, Burchard of Cambrai, and Bartholomew of Laon—were horrified by his physical condition: on his return from Provence, accompanied by his little group of followers in the very harsh winter of 1118–19, barefoot and worn out with fasting, three of his disciples died of exhaustion, while he himself fell seriously ill. Bartholomew took them to spend the winter in Laon and in the spring of 1120 he arrived in the forest of Voix where he established his group, including some women. There were already some other hermits there, in particular a Breton. In 1121, the master, having wavered between several orders, chose for the group the order of Saint Augustine. At Christmas the members of the community entered the canonical life. This step caused some problems, the details of which are obscure. In 1125 a bull approved the foundation of the order whose statutes were to be codified in 1131–34. During this time Norbert continued "as was his habit" his preaching, though now with some modifications: he passed the winter in Prémontré, and he traveled on a donkey and wore sandals. Soon he went north from where he had come, to Cambrai where he had friends, to Nivelles where he met unfaithful and critical disciples, to Cologne or perhaps Antwerp. Shortly after this he went to Champagne where he preached to the count. The noble vagabond was to end his life as bishop of Magdeburg. The Premonstratensian order had come into being.[86]

The life of Robert of Arbrissel has many parallels with that of Norbert of Gennep. His past clerical life was not without reproach; he was the son and grandson of priests serving in a Breton parish that had become hereditary in his family under the patronage of the castellan, the lord of La Guerche. The latter was also the bishop of Rennes. At thirty, Robert was ousted by the Gregorian reforms and went to Paris where he studied. There, this "eternal student" became aware of the sinful nature of the clerical marriage, or nicolaism, of which he was the product and of the simony that he had formerly practiced. He returned to his home diocese and there became one of the most zealous agents of the reform—too enthusiastic even, and he was forced to take refuge in Angers. Beneath his elegant clothes he was henceforth to conceal a hair shirt. In 1095 he went with a companion into the wilderness of the forest of Craon. Here he gathered around him disciples and founded a community. The pope, traveling to Angers the following year, gave him authorization to preach, but with a warning "not to say anything controversial." For his part, Robert was cautious with regard to this bestowal of a *licentia predicandi*. He left his community, determined, according to his biographer, not to settle anywhere. But once again he attracted disciples, among them prostitutes— those women without family abandoned on the outskirts of the towns by the wars in the west. The nights of prayer and meditation that Robert spent with them gave rise to the usual gossip. In 1101, as a result of pressure from the bishops, he set up again with his mixed community in a forest area at Fontevraud. Soon two distinct groups coexisted without mixing: on one side the noble women, three hundred contemplative nuns enclosed in the "big cloister," and on the other the disparate troop of repentant prostitutes, working laymen, clerics, lepers, the sick, each group in its own place. Robert set off again preaching and the younger daughters of the nobility took over the convent.[87]

Thus we see that the histories of the new foundations' origins are often quite similar. A cleric who until then had been moderately secular is converted—the word is no exaggeration—to the apostolic life. He retires to the forest where hermits are already living. Soon he comes out in order to preach in the squares and at the crossroads, soon too disciples and listeners press round him: clerics who abandon their prebends, laymen, families who have sold everything in order to follow the ways of the gospel, solitary people, the sick or knight-brigands, often women, widows or prostitutes, seeking in asceticism and the words of peace what the world denied them. These spontaneous and heterogenous communities are not those informal groupings of hermits mentioned above, but groups tightly gathered around the master, which depend on him and at first have only his example for their rule. This gives rise to the first problem: the master cannot continue to preach while dragging behind him the ever-increasing group drawn to him by his preaching. The problem is solved by settling the group, and the more or less firm pressure of the bishops often played an essential role here. Disciples and listeners would then clear a part of the forest and support themselves, imposing on themselves fasts and denials, going without meat.

But there were some backsliders and doubters and these were indicative of a second problem: the divorce that tended to occur between the master, who would continue traveling and preaching, and his community, partly, sometimes almost totally, left to itself. For this is the astonishing fact: those considered by their successors as the founders of their order and whose histories they would consequently write generally showed a marked indifference toward the institution they patronized. These founding fathers were less interested in their legitimate but peacefully settled offspring than in those who remained to be conquered. The story ends in a variety of ways: the community may adopt traditional customs and become more or less assimilated into one of the old *ordines*, Benedictine monks or regular canons; it may join a stricter rule such as that of Cîteaux; it may establish harsher and more austere customs within the canonical framework, as at Springersbach. Thus ultimate developments may mask a similarity of origins. Last, the community may simply collapse and disappear. This was the fate of the community of Odo of Tournai or that of the "fallen women" at Fontevraud.[88]

The success of these establishments is thus the reverse side of the coin of the more or less pronounced collapse of the true apostolic life. What remained thirty years afterward among the ladies of Fontevraud? Is it in the history of the new orders that we should seek the continuation of this powerful current of fervor that had launched out on the roads, among so many other barefoot preachers, the few men whose steps we can follow, because they have left behind them a monastery or college, and follow its course? What is there in common, to take an admittedly extreme example, between the feverish world of Robert of Arbrissel, his disreputable followers and prostitutes, and the majestic organization of the favorite abbey of the Plantagenet ladies? Robert did not die at Fontevraud, but while on his wanderings in Berry. His path and that of the noble ladies had already diverged and soon they would forget him. And yet his history continued; where would it lead? Let us leave this question unanswered for the moment. Suffice it to say that the entry of the new orders into the established Church was not accomplished without some bitter disputes.

The new religious orders were often explicitly critical of previous rules: what kind of monks are these, who, despite their name, live in the middle of towns and populous castles, "who impose laws on their men and take their property . . . who sit in judgement in their tribunal just like secular judges . . . who sometimes throw them in prison or have them beaten . . . who have taxable land and demand revenue from it . . . who have male and female serfs—*servi capitales*—and who raise the children of their serfs to make them serfs also? All this is worldly and has nothing spiritual about it."[89] This criticism clearly rejects lock, stock, and barrel all that the power and the wealth of the great abbeys had done and was still doing. It bears the characteristic imprint of that dislike of constraint that we see in Norbert of Gennep when he suggests that the canons of Saint-Martin in Laon should henceforth support themselves with their own work and should never defend their property by means of trials or excommunications. The new religious orders rejected the lordly role: let others demand tallage and have men beaten, not them. The explicit reference to those who raise up the children of their *servi capitales*, thus perpetuating servitude, is a clear indication that freedom, far from being just a word, was always present in the heart of the "poor," of whom the new regular orders had at one time been the brothers in poverty and for whom they were now the spokesman. Let there be no masters and no serfs, and let each man support himself; even if some people do not do this, those in holy orders at least should.

But does not this rehabilitation of labor—what we would call today productive work—date from an earlier period? Abbo of Fleury had already remarked on the hard lot of the peasants who "sweat and toil"; later Adalbero exclaimed: "The lord claims to feed his serfs, but it is they who feed him." Above all, those who attacked it—"I have not learned how to work the land . . . what I do not know is sought after"— shows that peasant labor was already esteemed by the movement of peace. For the moment, however, it was the monks, who had formerly been the promoters of this line of thought, who were to become the chief targets for the criticism of the supporters of labor.[90]

Moving on to the domestic life of the great monasteries, the new orders criticized its relative comfort. Some exclaimed: "What kind of order is this, where they dine so well, where they fast so little, where there is so little silence, where there are so often so many dishes!" Emaciated disciples of wandering masters, they had nothing but scorn for the large rations of the monks and canons of the old rule, for all the white bread, pork, beer, or wine and the extra rations on feast days.[91]

On all these points, the traditionalists attempted to justify themselves. Monks are reproached for their seigneury, they said, so be it; but it was not

from greed that they began to exercise it, but for the good of the serfs and the *hospites*; do we not see how many of those who flee from harsh lords take refuge in the seigneury of the Church? To protect them and defend them— this is not greed but charity, the highest charity! And if a man says to me that this is not the way in which monks should be involved in secular affairs, let me warn him to be more restrained in his criticism. . . . : it is not for those who have tasted the sweetness of the contemplative life, but for those others who have returned in the direction of the works of the active life, and there is as much charity, it seems to me, in defending the poor from unjust men as there is in feeding and sheltering them. And if they are reproached for receiving goods from the poor and from their *hospites?* Let them read again the words of the Lord: Render to Caesar the things that are Caesar's and to God the things that are God's, and let no one be surprised if they give the monks what is Caesar's, these fugitives who have made them into Caesars for the protection of themselves, their wives and their children and of their property. . . . [As for prison and beatings], this rule should be observed, that those who are thrown into prison do not go without, that those who are beaten do not die of it, and that such practices are not carried out in a spirit of vengeance, but for the correction of all their other serfs or dependants, so that seeing them all shall be afraid and will fear henceforth to commit bad deeds. For indeed, it is more valuable, both among the religious orders as in the secular world, that one man, having been whipped, makes his peace with many others, than to see unbridled mankind, scarcely able to restrain itself, even when evils and scourges are sent to punish its crimes, perish because through charity it has been given a licence to sin.[92]

It is clear that in this answer there is a fundamental clash of attitudes and not exclusively on a religious plane.

Lying at the heart of the debate is the emergence of banal seigneury and the breaking up of the allodial communities. Raimbaud, the cleric from Liège who wrote between 1125 and 1130 the *Liber de diversis ordinibus*, puts the problem well; the religious orders cannot remain indifferent to the fate of the "poor"; something must be done for them. The Benedictines have opted, in order to protect them from the seigneury of the lords, to play the same game but putting it, he insists, on a different basis of moderation and the common good; the innovators have made a different choice: to set an example of sanctity and disdain for the material world, to give shelter and relieve suffering, to forgive sins. A dangerous choice in the eyes of Raimbaud: if this line is pursued, he thinks, social life will soon break down.[93] We may or may not share the conclusions of Raimbaud of Saint-Jean, but we cannot fail to admire the fairness and force of his analysis.

Alongside this, the other responses—equally interesting to the clerics of the time—seem less substantial. The traditionalists pointed out that on the path of perfection not all could advance at the same speed, that some, congratulating themselves on their fasting, became proud, others, unable to fast, envied the first, and the resultant quarreling could destroy communities—hence the merit of a moderate rule. They stressed that plainness of food did not necessarily prevent greed, still less the desire that one could have for it. They criticized the strange nature of this or that new liturgy, or else the vestments.[94] With the disappearance of the most serious stumbling block, the presence of men and women together in the evangelical groups, other criticisms inevitably subsided, and the idea began to spread that "in my Father's house are many mansions," and that consequently many orders were possible in the Church.

Pushed further, this idea led to thoughts about the diversity of the human condition and the different ways of obtaining salvation. At the end of this evolution, the schema of the *tres ordines* was obviously in tatters. It is possible to trace in the texts the successive efforts of those who used it to integrate into it the changes that seemed to condemn it more and more to abstraction. Minute alterations in terminology, interpolations and glosses give evidence of a significant degree of social change. What had become of the peasants? In the mid-tenth century, Rather of Liège was still making a distinction among the *laboratores* between those who were free and those who were not. In the 1020s, Adalbero of Laon only speaks of serfs and he identifies nobles and freemen. The nobility? At the end of the eleventh century, Anselm of Canterbury replaces the now archaic *bellatores* and *pugnatores* with "knights," *milites*, which was to become the standard usage. As for the *ministeriales*, Honorius Augustodunensis reviews, as we have seen, another tripartite division, that of the three just men, Noah, Daniel, and Job, and in describing the descendants of Noah he makes his three sons the models for the nobles, the *milites (ministeriales?)*, and the serfs, the condition of the last being justified by the curse of Noah on Ham. Artisans and merchants intruded into the schema; Alger of Clairvaux and St. Bernard place them in a fourth order. Even those who clung to the old ternary division clearly see their social rise: John of Salisbury, listing the peasants, feels obliged to add: "To these can be added numerous types of workers in wool and the mechanical arts of wood, iron, bronze and the other metals. There are also the domestic trades and the many different ways of obtaining one's bread, earning one's living or improving one's situation." Honorius Augustodunensis elected to celebrate these merchants and artisans. And women were not left out of this system: in describing in the early twelfth century the triangle of the *ordines*, where the *oratores* occupy the summit, the *aratores* the left corner, and the *bellatores* the right, one author explains that women have their place in the triangle, since they are either the wives or the servants of the men in each order.[95] Stretched to its utmost, the schema is swept away by the violence of a new social critique.

This critique appears in the complaining homily of a court prelate, the Bishop of Rennes, Stephen of Fougères. His origins and his see made him no doubt more than usually aware of a dispute that the preachers of the west would not let him ignore. Between the traditional passages on the condition of the knight and the inevitable couplet on the need for obedience from the peasant, the bishop admits the unreasonable demands of the knights:

When the poor are gasping with hunger, they pillage and exploit them, they load them with work and spare them no labor. They receive their duly paid taxes which they eat and they drink, and then they persecute them and trick them without taking care to protect them as they should. The lord owes greater faith to his man than the man to his lord and master. God, what shame! He calls himself Lord and yet does not hesitate to do him harm. For the slightest mistake, he will strike him with his fist and his stick, then throw him in his prison and deprive him of all his protection. He is not afraid to hurt him, he takes all his possessions and leaves him there to die without a thought.

Turning to the peasants, Stephen cannot resist returning to the attack:

> To work the land and feed the livestock is, for the vilain, a struggle. He has much work and hardship even on the best day; he sows the rye, he harrows the oats, he scythes the meadow, he shears the wool, he makes hurdles, puts up fences, digs fishponds, does his labor service, suffers pillaging and pays a hundred customary dues. He never eats good bread, for we take the best corn, the finest and the healthiest, while the vilain is left with the tares. If he has a fat goose or chicken, he sends it to his lord, or to his lady in childbirth. If he has wine from his grapes, his lord tricks him out of it. He never gets a good morsel to eat, whether game or fowl. If he has black bread, milk and butter, he has had more than enough.[96]

And so too Stephen deploring . . . the ingratitude and impatience of the peasants.

Banal lordship, it was obvious, had scarcely improved the situation of the *laboratores*, and the clerics were aware of this. So too were the kings: while the king of England slept, he had a nightmare that the three orders were attacking him, and the first to strike were the *laboratores*. The monarchy no longer dominated the tripartite schema. The harmony is broken, social violence, unleashed, bursts forth, the smiling masks turn hostile and the king, a powerless magician, does not know what to say to them as they advance on him. In the mid-twelfth century, the *tres ordines* were by now no more than an appearance, and everyone knew it. The nobility denounced the parvenus, petty knights or *ministeriales* who attempted to join its ranks by way of royal service; the clerics, torn between irreconcilable demands, hesitated over which side to join; the third order had become a shifting and hostile world. The merchants and *ministeriales* attempted to escape, leaving the serfs to their problems and their revolts.[97] Soon the Plantagenets and later the kings of France revived for their own reasons the tripartite system, giving it a new direction: the maintenance of the balance at court and more generally in society between three privileged categories, clerics, knights, and merchant-financiers. Their power rested at the end of the twelfth century on this balance. The *tres ordines* ceased to be a mere abstraction and became a social reality.[98]

In the face of the weakness of the monarchy and the secular Church, staggering under the assault by the nobility, the Cluniacs had boldly combined the powers of the judge and the sanctity of the monk, thus laying the foundations for a new theocracy. Whether it be royal or pontifical, could a theocracy still resist the onslaughts from a period in which the relations between God and the material world could not be posed as in the past? The Cluniac peace, as also the other evangelical movements, revealed ever more urgently a basic need of the time, without for all that completely satisfying it.

The Gregorian reform progressed with the same momentum, but, unlike the movements that preceded or accompanied it, it offered a global reply to the problem of social order and more generally the world order. Because of its finality, because it arose in the same areas and same milieux as those where these preceding movements had developed, it was able to express at least a considerable part of their aspirations, but also of their contradictions. And these contradictions, lying dormant in the other movements, here became manifest.

This explains the controversies of these last decades. Different lines of research, examining the roots and developments of this rich phenomenon, have attempted to explain its apparently contradictory aspects. Sackür insisted on the divergences between the Gregorian reform and the Cluniac movement and Gerd Tellenbach today takes a very similar position. By contrast and because he differentiated, perhaps a little too much, between Gorze and Cluny, Kassius Hallinger stressed the common origins and the relationship between the Cluniac and Gregorian movements. The most recent research has revealed both the agreement at least in fundamentals between the great Burgundian abbey and the Roman pontiff and the superficial character, under the abbacy of Odilo, of the relations between Cluny and the emperor.[99] Cinzio Violante sheds light on both the reform and Cluniac monasticism in his masterly description of them against the complex background of the feudal society of the time, in which he highlights the extent of their influence.[100]

An analysis of the Gregorian reform, in the strict sense of the term, has long been used to try to explain eleventh- and twelfth-century society. Here we can take the opposite course, better to understand the hesitations and waverings of the reform, from Canossa to Worms, from Gregory himself to Urban II and Calixtus V. The reform relied, or hoped to rely, on the Cluniac network of exempted abbeys. But does not the intransigent affirmation of the authority of the sovereign pontiff not clash with the Cluniac concept of liberty, or, if one prefers, the habits of independence developed in these abbeys? The Gregorians tried to regenerate the episcopal churches by appointing monks to them. But this strengthening of the cathedral churches could only demolish a Cluniac power that had established itself to their detriment. Monastic exemption and private churches had for too long been linked for them now to be separated.

The reforming papacy depended also on the evangelical movements, while these were often reacting against the involvement of monks in feudal society. But Cluny, which in the 1020s had passed in the eyes of the traditionalist prelates for the enemy of the lords and their men, had by containing the violence of the knights contributed to justifying their existence. Worse still, Cluny and its imitators had built up seigneuries that were much too secular in the eyes of some, critics who publicly rebuked the desire for power and wealth of the old order. And the Gregorian bishops, concerned with good management, were bringing back under their control and even extending the episcopal seigneuries created by their predecessors.

The bishops in the north, for the most part long opposed to any extension of papal authority, by rallying to the reform brought to it a more flexible vision of the *libertas ecclesiae* than that of the first Gregorians. For the latter, the canonical demand for elections *a clero et populo* had been able to adapt itself to more effective practices: the pope would choose and consecrate the new reforming bishop. The former could not ignore the intervention of royal or imperial power. The concordat of Worms, which was supposed to resolve this difference, in fact left the two powers in competition.

It was the bishops who had inspired the distinction between spiritual and temporal realms, of which the concordat was the practical application. Let us make no mistake though; it corresponded to a much wider and deeper need, to which the ascetic and worker hermeticism of the founders of the new orders had failed to provide a satisfying answer. Others offered a more radical solution to the problem. And the reforming bishops, by limiting the distinction to problems posed by their investiture and by their powers, considerably restricted its extent. This arrangement, this desire for conciliation, was in fact preparing the way for and justifying a new form of royal power. They opened the way to a royal power that was less sacred but perhaps more magical, using to its advantage a popular religiosity containing elements of the supernatural, which doctrinal disputes all too often conceal from us.

Notes

1. Guibert de Nogent, *De vita sua* [46], 1:11, p. 30.
2. Fulbert, *Letters* [38], no. 56. More generally, Amman and Dumas, *L'Eglise* [323].
3. Poly, *La Provence* [87], p. 250. For a less critical view, see Magnou-Nortier, *L'introduction* [388] and *La crise* [389].
4. Congar, *Les laïcs* [350].
5. J. Le Goff, *La civilisation de l'Occident médiéval* (Paris, 1967), p. 369. The leagues of peace in Bourges had already provided an example.
6. David, *Les laboratores* [352]; Batany, *Des trois functions* [324]; Congar, *Les laïcs* [350]; Le Goff, *Note* [381]; Chelini, *Les laïcs* [348]; Duby, *Les sociétés médiévales* [476], p. 370; Le Goff, *La civilisation*, p. 325.
7. This problem has been examined by Georges Duby, *Les trois ordres* [616], which, using the schema of the *tres ordines* as a framework, embraces in fact the whole subject of the "ideology of feudalism."
8. On the world of the scholar and on this "genesis," Duby, ibid., pp. 85–104.
9. The date is not certain, cf. Carozzi, *La tripartition* [345], and Duby, *Les trois ordres* [616] p. 210. The dedication to a *fraternitas*, the accent on the priests who serve their own king—that is, God—the additions to the royal genealogy clumsily interrupted at Charles Martel, the allusion to Melchezidech are more typical of the tenth century than the end of the eleventh.
10. The schema was to be revived by the monk Aelfric of Canterbury (1005–1006) and Wulfstan of York (1005–1010) with the image of the

three pillars, *oratores-bellatores-laboratores*, which support the royal throne, Batany, *Des trois functions* [324], and Le Goff, *Note* [381]; Duby, *Les trois ordres* [616], p. 131.

11. *Miraculi sancti Bertini* [56], 7, p. 512; Carozzi, Introduction, in Adalbero, *Carmen* [23]; Duby, *Les trois ordres* [616], p. 123.

12. Rather, *Praeloquia* [65], 3:12, col. 236. On the author, G. Miccoli, *Raterio di Verona* (Todi, 1971); Taviani, *Naissance* [593]; Poly, *La Provence* [87], p. 35.

13. *Vita Geraldi* [34], 1:8, col. 647; Schneider, *La société* [512]; Duby, *Les trois ordres* [616], p. 125.

14. This bishop Turpin and his brother Aimon, the lay abbot of Saint-Martial in Limoges, were members with Berno of Cluny, Ebbo of Deols, Gerald of Aurillac, and Odo himself of the entourage of William the Pious. Odo describes Turpin, in his *Collationes, PL*, 133, col. 517, as "almost always in arms in the midst of a struggle"; he is supposed to have taken part around 930 in the crushing of the Vikings in Aquitaine. It is interesting to see that in the fifteenth century he was considered to have been associated with Charlemagne in the founding of Eymoutiers, Becquet, *Les évêques de Limoges* [329].

15. Batany, *Abbon de Fleury* [325]; Lemarignier, *L'exemption* [383], and *Le monachisme* [386], with an appendix by Olivier Guillot, *Un example . . .*, p. 399; Duby, *Les trois ordres* [616], p. 112.

16. Duby, ibid., p. 139.

17. See pp. 23–24 above.

18. Duby, *Les trois ordres*, p. 60.

19. Le Goff, *Note* [381].

20. See pp. 333–34 below.

21. Carozzi, Introduction in Adalbero, *Carmen* [23].

22. *Gesta episcoporum Cameracensium* [44], 3:52, p. 485; Adalbero, *Carmen* [23]. See the definitive commentaries of Georges Duby, *Les trois ordres* [616], pp. 25–81, and Claude Carozzi, *Les fondaments* [346].

23. Duby, *Gérard de Cambrai* [363].

24. He describes them as Crotoniates (v. 33), that is, as Claude Carozzi, in Adalbero [23], explains, as people who wish to substitute for nature an ideal, but an artifical and forced image.

25. A similar idea can already be found in Abbo of Fleury; can it have come from the teachers in the cathedral schools?

26. Adalbero's nickname.

27. Bonnaud-Delamare, *Les institutions . . . en Aquitaine* [338], which sees a Gascon influence; Hoffmann, *Gottesfriede* [373], pp. 24ff. and 46. Besides the old general works of Mansi and Labbé, the texts can be found in L. Huberti, *Studien zur Rechtsgeschichte der Gottesfrieden und Landfrieden*, vol. 1, 1892. On the meaning of the movement, see Duby, *Les laïcs* [362].

28. Fournier, p. 371; Poly, *La Provence* [87], p. 172.

29. See p. 7 above. Bonnaud-Delamare, *Les institutions . . . en Aquitaine* [338].

30. Is this quite certain? The peace in the diocese of Vienne should be examined more closely, where Odilo almost became archbishop.

31. For the dating of the council of Verdun-sur-le-Doubs, see n. 66 below. The date of the peace of Vienne, perhaps earlier, is uncertain, see Hoffman, *Gottesfriede* [373], p. 47.

32. On the assembly of Compiègne, Lemarignier, *Paix et Réforme* [385]; Fulbert, *Lettres* [38], nos. 62 and 149.

33. Poly, *La Provence* [87], p. 177.

34. Sassier, *Recherches sur le pouvoir comtal* . . ., p. 63; Hoffman, *Gottesfriede* [373], p. 53.

35. Recent edition, in Bonnaud-Delamare, *Les institutions* [335], p. 148.

36. There are numerous later councils that seem to fit in with this seven-year pattern, which may have been a penitential period.

37. Duby, *Les trois ordres* [616], p. 171.

38. *Gesta episcoporum cameracensium* [44], 3 : 40, p. 481.

39. Bonnaud-Delamare, *Les institutions* [335].

40. Bonnaud-Delamare, *Les institutions* [335], and *La paix en Flandre* [337]; Ch. Pfister, *Etudes sur le règne de Robert le Pieux* . . . (Paris, 1885), p. 175, gives 1030 for the peace of Amiens.

41. Boüard, *Sur les origines* [340], and *A propos des origines* [341]. On the same folio that gives the formula is a list of the nuns of Notre-Dame de Metz in the time of the abbess Odile, Bonnaud-Delamare, *Les institutions* [338].

42. J. Chelini, "La pratique dominicale des laïcs dans l'Eglise franque . . .," *RHEF*, 1956, p. 161; Cambrai, *Gesta episcoporum cameracensium* [44]; Toulouges, *Mansi*, 19 : 483.

43. Poly, *La Provence* [87], pp. 187 and 191; Bonnassie, *La Catalogne* [72], p. 656, following Abadal, *L'abat Oliba* [322], p. 270, sees the spread of a Catalan truce in 1033; Bonnaud-Delamare, *Les institutions* [335]. For the links between Normandy and Saint-Vaast, see Lemarignier, *Paix et Réforme* [385]. There are no traces of a council of peace at this period in Champagne, Bur, *La Champagne* [74], p. 183; the first traces appear in 1063, p. 209.

44. Poly, *La Provence* [87], p. 197, n. 157, incorrect on the dating of the Narbonne example.

45. Bonnaud-Delamare, *Les institutions* [335], p. 185.

46. On the chronology of this material, see Duby, *Gérard de Cambrai* [363]; Poly, *La Provence* [87], p. 195; Abadal, *L'abat Oliba* [322], p. 256; Bonnaud-Delamare, *Les institutions* [335].

47. On this letter, cf. the reservations of Hoffman, *Gottesfriede* [373], p. 76; on the council of 1033, p. 260, those of Poly, *La Provence* [87], p. 198. For the dating, Abadal, *L'abat Oliba* [322], p. 113, is content to refer to the work by P. Albareda, *L'abat Oliba, fundador de Montserrat* (Montserrat, 1931), p. 137, which is not very convincing (cf. the question of Wilfrid of Besalù).

48. Georges Duby, *Les trois ordres* [616], p. 41, takes for formula (B) the dating of Bonnaud-Delamare, which is based only on one point, though an important one: the clearly "episcopal" character of the arrangement of the text. The contrast between the Burgundian or southern truce and the Cambrai truce is undeniable; but it may be explained with a later dating.

49. *PL*, 146, col. 1413, and Hoffman, *Gottesfriede* [373], p. 186, which makes the comparison.

50. Platelle, *La violence* [398], to which can be added an example of 1068, in J. Rouquette, *Cartulaire de Béziers* (Paris, 1918), no. 76, p. 94.

51. Bonnaud-Delamare, *Les institutions* [335], and William of Poitiers,

Gesta Willelmi [47], 1:48, p. 118. It was perhaps also at this time that the *conventio pacis* of 1030 between Amiens and Corbie was replaced by a *decretum* of the bishop.

52. See p. 161 above.

53. Joris, *Observations* [377].

54. Ivo of Chartres, *Letters*, no. 90, *PL*, 162, col. 111.

55. Platelle, *La violence* [398], which shows this Flemish "savagery."

56. *Miraculi sancti Ursmari* [57], cap. 5, 6, 12, pp. 838–40. References in the text seem to indicate a date of 1062; the editors, in *MGH*, incline toward 1060.

57. As was said at a council of peace in Aquitaine: "Admirable is the name of Peace and beautiful the thought of the Unity which the ascending Christ left to his apostles," Bonnaud-Delamare, *Les institutions . . . en Aquitaine* [338].

58. Duby, *La diffusion* [236].

59. Duby, *Les trois ordres* [616], p. 228, which describes the affair of the peace militias of Berry in 1038.

60. Lemarignier, *L'exemption* [383]; on Abbo, see pp. 146–47 above.

61. On the date, see Bautier, in *Vita sancti Gauzlini* [25], p. 22.

62. Fulbert, *Lettres* [38], no. 8, p. 18.

63. Hallinger, *Gorze-Cluny* (Rome, 1950 and 1951); Lemarignier, *Les institutions ecclésiastiques* [384], p. 29; Wollasch, *Gérard von Brogne* [412]; Bulst, *Untersuchungen* [343].

64. In 1108, a knight became a monk "in the hands" of the abbot, *Cluny*, no. 3873. On the links between Cluniac liturgy and chivalry, see Vauchez, *La spiritualité* [407], p. 58.

65. On the justice of Cluny and its links with the peace movement, see Duby, *Recherches sur l'évolution* [112].

66. The date of the council of Verdun-sur-le-Doubs is determined by the very unusual signature of Oury, the future bishop of Orleans; his predecessor, Thierry, still in Orleans in 1021 (J. Thillier and E. Jarry, *Cartulaire de Sainte-Croix d'Orléans* [Orleans, 1906], no. 65), died on 27 January 1021 (ns. 1022), since Oury is already bishop in December 1022, Bautier, *L'hérésie* [564]. And we know that Oury became a priest only shortly before being made bishop, Fulbert, *Letters* [38], no. 42.

67. For Tours, see Fulbert, *Letters* [38], nos. 71 and 72, and Halphen, *Le Comté* [82], p. 38, n. 2; for Cluny, the bull of Benedict VII (Jaffe, no. 4013), traditionally dated to 1016, is addressed to among others the mother and the widow of the count of Provence, William, who died on 4 March 1019 (Poly, *La Provence* [87], p. 175). It is possible moreover to consider the charters of restitution to Cluny of 1023 and 1023–1024, *Cluny*, nos. 2782, 2784, 2848, as the results of the papal threat. The *Carmen* . . . speaks of a "battle" fought by the monks of Cluny in December and does not necessarily imply a journey by Odilo to Rome (*Hic petit Romam orare salutem*, he asks Rome to pray for his salvation-safety-health).

68. See p. 152 above; Fulbert, *Letters* [38], no. 94, p. 170; Duby, *Gérard de Cambrai* [363]; Hourlier, *Saint Odilon* [374].

69. Duby, *Les trois ordres* [616], p. 179.

70. *Gesta episcoporum cameracensium* [44], 3:52, p. 485; Duby, *Gérard de Cambrai* [363]. On the formula of the oath, see pp. 154–55.

71. Adalbero, *Carmen* [23], vv. 393, 114 and 115. We find the echo of these accusations against Odilo in an otherwise flattering letter where Fulbert calls the abbot "archangel of the monks," *Letters* [38], no. 64, and in his own biography of Odilo: "You would have taken him not for a duke or a prince, but for the archangel of the monks," Duby, *Les trois ordres* [616], p. 248. There was in Cluny from the middle of the tenth century (?) a manuscript of the celestial hierarchy, John Scot Eriugena, *Expositiones in ierarchiam cœlestem*, ed. J. Barbet (Turnhout, 1975), p. xviii. On the relations between Cluny and chivalry, see p. 106 above.

72. Carozzi, *Les fondements* [346], sheds light on the underlying structures of this text, the "unconfessed links between food, bestiality and sexuality."

73. Duby, *Gérard de Cambrai* [363].

74. Adalbero, *Carmen* [23], vv. 178–79.

75. Adalbero, *Carmen* [23], vv. 71–73. Eudes, count palatine, Bur, *La Champagne* [74], p. 156. Dreux, Pfister, *Etudes sur le règne de Robert le Pieux*, pp. 212, 214, 236, and Raoul Glaber, *Historiarum libri quinque* [64], 3:9, p. 84. Eudes's letter, see pp. 78–79 above. The Italian affair, Bur, *La Champagne* [74], p. 169, and Fulbert, *Letters* [38], nos. 102, 103, 104, 109, 110, 111, 112, 113. The Burgundian heritage, Poupardin, *Le royaume de Bourgogne (888–1083)* (Paris, 1907), p. 153.

76. Deeds for Baume, Poupardin, *Recueil des actes des rois de Provence* (Paris, 1920), no. 28. Bernon, Bollandists, *Acta sanctorum*, January, 1:824. Claude Carozzi is further developing work in this area.

77. Lemarignier, *L'exemption* [383].

78. Dereine, *L'école* [359].

79. Fulbert, *Letters* [38], no. 7; Guillot, *Le comte d'Anjou* [83], pp. 154 and 181. Lanfranc thus distinguished between Odo of Bayeux's status as cleric and his feudal status, Bates, *The Character* [326].

80. Duby, *Les trois ordres* [616], p. 272. On Cîteaux, see Mahn, *L'ordre* [390]; Pacaut, *Les ordres* [394], for Burgundy, Locatelli, *L'implantation* [387]; for Lower Lorraine, Despy, *Cîteaux* [361]. On the Carthusians, there is a bibliography in B. Bligny, "Les chartreux . . ., Aspects de la vie conventuelle aux XIe–XIIe siècles . . ." *Cahiers d'Histoire*, (1975) 20: 29.

81. Vauchez, *La spiritualité* [407], pp. 81 and 92; Chenu, *Moines* [349]; Génicot, *L'érémitisme* [368], which gives the social framework; Pacaut, *La notion* [395]. On the regular canons in general, see Dereine, *Vie commune* [353].

82. Kapferer, *Banditisme* [629], which unfortunately limits itself voluntarily to the historical aspect only. On the hunters' fear, see Guibert, *De vita sua* [46], 3:19, p. 224.

83. In the west, Becquet, *L'érémitisme* [328]; Bienvenu, *Aux origines* [332]; Bonnes, "Un des plus grands prédicateurs du XIIe siècle, Geoffrey du Lorroux," *RB* (1945–1946): 174; Morin, "Rainaud l'ermite . . .," *RB* (1928): 99; Le Clercq, *Le poème* [380]; Chédeville, *Chartres* [76], p. 128. In the east, Dereine, *Les origines* [354], *Le premier ordo* [355], *Les coutumiers* [356], *Odon de Tournai* [357]. Charles Dereine has shown that the bishops of imperial and Carolingian tradition like those of Liège preferred the order of canons to the monastic order. Was it not against this background that the new spirituality of the founders of the late eleventh and early twelfth century developed? *Clercs et moines* [360].

84. Becquet, *L'érémitisme* [328]. And for Grandmont, "Les institutions de l'ordre de Grandmont au Moyen Age," *Rev. Mabillon* (1952): 31; Musy, *Mouvements* [587]; Devailly, *Le Berry* [77], p. 274, which shows that in this region the communities often rallied to Cîteaux. The same thing in Besançon, Locatelli [387]. In the south, an order like that of Saint-Ruf implies a very different kind of spirituality, Dereine, *Saint-Ruf* [358].
85. Huyghebaert, *Moines* [373].
86. Dereine, *Les origines* [354].
87. Bienvenu, *Aux origines* [332].
88. Dereine, *Odon de Tournai* [357]; Bienvenu, *Aux origines* [332].
89. *Liber de diversis ordinibus ecclesiae, PL*, 213, col. 822. On the probable author, see p. 176 above. Criticism of bishops who go to war in a pseudo-letter of Fulbert, Fulbert, *Lettres* [38], p. lxi.
90. See below.
91. *Liber de diversis ordinibus*, col. 821. On the rations of Carolingian canons, Rouche, *La faim* [550].
92. Letter from Peter the Venerable to St. Bernard.
93. *Liber de diversis ordinibus*, col. 822. For the identification of the author with Raimbaud of Liège, see Chenu, *Moines* [349]. Peter the Venerable used the same type of reasoning to justify himself in regard to the Cistercians, *Letters* [60], no. 28, p. 86. On the vigor of the canon law school in Liège, see Dereine, *L'école* [359].
94. *Liber de diversis ordinibus*, col. 821; Dereine, *Le premier ordo* [355] and *Saint-Ruf* [358].
95. Congar, *Les laïcs* [350]; Duby, *Les trois ordres* [616], p. 346.
96. Etienne de Fougères, *Livre des manières*, ed. L. Gothier and R. Troux, *Recueil de textes d'histoire* vol. 2, (Liège-Paris, 1961). On Stephen and his milieu, see Duby, *Les trois ordres* [616], p. 340.
97. Le Goff, *Note* [381]; Duby, *Les trois ordres* [616], p. 346.
98. Duby, *Les trois ordres* [616], pp. 327 and 403.
99. Cowdrey, *The Cluniacs* [351], particularly pp. 141 and 157; and Benz, *Heinrich II* [330].
100. Violante, *Il monachesimo* [411].

CHAPTER

6

Celestial Hierarchy
Terrestrial Hierarchy
Feudal Hierarchy

It is impossible for our spirit to raise itself to the immaterial imitation
and contemplation of celestial hierarchies if it does not possess the
material guide suited to it.

—Pseudo-Dionysius

Politically the twelfth century is characterized by the reconstruction
of stronger principalities, effective centers of power around which
there gradually grew up increasingly elaborate structures and hierarchies. This change can be observed very early, after the crisis of
feudalism had passed, in Normandy, Flanders, and Catalonia.[1]

But nowhere did these developments appear with more clarity than
in the case of the Capetian monarchy at the end of the eleventh and the
beginning of the twelfth century. The Capetian king, however weak he
might have become, was never on the same level as the territorial
princes, his neighbors and his rivals. Even if his material power was
sometimes inferior to theirs, he retained that supernatural quality that
even at the moment of their greatest strength the princes never
dreamed of challenging, that royal mystique symbolized in the ritual of
coronation, the affirmation of a continuity that would be confirmed
one day as the "return to the line of Charles."[2]

The material weakening of the monarchy did not therefore imply the
weakening of the idea of monarchy. It has been pointed out in recent
years that the narrowing of the monarchy's areas of action and influence did not have the purely negative character formerly attributed to

186

it. Quite the reverse: it was from this very decline that the monarchy was to derive a new energy.[3]

After the appearance of the territorial principalities, the royal entourage differed little from those of the princes except for the fact, important admittedly, that the princes themselves appeared at court on certain solemn occasions. There also the title of count was assumed by men who were scarcely more powerful than ordinary castellans.[4] The documents increased this resemblance; in the kings' charters as in those of the princes, the entourages would henceforth be involved in confirming the decisions of their leaders. It is this alteration in the conception of a royal act that conclusively demonstrates the quantitative changes taking place in the king's retinue, where a difference in the social level of those forming the royal entourage implied also an alteration of structure and thought. Thus, we meet again Abbo of Fleury's question, posed in quite different terms, which now help to answer it: how can the king fulfill his function if the great men of the kingdom do not provide him with aid and counsel?

The Royal Household

In the course of the eleventh century, an important change took place in the royal court. Up until 1028 it had still been almost exclusively composed of bishops and counts, above all from Francia. After this date, castellans began to enter into the royal entourage. By 1077 the transformation was complete. The magnates, both secular and ecclesiastical, had abandoned the court. The mainstay of the Capetian court was petty knights from the Ile-de-France and particularly the royal household, the *familia regis*.[5] The king's house, originally no different from that of other great men, was to know a unique destiny.

Salary and Office

The structure of the *familia regis* at the beginning of the twelfth century seems at first glance hardly different from that of the Carolingian palace described by Hincmar or those of the households of the territorial princes. It consisted of a collection of domestic offices, groups of servants united around a certain number of necessities: bread, meat, wine, horses, writing, prayer, sleep. On closer inspection, however, we see the numerical importance—one could even say the hypertrophy—of two of these groups: the chamber and the chapel.

The chamber, the group of chamberlains, was an elite armed guard. This was already the case in the eleventh century with the *camera* of Count Bouchard the Venerable, which looked after the castle of Vendôme during the two months when the master resided there. The chamber of the king was certainly bigger. A text that we shall return to later, the Pseudo-Turpin, describes the chamber of a legendary Charlemagne, the model of kings. It numbered twelve hundred men who in groups of forty took watch in turns to keep guard each day of the month. At the same time as assuring the security of their lord, the chamberlains guarded his treasure. But their principal task, their *"mestier"* as a charter from Saint-Denis was to put it later, was to "sleep at his feet," exorcizing nocturnal fears, real or imaginary. Suger, writing the life of the King of France, Louis VI, contrasted his serenity with the anguish of the King of England, Henry I, terrified by the plots of his chamberlains: he feared the night above all, often changing his bed and multiplying the armed guards in order to be more sure of his safety. The symbolic and exceptional reward for this night watch in the dark was for a chamberlain to be buried when he died at the foot of the royal tomb.[6] A curious text appears to associate the royal chamber with the abbey of Saint-Denis. Certainly the majority of the kings took their last rest there, and the tradition had arisen of keeping the crown, the most precious item in the royal treasury, in the abbey.[7]

Another group, also very large, contributed to the security of the prince: the chaplains. They watched over his salvation and that of his family, they drafted his deeds, were his ambassadors, preached to his knights, and prayed in his battles. In return, the king provided them with chapels in the town where he lived. He also distributed the cathedral benefices in his gift in their favor, and an accumulation of prebends was often the sign and the measure of familiarity with the master. The *capella* was quite as prestigious as the guard of the chamber: to appoint this or that canon fictitiously as a member of it was to honor him and obtain for him closer royal protection. Soon bishops and abbots were laying claim to the chapel.[8]

Who were these people of the *familia?* Many were "youths" who early on became part of the household and who must have been brought up with the young prince. They had to remain "youths" for a long time before becoming established, sometimes as late as forty. Many were younger sons, and as with their equivalents in the princely households, the hunt for an inheritance and for bags of gold was a matter of some concern for these companions of the king.[9]

The young warriors were not the only ones to belong to the royal *familia:* we find also the bailiffs of the royal estates and no doubt also other more humble servants. There seems little in common between the king's knights and the groups of farmhands in the *curtes* and yet the same legal term unites them, and we may seek in vain in the documents for a distinction between a military *familia* and a servile *familia.*[10] Thus the *familia* appears to imply a sort of identical status for all its members, younger sons of knightly families or villeins. Should we deduce from this that both groups were of servile origin? Here we come up against the problem of the knight-serfs and the *ministeriales* in France. In fact, there are certain indications that still in the twelfth century the *milites* in the royal entourage were not free of the taint of servitude.

This is the case with those who are described in the documents as born in the *familia*, as for example the chamberlain Vulgrin. When he felt death approaching, Vulgrin, who had left no successor, left his possessions to Morigny: heedless of charity, the king seized the goods. To the fury of the monks, Louis VI replied that Vulgrin, born in his *familia*, had died without an heir; the succession returned to him. Two texts shed a curious light on the situation of another member of the *familia*, one Henry of Lorraine. In 1112, envious informers suggested to the king that Henry *servum nostrum debere esse et matre quidem illius libera existente ex paterna tantum origine servitutis maculam contraxisse* ("ought to be our serf for, while his mother was freeborn, he contracted the taint of serfdom from his father's side"). The affair reached the point where the king summoned Henry to appear before the royal court, and the *servitutis obsequium* was demanded of him. In his defense, Henry denied that his father had been a serf or should have been one; he swore also that he was a free man and that his father and grandfather before him had been free. Thus we see that the accusation of servitude against a member of the royal household was neither impossible nor absurd; Henry's memory only went back to his grandfather, yet at the same period the memory of the canon of Cambrai, Lambert of Wattrelos, reached back to the fourth generation. Was Henry afraid of looking too far back? He does not mention his grandmother either. Shortly before his trial, as if to avoid the shameful accusation and end the matter at the risk of death duties, Henry had asked the king to confirm him in his possession of his benefices and to do the same for his son, on condition that he gave homage. *Beneficia, hominium:* the vocabulary here is that of knighthood.

In fact, since the end of the tenth century the knights of the royal cities had not disdained to claim kinship to serfs. In 987–996, Rothold, one of the *milites* of Senlis, laid claim, despite Saint-Bertin, to the inheritance of a rich estate in the Beauvaisis belonging to a certain Renaud; "he called himself his successor, through kinship, and above all because Renaud was his serf." Again, around the middle of the twelfth century, the royal serf Eremburga—*de familia et ancilla nostra*—was the daughter of a knight. Her son may also have been a knight.[11]

Guibert of Nogent was probably thinking of the humble origin of many of the king's household when he claimed that the king "listened too much with his ears and his mind to people debased and corrupted by the temptation of gain." For the king's household was mercenary and greedy. How could it be otherwise? Its wealth was not derived from land. Its fortune came from closeness to the prince. The entourages of the king of England or the pope acted in just the same way.[12] A greater circulation of deniers and precious metals can be seen around the princes. All petitions were accompanied with gifts. As for the coinage, it came from an increased number of mints given in benefice or from the control of the great fairs. These fairs—the Lendit fair at Saint-Denis is a good example—had close links with popular piety. Princely households, the circulation of money, and the fairs are complementary structures.

All taken into account, these were occasional profits. More illuminating for understanding the mentality of the *familia* is another relationship, this time regular, which established itself between money and the king's house. In the second half of the eleventh century, the domestic knights of certain great households were receiving a wage.[13]

When Dudo of Saint-Quentin in the early eleventh century is describing the promises made by William Longsword, duke of Normandy, to the knights of his household, he mentions all the pieces of the military equipment, the moveable goods, but not a wage. By contrast, when in 1059 William the Bastard chooses fifty elite knights for a daring assault on the castle of Domfront, he promises to increase the wage that they receive—*acceptum stipendium augere*. It is very unlikely that he entrusted himself to mercenary knights, *conducticii*, so this must mean people of his household. At the same period—from 1045—the count of Barcelona began to take on knights to whom he accorded in fief an income of five to seven ounces of gold, payable at Easter or Michaelmas.[14]

An important text by William, the biographer of Suger, shows that the knights of the royal house received on a fixed date each year along with clothes and presents a wage, *stipendium*. Other texts reveal the same thing at the churches of Beauvais and Arras, where the *stipendia* were assimilated into the money fiefs, *beneficia denariorum*.[15]

Thus we see that the system of money fiefs was customary in the king's house by 1147–49—therefore it must have started sometime earlier. An example from Arras fixes the chronology more precisely. In a tribunal in 1132 the knight Eustace of La Longue claimed the money fief held by his father from the bishop, Robert (1115–31), thus dating the granting of it to a little after 1115. But the text also shows that the fief was newly created, which would seem to indicate not the creation of a system of wages in Arras, but its extension through new money fiefs.

Traces of the same system can already be found from the mid-eleventh century at Saint-Florent-de-Saumur, which belonged to the count of Anjou, where we find a *miles stipendiarius*, and in the entourage of the count of Blois-Champagne who had granted to a knight between 1102 and 1128 a *casamentum-feodum* of ten livres on the fair of Bar-sur-Aube. At the end of the eleventh century, the archbishop of Rheims, Manassès, distributed the gold plate from his church piece by piece to the knights of his household in order to bind them to him. But such gifts of precious metal seem not to have been a regular practice; on the other hand, it was certainly a money fief that the brother of

Guibert of Nogent had at the castle of Clermont in the Beauvaisis at around the same period. Outside "France" we find examples of money fiefs in 996 in Utrecht—held from the bishop, in 1023–1026 in Aquitaine—held from the duke, in 1048 in Fulda and in 1087 at Saint-Bertin. But there is nothing to prove that this was a regular or constant practice or that they were real wages. Rather the contrary in the case of Fulda: it is specified that the income will allow the vassal to wait for the granting of a piece of land in benefice. At Saint-Bertin, the knights who guarded the castle of Saint-Omer for the count were still in 1127 only receiving rations.[16]

The word *stipendium* itself, a learned but technical term, frequently used, is a borrowing from the vocabulary of the Roman army, perhaps by way of the gospels. Thus the Bishop of Chartres, John of Salisbury, who was quite ready elsewhere to apply the texts of classical antiquity to the knighthood of his time, recalls, quoting Luke, the words of St. John to the baptized *milites:* "Do violence to no man, neither accuse any falsely; and be content with your wages—*stipendiis vestris.*" An apt piece of advice for the *ministeriales!* Later in the bishop's text he shows that he considered these *stipendiae* to be public in nature.[17]

These paid military *familiae,* when attached to a church, were no less dependent on the king. When in the twelfth century the reforming bishops tried to dispense with them, the king reacted very violently, revealing the interest he had in the institution. The system of money fiefs in the episcopal households of *Francia* worked to the advantage of the monarchy just as it reflected its structures.

It is probable that this kind of organization derives from the *familiae* of the dependants of humble origins with whom the bishoprics and great abbeys surrounded themselves and who occupied the offices or *ministeria.*[18] In a letter addressed to the king, Fulbert complains of a custom, a bad one in his eyes, which obliged him to support and feed "superfluous servants," while other letters from him show that these *domestici* formed his usual armed escort. Thus at Chartres as in other churches in Francia, there existed alongside the *milites casati* a group of servants who were employed along with others in military tasks. The same word, *domestici,* was used to refer even to the *milites regii.*[19] Since the Carolingian era, the churches had sometimes armed their serfs or *coloni.* It seems possible, as Ganshof proposes for Flanders and Lorraine, that the replacement of the free *vassi* with *ministeriales* in the entourages and armed escorts of the bishops and the great abbots is a characteristic of the late tenth century.[20] Then, no doubt, the fief retreated before the giving of "provisions," later to be replaced by the *stipendium.*

This *stipendium* of the *milites* can be compared to the income granted by the king to his chaplains. The king's clerics often served the royal chapels and in these different sanctuaries he accorded them a proper wage that varied very little from place to place. When Louis VII founded a chapel in Paris, he exacted two hogsheads of wheat every year from the barn of Gonesse, six hogsheads of wine and thirty sous parisis from the tax of Bagneux. It was the same for the chaplains of Compiègne and Laon. The chaplain received in addition offerings, and when the king, the queen, or their children stayed in the palace in question he was provided with a supplementary allowance for each day of the royal visit.[21] Thus from the early twelfth century in the entourage of the kings of France and of England, salaries and offices strengthened the feudal-vassalic bond.

Help and Counsel

Abbo of Fleury's question—how is the king to govern if the great men of the kingdom do not give him help and counsel?—could now be answered. The royal household was now sufficiently strong and self-confident to replace, when necessary, the weaker princes.

Let us examine this help first of all. It was the royal knights who, apart from appropriate allies, made up the troops of Prince Louis in his struggle with the lords of Francia. Indeed, at times of need the king often had only his *familia* to fall back on. To teach Humbaud a lesson, the knights of the king's household—*domestici*—ventured alone into Berry. When the people of Corbeil implored help it was a small group of *curiales* that hastened to their aid. In order to deliver Touri from Hugh of Puiset there arrived "men in arms, of the royal household," gathered by William of Garlande.

How many were they? In 1097–98 the army of the young Prince Louis consisted at various times of between 300 and 500 knights. In 1102 and 1103 it was as many as 700. A little later the vanguard of the king's house numbered only forty knights. When we compare these figures with those given by Suger for the army gathered at the time of the invasion of 1124 they seem derisory.[22]

Despite their small numbers, however, the "king's knights" charged into the thick of the battles. In their midst the king was safe: "These are my fellow countrymen, I was brought up amongst them. In my life they will help me. When I die they will keep my body and bring it home," said Louis VI when he led the army of Saint-Denis—an army that was "numerous and devoted to the crown, *corone devoto.*"[23]

Their daring was legendary and if they fought bravely it was to be worthy of their reputation. Legendary—the word is not too strong. More than any others, the royal knights lived the Carolingian *gesta*. When the moment came to give their war cry, it was—at the same time as to God—to the great emperor that they commended themselves: "Mountjoy," Charlemagne's legendary banner, given according to the *Chanson de Roland* by the pope, a red-gold banner that was also known as the *oriflamme.*[24]

In Limoges were preserved in the twelfth century the standards from Waïfre that Pepin after his victory had given to the church of Saint-Martial. A similar veneration for a standard, associated also with the cult of relics, could be found at Liège, where the knights, before raising the banner of St. Lambert for the assault on the castles rebelling against the bishop, insisted that the latter send the saint's relics to accompany them. The very same ritual was performed by the king and his followers when, at the raising of the banner of St. Denis, they had the relics of the martyr and his companions placed on the altar.[25]

Can this vexillum sancti Dionysii be identified with Charlemagne's oriflamme? This is a much-debated question. It is only at the end of the twelfth century that the texts equate them. In 1119, in a battle against the Anglo-Normans, the French shouted "Mountjoy"; they probably carried with them the standard of Charlemagne. In 1124, according to Suger, they marched behind that of St. Denis. It seems unlikely that they would have changed banners in that interval of time. So why does Suger not name the oriflamme? Perhaps because in the eleventh century it was associated with the preeminence of the papacy. As the Chanson de Roland says of the banner—and what is more has it carried by a Geoffrey of Anjou: "It was the banner of St. Peter and was called Roman." We know too that in the eleventh century the pope had similarly given banners to the Norman princes of Italy and to William the Conqueror. But possessing a standard of Roman origin could be interpreted as a sign of submission to the holy see; hence it was advisable to forget a similarly inconvenient fact and to associate the old standard of Charles with the cult of Denis, while affirming at the same time the connection between the saint and the Capetian.[26]

What here is legend and what is reality? When they heard the singing of The Coronation of Louis, which exalts William's fidelity toward the young crowned king against all and stigmatizes the selfishness of the magnates and sometimes their cowardice, the companions of a new Louis could hardly fail to recognize themselves. Mercenary definitely, coarse perhaps—but what of it? The new royal entourage drew from its humble origins the reasons for a devotion that raised it, in its own eyes at least, to the level of the epic poem.[27]

The king relied on the counsel of his companions in arms and on his clerics. It was now "low people" who, whether the magnates liked it or not, decided policy with the king. He would remind them, should it be necessary, that "they owed their power to their closeness to the king": they were the ones to form his true council, and in return his council alone made them what they were. The fidelis now made way for the familiar. The familiars of the king arranged the young prince's coronation. Through them rebel counts could be pardoned, and hired assassins could escape the courts. With their advice the king agreed to the wish of the duke of Aquitaine to watch over his lands, to have the care of his heir, and, later, to marry his son to Eleanor. With them the king could give vent to his troubles, and with them he could joke: "The emperor of Germany has good men at arms and warhorses. . . . The king of England lacks for nothing; men and horses, gold and silk, precious stones, fruits, game—he has them all. But we in France have nothing, except bread, wine and joy." Or again, showing his backside to the ambassador of the Holy Roman Empire: "Take that, German!" To know what the king was going to do, it was enough to watch his entourage: Peter the Pisan, the friend and informant of Pope Alexander III, informed him in 1162: "My lord the king is troubled, too much so, and as he has become attached to new princes and new 'youths,' it is much to be feared that his arrangements will change."[28]

From the very heart of his *familia* at the beginning of the twelfth century the king drew men to help him in his political decisions. The old solemn assemblies still remained, of course, but the absence or removal of the upper aristocracy and the growing influence of the members of his entourage made this government by enlarged council illusory. The real power lay in the hands of the officers, the royal knights, and the palace clerics.

The king's familiars, those petty knights of the Ile-de-France with their many kinsmen, abandoned by the magnates and the bishops, had to steer the royal ship on their own. It was they who spoke now, through the mouth of the king. And their words and their ideas were those of men like themselves, from the *familiae*, men who served. Under their influence the face of royalty was remodeled. Corresponding to the social changes taking place in the king's entourage was a change in the "idealizing" literature. Once the noble descendants of the nobility of the empire had disappeared from the palace, their utterances were replaced by new ones. Because neo-Carolingian theories and the traditional *Mirror of Princes* no longer represented the mental habits and ideological needs of the royal knights, they needed to redefine from their own social experience the relations of the royal figure to the sacred and reinterpret the old vassalic relationships. They had to create a new image of power.

Royal Power and Feudal Hierarchy

For a long time the ceremony of coronation had made the king a person apart from others. But the Carolingian scholars had produced little more than rather cerebral treatises to describe the position of the king in relation to the divinity: a learned and almost rational divinity that fixed the king in an inaccessible majesty, just below God.

Paradoxically, it was just at the moment when the "return to Carolingian origins" became a major, almost obsessive, theme of the Capetian monarchy that it turned its back on what now appears to us today as the Carolingian theory of power—or at least the official theory.

The strength of the new monarchy was in fact to abandon the old habits and to base its legitimacy on the coming together of the two major currents of the twelfth century. The first was that which brought to the fore the ancient devotion of the country people and the petty knights toward the saints, who only partially concealed the presence of rustic divinities, protectors in war, the hunt, and at harvest. The second was that which merged together in the same epic poem ancient songs and legendary themes and which held up to Europe the heroic model of an ideal monarchy incarnated in the figure of the emperor with the snowy beard.[29]

The Reality of the Legend

In order to understand this movement, we have to penetrate into those places where it developed, in that stronghold of the new royal counsellors, the abbey of Saint-Denis. St. Bernard who did not love them overmuch, knew what he was talking about when he recalled in 1127: "This place had been ennobled and raised to royal dignity in the earliest times. It was the arbiter of the judgements of the court and the army of kings; there what was Caesar's was rendered unto Caesar without hesitation or deception, but the same care was not taken to render unto God what was God's." He accurately called the abbey "Vulcan's workshop." The theories and the false charters forged at Saint-Denis were not those of the abbot and the monks but rather those of the new court.[30] Inspired by this court, the skillful workers of the Saint-Denis workshops got to work without delay: taking the Carolingian legend, they altered it, rectified it, adjusted it, cutting here or adding there, until the statue, the "sign," thus forged could in its perfection bind to it men's souls to the profit of their king.

We can see the beginning of this slow and patient work around the years 1080–95. A monk of Saint-Denis at that time composed the first historical account to draw widely on legend. This was the *Descriptio qualiter Karolus . . .* , which tells how Charlemagne liberated the city of Jerusalem and brought back from Constantinople the relics of the passion; these relics, first brought to Aachen, then passed in part to Saint-Denis through a donation by Charles the Bald. The immediate interest of this work was to affirm the authenticity of the relics possessed by the royal monastery and, more generally, to contribute toward the sanctification of a certain number of standards and reliquary-weapons, presented rightly or wrongly as belonging to the great emperor, as was the case with the sword, first given to Saint-Riquier, the lance, and the standard, the importance of which we have discussed earlier.[31]

A few decades later the Saint-Denis faction went much further, reworking an apocryphal text that, when translated, was to become the most famous of the histories of Charlemagne: the *Historia Karoli Magni et Rotholandi*, presented as the work of one of the legendary companions of Charles, Archbishop Turpin, and for this reason known by historians as the Pseudo-Turpin.[32] The enormous success of the work is attested to by the number of manuscripts of it existing and, particularly, at the end of the century, by the number of translations of it into the vernacular. At this time, the false had become to contemporary eyes the only, the true, and the authentic history of the model emperor. It is interesting to see how this situation came about.

The writing of the Pseudo-Turpin covered almost a century, and it was the work of several workshops, each one of which endeavored to surpass the previous one. Contemporary accounts reveal these workshops clearly when, at the end of the twelfth century, they cite as guarantors of the authenticity of the Pseudo-Turpin the three abbeys of Saint-Martin of Tours, Cluny, and Saint-Denis.[33] The first stage could well have been the work done at Saint-Martin, which can be found at the dependent abbey of Saint-Yrieix in the Limousin, and more generally on the road between the Loire and Spain. From this period there were added legendary Carolingian elements and others connected with several Alfonsos, kings of Spain, and particularly Alfonso III the Great (838–910) and Alfonso VI the Valiant (1049–1109). It was remembered at Saint-Martin that Alfonso III had bought a "crown of Charlemagne" owned by the abbey; in the Limousin they remembered a Bishop Turpin famous for his bravery.[34]

Did all these elements yet form a single whole? The fusion took place in any case when, in a second stage, a forger resolutely centered the Pseudo-Turpin around the glorification of St. James of Compostella. This forger was very probably a Cluniac, and the influence of Cluny was at its height in the kingdom of Leon at the beginning of the twelfth century. In 1087 the Bishop of Compostella, Diego Pelaez, who had supported the revolt of the Galician nobles against Alfonso VI, was deposed by this king; the pope rejected his successor, and the king, after negotiations with the abbot of Cluny—the Burgundian Hugh of Semur (1049–1109)—appointed in Compostella the Cluniac Dalmatius (1094–1100), very likely Hugh's brother. It is unlikely that he came alone to Galicia. At the same period the count in that area was Raymond of Burgundy, son-in-law of King Alfonso, while his cousin Henry was count of Portugal. A few years later there mounted the papal throne, under the name of Callixtus II (1119–24), the Archbishop of Vienne, Guy of Burgundy, brother of the Count Renaud of Mâcon who had gone to the crusades in Spain in 1090, and successor in the see of Vienne of a Cluniac.[35] Thus a far-reaching plan was born: to take away from Toledo, which had been reconquered in 1085, its old primacy over all the churches of Spain. The Cluniac rewriter's task was clearly defined: to establish the primacy of Compostella, prestigious heir, thanks to St. James, to the obscure bishopric of Iria Flavia. He tells us that after reconquering Galicia and reinstating its bishops, Charlemagne "established that all the bishops, Christian princes and kings of Europe and all the Galicians present then and in the future owed obedience to the archbishop of Monseigneur St James." Then the text, having dealt with any possible claims from Iria Flavia, the former seat of the bishopric, specifies that Charles submitted all the land to Compostella and commanded that each house in Spain and in Galicia should give annually to the church of Monseigneur St. James four deniers and that thereafter they were free of any other services. Finally, Charles ordered that the church of Compostella, since it was established by St. James himself, should be called an apostolic see. As a consequence, councils of all the bishops of Spain would be held there, the crosiers given to the bishops at their investiture would be given by the hand of the archbishop, as would the crown at coronations of kings. If the Christian faith should disappear in certain places, these could only be reconciled with the Church through the offices of the archbishop. This was clearly aimed at the territories liberated by the *Reconquista* and at the foundation of new bishoprics. The system proposed in this text makes Compostella the true metropolis of Spain at the expense of Toledo. And the Pseudo-Turpin was to finish with the death of Turpin in Vienne and the exalting of St. James, the "headless Galician," protector and savior of Charles before the court of heaven. This false document had two very real results: a papal privilege in 1120, making St. James an archbishopric subject only to Rome, and the "Archbishop" Diego Gelmirez a papal legate. Turpin's tomb can be found in Vienne, near the old funerary basilica in the city, Saint-Ferréol, where there was no shortage of beautiful marble sarcophagi.[36]

The third stage occurred in the 1120s when the Saint-Denis faction got wind of Charles's Spanish donations. One of the merchants who was going to Spain to sell the cloths of St. Denis must have brought back this news. Here too the monks set to work and soon the Parisian abbey had its *Historia Tilpini de Hispania*, considerably reworked, as we shall see, in the interests of the cause.[37]

The last stages were those of the consolidation and the diffusion of the forgery. The fourth stage takes us to Vézelay, to an environment very similar to that of Cluny. Living there was Aimery Picaud, of Parthenay, who it appears ran the hospital Saint-Jacques d'Asquins, near the abbey and dependent on it. He had a female companion, *socia*, called Gerberga of Flanders. Probably at the request first of Abbot Aubry, now cardinal-bishop of Ostia, and then of the latter's successor, Ponce of Montboissier, brother of the abbot of Cluny, Peter the Venerable, Aimery seems to have undertaken, around 1139–40, the integration of the Pseudo-Turpin into a more general compilation of five books. The first dealt with the liturgy used in honor of the apostle, the second described his miracles (many of them Burgundian), the third his preaching in Spain, his martyrdom in Palestine, and his translation to Galicia. The fifth book was the famous *Guide for the Pilgrims of St. James*, while the fourth book was our Pseudo-Turpin. Aimery placed his collection under the authority of the deceased Pope Callixtus and—an inspired move—lodged it at Compostella where it became the *Liber Sancti Jacobi* of the cathedral and was thus guaranteed against any future interpolations.[38] It was here that the Catalan Arnalt de Mont came to consult it in 1173–74, and Geoffrey of Vigeois from the Limousin came in 1171–72. In a final stage, the Pseudo-Turpin gained the heartland of Carolingian territory proper, Picardy, the Boulonnais, and Hainault, where it was translated into the vernacular. It was from the count of Hainault in Mons that the envoys from the German court of the Holy Roman Emperor, who had tried to draw the legend there by canonizing Charlemagne at Aachen, had to get hold of the book. Thus St. James and St. Denis shared out the posthumous gifts of Charlemagne.

The Saint-Denis reworking of the Pseudo-Turpin was then a plagiarized version of the Compostella system, but a plagiarism that was remarkably well adapted. The old emperor assigns to St. Denis in France the place held in the Iberian kingdom by the apostle James Matamoros (the Moor Slayer). This parallel is awkward because "Turpin," at the end of his description of the restoration of Compostella by Charles, had insisted on the fact that there are in the world only three principal sees, Rome (because of St. Peter), Ephesus (St. John) and Compostella (St. James). The Saint-Denis forger, not able to make St. Denis an apostle, gets round the problem neatly by declaring that "the king has given the whole of France to Monseigneur St. Denis, as St. Paul the apostle and St. Clement the apostle had before given it to Monseigneur St. Denis." The descendancy was assured.[39]

Finally, around 1156 Saint-Denis put the final touch to its construction. They "invented" the document of the donation of Charlemagne, closely copied from the passage in the Pseudo-Denis.[40] The "Pseudo-Charlemagne" presents us with the final expression of the theory of royal power according to Saint-Denis. What does it tell us? First that the abbey, the royal church par excellence, is in consequence the first church of the kingdom. All the churches of France are attached to it and it becomes the head—*caput omnium ecclesiarum regni*. At the same time the abbot took precedence over all other prelates; without his consent and advice, the archbishops and bishops could not be confirmed, received or condemned in Rome. There was a precedent that could authorize these arrangements: the regency of Suger at the time of the second crusade. But now an exception had become a general measure. It could not have been just the monks of Saint-Denis who could lay claim to so much; we can guess at the actions of certain royal counsellors known for their hostility to the Gregorian reform and the reformers.[41] The prerogatives transferred to the saint, to the benefit of the Capetian king, were no other than those of the old royal power over the bishops of the realm; as such this measure also aimed at the princes. Under the powerful and combined patronage of Denis and Charles, the monarchy laid claim to a return to a total control over the Church in France. Another measure came to undermine the Rheims privilege, specifying that the king, after the ceremony of anointing, could be crowned nowhere but at Saint-Denis, perhaps in order to forestall future problems in the case of a difficult succession.

Finally, and above all, the text puts forward a veritable theory of *chevage* (the "head tax"). The king, it is said, holds his kingdom from

God through the intermediary of St. Denis. It is in sign of recognition of the lordship of the martyr that the king places his crown on the altar. From this the practice, probably much older, which had made the abbey the depository for the royal insignia, was explained. But the Pseudo-Charlemagne does more: on the altar he places also the *chevage*, the four ritual coins—in this case gold besants. A daring image at a period when the four deniers were more and more frequently interpreted as the mark of servitude. The Pseudo-Charlemagne in fact feels the need to justify this: "I beg and pray all the kings our successors that they should do the same each year and offer these four besants . . . bowing their heads and prostrating themselves; this is not to submit oneself to a human obedience, but rather to divine obedience which we should call sovereign freedom since to serve God is to reign." An extraordinary manifesto, where the Capetian king is given the model of a serf king who humbles himself to conquer![42]

After the king, the magnates and nobles were invited in their turn to do the same. Each, for his house-*domus*, had to give four gold coins. Finally, playing on the ambiguity of the ritual of the four deniers, the Pseudo-Charlemagne "emancipated and made free for ever all men reduced to servitude" who would make the same offering; henceforth they would be called the Franks or Freemen of St. Denis. We see a link with the aspirations of the most powerful and rich of the abbey *familiae*, and particularly of the *familiares regis* "devoted" to St. Denis. The four coins, with their ambiguous symbolism, created both the freedom of the serfs and royal submission to the most powerful of the saints—a freedom and a submission that were both equally honorable. Monarch and *ministeriales* found themselves daringly united in the same ideology of service.

But we should not imagine that these were mere monastic dreams; we are dealing here with the renaissance of the monarchy. We can be sure that at least from the time of Philip-Augustus the king gave St. Denis his four besants on the occasion of a solemn feast day.[43] The king of France became henceforth, as in the epic poems, "the king of St. Denis." We should understand this as meaning the king of the saint his patron, not the king of the abbey of Saint-Denis. The saint correspondingly became, as Guibert of Nogent says, "the lord of all France."[44] To complete the picture, it only remained to give this new Charlemagne peers and barons, as the previous Charlemagne had had. This was done during the second half of the twelfth century.

The word "baron" originally meant "man" as opposed to "woman." The word survives into the thirteenth century in this meaning, when Beaumanior, for example, writes: "The husband (*mari*) is the man (*bers*) of his wife/woman (*femme*)." But early on, from the end of the Merovingian period, "baron" takes on the meaning of "servant" and was to have from then on a history similar to that of *vassus*, which had also originally meant "man." At the end of the tenth century in the

Limousin, *barones* referred to the knights living near the monastery of Uzerche. In the eleventh century the term was applied to the men of a castle, "barons of the land" and vassals of the lord. A good example from 1099 is that of of the barons of the castle of Talmond in Poitou. They made up the court of the castellan and the charters attach them expressly to the castle—*barones castri*—and to the region—*barones hujus terrae*. These were people of little importance with significant surnames: The Bald, The Bastard, Pagan, Swineherd. But from this period the word begins to be used by the chanceries of certain territorial princes—the duke of Normandy and the counts of Anjou and Flanders—to refer generally to all those dependent on them. Suger reinforced this meaning of "vassal" when he was to speak of the "feudatory barons" of Saint-Denis.[45]

Thus "baron" was popularly used to refer to the strong men of the lords and consequently it fitted well into the *Chansons de Geste* with its two meanings: virile, brave man, and man of another. And as the chief figure—whether good or bad—of these epics was the king, he too was represented as surrounded by his barons "the Frankish barons," who gave without stinting their aid—*"Barons français, vos estes bons vassals, /Tantes batailles avez faites en camp"* (French barons, you are good vassals who have fought so many battles in the field)—and their advice—*"Desuz un pin en est li reis alez, /Ses barons mandet pur sun conseil finer"* (Under a pine the king did go, sending for his barons to finish his discussion).

Paradoxically, at the same time and despite the lowering of social levels that had taken place in their master's entourage, the royal notaries, preserving tradition, continued to employ the old terminology formerly used to refer to the great men of the kingdom, *proceres, optimates, fideles*. This resistance weakened just at the time when the king reestablished relations with the most important men of the feudal world. Only then did *baro* begin, in the deeds of the royal chancery, to take the place of the old terms, which gradually disappeared. In 1150 for the first time the expression "barons of the kingdom" replaced *proceres regni*, used up until then without distinction. Where in the past there had been reference made to the council of bishops and magnates, now it was to the prelates and barons.

But although "baron" replaced "prince" and "magnate," it was not an equivalent. In royal deeds, baron was not used only of the magnates but was used to refer both to the most powerful princes and to the most petty of lords. Even a simple *castellanus*—the officer looking after a castle for a lord—could be given this name. However, it was hardly appealing for men of the importance of the duke of Burgundy or the count of Flanders to see themselves given the same name that they reserved for their own vassals. But then they were also confused with the royal knights, so what did it matter? It seemed as if even in the vocabulary there was a desire to establish the idea that the king did not have a special relationship only with the great, but with the whole of the nobility.[46]

It was hard to maintain this fiction when it came to the princes. There too the Carolingian legend provided a model. Among Charlemagne's barons, the poets distinguished those who had a special right to speak at the council because they were the most noble and powerful. It had become habitual to depict the monarch surrounded by a group of twelve heroes, twelve of the most faithful and noble peers, or sometimes twelve of the king's nephews. The number twelve was of course symbolic, among other things, of Christ's twelve disciples. This imaginary structure now had to be applied to the reality of the relations between the great territorial princes and the king, to make them play their part in the solemn scene that was being created around him. The great princes of the Church were, it appears, the first to accept a place that satisfied their pride, even if it was not strictly canonical. Had not "Turpin of Rheims" before them pointed the way? Was it a coincidence that the first known peer was Henry, duke and archbishop of Rheims and also the king's brother?

We find the first mention of the title in 1171, but it probably dates back to the election of Henry and the ceremony of his investiture by the king in 1162 at the time of the awarding of the *regalia* to the new bishop. On the other hand, the peerage seems not to have existed in 1153, when a dispute between the duke of Burgundy and the bishop of Langres was decided without any reference to peers. Revealing too are the terms of the treaty of 1177 between the king of France and the duke of Normandy. A court of arbitration was provided for in the case of disagreement between the two princes; it was to include twelve members, six bishops and six barons, half of each group being chosen by the other group. In 1180, the count of Champagne is called "peer of France."[47]

From the idea of a special position for six ecclesiastical peers—the bishops of Rheims, Laon, Langres, Châlons, Beauvais, and Noyon—and six lay peers—the dukes or counts of Flanders, Aquitaine, Burgundy, Normandy, Toulouse, and Champagne—the idea developed a little later into one encompassing judicial privileges.[48]

In order to establish their legitimate existence, some magnates were obliged to claim a place—purely honorary—in the royal entourage. Hugh of Clers, a member of the suite of Henry Plantagenet, composed in 1158 a small treatise to claim for his master the post of seneschal when he was at the court of France. And it will be recalled that the count of Anjou in the *Chanson de Roland* was Charlemagne's standard-bearer. Hugh dwells on concrete actions—cutting the bread and bringing the food. Reality once again has to be adjusted: in 1169 and 1179 Henry the Younger, son of the king of England, serves the king on his knees and cuts his meat for him, when sixty years before another Henry, his ancestor, had refused to pay homage.[49] The function is obscured here by the ceremony.

Through these symbolic gestures of the provision of nourishment, the upper aristocracy tried in vain to reestablish a bond with the person of a king, who once again dominated them, to revive between them, even if only for a few days of pomp, the long-lost complicity and familiarity. In the liturgy of the monarchy that was taking shape at that time,[50] the magnates were forced to play their role; they had to learn, like it or not, "the taste of household bread," which lay at the origins not so much of vassalage as of the *familia*.

The symbol was powerful. From the 1150s the monarchy, by incarnating the Carolingian legend, forced the actions of power to conform to an imaginary model that it represented. The thousands of petty knights in the castles and towns of France had no difficulty in recognizing this model, for it was within them. The royal entourage gradually organized around this solid mental image the feudal bonds that had become widespread in the previous century. Little by little the lords and princes were caught in the net of a fealty that was more restricting because it was more tightly structured.

A "Real" Hierarchy

Although it unfolded in the illusion of a Carolingian *Renovatio Imperii*, the history of power in the twelfth century cannot be seen as one of a monarchy that, discarding the "mistakes" of vassalage, was rediscovering a purer conception of the state. Quite apart from its obvious anachronism, such an idea would be to look at the result without considering its development in reality. Far from being able to combat or deny the bonds of feudalism, obedience to a general power, to a "public authority," could only be established through those bonds. What was needed was to give them a hierarchical form. The Carolingians had glimpsed this path when they encouraged the magnates to develop vassalage for the royal service. But in the twelfth century it was no longer, as it was in the ninth century, a matter of keeping control over a particular structure, but of mastering social relations that had now become dominant. The strength of the movement of ideas that carried forward the new monarchy lay in the rejection of useless laments and the complete reinterpretation of the feudal-vassalic relationship in order to establish through this a political hierarchy that can properly be called a feudal hierarchy.

There had of course been chains of inherited vassalage since the tenth century and it was of these that the monarchy was to make use; but their mere existence, here and there, did not imply a proper hierarchy. For this a combination of two things was needed. First these chains needed to be greatly multiplied so that every man and every piece of land was included in them. It mattered little whether or not the king was at the head of one of these chains if they involved only a few people in one country. Second, each of the links had to remain in the same position in the chain—in other words, people of the same social level should always occupy the same place in the succession of homages. Otherwise similar bonds could quite well conclude impermanent alliances rather than sealing a firm domination. For what did the spread of chains of vassalage matter if the king could be vassal of a prince and the prince of a simple knight?[51]

The spread of relationships of submission linked to land had been the work of the princes and the important castellans, but this was a long way from being a system of chains of vassalage established in homologous and immutable sequence. The major problem was to be found at precisely that social level of the princes and lords where the most negative concept of homage dominated. In 1108 at the accession of Louis VI, three of the most important princes, pursuing a policy of humbling the monarchy to its extreme limit, had refused to pay homage to the new king.[52] The Capetian king had to fight hard to obtain it. But the reestablishment of a superior power in what was to become the kingdom of France cannot be reduced merely to a list of castles captured or lances lined up for battle; power is not just a matter of large battalions. Nor did vassalage become the same thing as the homage of peace, even when the latter was imposed, reinforced, and multiplied. Between the disquieting excuses of Eudes II of Blois or the refusal to give homage of 1108 and the famous adage of a thirteenth-century customary: "Duke, count, viscount and baron can be vassals of one another . . . and all are in the hand of the king," an extraordinary ideological upheaval took place.

To understand the origin of this change, we need to return to those petty knights of the Ile-de-France who made up the royal household. What did holding in fief mean to them? We are here in an area where more than elsewhere the fiscal estate and the estates of the great royal abbeys, of which Saint-Germain and Saint-Denis were the most prominent, were predominant. Part of the peasantry, both dependent and warlike, had for a long time become accustomed to living on the *casamenta*, the tenements of domestic knights carved out of some monastic estate. Here, although the advent of banal lordship sometimes broke up this structure into smaller elements, it did not substantially change it. The most immediate fiscal rights appear to have decayed early on, perhaps because they had been for a long time combined and confused with the manorial taxes: hence those *vicariae* that applied to certain pieces of land. The tenements of the *casati* differed from the strictly peasant tenements, and at the same time resembled them in the basic idea that the land of a family is its *casamentum*, and nothing else. There is a significant time lag in the chronology of the use of the word feudatory, which places the accent firmly on relationship to the land: in 1069 a charter of Philip I speaks of *fevati milites*, while we have to wait until the end of the century for the word to spread to the Mâconnais, Auvergne, and the Dauphiné.

But the family, even having adopted direct descent, is not a relationship. The inheritance of a fief and the successive breaking up of pieces of land multiplied the bonds of vassalage even within the lesser families of knights in the Ile-de-France. A tangled network was created where fealty, kinship, and friendship piled up on one another. With this degree of proliferation, the *casamentum* became not just a tenement but a way of thinking. But at this point too the network would have lost all coherence if tradition had not modeled it closely on the mosaic of the small fiefs that made up the patrimony of the "French" noble families. In this enfeoffed area, the relationships of one man to another copied those firmly established relations that existed between lands; a man might break his word or disassociate himself from an alliance, but it was not easy to separate a piece of land from an estate or a tenement from a manor when they belonged to a saint. The church held in mortmain; the martyrs, jealous of their property, would not give up what they held.

It has become customary to define these immutable relationships in terms which, ironically, imply movement: one piece of land "moves from" [*meut de* = is subinfeudated to] another. After 1130 such expressions become frequent in the deeds of the Paris area: a certain woman holds two acres [*arpents*] of vines from her brother "from whose fief these two acres 'move' "; a man concedes a tithe with the agreement of his uncle "from whose fief the aforementioned tithe 'moved.' " From these documents the expression spread to royal charters: in 1139 a royal notary uses it quite naturally in drawing up a deed of confirmation.[53] What strange movement was this which, far from removing family lines, fixed lineages of direct descent? It brings to mind one of the old expressions used to express the dependence of the *coloni* or the serfs and their tenements on the manor: *spectare ad, adspicere ad, obsequere*, forceful reminders of the power of the master. They had to keep their eyes on him, follow him, only move at his command. And in the pompous style of the notaries, their tenements had to behave in the same way in relation to the manor. It is also interesting to note that when it appeared, the expression was used in descriptions of movement from one lineage to another. So we may have an imitation of the genealogical systems of the time, where individuals "descend" from a single author.

It was this truly "feudal" vocabulary that the royal entourage, and particularly Suger, was to apply to the relations of the king with the magnates. The abbot of Saint-Denis, breaking with his former usage, now uses the term *feodum* to mean the principalities, and describing the relations between the king and the Norman duke, he specifies: "The king of France, strong in his high position . . . raised himself above the king of England, duke of Normandy, as above a feudatory." In another famous passage he has the duke of Aquitaine address Louis VI as follows: "If the count of Auvergne has committed some fault, then I should present him at your court on your order, since he holds from me the Auvergne that I hold from you."[54] The important thing here is the fief, the basis of the vassal bond, and not fealty.

Naturally there was an attempt to preserve the old personal concept among the territorial princes. In a letter written by St. Bernard in 1143 in support of Count Thibaud, the latter is described by Bernard as the man and the *fidelis* of the king, ready to serve him like a vassal does his lord. The vocabulary itself remains antiquated, and we have seen how the count of Blois-Champagne, like his peers, had no hesitation in swearing multiple fealties.[55] But, like it or not, they had to adopt the new ideas.

One feature is significant. In the eleventh and early twelfth centuries the princes paid homage in the name of their *honores* or for this or that town or castle. In the second half of the twelfth century, a prince paid homage for the whole of his principality, defined as a single territorial entity and seen more widely as a fief "moving" from the monarchy.[56]

The sense of the word kingdom itself had to adjust to the new structure. At the same date around 1140 an English chronicler, Henry of Huntingdon, wrote that Normandy touched the kingdom of France, and Suger himself sometimes used the word *regnum* in the sense of *Francia*, the Ile-de-France. But a few years later, Robert de Torigny, even though he sometimes criticizes such passages, is forced to admit that the duchy of Normandy "is of the kingdom of France." In 1163 and 1168, several letters name Forez, Narbonne, Burgundy, and Toulouse as *de regno*. The terms used by Abbot Stephen of Cluny to the king in 1166 are revealing: "Consider all your kingdom as one body. . . . It is not only France which is of your kingdom, although the title of king refers to it more particularly; Burgundy too is yours." And he develops the old theme of the sick member that compromises the health of the whole body. The kingdom of France has become the mystic body of the theologians, after the fashion of the Church.[57]

Thus, in the 1160s a hierarchy of land, a "real" hierarchy was established in France, which duplicated and territorialized the hierarchy of individuals. The king stood in theory at the pinnacle. However, the logic of the new system led to a significant difficulty: if the king were to hold a fief moving from (subinfeudated to) another, was he thereby enfeoffed? The question was raised, for the first time it appears, à propos of the county of the Vexin, which was land belonging to the abbey of Saint-Denis.[58]

The Vexin had been held until the end of the eleventh century by counts who were no doubt also advocates of the abbey for its many immunities in that area. It is even possible, as in the case of Saint-Riquier in the mid-eleventh century, that in the absence of a true county (estate of a count) it was the chief advocate of the abbey, appointed by the king, who took the title of count. The importance of this county, a natural defense for the king's lands against the Anglo-Normans, and its wealth were such that the monarchy was resolved to strike a blow and take it over. This was not easily accomplished. The heir of the Vexin, an orphan, was stripped of his possessions. But after King Philip had awarded them to Louis, still only a child, the royal entourage had a hard battle up to 1119 to take real possession of the region and rid it of, among others, the subadvocates who existed in large numbers. The monarchy derived an obvious advantage from the patronage of St. Denis over the former county: anyone who attacked it would be exposing himself to the anger of a protector who was widely venerated by the local peasantry. The royal usurpation was concealed beneath the powerful aegis of Denis. But the very fact of placing the accent on the seigneury of the saint rather than on that of the abbey meant that the king's legal position was delicate. He had to preach from example, showing that he too respected the sacred nature of the land of the martyr.

The problem was solved on the army's return in 1124, when the king managed to gather almost all the princes beneath the magic banner, conquering without a fight. It was a propitious moment for Suger, and the chancery drafted at his instigation a charter in which the king recognized that the county of the Vexin depended—*spectare*—on the altar of St. Denis and that he held it in fief from the martyr and his two companions. He linked this recognition with a symbolic gesture, the taking of the standard from the altar in the role of natural standard-bearer of the abbey. Thereafter the ceremony was interpreted as a ritual of investiture. Some twenty years later, when writing texts that are both a reasoned interpretation of the past and his own apologia, Suger was to make this clear. The king had "received the standard as from his lord," but, a few years later he adds to his third description of the famous scene the famous formula: "The king had recognized that he was a vassal of St. Denis and that, if he had not been king, he would have been bound to do homage to him."

The desire of Suger, a reluctant reformer, to justify the administration of an abbey in which the king was too much involved has been stressed. But whatever may have been the reasons that motivated the abbot and the royal entourage, this feudal construction of the relations of the king and the Vexin is less daring than it might appear. What is new here is not the assertion that the king will never kneel before any man, but rather that he admits to being a feudatary of an abbey. We see here, adapted to the person of the king, the position that the council of Clermont had wished to assign to the bishops, in which prelates were permitted to hold land in fief but not to do homage. The paradox is that the king, going further, demanded from his bishops not only the oath but also the giving of hands.[59] Thus only the king in France was excused homage; yet nevertheless he took only second place in the chain of vassalage. One could of course see the personal relations between saint and king as standing outside this problem. But in 1185 the thesis was once again affirmed, and this time unambiguously, since it involved the church of Amiens. Philip Augustus, taking direct control of the county of Amiens, declared that he held it from the Church, and he stated: "It consented willingly to let us hold the aforementioned fief without doing homage, since we neither owe nor can do homage to anyone."[60] This marks an intermediate stage in the setting up of the "sovereign suzerainty" of the king: he cannot do homage, but he can still hold in fief.

A few years later the decisive step was to be taken. The castle of Luzarches was held by the lords of Beaumont in fief from the counts of Clermont; the latter held it in turn from the church of Paris. On the death of the count of Clermont in 1192, Philip Augustus seized his estate, or at least as much of it as he could. The count of Beaumont then came to the king and offered him homage for the castle of Luzarches. The king answered that "he would not receive his homage, for he did not wish to be the man of the bishop of Paris; he answered in addition that the aforementioned count should go to the bishop of Paris and do homage for Luzarche to him." Philip preferred to forego the count's homage rather than enter into the chain of vassalage.[61] Henceforth the king was to be found only at the top of the system of subinfeudation; he did indeed occupy a place in the feudal hierarchy—but the only one that he could contemplate, the summit.

What were the theoretical paths that led to the formation and then justification of a "real" ladder of subinfeudation with the king at the top? We should look first at the extraordinary success of the Cluniac order or at that of the Cistercians, with their arrangement of mother houses and daughter houses, and, more generally, at the success of the hierarchical idea developed throughout the Church by the Gregorians.[62] We should look too at the development at this same period of the scholastic movement. Did the new ideas find an echo here?

The time lag between the north and the south is once again noticeable. It would have been possible, as it was later, to back up the renaissance of royal power with that of Roman law. From the first half of the twelfth century, Justinianic law had spread vigorously in the south of the kingdom in the circles of bishops and magnates and in the merchant cities.[63] The development of the episcopal estates, the influence of the papacy, and the activity of the regular canons had made it a necessary science. In the Languedoc it became what theology and canon law[64] had become in the north: a means of succeeding in princes' councils, in cathedral chapters, and even in the Roman curia. Used appropriately, the new law could be a powerful weapon in the hands of a prince. In 1162 the count of Barcelona, advised by one of the four doctors of Bologna, the famous Bulgarus, had invoked lèse-majesté at the meeting with Hugh of Les Baux, a great lord of Provence and his vassal. It was at just this time that the king of France drew up a policy for the south. In 1155, on his return from Compostella, Louis VII stayed in the Midi. While in Montpellier, renewing a tradition that had long fallen into disuse, he granted several charters. Sooner or later the royal entourage was going to find itself in a difficult confrontation with the new law.

In Paris, in fact, Roman law seemed to be little in favor. Naturally, here and there, there were masters who showed a knowledge of it— some of them indeed had come from Bologna—but it is only around

1170 that we find the first indications of the teaching of law in the Parisian schools. We can imagine the confusion of the royal court when in 1164 southerners addressed it invoking Roman law.[65]

A knight of the city of Narbonne, Berengar of Puiserguier, was in dispute with the lord of the town, Viscountess Ermengarde, over the toll. Berengar rejected the jurisdiction of the viscountess's tribunal on the grounds that Roman law forbade women to be magistrates. The dispute was also political; behind Berengar and a party of citizen knights stood the count of Toulouse, eager to reestablish his position of power over a dynasty of viscounts that had long favored his rivals in Barcelona. The viscountess was supported by an old adversary of the count's, the lord of Montpellier, and the latter's patron, the pope. The viscountess sent as advocate to the king the abbot of Saint-Paul-de-Narbonne, a collegiate abbey whose precentor at least was a Romanist. In the king's council there figured another Romanist, Master Mainier, also protected by Alexander III. The court, with some misgivings, set aside the imperial laws in favor of the usage of the kingdom; this seems in fact to have been the position taken by several southern jurists.[66]

The reasons for the monarchy's rejection of a Roman law that could have helped it are obvious. At the beginning of the eleventh century, a French bishop, Fulbert of Chartres, could without any difficulty call on the texts concerning lèse-majesté in support of King Robert.[67] In the twelfth century, the use of the *leges* had become practically impossible for the monarchy, because they had become one of the most useful tools of propaganda for the emperor, protector of the school of Bologna and the "holy laws." His imperial legislation, added to the end of the old *leges*, was a clear demonstration of the continuity of the imperial tradition.[68]

In fact, at the moment when the royal entourage was discovering Roman law, the emperor's counsellors had been aware of it for at least a generation. In 1116 and 1118, imperial charters mention consultations with Bologna. The chancellor of Conrad III since 1138 was a Romanist. He was Wibald, abbot of Stavelot, son of a family of *ministeriales*, and it was he who introduced into the deeds of the chancery the epithet *augustus* attached to the title *rex* and the systematic use of the word *imperium* to describe the power of the German sovereign.[69] The imperial faction had not been pleased to see the French monarchy adopt the Carolingian myth and they had tried in vain to recapture it. On the other hand, in the field of Roman law, their domination was too well established for anyone to dream of challenging it. The laws remained with the empire.

So it was no accident that the attempt to rearrange feudal relations in a hierarchical order sought its justification not in the arsenal of Roman laws, but in that of theology, of which Paris was to be the queen.[70] And this brings us back to Saint-Denis.

The veneration of the abbey since Carolingian times of what was believed to be a treatise by the thrice-blessed Denis is well known.

This was a neo-Platonist work, earlier translated into Latin and commented on by John Scotus Eriugena. In the cosmic vision of the Pseudo-Dionysius, the world was conceived as a succession of steps leading to God, in a pyramid of light. But this mystic work was not always well understood by hasty readers and some retained little more than the grandiose vision of the army of angels. This appears to be the use made of it by eleventh-century scholars like Gerard of Cambrai and Adalbero of Laon (where the cathedral library had a copy of the Latin translation).[71] Was it through them or their Cluniac abbot Vivien that the monks of Saint-Denis renewed contact, at the restoration of the abbey, with a text that would by now have been unfamiliar? In any event, from this date the rights of the saint to be the exclusive patron of royalty are affirmed. The treaty could not fail to be of interest to the king to whom the *laudes regiae* had long accorded the assistance of the celestial hierarchy.[72]

The twelfth century reveals the growing interest in the Pseudo-Dionysius. First of all at the abbey itself: its influence on the architecture and liturgy has been amply demonstrated. The exhibition of the relics became a pretext for astonishing public displays where innumberable Church dignitaries, dazzling in their white chasubles, ornamented with mitres and gold, processed right round the nave "more like a celestial than an earthly choir."[73] But Pseudo-Dionysius was regarded with just as much reverence by the royal house: Abelard fell from the king's favor and had to flee from Paris for having doubted the identification of the author of the treatise with the saint. A few years later, Hugh of Saint-Victor, defender of royal power, undertook a commentary.[74] In the 1160s a team of translators went to Constantinople in search of texts about their patron saint. Among them were a doctor from Avignon, Master William of Gap, who had perhaps learned Greek in Montpellier, and Master John Sarrazin, who may have been related to the royal clerk Philip Sarrazin. In 1167 they returned, bringing with them a life of the Areopagite and several other manuscripts that they began to translate. We see John of Salisbury several times pressing John Sarrazin to finish his work. The work done by this team was to serve as a basis for the Dionysian *corpus* that the Parisian schools commented upon. The new theology helped to reinforce the power of the king. The king showed his gratitude and William of Gap became abbot of Saint-Denis, the church whose patron saint he had so well served.[75]

All that remained now, "in order to allow the human spirit to raise itself up to the imitation of the celestial hierarchies," was to provide it with a symbolic object, "a fitting earthly guide," to bind the kingdom beyond the person of the king to the precious treasure guarded by the monks of Saint-Denis, the crown. In 1149 Abbot Suger described each fief of the kingdom as one floweret of the crown, with the archbisopric of Rheims as the jewel decorating its summit.[76] This was not just a pleasing image, coming as it did from a man who, recalling the Pseudo-Dionysius, wrote: "When the beauty of the different coloured stones calls me away from external cares and an honourable meditation leads me to reflect, by transposing what is material to what is immaterial, on the diversity of sacred virtues . . . I believe it is possible, by the grace of God, to be transported in a similar way from this world below to a higher world."[77] The theoretician's thoughts draw their inspiration and energy from a hypnotic ecstasy and dream. By the end of the twelfth century all the elements of the royal liturgy are in place. At the great annual festivals the ritual of coronation was repeated and royal power was revived. The Pseudo-Turpin, in describing the crowned courts of the legendary Charlemagne, is only reproducing the model before him in the courts of the king of France.[78] Are not these solemn courts, where the peers and important officers publicly performed the ritual gestures imparted to them, like a replica of the great liturgies of Saint-Denis and, beyond that, like an earthly vision of the celestical hierarchy? They are a royal mystery where the crown takes the place of the apostle's head. The crown, glittering symbol and perfect circle, reminds all those whom it dazzles with its many splendors that power is something more than the mortal person of the king.

The renaissance of royal power in the twelfth century, far from opposing the feudalization that had led in the previous century to the setting up of banal lordship, existed only through it. It completed the process by controlling it. The principal protagonists bear witness to this—the royal entourage of counsellors, petty knights trained for service by their dependent origins, who surrounded the crown as the representatives of a new and autonomous social group, that of seigneurial officers.

Strengthened by their support, the king of the four pennies emerged at the head of the feudal imagination, or rather, of a properly feudal change in the collective imagination that visualized society as a great *familia* and a collection of interconnected vassalages. The kingdom was indeed now one estate. The realization, in both senses of the word, of feudalism, the transposition and the attachment to the land of social relations of submission fix them and thus hierarchize them. Dependency is no longer discussed, it no longer needs to justify itself, it expresses itself in the space it has taken over. A vast movement of alienation gives it the strength of a natural self-evidence.

Notes

1. Boüard, "Le duché de Normandie," in Lot and Fawtier, *Histoire des institutions françaises au Moyen Age*, vol. 1 (Paris, 1957), 1 : 13; Ganshof, *La Flandre* [128], p. 400; Bonnassie, *La Catalogne* [72], pp. 685, 705, 779.
2. Werner, *Die Legitimität* [570]. On anointing, see Bloch, *Les rois thaumaturges* [607], Appendix 3, p. 462, and more recently the Rheims symposium of 1976. The Rheims legends, particularly that of the Sainte

Ampoule, no doubt helped to maintain the tradition, Bloch, *Les rois thaumaturges* [607], p. 226.
3. Duby, *Le gouvernement royal* [427].
4. Lemarignier, *Le gouvernement* [455], p. 126.
5. Ibid., pp. 67 and 146.
6. Bournazel, *Le gouvernement* [418], p. 90; *Pseudo-Turpin* [63], c. 49.
7. Spiegel, *The cult* [467]; Erlande-Brandenbourg, *Le roi est mort* [430], pp. 68 and 81; for the anniversary mass of Dagobert, Abbot Adam in the early twelfth century had the Church of Saint-Denis decorated with crowns "like the royal chamber." On the crowns, see Schramm, *Der König* [465], p. 206.
8. Bournazel, *Le gouvernement* [418], p. 100; Graboïs, *La royauté capétienne et l'Eglise au XIIe siècle*, thesis Dijon, 1963, p. 391; Duby, *La noblesse* [230] and *Bouvines* [429], p. 158.
9. Duby, *Les jeunes* [428]; Bournazel, *Le gouvernement* [418], p. 102ff.
10. Bournazel, *Le gouvernement* [418], p. 108.
11. Ibid., p. 109; Duby, *Structures* [232].
12. L. Musset, *A-t-il existé en Normandie au XIe une aristocratie d'argent?* AN, 1959, p. 285.
13. Sczaniecki, *Essai* [466]; Lyon, *From Fief* [456], despite the broadening of the field of observation, leaves aside Catalonia and Castile, where however the fief money was flourishing very early on, see Bonnassie, *Les conventions* [178a] and *La Catalogne* [72], p. 755.
14. Ganshof, *La féodalité* [189], p. 127; William of Poitiers, *Gesta Willelmi* [47], 1:16, p. 36; Bonnassie, *Les conventions* [178a]. These annual payments should not be confused with those made to mercenaries who appeared from 990 onward. The term generally used is *conducticii*, see Boussard, *Services féodaux* [95].
15. Bournazel, *Le gouvernement* [418], p. 106.
16. Boussard, *Services féodaux* [95]; Bur, *La Champagne* [74], p. 395; Lyon, *From Fief* [456], pp. 28–31; Ganshof, *La féodalité* [189], pp. 149 and 159; Guibert, *De vita sua* [46], 1:7, p. 19, and 11, p. 32.
17. John of Salisbury, *Policraticus* [51], 6:10, p. 25. The clerics of Rheims could in any case find very precise allusions to the system of the *stipendia* in antiquity in the works of Archbishop Hincmar, cf. *Pro Ecclesiae libertatum defensione PL*, 125, col. 1050.
18. Sczaniecki, *Essai* [466], pp. 24 and 44; *contra* Lyon, *From Fief* [456], p. 183.
19. Fulbert, *Letters* [38], no. 59.
20. Ganshof, *Les ministeriales* [306], p. 241.
21. Bournazel, *Le gouvernement* [418], p. 100.
22. Ibid., p. 103.
23. Suger, *Vita Ludovici* [67], 28, p. 224.
24. Diament, *La légende dionysienne* [426]; Hibbard-Loomis, *L'oriflamme* [445]; Contamine, *L'oriflamme* [423].
25. Geoffroy de Vigeois, *Chronica* [40], cap. 59; Gaier, *Le rôle militaire* [434]. On the standard of Sainte-Foy-de-Conques and its military virtues, see *Miracula Sanctae Fidis* [29], 3:18, p. 159.
26. During the siege of Paris in 885, it seemed as if the tower of the great bridge was about to collapse under the Viking attack; "Frenzied Mars was

increasing in fury, when suddenly there ran out of the sweet city a standard-bearer to equal him, who climbed up the tower, waving on a double lance a saffron cloth with wide ears [*oreilles*], the terror of the Danes," Abbo, *Le siège* [21], vv. 152–54. Edouard Favre, *Eudes, comte de Paris et roi de France* (Paris, 1893), p. 39, understood this, correctly in our opinion, to mean the "auriflame," i.e., the flame with ears, but he was hampered by a translation that confused the standard-bearer and the banner. It is known furthermore that there were links between Eudo, the defender of Paris, and the abbey of Saint-Denis where he had wished to be buried, ibid., p. 151. In their hour of danger, the Parisians turned to a guardian banner, the sight of which was believed to terrify the enemy. As much as of Charlemagne, one thinks of the ritual processions where banners were carried, attested to only in the twelfth century it is true, but the origin of which may have been much older, Le Goff, *Culture ecclésiastique* [635], p. 275.

27. See chapter 10 below.
28. Bournazel, *Le gouvernement* [418], p. 148ff.; Walter Map, text quoted ibid., p. 125, n. 26; Peter of Pisa, *PL*, 200, col. 1365.
29. See chapter 10 below.
30. St. Bernard, *Letters* [30], no. 78; Bournazel, *Le gouvernement* [418], p. 112. Abelard said *à propos* of this reform: "It was the king's opinion that the less regular this abbey was, the more useful and submissive it would be to him," *Historia calamitatum* [22]. On St. Denis *caput regni* in 1124, see Schramm, *Der König* [465], 1:135.
31. Ibid., 1:131; Kienast, *Deutschland* [450], p. 504; Hibbard-Loomis, *L'oriflamme* [445].
32. Cf. the preface to the edition by Meredith-Jones [63] and the comments and theories of André de Mandach, *La geste de Charlemagne* [677], particularly pp. 56ff. and 81ff.; see also Horrent, *Notes de critique* [446]. On its French tradition and wide diffusion, see Walpole [63].
33. Mandach, *La geste de Charlemagne* [677], p. 92, which quotes the declaration of the count of Hainault to the Roman-Germanic emperor.
34. See chapter 10 below.
35. Défourneaux, *Les Français* [613], pp. 75 and 141; Cowdrey, *The Cluniacs* [351], pp. 214ff. and 245. On Hugh of Semur and St. James, see Poly, *Le diable* [645].
36. *Historia Karoli* [63], 19, p. 168ff.; Mandach, *La geste de Charlemagne* [677], p. 81ff. It was in 1104 that Bishop Diego Gelmirez received the *pallium* and called himself archbishop, having first consulted Abbot Hugh of Cluny; the apostolic character of his church is mentioned in 1117, R. Pastor, *Diego Gelmirez; Mélanges René Crozet* (Poitiers, 1966), 1:597.
37. Bonnassie, *La Catalogne* [72], p. 415.
38. Mandach, *La geste de Charlemagne* [677], p. 114. On the question of dating, see P. Le Gentil, *La Chanson de Roland* (Paris, 1967).
39. *Historia Karoli* [63], 30, p. 216ff.
40. Barroux, *L'abbé Suger* [414]; Van de Kieft, *Deux diplômes* [469]. Barroux dates the charter to c. 1124 with reference to Suger's action; Van De Kieft, using evidence from the text itself, suggests c. 1156, during the abbacy of Odo of Deuil.

41. A. Fliche, *La querelle des investitures* (Paris, 1946), p. 143.
42. Cf. also the practice of the dues paid to the Roman Church by certain princes, Lemarignier, *Hiérarchie monastique* [454]. In *Doon de Mayence*, we also find the king of Denmark paying four "gold deniers" to Charlemagne in sign of submission, Aebischer, *Des annales* [659], p. 209.
43. Spiegel, *The Cult* [467]; for Louis IX, see Erlande-Brandenbourg, *Le roi est mort* [430], p. 86. From 1179 we can be sure that the coronation insignia at Rheims comes from Saint-Denis. The Rheims privilege that they dared not abolish was nevertheless destroyed because the queen was then crowned at Saint-Denis, ibid., p. 85.
44. Kienast, *Deutschland* [450], p. 503; Guibert, *Histoire* [46], 3:20, p. 233.
45. Normandy, 1032; Saint-Bertin, 1056; Saumur, 1086–89; Aragon, 1072; the Mâconnais, Septimania, Provence, twelfth century. Hollyman, *Le vocabulaire* [194]; Garaud, *Les châtelains de Poitou* [81], p. 90; Fauroux, *Recueil des actes des ducs de Normandie (911–1066)* (Caen, 1961), p. 195; Duby, *La société* [78], p. 348; Poly, *La Provence* [87], p. 355.
46. Bournazel, *Le gouvernement* [418], p. 152ff.
47. Lot, *Quelques mots* [457]; Lemarignier, *L'hommage* [197], p. 99; Schramm, *Der König* [465], p. 172, Köhler, *L'aventure* [668], p. 22.
48. Boulet-Sautel, *Le rôle juridictionnel* [417].
49. Bournazel, *Le gouvernement* [418], p. 122ff.; Boussard, *Le gouvernement* [420], p. 533.
50. Duby, *Bouvines* [429], p. 178.
51. Lemarignier, *Le gouvernement* [455], p. 172; *contra* Bur, *La Champagne* [74], p. 218.
52. Lemarignier, *La France médiěavale*, p. 159.
53. *Cartulaire du prieuré de Notre-Dame-de-Longpont*, ed. A. Marion, (Lyons, 1879), nos. 334 and 10; Luchaire, *Etudes sur les actes de Louis VII* (Paris, 1885), no. 39.
54. Lemarignier, *Le gouvernement* [455], p. 174.
55. Bur, *La Champagne* [74], p. 397.
56. Lot, *Fidèles* [201], pp. 18, 45 and 81.
57. Henry of Huntingdon, *Historia Anglorum*, ed. Arnold, (London, 1879), p. 260; Robert de Torigny, *Chronique*, ed. Delisle (Paris, 1871–73), 1: 207; Wood, *Regnum* [471]; Duby, *La société* [78], p. 405ff., which gives the circumstances of Stephen's letter, *RHF*, 16, 399, p. 131.
58. Lemarignier, *L'hommage* [197]; Barroux, *L'abbé Suger* [414].
59. Lemarignier, *Le gouvernement* [455], p. 175.
60. Halphen, *La place de la royauté* [444].
61. Douet d'Arc, *Recherches . . . sur les comtes de Beaumont* (Amiens, 1855), no. 217, p. 221.
62. Pacaut, *Structures monastiques* [396]; Lemarignier, *Le gouvernement* [455], p. 172; Duby, *Le gouvernement royal* [427].
63. Gaudemet, *Le droit romain* [436]; Gouron, *Les étapes* [437]; Poly, *Les légistes* [463].
64. Gouron, *Autour de Placentin* [440], *La date* [439], *Le cardinal Raymond* [442]; Poly, *Les maîtres* [464], and *La Provence* [87], p. 353.
65. Lebras, *Histoire du Droit* [379], 7:27. One should not of course exaggerate the contrast between Roman law and canon law, cf. Legendre, *La pénétration* [452]. On the social milieu, see Baldwin, *Masters* [413].

On the position of those who seem to have been called the *moderni*, see Benton, *Philology's search* [415] and M. T. Clanchy, "Moderni in Education and Government in England," *Speculum* (1975): 671.
66. Bournazel, *Le gouvernement* [418], p. 169ff. St. Bernard's hostility to Roman law is well known, Jacqueline, *Saint Bernard et le droit romain* [447].
67. Lemarignier, *A propos* [455a].
68. Bloch, *L'Empire et l'idée d'Empire* [416]; Folz, *L'idée d'Empire en Occident* . . . (Paris, 1953), p. 103. On the Bolognese revival and its links with the empire, see Calasso, *Medioevo* [421], p. 503.
69. Joris, *Wibald de Stavelot* [449] and, more generally, *Notes sur la pénétration* [448]; Kienast, *Deutschland* [450], p. 282. Many *magistri* of Lower Lorraine seem to have come from the background of the *ministeriales*, F. Vercauteren, "Un clerc liégeois du Xlle siècle, maître Benoît de Saint-Jean," *MA* (1967): 35.
70. We should remember also the canonists, such as Stephen of Tournai, Kienast, *Deutschland* [450], p. 422.
71. For a commentary in depth of this usage, see Duby, *Les trois ordres* [616], p. 141.
72. Kantorowicz, *Laudes regiae* [630].
73. Panofsky, *Architecture* [461], pp. 31 and 59.
74. Abelard, *Historia calamitatum* [22]; Hughes de Saint-Victor, *Commentarium in hierarchiam coelestem, PL,* 175, col. 130; Duby, *Les trois ordres* [616], p. 296; Kienast, *Deutschland* [450], p. 388.
75. William, Abbot, *CCN,* 7, col 380. On him and on John, see *Histoire littéraire de France,* 14:191 and 374. On Philip, Bournazel, *Le gouvernement* [418], pp. 25 and 170. Correspondence of John of Salisbury, *RHF,* 16:522, 550, 551, 570, and 578.
76. Bournazel, *Le gouvernement* [418], p. 172.
77. Panofsky, *Architecture* [461], p. 41.
78. Schramm, *Der König* [465], pp. 140, 167 and 173.

PART

II

NEW INTERPRETATIONS

"One day the chariots of the barbarians stormed the barricade placed in their way by the Roman armies. . . . This was the beginning of the Middle Ages . . . through the meeting of two societies of similar structures . . . both rural, both dependent on slaves, both dominated by strong aristocracies and a similar brutality."* The last great victory of tribalism did indeed mark the beginning of its more or less total disappearance in the West. The society of tribes was followed irrevocably by a society of orders and classes. The political form that claimed to watch over its conflicts was the one whose decline marks the threshold of this book: the Frankish state. The problems connected with the existence as well as the disappearance of this state and with the social tensions and cultural diversities that sustained and determined it will be described in Chapter 7. The following chapter considers the problems raised by the existence and transformation of different forms of land ownership in their most material aspect. Chapter 9 returns to one of the most controversial aspects of the spirituality of the eleventh and twelfth centuries—heresy, and the social upheavals that it exposed. Finally, Chapter 10 deals more broadly with the question of beliefs and ideas.

*Duby, *Les sociétés médiévales* [47].

CHAPTER 7

Political Unity
and Ethnic Opposition

History teaches us that Romulus, who gave his name to the Romans,
murdered his brother and was born of an adulterer. He created a refuge
where he took in insolvent debtors, runaway serfs, murderers and all
those whose crimes deserved capital punishment, and to this collection
of people drawn around him he gave the name of Romans. It was from
such a nobility that those whom you call "Cosmocratores," Masters of
the World, are descended!
    —The Lombard Liutprand of Cremona to the
    Byzantine emperor, Nicephorus Phocas

It has long been noted that these two opposed worlds, barbarian and
Romanizing, were not so dissimilar. The Franks, led forth by the
Merovingians, had formerly taken their places in the battle lines of the
Roman armies; and beneath the worn veneer of fifth-century Greco-
Latin culture, the native peasantry revealed the underlying traces of a
barbarism that owed nothing to the Germanic legacy. Already many
parts of the countryside had been repopulated by small groups of
barbarian prisoners who had started to farm the land.[1] But we know
little about this fusion of races and so also little of the cultures among
those working on the land. To learn more, an archaeology of humble
and everyday life is needed. The problem takes a different form at the
level of the aristocracy, the old senatorial nobility, and the new war
chieftains. Here, setting aside a few exceptions,[2] or nuances,[3] historiography seems generally unanimous: in the seventh century little
remained of the Roman world. In 1891, Fustel de Coulanges declared:
"Franks and Gauls lived together; the families intermarried and
merged. After two or three generations it had become very difficult to

tell one from the other. In the seventh century there were few people of whom it could be said with certainty that they were of Gaulish or Germanic blood."[4] It could not be said . . . yet with an annoying obstinacy it was said, and it went on being said until the tenth century. Was it archaism, conservatism, or tradition? These words describe rather than explain the phenomenon. The old question now reemerges in another form: were the social structures of the first feudal period more or less identical in the north and the south, or were there, on the contrary, significant differences?[5] In asking the question in these terms, undoubtedly broader and more accurate terms, we are inevitably brought to consider in a rather different way the matter of the fusion of the aristocracies. But by calling into question the unity of the "Frankish" structures, we destroy at the same time the idea of a single dominant class in the kingdom of the Franks. If we consider the duality of the aristocracy, then this raises the problem of the destiny of the "Carolingian state" and its meaning.

Nation and Nobility

There is no doubt that from the time of Clovis the elements for a process of fusion existed: the royal entourage, marriage, and the army gave Franks and the "Romans" the opportunity to mix and become one. But we need to know when this fusion was accomplished and to what extent. There are two directions worth examining: a reconsideration of the problems of the origins and nature of the nobility in the light of cultural differences, and a reexamination of the juridical expression of these differences—the old question of the personality of laws.

It is clear that in the seventh century the texts still carefully specify the "nation" of the magnates of whom they speak: some are Franks, or more poetically Sicambri, others Romans or Aquitainians, and also Alamans, Saxons, Thuringians, and Bretons. And it is particularly striking to see how an awareness of their different origins is preserved very distinctly among small ethnic groups, which had arrived from other areas two centuries earlier.

A certain abbot of Burgundy was the son "of a noble family of the Attici," by which was meant the old Chattuari contingents, living in the fifth century alongside the Chamavi of Amous, Scotingi of Escuens, and Warasci of the Varais in order to guard the way through the Belfort gap. Another man was said to be "of a Theifali family," a reference to the contingent of barbarian horsemen stationed in Poitou in the late empire; they left behind them their funerary stelae and the name Tiffauges. As late as the eleventh century there were still found near Courtrai the Swabians of *Suevengau* and the name Noble Saxony—*Otlinga Saxonia*—was still given to the region of the Bessin. These were in each case small contingents that preceded the great invasions and the survival of their ethnic names is all the more surprising.[6]

But this consciousness of belonging to a particular race persisted beyond the seventh century. The clearest example of this is found in the *Acts* of the bishops of Auxerre and those of the bishops of Le Mans, which until the ninth century carefully indicated the "nation" of the prelates mentioned, independently of their places of birth.

At the beginning of the ninth century there appear on the list of bishops of Auxerre the names of three bishops named as Bavarians, without having come from Bavaria. They are descendants of those six "princes of the Bavarians" to whom Pepin the Short, two generations before, had distributed practically all the estates of the bishopric. The following bishops are respectively Alaman and Frankish. But from Wala (d. 877) onward the list, which is no more than a continuation, seems to hesitate: the first successor of Wala comes from Cambrai and is called "of French nation—*natio francigena*"; the second is "from Chartres by nation . . . son of a very noble lineage from the Marches of Armorica"; the third, from Soissons, is called a Frank; the fourth is Burgundian by nation, "from our Burgundy" and his mother is *francigena*. Further on, from the mid-tenth century, only the place of birth is indicated, Auxerre or Sens.[7] The same practices existed in the Midi: at the beginning of the tenth century in Valence a collection of miracles specifies that the bishop, Regemar, ordained in 911, is *natione francus*. Since the kingdom of Vienne was at that time autonomous, it is unlikely that Regemar came directly from Francia; *francus* here cannot be an indication of geographical provenance but rather an ethnic survival.[8]

Obviously we have no desire to revive the thesis of ethnic purity or of biological continuity through the tightly knit aristocratic families of the Frankish kingdom. Different bloods had already for a long time been mixed by marriage. But quite apart from not knowing the frequency of these marriages, the question posed in these terms has no interest for us. It matters little whether this or that nobleman from Auxerre or Valence was really the descendant of Frankish or Roman ancestors; the only thing that matters here is what he thought he was. We are dealing here not with a biological but with a cultural phenomenon.

One of the fundamental elements of this culture is its naming patterns. It is one of its very obvious manifestations although it has yet been only partly exploited, despite much research over the years. We have seen that the mechanisms governing the division of names were not arbitrary and that the bearing of a name indicated not only a biological reference to an ancestor who was close or at least known, but also a choice among the names available.[9] The progressive elimination of Gallo-Roman names in favor of Germanic names is thus of great significance. It does not mean the disappearance of the old senatorial families, but it constitutes just one of the elements of their assimilation into barbarian culture. The reverse phenomenon, members of great Frankish families reviving Roman names, seldom if ever occurs. This is the clearest indication of Frankish dominance.[10] If it is difficult to know how many Gallo-Roman nobles took German names, it seems by contrast quite possible to assess the survival of names the masters in power had not used for a long time. From this point of departure we should also ask what is the significance of such a survival: nostalgia or open hostility and active resistance?

In this context we await with impatience the systematic prosopography of the eighth, ninth, and tenth centuries. The only properly established lists are those of bishops, and these could be improved. Lists of counts, viscounts, and *vassi regales* could follow.[11]

It is worth looking more closely at some of the episcopal lists, which are among the most assured and most interesting from the geographical point of view, because they come from an area of contact between the north and south.

Let us return to the Auxerre list where we can compare the names of the prelates and their nations of origin. It is easy to detect the characteristic entry of the Bavarians and Alamans in the first years of the ninth century. Up until 700, on the other hand, the names and nations are undeniably Roman. That leaves the eighth century. It opens with a Foucaud-*Folcoaldus*, a name evoking the ancestor of the Frankish counts of Toulouse. After him come three people, the uncle, the nephew, and the protegé of the latter, one of whom, the famous *Savaricus*, bears a Germanic name found particularly in the Midi. Their successors on the other hand have ultra-Roman names: Quintillian, son of another Quintillian, Cillianus or Clement, and the century closes equitably with an Aidulfus followed by a Maurinus. One is tempted to think that the Germanic names of the bishops of Auxerre in the eighth century were brought by members of the Gallo-Roman aristrocracy. Let us now compare the Auxerre list with those of Lyons, Vienne, Grenoble, and Geneva. Up to the middle of the seventh century the senatorial names reign without interruption; after 650 a few Germanic names appear, but only one is borne by a bishop described as being of the family of the Frankish kings. In the eighth century, by contrast, Frankish influence is clear, with a Lambert, former abbot of Fontenelle, and two Austreberts, one of whom is buried at Vesly near Les Andelys. An Elduin of Vienne, successor to his uncle Ado, took refuge in Lérins, while Wiliachaire of Vienne retired to Agaune. Around 800 the Bavarians and Alamans appear: Leidrade in Lyons, Vulferi in Vienne, and Arding in Grenoble.

In the ninth century the Roman names begin to make way for the Germanic names, of which only some are typically Frankish. It is probable that the Germanic infiltration occurred in successive waves: the Franks of Neustria first, as a result of the upheavals of the end of the seventh century; then the Bavarians, around 800, sons or grandsons of the contingents established by Pepin; lastly the Franks, probably Burgundians, at the end of the ninth century. The atypical Germanic names were no doubt those of local families who were very Romanized if not entirely Roman.[12]

Something similar can be seen to take place in the case of counts or viscounts, even if the Roman names are less frequent here—which is no coincidence. We remember how the Astronomer describes how Charlemagne regained control of the Midi after the battle of Ronces-valles and replaced the disloyal counts with others, generally pre-sented as Franks. In reality, more is read into this text than it actually says. The text mentions counts, abbots, and *vassi*, but the qualifica-tion, "of the Frankish race," only applies unambiguously to the latter. For the counts it is not at all certain: Ithier of Clermont has a name with various spellings, but which is probably the Roman Aetherius; Roger of Limoges was to make a will in Roman form and his wife was called Euphrasia. We find among the names of the counts that of the count of Maguelonne, Amicus, probably the father of Benedict of Aniane, alias Witiza, alias Euticius, of the old Roman-Gothic nobility, and those of Donatus, count of Melun and of his viscount Genesius.[13]

This kind of data must be interpreted with caution. Despite every-thing, in the face of so many Bernards, Williams, Lamberts, and Thier-rys, the persistence of such a divergent pattern of names must indicate the continuation into the ninth and tenth centuries of a "Roman" nobility even at the level of count, although it is a level increasingly monopolized by the Frankish aristocracy. The lists register this phe-nomenon of survival and indicate its degree. A proper study of south-ern families would help us to understand it further.

Does the continuity of this or that name in these families really imply a consciousness of genealogy, or indeed a reference to real gen-ealogies? Since the research done by Michel Rouche,[14] it would be hard to deny the existence in early eighth-century Aquitaine of a nobility proud of its "Roman" origins. These conclusions can be extended to embrace the whole of the Midi, an area beginning at Lyons or Vienne. Indeed, the best example comes from this area. This is Abbo's will, which allows us to reconstruct a network of kinship and friendship woven around a noble of senatorial family in the first half of the eighth century.

Abbo, founder of the Piedmontese abbey of Novalese, was the gover-nor, *rector*, of the Viennoise; his collaboration with the Franks gave him for a while the governorship of Provence. His personal estates stretched from Lyons to Marseilles in three groups, to the east of Lyons, near Grenoble around Vizille, and in Provence on the right bank of the Durance between Gap and Digne. The oratory founded by his family at Suza is dedicated to St. Veranus, son of St. Eucherius, bishop of Lyons and the brother of Salonius, bishop of Geneva. Through his father he would appear to be Genevan, while through his mother he is connected rather with Provence. A very high proportion of Roman names are found in his family: Maurinus and Marro, his two grand-fathers; Felix and Rustica his parents; Symphorianus his uncle and Honoria his cousin and his "most sweet" Virgilia. But this obvious Romanism in Abbo's family is tinged with Germanic influence. His grandmother was called Doda-Dhuoda; an uncle, Doon; an aunt, Ep-tolena; a female relation, Goda. Among the witnesses who signed his will—in conformity with Roman law—three, Rusticus, Symphorianus, and Vitalis, have Roman names, and only two have Germanic names. They all give themselves the title of *vir clarissimus*. If we add those people with connections with Abbo or his family we find that there is an equal number of Roman and Germanic names.[15]

It is clear that the partially Germanic—rather than "Frankish"—origins of the names in this aristocratic group do not at all signify the absence of a Roman consciousness, as demonstrated here by the use of the Roman will, the usage of noble titles fixed by imperial protocol, and the devotion to saints descended from old senatorial families—saints who were probably also their ancestors.

It appears that this continuity of the senatorial families was not disturbed by the arrival in the Midi of the Carolingians. But to look closely at this phenomenon we must leave aside the rich northern documentation, too much influenced by the Carolingian palace, al-though hitherto it has provided the chief resource for studies of this period. To learn about the southern families we must look at docu-mentary remnants, poor copies of deeds, legendary lives—all those scraps of memory that, despite the Frankish hegemony, persisted among the impoverished religious foundations of the descendents of the *clarissimi* of the late empire. Thus in the marches to the north of Aquitaine, at Deols in Berry, there was the tomb of St. Ludres [Lusor], son of the senator Leocadius, who was supposed to be one of the founders of Christianity in Bourges and whom Gregory of Tours was proud to number among his ancestors. In the tenth century, the place was in the hands of a powerful family of lords of Berry who borrowed his name and considered themselves too to be descended from Leocadius.[16] At the other end of Aquitaine, a certain count Auriol died in 809 fighting against Huesca and Saragossa; when Adhemar of Chabannes commented on the text of the royal annals two centuries later, he added to the passage this clarification—legendary, but no matter—"the count Auriol of the family of Felix Auriol, count of Périgueux," making a clear reference to the house of St. Cybard [Eparchius] of Angoulême (d. 581) whose burial place was the little abbey of Trémolat in Périgord, established on a family estate.[17] When Gerald "the Aquitainian" (d. 909), founder of Aurillac, spoke of his family, he would boast of the saints among his ancestors, Cæsarius of Arles (d. 543) and Aredius [Yrieix] of Limoges (d. 591).[18] So here we have three Aquitainian families still claiming a connection in the tenth and eleventh centuries with the Gallo-Roman *senatores*.

Further evidence is provided by some supplementary pieces of information. They all concern the Limousin, which was probably one of the chief centers of continuing Romanism. In the twelfth century the area appears to have been widely scattered with those venerated places that sheltered the remains of aristocrats who had been made saints. The local families certainly looked on these saints as their forebears. The Lastours knew, in the eleventh century, that they were descended from the founder of Guérêt in the eighth century—the senator Lantarius? The shrine of St. Pardoux [Pardulphus] was evidence of the family's ancient origin and they considered it as their personal property. They had also appropriated the relics of Ferreolus, bishop of Limoges in the sixth century, and they had transferred the bodies of "their" saints to the two small abbeys of Arnac and Nexon that housed their family tombs. At the same period, the lords of Malemort, allied to the Lastours, said that they were descended from Gerald of Aurillac. One of the family was considered a saint.[19] But the most astonishing case is that of Carissima, founder in the seventh century of the little abbey of Moutier-Rozeille close to Aubusson.

We know of Carissima from a text composed by a forger, probably at the end of the eleventh century. In Limoges as elsewhere the tenth-century bishops, such as Turpin of Aubusson, had been forced to make many concessions to their *fideles* and this document, presented as the will of a lady, appears to have been an element in the reestablishment of the estates of the abbey of Saint-Yrieix, which was attached to Saint-Martin in Tours.[20] In order to give veracity to a crude forgery, the scribe supports the document with reference to two monuments that his contemporaries could not impugn: the tomb of Carissima, at Mouton-Rozeille, which may have been of Pyrenean marble,[21] and a genealogy that mentions Aredius, the great saint of the Limousin. The first scholars to study this genealogy could only consider it to be false, because of elements that paradoxically today prove its authenticity.[22] The genealogy extends over ten generations and includes no less than forty-five names, all Gallo-Roman except for five. In this family we find a Frankish king before Clovis, three bishops of Limoges, Bourges, and Le Puy, two Spanish martyrs, and some important people, *principes*, whose names evoke Trèves, Ravenna, Bourges, Périgueux, and Limoges.

Thanks to this exceptional document, we know not only the kinship of a noblewoman of the Limousin around the middle of the seventh century, but also we see that the *stemma*, or family trees, that underlay the noble consciousness still existed in the eleventh century. Thus the family references of a Gerald of Aurillac or a lord of Lastours can be explained as more than just vague reminiscences.

We could quote other examples. For the moment it is enough to establish the phenomenon. Even if some genealogical details are legendary, they reveal a clear desire to establish links with certain ancestors, all of whom belong to the senatorial order, or to what remained of it in the sixth century. Concrete details helped to fix and retain the noble origins: venerated places where lay the heavy marble or stone sarcophagi of their ancestors or stelae preserving funerary inscriptions that commemorated their names, their virtues, and sometimes their titles and offices;[23] lives of saints, collections of miracles sometimes composed from the evidence of the stones, legends that augmented the memory in the popular consciousness; lastly, at least in certain families, veritable genealogical *stemma.*

This persistence of a consciousness of "Roman-style" nobility leads to a rather different view of the origins of the nobility. We can glimpse the triple sources from where, as late as the tenth and eleventh centuries, the southern *principes* drew their *nobilitas.* First of all perhaps in the legend of the Trojan foundation of Rome.

Lucan had already written that the noble Arvernians claimed to be the brothers of the Latins through a common Trojan ancestry. Sidonius Apollinaris boasted of Auvergne, his native land "nourished with Latin blood." Ammianus Marcellinus recalled: "Some say that a few Trojans, fleeing from the Greeks after the Sack of Troy . . . had occupied these still uninhabited places (Gaul)." The *Albini* in the fifth century traced their ancestors back to the ancient kings of the Rutules. The epitaph of the two bishops called Rurice of Limoges, grandfather and grandson, recalls their ancestors the Anicii who dominated in Rome. This is a magnificent procession of mythical ancestors: Agamemnon, Aeneas, Valerius Publicola, the Julii, Fabii, Scipios, and Gracchi.

The nobility of Gaul had earlier based its loyalty and its attachment to the *communis patria* on this identification with the origins of Rome. And when they opened Virgil, the Gaulish senators believed that they were reading in it the wonderful history of their ancestors.[24]

We have found no source that attests directly to the continuation of the legend among their descendants, but, paradoxically, it was the Franks who next laid claim to this mark of *nobilitas romana.* The Trojan origin of the Frankish people is absent in the late sixth-century history of Gregory of Tours. It appears in Fredegar after 642. We find it in the early eighth century in the *Liber historiae francorum;* a little later it reaches the chronicle of Moissac and Paul the Deacon and it was to feature prominently in royal genealogies.[25] The content of the legend is unambiguous: both in the title given by Fredegar, "The Taking of Troy and the beginning of the Franks and the Romans," and in the choice of king, Priam, thus superior even to Aeneas, who was so dear to the Romans, or in the exploits of the Franks whose relations with the empire are described to their advantage. They help the Roman army, but are exempt from paying tribute; when the emperor sends tax collectors among them, they kill them. The desire to reinterpret history and to establish Frankish domination over the ancient nobility is obvious. There were many other sources in old Germanic folk law that they could have drawn on. That they too felt obliged to look to the shores of Troy appears to have been a response to the pretensions and pride that still existed intact in the great senatorial families. And was it not also—and the aggressiveness of the tone seems to confirm it—a forced homage to a nobility that they otherwise despaired of attaining? An involuntary admission: a person is not truly noble unless Trojan, which is to say Roman. We only have to recall the efforts made by the Carolingians to connect themselves to the senatorial families.[26]

The Gaulish senators found a second source for their nobility in the coming of Christianity to Gaul. Sidonius Apollinaris recalled proudly in the epitaph of his ancestor of the same name that he had been one of the first to be converted to the new religion. We have seen above how Gregory of Tours recalls the senator Leocadius, descendant of the martyr from Lyons, Vettius Epagathus.[27] The sanctity of the beginnings had been reinforced, generation after generation, by the succession of bishop-saints whose tombs made certain urban chapels into veritable family mausoleums.

When, from the ninth century onward and even more in the eleventh century, the churches tried to establish their foundation in apostolic times, the inscriptions on these tombs provided rich material. So it was in Limoges where the geography of the tombs at Saint-Martial gives the legend its structure. In Sens a group of epitaphs provides the framework for an elaborate missionary history with local interests in mind, the touching and triple martyrdom of some disciples of St. Peter with very exotic names more reminiscent of the fourth to fifth centuries than of apostolic times: Sabinianus, his friend the rich Victorinus, and the latter's son Serotinus; Potentianus, Altin, and Eodald. The magistrates who arrested or executed them were called Quirinus, Agrippinus, and Severus Gallus. These ingenious constructions sometimes provoked bitter criticism from contemporaries. A monk from Sens complained: "We did not have these stories before, they had existed but our ancestors lost them. . . . You have given them back to us. But envy attacks these writings. Jealous men claim that you have served us up with fictions in the name of old traditions." But regardless of the criticism, the legends won the day. What was accomplished by the sanctity and nobility of a few great families was henceforth used to establish the apostolicity of the chief churches and to assert their power over the others. We can only guess at how many other churches copied Sens. All these legends need to be reexamined, not to reveal their falsity as did the scholars of the nineteenth century—quite rightly as a first stage—but in order to shed light on this phenomenon of the transference of sanctity.[28]

The "Roman" pretensions to a family monopoly of the sacred were sufficiently widespread to force the Frankish nobility to combat them. The prologue of the Salic law, in its eighth-century version, is here very revealing, "the bodies of the holy martyrs whom the Romans had burned, mutilated with irons or thrown to the beasts who tore them to pieces, were found by the Franks and covered with gold and precious stones." Here too we see a hostility to the Gallo-Roman nobility at the time when the Frankish aristocracy, by supporting the spread of the gospel in northeastern Gaul and then beyond the Rhine, was beginning to dominate the Church and to raise itself up in turn to Christian sanctity.[29]

There was a third ground on which the two aristocracies could perhaps meet. Traditionally Roman nobility had also been acquired through the exercise of public office. But there were others who were even more noble: all those who could claim to have among their ancestors an emperor, whether or not he was a usurper, like Claudius Albinus, Eparchius Avitus, or Heraclius.[30] In the seventh century or in the ninth century such a relationship takes the ambiguous form of a reference to royalty. Thus Aredius of Limoges is *ex regia parentela* and Menelas of Ménat, *regio de semine ortus*. But where it is possible to shed light on these references with other documents, they take on a different meaning. We know from Carissima's genealogy that Aredius claimed kinship with a Frankish king; on the other hand the life of Menelas, written in Carolingian times, relates him to the Emperor Heraclius. The mantle of monarchy united two traditions with very different beginnings.[31]

Given these facts, it would seem wise to reassess the "appearance" around the year 1000 of the titles of nobility in certain castellan families, at least in the southern half of France. When in the early eleventh century, Hugh of Lusignan or Rostaing of Sabran gave themselves the title *vir clarissimus* or *illustrissimus*, should we imagine that they had only then reached the ranks of the nobility?[32] It seems more likely that this was the reaffirmation of a sentiment that they had always had at the moment when their humbling by the aristocracy of the empire ceased. It was not in the circles of the Carolingian monarchy that Gerald of Aurillac or the lords of Déols sought their nobility.

We are not here questioning the suggestion of most recent historiography, where nobility means both kinship with the "royal race" and from the tenth century the building of one's own house, of a lineage in the proper sense of the word, with all that it involves in the restructuring of family relationships. We should perhaps qualify this position a little: the image of kinship given by the *libri memoriales* is a precious piece of evidence, but the problem is that these *libri* are not found everywhere; they too are part of one particular cultural model. It is striking to see that the only source for anything like them in the Midi is the cartulary of Vabre, an abbey founded by the Frankish counts of Toulouse and more generally a Frankish refuge.[33] One hypothesis is as follows: the consciousness, among some of the southern nobles, of having a place in a genealogy precisely set out in time had not completely disappeared in the course of the ninth century. Rather it had been obscured by the dominant sources that systematically favored the Frankish aristocracy, whose kinship could be displayed less easily in rational historical time. This documentary deformation is further increased by our own historiographical tendencies. As a consequence, the schema proposed, particularly by the Freiburg School, undeniably applies to the *Reichsaristokratie* of the ninth century, which, doubtless because it dominated the "Roman" families at this period, puts up a screen between these families and us, obscuring them. The opposition between two types of nobility, between the truly Carolingian *Hausadel* and the *Senatorische Adel* was to be resolved in the tenth century, when the origins of the latter were at least partly forgotten, and when the former, by adopting lineal descent, formed proper genealogies in which the position assigned to each of the ancestors gradually took the place of myths of collective nobility and heroic legends.[34] Myth and legend were pushed back to the origins of genealogies. They begin where the genealogies end. In this diffusion of a model that was both genealogical and lineal, the new princely dynasties, which were establishing themselves throughout the empire of the Franks, seem to have played an important role.

One of the most awkward obstacles to the theory of the fusion of the two nobilities, and more generally of the fusion of the two cultures, is the phenomenon known as the personality of laws. Until the tenth century the accounts of tribunals are careful to say whether they follow Roman law, Salic law, Gothic or Burgundian law. This would be a surprising survival if the races had been unified for at least two centuries. Some historians recognize the fact without attempting to explain it. Thus Lucien Musset cautiously states that in the early eighth century the division between "Roman" and barbarian "fades or more exactly survives only in the field of law." For other authors the distinction is purely theoretical: Roman law invoked here or there is according to them "an artificial ornament . . . a fossilized remnant."[35]

Account should be taken of time and place. As late as the beginning of the eighth century it is clear that a Roman legal culture was maintained even in the royal palace. A degraded culture, it will be said, if by this we mean that we are a long way from the firm conciseness of the *veteres* or the magistral elegance of Ulpian. But to leave it at that would be to rely on evidence that is both banal and insufficient. It still remains to explain what is the practice of this "degraded" law. In these terms, the problem can be posed well before the eighth century, and for certain regions of the empire or certain social classes, right in the middle of the classical period: we have here the whole question of vulgar Roman law.[36] To speak of the degradation of the law does not therefore remove the need to examine legal practices that still claimed to be Roman. In this respect it is clear that not all the regions of Gaul developed in the same way. It cannot be denied that references to Roman law in northern Gaul after the eighth century become very uncertain. The references to Roman law or Salic law seem to apply to identical practices.[37]

Let us look at one topic of great interest to contemporaries, that of slavery-servitude. There are charters from Cluny that describe the voluntary entry into slavery of a free man, justifying it with reference to Roman law. This may seem surprising: one of Diocletian's constitutions in fact forbids free men from becoming *servi* as a result of a voluntary agreement. However, when the charters clarify the reference, it is not this text to which they refer, but to a fragment by Paul on the hiring of service in the version by Benedict the Deacon, "free men can improve or worsen their state." Was this clumsiness or a clever adaptation in order to alter dispositions inadequate for an age where the sources of slavery were drying up? In the same spirit, the old formula of the guarantee of contract of sale for a slave is changed: the epileptic, *caducus*, is transformed into a prisoner of war, *captivus*, in order either to set aside this quality or to make it more precise. But in the old formula the clause *non caducus . . .* was an alternative for *mente et corpore sanus*, which was retained in the charters of the tenth century. So the accent has simply been placed on the quality of being captive, perhaps because Burgundian law freed certain captives according to their origins.[38]

In the north of Burgundy we are still close to areas where a Frankish culture dominated. The further south we go, the more frequent and the more firm become the references to Roman law. In Poitou vulgar Roman law—that of the *interpretatio* of the Breviary of Alaric—was still familiar to some writers of charters of the ninth and tenth centuries, and it appears that they did not always apply it erroneously.[39] In Limoges in 851 the different parties at a tribunal were asked what were their laws. The plaintiff and the defendant, a vassal of the bishop, said that they were Romans. In Vienne, from 870 to 928, Roman law and Salic law were carefully distinguished. In Nîmes, the region of Agde-Béziers and Provence, precise mentions of Roman law continued into the middle and even to the end of the tenth century. The thirty-year order, the public opening of a will, the public renewal of damaged charters are among the most obvious characteristics of this persistence. Conversely, the Franks used Salic rituals and vocabulary: the throwing of the straw—*festuca wadium* and *andalang*.[40] Even more than in the Midi, Catalonia provides the example of the astonishing survival of the Romano-Gothic code of Recceswinth of 654, the *Liber judiciorum*. Pierre Bonnassie has amply demonstrated that this was, as late as the tenth century, fully in force.[41]

Even if this were all, the manuscripts that have come down to us of Alaric's Breviary would be enough to reveal the survival of Roman law. In Orleans, Lyons, Clermont, Narbonne, Poitiers, and Massay in Berry the scribes continued in the ninth century to recopy the *codices* of the *lex*, sometimes on the order of the count. It should be said, though, that in competition with these integral editions there began to appear in the ninth century shortened versions that reduced the breviary to its *interpretatio*. These *libri decurtati* were still being copied in the tenth century.[42]

The most conclusive proof of the interest paid by contemporaries to the distinction between laws is provided not by the charters but by the accounts of tribunals. Up until the tenth century, all over the south care was taken to ask the parties in dispute under what law they lived, and the judge's advisors were carefully divided into *romani, salici,* and *gothi.*

It has sometimes been thought that the principle of the personality of laws disappeared before the principle of territoriality. That would be a very clear indication of cultural fusion in the different regions under consideration. We have still to see in what direction that operated. Thus, at the beginning of the ninth century at a tribunal where the abbey of Saint-Denis was in dispute with that of Fleury, there was no longer anyone in the Paris region who could apply Roman law—or what contemporaries understood by Roman law. We find only "judges of the Salic law" who, according to the text that tells us of this, cannot decide correctly on the devolution of ecclesiastical goods regulated by Roman law. The tribunal had to be moved to Orleans, and it is significant that there appeared at it a count of Melun called Donatus and a viscount by the name of Genesius. In Orleans a *legis doctor* from the Gâtinais gave judgement against Fleury.[43]

These *legis docti* were the successors of the scholars of the seventh century who knew the law. One was Didier, bishop of Cahors, and there were the three successive bishops of Clermont, Prejectus, Avit, and Bonet. At the end of the ninth century, Gerald of Aurillac quoted the Breviary to excuse the limited number of freed men he had made. His friend Abbo, a Romanized Frank who lived in the Limousin, claimed to read Justinian's *Novels.* In Angoulême, Robert, viscount of Marcillac, was *legis doctus.*[44] But such references must be treated with caution. In some cases they are mentioned in the text because they are exceptional. In the areas where *judices romani* were still numerous, there are no such mentions. By the eleventh century only a few clerics still had a knowledge, and that rather limited, of Roman law.

By contrast, we know from Agobard's invectives that the personality of the laws was still very much alive and sometimes inconvenient in Lyons at the beginning of the ninth century. Lyons was one of those towns where equal numbers of Franks, Burgundians, and Romans lived side by side. The edict of Pitres in 864, on the other hand, speaks of lands where Roman law is applied; in 865 the assembly of Tusey in Burgundy recalls the measures of the Theodosian Code, via the Breviary, which declared void any citations of law that had no date or consulate.[45] Thus there were regions in the kingdom where Roman law was the norm for the population, and where this law was still that of Alaric's Breviary. This was the period when there were uprisings in Gothia, when Charles the Bald was trying to make inroads in Provence, and when the royal *missi* were reorganizing the Midi. The texts from Pitres and Tusey are thus chiefly concerned with the southern regions; those same regions where, as we have seen, the quotations of *lex romana* are most frequent in the charters. This does not mean that Roman law had become territorial, which is to say applicable to all the residents regardless of their race—quite the opposite. The king and his counsellors did not refuse their Salic law to those Franks, counts, or *vassi regales* living in the Midi, as can be proved by the notices of tribunals. They simply recognize one fact: the primacy in the Midi of Roman law, which is the law of the majority of the population and thus appears as the national law of the people of the south. We should be wary of a false symmetry: the territorialization of personal law was probably complete in the Paris area and further north, that is, basically in Francia. To the south of the Loire, by contrast, Frankish law and Roman law, or Romanized laws like the *loi Gombette* in Burgundy or the *liber judiciorum* in Catalonia and to a lesser extent in Gothia all coexisted until the tenth century. In Gothia the Franks were in a minority and their domination was superficial: they controlled the cities but they did not change in any perceptible way the content of the law. In their own eyes, Franks and Romans coexisted, they did not mix. Their laws resembled one another's perhaps, but they still did not merge.

It was only at the beginning of the tenth century, in Poitou, that reference is made to regional custom—a much more definite indication of a true territoriality.[46] It was to appear still later in Gothia. In 933, the count of Toulouse, when asked in Toulouse *qualem legem vivebat* [what law he lived under], was still sure that he was ruled by Salic law. Six generations later, in 1095, the scribe writing the account of the *sponsalicium* of the count of Toulouse to his new wife has no hesitation in placing him under Roman law. The fusion here has come about under a Romanness that had at the same time been deprived of a great part of its content, since the law that was applied in the Midi in the eleventh century was now much more that of the *convenientiae* than that of the Breviary.[47] But this memory of Roman law, reduced to its mere evocation, surely helps to explain in part the early spread in these areas, at least among the nobility, of the Justinianic law from Italy.

Until the tenth century the distinction between laws continued to be a living phenomenon in a large part of the territory making up present-day France. It is in an important sector of social life an indication of the existence of separate cultures. The law, by dividing between "nations" and not, as the customaries of the thirteenth century do, between nobles and commoners, shows that the chief social divide on the level of the kingdom was still between "Romans" and "Franks" and not between the different aristocracies and their respective "people."[48]

This opposition between the nobilities of different origins and cultures would appear to be one of the most fruitful areas for future research, as long as its limits are clearly seen. On the one hand, the errors of an old historiography should not be revived by encouraging the idea of the continuation in the state for several centuries of the nobility of the late empire confronting barbarian princes straight out of Germanic sagas. Continuity does not exclude change and a partial reciprocal adaptation to other cultures. The coming together of legal structures, linguistic borrowings (always difficult to interpret, as in the case of *fevum*), and the influence of Germanic names are all undeniable phenomena that should not be forgotten in order all the better to be able to measure their extent.

On the other hand, it seems equally impossible nowadays to maintain the theory of the complete fusion of the aristocracies from the seventh century on. To do this is to ignore a whole section of our documentation, either because one cannot interpret it or even because it has not been considered. It is also to fail to understand and get to know better one of the most important contradictions in prefeudal society: that the specificity of the southern institutions, which is becoming a frequent theme of present-day historiography, cannot be explained as a southern particularism any more than the properties of the poppy can be explained by its sleep-inducing powers. The contrast between "southern culture" and "Frankish culture" seems to us to be inseparable from the duality of the dominant groups. This seems almost to be a tautology: it is because the separate groups existed that the cultural models we glimpse today were produced; and insofar as the cultural characteristics that can be gleaned from the documents are ordered into distinct structures we can speak of these same groups.

Is this to say that these groups are the sole bearers of the cultural characteristics that we are able to perceive? This raises the whole problem of the relationship between the aristocracies and the peasantry about whose culture we know very little, and which appears to have been divided at this time into clearly defined social levels. Our texts differentiate between those following Roman and those Salic law; can one infer that no cultural characteristics distinguished the great Gallo-Roman landowners and their households from a village community? That the preoccupations of the *vassi* of the Frankish *scarae* were the same as those of the powerful governor in the southern Marches?[49]

With these reservations in mind, it is necessary, if one is to admit the survival of distinct aristocracies, to reexamine from this point of view the issue that appeared at the very beginning of this study: the decline of the Carolingian "state."

Grandeur and Decadence of the Carolingian State

The clearly heterogenous nature of the Carolingian Empire poses *a contrario* the question of the meaning and the content of what is called, with occasional reservations, the Carolingian state.[50] Since the war it has become usual to stress to a greater or lesser degree the precarious, almost imaginary, nature of this structure.[51] Most importantly, a few, all too rare texts show that the ethnic tensions of the Merovingian period were still alive in the eighth and ninth centuries.

One only has to think of the proud accents of the prologue to the Salic law or the heavy irony of the Cassel gloss insisting on the stupidity of the Romance speakers. We should not forget also the systematic scorn of the Frankish poets and annalists, Abbo of Saint-Germain and Flodoard of Rheims, for the Aquitainians, cunning people, inconstant and untrustworthy. The monk of St-Gall at the end of the ninth century looked back with nostalgia to the time when "Gauls and Aquitainians were honored to be called the serfs of the Franks." The Lombard Liutprand of Cremona, enraged at the reception accorded to his embassy by the Byzantines, cries from the heart: "We Lombards, Saxons, Franks, Bavarians, Swabians or Burgundians despise the Romans so much that the very name (Roman) is the worst of insults that we can hurl at our enemies." And Nithard speaks proudly of the ferocity of the "hearts of steel of the Franks which even the power of the Romans could not tame."[52] The logical consequence of this tension was that turmoil and invasions from outside were regularly attributed by the Frankish chroniclers to the disloyalty of the southerners of Aquitaine or Provence.

St. Boniface speaks of "rebellions, attempts and Saracen threats which have been revealed among the Romans." The writer who continued Fredegar's work develops the theme of the betrayal of Duke Eudes and the patrician Mauronte, while the annals through the years take up and amplify the same accusation. For many Franks, any Aquitainian, any Roman, was a traitor in power who at bottom was no better than the Saracens, his allies.[53]

Michel Rouche is right to point out that these accusations reveal a certain way of thinking rather than any real alliances between southerners and Muslims. But it is clear that attempts at revolts existed. "Betrayals" and "inconstancy" had a foundation in truth, first in the rejection of Frankish domination by certain southerners and later in the suspicion of such a rejection by the Franks. This profound defiance—which was not without reasons—is revealed without evasions in the life of Benedict of Aniane written by one of his fellow Septimanians. The countryside around Nîmes, Maguelonne, and Lodève had been devastated after the Frankish liberating raids and the inhabitants reduced to famine and despair. Benedict, son of the local count, a Goth who had rallied to the Franks, founded a monastery and attempted to relieve the poverty around him. That was enough to raise accusations in the Frankish palace: Benedict was a traitor, he was becoming the spokeman of his own people, he should be called and judged. Luckily for him, he was supported by one faction of Franks and was saved.[54]

So there still remained antagonisms between the Franks and the "Romans" that it would be hard to overcome and would remain sufficiently strong to imprint on men's ideas psychological types and roles that would for a long time determine reciprocal behavior. Is it not this tension, in fact, which disguises and conceals from us all the others? Should it not be in relation to this tension that we should understand

and define the Carolingian state first and then the territorial principalities?

Jan Dhondt has emphasized, somewhat mischievously, that the weighty machine of the Carolingian army was used not only to fight the foreigner but also—and perhaps above all—to ensure Frankish dominance inside the empire.[55] This is certainly how the writer of the *Annales Mettenses priores* describes the political world of the Franks: first there was the land of the Franks themselves, then the lands of the peoples who had formerly been part of the kingdom and whom the Franks subjugated again, and then finally the foreign nations.[56] Among the faithless *gentes*, the Aquitainians obviously had an important position. Looked at from this point of view, the relationship that joined the *principatus francorum* to the peoples of the empire was often one of conquest and military occupation, a brutal and plundering domination.[57] But alongside this "semicolonial" view there is a more serene vision of an empire "where there is no . . . Aquitainian and Lombard, Burgundian or Alaman . . . but in everything and in everyone, Christ." The Spaniard Agobard exclaims: "Would to heaven that united under a single most pious king all would be ruled by a single law, that same law under which the King and his men live. . . . But that is something considerable and perhaps impossible for man."[58] Royal power at least should allow concord and peace to reign among all in the city of God. These two concepts of power clashed and dominated one another in turn.

The most concrete continuation of this duality can be found in the two faces of Frankish power: that of the expeditions, ever and again revived, of the old *scarae* of the north to a Midi whose loyalty was still suspect, and that of the *tres placita* where the Frankish count would arbitrate on disputes under the supervision of envoys from the palace. Royal power, originally founded on the decree of the Austrasian hordes, thus began to become established on the balance between the warrior groups—the count and his *vassi*, to whom was entrusted through the intermediary of their leader the management of the great governments—and the local potentates who had joined the monarchy to a greater or lesser degree or who were often protected by immunity and their position as royal vassals.[59]

This balance, expressed in the court formulae distinguishing between the *salici* on one side and the *romani* or *gothi* on the other, was not a stable one. It could tip in favor of the locals as a result of the cultural integration of the Franks who governed them.

The best example of such an occurrence is that of the William dynasty. This great Frankish family had always attempted throughout the ninth century to establish an almost autonomous domination in the Midi, and its collusion with the southerners is clear. It was this family that furthered the career of Benedict of Aniane, partisan of entente with the Franks; it was for this family that the people of Toulouse murdered their count, Bernard "the Calf"; it was probably in their favor that the Goth Miro of Conflans rebelled against the marquis of Gothia. In the household could be found Romanized Franks like Abbo, who prided himself on his knowledge of Roman law, or like his son Odo of Cluny, who went into raptures over that model of Romanness, Gerald of Aurillac. And what of those kings' sons given to the Aquitainians who wore their costume or were influenced by their bad counsel?[60]

The integration of the Frankish chiefs into the local aristrocracy merely conceals the latter's underlying desire for autonomy. One of the characteristics of some of these chieftains was indeed a tendency to autonomy. Jan Dhondt has rightly described the *Reichsaristokratie* as a "syndicate of the powerful," which chose a leader to lead the fight; its constant dream "was an oligarchy where each magnate would be largely independent, while still paying lip service to a *primus inter pares*, because that was necessary in the face of the threat from outside," and, we could add, to obtain rich plunder. But this oligarchy was to bear within itself the seeds of its own destruction: in this group each chieftain and his men struggled to overtake the others in order not to be overtaken themselves.[61] They were consequently tempted to play a decisive trump card—friendship with local nobles. These were dangerous alliances, which upset the sentiment of Frankish superiority so firmly rooted among the warriors of the north and which even more deeply sapped the very cohesion of the group, threatening its position of dominance. The ambition of the few was a threat to the power of the Frankish *populus* as a whole over the other peoples. This brought about the need at the time of the punitive expeditions to carry out the elimination of compromised groups and to replace them.[62] The cohesion of the *Reichsaristokratie* could only be preserved at the price of a permanent invasion inside the boundaries of the empire. The balance that tipped in favor of autonomy was thus each time corrected in favor of the Franks and each time too the local nobility paid a heavy tribute to Frankish greed and became a little weaker.

In this scenario, the king appears not only as the arbiter of internal conflicts in the empire's aristocracy,[63] but also equally as the regulator through these conflicts of the chief tension that set the Frankish warriors—the chosen people—against the subjugated peoples, which is to say the local nobles who had now become the defenders of the local allodialists. Among the theoreticians of the royal court who contributed the most to the exaltation of the majesty of the monarchy by insisting at the same time on the abstract nature of the function of royalty—*ministerium regis*—and by resuscitating a whole ancient vocabulary attached to the idea of *renovatio romani imperii*,[64] it is curious to notice that there are numerous southerners, Aquitainians, Goths, and Spaniards: the chancellor Helicassar, Benedict of Aniane, the Bishops Claudius of Turin, Theodulf and Jonas of Orleans, Agobard of Lyons and Prudentius of Troyes.[65] It is curious too to find in the work of the Auvergnat Gerald of Aurillac a very particular concept of the fealty owed to the king, and one that reappears nearly a century later in the work of his compatriot Gerbert.[66] And finally it is curious to note, in those areas of the Midi least influenced by the Franks, the persistence into the tenth century of solid knots of Carolingian legitimists who continued to ask for royal confirmations and who refused to calculate the date according to the reign of the usurpers.[67]

How can we reconcile such an attachment to the monarchy with the tradition of Aquitainian disloyalty? It would appear that at the same time as nourishing a desire for autonomy, the southerners, or at least the more prudent of them, were using the idea of monarchy—detached from the Frankish context and interpreted in their own way—as a shield against the demands of the warriors from the north.[68]

We have referred to the constant discrepancy in the Carolingian state between a grandiose theory, understood by only a small elite, and the greed of the dominant aristocracy. It is tempting to deny the importance of what to some historians seems rather illusory. This is, however, a rather debatable way of resolving such a contradiction, and for two reasons. First, because by proceeding in this way we fail to consider the social utility of an abstract construction. To speak of illusion at a precise historical moment in the face of a phenomenon of this importance basically resolves nothing, because it is still necessary to explain why the illusion was formed. Particularly because it is precisely the existence of such a theoretical construction of public order—however incomplete and fragile—which allows us to speak of a state in the strict meaning of the word; that is, as an abstraction apparently placed above social divisions, an essential element of power that claims to resolve the contradictions in society. However, the way in which this system is perceived or applied is only one aspect of the question: are we quite sure that such a discrepancy between doctrinal theory and governmental practice is peculiar to Carolingian society?

Even though they coexisted, so long as a cultural divide separated the Franks and the Romans, they each had in their own way need of the monarchy. Carolingian power, in the form in which it had existed at its height—the juxtaposition of a heavy military structure and a providential theory of the state—would lose its *raison d'être* on the day when they resolved these differences.

The surest mark of the end of Frankish preponderance in the kingdom was the halt in the early years of the tenth century in the great armed expeditions into the southern regions. The last important campaigns were those of the Robertians in Berry and Auvergne against the William dynasty of 892–927 and the Burgundians in Provence in 896–916. It was in the years 920–930 that the vast *pagus* of Bourges found itself divided into two areas, one looking toward the north of the kingdom and the other to the south, divisions that were to last for many centuries and leave a profound mark on the region.[69] When the king came henceforth to the Midi, it would be, for Louis V, as a rejected husband, or for Robert the Pious, as a pilgrim. The bond that united the north and the south was broken and each went their different ways. In the north the monarchy was to be transformed, while the Midi was to become a land without a king. The tradition of the public assemblies died out; the great royal abbeys of the north, strong pillars of Carolingian power, declined and almost disappeared. But the end of Frankish domination was also to be the beginning of what have become known as the territorial principalities "of the first type."

One of the few theories to have sought to explain the appearance of these territorial principalities is based on two ideas. First, Carolingian unity was nothing more at bottom than an idea of thinkers who did not take account of economic contingencies and types of government; the socio-political entity that corresponds to these historical conditions is the territorial principality. The failure of Charlemagne was inevitable in the face of this basic reality. What gave the territorial principalities their particular strength was the homogeneity of an ethnic substratum. The sense of local identity resulting from the invasions had been resisted by the Carolingians in the name of unity; this sense was to reappear, at least in part, after the fall of the monarchy. This kind of approach has the great merit of stressing the heterogeneous cultures in the period in question, in reaction against the idea, rather too easily accepted, of the total fusion of groups and cultures within the empire. It also has the advantage, in relating the survival of local identity to the principalities, of putting forward an explanation of their origins that is both universal and profound.[70]

This theory is open to several criticisms. The first is that this type of explanation is chiefly true for the marginal regions: Brittany, Gascony, and probably Normandy and Flanders certainly corresponded to distinct *populi*. But it becomes less convincing in the case of the areas that are the most important by far in the whole of the western kingdom. For Francia (in the narrow sense) first of all, the historical phenomenon did not occur either so early or with such strength as it did on the borders of the kingdom. We could even question whether it was of the same nature if we look at the relations between the king of France and the count of Anjou. Next, in the Midi, to note that Aquitaine corresponds to the region formerly conquered by the Visigoths is not in itself convincing.[71] It seems probable in fact that Aquitaine, Gothia, and Provence scarcely differed culturally; the same Roman stratum survived in them, modified here and there by the contributions of Frankish garrisons or of the Goths fleeing from Spain.[72] But the strongest argument against this theory is that the principalities were formed at precisely the time when the personality of the laws was disappearing and when there was a move toward local customary law, which implies the disappearance of or at least a significant decline in ethnic criteria. This was the moment too when, as a result of the activities of the reforming monks encouraged by some of the princes, many differences became blurred and so consequently did many antagonisms.[73]

The explanation should perhaps be reversed. It is true that the principalities were often formed on the basis of old decrees that must have taken account of preexisting socio-cultural divisions.[74] But what allowed the formation of the principality may precisely have been the weakening of a consciousness of local identity as a result of the final fusion between the Frankish rulers and their dynasty on one side and the local nobility on the other. It would be worth looking a little more closely at the names of families to the south of the Loire and on the Langres plateau and from this starting point, investigating the dominant matrimonial system in the princely families. To what extent does the image of the *Reichsaristokratie* as presented to us by the Freiburg School imply a marked endogamy by this group? How far, on the other hand, does the branching of the princely dynasties correspond to the abandonment in part at least of such a practice?

When, at the end of the ninth century, the insolence of the marquises extended to demanding the submission of the royal vassals, William of Aquitaine not only asked Gerald of Aurillac to make to him the oath of fealty due to the king, but he also offered him his sister in marriage. Gerald refused this most advantageous offer. How many men did as much? It is striking to see in the contemporary list of family names of the counts of Toulouse, until then typically Frankish—Fredol, Raimon, Bernard, Arbert—the name of Pons, associated furthermore with the old name of Raimon. The son of this Raimon-Pons, another Raimon, married Azalaïs of Anjou, widow of a certain Stephen, viscount in the region of Mende or Brioude, by whom she had had a son called Pons; and it was precisely at the beginning of the century that Raimon-Pons had come to southern Auvergne to claim the title of duke of Aquitaine. It all happened as if the taking of an illustrious Gallo-Roman name by a Frankish family was linked to its influence accrued in a region where Romanness had never disappeared.[75]

If we could form such hypotheses with more certainty, we would have to conclude that the territorial principality was not so much the finally revealed expression of an awareness of local identity that had remained active in the face of the customs and institutions of the Franks, as the result of a fusion of cultures in the aristocracy of any one area. The precise content of such a fusion in one place or another would have to be considered. In this sense the principalities would constitute on their level the final achievement of the Carolingian plan, if we accept that its aim was limited to concord between the races. It was a precarious achievement for all that, for the territorial principality, a social form that we are told was in keeping with the time, only survived in its first form for the space of a few generations, between the great crisis of the early tenth century and the rise at the end of the same century of banal lordship.

We speak of the "failure" of Charlemagne, so what can be said then of the principalities founded on the ruins of the empire? Certainly it will be said their borders were often to be those of the principalities of the twelfth century. But can we be sure? In the intervening period in many cases an important phenomenon had taken place: the break-up of the *pagus*. Any medievalist knows that the map of this or that principality in the tenth century—and the false coherence of these is often confusing—will resemble very little the map of the same principality two centuries later, with inroads made into its borders, punctured by enclaves, and sometimes wavering and uncertain in areas. The principality of the twelfth century was to be based on different foundations from that of the tenth century. The twelfth-century principality was a social form destined to perpetuate itself through the centuries in a slow movement of reassociation that was to culminate in the absolute monarchy. The tenth-century principality was a transitory form between the collapse of the Carolingian order and the feudal crisis of the year 1000.

However it is seen, the break-up of the *pagus* was closely linked to the appearance of the *consuetudines* in the widest sense of the word. They are the double representation of a phenomenon that was both unique and important that occurs on the very edge of the strict dividing line between the periods called Carolingian and feudal.

The upheavals around the year 1000 and later that rocked the principalities show that social tensions had shifted level and hence meaning. Disputes now arose within the ranks of the lords: encastellation, the dragooning of the local allodial squires, the militarization of the countryside, and the terrorism of the knights denounced by the clerics are all evidence of this resituation.[76] Now that the antagonism between the nobles had disappeared, violence welled up elsewhere. "Stealthily a movement now began which turned the whole military system in on itself, acquiring a taste for seizing by force."[77] A newly unified aristocracy began to extend its domination totally and absolutely over the countryside, a task that had probably never before been achieved. Just like the parish, banal lordship was the final stage in the enclosure of the peasants.

This is the probable explanation for the apparent initial drop in the size of military contingents.[78] The great armies, having no longer any *raison d'être*, disappear. Fighting was now the business of small groups of *milites castri*. The enemy was no longer a rebellious *populus*, but the allodialist who refused the lord's demands.

The break-up of the principalities and the establishment of banal lordship are two faces of the same crisis, which can fairly be called feudal because it introduced new social relationships that were increasingly to be crystallized around the fief. The knight's *casamentum*, the lord's castle, the territorial principality and sometimes even the peasant's holding were all fiefs. When the arbitrariness of the lord lessened and the violence of the knights calmed down, a new balance was established. Custom expressed and determined, for a while at least, a relationship of strength that did not always operate against the interests of the peasant. Just as the uneasy coexistence of the *leges* had been the chief problem of ninth-century society, so customary law showed in its diversity the area where social antagonisms were now being resolved.[79]

Both the provisional success and the decline of the first principalities would thus seem to indicate the appearance in the Midi of a new aristocracy intermingled with the ancient nobility. But a unification of this sort was not accomplished without clashes and hesitations. Once again let us return to one of the key pieces of evidence of the period, the life of Gerald of Aurillac. It shows us the kind of attitude that could be found in one of the last great southerners who refused the new order. Gerald was in fact surrounded on almost all sides. To the north, his friend Duke William pleaded with him insistently; to the west, Adhemar of Poitiers, brother-in-law of the count of Périgueux, and his *fidelis* Geoffrey of Turenne attacked him ceaselessly; to the south, Raymond of Toulouse was holding his nephew prisoner. Although he was a royal vassal, the palace abandoned him.[80] His only heirs are his nephews. Reading his life, we cannot fail to see in his behavior a certain detachment from the affairs of the world at the very time when he is involved in them—a sort of disillusioned indulgence. As a judge he does not condemn men to death, as a warrior he does not personally strike. As a lord, he allows discontented *coloni* to run away from his land. Around him moves a brightly colored world of brutal knights, sorcerers, pickpockets, obsequious merchants, debtors and grateful peasants who offer candles and sometimes their daughters. Gerald remains detached—his interests lie elsewhere. On the roads of Rome his horse moves at walking pace, well ahead of the master's escort. Gerald, beneath his hood, meditates alone. Before him they carry his sword. Odo of Cluny, his admirer and biographer, hesitates. His sanctity is neither humility nor great charity. Debts owing to him are collected, servants chastised, brigands punished, and serfs set free only in so far as it is required by law. His apparel reflects the man, "neither too rich nor too poor." What makes the sanctity of Gerald is rather this mixture of external moderation—the sense of what is reasonable and right—and of internal detachment, which recalls the aristocratic and disabused stoicism of the first-century patricians.[81] But he is the exception in his time, and as such he has no future. What was to happen after his death to the well-regulated estate in which he lived, this little world over which he ruled? It was important to protect it and preserve it. Since there was no king, Gerald remembers that he is Roman, he founds a monastery, and like many others before and after him he turns to Rome and places his property under the protection of St. Peter. For Gerald's peers, Rome was still in Rome, *caput mundi*.[82]

At the same period, the mother of Odo of Cluny gave her lands to the Abbey of Saint-Pierre of Mauriac "in honor of St Peter's in Rome."[83] In the year of Gerald's death, his lord and friend William the Pious also made donations to the prince of apostles and to Rome. We find here one of the origins, and a not unimportant one, of exemption. It was the strength and grandeur of Cluny to have recuperated and organized this current of veneration, which caused all or some of the property of worried or threatened great families of the Midi to be transferred to the patrimony of Rome.[84] It is tempting to see Cluny at the dawn of the tenth century as the last heir of Romanness in Gaul. Furthermore, the initial core of Cluny's possessions show this: lands in Auvergne and Berry come from the entourage of the vanished William family, and lands in Provence are the broken-up inheritance of a powerful clan massacred by the Burgundians. Is it coincidence that the biographer of Gerald is the abbot of Cluny? Is it a coincidence that the peace movement was to appear in the Limousin and in Auvergne before being taken up and spread by Cluny?

Notes

1. Musset, *Les invasions, Les vagues germaniques* [502], p. 222ff.
2. Thus Michel Rouche, *Les Aquitains* [510] and *L'Aquitaine* [511], p. 468. Eugen Ewig believes that the fusion was only completed around 700, in *Volkstum* [478] and *L'Aquitaine* [477].
3. Musset, *Les invasions* [502], p. 208.
4. Fustel de Coulanges, *Histoire des institutions politiques de l'ancienne France*, quoted by Tessier, *Le baptême de Clovis* (Paris, 1964), p. 366, which takes up the theme of fusion. The whole structure of Fustel's argument supporting the idea of a fusion needs analyzing. For the historiography of the question, see Bloch, *Sur les grandes invasions* [474].
5. Schneider, *Ouverture au Colloque: Les structures sociales de l'Aquitaine;* cf. *Structures . . .*
6. Ewig, *Volkstum* [478].
7. L. M. Duru, ed., *Gesta pontificum Autissiodorensium*, Bibl. hist. de l'Yonne, vol. 1 (Auxerre, 1850). On the different editions of the *gesta,* see L. Duchesne, *Fastes épiscopaux de l'ancienne Gaule* (Paris, 1899), 2:427. Walther Kienast, *Studien* [494], p. 21, which looks at the Le Mans list, revealing in the late eighth century one mention of birth in Chartres and in the early ninth century the qualification *natione francus, ex Francia natus.* For a new reading of these *Acta,* see Sot, *Historiographie* [267], which compares them to the model of direct descent.
8. U. Chevalier, ed., *Miracula sancti Apollinaris, Bull. d'Hist. eccl. et d'arch. relig.,* 15:38.
9. One can see the advances made in the study of names when we compare the brief essay of Ferdinand Lot, "L'anthroponymie française," *Recueil . . .,* 3:441, and the recent studies of Karl Ferdinand Werner, *Bedeutende Adelsfamilien* [518], *Liens de parenté* [279] and *Problèmes de l'exploitation* [16]. Georges Duby has shown what can be gleaned from a study of the names of the knights of the Mâconnais in the eleventh and twelfth centuries, in *Lignages* [235]. For an urban milieu in the twelfth century, see Kedar, *Noms de saints* [493]; on two peasant milieux in the ninth century, see Rosellini, *Les noms de personne* [509]. With reservations, one can also use Morlet, *Les noms de personne* [501].

10. On the Germanization of the names of bishops, see Musset, *Les invasions* [502], p. 190. The process in reverse in Visigothic Spain, Abadal, *A propos du legs* [472]. Tables for the sixth and seventh centuries, Rouche, *L'Aquitaine* [511], p. 171ff.

11. Available soon on the bishops will be Engels and Weinfurter, *Series episcoporum* [15], which will bring up to date the older lists of Gams. For the royal officers in the seventh century, see H. Ebling, *Prosopographie der Amtsträger des Merovingerreiches von Chlotar II bis Karl Martel* (Munich, 1974). On the senatorial nobility, see Stroheker, *Der Senatorische Adel* [514]. For the counts, G. Kurth, "De la nationalité des comtes mérovingiens," *Mélanges, Paul Fabre* (Paris, 1902), p. 23. On methodology, see R. Chastagnol, "La prosopographie. Méthode de recherche sur l'histoire du Bas-Empire," *AESC* (1970):1229. For the period we are concerned with, it is not always easy to separate prosopographical studies from genealogical studies, cf. for Italy, Hlawitschka, *Franken* [491]. We await the results of the *prosopographia regnorum orbis latini*, being produced by the German Historical Institute of Paris [Institut historique allemand].

12. Duchesne, *Fastes épiscopaux*, 1:146, 221, 225 and 2:161, 440. On the survival of Roman names in Provence, Poly, *La Provence* [87], p. 52. On the impression of direct descent given by these lists, Sot, *Historiographic* [267].

13. Text quoted above, p. 51. Of the three categories listed in the text, counts, abbots, and vassals, the only ones that from the grammatical structure of the sentence are definitely *ex gente Francorum* are the latter. Walther Kienast, *Studien* [494], p. 53, takes the reference to include the counts and abbots. For a critical study of the will of Roger, see R. de Lasteyrie, *Etudes sur les comtes et les vicomtes de Limoges* (Paris, 1874), p. 14. Amicus: *Vita Benedicti* 1, *MGH*, 16:201; Donat: Adrevald, *Miracula sancti Benedicti* 27, *MGH, SS*, 15:490, and Werner, *Untersuchungen* [278], 2:157.

14. Rouche, *L'Aquitaine* [511], especially, pp. 168 and 341ff.

15. Deed known from the confirmation of it by Charlemagne. J. Marion, *Cartulaires de Grenoble* (Paris, 1869), p. 33, and G. de Manteyer, *La Provence du Ier au XIIe siècle* (Paris, 1905), p. 72. Abbo mentions among his relations a bishop, Wandalbert (successor of a Bishop Abbo in Besançon, Duchesne, *Fastes épiscopaux*, 3:201), which recalls another family of senatorial origin, that of Duke Waldelen, described by Werner, *Bedeutende Adelsfamilien* [518].

16. Wollasch, *Königtum* [522].

17. Adhemar de Chabannes, *Chronicon* [24], 2:22, p. 100. Cybard's relations were buried there *velut in proprio jure paterno*, Adhemar tells us in the eleventh century, Rouche, *L'Aquitaine* [511], p. 217.

18. Schneider, *Aspects de la Société* [512]; on the adjective *aquitanus*, Rouche, *L'Aquitaine* [511], p. 417.

19. Cf. the long list of holy places given by Geoffrey of Vigeois, *Chronica* [40], cap. 2, 3, 4, 15; Adhemar de Chabannes, *Chronicon* [24], 3:48, p. 171.

20. The document, discovered by Duchesne in the archives of Saint-Martin in Tours, was discussed by Lecointe, *Annales*, 3:711, then by Krusch, who follows Lecointe, *MGH, SS Rer. Merov.*, 3:611. The forgery is dated 741, while according to the genealogy Carissima lived in the first half of

the seventh century; the formula of the dating recalls the legend of Waïfre and Pepin, already found in Adhemar de Chabannes, Rouche, *L'Aquitaine* [511], p. 119; he speaks of *bordariae*, and the list of witnesses would indicate the early tenth century. In the twelfth century, Saint-Yriex had certainly recovered Rozeille, *GCN*, 2, instr. col. 177.

21. The *Pseudo-Carissima* of the will indicates that she bought her tomb from a count of Narbonne. On this type of sarcophagus used until the end of the seventh century, see Rouche, *L'Aquitaine* [511], p. 321. For the genealogy should we imagine a *stemma* painted on a wall?

22. The bishop *Astidius* of Limoges who according to the list of bishops lived in the second half of the fifth century, Duchesne, *Fastes épiscopaux*, 2:47 and 50, had for maternal grandfather a king Childebert. Some lists of Frankish kings do mention a King Childebert, *MGH, SS Rer. Merov.*, 2:307. The other elements of the commentary will be found in an article that we hope to devote to this document.

23. Pierre Riché, *Education* [508], p. 223, comments on the southern character of this area of lapidary inscriptions. Such tombs are mentioned several times by Gregory of Tours; an archaelogical example in Saint-Maxim and in Poitiérs, Salin, *La civilisation mérovingienne* 2, *Les sépultures* (Paris, 1952, repub. 1973), p. 36ff. On the link between genealogy and funerary foundations, see Duby, *Remarques* [233]. For Germany, one thinks of the *handgemal*, but it is curious to see the *Staufen* boasting of their Merovingian origins through *Hlodio*, using the funerary inscription of a probably Roman tomb, erected by a certain *Clodius* to his wife near the village of Waiblingen, Schmid, *Remarques* [266].

24. Stroheker, *Der Senatorische Adel* [514], p. 20 and n. 1, which shows that in fact the genealogical memories of these Gallo-Roman families did not go back much before the fourth century. Macrobius, *Saturnalia* 5, 18–19, ed. F. Richard, (Paris, 1937), 2:44.

25. Fredegar, 2: 4, *MGH, SS Rer. merov.*, 2:45; *Historia Daretis Frigii*, ibid., p. 123; *Liber Hist. Franc.*, ibid., p. 244; Sot, *Historiographie* [267]; Génicot, *Princes territoriaux* [138]; E. Zollner, *Geschichte der Franken* (Munich, 1970), p. 5. On the development of the theme, see Guénée, "Etat et nation en France au Moyen Age," *RH* (1969) and Poliakov, *Du mythe* [505].

26. Hlawitschka, *Die vorfahren* [492].

27. Stroheker, *Der Senatorische Adel* [514], no. 20, p. 145 and no. 214, p. 188.

28. Duchesne, *Fastes épiscopaux*, 2:401 and 405.

29. Long prologue to the Salic law, A. Holder, *Lex salica emendata (Codex Vossianus)* (Leipzig, 1879), p. 1; Werner, *Le rôle de l'aristocratie* [521]; Ewig, *Les missions* [479]; K. A. Eckhardt, ed., *Lex salica, 100 Titel-Text* (Weimar, 1953), p. 88.

30. Stroheker, *Der Senatorische Adel* [514], p. 10.

31. Boll. jul., 5:308; Ardon, *Vita Benedicti MGH, SS*, 15:214; *PL*, 133, col. 643; *MGH, SS Rer. merov.*, 5:129.

32. Garaud, *Les châtelains de Poitou* [81], p. 217; Poly, *La Provence* [87], p. 137.

33. See p. 91 above.

34. How far did the confusion between freedom and nobility, characteristic of the northern regions of the old Frankish empire, stem from this distant awareness of their collective nobility?

35. Musset, *Les invasions* [502], p. 208; Flach, *Le droit romain* [481].
36. Gaudemet, *A propos du droit vulgaire* [487].
37. Gaudemet, *Survivances* [486]; Riché, *L'enseignement* [507].
38. Jacques Flach, *Le droit romain* [481], interprets these changes as accidental; contra, Blok, *Les formules* [474a], which shows that they were often due to the adaptations of ingenious scribes or chancellors. For escaped slaves in Burgundian law, see Verlinden, *L'esclavage* [321], p. 642.
39. Garaud, *Le droit romain* [485].
40. Font-Réaux, "Cartulaire de Saint-Etienne de Limoges," *Bull. de la Soc. Arch. et Hist. du Limousin*, t. 69, 1922, no. 3; *Cluny . . .*, nos. 15, 23, 30, 88, 272, 276, 358; Stouff, *L'interpretatio* [513]; Kienast, *Studien* [494], p. 152; Poly, *La Provence* [87], p. 44.
41. Bonnassie, *La Catalogne* [72], pp. 194, 258, to which can be added Bastier, *Le testament* [222]. The same interpretation is supported by Pierre Toubert, *Le Latium* [89], p. 1229.
42. Mommsen, *Theodosiani libri XVI, Prolegemena*, p. lxv ff. and xcv.
43. Adrevald, *Miracula sancti*, see note 13 above.
44. Riché, *L'enseignement* [507]; Schneider, *Aspects de la société* [512]; on Abbo, father of Odo of Cluny, *Vita Odonis* 1:5, PL, 133, col. 48; Robert of Marcillac, Adhemar de Chabannes, *Chronicon* [24], 3:20, p. 138.
45. MGH, *Capitularia*, 2:310 and 330; Ganshof, *Contribution* [483]. It is significant that even those of the *libri decurtati* that reduce the Breviary to the *interpretationes* retain the mentions of the days and the consulates.
46. Garaud, *La droit romaine* [485].
47. HGL, 5, cols. 160 and 738; Ourliac, *La convenientia* [503].
48. *Lex nobilium*, from the end of the twelfth century, see p. 96 above.
49. Should we see a connection with the emergence of popular elements in literature from the twelfth century? See chapter 10 below.
50. On the use of the concept and its validity, see Ballandier, *Anthropologie politique* (Paris, 1966), p. 145ff. Cf. also Dhondt, *Le haut Moyen Age* [475], chapter 3.
51. The same idea with a different approach in Halphen, *L'idée d'Etat* [489]; F. L. Ganshof, "L'échec de Charlemagne," *The Carolingians . . .*, (London, 1971), p. 256; Fichtenau, *L'empire* [480], p. 214; Perroy, *Le monde carolingien* [504], p. 191.
52. Bloch, *Sur les grandes invasions* [474]; Dhondt, *Le haut Moyen Age* [475], p. 40; Kienast, *Studien* [494], pp. 22, 39 and 52; Poly, *La Provence* [87], p. 53.
53. Rouche, *Les Aquitains* [510].
54. *Vita Benedicti*, c. 29, MGH, 15(1):211. Conversely, the alliance between the little kingdom of Asturias and Charlemagne came up against an anti-Frankish reaction in the early ninth century. J. Perez de Urbel, "Los primeros siglos de la reconquista," in R. Menendez Pidal, gen. ed., *Historia de España*, vol. 6 (Madrid, 1964), 6:51.
55. Dhondt, *Le Haut Moyen Age* [475], p. 52.
56. Werner, *Les principautés* [530].
57. Dhondt, *Les principautés* [108], p. 232. On the question of military occupation, Bloch, *La société du haut Moyen Age* [473].
58. Lemarignier, *La France médiévale*, pp. 66 and 67.
59. On these groups, see p. 52 above. Fichtenau, *L'empire* [480], p. 140;

Dhondt, *Les principautés* [108], p. 42.

60. Dhondt, *Les principautés* [108], pp. 213ff. and 293ff.; Abadal, *Els primers comtes* [90]. p. 59; Perroy, *Le monde carolingien* [504], p. 210.

61. Dhondt, *Le haut Moyen Age* [475], p. 42; Tabacco, *La connessione* [269].

62. On the replacement of local aristocrats by Frankish counts, see Hlawitschka, *Franken* [491], and Poly, *La Provence* [87], p. 23.

63. He appeared then as the representative in the full sense of the word of the Frankish aristocracy as an entity, and it was through the intermediary of his *gratia* that the pressure from the different families was kept in balance. On this *gratia*, see Ganshof, *La gratia* [482]. A similar characteristic in Leon, Grassotti, *La ira regia* [488].

64. On the central idea of *respublica*, Halphen, *L'idée d'Etat* [489], or theology, Fichtenau, *L'empire* [480], p. 74.

65. On the southerners in the royal entourage, see Kienast, *Studien* [494], p. 87; Ewig, *L'Aquitaine* [477]; Wemple, *Claudius of Turin* [517]; Rouche, *L'Aquitaine* [511], p. 461.

66. Schneider, *Aspects de la société* [512]; Gerbert, *Letters* [42], no. 159.

67. Lemarignier, *Le gouvernement* [455], p. 32; Abadal, *Els primers comtes* [90], pp. 271ff. and 297; Dufour, *Recueil* [19], p. cv.

68. This explains the alternation in Aquitaine between isolation and domination, Rouche, *Les Aquitaine* [510], p. 480.

69. L. Auzias, *L'Aquitaine carolingienne* (Toulouse, Paris, 1937), p. 431ff.; Poly, *La Provence* [87], p. 13ff.; Devailly, *Le Berry* [77], pp. 122 and 172ff.

70. Dhondt, *Les principautés* [108], p. 234ff. In Germany, the matter hinges on the much more ideologically loaded question of the *Volksstämme*, particularly developed by Kienast, *Studien* [494], p. 11ff., and *Der Herzogstitel* [495]. Walther Kienast perhaps does not distinguish sufficiently between the affirmations of strictly "national" origin—*natione Burgundio*—and the later references that lay much less emphasis on it. He quotes for example in *Studien* [494], p. 39: *Betto episcopus natione hujus nostrae Burgundiae Burgundio, Senonicae urbis indigena, patre Alberico aeque Burgundione editus, matre vero vocabulo Angela Francigena.* But the passage changes in the development of his argument to "the *natio nostra Burgundiae* spoken of by the biographer . . . of the bishop." In fact, the text, which conforms by adaptation to an earlier biographical model, is more ambiguous than at first appears. Are we to understand that there were in Burgundy people other than Burgundians— Franks for example? Then we would indeed be dealing with the consciousness of belonging to the old families of the *Burgundiones.* Or does it simply mean that Betto was born in the duchy of Burgundy and not in the kingdom of Burgundy? The study of the *Gesta* as a whole shows that the mention of *natio*, a standard practice, was at just that time—the end of the ninth century—changing its meaning.

71. Besides the now rather out-of-date remarks of Ferdinand Lot in his account of the work of Dhondt (*Recueil* . . . 3 : 155), see also Manteuffel, *Problèmes* [500], Ganshof, *A propos de ducs* [484] and Werner, *Untersuchungen* [278], 2 : 256ff. The debate clearly centers on the question of the formation of a feeling of nationhood, so important for the historiography of the nineteenth and early twentieth centuries. Auguste Longnon was able to speak of "the wonderful history of the formation of French unity." For a critique of such models: see Labuda, *Tendances* [496],

Werner, *Les Nations* [519]. By contrast, Poliakov, *Des mythes* [505], points out that the fear of racism has led certain historians to reject rather too swiftly the queston of relations between race and dominant class.

72. On the Mozarabs of Catalonia, see Udina, *L'évolution* [515].
73. Lemarignier, *La France médiévale*, p. 112.
74. On the problem of the *regna*, see p. 11 above.
75. *Vie de Géraud* [34], 1:32, col. 660.
76. See pp. 33 and 136 above.
77. Duby, *Les trois ordres* [616], p. 188.
78. See p. 21 above.
79. See pp. 107 and 230 above.
80. *Vita Geraldi* [34], 1:35, and 2:28, col. 663 and 685; Adhemar de Chabannes, *Chronicon* [24], 3:21, p. 140.
81. The words of Odo of Cluny bring to mind the eulogy of Agricola by his son-in-law Tacitus: "He was preserved from the seductions of vice by his innate goodness and purity. . . . He fulfilled . . . the vain obligations of his office by keeping a just measure between economy and profusion; avoiding luxury, he earned the esteem of all. . . . When he was required to attend assizes and audiences, he was serious, assiduous, grave and almost always merciful. . . . His good-heartedness did not detract from his prestige, nor his gravity from his popularity. . . . He retained that part of philosophy which is the most difficult, a sense of moderation," Tacitus, *Agricola*, ed. E. de Saint-Denis (Paris, 1956). The theme of the magistrate opposed to the death sentence is commonly found among the educated men of the late empire.
82. Schneider, *Aspects de la société* [512]. As late as the beginning of the twelfth century, Hildebert of Lavardin was writing of the continuity of Rome through its many vicissitudes: "The standard bearing the Cross brings me more than that bearing the eagle, more Peter than Caesar, more the unarmed people than the chieftains in armor. Standing I dominated many lands, ruined I hold back Hell," Hauréau, ed., *Les mélanges poétiques d'Hildebert de Lavardin* (Paris, 1882).
83. *Cluny*, no. 532. The rarity of this type of piece in the cartulary, the importance of the property bequeathed, the date and the name of the husband of the deceased woman, Abbo, seem fairly certainly to indicate that it refers to the mother of the famous abbot. Cf. Bournazel, "Frotaire de Bourges et Eudes de Cluny, note sur quelques familles du Limousin méridional," article forthcoming in *Bull. de la Soc. Arch. et Hist. du Limousin.*
84. So too the Bourbon family for Souvigny or the Déol family for the abbey of the same name, Devailly, *Le Berry* [77], pp. 154 and 156. On the links between this entourage and the successor of Odo of Cluny, the Provençal Maiolus, see Poly, *La Provence* [87], pp. 21 and 33.

CHAPTER

8

Power and Production

The master is nourished by the serf, yet it is he who claims to nourish him.

—Adalbero of Laon

The constructions of the mind always take account, one way or another, of material life. Nevertheless, the history of ideas cannot be separated from that of the human environment at its most immediate, concrete, and mundane. An obvious fact, perhaps, but one of which we need sometimes to be reminded.[1] Institutions and economics are only separated in university courses. For a long time now the very nature of research in these fields has meant that medievalists these days pay little attention to a division that they consider irrelevant. At the very heart of this period, a social phenomenon of considerable importance, seigneury, was obstinately resisting artificial dichotomies. We are not concerned here with the economic approach to social phenomena, but with an inverse and more limited development: What are the possible connections between the institutional and social structures as described by historiography and this complex, central phenomenon of seigneury? Such an approach would shed further light on the origins of what can be called, following Georges Duby, the seigneurial mode of production.[2] This brings us to a question left to one side until now. We have seen how the establishment of judicial lordship, materially expressed in the phenomenon of "encastellation," was the essential phenomenon of the so-called feudal period, but we have ignored the forms of "agrarian power" that preceded it. Before being judicial, or banal, what was lordship like? The idea that European feudal society depended at least in its period of development on the manorial system is an old one. This idea depends on two postulates: first, the crushing predominance of the large estate in the west, only a few border areas

246

escaping,[3] and second, the existence on this large estate of labor service as the fundamental link between the land cultivated directly under the control of the master or his stewards, the demesne, and the small farms where the dependent peasants lived—tenements, manses, and the smallholdings of the *coloni*. This theory has recently come under increasingly fierce attack,[4] making it necessary to reexamine first the question of the manorial forms in the ninth and tenth centuries and then the question of lordship and its relationship to the town as a center of power.

Manor and Power

Pierre Toubert must have been thinking of medievalists when he exclaimed "even if there is no one left today who believes in the existence, even in the heart of the Frankish Empire, of a 'classic manorial system,' it is important not to replace the old theories with the convenience of confusion."[5] Nevertheless, it took more than this caution, outside of a restricted circle of specialists, to persuade people to abandon this purely abstract concept, produced *a priori* by a "combining method" whose chief fault is to amalgamate disparate elements borrowed from sources that are sometimes irreconcilable. We shall see further how this economic model works for historiography—and nowhere else. Today we need to substitute a richer and more flexible typology of the manorial system, which without too much oversimplification can be applied to a society whose cultural diversity is increasingly intelligible to the historian. It is only within the framework of such a typology that we can reconsider the question of the productive possibilities of the peasantry in the ninth and tenth centuries.

Research today seems to be moving toward a tripartite typology arranged around two traditional starting points: the structure of the manorial demesnes and their relationship to the tenements. Two versions have been offered, one for Lombardy and central Italy, the other for Flanders.

Pierre Toubert describes in Lombardy a first type, which he calls the "pioneer *curtis*". This estate is characterized by the weakness or even the absence of a proper *casa dominicata*. There are neither important manorial buildings nor large arable areas farmed by direct labor. The pioneer *curtes* were content to juxtapose two distinct economic sectors: one of direct manorial profit that was essentially derived from grazing and winegrowing; the other of peasant labor on tenements set up on the cleared woodland where a portion of the harvest went to the master. This system evolved through the increase in the number of peasant tenements at the expense of a demesne that was chiefly forest and grazing land.

A second type is that of the better established *curtes*, perhaps because they were older, which concentrated direct exploitation into areas of specialized profit: most importantly, the domestication of water, the mills and their annexes; the fishponds; particular crops, such as vines, were greatly developed; forests and grazing land, though still present, became less important than in the pioneer *curtes*. The tenants' labor service was limited to a few days' or at maximum a few weeks' work a year. This second type of estate is thus characterized by the complexity and variety of the profits of the demesne and by the secondary importance of cereal crops in the overall production of the estate.

A third type corresponds better to the classic model: here the demesne is made up essentially of vast fields growing cereals—where the labor service performed by the tenants made an important contribution.

At the other extremity of the Frankish Empire, in present-day Belgium, Adriaan Verhulst also distinguishes three types of estates.[6] First the *akker*, pieces of land resulting from Frankish forest clearance and that formed areas characterized by agricultural variety. Then the *kutter*, medium-sized demesnes sometimes created—as in the case of that of Saint-Bavo in Ghent—from the regrouping of land combining newly acquired land and tenements whose links with the demesne remained weak and where collective habits were strong. These estates often corresponded to areas considered typical of the old German structures, which had names ending in *gem*. Lastly, the *gewanne*— possibly an evolved stage of the *kutter*—where the demesne consisted of large areas of land operating a triennial rotation of crops and that here corresponded to the classic estate. These two typologies—and this comes as no surprise—do not coincide exactly, but by their simplification they allow us to envisage the coexistence in Western Europe of three manorial systems. One classic type where demesnes and tenements are equally balanced by the intermediary of labor service, which is, as Georges Duby stresses, the "crux of the system," and two other types where this balance is broken, either in favor of the tenements— the pioneer *curtes*, the *akker*—where the master is essentially a landlord, or else in favor of a demesne that makes up for its small size by the profits derived from the sharing of equipment.

A geographical division of these three types has begun to emerge. The classic estate appears to be well-established in the ninth century in the center and to the north of the Ile-de-France, in Picardy, southern Flanders or Brabant, Lorraine, Alsace, and northern Burgundy. A weaker version of this system appears in the Rhineland. The non-classic systems, on the other hand, appear in Flanders, to the west of the Seine in the Chartrain, in the Limousin and Auvergne. It is likely that the Le Mans region and southern Burgundy were part of the same zone.[7]

It remains to investigate the question of the relationships--particularly that in time—between these different methods of farming.

One might think that the nonclassic models were the result of the decay of the classic model. The most recent studies show this not to be the case, seeing the classic estate as a creation of the seventh century.[8] The only southern source of any substance is the *polyptique* of the Church of Marseilles, written in 813–814 by Bishop Wadalde. This inventory, general or almost so, was one of a series of polyptiques from Marseilles, now disappeared, going back to the eighth century. Wadalde's investigators only mention one field belonging to the demesne and seem to be more concerned with tenants than tenements. He is content to list these tenements, without ever giving the size, calling them *colonicae*, whatever the legal status of the occupant. The only specified dues, still irregular, are pasturage (one or two sheep), pannage (one pig), *tributum* (one penny), hens and eggs, probably the traditional *eulogiae*.[9] Pannage and pasturage were already customary and linked to the tithe in Gothic law; they will reappear in the tenth century. The *tributum* too had ancient roots and an astonishingly long life.[10]

It is unlikely that these were the only income that the church in Marseilles derived from its estates—some fifty pigs, thirty piglets, four hundred hens and chickens, and a hundred and forty-five dozen eggs; if these were their only resources the bishop, clerics, and poor people of the church must have often had to fast. Thus we may suppose that, in the absence of a large demesne, the *coloni* had to give in addition the customary dues, a portion of their produce as was specified in the old Roman *codices* that were still in force, that is a tenth of the harvest. This was called *taxa* in the tenth century, at other times *agrarium*.[11]

Wadalde's polyptique is basically in the mainstream of a tradition that probably extended back beyond the barbarian kingdoms to the end of the late empire. The fiscal registers or *polyptyca publica* had begun in the fifth century to mention taxes and services. From this time too palace officials had these fiscal lists put in their names. We know that in the seventh century the churches of Rome and Ravenna had polyptiques, and a fragment of the Ravenna register reveals dues that partly resemble those of Marseilles. The presents, *xenia*, consist essentially of pork, poultry, and eggs, but the dues in coin seem larger and in addition there is also in some cases the three days labor service a week, here called *opera*.[12]

The areas in the north with the system of *colonicae* seem to date from early on. At the end of the seventh century, the estates of the great Abbey of Saint-Martin of Tours consisted for the most part of *colonicae* that owed dues in wheat and wood—*agrarium* and *lignaticum*. Obviously it is not possible to prove that the abbey did not have also a demesne. But the enormous quantity of corn owed would generally be sufficient to compensate for its possible absence. The similarity to the model that emerges from Wadalde's polyptique is obvious, with one exception: the *agrarium* is fixed, being no longer a share of the harvest but a set amount. We find this changed form of the southern model in the ninth century at Mauriac in Auvergne and at Montierender in northern Burgundy.[13]

The system of *colonicae* of the early Middle Ages seems to have derived directly from the public estate of the late empire, which passed into the hands of the Church or of some important personage. Land rent, due from each *colonus* to the master of the land was, as was normal, passed over in silence in the register dealing chiefly with registering fiscal dues. The latter—dues, grazing rights, *eulogiae* or *xenia*—were in addition to the rent and increased to a greater or lesser extent without significantly altering the bond that linked the master, the owner of the land, to his tenants.

On this first type of estate we can perhaps juxtapose a second. Following the Roman agronomists who recommended direct working of the land, there appear to have been estates where the master himself farmed the land with his slaves. Here the *colonica* played only a marginal role, being a reward for freed slaves. The will of the patrician Abbo in the eighth century shows what happened to such a system when it was subject to inheritances, divisions, or acquisitions and when slaves were becoming scarce. The mention of *curtes* does not conceal the extreme fragmentation of this estate and the weakness of the demesne. In one such *curtis* in Tallard, the *colonica* is occupied by a freed man, while elsewhere, at Valernes, the text gives the impression that several families of freed men were living in the *curtis*.[14]

There is nothing to indicate that on such estates the owners were yet collaborating with the fisc to draw up proper polyptiques. It is possible that these polyptiques were from this time limited to a description of only public estates, even if on the order of the prince the name of this or that magnate might be included on the roll to note his quality as beneficiary of dues. It is striking to note that some of the polyptiques from Marseilles were drawn up precisely at the moment when the estate described was conceded on the order of the governor—patrician or count—to one of his lay agents. At the moment when the estate changes master and comes into the hands of a magnate, a new polyptique is therefore drawn up, both so that the recipient is aware of his rights and so that the conceder can retain his in the future.[15]

According to this hypothesis there would be on the one hand the estates mentioned on a polyptique where rent predominated and that could be leased out,[16] and on the other hand, the private estates that had been chiefly farmed by the owner and that from the sixth century must have been in difficulties. But as early as the sixth or seventh century, the fragment from Ravenna shows that the public authority or its representative, here the Church, had begun the habit of having included in the polyptique the *opera* owed by people who were probably *servi fiscalini*. The status of these farmers, as Verlinden shows, could not be compared with that of private slaves.[17] For them, as for the freed men, the problem was the definition and limitation of the *opera*. But through this we see a link being forged between the tenements and the land that the master farmed directly with his domestic slaves.

We move now far from Rome and Ravenna to the land between the Seine and the forest of Charbonnière. Between 623 and 639 an edict of the Frankish King Dagobert I fixed the respective obligations of the *coloni* and the *servi* on the public estates and perhaps also on those of the Church.[18] We see that the free tenants owed dues consisting of tithes, hens and eggs—the *eulogiae?*—the harness for a horse, carts, and the maintenance of the royal houses. But they owed also "piece-work," later called "furrow" (*riga*), in the fields, meadows, and vine-yards of the demesne. Alongside them lived other tenants who were *servi*. They were not particularly expected to pay dues, which are scarcely mentioned, but rather to "serve on the estate three days a week." The link between the demesne and the tenements that was first established with the *servi* was beginning to extend to the *coloni*, though admittedly in an attenuated form. This seems to be something new.

At the same period, as François-Louis Ganshof has shown, the term "manse" appears in the Paris region, spreading later to the north, to Artois and Hainault, to the east to Burgundy and Lorraine, and to the south, in the Orleanais.[19] The new term may indicate three things: first, the abandonment or the fossilization of the *agrarium* charac-teristic of the *colonica;* second, the attachment of duties, henceforth obligatory—service and labor—to tenure; last, the accent placed on the residence of the tenant. The tenement is now not so much the land that the tenant works as a sharecropper—*colere-colonica*—as the land where he lives—*manere-mansus*—in order to receive his master's or-ders. We could go so far as to say that the *mansus* was more a house, *mansio*, than a piece of land. There were still *coloni*, but in the north no longer a system of *colonicae*. In the Midi, on the other hand, the vestiges of the rent system tipped the balance in the other direction: the domiciled *servus* worked on a *colonica* just like his free neighbor.

Adriaan Verhulst has correctly pointed out that the classic *villa*, with its fairly compact estate so that those doing labor service could be near at hand, implied a vast amount of forest clearing. But he reminds us also that the hypothesis of land clearance in the early Middle Ages is controversial. Could there not be an explanation taking a middle way, which could also take into account the problem of the continuity, or lack of it, of the large estate between the fifth and ninth centuries? We know that at Palaiseau in the Ile-de-France, as also at Fontaine-Valmont in the south of present-day Belgium, the fiscal estate had succeeded the large Roman *fundi*. But in these cases as in many others these *fundi* had for the most part returned to the wild and the forest. The land clearance that would have had to accompany the setting up in the seventh century of the "classic" manorial system would have been carried out in the great *fundi* of the late empire, now passed into the hands of the Frankish king and his followers.[20] What we do not know is where the necessary labor for these clearances came from. It is perhaps no coincidence that associated with the reign of Dagobert is the story of Samo, a Frankish adventurer and slave dealer in the Elbe area.[21]

The "classic" manorial system, as described in the Carolingian polyptiques, thus appears to be the consolidation from the seventh century of the old slave system, which was by now in difficulties on the public estates. This consolidation was effective in its time, as can be seen from the vast demesnes under cultivation in the Carolingian period. But it was a system that was limited in space and time—in space because it presupposes a particularly strong and constricting *bannum*. This explains how the large classic estates are found chiefly in the same areas as the dependent Frankish warriors. The historical importance of the large estates should not let us forget that in the greater part of Western Europe it was unknown to either masters or peasants. As a model it only extended, despite Frankish domination, to the south of the Loire and the Langres plateau, another indication that this domination was far from being as total as has been imagined. As for the "Roman" aristocracy, whose survival we have discussed, it failed to carry out this "manorial consolidation," and its relations with the peasantry were probably little different from those that characterized the estates of the last empire. Similarly, the southern fiscs, carved out of the Church's estates by the Carolingians after the reconquest of the Midi, did not, it appears, benefit from a system created in the framework of the royal fisc at a time when the latter was restricted to the northern estates.

A good example of the profound diversity of the public estates is provided by the immunity of the great abbeys of the Midi and the north. In the north, immunity already signifies a true territory of power where the immunist, helped by his lay representative, maintains a garrison. In the Midi, immunity only excuses the dependents of the abbey from a certain number of obligations, without however removing the restrictions of public laws.[22]

The fiscs of the Midi, held by the Frankish counts or their men or by certain Romans loyal to them, were soon to establish the possession of public rights in a determined jurisdictional area. They did not succeed in making the southern farmers perform labor service.[23] Circumscribed in space, the classic manorial system is also limited in time: the majority of the Carolingian polyptiques describe a structure in decline, not one at its peak. The relative failure of the classic estate brings us inevitably back to the question of the situation of the peasantry in the period that precedes the setting up of banal lordship. Since 1960 historians have been almost unanimous in painting a rather black picture of the material conditions of the peasants up to the eleventh century.[24] It must be admitted that the few all-too-scarce texts that tell us about agricultural production and peasant demography are often disturbing. And the general impression that we receive from these documents is unlikely to let us imagine the peasants of the time living in abundance. For all that, should the already somber picture so vividly drawn by Georges Duby in his *Rural Economy* be further darkened? Can we be content with a phrase like: "Carolingian man was a starveling living in the woods"?[25] Such an analysis is based essentially on two areas of research: one that takes a fine-tooth comb to the texts to produce precise data on productivity, the other that tries to reconstruct the peasant demography of the period.

An analysis of the essential cereal production reveals the horrifying figure of 2 to 1 as the average yield of the period. However, this figure has only recently been established and is already being challenged, since the productivity of the fields varied enormously from year to year.[26]

Indeed, it appears that one of the texts, now the most frequently quoted, the inventory of the royal estate of Annapes, was written after a bad harvest. Raymond Delatouche notes that yields similar to that of Annapes that year—1.6 to 1—can be found again in the thirteenth, fourteenth, and even eighteenth centuries. The yield of the preceding year appears to have been 4 to 1, a figure little different from those from the twelfth century. The same author questions other known examples, such as Maisons in the Ile-de-France, where the average yield, as far as one can calculate it, falls to 0.6 to 1, which is obviously impossible, or Porzano in Lombardy, where he estimates the yields to be 3.5 to 1 for the winter grain and 2.5 to 1 for the spring grain. In these two cases, the sowing area, an essential part of the calculation, is the area capable of being sown and not necessarily the area actually sown. Only the latter figure would indicate the quantity of seed used. It is thus difficult to compare this with a stock of seed, especially when we are not even sure if this represents the entire harvest.[27]

We should probably raise the more pessimistic figures.[28] But above all, we know almost nothing about one fundamental area: did the small plots of land, tenements or allods, give similar, smaller, or greater yields than those of the demesnes on the large estates?

There are a few indications that lead one to wonder whether the yield from a smallholding was not greater. An example is a tenement, a manse of the *villa* of Villemeux near Nogent-le-Roi—twelve hectares of land supporting five adults and thirteen children. If the yields calculated for the demesne are applied to them, they would have about 220 grams of corn per day per head, that is, about 150 grams of bread. Let us now look at a small, well-established allodial estate belonging to one Ainhard, near Mortagne-au-Perche. His descendants—six adults and thirteen children—cultivate seventeen *bonniers* of land on a sharecropping basis and have four others free of dues. If we assume, as would be normal, that some land lay fallow, they have scarcely more to eat than the tenants of the large estate of Villemeux. With such rations it would be impossible to work at all. So we must assume that there were better yields or perhaps a diet that was less dependent on cereal. It would be interesting too to envisage a third level within the estate, like the medium-sized plots of land—thirty to sixty ploughed hectares—included in the estate of Saint-Bertin, where a system of direct intensive farming predominated under the personal direction of the beneficiary, who himself worked with a team of *mancipia,* sometimes of twenty or more. It is to be hoped that their laboring was not the only resource of these small *familiae,* or else that here too the yields were greater.[29]

Other indications, such as the pasturages and number of mills, point in the same direction. Villemeux had twenty-two mills, which were still there in the nineteenth century. That is a lot for fields with such bad harvests, and we know that the mills gave a good return. The mills of Annapes yielded quantities of grain almost equal to the harvest. The tenants or their allodial neighbors must have produced sufficient corn to justify the large number of mills.

It seems probable that the smallholdings gave a yield superior to that of the manorial demesnes, 5 to 1 or even sometimes perhaps 7 to 1. The possible low yields of the demesne could be explained by the lack of enthusiasm of those performing labor service and by insufficient or nonexistent manuring on overlarge fields.

If we accept that the yields of the ninth and the twelfth centuries were more or less similar,[30] one whole type of explanation of historic movement collapses. This is the theory that the expansion at the end of the eleventh and beginning of the twelfth centuries was due almost entirely to a series of technological revolutions, or in other words, on a development of the productive forces.

This view has been particularly developed by the Marxist historians, or those who considered themselves such. So Charles Parain writes: "At the beginning of the ninth century technical innovations had been acquired or introduced which ensured the economic superiority of feudal agriculture over Roman agriculture."[31] To use this kind of statement to explain the upheavals of the year 1000 is far from convincing. The heavy plow, its Nordic or Slav origins still unclear, probably existed in northern Italy and perhaps in the Rhineland and western Germany from the seventh century. It is the same for the horse harness: if the modern harness was known in Europe since 800, why was it necessary to wait nearly three centuries for the spread of the use of horses for working in the fields? Because of the institution of the triennial rotation of crops that produced oats? But that had been known for a long time. We hardly need mention the mechanical harvester known at the end of antiquity in northern Gaul and later abandoned. As for the individual tools—sickle, scythe, spade, axe—here too things are not clear. Was there a development in the usage of iron from the Carolingian period or on the contrary did it remain rare? Raymond Delatouche has remarked that "the simplest, most primitive tool, the hoe, is still the tool used for the most intensive work, gardening."[32] But the most striking example is still that most famous one of the watermill. As Pierre Toubert says: "since Marc Bloch, it has been obligatory for all those who write about the large estate to wax lyrical about the watermill."[33] Although a very ancient invention, it cannot be denied that the mill spread considerably during the early Middle Ages, and there seems no doubt that the end of the tenth and especially the eleventh centuries were an important stage in this evolution, though with slight differences according to the region in question. At the beginning of the ninth century, the lands of Saint-Germain, for example, were well provided with mills: 83 or 84 for 16 estates.[34] But the building of new mills in the eleventh century shows us perhaps more about the progress of the nucleated settlement than it does about the setting up of judicial lordship,[35] particularly since the wave of building of the eleventh century is chronologically out of step with this development.

The debate on technical innovations is in any case vitiated by the bizarre idea that the lord was the entrepreneur and the large estate the context. The peasantry on the other hand, and no doubt not deliberately, is depicted as being a weak and anaemic class without resources or initiative. The peasant is too rarely credited with any sophisticated technical knowledge. If tenants have vines, they must have learned to cultivate them on the demesne. But from whom? It was often they alone who worked on the demesne, and in the tenth century the planting contracts are a clear demonstration of the confidence of the great landowners in the ability of the peasants. If they pay their dues in honey and wax, these historians presume that they must have found a little in the woods. And yet the barbarian laws speak of apiculture and the polyptiques and inventories mention dues paid in hives; and it is well known what skill and attention to detail is required for beekeeping. Much could be said also about the origin of the techniques of clothmaking. Did the Frisians, who wove brightly colored and precious cloth, learn how to do it in the workshops of the estate? But there were no large estates in Frisia! The southern peasants brought to the judges leather dyed red in imitation of Cordoba leather; in the twelfth century they were forced to hand over their store of vermillion to the town tradesman.[36] In many things the towns learned from the countryside, and perhaps the men learned from the women. It is an anachronism that few medievalists would uphold to present the lord in the ninth, tenth, and eleventh centuries as an entrepreneur concerned with "technical progress." On the other hand, the lord's officers, drawn from the peasantry, were a different matter, and they were to a certain extent able to play such a role, and increasingly as their social position became established.[37]

Thus the origin of technical innovations is as problematic as their chronology. In so far as recent research has been able to date them, they appear to lag considerably behind the movement of agrarian and cereal growth that can be detected after the year 1000 and becomes established from the last quarter of the eleventh century. "It seems likely that this continuous . . . extension in the growing of cereals suitable for bread was accompanied by a marked improvement in farming practice. . . . Progress lay no doubt in the spread of these procedures, but it does not seem to have relied on their perfection."[38] The relationship between a possible "technical agrarian revolution"—hard to pin down in time—and the improvement in production of the eleventh century is still far from clear. We might do better to remember the words of Raymond Delatouche:

> There is no such thing as Carolingian agriculture, any more than there is Gaulish, Roman, barbarian, medieval, renaissance or modern agriculture. There is a traditional agriculture which appears at the dawn of history equipped with its procedures, vegetables and animals and which lasts until the only agricultural revolution in history, that which became apparent in the nineteenth century and which has been gathering pace in the last thirty years. Before this revolution no material invention had any really revolutionary consequences. . . . In this agriculture almost the only factor is man at grips with nature, his intelligence, his spirit of observation, initiative and enterprise, his effort and his numbers. This agriculture, based only on natural resources and actions, has only one method of intensifying: the increased use of human physical labor.[39]

According to this point of view, the only innovation that could increase production is demographic growth. Although this is difficult to measure precisely before the thirteenth century, it is indisputable.[40] The point of departure is the low population of the ninth century.

Corresponding to the poverty of production in a pessimistic analysis of prefeudal times is a poverty in reproduction. Certainly, even giving a favorable interpretation to the few uncertain pieces of information gleaned from the documents, the demographic picture for the period is not very cheerful: appalling child mortality, much celibacy, high female mortality, and a low life expectancy.[41] But this information can be qualified when we look at it in the broader picture. The demographic structure that we glimpse here is that of the tenants of the great estates. Now we know to what degree at later periods seigneurial constraints and familial customs are linked.[42] But can we be sure that the small allodialists lived their family life in the same way as the tenants? As with the crop yields, it might be wise to distinguish here between different types of farming. We should above all try to take account of the existence of different types of estates and, rather than making a direct link between the level of production and low population, raise the question of the relationship between the demographic structures and the structures of the estates and more generally of agriculture.

The same documents that show us different types of estate also reveal considerable demographic divergences. For example, the numerical relation of women to men: if compared with the biologically normal sex ratio, it is strongly tipped in favor of men in the large estates of the north. But infant mortality, always significant in ancient societies, affects more boys than girls. To reconcile these two pieces of information one would assume a very high mortality rate among adult females as a result of childbirth. That would be biologically "normal." But more detailed study reveals that the sex ratio is unbalanced from childhood. Thus there must be a higher rate of mortality or even of stillbirths among girls than among boys—in other words, a reversal of the normal biological ratio. The only explanation that seems possible in our present state of knowledge is infanticide—deliberate or semi-deliberate—of girls.[43] In the Midi, by contrast, the sex ratio among children is clearly in favor of girls, which corresponds to the normal mortality among boys. Can such a fundamental disparity of structures be explained by a different development of "productive forces" in the north and in the south? The tenants of Saint-Germain or Saint-Rémi of Rheims would be forced to sacrifice their girl babies not only because of the certainty of not being able to feed them but also because of a determined social relationship, the one expressed by labor service. To plough the master's fields, the tenement must supply men; working the land is harder for women and it is above all for contemporaries "contrary to nature."[44] In the south, where the tenant only had to give a tenth of his harvest, the laboring duties were lighter. It would be interesting to consider other variations if they could be established; for example variations in fertility according to the legal status of the parents. Would *servi* have as many children as free tenants? We know that status is an important factor in the allotment of peasant marriages, and that female serfs appear to have had difficulty in marrying anyone other than serfs.[45] We should not expect too much from this line of research,[46] but we could at least learn from it that within a general framework some significant differences in demographic structures could exist.[47] These demographic structures would be related more to the different types of productive relations than to a general level of productivity, which is in any case not well established. The end of the period of low population is probably connected with the great social change that embraced both the changes in the "classic" manorial structures and the end of the wars in the south.

Between production and demography lies another area to be investigated—diet. This often appeared to medieval man in its most negative aspect: famine, and its corollary, the rise in the deathrate. We know that in traditional agriculture one harvest out of four was bad, two average, and one good, with deviations ranging from 50 percent to 170 percent. Famine was the result of a succession of bad harvests. With or without effective methods of production, the Carolingian harvests, like those of the eleventh and twelfth centuries, could not fail to be affected by considerable variations, which would be enough, even on their own, to explain the famines.

Pierre Riché lists some dozen famines for the ninth century, without counting other direct or indirect factors of mortality—floods, cold winters, epidemics or diseases among animals—which added to the

famines give a figure of about thirty-four bad years. Raymond Delatouche, basing himself on the work of Marie-Jeanne Tits-Dieuaide,
gives twenty-six years of famine in Western Europe in the ninth century, as against ten for the tenth century, twenty-one in the eleventh
century, and thirty-two in the twelfth century. If we accept these
figures, we see that famine, as such, is not a phenomenon peculiar to
the Carolingian period: it ran all through the period of economic
expansion of the late eleventh and the twelfth centuries. It remains to
be seen whether its causes were always the same.[48]

Were all the famines really the inevitable consequences of poor
harvests? This brings us to the problem of the peasant surplus. We still
leave aside the case of the *servi* who were severely handicapped by
their thrice-weekly labor service. In any case we know very little about
the fate of their property, and it has perhaps been too hastily supposed
that the situation of the Carolingian *servi* was the same as that of the
serfs in the twelfth century. But there remains the cases of the other
tenants and the small allodialists. Normally, they had a surplus: the
tenants of some estates sometimes went to sell it at the market.
Should we conclude that they could not or would not stockpile it?

The magnates certainly stored the surplus. On the fisc of Annapes
the harvest from the previous year was kept, or at least a large part of it
was. This was one of the lords' virtues, at least in theory: to have
demesnes to aid the poor when they were in difficulties. Already at an
earlier date the Merovingian bishops had set the example. Did this
tradition of charity continue as it should have done, and did the rich
landowners not begin to demand from those whom they had "obliged"
much more than just entry into their *mundium* and the payment of a
chevage?

Certain capitularies condemning usurers seem to be directed more
at the merchants—"those who buy . . . in order to sell"—than at the
magnates. Was this a protection for the poor against the worst abuses or
a limitation of the role of the merchants who were in competition with
the magnates? In either case, the ban is a good indication *a contrario* of
the important role played by the big landowner's reserves of corn,
which allowed him to offer or withhold aid for his neighbors, the small
independent peasants.[49] Thus, Gerald of Aurillac, who was a saint,
lent money at interest, and those who were not among his admirers
harshly criticized him for it. Even his hagiographer, Odo of Cluny,
found only this to say in defense of his hero: he sometimes excused his
debtors from paying the interest, and sometimes even the capital.[50]
Sometimes . . . lucky debtors! But what about the others? In such a
system, bad harvests, as long as they did not happen too frequently,
were a good thing for the big landowner since they allowed him to
exercise his generosity and thereby increase his influence and power. In
the Carolingian period as in preceding centuries, there was a connection between monopoly and famine, and the schemes of the magnates
were probably just as responsible for shortages among the peasants as

were poor yields and natural variations in production. This very ancient usurious link that joined and opposed, in the Midi at least, the peasant allodialists to the landed aristocracy was still as important at the end of the ninth century—except in certain "privileged" places—as the strictly speaking manorial structures.

The "classic" estate, the most solid of the manorial systems, which had developed in the context of Frankish royalty, was already in decline almost everywhere in the ninth century. Its rigor, even its rigidity, should not deceive us: the majority of the polyptiques "describe an organism which had partly collapsed, a disintegration which they were struggling vainly to slow down."[51] The system of labor service, successor to the ancient system of slavery that had long ago been compromised but was always ready to spring up again, slowly declined, undermined by the muted but obstinate resistance of all those men written off in the documents as very poor and very humble. The system aimed to dominate them from above, and it is true that on the fiscs as on the lands of the great royal abbeys the gangs of *vassi* and the blows of immunist justice served to remind the recalcitrant of their weakness and humbleness. But it came up against those spontaneous tendencies that have always given life to the collective action of oppressed peasantries: the sabotage of forced work, flight, and incessant dealing in land or goods stolen from under the nose of the master and his stewards.[52]

Whether of the classic type, based on labor service and duties, or merely the heir to earlier models, the great estate of the ninth century did not succeed in effectively dominating the countryside. In the north, the system of labor service was both difficult to maintain and too inflexible. The establishment of a "medium" tenement, designed to maintain without a large surplus a family of laborers, came up against the problem both of variations in agrarian production and of peasant exchange. Fixing the tenements at too small a size was to expose the estate to repeated shortages. To make them bigger was to risk seeing the peasants selling the surplus in good years only to entrust themselves to the master again in bad years; we belong to the master, let him feed us. In the south, it is probable that the majority of estates did not have the *bannum*. The master had either to content himself, in a system of *colonicae*, with the portion of the harvest due to him by custom, or undertake with teams of domestic *mancipia* direct farming, necessarily limited by the increasing scarcity of servile labor.

Above all, the presence, greater or smaller but universal, of groups of allodial peasants who were partly able to escape the embrace of the estates made it difficult for the lord to control his own dependents. Freedom is an inconvenient neighbor for servitude and there were too many villages where *coloni* and serfs escaping from the *bannum* could take refuge. The only really effective way to prevent runaways and rebels was to suppress these islands of safety and to extend the manorial system in order to encompass completely the peasant masses.

That could only be accomplished on two conditions: first, the differences separating noble groups of different cultures had to be resolved and the masters united into a single aristocracy; second, a section of the peasantry itself would have to participate actively, even militantly, in this process.

Seigneury, Country, and Town

The disintegration of the "classic" large estate with its system of labor service is thus like the collapse of the Carolingian state, which is generally taken to be the threshold of the period where feudal relations became established and general, or when feudal-vassalic relations really became the dominant social relationship. But how do we reconcile this introductory phenomenon with the appearance of the chief structure of the eleventh and twelfth centuries, judicial or banal lordship? Did it emerge in an area where the classic estate predominated, or did it establish itself in regions where that system had never existed? Again with reference to the same situation, how should we analyze another phenomenon, also characteristic of the period, the establishment or reestablishment of the power of the towns over the countryside?

For a long time the problem of the transition from a period characterized (or presumed to be) by the large estates to a period dominated by banal lordship was ignored by historians for the simple reason that they made little distinction between the two structures.[53] Modern historians, by contrast, have firmly emphasized the rupture represented by the end of the tenth century, with the move from a decaying and limited system to one whose energy and extent we know.

The continuity of lordship—there had always been more or less "great" estates and peasant tenants—should not obscure the essential differences in the periods: the strengthening of the *bannum* or the lord's command in the decades that preceded the year 1000 was not successful in establishing a system of labor service where it had not previously existed, nor did it manage to reinforce it where it did exist.

Let us take the example of Lorraine. This was one of the areas favoring the classic great estate. From the tenth century, the old *villa*, a large estate held by one person, broke up without the relationship between the demesne and the manses being respected. Sometimes the alienated part was reduced to a few manses with no remaining *indominicatum*; sometimes it was limited to a portion of the demesne without adjoining manses; and sometimes the manses handed over were too far away from the demesne to be able to collaborate in a regular and workable way with its cultivation. All these cases meant sooner or later the collapse of the traditional services and the disappearance of the old status of the estate. Similarly, though the breaking up of the manse into quarters may initially have allowed the lord to demand services from a larger number of tenants than the former single tenant, it was to lead eventually to the diminution or even the disappearance of these services. And the reduction of the demesne through division into separate plots was much more the consequence than the cause of the slow process of erosion of the system of labor service. From the end of the tenth century lay lords were transferring *mancipia* to the abbeys—men who had been formerly attached to the demesne and who now swelled the numbers of the *mundiliones*. Rent began to replace labor services. Simultaneously, we see in the eleventh century the beginning of *banalités*, or, in other words, the use of the *bannum* to augment land rent, whether in kind or in money.[54]

The evolution that we have seen in Lorraine was not very different in the Midi, despite the different origins of the estates. Here little or no use was made of labor services, and the lord was already as much a landlord as a farmer. When banal lordship was established at the end of the tenth century, it did not set up labor services but instead extended and increased the levies made by the lord on the peasant households.[55] From the year 1000 in both the north and the south rent became more important than services.

It has been known for a long time, however, that the *banalités* did not have the same force in different areas. There is no better example of this disparity than the two *banalités* with a bearing on men's daily bread: the mill and the oven. Manorial mills had already been in existence for a long time when in the northern estates it became obligatory for the peasants to have their corn ground in them. Marc Bloch has stressed how unpopular this obligation was and has shown the resistance, or rather the veritable war, which it provoked among the peasants who obstinately continued to use their own hand mills and the lords who had them sought out and broken.[56]

An economist who is also a historian, Pierre Dockès, has investigated the attitude that the small peasant may have taken in the face of these two possibilities—milling by hand or taking the corn to the lord's mill—and has calculated the average cost in either case. With the hand mill it would take two people about one hour to grind 7 kilograms of corn, or enough for seven people. The due for use of the lord's mill could be anything from 10 to more than 16 percent of the corn. The time of transport has also to be taken into account. In other words, for a peasant producing only a little corn there was no advantage in going to the lord's mill. On the other hand, a peasant producing a lot—either because of the size of his holding, or because of high yields—would benefit from taking the corn to the mill. Here there was no need of a *banalité* to force him.[57]

The original reason for the building of the large manorial mills was the lord's need to cut down on the large number of women making the bread that was distributed to the members of his household. By allowing the local allodialists, and more generally the wealthier peasants, to come and use his mill, the lord was merely making an expensive installation pay for itself. Furthermore, there is nothing to prove that the poor tenants brought the corn used for their own consumption to the mill. When the mill became banal, they were forced to do so. We saw earlier how these tenants had succeeded in lessening the burden of their services by farming divided-up portions of the manse, that is by accepting tenements that became ever smaller. More intensive work was probably unable to compensate entirely for the reduction in cultivated area. The *banalité* of the mill was probably aimed at these peasants farming on small divided-up plots who had been partially successful in getting out of labor service.[58] The absence of such an obligation in the south implies a less strict lordship and larger tenements having a direct contact with the market.

Thus in the twelfth century the lord's *bannum* was the instrument for a general extension of an adaptable and effective land rent, which now affected almost the whole of peasant society. It is interesting to compare this extension with the long history of the use of the *potestas publica* by the landowners. This brings us to the relationship between immunity, the fisc, and the beginnings of banal lordship. This is a matter not so much of the delegation or usurpation of the *bannum* but of the habitual, customary exercise of "public" rights, intermingled with landlord's dues levied on determined pieces of land.

This confusion between estate and jurisdiction, so characteristic of banal lordship, had as its immediate precedent the royal estate itself, or more generally the fiscal estate. And we can perhaps now get a better idea of the succession of the relationships that were established between the large public estates—fiscal in the late empire and then royal—the peasantry, and the aristocracy, or rather, aristocracies. A first stage might have been, in the last years of the Roman Empire, the appropriation by certain magnates even if only temporarily of public rights such as the *tributum* following their appearance at the beginning of fiscal lists—the original polyptiques.[59] In many ways this system appears to underlie the Church's great southern estates. But the example of the polyptique of Saint-Victor would indicate the weakening in some cases of this type of levy.

A second stage is probably represented by the system that arose in the second half of the seventh century on the estates of the Frankish monarchy and then spread to the great royal abbeys, and more generally to the neighboring churches. This was a significant grouping of large estates where the old public laws, given new life by the Frankish royal *bannum*, were used not to increase taxes but to extend services. At the same time, the essential public functions of justice and military command were attached to these estates to become, within their limits, the adjuncts of the landlords' powers. This group of estates, once formed, became the essential support not only of the king and the royal churches, but above all of the Frankish high aristocracy—that class that would undertake the reconquest of the lands once held by their ancestors and form the *Reichsaristokratie*. This class, whether the sons were clerics—bishops or great abbots—or laymen—counts and secular abbots—now had estates that were infinitely more firmly established than their own allods, which could be divided up or sold at will.[60] One of the conditions of this system was evidently the affirmation of the public character of these estates, which guaranteed their stability and by preventing their individual monopoly maintained the collective domination of the Frankish masters and gave their group, despite friction and rivalries, its impressive cohesion. This was the point of the immunity of the great ecclesiastical estates of the north, which conferred on any new piece of land, even one of allodial origin, given to the Church the characteristics of a fiscal estate and thus integrated it into those public lands that the Frankish nobility "passed down from hand to hand." This explains how the property of the *comitatus* and that of the *episcopatus* were considered as "forms of the royal estate" and could pass freely from one to the other. Logically the system comes to an end when all royal prerogatives are consigned to the immunist on at least a small portion of the estate, a concession that was soon to be considered as being the gift of a true *comitatus*. As Jean-François Lemarignier stresses, immunity was sliding unnoticed toward banal lordship.[61]

This fiscal system, though incomplete, was introduced into the south by the Carolingians in the eighth century by transforming some of the estates of the great southern churches into fiscal property that they awarded to their counts. The latter did not establish the draconian labor service that had been imposed on the fiscal estates of the north, but they certainly required the performance of public duties. At the beginning of the tenth century these duties had become so much connected to the estate that if it changed hands they too were transferred.[62]

The third stage of the confusion of public duties and landed rights is that of banal lordship. As such, and only as such, the great fiscal estates of the ninth century continued. But, as we have seen, the spread and extraordinary extension of the fiscal model at the end of the tenth century was in the long run to bring about the abandonment of services in those places where they had existed and to bring about also an increase in rent. Thus the establishment of banal lordship seems to be both the outcome of a very ancient tendency among the great landowners to make use of elements derived from what can rightly be called public power and at the same time a quantitative leap in this evolution. From this time onward the small peasant allodialists were integrated, almost everywhere, into the manors. Thus for a time the movement that for centuries had opposed the landed aristocracy and the independent peasantry came to a halt.

The end of the military exploits of the Austrasian aristocracy within the Frankish Empire and the disappearance of this distinctive social group implies two different versions of the same movement for the north and the south. In the north the local aristocracy, by entering definitively into the Frankish system of vassalage, was finally able to exercise the power of the *bannum*, using it to consolidate its insecure domination over the land. At the same time, as we have seen, this aristocracy enabled the Frankish princes and their men to establish themselves in a way that would otherwise have been impossible. In the south the awe-inspiring Frankish war machine, which had upheld the classic estate, was dismantled. Banal lordship was then built up on the remains of the ancient public estate. This accounts for the many advocates and vidames formerly attached to the royal abbeys and the northern bishops, who were now aspiring to act on their behalf. With the *bannum*, the fiscal estate was able to transfer to banal lordship that indivisibility which had assured its strength and balance. It was easy to divide up an estate, formed either of tenements scattered here and there or of pieces of land farmed by the master with his domestic slaves. A true lordship cannot properly be divided up. In order to dominate the peasantry the nobility had to dominate its own members and control its daughters and younger sons.[63] The nobility would extend this family structure to those peasants who joined with it to establish and share in its ascendancy.

The importance of this intermediate layer of society now begins to be clear, but we need to identify its origins and from these its manner of formation. In the Frankish lands, we see with greater or lesser clarity depending on the state of research the "semi-servile" (once again only a stopgap term) origin of many knights. Going south, however, the group of *milites* appears to have developed from the upper levels of the small allodialist peasantry. For the historian of ideas, this is an important distinction. The former, descendants of the great monastic, episcopal, or princely *familiae*, had been brought up in the school, if not of servitude then at least of dependence and of service; the others had not.

Is it a coincidence that in the places where we see the phenomenon of the renaissance of the towns earliest and most markedly,[64] it appears to be linked to this intermediary class of the *ministeriales*?

For a long time the history of feudalism and that of the towns appeared to historians as an antithesis—an echo perhaps of a time when the triumphant bourgeoisie liked to contrast feudal obscurantism with the urban freedom that it claimed to inherit. They painted a romantic picture of the town belfry defying the keep and striking the hour of future freedom. In more recent times, the division was continued between historians of towns, more concerned with economics, and those of the manors, who, sometimes descendants in their way of the feudists of the ancien régime, saw social phenomena in a more legal or political light. It was an unfortunate division in so far as the reader sometimes had the impression of two quite different Middle Ages, but which is today a thing of the past, or soon will be. What should concern us here is not the town per se, but the link that might exist between the countryside dominated by banal lordship and the urban renaissance of the late tenth and the eleventh centuries in its political aspect.

For what is a town? "That which calls itself a town"? This is a definition that wittily reminds us that the same word can apply to very different historical realities. Or from the economic point of view, "any group of men who depend for their subsistence on agricultural products from outside"? But any definition of this sort in its desire to be general is of course a result of hindsight. Our European towns had their origins in the Middle Ages more than in any other period. "The original characteristic of medieval towns is their situation in feudalism."[65]

For several years now historians concerned with the renaissance of the towns have insisted on the continuity of occupation of certain sites. Anne Lombard-Jourdan has recently emphasized the continuity of use of certain urban, or more precisely, suburban, sites.[66] She shows that many of the medieval fairs were undoubtedly the successors in time and place of the great gatherings of the cities of Gaul. The fair of La Pierre-Levée in Poitiers was for a long time held outside the town on a site near which were megaliths and burial places. The great fair of Autun is held at Mont Beuvray. The names themselves are revealing: Lendit and Chalendemai (Calendamaia) in Auxerre, Lendit again at Saint-Denis. The dates are those of the great Gaulish festivals, around 24 June and 1 May, more or less successfully Christianized by dedication to important saints, the usual disguise for ancient divinities, or to local saints whose days coincided approximately with these festivals. Sometimes only the opportune translation of relics allowed this coincidence: thus in 946 the remains of St. Eloquius, originally buried in a mound at the confluence of the rivers Oise and Sommeron, were transferred to the Abbey of Waulsort in the Namurois in order to reform the custom of the people there of coming from far away with their goods. The market at Ardres, which was to give rise to the town, was held at the foot of a mountain that was known as *Heiligoland*, sacred land. And in the ancient Roman cities, fairs were held outside the walls near the old cemeteries, as at Auxerre at the mountain *Autricus*, near the fortress, and the tomb of St. Amator, whose feast day was celebrated on 1 May.

The suburban abbeys, often dedicated to a local saint, continued the cult alongside episcopal mausoleums, but they also established a presence in places that it would have been dangerous to leave unattended, where mounds, stones, trees, or springs had long attracted the devotion of the peasants. This, despite the attempts at Christianization, explains the clearly pagan character of so many suburban cults.[67] These great festivals, which on a fixed date brought the peasants of one *pagus* together in their ancient religious places, were not just the occasion for trading goods but were also places for social exchange. A capitulary of Louis the Pious indicating the place where oaths of fealty should be made states: "In that place where from time immemorial the custom was to prove one's freedom by oath and by *adchramitio*, there should the *mallum* be held and there the oaths should be made. However, the *mallum* should not be held in a church nor in its forecourt."[68] So there were places, often close to a church, which custom consecrated to the assembly of free men. Indeed, local traditions in many places attest to the faithfulness of communal meetings to the original meeting place. In many medieval towns a church—and only one—would add the qualification *de foro* or *in foro* to its dedication.

In Tournai the *mallum* was outside the precinct, not far from the Church of Saint-Quentin *in foro* where fairs were held in May and September. The communal meetings in Liège, Namur, and Huy were held outside the walls, near some "steps" symbolizing communal liberty. These steps are generally considered to have derived from the market crosses, and it is possible that these crosses were erected on megaliths, "stones of justice," in order to Christianize them.[69]

Thus the restricted space of the towns of the very early Middle Ages often lay next to a traditional place where, despite and throughout political upheavals, the inhabitants of the *civitas,* in the old sense of the word, would gather.[70] The *urbs* may have taken over the term, calling itself "city," gathering within its walls the bishop and his clerics and a few magnates and their soldiers, but nevertheless the simple freemen of the countryside continued to hold their secular assemblies.

It would be interesting to compare these central places, where the social cohesion of a group, the cult that sanctified the places, and the oaths made in them were all reinforced, with those other meeting places, equally traditional but places of encounter and passage where alliances between neighboring groups were forged. Equally interesting would be to compare them with the "trading towns" found on the northern borders of the Carolingian Empire, such as *Haithabu-Hedeby,* with their wooden enclosures that surrounded areas for bartering and cemeteries.[71] These were all places of peace.

The *urbs* of the very early Middle Ages seems to be the juxtaposition of a *castrum* that protects the local magnate and over which he is master, and a place of assembly that he controls but does not command. The character of this second social group, both peasant and pagan, is well expressed by St. Boniface when he writes that Erfurt in Hesse "formerly took the place of town for the pagan peasants."[72]

In the tenth century a number of important changes altered this balance. There appeared, or reappeared, in Aquitaine and the Loire Valley, around towns whose walls had been restored, suburban jurisdictions that were both military and judicial, the *quinte* or *septaine,* also called *defensaria.* Late texts suggest that those who lived there had to contribute to the maintenance of the fortifications of the city, within which they were allowed to come to take shelter. In the north the *banlieue* was to play the same role. It is notable that when new inhabitants came to cluster around the base of the walls in *burgi* surrounded by palisades—places hitherto used only by traders—the majority of them were from this area.[73] Henceforth the town was to drain off the nearest country people. The rich *mundiliones* of the great monasteries, merchants or abbey officials in the north like the *boni homines* of the southern cities were to become the aristocracy of the city.

In the second half of the tenth century there are clear signs in several places of the decline of or the move away from the *mallum* as places of justice. The counts, if they still lived in the towns, sat in judgment over those who were still dependent on them. The others were subject to castellan justice. Where the judicial *mallum* still existed, it involved only townspeople and not all free men. The very freedom of citizens was put in question. Thus, for perhaps the first time, there came about a separation of the economic and the political realms. The peasants still gathered at the *feriae*, but now they were nothing more than fairs. In Dijon and Autun, the *placitum generale* had become simply the right to hold a market. For all that, even here the peasants are not completely at home. The townspeople mistreat them and cheat them, or at least that is their impression.[74] The princes and lords took over the organizing of the fairs, supervising them, protecting them, and taxing them. The clerics, guardians of the old tutelary sanctuaries, were forced to forge false documents to claim rights based only on ancient custom.[75] Thus little by little there emerged in the revived towns, despite opposition that has perhaps been exaggerated, an agreement between the princes, a clergy that was often rather irregular, the citizen knights, and the richer burgesses. This firm alliance was to establish definitively the power of the towns over the country.

Naturally, there were uprisings against the local lord, the revolt in Laon being a famous and bloody example. There are also examples of conflict between the town and some lord of the countryside, such as that between Bruges and the lords of Straten. But these tensions should not conceal the reality. In Arras, it was not always possible to distinguish knights from burgesses. In Paris the royal knights did not disdain becoming involved in trade. The moneyers of the entourage of the duke of Normandy were part of the landed aristocracy. In Arles, the knights were also tradesmen and were not opposed by the burgesses until the end of the twelfth century.[76] These groups of town knights were often the most determined promoters of an ordered and hierarchical conception of feudal relationships. In such cases the town, far from opposing feudalism, in the strict sense of the word, became the agent of its diffusion and generalization.

Thus, throughout the history of material structures we find the same major change as are seen in the history of public institutions or in the aristocracy.

Until the eleventh century, rural productivity had remained . . . low, while growth had been principally that of a war economy, with slavery and pillage as its foundations. But in the feudal peace which followed, the decisive conquests had gradually become those of the peasants, incited by the restrictions of the lords to become increasingly productive, to become more numerous also, and for this reason to become increasingly free to order their labor in their own way and to sell the fruits of this labor.[77]

Curiously, this relative liberation of the countryside led to the domination of the towns; and it is well known how much certain free towns or those administered by a council were hated by the neighboring peasants. There is no doubt that the subordination of the peasant economy meant a significant increase in the production of goods. But it would be well to remember that it also implied another way of using and distributing them. The town had not taught the peasants how to "hold fairs," but it taxed them and profited from them. Naturally, compared with the magnates, the town merchants had "the spirit of enterprise." But is that to say that the peasants did not? We cannot forget that the activity of many of these merchant groups was originally almost indistinguishable from the war of which it was the product. Servants of the great, these western merchants owed their position to the horses, weapons, silks, and furs that they obtained for their masters—and to the slaves above all, those products par excellence of the war. The nobles, incapable of producing, needed—as Adalbero was only too aware—intermediaries. Another thing that begins to change from the eleventh century on is the social importance of this latter group.

The town reinforced what banal lordship had begun. One enclosed the country allodialists in their daily life; the other controlled their old assemblies and attempted to reduce their old society to mere buying and selling. They were robbed even of their legends, which were reworked by crafty clerics who forged out of them the mental foundations of a veritable ideology of power: through the Lendit fair of Saint-Denis, devotion to the Areopagite was to spread loyalty to the feudal king the length and breadth of the countryside.

Notes

1. For the question as posed by Georges Duby, see p. 2 above.
2. Duby, *Les trois ordres* [616], p. 189.
3. Bloch, *La société* [78], pp. 337, 344, and 609.
4. Duby, *L'économie rurale* [300], 1:120ff., *Guerriers* [532], pp. 105 and 111.
5. Toubert, *L'Italie rurale* [558], and *Le Latium* [89], p. 464.
6. Verhulst, *La genèse* [559].
7. Ibid.
8. Ganshof, *Quelques aspects* [533].
9. On these *eulogiae* or *xenia* and their use, see p. 251 above and p. 313 below.
10. Sanchez-Albornoz, *El tributum* [552].
11. Poly, *Régime domanial* [548]. The tax of a tenth was owed by the *colonus* in the Visigothic and Ravenna estates, Doehaerd, *Le haut Moyen Age* (Paris, 1971), p. 196. It was still paid in Catalonia in the eleventh century

(see Bonnassie, *La Catalogne* [72], p. 819) and in Italy (Toubert, *Le Latium* [89], p. 470). We shall see later what happened in the north (pp. 249–50 above).

12. Goffart, *From Roman Taxation* [536]. On the dating of the fragment from Ravenna and on the *operae*, Toubert, *Le Latium* [89], p. 466, who thinks they only took root in Latium and not everywhere in the eighth century. The labor services (*opera*) owed by the freedman to his master probably relate to such a period and milieu, rather than being public *angariae* that appear later in this type of documentation and seem to have been less onerous.
13. Gasnault, *Documents comptables* [534]; Rouche, *L'Aquitaine* [511], p. 209; Lot, *Note* [542].
14. References, see pp. 221–22 above.
15. Goffart, *From Roman Taxation* [536].
16. Doehaerd, *Le haut Moyen Age*, p. 183.
17. See pp. 120–21 above.
18. Beyerle, *Die beiden . . . Stammesrechte* [523], whose conclusions are taken up by Ganshof, *Quelques aspects* [533], and Verhulst, *La genèse* [559].
19. Ganshof, *Quelques aspects* [533].
20. Verhulst, *La genèse* [559]. The shifting of habitation between antiquity and the Middle Ages indicates also the internal breakdown in the great estates.
21. Verlinden, *L'esclavage* [521], p. 668. The movement inevitably became more accentuated with the crisis raging in England in the eighth century, Dufermont, *Les pauvres* [502].
22. Cf. p. 35 above.
23. Duby, *L'économie rurale*]300], 2:427.
24. For a critique of this historiography, see Delatouche, *Regards* [527].
25. Dhondt, *Le haut Moyen Age* [475], p. 104.
26. Duby, *L'économie rurale* [300], 1:84 and 86, himself queries this figure.
27. Delatouche, *Regards* [527].
28. Slicher Van Bath, *An Agrarian History* [556] and *Le climat* [557].
29. Delatouche, *Regards* [527]; Duby, *L'économie rurale* [300], p. 307; Genicot, *Sur le domaine* [535].
30. Duby, *Guerriers* [532], p. 223, and *Un inventaire* [529].
31. Quoted and queried by Dockès, along with the other "mechanisms," *Libération* [528], p. 187ff.
32. White, *Technologie* [561], pp. 57ff. and 76; Doehaerd, *Le haut Moyen Age*, p. 66ff.; Delatouche, *Regards* [527].
33. Toubert, *L'Italie rurale* [558].
34. White, *Technologie* [561], p. 104; Delatouche, *Regards* [527].
35. Toubert, *Le Latium* [89], p. 460.
36. Vines: Toubert, *Le Latium* [89], pp. 289 and 516; Violante, *La società milanese nell'età precomunale* (Bari, 1953), p. 76; Magnou-Nortier, *La société laïque* [86], p. 204; Bonnassie, *La Catalogne* [72], p. 442; Poly, *La Provence* [87], p. 107. Beehives: Delatouche, *Regards* [527], chapter 9, p. 425. Cloth: Doehaerd, *Le haut Moyen Age*, p. 234; in 70 B.C. the Batavian rebel Civilis, ally of the Frisians, had fitted ships captured from the Romans with multicolored cloth as sails, Tacitus, *Histoires*, 5:23, ed. H. Goelzer (Paris, 1965), p. 310. Cordoban-style leather: Poly, *La Provence* [87], p. 224.

37. Duby, *Guerriers* [532], pp. 267 and 299.
38. Duby, *Guerriers* [532], pp. 296, 202 and 214.
39. Delatouche, *Regards* [527], and the comment by Kula, *Théorie* [538], p. 52, "it is the number of hands which limits the dimensions of production."
40. Fossier, *La terre* [79], p. 274, tables pp. 285 and 288.
41. Duby, *Guerriers* [532], p. 92, summarizes the question.
42. Ibid., p. 45.
43. Coleman, *L'infanticide* [526].
44. *Vita Geraldi* [34], 1:21, col. 656. The Polish masters of the seventeenth century also preferred male labor, Kula, *Théorie* [538], p. 53.
45. Coleman, *Medieval marriage* [525], *L'infanticide* [526]; Génicot, *Sur le domaine* [535].
46. Starting with the study of cemeteries, Russell, *Medieval cemetery* [551].
47. A possible southern demographic model, Poly, *Régime domanial* [548].
48. Riché, *La vie quotidienne* [646], p. 294; Delatouche, *Regards* [527], Slicher Van Bath, *Le climat* [557].
49. Duby, *Guerriers* [532], pp. 110 and 124; Doehaerd, *Le haut Moyen Age*, p. 227.
50. Schneider, *Aspects de la société* [512].
51. Duby, *Guerriers* [532], pp. 104 and 111. Compare, however, the case of the estate of Saint-Bertin, which seems more secure, pp. 253–54 above.
52. There are striking resemblances between a large number of the acts of resistance described by Georges Duby and those described by Witold Kula for the great estates in sixteenth- and seventeenth-century Poland, see Kula, *Théorie* [538], p. 146.
53. Interestingly, the lacunae in ancient historiography can be found in the work of several historians considered to be Marxists and who appear even today not to distinguish between Carolingian and twelfth-century serfdom. They seem similarly to have some difficulty in integrating banal lordship into a chronology that made feudalism "flower" well before the advent of the former. See for example, Charles Parain, *Sur le féodalisme* (Paris, 1971), p. 24 ("modern" chronology) and p. 27 (old analysis); cf. also the summary by Lyon, *Encore le problème* [543].
54. Perrin, *La seigneurie rurale* [156], pp. 637, 649, 652 and 668. Light labor services were established in Picardy from the eleventh century; they were to become even less onerous by the end of the twelfth century, Fossier, *La terre* [79], pp. 586 and 588.
55. Duby, *La société* [78], pp. 79 and 254; Bonnassie, *La Catalogne* [72], p. 590; Poly, *La Provence* [87], p. 133.
56. Banal mill at Saint-Ouen c. 1023, Fulbert, *Letters* [38], no. 83. M. Bloch, "Avènement et conquête du moulin à eau," *Melanges . . .* , p. 800.
57. Dockès, *Libération* [528], p. 229; this explains why the banal mill was a relatively late occurrence and limited geographically. We can conclude with Pierre Dockès, p. 225: "Did the mill eventually bring about a growth in the total production through the saving of time which it represented? Perhaps. . . . It was above all a way of redistributing this production between the surplus and the remainder."
58. Fossier, *Histoire sociale de l'Occident médiéval* (Paris, 1970), p. 200. On the inn, see Kula, *Théorie* [538], p. 102, which shows how this was a means of accumulation.

59. Goffart, *From Roman Taxation* [536].
60. On the origins of the allod, see the interesting comments of Gurevic, *Représentations* [537].
61. Poupardin, *Le royaume de Bourgogne* (Paris, 1907), p. 373; Lemarignier, *De l'immunité* [150].
62. Poly, *La Provence* [87], p. 115.
63. See p. 110 above.
64. Duby, *Guerriers* [532], p. 296.
65. Keyser and Sombart quoted by J. Le Goff, "Ordres mendiants . . .," *AESC*, 1960.
66. Lombard-Jourdan, *Du probléme* [539], *Oppidum* [540], to which should be added Mitterauer, *La continuité* [545].
67. For example the dragon of Saint-Marcel in Paris, Le Goff, *Culture ecclésiastique* [635].
68. 818/819, c. 14, *MGH*, capit. 1:284.
69. Lombard-Jourdan, *Du probléme* [539].
70. J. Gaudemet, *Institutions de l'Antiquité* (Paris, 1967), p. 356; Le Goff, *Ordres mendiants*, which recalls the definitions given by St. Augustine and Isidore of Seville.
71. On *Hedeby*, see Jankhun, "Frühe Städte im Nord- und Ostseeraum," *Settimane di studio . . . di Spoleto* (1973), p. 92.
72. Lombard-Jourdan, *Du probléme* [539].
73. Lombard-Jourdan, *Oppidum* [540]; Schneider, *Aspects de la société* [512]. For Arras and Amiens in the thirteenth century, cf. maps in Fossier, *La terre* [79], p. 297.
74. Guibert de Nogent, *De vita sua* [46], 3:7, p. 155.
75. Lombard-Jourdan, *Du problème* [539].
76. Dhondt, *Les solidarités* [295]; Lestocquoy, *Les villes de Flandre et d'Italie sous le gouvernement des patriciens* (Paris, 1952); Bournazel, *Le gouvernement* [418], p. 89; Poly, *La Provence* [87], p. 301.
77. Duby, *Guerriers* [532], p. 300.

CHAPTER

9

Psychomachia

They say that there were since all eternity two opposite and opposing principles, one good, the other evil . . . and that from them all things were created .

—Eckbert of Schönau

When we examined the conflicts that in the eleventh century brought into opposition different concepts of the social order, we encountered the problem of heresy. To speak of heresy, even after so many centuries have passed, is neither so simple nor so innocent as one might believe. The manifestations of heresy in the eleventh and twelfth centuries gave rise, and still do, to many controversies, and the scientific rigor of today's historians cannot and must not allow the passion that animated them to be forgotten. Since this is a passion whose roots go deep and far into the cultural past and into the mental universe of each and every one of us, it is a particularly difficult subject to assess. Historians still do not agree about the heretical movements—those important social and religious phenomena of the eleventh and twelfth centuries—their origins, their meaning, their transmitters, their doctrinal contents, whether or not there was a single movement or if they occurred in isolated centers, and if indeed there even was any heresy.

The best procedure is to start with what is most factual and obvious: an external description of what was considered to be heretical by contemporaries. Only then can we posit the double question of the content and the external origin of heresy. Finally we will look at the social interpretations put forward by modern historians.[1]

272

The Wheat and the Tares:
The Development of Heresy

The dominant trend in today's historiography has until now contrasted two waves of heresy, and it has cast doubt on their being closely linked.[2] The first wave, in the eleventh century, was a brief emergence of religious expressions of a pietistic rather than truly heretical nature. Only the second wave in the twelfth century could properly be considered a deviant movement, and then only from the moment when the texts explicitly revealed the presence of eastern missionaries, that is, in the last decades of the century. Even, and particularly, if one does not agree with this analysis, it is useful to follow this chronological pattern and to distinguish between these two chief moments of the heretical movement.

Let us approach heresy in the way that most contemporaries did: by observing the scandal that revealed it to all, and then by trying to follow the movement back through its ramifications to the place where it had first emerged.

Before the eyes of all the scandal broke at Christmas 1022 in Orleans. Shortly after the year 1000 King Robert had inaugurated a policy of reform by entrusting bishoprics and abbeys to particularly pious and educated clerics, without regard for their social origins. It seems probable that the influence of his master Gerbert, a good example of such a man, had something to do with this attitude. Whatever the case, in so far as many of these clerics were either fellow-disciples of Gerbert or their pupils, Robert could hope for their loyalty. This policy had been much attacked, and he was reproached for choosing humble people to elevate to the great ecclesiastical posts. It was in these circles that heresy emerged.

Fulbert of Chartres was of humble origin, born perhaps in Picardy or in the diocese of Châlons-sur-Marne, and he was a pupil of Gerbert. Enguerrand of Saint-Riquier, who was also not an aristocrat, had also been a pupil of Gerbert. Gauzlin of Fleury, although from a family of Frankish *principes*, was a bastard. But we should be careful not to oversimplify. Thierry the royal notary, brought up at Saint-Pierre-le-Vif in Sens, was of an illustrious family. His grandfather had built Château-Thierry; one of his uncles, Seguin, had been archbishop of Sens and the other, Renard, abbot of Saint-Pierre-le-Vif; the lord of Tonnerre was his cousin. Azenaire-Asnar, abbot of Massay, belonged to the family said to be that of the abbots of Micy, related to the viscounts of Châteaudun and the lords of Bellême.[3]

The discovery of the scandal has a double history. The first is obvious. A Norman cleric, Herbert, having gone to study in Orleans, is supposed to have come home with some strange ideas. His lord, Arfast, listening closely to his words, realized that he was departing from the true path. He alerted Duke Richard, who brought the affair to the attention of the king. He, we are told, "sent to our man [Arfast], telling him to go to Orleans with his cleric [Herbert], seeking his help in this matter by whatever means." Arfast made contact with the heretics, introduced himself into their group, and finally denounced them before a synod of only five bishops. After a few specious attempts to hide their heresy, the accused, mortified by the accusations of their false disciple Arfast and the questions of the bishop of Beauvais, admitted their crime and even claimed its correctness. They were burned. Who were they? Ten canons from the cathedral of Saint-Croix, the master of the school of Saint-Pierre-le-Puellier and two lay nobles. A canon and a nun retracted their heretical assertions in time. All our texts insist on this point: these clerics are among the most noble and learned of the city; of their number is the queen's own confessor and the favorite of the king, Lisois, whose name evokes the family of the lords of Amboise. For good measure they even disinterred the corpse of the former precentor of the cathedral, Deodatus, who had been their master. He died in 1019, so heresy in Orleans must have dated back at least to the first years of the century.[4]

This act of posthumous vengeance reveals that the scandal of 1022 had long been expected and that it was deliberately provoked. There is another version of this story. Just as Herbert had tried to convert Arfast, so Deodatus well before 1006 had raised with his colleague Fulbert, then the master of the school of Chartres, some very worrying topics. The subjects touched on by Fulbert in his answer and the tone that he uses reveal both the dangerous path down which Deodatus was traveling and Fulbert's awareness of it.[5]

In the following years we can see in the correspondence of the bishop of Chartres how the net was tightening around the heretics of Orleans and their protector Bishop Thierry.

In the years from 1009 to 1012, a first letter to Thierry, who was recently consecrated, expressed reservations about his profession of faith. A second, addressed to Raoul, the bursar of the cathedral of Orleans, discusses what to do in the case of a priest who at mass refuses the Eucharist. Having carefully reviewed all the possible reasons—including indigestion—for such behavior, Fulbert mentions heresy and the degradation that would follow from it. In 1021 Bishop Thierry was attacked by the supporters of his rival, Oury of Broyes-Pithiviers, and these men, threatening him with their lances, made him promise to abandon the bishopric. Fulbert was content to send a short letter to Thierry, advising against the excommunication of the guilty parties. It should be said that at least two of the group, the aforementioned Raoul and the dean Herfrid, were among his friends and correspondents. In the same year he refuses, with ironic thanks, Thierry's suggestion of a joint procession of the clerics of the two churches of Chartres and Orleans. A threatening letter to Lierry (Leothericus) of Sens probably dates from the same period and should be compared with that King Robert wrote to the archbishop forbidding him to doubt the real presence of the body of Christ in the Eucharist. When Oury wanted to replace Thierry, even before the death of the latter, it was Fulbert who ordained Oury priest. When the denouncer Arfast came to Orleans, he passed through Chartres to clarify how he should proceed. Finally, the council of 1022, which tried the heretics and at which Fulbert was not present because he had gone to Rome at the precise moment when the deposed bishop Thierry was on his way there, consisted of three of Fulbert's friends, Oury of Orleans, Franc of Paris, and Guérin of Beauvais (though he was actually from the province of Rheims), all three very much involved in temporal matters. With them was Lierry of Sens and Gauzlin of Bourges, whose sympathy forced them to remain silent. Adalbero of Laon was to protest at the composition of this court.[6]

With the heresy unmasked, we can now pursue the agitators and the sympathizers. Robert-Henri Bautier has described the "witch-hunt" that was unleashed in 1023 among the educated clerics. Gauzlin in Orleans recited in the nick of time an old trinitarian profession of faith from the fifth century, which he had from his master Gerbert. Lierry, threatened by the letters from Fulbert and the king, moved away just in time from "an evil doctrine which was growing in the world." Helgaud, the precentor of Fleury, had had some problems with his teaching and the ghosts of burned heretics were seen prowling round the abbey. Odoran, the precentor of Sens, only survived thanks to protectors in high places, an opportune retreat to Saint-Denis, and to a satire— directed at one of the orthodox of Orleans—in which in justifying himself he accuses in turn his adversaries of regarding God as like a human being, the anthropomorphic heresy. Aznar, abbot of Massay and canon of Orleans, saved himself by handing over his prebend to the new bishop at the time of a second synod in 1023–1025 and leaving for Jerusalem.[7] Adalbero of Laon, who had shown his hostility to the council of Orleans, also thought it wise to justify himself, addressing to King Robert a little poem where he holds a dialogue with an allegory of Faith: "Faith:—Now that is enough, my son, disturb me no longer; Carthage calls me, and rich Babylon; they invite me, they press me; there heresies reign. . . . The Bishop:—Go in peace, Faith, and preserve the king for all time, this king who forced me to discourse on the difficulties of the celestial world, trampling under foot the heresy which he thought I harboured."[8] At this time of uncertainty, old alliances still operated, counterbalancing the settling of scores that were both political and religious.[9]

By contrast, some rapprochements were taking place, between Fulbert of Chartres and some very secular prelates like Oury of Orleans and Franc of Paris on the one hand, and between Odilo and his monks on the other. The support of the abbot of Cluny was invaluable and he supported Fulbert with his letters, advised the repentant bishop of Sens, Lierry, and thundered from his throne, borrowing the voice of Christ: "God the creator of man and son of man says: Who is it who troubles you about my birth. . . . The one whom you despise, Manichean, she is my mother, but she was made by my hand. . . . You, Manichean, are trampling under foot the mother of Christ, you are not defending Christ."[10] These were the same men who in the theory of the *tres ordines* and heretical asceticism opened a middle way: that of the Peace of God. The number and the quality of those whom they suspected and persecuted show instantly how widespread was the scandal and how important the stakes.

Not only the royal bishops were involved. In the years following the first synod of Orleans, heretics were pursued at Charroux in Poitou, at Toulouse, and at Arras. If we know little or nothing about Charroux or Toulouse,[11] that is not the case for the synod of Arras, whose chief merit is revealing to us the seat of heresy in the France of the 1020s. The heretical missionaries arrested in Arras had stayed previously with a community living in the diocese of Châlons-sur-Marne. There was nothing unusual about that. In 997 a peasant from the village of Vertus, Leutard, professed the same heresies. In 1015 the bishop of Châlons, Roger, held a synod against the heretics. In 1042–1048 his successor of the same name wrote to the bishop of Liège, Waso-Gasce, famous for his knowledge of canon law, to ask him if with the heretics of his diocese he should follow literally the parable of the wheat and the tares—in other words, burn them. We learn on this occasion that it was the peasants of the diocese who were infected by the evil, so much so that they were arrested on account of their pallor—the sign, it was believed, of heretical fasting—and massacred where they stood. In 1049 a general council of the province of Rheims once again condemned the heretics. It would appear that from the 1040s on heresy had become dominant in part of the diocese of Châlons.[12]

Nor had it disappeared in Arras, despite the oratorical efforts of Bishop Gerard, as we can see from a letter that he sent to Leduin of Saint-Vaast in 1031 after the fire at the church of Notre-Dame caused by lightning. Despite his frankly admitted discouragement and bitterness, Gerard invites the monks to reject "the foolishness" of those who saw the fire as a manifestation of divine anger.

> They say of us who are the ministers of the church:—behold the pastors of the people, they are not pastors but wolves; do they not feed themselves on the sins of men when they receive revenues from the Church as a daily salary—. . . and in this way they say that everything bad which happens in the world, death, plague, famine, benefits the sanctuary and derives from it . . . to him, heretic or false Christian, who says that to the faithful, we must reply . . .[13]

A few years later in 1051 the duke of Lower Lorraine captured some heretics whom he brought before the imperial court at Goslar, where they were hung.[14] The agreement of the texts on a subject where they are scarce leaves little room for doubt. Heresy first became established in Champagne; this was where it was strongest, reaching even to the peasants.

The very ancient castle of Mont-Guimer, from which came the missionaries of the 1130s and that was to be the seat of the Cathar bishopric of "France," lies only a small distance from the village of Vertus, which it overlooks. The legends of the heretics of the thirteenth century say that it was here that a Cathar "bishop," Fortunat, came, having been driven out by St. Augustine, and where he was supposed to have converted the lord, Guimer. It was in Mont-Guimer in 1239 that the last northern Cathars were to die, 187 of them with their bishop—a tragic replica of Montségur, which is curiously little known in popular history. Today Mont-Guimer is called Mont-Aimé.[15]

It would appear then that there was a contrast between the Orleans heresy, established among the learned but with a small number of adherents, and the Châlons-Arras heresy that was followed by large numbers of ordinary people. But there are a number of curious similarities. The trinitarian profession of faith used in Orleans by Gauzlin had already been used by his master Gerbert when he became for a time archbishop of Rheims in 991. This fifth-century text had been used to combat the Priscillantists. There seems no reason for Gerbert to have unearthed it if he had not wanted to affirm his orthodoxy—justification or call to order—in an environment where ancient heresies seemed to be rising to the surface. Furthermore, a royal charter of 1028 confirms the foundation in Châlons by the cleric Beuve of a church dedicated to the Trinity and indicates that this decision had been taken at a previous synod held in Orleans. Finally, Bishop Thierry of Orleans, brought up in Sens, came from Château-Thierry, which is only about fifty kilometers from Vertus.[16] The popular character of the Châlons movement, due perhaps to the fact that the heresy there was older than in Orleans, does not for all that exclude the possibility of a learned origin for it; this would explain the relative gentleness with which the heretical current seems to have been treated at the beginning.

Thus, as far as we can tell, the first wave of heresy occurred between 991 and 1052. These were not isolated sects; on the contrary, we can identify a stronghold of heresy in Champagne, with certain ramifications in Arras and Liège, and probable branches in Orleans. Traces of heretics have been discovered in the Aquitaine and Toulouse areas. The period that followed is considered to be a "heretical void," an expression that should not mislead us. The disappearance, which in any case was not total, of heretics from the texts does not necessarily mean that they had abandoned their beliefs and deserted the villages where they taught them.[17] The stakes of Orleans, the gallows of Goslar, and the summary executions of Châlons not only eliminated a few leading heretics; they must have made the followers more cautious in their proselytism and shown them forcibly that the general conversion of the kingdom was not so close as their brothers in Orleans had rather naively believed.[18] One or two generations later, a second wave of heresy was to begin.

Between 1064 and 1104 heretics were detected in the monastery of Saint-Germer-de-Fly in the Beauvaisis. In 1114 some peasants were arrested in Soissons. They came from Bucy, not far from the city, and from Dormans, between Château-Thierry and Vertus.[19] The network that was to emerge as the years passed coincides at the beginning with the one that had developed in the eleventh century. In 1135 a community was being hounded in Liège and the cathedral canons knew full well a few years later that it had come—but when?—from Mont-Guimer. By this time heresy had reached the Rhine; in 1143 heretics were arrested and burned in Cologne, they had supporters in Bonn, and were natives of Flanders. More were burned in 1163; some thirty survivors escaped to England where they were captured. The council of Rheims of 1148 stated expressly that the centers of the movement were in Champagne and Flanders. In 1157 a second Rheims council renewed the condemnations. In 1162 the heretics of Champagne were powerful and audacious enough to try to buy the archbishop, Henry, the king's brother, for a price of six hundred silver marks. St. Bernard, by denouncing this practice, shows that it was not exceptional. When in 1167 a bishop of "France" came to the heretical council of Saint-Felix of Caraman in the Toulousain, his name evoked Champagne, as did also that of his successor who was burned in 1239.[20]

Not only do we see heresy reemerging in its original territory, but now we also know how it spread, carried by zealous preachers. The texts agree in their description of the bearded vagabonds, barefooted and dressed in a long black hooded cassocks, accompanied by groups of women and weavers.[21] We know some of them and can reconstruct their itineraries. Very early on, in 1112, an ex-monk, Tanchelm, preached openly in Flanders, Brabant, and as far as Zealand. His passionate sermons won him the sympathy of quite large popular crowds. Calumny was heaped on him and he was accused of unchaste behavior, even as he was denouncing priests who took concubines. Among his disciples, it was true, there was a priest who had formerly been married. His enemies could find no other means of halting the heresy than to murder him in 1114. But his supporters continued his work.[22] A few decades later we read in the sources of Jonas, a cleric who was active in the old heretical areas of the north. He had been condemned for Catharism in Cologne, perhaps in 1143, at the time of the discovery of the heretical community there. He was condemned in Trèves and in Liège between 1145 and 1164 and again in Liège in 1165–1167. He then had the effrontery to lay claim to a parish at the tribunal of the bishop of Cambrai; it was refused.[23]

Peter, a priest of Bruys near Bucy in the Soissonnais, left home to preach in the south between 1115 and 1118. He may have stopped near Vézelay and La Charité-sur-Loire and also at Vienne, where a little later

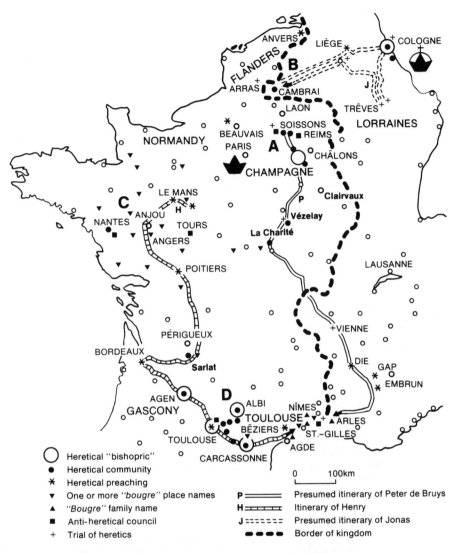

Map 5. Heretical Preaching (First Half of Twelfth Century)

A. Original area: bishopric of *Francia*. Repression only around 1170?

B. Extensions to north (Flanders–Rhine). Harsh repression 1140-60. Bishopric (subsequently disappeared), Cologne?

C. West area (Angevin?), result of Henry's preaching. The communities have not been exterminated, but rather dispersed after 1145? (place names still refer to cleared land, often forests, particularly the forest of Craon). There was a "heresiarch" not far from Nantes.

D. The notorious southern area. The "heresiarch" of Périgueux died in 1145. The bishopric of Agen must correspond to a Gascon preaching.

Notably absent: Normandy (failure of preaching at Saint-Germer-de-Fly), Burgundy, Auvergne, Lower Provence.

there were to be found the *Publicani,* or dualist heretics. But it was in the mountain dioceses of the Dauphiné and Provence that he gained the most support, in Diois and then around Gap and Embrun. Actively hunted by the bishops of the region, he dared to go down to Arles, to Saint-Gilles and the coast of Septimania. He was burned shortly before 1137–38, perhaps in 1134.[24] One of his disciples was Henry whose itinerary we also know from a letter from St. Bernard to Anfos of Saint-Gilles of Toulouse in which the abbot reproaches him for his leniency toward the heretic. Henry was a deacon, he was hunted out of Lausanne—or from Laon—then came to Le Mans in 1116, from which he was expelled by the bishop, Hildebert of Lavardin. From there he went to Poitiers, Bordeaux, and then Toulouse (in 1119?); a little later he joined his master Peter of Bruys in the area around Béziers and Saint-Gilles. There he was arrested and in 1135 brought before the council of Pisa.[25] At the instigation of St. Bernard he became a monk; then he was freed, but he hastened to return to his "errors" and to his refuge in Toulouse. Henry was still active in 1138 and 1142, even writing a treatise. He seems to have disappeared in 1145, at the time of the purge unleashed by the journey of St. Bernard to the Midi. The Manicheans of Nantes like the *Enriciani* of Sarlat in Périgord in 1145 were his disciples; the "Arians" of the Toulouse and Albi areas were considered to be his followers.[26] Henry, like Peter, had begun his pilgrimage around the years 1114–15; should their departure not be seen in relation to the persecutions known to have taken place at this period in Soissons and in Flanders?

We shall return to these events. Suffice it here to signal the change in our documentation and note its meaning. For the wave of heresy of the eleventh century, our information mostly comes from fragments of the reports of councils and from the monastic accounts that followed from them. For the later wave our information is largely drawn from the letters or even from full-scale treatises written by those who were alarmed by the by-now-obvious progress of heresy. To combat effectively the spreading network of heretic missions, an opposing network of correspondence arose between the great names of Christendom and their informants and friends, such as Bernard of Clairvaux, Peter the Venerable of Cluny, Hugh of Boves, the archbishop of Rouen, William of Saint-Thierry, William of Rheims, and also Evervin of Steinfeld, Eckbert of Schönau, the canons of Liège and those of Utrecht. They describe the heretics, indicate their movements, recall their previous condemnations, give ways of answering their arguments. This new type of evidence corresponds to a different expression of heresy—no longer do we have the isolated heretic before his inquisitor, but the public preaching of a heresiarch before crowds of peasants or even towndwellers in the markets and the fairs.

But was it still the same heresy as in the eleventh century? Was it not perhaps just a pietist and evangelical deviation in the face of a too-worldly Church? Should we see in it "a simple and strong protest at the clerical and lordly society then emerging"? We have just shown that the notion of small scattered groups, without links between them other than those of historic conjuncture, does not stand up to examination. Now we should consider the most difficult problem: that of the content of the heresy and its origins.

The Two Principles
and the Way to Perfection

To investigate the content of the heresy is no longer to define it from the outside but to try to examine it from inside—a much more delicate task. There are three pitfalls to be avoided here. First is imagining this heresy, or others, as a precise and uniform body of doctrine.

One of the values of the reports of the Inquisition in the thirteenth and fourteenth centuries is that they show us both the extraordinary richness and the astonishing diversity of a heresy at the point where it becomes a widespread and popular movement, or what we would today call a mass movement. Among the peasants of Montaillou considered to be Cathars, there were agnostics, pagans, or almost such, and even sometimes materialists. The discussions in the mountain huts brought together the shepherds of Aragon, Muslims, Catholics and Cathars.[27]

Thus we should beware of trying to find in the statements of the heretics a single monolithic doctrine, which would have been an impossibility. But diversity in a community does not necessarily exclude cohesion and unity.

The second pitfall is equally obvious. We only know of this vast ideological upheaval through the evidence of those who were hunting it, in other words, through the theological lens of inquisitors whose job it was to examine the doctrine and the work of the accused.[28] Or still worse, through the tittle-tattle of the propagandists.

Robert-Henri Bautier has demonstrated the stereotyped nature of the accusations brought against the heretics of Orleans both by Paul of Chartres and Adhemar of Chabannes—the same allusions to scenes of diabolic incantation, wild nocturnal couplings, and magic powder made with the ashes of newly born babies. It is not difficult to recognize here the witches' sabbath, and Bauthier suggests that the chroniclers exaggerated for the sake of propaganda. We are able to compare the grotesque but passionate calumnies of Raoul Glaber against the heretics of Monforte d'Alba and the interrogation by the archbishop of Milan of one of their number. There is little in common between Glaber's accusations—sorcery, the worship of idols mixed with Judaism—and the calm statements of Gerard of Monforte.[29]

Even if we ignore the obvious forgeries, it is still the case that the words of the heretic in even the best documents are not his own, but constitute a forced response to a model imposed upon him, or rather that part of it which the interrogator wanted or was able to retain.

Finally, and especially, the answers of the heretics may always have a double meaning, and their apparent conformity to dogma is always suspect. Like it or not, the historian is condemned to the same wariness, since the Inquisition is his source. When faced with torture and the stake, can one be sure of sincerity?

This is the main problem with the "evangelical" interpretation of the eleventh-century heresies. This interpretation insists on the relative agreement, here or there, between a certain text of the Gospels and the declarations of the heretics. But how can we know what this agreement conceals? When Gerard of Cambrai tells us that the heretics of Arras rejected the cult of the confessors but agreed to venerate the apostles and the martyrs, we can guess through his response that they had attacked the cult of saints as a resurgence of paganism. But what did they understand by apostles and, particularly, by martyrs? They claimed, according to Gerard, to be the imitators of the apostles, but we shall see later what we might think of this. As for the martyrs, they said that they too should be imitated: and we recall the torments to which the heretics of Monforte voluntarily exposed themselves before dying. In the fourteenth century, the inquisitor's manual lists the different devices used by the heretics to evade the questions of their judges; it is remarkable to see that in the eleventh and twelfth centuries the heretics of Monforte and Soissons used the same methods. The exchanges of heresy and dogma are thus at best verbal fencing and at worst a dialogue of the deaf.[30]

The historiographical procedure that consists in comparing the negations offered here and there by the heretics with the affirmations of dogma, without forcing itself to penetrate the internal logic of the exchange and restore its positive content, almost inevitably comes to a dead end. A necessarily superficial catalogue of the heretics' denials cannot be convincing either in its similarities—for these can be put down to the uniformity of the questioning—nor by its dissimilarities, which are often no more than the consequences of the profound inability of heresy to provide an adequate reply to the question put. Having said this, let us reexamine with hypercritical eyes the ideas of two different periods of heresy.

The list of heretical deviations in the eleventh century in relation to the Credo is well known: the rejection of the Incarnation with the consequent scorn for the Eucharist, the cross and marriage, and the refusal of the sacraments. The similarity of this with the Bogomil doctrine as described, very imperfectly, in the tenth century by its chief critic, Cosmas the Priest,[31] has rightly been underlined. In both cases, the insistence on the spiritual character of the divinity and a hostility to the idea of Incarnation are obvious, but they are not enough to allow us to speak of dualism. But two matters of great importance for the heretic, and thus more revealing, require a closer look: the relations between God and the material world in the ideas of the Orleans heretics, and the refusal to eat meat.

In Orleans, controversy arose for a time around the problem of creation. It has been shown how in their defense the heretics would use the phrase: "We know only what we have learned from God, *omnium conditor.*" As a result, the evidence of Raoul Glaber has been rejected, although he went to the trouble of writing a long and verbose reply to the heretics. Here he said:

That which best characterises the stupidity of these heretics . . . is that they deny the author of all creatures, that is, God, since it is clear that if all things . . . are dominated by the greatness of another, we can recognise from this that everything proceeds from the greatest being of all, and this reasoning is valid both for corporeal things and for incorporeal things. It should be known also that though all corporeal or incorporeal things can be modified by some accident, impulse or action, they no less evidently proceed from the immutable Master of all things, and it is through Him, if this thing should cease to be, that it will find its end.

And Raoul adds a supplementary proof of the harmony of the material world with God its creator: "Nothing in the universe has been destroyed by the Creator, unless it was that which blatantly transgressed the order of Nature, established by Him." So Raoul is not really saying that the heretics deny the existence of God, he claims only to trap them in the following argument: if you deny the creation of the material world by God, you deny the Divinity. He had in fact maintained that the heretics of Orleans "asserted that the Heaven and the Earth as we know them had always existed without the Creator."[32] The monk Paul of Chartres has preserved for us a fragment of the deeds of the council. When Guérin of Beauvais asked the heretics, "Before anything was in Nature, do you not believe that God drew all things from nothing?" the heretics refused to say any more at the interrogation, opposing to "the earthly wisdom with its signs inscribed by men of flesh and blood on parchment"—that is the Scriptures—"the law written within man by the Holy Spirit. We know nothing but what we have learned from God, *the creator of us all.*" Two different ways of thinking clash here without being able to meet or understand one another in a tragic dialogue of the deaf. We retain, nevertheless, the impression that the heretics of Orleans were proposing a clear distinction between God on one side and corporeal things, or Nature, on the other. But who had created the material world, "the heaven and earth *as we know them*"? What were the relations of God to this creation, or with that creator, "before anything was in Nature?" What "accident" could have separated "the Master" and material creation? We will never know the answers to these questions. But the very fact that they were asked is in itself revealing: one way or another, for the heretics of Orleans, God was at a certain moment separated from his creation.

And then there is the matter of the rejection of meat. This was the characteristic that first struck the earliest and least-well-informed of our informants. Adhemar of Chabannes, speaking of those whom he calls the Manicheans of Aquitaine, says as if in passing: "In abstaining from certain foods they seem like monks and simulate their chastity." The same is said of the people of Orleans, and it is curious to see that the holy Archbishop Sequin (977–999), uncle of Thierry of Orleans and protector of Lierry of Sens, had not touched any meat since the day he had been ordained; his biographer sees this simply as a mark of sanctity. At this stage the food taboo had nothing shocking about it. Less than half-a-century later, in Châlons, pallor alone was enough to accuse a man of being a heretic who abstained from meat, and it meant execution. In the twelfth century, the rule of Hérival in Lorraine was to forbid the exclusion of meat from meals, "in order not to imitate the *populicani* or the Albigensians." What had been a way to asceticism had now become a sign of heresy. Henceforth abstention from meat among the heretics was not just an imitation of the harshest of monastic asceticisms, but the visible part of a broader and more profound interdiction: not only disgust for flesh but also, and Wazo of Liège stresses this, the refusal to kill. His letter indicates that the heretics of Châlons "misunderstood the 'thou shalt not kill' of the Old Testament," but his biographer Anselm of Liège puts it more clearly, "they tried to conceal their error with the Lord's words in the Old Testament." The heretics taken to Goslar preferred to be hanged rather than strangle the chicks presented to them. Conversely, the people of Monforte did not hesitate to kill those among them who were ready to yield up their souls. How can this contradiction be resolved? Either by postulating that there is nothing doctrinally in common between the heretics of Monforte and Châlons. Or by attempting to reconstruct the underlying ideas that gave logic and coherence to the actions of the heretics. To give death to a brother, when after a life of good works his "consoled" soul is ready to leave its material body, is to prevent a last slide into sin that might compromise his salvation. The chick, on the other hand, should be allowed to live in order that the way of the Spirit can be accomplished through it. Could not the explanation for and the link between the chicks of Goslar and the "suicides" of Monforte be the doctrine of metempsychosis?[33] Metempsychosis in Châlons! It seems extraordinary, and yet . . . At the end of the tenth century, Folcuin, a monk of Lobbes who had studied in Rheims at the same time as Gerbert, wrote a history of his monastery, drawing on the old biographies of the abbots. Recalling that the sanctity of one of these abbots had been equalled by that of his successor, he makes this curious comment: "If one were allowed to believe, as did the Epicureans, in the transmigration of souls into other bodies, one would think that he was reincarnated in him." A little further on, in explaining the absence in the list of bishops of Rheims of an abbot of Lobbes who had become archbishop, he puts forward the hypothesis that the missing bishop might have been a heretic, or rather had not resisted the heretics, "which is almost the same thing." Then he rejects this possibility: "The men of the time would not have allowed heresy to creep in." It

seems that this former pupil of the Rheims schools was very preoc-
cupied with heresy. His allusion to the Epicureans is strangely reminiscent of the qualification applied by Raoul Glaber—without properly
understanding it—to the heretics of Orleans. By the twelfth century,
the link between the refusal of meat and the transmigration of souls
was known and denounced. Alain of Lille correctly noticed the profound difference between fasting among Catholics and among heretics;
the former abstained from meat on Fridays because eating it encouraged concupiscence, the others went without it because of their doctrine of metempsychosis.[34]

Adhemar of Chabannes, like Alan of Lille, linked in part the eating of
meat and the pleasures of the flesh. Huguette Taviani, studying the
question of marriage and heresy in the year 1000, has shown how the
content of heretical teaching on chastity was twisted to show a negation of Catholic dogma. The Catalan John of Ripoll, who was staying at
Fleury at the time of the trial in Orleans, notes: "They despised marriage." With Andrew of Fleury, the remark becomes: "There should not
be any marriage with a benediction; let each man take a spouse as he
wishes." Finally Raoul Glaber says: "They were like the Epicurean
heretics in that they did not believe that amorous debauches were met
with an avenging punishment." Finally, with Adhemar of Chabannes
and Paul of Chartres, as later with Guibert of Nogent, we come to the
well-known description of the heretics' orgies, with incest and the
eating of the ashes of the newly born—in other words the traditional
picture of the witches' sabbath.[35] Here too the calumny was probably
only the distorted reflection of a doctrine that taught that incest was
no worse than marriage or copulation in general. The contradiction
between the evidence of Raoul Glaber and that of John and Andrew,
which indicated that "once the infamous acts of vice were perpetrated,
they denied that one's sins could be forgiven" is only apparent. Raoul's
"avenging punishment" probably refers to a divine intervention on
earth, without meaning for a heretic; Andrew and John's "forgiveness"
no doubt refers to the irremediable loss of the Spirit by the one who
committed the sin of the flesh.

Many other contradictions should be resolved in the same way. A
good example comes once again from the events in Orleans. According
to Paul of Chartres, the heretics had promised their false disciple
Arfast: "We will reveal to you the door to salvation; by crossing over
through the laying on of our hands you will be washed clean of all your
sins and you will be filled with the gift of the Holy Spirit." But when
the monk Andrew of Fleury describes "the mad aberrations" of the
leading heretics he says: "They counted for nothing the laying on of
hands." A contradiction? Perhaps, but everything depends on the context of the question: were they talking about the benediction of Catholic priests or of a Cathar ritual, similar to the *consolamentum?* And
this is what we gather from the interrogation of the Arras heretics:
they differentiated between the *manus impositio* by which priests and

bishops were ordained and those which they performed.[36] Another contrast that is often mentioned was the differing attitudes of the two groups of heretics when faced with the question: do you believe in the Old and New Testaments? The varying replies were not very significant because the heretics in any case subjected all these texts to an exegesis that generally deprived them of their literal meaning. This is what is meant by the accusation of hypocrisy that was often made against them. Gerard of Monforte stated at first that he believed in the Trinity. But the archbishop of Milan pressed him "to show clearly what they thought, he and his companions, about each word which he had said." Then he joyfully replied: "That which I called the Father is eternal God . . . that which I called the Son is the human spirit . . . that which I called the Holy Ghost is the knowledge of the divine sciences." And as the bishop continued: "My friend, what do you say of our lord Jesus Christ who was born of the Virgin Mary?" he received this answer: "This Jesus Christ of whom you speak is the spirit born in the flesh of the Virgin Mary, which is to say the Holy Scriptures." To the same question about the birth of Christ, the heretics of Orleans, "these snakes' tongues", replied ironically: "A mother like that of the son of God—we all have one" or again: "As for us, we were not there and we cannot believe that all this was true." Guérin of Beauvais thought himself cleverer than they when he pointed out to them that they believed that they had been born of their own earthly parents without however having been witnesses of the scene. Infuriated, they replied scornfully: "You can tell that to those who believe in the letters traced by earthly men on the skins of animals; we have our own law, which is written within man by the Holy Spirit . . . you utter useless things in vain . . . cease your words."[37]

So there are several positive points of contact between the western and the eastern heresies. Is this because they developed in cultural areas that were originally quite close, and were influenced particularly by neo-Platonism, which predominated among the intellectuals of both Byzantium and Francia? It is very possible.[38] But does this exclude a closer influence? Let us look in another way at the question of the relationship between the heresy in Champagne and Orleans and the one in the east with reference to the terms and the origins attributed to them by contemporaries. Whether rightly or wrongly, giving a name to the heresy was, for many, the essential task. Around 1040, Adhemar of Chabannes had no hesitations: they are Manicheans. The historian is right to have reservations about this oversimplification; these monks, it has been said, had read St. Augustine and seen there analogies with the heresy that was worrying them, and they also found there a name that suited it. Heresy is a crime and, like all crime, it must have a name. The inquisitor, as a good criminal prosecutor, attached the act of heresy to one of the articles in his code, to one of the named crimes in his list. To name is to condemn.[39] Hence arises the tendency that seems to predominate today by a legitimate reaction, to dismiss from the eleventh century both the idea of dualism and that of an eastern, pseudo-Manichean influence by way of the Paulicians of Armenia and the Bogomils of Bulgaria.

The Docetism of the Orleans community has often been commented upon, supported by the phrase that we have already mentioned: "We know nothing other than what we have been taught by God, *omnium conditor.*" It has been concluded from this, rather surprisingly, that the matter was closed and that there were no Bogomils in Orleans.[40] That may be. The Bogomils were half-hearted dualists and did not deny that evil might have originally come from God. We know from the very metaphor that they used to enlighten Arfast—the tree which is cut down—that the clerics of Orleans contrasted Catholicism, this insipid doctrine, with "ours, which comes to us from the Holy Spirit." Thus they considered themselves to be the bearers of a completely different religion. A generation after the scandal, we find in the chapter a canon called Stephen, who was, incidentally, one of the victims of 1022. A deed of 1063 includes his nickname that he had acquired, *bulgarellus (bougrel*—little *bougre,* i.e. little bugger or Bulgar), a clear allusion to his suspect kinship.[41] In Orleans in the eleventh century as in France in the twelfth century, to be a heretic was to be a Bulgar. There may not have been any real Bogomils in Orleans, but in the middle of the eleventh century the people of Orleans were convinced that there were.

In Châlons the inheritance is expressed in an even more extraordinary way. We have already seen how the term Manichean had been applied to them. The calumny of the learned one might think. But the text of 1042–48—Anselm of Liège's account of the letter sent by Roger of Châlons to Wazo of Liège—says a lot more. The bishop writes not only that "in part of his see there were peasants who followed the dogma of the depraved Manicheans in secret meetings," but he adds: "They claimed to give the Holy Spirit by a sacrilegious laying on of hands; and to give greater credence to their error, they falsely claimed that It (the Holy Spirit) had not been sent by God anywhere other than into their leader Mani, as if Mani was no other than the Holy Spirit." Thus, according to Roger, the heretics of Châlons were well-acquainted with Mani and considered him to be either their founder or one of the founders of their heresy, the first of the elect who, filled with the Holy Spirit, was worthy of their identifying with him at their death. This error is not for Roger merely hearsay, it is the worst of all that he has found out about the Châlons doctrine, "a blasphemy," he exclaims, "which can never be forgiven." Can we dispute such evidence?[42]

The Arras missionaries who came, as we have seen, from Châlons, and so who brought the same heresy as that of the peasants described by Roger, confessed that "they came from Italy" (which does not necessarily mean that they were Italians). Their master was Gandolfo, "a man of Italy," and nothing indicates that he ever left that country. Raoul Glaber believed, rightly or wrongly, that the heresy had been brought to Orleans by a woman who had come from Italy. When the Torinese Gerard of Monforte was asked: "Is the absolution of sins to be found from the pope, the bishop or a priest?" he answered with a clear allusion to the Holy Spirit: "We have a pontiff, not the Roman pontiff but another who each day visits our brothers scattered over all the world." Thus Gerard did not consider himself to be a member of an isolated community, but rather of a universal church. And Landolf of Milan, who reports this interrogation, implies that the heresy had come from elsewhere. The Italian Gerard, first bishop of Csanad (Marosvar) in Hungary, declares bluntly: unfortunate Greece has always had heretics, Italy abounds with them in some regions, Ravenna, Venice, and Verona, "Gaul is wavering"; he denounces the "unbelievable heresy of this age: to ask for the restitution of alms given for the souls of the dead," and he reports perfidiously that "the heretics, they say, invoke the angel Uriel, which in Greek means Fire of God."[43]

It is known that a few years before 872 the Byzantines had deported the survivors of the Paulician communities defeated in Armenia to the south of Italy, where they used them as mercenaries. Around 975 they had installed others in Thrace, around the fortress of Philippopolis, reconquered from the Bulgarians. Thus there were Paulicians in both Bulgaria and southern Italy in the tenth century, and the Bogomils must have been in contact with them. And that is not all. We have seen that a certain number of the inspirers of the hermit movement of the eleventh century came from the south of Italy and particularly from Calabria. In 1087 the most famous of the Calabrian anchorites, Nilus of Rossano, was condemned by a Byzantine council. To obtain absolution he was forced to utter the same abjuration that had been imposed on the Paulicians in 1027. The text mentions the dualist belief in the two sons of God. This does not make Nilus a Paulician, but it shows rather how wary people were of this heresy in the area. Finally, the possibility cannot be excluded that missionaries came to France from faraway Armenia, since a hermit from this country is mentioned in the eleventh century.[44]

The Châlonnais missionaries in Arras "said that they followed the evangelical faith and the apostolic tradition." But if we examine Gerard's words closely, it is clear which apostle they favored: "Paul, whose doctrine you claim to hold . . . The apostle Paul whom you falsely say is your Doctor . . . Paul, whose pupils you claim to be . . . Paul whose imitators you say you are. . . ." Seven times the bishop apostrophizes them in these terms. He had, of course, no difficulty in demonstrating that the apostle Paul said the opposite of what was claimed by the heretics, and he stresses this. But was it the same Paul?

Steven Runciman has shown the Paulicians' affection for a St. Paul who had become for them something clearly unorthodox. They probably used the apocryphal writings of the apostle, which were found also among the Bogomils.[45]

Bulgarellus (*bougre*) or Manichean are the expressions of the sense of the foreignness of the heresy in the eyes of both the heretics and their adversaries in the eleventh century. We shall probably never be completely sure, unless some new discovery is made, whether or not the heresy in Châlons from the year 1000 was really a form of that major heresy, dualism, here probably "watered down," which opposes in a gradiose dialectic Good and Evil, God and Nature, Spirit and Matter. But the little that we do know of the heresy of the eleventh century does not mean that we should exclude the possibility—quite the opposite.

Let us now pause to look at the preachers of the early twelfth century, those sometimes called by the historians "demagogues," leading "fanatical crowds" and setting up "substitutes for the Church . . . dominated by the muscular power of the masses." These wandering preachers of the years 1114–1115 are contrasted with the "true Cathars" who had come from the east, either after 1143 when Manuel Comnenus began to expel them from Byzantium, or after 1149 at the end of the second crusade.[46] This analysis conflicts with some of the evidence.

We know of heretics in Cologne at the time of the persecutions of 1143 and then in 1163 from the evidence of Evervin of Steinfeld and then of Eckbert of Schönau. The heretics set up an organized church, with an "elect" and "auditors," a baptism "not with water but with fire and the spirit," communal meals where the Lord's prayer was recited, a taboo on meat and "all that which comes from coitus." The heretics claimed that their religion had existed since the time of the apostles, of whom the "elect" were the continuation, and that it came from Greece, which did not mean, in that context, that it had just arrived in Cologne but rather was a sign of its ancient origin.[47] The statements of Eckbert confirm those of Evervin. He had known those whom he calls "the Cathars" when, before 1155, he had been a canon in Bonn and he had had many an argument with their supporters. He had advised the archbishop of Cologne when the latter had interrogated the accused. And it was doubtless at this period that the preacher Jonas was convicted "of Cathar heresy." So Eckbert knew the heretics well when he declared in 1163–1166: "They taught that there are two creators, one good and the other evil, God and some terrible Prince of Darkness. . . . They say that there were, from all eternity, two principles—naturae—contrasted and opposing, one good, the other evil, and they say that from these two all things were created."[48]

Are we to suppose that between the evidence provided by Evervin and that of Eckbert the heretics of Cologne had moved from a "watered down" dualism where God was also the creator of the "creator of evil" to a "radical" dualism? This radicalization would have occurred between 1143 and 1163 and can thus be seen in relation to the return from the second crusade. Or, alternatively, should we take Eckbert's evidence at the trial of 1143 and accept that Evervin, as Caesarius of Heisterbach and Hildegard of Bingen later, was less successful in penetrating the secrets of the doctrine than was the canon of Bonn?[49] Was it Eckbert who, in order to implicate them further, "radicalized" the dualism of his interlocutors? Above all, is it really one specific heretical church in Cologne that is being described? In a fragment of a work dedicated to the archbishop Arnold, Eckbert urges the citizens to close their doors to heresy, and he entitles this passage *de malis Francigenis*, which clearly refers to people come from France, in the restricted sense of the word. This piece of evidence is confirmed by the chronicle from Cologne, which tells us à propos of the trial of 1163 that "those who are called Cathars" had come from Flanders. So did the Cologne dualism come from Arras and before that from Champagne?[50]

With Champagne we have returned to the original center of the heresy and hence to the wandering missionaries of the early twelfth century. A rapid look at the texts that mention them only provides the usual succession of "external signs of heresy"—rejection of the sacraments, of marriage, of the Church, and sometimes the same accusations of witches' sabbaths as were made in the eleventh century.[51] Once again we need to look closer. The treatise by Peter the Venerable against Peter of Bruys and his disciple Henry contains several major points. Peter was accused of denying the baptism of children and of rebaptizing adults. He then quoted Mark 16:16: "He that believeth and is baptised shall be saved; but he that believeth not shall be damned." But by linking the performance of baptism to the desire for faith, Peter goes much further than the simple rejection of infant baptism. And he reveals what lies behind his words when he adds ironically: "We are not rebaptising, as you claim, a person who has never been baptised: the baptism which washes away sin is not a bath." So the "baptism" given by Peter to certain adults was a baptism without water, a baptism by the Spirit, like that of the heretics of Cologne. We can compare this with Guibert of Nogent's interrogation of the peasants in Soissons. He asked the direct and embarrassing question: What do you think of the baptism of children? They replied by quoting the very same text from Mark—definitely a useful verse. But Guibert is obstinate and presses them. They reply: "For God's sake, do not examine us so deeply" and then they use the heretics' well-known "device": "We believe all that you say"—meaning, we believe that you say it. If we look to Flanders we find the supporters of Tanchelm making jokes about bathwater.[52]

Hostility toward the cross had been a characteristic of the "Manichean" heretics since the end of the tenth century. Peter of Bruys is found here, for he hated the cross. If his mission ended so tragically at Saint-Gilles, it was because he had dared to organize a public scandal: his supporters lit a huge bonfire of crucifixes and calvaries and roasted meat on it. When he fulminated against the cross before the crowds he shouted at his listeners: "The noose which killed your father, the sword which slew your brother—would you adore that?" We can gauge the emotion felt by the audience from the anger of the abbot of Cluny when he described this scene. This extraordinary oratorical device was the same as that used by the Bogomil preachers of the tenth century: "If someone killed the king's son with a cross of wood, could this piece of wood be dear to the king?" and in the eleventh century: "If someone killed your father by attaching him to a piece of wood, would you respect and glorify it?" Peter's lessons did not go unheeded. As late as the fourteenth century, the Cathars of the Midi were using the same image: "If someone had hung your father from a tree, would you love that tree?"[53]

To back up their arguments, the heretical preachers had recourse to certain artifices, such as fighting. At Saint-Germer-de-Fly, one of them, one of the barefoot *deonarii*, accompanied by his "son," tried to persuade an elderly and ascetic monk: "What are you doing here at the infirmary, you a layman and a stranger?" said the monk harshly. The other replied: "I had heard, Messire, that there were in this monastery very holy men, and I had come to be instructed in religion; do not take it badly, I beg you." "It is not here that you can be instructed in the rule and in religion; if you want to be taught, go and see those who are in the cloister . . . Go on, out of here!" and the old man pushed the two of them toward the door. On the threshold, the preacher turned round: "You are wrong to chase me out of here; you should listen to me! . . . One of your servants is guilty of theft, and if he tries to deny it, I will fight him and you will benefit greatly." The monk did not let him finish, but burst out laughing: "Well, now it's clear, I see the danger concealed beneath your lies; you said you had come for religion, and here you are talking about fighting. One should neither heed nor detain a liar like that!"[54]

What did this fight mean? The fight between good and evil? And the thief? Satan, the thief of souls? Once again we are confronted by one of the oratorical devices, common among the heretical preachers. Orators of the marketplace, used to speaking to crowds of peasants, they knew how to frame their parables in images from daily life: vehemently, "if your father had been killed . . ."; intriguingly, "there is a thief here, I will fight him . . ."; derisively, "since the time that people have been eating the Body of Christ . . ."; mockingly, "baptism isn't a bath . . ." The audience weeps, shouts, laughs; the preacher is halfway there. And he can go further; he explains the Gospels in his own way. He translates, without any scruples, *beati eritis*, blessed are the heretics, or blessed are the inheritors, it is the same thing, heretic, to inherit, you will inherit from God. When a peasant calmly produced this translation before the bishop and Guibert of Nogent, they thought: "He is illiterate . . . and they claim to lead the life of the apostles and follow the *acta!*"[55] So they may have done, but we can imagine the effect upon the villagers of this little phrase, interpreted to mean "happy are the heretics."

With more educated heretics, the argument followed a different route. Peter of Bruys and Henry preferred the Gospel of Matthew to that of Luke, which they believed to be at least partly apocryphal. It seems likely that when they recited the Lord's Prayer the Bogomils, and later the southern Cathars, always chose the version in Matthew 6:11: "Give us our transubstantial daily bread" (*panem nostrum superstantialem*), instead of the version in Luke 11:3: "Give us this day our daily bread" (*panem nostrum quotidianum*).[56] Another not insignificant clue: the heretics of Sarlat of 1145 used, as did the Bogomils and then the Cathars, a doxology of Greek origin at the end of the Lord's Prayer: *Gloria Patri quoniam regnum tuum . . . Tu dominaris universis creaturis in saecula saeculorum, Amen.*[57]

Peter and Henry baptized by the Spirit, they took up the Bogomil invectives against the cross, they preferred Matthew to Luke, they also loved St. Paul, but they appear to have quoted him in an unusual way. All this does not make them into out-and-out dualists. But could dualism always and everywhere be admitted? Others at this time sometimes allowed themselves to be drawn into dangerous waters. The Archbishop of Rouen, Hugh of Boves, a former pupil of Anselm of Laon and at one time a legate in the Midi, wrote a treatise against the heretics of Nantes. Here we find attacked the same heretical rejections supported by the same arguments, particularly that of baptism, justified by Mark 16:16. But after the usual long and detailed refutation, we find this: "Satan, source of falsehood, origin of sin, created good by a Good Creator, but immediately perverted by his own will." "Satan is that Lucifer created noble and excellent by God, but immediately depraved by his own will." Against whom was this affirmation of the free will of Satan directed if not to people whose theology had an alternative explanation for the problem of the creation of evil?[58]

This helps to explain the terse insinuations of the abbot of Cluny: your dogma is a foreign dogma, or again, à propos of Peter's rejection of the Church Fathers: "You have banished the Latins from the throne and from heaven, but perhaps you spare the Greeks," and having shown that one cannot separate the Old and New Testaments, he concludes: "If you reject the Old Testament and the Church, you also lose the Gospels; if you do not have the Gospels, you do not have Christ, if you do not have Christ, you are not Christians. Here is the abyss, here the trap! You are not Christian heretics, but pagans and publicans!"[59] *Ethnici et publicana*—the insult was not new, and the heretic Henry had himself hurled it at the unworthy clerics of Le Mans. But here it sounds strangely. A few years later, publican was to become a synonym for heretic.

It took the abbot of Cluny a long treatise to conclude that Peter of Bruys and his disciples were not Christians. Others had no hesitation in saying it from the outset. We have already encountered one *bulgarellus* (*Bougrel*) in Orleans in 1063; we find another at the end of the century in Nîmes, another in 1147 in Agde, a wine grower in Melgueil in 1179, and in 1195 a townsman from Arles. The nickname, even softened with the diminutive, must at this period have become a serious embarrassment. In the vulgar tongue the term *bougre* became pejorative, but apparently in different ways in the north and in the Midi. In the north, *bougre* means sodomite (cf. English "bugger"); the heretic is first and foremost a debauched person. In the south, *bigro* means crafty; the heretic is a hypocrite.[60] The list of names that were used from now on in the twelfth century to qualify or disqualify heretics was long and indicative.[61] Arian, of learned origin, seems to have become popular, perhaps because of the legend of Arius. We know that a heretic reconciled with the Church in Toulouse had been given this nickname by the canons. Later a link had been established between *arriani* and *Castenau d'Ari*. There seems to have been a confusion, deliberate, between *Ari* and the southern form of Henry, *Enri*.[62] In "France" and Burgundy, they preferred to call the heretics "publicans." During the first crusade, the French knights had encountered in Asia communities of Paulician Armenians and the Greek name *pavlikianoi* had been converted into the Latin *publicani*. Common pronunciation gave *poplicani* or *populicani*—deliberately mischievous distortions that could be understood as "the dogs of the people" or as referring through the biblical publicans to the wealth of the Cathar city communities. But among the weavers, whose name had become synonymous with heretic, the French word *policien* was the name for a carding comb.[63] By contrast, neither "Manichean," *katafrigae,* nor *circumcelliones* were or were to become popular forms: those who used them must have taken them from Isidore of Seville.[64]

The problem is quite different in the case of a number of words whose origin is undeniably learned but that were in the twelfth century in current popular usage. An example is *cathari*, meaning those who are cleansed, the purified. The term is in Isidore's list, but it did not refer precisely to Manicheans. In the eleventh century, Landolf of Milan used it to mean the people of Monforte. In the twelfth century, Eckbert of Schönau reveals that the word was part of the common language in Cologne: "They are those who are called in the vulgar tongue Cathars."[65] In Italy as in the Germanic-speaking countries the term did indeed pass into the vulgate, *gazzaro* and *ketzer*. The assonance *Cathari-patari* invites a closer look at the word *paterin*. Contemporary authors had commented on the malicious play on words Patarins-*Patari*, secondhand clothes dealers, rag merchants, ragamuffins. A *pâte* is in the south a rag. But Arnolf of Milan warns: "Patarin is ironic . . . in reality it does not refer to the trade, but [means] offered to death," and a decree of Frederick II confirms: "Following the example of the martyrs . . . they called themselves patarins, which means exposed to martyrdom." We perceive too beneath the hostile pun a Greek form: "Those who are chosen for suffering," which could well have come from the vocabulary of the heretics themselves. The evolution of the word is no less significant. In the twelfth century, the Assises of Jerusalem were still envisaging the possibility of the knight or baron "who becomes a Patalin or non-believer in Jesus Christ." At the beginning of the fifteenth century, "M. Pierre Patelin" has become the stock type of the flattering hypocrite.[66]

And this is not all. From the end of the eleventh century, the heretics of the north referred to themselves with the word *Deonarii*, where it is not difficult to recognize the Greek *theonearioi*, those who are born again in God, a reference to the baptism by the Spirit. The name *piphli* or *piphles* is no less interesting; we can see in it the form *pipleis*, he who is filled, another reference to the baptism through the Spirit; the vulgate form was *piffre*, which means glutton.[67] All these forms, Greek in origin and therefore learned, became popular in the mid-twelfth century, and it is clear from the way in which they are reported that our informants were neither the authors nor the propagators of these words. There is only one possible hypothesis: these forms were introduced by the heretics themselves and it was through them that they became popular. They are a clear indication of the eastern influence on heresy from before 1104, indicated by Gerard of Csanad, later admitted by the Cologne Cathars, and well known to the inquisitors of the thirteenth century.

When Niketas came from Greece in 1167 or 1172 to the assembly of Saint-Félix in Caraman in the Lauraguais, when in 1177 the count of Toulouse declared, horrified, that "two principles have been introduced,"[68] when the heretic leaders in his city confessed to having believed that there was "another god," we can be sure that we are dealing with dualists. But was this late twelfth-century dualism the outcome, as a result of recent contacts with the east, of a heretical tradition that was in origin very close to an evangelical Christianity? Was it the confession, now made public, of a heresy that had become sufficiently strong to dare to admit its existence? Did our informants see dualism arriving or did they simply learn how better to recognize it? Was there a development in the heretical doctrines, or did the believers merely become more forthcoming and the interrogators more informed? These propositions are only contradictory when we come to that part of historiography that insists on reducing heresy to a minor and diffuse deviation, or at best to a secondary successor of the great movement of ideas represented by the Gregorian reform. If on the other hand we accept the continuity of the heretical movement and its doctrinal originality, we can look at the problem in different terms: in the heresy of the eleventh and twelfth centuries, as in any social movement, belief and knowledge were not everywhere the same. Among those who were heretics, some could have been perfectly aware of dualism, others would have been content with its external manifestations; and there were many possibilities between these two positions. What is really of interest to us in medieval Manicheanism is the relationship between the learned doctrine, of necessity esoteric, and the meaning it takes on as it gradually takes root in ever-broader social groups.[69]

The Meaning of a Heresy

Starting from the idea of a profound separation, around 1020 and probably from the year 1000, between Catholic doctrine and heresy, we must now investigate the social meaning of the latter. This is an even more thorny problem than the question of heresy's origins and content. It seems wise to discard the argument that "religious movements" and "social movements"[70] are two different things. Such a division, at least in the medieval period, seems hardly conceivable and is really only explained by the fact that they are separated into different schools of research. It would be better too to avoid as much as possible a too formal and mechanical interpretation of the relations between a doctrine and the social groups that inspired or adopted it.[71] The plurality of these relations should not be diminished. Let us look then at the meaning that heresy may have held for the three great categories of people in medieval society, the nobles, the clerics, and the peasants.

The involvement of the nobles in the heretical movement raises a problem for those who would like to interpret medieval Manicheanism as a protest against the nobility. Examples of passive complicity and sympathy are undeniable. It is hard to imagine that the count of Champagne and lord of Vertus[72] was ignorant of what was going on at Mont Guimer. It is unlikely that a century later the count, Anfos of Saint-Gilles, needed St. Bernard's letter to inform him that the preacher Henry was straying from the straight and narrow. These princes cannot have been sorry, at least at first, to see a desire expressed to strip the Church of some of its wealth. Saint-Gilles and Vertus were both lands held from the Church, as were many other manors in these two areas. We can imagine the nobility's vicarious pleasure.[73] But this type of explanation does not take into account the more active sympathies, such as those of the lords of Château-Thierry, still less the total involvement of the lady of Monforte, a minor noblewoman, or the noble canons of Orleans. This becomes even more the case at the end of the twelfth century in the Midi, where many petty lords supported the cause of heresy. It is true that at this time Catharism was the dominant religion in this area.

By contrast, it should be pointed out that in several cases it was not so much the Church authorities who were merciless toward heresy but rather the lords. Duke Richard and his family were active in the unmasking of the Orleans heretics. The *capitanei* of Milan put pressure on the archbishop to kindle the stakes. The duke of Lower Lorraine, Godfrey, dragged some heretics as far as Goslar to have them hung.[74] The attitude of the majority of the lords in the north seems to have differed from that of the southern nobility. We have already seen the gap between the minor lords of the south and the great retinues of "France." A distinction also needs to be made between the upper and the lower nobility and, in Picardy, Flanders, and Lower Lorraine, between the nobles, strictly speaking, and the *milites*. Finally, we need to consider whether heretical influences, where they are found among the nobles, slip in via clerics and women?

In contrast to the declared hostility of the majority of the great princes is the extraordinary leniency of a certain number of clerics, principally in those regions where heresy first originated. The bishop of Châlons had at first been content to reason with Leutard of Vertus. Gerard of Cambrai must have been told of the activities of the heretics by Guérin of Beauvais in 1023 at the assembly of Compiègne, but it took him more than a year to uncover the little community in Arras. The people of Arras seem to have been more fortunate than those in Orleans: a little torture, a learned sermon from the bishop—though it did last for a whole day—a cross at the bottom of a parchment. . . . They certainly showed themselves to be more adaptable than the masters of Orleans, and their humble positions and status as "illiterates" made the scandal less serious. In Liège, the ex-master of the cathedral school Wazo categorically condemned the repressions in Châlons. His biographer, Anselm, adds that if he had still been alive at the time of the Goslar affair, he would have disapproved of the sentence and interceded on behalf of the condemned men, as St. Martin had done for the Priscillianists. The Lorrainer Adalbero of Laon was of the same mind when he protested against the council of Orleans. The common factor among all these people is their education, which was that of the scholars of the Carolingian tradition, and more particularly of Rheims. The clerics of Orleans were not only the most noble of the city, but also the most learned, and it is not hard to find among the heretics and their sympathizers a significant number of precentors and masters of the cathedral school. Could there perhaps be a link between the old clerical Carolingian culture, the milieu of the masters of the school, often of humble origin, and heresy?[75]

A good example from this social group is the Liège cleric, Rather of Lobbes, who became bishop of Verona in the mid-tenth century.

Huguette Taviani, who rightly stresses the latent currents of heresy among the Carolingian theologians and particularly John Scotus Erigena, has worked on Rather. She has shown how, in wanting to criticize the priests of the diocese of Vicenza attached to an anthropomorphic representation of God, he was drawn to an insistence on God's spiritual nature. Taking his theme from Paul's First Epistle to the Corinthians, he had developed the idea of the preeminence of the soul over all that which is material, and of the identity between God and the Spirit. This homily provoked a sharp reaction from the Italian clergy and Rather was accused of leaning too far in the direction of the opposite error to the one he wished to attack.[76]

Like Wazo, Rather was of humble origin and it cost him many setbacks and the loss of his bishopric. Insisting forcefully in his *praeloquia* on the equality of men, he criticizes the arrogance of the nobility and its pretentions. Let us take, he says, "the son of a prefect—a count—, his grandfather was a judge, his great-grandfather a local official—*sculdahis*—, his great-great-grandfather was a *miles*, but who was the father of this *miles*? A bath attendant, a birdcatcher . . . a tailor, a butcher, a muleteer? Soldier or peasant, serf or freeman, who can remember anyway?"[77] For Rather there is no such thing as nobility *per se*, but rather a series of social steps that one can ascend and no doubt also descend. It is not hard to find a parallel between Rather's ideas and his own social position. But this vision of a world traversed by an ascending path has as its spiritual correlation the vision of salvation that is also gained through stages.

There were many clerics like Rather at the end of the tenth century. It was they who like Gerbert set the tone for learned circles. Did the sometimes difficult climb up the social ladder correspond in their eyes to the ascent in the stages of the Spirit? A career and the road to perfection are two different paths that can nevertheless be related. The heresy of the eleventh century is a theory of progress through the intelligence, *mens*. It is also a doctrine that in so far as it separates Spirit from Matter, is no longer obliged to see in the latter the intervention of God but rather the laws of nature and those of reason. Thus it opens the way to scholastic dissertations, and it is no accident if the ideas of Berengar of Tours or Amaury of Bène and their disciples were sometimes considered by their contemporaries to be continuations or faint echoes of the heresy that has preceded them.[78]

It is, not surprisingly, more difficult to establish a correspondence between heretical teachings and the mentality of the peasants, and yet the heart of the problem lies here. Among the *rustici* we sense a veritable liberation of expression, and Roger of Châlons was one of the first to have noticed this: "If illiterate or taciturn men joined the sectarians of error, they immediately became more articulate than the most learned Catholic, to the point where the sincere eloquence of the scholars was scarcely able to dominate their loquacity." But we should be cautious: beyond the formal doctrinal identity, their speeches did not always have the same meaning for those who uttered them and those who heard them. What meaning did the peasants' heretical words have?

The most obvious characteristics have been known for a long time, the refusal to pay tithes or taxes on the occasion of a burial in order to support a Church that had no longer any *raison d'être* as a material organization. This attitude appears very early, before 997 in Leutard of Vertus and in 1025 among the missionaries arrested in Arras. Another theme is work and the communal ownership of property. In Arras and later in Cologne and Rheims, the heretics supported themselves by their own hands; at Monforte they owned their property communally. Was this simply evangelical poverty? Perhaps, but it must be realized that work for the peasants was not just a penance, a form of asceticism, but a daily reality. The same could be said of their food: it was probably easier for a peasant, used to bread and gruel or cabbage, to go without meat than for a noble, a hunter fond of venison.[79]

To leave the world, to repress the desires of the flesh, to support oneself by the labor of one's own hands, to do no harm to anyone and charity to all—was there room in this program for the payment of the tallage and other dues owed to lords? No sacraments, no oaths—could feudal society accept such affirmations?

The heretic is not of this world; but could the peasants be allowed to ignore the world and confine themselves to cultivating only what was strictly necessary for their own wants? When banal lordship was established—and in such harsh conditions—the old heretics' question, "Where does evil come from?," must have become very significant for the peasants. And the preachings of the heretics would have awakened in their simple believers aspirations that the heretics themselves had not looked for nor desired![80]

It would be a mistake to imagine the peasant heretics as paupers. Those in Bucy, whose insolence is denounced by Guibert of Nogent in the first years of the twelfth century, were rich enough to make themselves heard by the count and to associate with him.[81] This may explain the simultaneous spread of heresy in the countryside and in the episcopal schools. Did the masters of the schools and peasant preachers have, if not the same culture, the same social origins? Once again we glimpse the decisive role played by the wealthier peasants, the laborers, and a peasant society that was less passive and more determined than some of our documents, charters, or inventories, would lead us to believe.

The similarities between the communities of peasant heretics and the groups of hermits have been rightly stressed, with the accent in both groups on work and poverty. Indeed the borderline between heresy and the life of a hermit could at times be very narrow. Engibaud (Engebaldus), a priest in the service of the nuns of Remiremont, had gone into retreat in the wilderness. He refused to build a church, celebrate the mass, sing psalms, or take communion—and no doubt also to eat meat. At the end of his life he agreed to return to the fold of the Church and thus became the founder of the community of Hérival.[82]

But it should be noticed that the craze for the eremetical movement in France and particularly among women appears at precisely that time that has been called the "heretical void" of the second half of the eleventh century. The last clear pieces of evidence about heresy are the massacres of Châlons spoken of by Anselm of Liège in 1042–48, the hangings in Goslar in 1051, and the council of Toulouse of 1056.

It is only around 1070 that Engibaud goes into the wilderness. It is only at the end of the century that eremetical movements develop in the west of France, and according to Bernold of Constance, there were formed in Germany lay communities of peasants, men and women, and also girls wishing to live in chastity. Envious men tried to harm them, criticizing their way of living, but, Bernold stresses, these communities were doing no more than returning to the early Church and they never stopped obeying the members of the Church, clerics or monks, to whom they were attached.[83]

It is striking to see to what extent the heretical or simply dissident movements were supported and carried on by women. This course gave rise to calumnies, such as that which overwhelmed Tanchelm in Flanders. Here too we need to ask in what way a certain type of doctrine expresses certain needs and what were these needs. The move of heresy into the towns also raises problems. In the two cases of which we know, Orleans and Arras, it was suppressed. In the twelfth century, by contrast, with the weavers and perhaps already the burgesses—had not the Paulicians of Flanders even tried to buy the archbishop of Rheims, the brother of the king?—heresy became a fact of town life also. This had been the case in Italy since the second half of the eleventh century. George Duby describes how an ideal of poverty could compensate for a guilty conscience felt in some social milieux about too recently acquired wealth.[84]

The similarity between heretical attitudes and the demands for reform of the Church has also been observed. We know of the links between Gregory VII in Italy and the Milanese *Pataria*. We know also that Gregory protested against the executions in Cambrai in 1077 of the priest Rainhard and of his disciples who refused to receive the Eucharist from any priest, abbot, or even bishop, accusing them of simony. A few years later the chronicler of Saint-André in Cambrai states, having talked of Rainhard: "Still today there are in some towns many members of this sect; the weavers all support it."[85] A fact that sheds a worrying light on the orthodoxy of the "Gregorian martyr," Rainhard, is that "weaver" is at this period synonymous with heretic.

In any case, it should be recognized that we have reached a second phase in the development of these ideas, still in this period of the "heretical void." The eremitical movement and reforming pietism had contacts with the current of heresy. But rather than considering the latter to be a deviation from the former, chronology leads us to see these movements as a weakening of more radical demands, a critique developing in the same area as heresy, which at this time had been silenced, replacing or sometimes concealing it. For in some cases it is hard to distinguish between the quasi heretics who had more or less repented—Engibaud is a good example—and the simple aspirants to evangelical purity. This does not mean that this phenomenon is any less important. From this time onward, the evangelical life was no longer the monopoly of the resolute opponents of the Church. When a truly heretical movement started up again, it was to find itself very close to other groups on the frontiers of orthodoxy, such as the evangelicals of Cologne or the poor people of Lyons,[86] and this parallel development, indeed this competition, was to be a dangerous weakness in the development of heresy.

Finally, we should examine the deep-rooted nature of this heretical radicalism. Hostility to a visible world that was itself becoming hostile is perhaps not a sufficient explanation for the development of heresy as a popular movement, that is, in the eleventh century at least, a peasant movement. As Georges Duby has said,

> almost always. . . , in the milieux which take up a heresy, there intervene as a distorting agent the latent collective attitudes which also greatly favoured the reception of the doctrine, those uncertain attitudes which the Churches call superstitions but which we can define as instinctive religious reactions, based on an extremely simple representation of life. It is on this level of consciousness that we need to seek particularly the origins of prohibitions, taboos, types of exclusion and division which can take on very clearcut forms, of a generally dualist nature. This dualism, the existence of which can be felt on this level of consciousness, participates in many instinctive drives, notably the feeling of sexual guilt, which explains the frequency, within the heretical groups, of the insistence on purity, if not in the believer himself, then at least in the intermediary, the Perfect.[87]

Among the important sources for this type of enquiry are the Apocrypha, whose adaptability and vein of legend provide a combination of individual learned concepts and collective "popular" concepts of heresy. Historians of Bogomilism have used them frequently and have established connections with certain folk motifs.[88]

It has been remarked how the theme of bees occurs in the early years of heresy, in Leutard of Vertus in 997 and Gerard of Monforte in 1027. Gerard sees them as an expression of chastity, or rather of chaste reproduction. For Leutard they incarnate the revelvation that inspires him and his preaching.[89] It is interesting to find the same motif at different periods. The songs of Flanders kept alive the memory of the thirteenth-century Kloeffers and of their persecution by the inquisitor Robert le Bougre. One of these songs says that beekeeping was very common in the heretic villages and has the heretics killed not by burning but by the stings of their bees let loose on them by the executors. It goes on, revealingly, to draw a parallel between the stings of the bees and the bite of tongues of flame. This image is also evocative of Pentecost, when the Holy Spirit came down to the apostles. Another song tells the story of a young heretic from Béthune, also a beekeeper and also subjected to the same torture, but who charms the bees with a song that he used to sing to them when he cared for them. They form a halo around his head, and, when his executioners stabbed him, the bees attack them with such violence that they do not survive their victim.[90] These stories may have a connection with the thirteenth-century French word used to refer to those peasants who set up swarms of bees in hives in the forest clearings and assarts: the word *bigre*, according to the etymologists, comes from the Latin *apiger*, but the well-known pair *bigre-bougre* leads one to suspect at least a significant contamination.[91]

Earlier, we find the astonishing story, told by Gregory of Tours, of a man "from Bourges who went into the depths of the forest to cut wood. . . . He was attacked by a swarm of flies and as a result he became insane and remained so for two whole years. He made his way to the province of Arles, and there, dressed in animal skins, he prayed like a man of the Church. To lead him astray, the enemy [the devil] gave him the gift of divination." The man declared he was Christ and had with him a woman whom he called Mary. Crowds flocked to him, he laid hands on the sick and distributed the offerings he received among the poor. More than three thousand people followed him, including, besides peasants, some priests. The bishop of Le Puy had him assassinated.[92] Here again we find a community where the leader is inspired by flies, probably here meaning "honey flies." The theme of bees must have long been connected with that of prophetic inspiration and, beyond that, perhaps to the idea of a transmission or reproduction of the Spirit and through the Spirit.

It is clear that the file, as it can be reconstructed today, is very rich. It can be further enriched and its meaning, above all, is far from being fully understood. We can show that Bogomils and Paulicians were able to preach in Italy and even in Champagne; we can describe an eleventh century in tumult with the immense and sometimes chaotic impact of new faiths—those of the hermits, the reformers, and the heretics. The place of heresy in these movements and its profound significance are still far from being understood. Between the apparent naïveté of the illiterate peasant, the subtle docetism of the skillful cleric, and the humility of the nobleman turned beggar, the shadow of heresy slips through our hands and keeps it secrets.

> Could heresy have posed even more of a threat to Society than it did to Faith? Putting the question like this is to ignore the fact that in the language of the Church, the only one which has come down to us, the two cannot be separated. The time of heresy was also the time of new thinking about the theory of the *ordines.* The deviation from Faith shook the Order in its theological sense and almost overturned, even if it was not its original intention, the setting up of an earthly Order considered to be indissociably linked to the Kingdom of God[93]

The question of heresy comes back inevitably to the social order and the concepts underlying it. From the moment that sanctity takes root in the renunciation of the world, how is it possible to justify that most worldly of institutions, that of power? The answer is clear: at the very moment when the Cathars of Cologne were preaching the Spirit and a rejection of the world, the imperial entourage produced the cult of the three kings in order to legitimize the power of the prince.[94] Already the Cluniac peace movement had only been successful by relying on the veneration of relics. More than any other, the eleventh century is the century of wonders and idols. The heretics did not err when they criticized the cult of images and of confessor saints. And Bishop Gerard was clearly feeling uncomfortable in his response to the heretics of

Arras: "In the places where miracles happen but where the memory of the ancients does not give us anything certain, the bishops forbid the homage due to the saints, so that the old temples of the idols are not venerated in the manner of pagans and divine honours are not shamelessly paid at those tombs."[95] However, when he had to justify against their criticism the necessity of the hierarchy in the Church, it is to one of these magic saints that he refers, Dionysius the Areopagite "who, raised to the third heaven, saw the secrets of heaven and wrote two books on the Hierarchy of the Angels and that of the Church." One vision confronts another in a silent battle.

The heretics of Orleans promised their disciples: "We will reveal to you the Door of Salvation. Passing through it with the laying on of our hands you shall be washed clean of all your sins and filled with the gift of the Holy Spirit. . . . Then, your hunger satisfied with celestial nourishment, reborn through an internal satiety, you shall often see angelic visions with us, and uplifted and sustained by these, go with them, without delay or hindrance, where you wish, when you wish."[96] This dream of flight, which is also that of knowledge, is countered by Gerard with another ecstasy, the vision of the Pseudo-Dionysius: Christ in majesty, surrounded by the army of angels, motionless in severe perfection. "The King of Kings, through whom kings reign, who rules over Heaven and earth and is the whole State, who arranges and disposes in distinct orders the universal host, both the spiritual in heaven and the temporal here below, who presides over the supreme court and those on earth, who, in a miraculous order, gives the angels and men their offices at the right and established time."[97]

Notes

1. Duby, "Conclusion to the Symposium Heresies and Societies," cf. *Hérésies* . . .
2. Characteristic of this current are the work of Rafaello Morghen, most recently *Problèmes sur l'origine* [586], and of Arno Borst, *Die Katharer* [567]. *Contra,* Dondaine, *L'origine* [572].
3. Fulbert, *Letters* [38], introduction, p. xvi and letter no. 15, p. 30; Hariulf, *Chronicle* [48], p. xxx and xxxii; Adhemar de Chabannes, *Chronicle* [24], 3:39, p. 161; Bautier, *L'hérésie* [564]; Musset, *L'aristocratie* [257].
4. The description and complete critique can be found in Bautier, *L'hérésie* [564], which perhaps underestimates the documentation which may have been available to Paul of Chartres. The changes in style in the latter's account nevertheless reveal the "recycled" passages.
5. Fulbert's tone becomes increasingly polemic and aggressive in the course of the letter, indicating that he certainly suspects his correspondent of falling into the errors that he is denouncing. *PL,* 141, col. 196, *epist.* 5, not published by Behrends; also Fulbert, *Letters* [38], nos. 23 and 42. It was before Herfrid that Odoran of Sens was to attempt to justify himself, Bautier, *L'hérésie* [564].

6. Fulbert, *Letters* [38], nos. 22, 123, 40, 18, 43; Adalbero, *Carmen* [23], vv. 56–57.
7. Bautier, *L'hérésie* [564], and ed. Helgaud [49], introduction, p. 23; in Odoran ed. [58], p. 14. On the problems of Helgaud, Andrew of Fleury in De Certain, *Miracula* [27], 7:11, p. 266.
8. Huckel, *Les poèmes* [23], vv. 308–26, p. 176.
9. The affair must have had links with the struggles within the royal entourage between the friends of Eudes of Blois and those of the house of Anjou, see Bautier, *L'hérésie* [564], which refers also to the persistence of hostile acts directed toward the winning side: the name of the bishop Oury scratched out on a deed that he had had drawn up in the famous Bible of Theodulf, the misfortunes in Chartres of the Chancellor Evrard who had been the counsellor of Arfast, the cult in Burgundy of Bishop Thierry.
10. *PL,* 142, col. 1028, which is clearly using the cult of the Virgin to combat heresy.
11. But see also the letter written in Fleury by the Catalan monk John to the bishop of Vich, Oliba: "Enquire diligently in your bishopric and in your abbeys." Helgaud [49], app. 3:182. Note also the presence of the notebooks of Arnulf of Montmajour, a pupil of Fulbert, of a list of apocryphal and forbidden works, taken from the decree of Pope Gelasius I, Poly, *La Provence* [87], p. 185. Arnoul was probably a counsellor of the countess Azalaïs, mother of the count of Toulouse; 1056, council of Toulouse, *Mansi,* 19:849.
12. Gerard of Cambrai was addressing Roger of Châlons, not Renard of Liège, Noiroux, *Les deux premiers documents* [588]; Raoul Glaber, *Historiarum libri quinque* [64], 2:11, p. 49 (the reference is to Gibuin the Old and not to his nephew and successor), and Duby, *L'an mil* [615], p. 121; Anselm, *Gesta* [28], p. 226; Council of Rheims 1049, Mansi, 19:742.
13. *Gesta episcoporum cameracensium* [44], 3:32, p. 478. The priests "who eat up the sins of the people" are taken from *Hosea,* 4:8; Abbo of Fleury had already defended the monks against this accusation, Lemarignier, *Le monachisme* [386]. In the twelfth century, the heretics of Soissons used to say: "Mouth of priest, mouth of Hell," Guibert, *De vita sua* [46], 3:17, p. 212.
14. Borst, *Der Katherer* [567], p. 71.
15. Grisart, *Les cathares* [573], probably following *Le dict de la jument du Diable.* The castle is mentioned in 691, *GCN* 4, instr. col. 43, and in 877, *Annales de Saint-Bertin,* ed. F. Grat (Paris, 1964), p. 218.
16. Bautier, *L'Hérésie* [564], *RHF,* 10: 619.
17. Georges Duby, *Les trois ordres* [616], p. 218, casts doubt on the reality of the "heretic void."
18. Glaber, *Historiarum libri quinque* [64], 3:8, p. 75. "We have been dedicated for a long time to this sect which you have only just discovered; but we await the day when you will come to it in your turn, you and all the others, of all religions and all orders. And now still we believe that this day will come"; and Duby, *L'an mil* [615], p. 126.
19. Guibert, *History* [46], 2:5, p. 122. For the date of their stay in Saint-Germer, pp. v and ix; commentaries, p. 291 above. For Bucy, ibid., 2:17, p. 212.
20. St. Bernard, *Sermones in Cantica,* no. 66, addressed to Evervin of

Steinfeld, *PL*, 183, col. 1101; Grisart, *Les cathares* [573]; Thouzellier, *Hérésie et croisade* [596]; *RHF*, 15:790; Borst, *Die Katharer*, p. 197; in 1167 Robert of Epernay, rather than Epernon? in 1239, of Morains, 6 kms from Mont-Guimer. For the end of the twelfth century, see Thouzellier, *Catharisme* [597], pp. 40ff. and 470.

21. Cf. Guibert, p. 291 above and Rheims, 1148 and 1157, *Mansi*, 21:843.

22. De Smet, *De monnik Tanchelm* [571].

23. Bonenfant, *Un clerc* [565]. The parish that Jonas disputed with the abbey of Jette had been in the gift of the monastery of St. Cornelius in Cologne. For 1143, p. 289 above.

24. Peter the Venerable, *Contra Petrobrusianos* [61], written shortly before March-April 1138 (date confirmed by the dedication to William of Gap, after 1131, and to Oury of Die, before 1145), reworked in 1141–42 and quoted in a letter from Peter to St. Bernard in 1143; Peter of Bruys had arrived in the Diois some twenty years before the first version of the treatise, see Peter the Venerable, *Letters* [60], 2:285ff. He had died by the time of this writing, perhaps before the council of Pisa to which only his disciple Henry was brought.

25. *PL*, 182, col. 434, letters 241 and 242. Henry is here shown as having been chased from the city of Lausanne; his subsequent appearance in Le Mans is thus rather surprising. Should we read *Laudunensis* for *Lausanensis*? The heresy was again denounced in Toulouse in 1119, *Mansi*, 21:226. In 1129, the dower of the lady of Montpellier specified in its preamble "that the apostle Paul considered those who forbade marriage to be heretics." Germain, *Cartulaire des Guilhems* (Montpellier, 1884), no. 128.

26. Possible for the heretics of Nantes. Very probable for those of Périgord. Geoffrey of Auxerre, biographer of St. Bernard, places the latter's intervention at Sarlat in the context of his mission against Henry and his disciples, *PL*, 185, col. 313, 337, 410, 415, 1325. The document that gives us this information, *RHF*, 12:548, written by a monk Herbert, must be the work of the Spanish disciple of that name who was in Bernard's entourage at this time, and who wrote the book of the saint's miracles. A twelfth-century interpolation in Adhemar of Chabannes says that the Orleans heresy was introduced by a peasant "of Périgord"; Adhemar [24], p. 184. The placenames confirm the localization in the Sarladais, at Calviac. On the heretics of Toulouse, see Thouzellier, *Catharisme* [597], pp. 19 and 38.

27. E. Le Roy Ladurie, *Montaillou, village occitan de 1294 à 1324* (Paris, 1975), p. 156.

28. The words of Gerard of Cambrai to the heretics of Arras tell us more about his attitudes than about those of the accused. For comment on this, see Duby, *Les trois ordres* [616], p. 45.

29. Bautier, *L'hérésie* [564]; Glaber, *Historianum libri quinque* [64], 4:2, p. 94, and Taviani, *Naissance* [593].

30. L. Sala-Molins, ed. N. Eymerich, *Le manuel des inquisiteurs* (Paris-The Hague, 1973), p. 126.

31. Puech, *Catharisme* [589]; Jean Must, *Mouvements* [587], having made a critique of the methodology concludes: "These resemblances impose themselves on every page and may mislead the reader." He might as well have gone the whole way and said they cannot fail to mislead.

32. Glaber, *Historiarium libri quinque* [64], p. 76; Duby, *L'an mil* [615], pp. 56 and 127, though we have slightly changed the translation; B. Guérard, *Cartulaire de Saint-Père de Chartres* (Paris, 1840), 1:108, and *RHF,* 10:537.

33. Seguin, *GCN,* 12:32; Hérival, Musy, *Mouvements* [587]; Wazo, references, n. 42 below.

34. Folcuin, *Gesta abbatum, PL,* 137, col. 552 and 553; these remarks are certainly additions by Folcuin since they are not found in the Carolingian *vitae,* Boll. AASS, 2:560; Alain of Lille, *Contra hereticos,* 1:74, *PL,* 210, col. 376.

35. Taviani, *Le mariage* [594], and earlier in *Naissance* [593]. We have slightly changed Taviani's translations.

36. Musy, *Mouvements* [587]; *Vita Gauzlini* [25], 56, p. 98, and the synod of Arras, *PL,* 142, col. 1294.

37. Musy, *Mouvements* [587]; Landolf, *Historia Mediolanensis,* 2:27, *MGH SS,* 8:65; Paul of Chartres, see p. 283 above.

38. This is the opinion of Huguette Tavianti and Claude Carozzi.

39. The list of heresies drawn up by Isidore of Seville was to pass into Gratian's *Decretum,* Dec. c. 39, C. 24, Qu. 3; then in the fourteenth century into the inquisitor's manual. Sala-Molins, *Le manuel,* p. 56. On the psychology of the inquisitor, see Duby, "Conclusion to the Symposium," cf. *Hérésies . . .*

40. Musy, *Mouvements* [587].

41. *GCN,* 8, inst. col. 494.

42. *Gesta episcoporum Leodicensium,* cap. 62, *MGH SS,* 7: 226.

43. Taviani, *Naissance* [593]; Gerard of Csanad, *Deliberatio supra hymnum trium puerorum,* 4: 1. 469 and 8: 76, ed. Silagi G. (Turnhout, 1978).

44. Runciman, *Le manichéisme* [590], p. 45; Thouzellier, *Le vocable* [599]. On the Armenian preacher, see Génicot, *L'érémitisme* [368].

45. Runciman, *Le manichéisme* [590], p. 48; Taviani, *Le mariage* [594]; it is interesting to note that the two oldest manuscripts of the *Passio sanctae Theclae,* a Paulician apocryphal text, come from Orleans (tenth century) and Le Mans (eleventh century).

46. Borst, *Die Katharer,* pp. 74 and 77. But Steven Runciman, *Le manichéisme* [590], p. 67ff., seems to indicate that the persecution under Manuel Comnenus was much less severe than under Alexis. As for the return from the crusade, it is rather too late to account for the apostolic heretics of Cologne of 1143. This is why Arno Borst seeks the explanation in hypothetical merchants. Anselm of Alexandria's text, often invoked, is too late and furthermore refers not to the second but to the fourth crusade.

47. Evervin, *PL,* 182, col. 677.

48. Eckbert, *Sermones,* 1: 4, *PL,* 195, col. 17. The mention of an archbishop named Arnold refers either to Arnold II (1151–1156) or to Arnold I (1138–1151); the texts only mention two trials, in 1143 and 1163.

49. Thouzellier, *Hérésie et croisade* [596].

50. Noiroux, *Les deux premiers documents* [588], which focuses attention on this text, but follows the old identification (Egbert of Liège, cleric, 1010-1027). The bishop *Aboldus* must be *Arnoldus.*

51. Guibert, *De vita sua* [46], p. 213.

52. Peter the Venerable [61], 10, p. 13; Guibert, *De vita sua* [46], p. 214.

53. Peter the Venerable, [61], 116, p. 69; Primov, *Les bougres* (Paris, 1975), p. 117.

54. Guibert, *De vita sua* [64], 2: 5, p. 122. The heretical nature of the people described emerges from the name given to them, *deonandi* corrected to *deonarii*; see p. 294 above.

55. Guibert, *De vita sua* [64], 3:17, p. 213.

56. Peter the Venerable [61], 16, pp. 16, 18 and 19; Runciman, *Le manichéisme* [590], pp. 139 and 149.

57. On these heretics from Périgord, see p. 280 above. Formula given in *RHF*, 12: 548.

58. I, 6, *PL*, 192, col. 1255. The heretics attacked by Hugh cannot be the supporters of Eon de l'Etoile; their heresiarch, unlike the latter, did not in fact appear before the inquisitors. Hugh's origins, his legation to Montpellier in 1134, his presence in Pisa in 1135, must have made him pay particular attention to heresy. If we are to believe Alain of Lille, the Cathars did not attribute free will to the fallen angels, Thouzellier, *Catharisme* [597], p. 85.

59. Peter the Venerable [61], 6, pp. 10, 12, 14, 31, 26 and 27.

60. E. Germer-Durand, *Cartulaire de Notre-Dame de Nîmes* (Nîmes, 1875), no. 171, where the nickname corresponds to the placename Bougarel; map p. 390; O. Terrin, *Cartulaire du chapitre d'Agde* (Nîmes, 1969), nos. 331 and 265; J. Rouquette, *Cartulaire de Maguelone* (Montpellier, 1912), vol. 1, no. 170; Albanés, *GCNN*, Arles, no. 2563. On the accusation of homosexuality, see Guibert, *De vita sua* [64], p. 212.

61. Elements in Borst, p. 204, and Runciman, *Le manichéisme* [590], pp. 168.

62. Thouzellier, *Catharisme* [597], p. 40. St. Bernard's biographer writes: "The weavers who call themselves Arians . . ." *PL*, 185, col. 411; and Peter of Vaux de Cernay attaches the name to the castle, Borst, *Die Katharer*, p. 212.

63. Runciman, *Le manichéisme* [590], p. 111; Borst, *Die Katharer*, p. 209, dodges the question. *Policien*, cf. Littré, *Dictionnaire de la langue française*.

64. *Circumcelliones*, which recalls St. Augustine, is used by Guibert, *De vita sua* [64], 2:5, p. 122, with the sense of "restless wanderer" to describe the itinerant habits of the *deonarii*. *Katafrigae* is only used in Cologne, Borst, *Die Katharer*, p. 205.

65. "Cathars" seems for a long time to have been used by the theologians to mean Novatianists. To find the sense of the dualists, it is necessary to look to Asia Minor in the fourth century, Thouzellier, *Le vocable* [599]. The use of the word by the western heretics to refer to themselves, n. 67 below, does not then seem to have taken root in the western theological tradition. The fact that Landolf says of the *Patari* that they are *falsi cathari*—Borst, *Die Katharer*, p. 73—inclines us rather to think that at this period certain Italian heretics chose to call themselves by this name.

66. References in Du Cange (1845), 5:137.

67. The synonym *Deonarii-Publicani* is found in 1167 in Vézelay, Runciman, *Le manichéisme* [590], p. 111; Borst, *Die Katharer*, p. 209, prefers to translate *"tonloyer"* (toll-collector) because of the publicans; but the form had already appeared in Guibert, see p. 000 above. Eckbert deliberately groups together "those whom our Germany calls Cathars, Flanders

Piphiles, Gaul, weavers," Thouzellier, *Hérésie et croisade* [596]. The council of Rheims of 1157 defines the *Piphili*: "The sect of the Manicheans" led by "abject weavers" who wish to appear "more pure and more clean, *puriores mundioresque*"; which recalls the definition, *cathari id est mundi*, given by Eckbert following the heretics themselves, *Mansi*, 21: 843; Borst, *Die Katharer*, p. 209, see *piphiles* as deriving from *popelicani* . . .

68. Thouzellier, *Catharisme* [597], pp. 13 and 19.
69. Violante, *La povertà* [600]; Duby, "Conclusion au colloque . . . ," cf. *Hérésies* . . . and *Les trois ordres* [616], p. 199.
70. Musy, *Mouvements* [587]; *contra* Taviani, *Le mariage* [594].
71. Cf. the comments of Raffaello Morghen in his assessment of Koch, *Frauenfrage* [577].
72. Bur, *La Champagne* [74], p. 109. See the "voluntary poverty" of Count Thibaud, Duby, *Les trois ordres* [616], p. 262.
73. On the accusations of St. Bernard against certain princes and bishops, p. 278 above.
74. On Godfrey, see Parisse, *La noblesse* [261], p. 41.
75. An old work, Pfister, *Etudes sur le règne de Robert le Pieux* (Paris, 1885), p. 327; Bautier, *L'hérésie* [564]. On this type of culture, see Claude Carozzi, introduction in Adalbero [23]; on the rivalry of this faction with that of the monks, see p. 163 above.
76. Taviani, *Naissance* [593]. On the hereticizing elements in Carolingian theology, cf. also Musy, *Mouvements* [587].
77. *Praeloquia* [65], cols. 166–67, and p. 145 above.
78. Musy, *Mouvements* [587]; Montclos, *Lanfranc et Bèrenger* [583]; Somerville, "The Case Against Berengar of Tours: A New Text." *Studi Gregoriani* (1972): 53.
79. Cf. pp. 177–78 above.
80. Thus in Le Mans, Henry's supporters threatened to kill the canons.
81. Guibert, *De vita sua* [64], 3: 16 and 17, pp. 211 and 212.
82. Musy, *Mouvements* [587].
83. Duby, *Les trois ordres* [616], p. 218; Chenu, *Moines* [349].
84. Duby, "Conclusion au colloque. . . ." cf. *Hérésies*. . . . and the remarks on usury in the thirteenth century in Borst, *Die Katharer*, p. 92.
85. Musy, *Mouvements* [587].
86. On Valdès, see Thouzellier, *Catharisme* [597], p. 16ff. The evangelicals of Cologne must have been distinguished from the Cathar community of the city; it is their very disputes that have made this clear.
87. Duby, "Conclusion au colloque . . ." Cf. *Hérésies* . . .
88. Ivanov, *Livres et légendes* [576], and the development of the theme of the evil son of God, the dishonest steward, Morghen, *Medioevo* [584], p. 260. The horse and metempsychosis, Le Roy Ladurie, *Montaillou*, p. 454; Bordenave and Vialelle, *Aux racines* [566].
89. The swarm of bees that penetrates the body of Leutard, "through his secret natural way," Duby, *L'an mil* [615], p. 121, reminds us of the obsessions of President Schreiber as described by Freud.
90. Primov, *Les bougres*, p. 19. The bee as God's messenger in Slav folklore, Runciman, *Le manichéisme* [590], p. 81. The idea of a cultural transplant, Le Roy Ladurie, *Montaillou*, p. 509.

91. Littré gives the form *"bigres à l'huile"* to describe in the fifteenth century the Minims, famous for their strict fasting, the southern origins of whose order required them to cook only in oil.

92. Gregory of Tours, *Historia Francorum*, 10: 25, *MGH, SS Rer. Merov.*, 1: 440.

93. Taviani, *Le mariage* [594].

94. See pp. 334–35 below.

95. Gerard of Cambrai [41], col. 1303.

96. Paul of Chartres, see pp. 283–84 above.

97. *PL*, 142, col. 1307.

CHAPTER

10

Feudal Attitudes

What think you of the idol, brother?

—Bernard of Angers

One of the phenomena that characterizes the mental and intellectual history of the twelfth century is the appearance in documents of the fantastic and legendary—what Jacques Le Goff called "the great wave of folklore of the twelfth and thirteenth centuries."[1] A careful study of the written sources shows that this tendency began around the year 1000. Georges Duby has contrasted the new language of the Burgundian monk Raoul Glaber with that of Richer of Rheims, which looks back to a historical culture that had flourished around the great Carolingian sanctuaries of the north.[2] For what we see of the culture before 1000 almost always follows this model, sustained by a clerical elite that was reviving and adapting an intellectual tool that had formerly been perfected by the didactic authors of the late empire. This elite placed at the disposal of the Frankish monarchy the cultural heritage of the great families of the Gallo-Roman aristocracy. Remote from this "Carolingian renaissance," popular culture retained its "traditional," "primitive" techniques, belief, and mentalities. But we begin to glimpse this only when ecclesiastical culture assumed some "popular" elements, notably as a result of its missionary needs. Ecclesiastical culture initially rejected these "folk" elements, obliterating them by imposing its own practices, and distorting them by profoundly changing their meaning. Thus two distinct cultural models coexisted, but without merging to any degree. One was "popular," based on beliefs in ambiguous forces, both good and bad; the other was "clerical," which followed a certain Latin rationality and attempted to separate completely good from bad, true from false. To understand the increasingly

309

obvious intrusion, during the eleventh and twelfth centuries, of whole layers of the old popular culture into the ecclesiastical culture and to grasp the establishment of new cultural types, we need to distinguish three cultural levels: that of the peasants and petty knights in the country, that of the entourage of the great princely families, and finally that of royalty.

Peasant Paganism and "Savage Thought"

Many traces have been found in the countryside, despite successive waves of rural evangelization, of practices and beliefs described for want of a better word as pagan survivals. Recent research, based chiefly on "missionary" sources, sermons, or penitentials from the ninth and tenth centuries, shows that there was in fact an astonishing permanence among the peasants of a truly pagan religiosity.[3] In the following century it was not so much the content of this religiosity that changed as its dress.

The first piece of evidence—negative—of the strength of paganism in the early years of this study is provided by the attitude of the Church with regard to some statues representing a supernatural lady. At the end of the sixth century, the deacon Wulfilaïcus, arriving at Ivois-Carignan in the diocese of Trèves, had been obliged to turn away peasants from the cult of Diana, who was worshipped in this place in the form of a large idol and several smaller ones. He had them pulled down. The statues were demolished, but the danger remained. It was still feared in the ninth century that the Virgin and Child might be confused with Venus carrying Aeneas. In the tenth century, however, in the south the attitude toward such "simulacra" changed. The first statue of the Virgin was made shortly after 946 for Stephen II, bishop of Clermont.[4] At the beginning of the eleventh century, the history of the master of the cathedral school of Angers, Bernard, shows perfectly the final change in attitude.

In 1010 Bernard, pupil of Fulbert of Chartres—himself the pupil of Gerbert of Rheims—was traveling in Auvergne and Rouergue. In Aurillac he and his companion stared with an embarassed irony at the reliquary statue of St. Gerald, "a statue remarkable for the fineness of its gold and its precious stones, which reproduced the features of the human face so skillfully that the peasants who saw it felt themselves transfixed by its farseeing eyes, in which they believed that they sometimes saw a sign of favor for their wishes." And Bernard said jokingly: "What think you of the idol, brother? Would not Jupiter and Mars have been content with such a one?" And later, praying before the statue of St. Faith in Conques, he confessed: "I despised it as if it had been a statue of Venus or Diana, I treated it as a simulacrum." St. Faith, a touchy and grasping virgin, soon taught him with her redoubtable miracles that she would not stand for such mockery.[5]

The fears of the educated were not without foundation. Other texts show that the worship of "simulacra" was still an expression of a cultural and religious system that was clearly on the edge of paganism.

In the mid-eighth century, the council of Leptines in Hainault had issued an impressive list of forbidden rituals and spells. Among them we find not only the usual practices of country magic but also the persistence of pagan temples, reduced, it is true, to "little houses," and the traditional Dionysian processions of idols, "the pagan race called the *gyrias*, with slashed clothes and shoes."[6] The hazards of documentation sometimes allow us a clearer glimpse here and there of the degree to which the "superstitions and paganisms" denounced at Leptines, far from retreating or being pushed to the edges of territories, were still alive and kicking. Thus it was with the rituals of moon worship in the countryside between Worms and Fulda.

The twenty-first prohibition of Leptines concerned "the eclipse of the moon, when people said: 'Moon, to you be victory.' " Nearly a century later, as night was falling, Rabanus Maurus, then abbot of Fulda, was quietly meditating in the calm of his house when suddenly he heard a general outcry so loud that it reached the heavens. He sent to find out the reason and the answer came: "It is to help the moon in her travail." The next day he made inquiries and was given a detailed description of the rituals of the *Vince Luna* by some informants who asserted that the same had been observed where they lived. An eclipse plunged the peasants into a kind of trance. Some blew horns, some imitated the grunting of pigs, while others shot arrows at the sky or threw torches; the hedges were cut down around the houses and pots were broken. The indignant abbot preached the peasants a vehement sermon—and here we find the cultural imperviousness described by Jacques Le Goff. Two steps away from one of the most important abbeys of the Carolingian world the peasants were openly flouting the prohibitions of the councils.[7] Furthermore, his informers told him that the aim of the different rituals they had described was to help the moon against "the monsters that attack her." He exclaimed: "But it is forbidden to believe that humans can change themselves into beasts." So the monsters attacking the moon are thought to be werewolves, frequently identified in European folklore with the spirits of unbaptized babies.[8] In the eleventh century, Burchard of Worms in his penitential asks: "Have you done what certain women are accustomed to do: when a child has died without being baptised they take the corpse of the child, putting it in some secret place and piercing the body with a stake, saying that if they do not do this the child will rise up and could do harm to many." What harm? The spirit of the father of Guibert of Nogent was even after death gnawed in the side by his dead bastard son who died unbaptized; the wound was as horrible to see as the cries of the child were to hear.[9] Peasant practices thus form part of a logical cycle of beliefs and express the relationship of man with a deified and ambivalent nature: an oppressive religion, for it was probably not with any lightness of heart that the peasants of the Rhine watched the village witch carry away their babies to pierce their hearts, but custom demanded it.

The same Burchard of Worms describes in detail the ceremony performed by the women of certain villages to bring rain. They would form a procession, away from the presence of men, to bring one of their number, a young girl, to a field where grew a henbane plant. The girl had to pick the plant with great care and then it was tied to the little toe of her left foot. Her companions would then take her to the river and plunge her in: she rinsed herself with water and sprinkled it on them; finally they took her back to the village, being careful to walk backwards and to keep their eyes fixed on the river.[10] The presence of the henbane, effective against the pains of childbirth—and also hallucinogenic and poisonous—is a clear indication of the meaning of the ritual: the miming of the fertility of the earth through heavenly rain. It should be noticed that the scene took place in broad daylight—there is no question of secret witchcraft. And the fact that it was the women of the village who performed the ritual gives us a good idea of their power in the community.

"Paganisms" are found as much in the south as in the north. Gervase of Tilbury, an acute observer of the peculiarities of his time, gives us an interesting custom of the inhabitants of the lower Rhône valley. They would put the coffins of their dead into the water and the current would take them to a bend in the river, near Arles, where they would run aground. The gravediggers would lift them out and bury them in the Alyscamps, that vast area of tombs that filled the land between the city walls and the marshes near the river. To pay for the passage of their dead, the peasants placed a penny on the coffin. If the coin had been removed, the coffins bobbed in the Rhône without coming to land. Here we have a paganizing funerary practice that recalls the coin paid to Charon, the boatman of the underworld. And the fame of the great cemetery of Arles in the twelfth century is an indication of the extent of the ritual.[11]

Many of the allusions that we find scattered by reticent authors in many texts probably refer to practices similar to those we have described, and which were, in the tenth and perhaps in the eleventh centuries, both more general and much more dominant than we might imagine. The difficulty lies in the invariably incomplete and damaged state of our information, since our texts are not interested in reporting the act of magic or the ritual either logically or in its entirety. A manuscript may have a magic formula scribbled in its margin,[12] but we know that it should have been "chanted," that it was probably accompanied by certain gestures, the use of certain objects, the sacrifice of certain animals, and that it was probably done at a certain time and in a certain place.[13] Once these elements have disappeared, how can this or that ritual be replaced in relation to the general concept of the world that inspired it and of which it was an expression? Here again, as in the case of the heresies but in a different way, the mirror of our documentation reflects back to us a broken image, and we should bear this in mind.

One might think that this type of reconstruction would be of only marginal interest to the historian, and that we should distrust precisely this "folklore" element. But might it not be the worst of anachronism to gloss over what was, at least for some, the essential? When we cast a prosaic glance at hedges, pots, horns, henbane, pigs, coins, or rivers, we should not forget that for the peasants of that time the relationship of man to his surroundings was very different from this relation in our day. And we should not be afraid to ask what was the meaning of this or that ritual: a society is defined as much by what is latent in it as by what it reveals.[14] Let us return to the theme of the moon's eclipse, banal though it may be. This is clearly a very emotional ritual and we might be surprised that there should be such intense fear of the newborn, turned into a ghost. But if we recall on the one hand that a very ancient custom seems to have obliged parents to delay baptism of their children until the age of two, and on the other hand that at this period one baby in two died before this age, then it becomes easier to understand the enormous sense of guilt felt by the parents and particularly by the mothers. And that is leaving aside infanticide.[15] The "superstition" clearly indicates in the group the tension that quantitative demographic study would lead us to expect. Going beyond the figures, here we are dealing with relationships between one person and another and with himself.

Let us now examine another area, that of customary gifts. Historians have always expressed surprise at the smallness of some of the most ancient dues: a few chickens, some eggs, a capon.[16] They are found particularly in the polyptyques and then later—but in a more precise and less scattered form—in the rent rolls of banal lordship, especially in the twelfth century, at a time when their meaning had no doubt been partially lost. Their survival, like their low economic value, inclines us to give them a psychological value, which the old jurists called when speaking of the rent a value indicating submission. These dues were called *oblata, oblationes,* presents, offerings, and in the oldest texts, *eulogiae* or *xenia.*[17] They were brought to the master's house by the peasant households on the great feast days—Christmas, Easter, Whitsun, with variations in date—and around the feastdays of certain saints, which corresponded to local habits. And we see a relationship between the animal offered and the festival. The rhythm of the seasons? But the Christmas capons, the "Shrove Tuesday" hens, the Easter eggs are not only that. What did the lord do with these presents? It is usually implicitly admitted that he added them to his provisions or ate them himself. But a few texts give us a clue: a certain pope, his ninth-century biography tells us, used to distribute them to the poor. An abbot from Le Mans of the seventh century on the day following the offering would invite the freemen to a great meal. A tax roll from

Lorraine of the twelfth century links the *oblata* with the *tria comitia*, the three customary assemblies.[18] So it seems very probable that at the beginning at least the lord redistributed the gifts on the occasion of a feast. This raises two questions. What was the meaning of the offerings, whose original "magic," or if one prefers "religious," character is not in question?

Macrobius, the "founder of the Middle Ages," and an excellent witness of the state of paganism in his time, stresses the religious significance of the egg, a symbol of cosmic perfection.[19] And to this day the innocent custom of Easter eggs is evidence of the vitality of the folklore of eggs. There has been a similar development in the offering of wax candles. Originally the freedmen had to bring them—probably with some food—to the tomb of their master as funerary offerings. In the seventh century, the Church, which did not approve of such practices, succeeded in having the offerings moved from the tomb to the altar of the funerary basilica. At the end of the ninth century, grateful peasants brought wax candles to Gerald of Aurillac. A century later the descendants of these same peasants venerated the statue of the same Gerald in a way that Bernard of Angers thought idolatrous. By contrast, in the twelfth century in the Limousin the bringing of wax to the lord had become something very common, even if wax was still scarce and precious.[20]

Thus it is possible that the value of the offering of such presents was still very strong in the tenth and eleventh centuries. The other problem is to know what the free peasants did at these same festivals. Did they too offer presents to the great, or to one another, or to some local saint? Were these presents consumed at a feast of which we still find traces in folklore?[21] If we knew this we could map out areas of collective conviviality and areas where this conviviality came under the control of the lord. The preeminence of the lord would appear to be based both in relation to the rhythm of nature and to the ritual exchanges of presents that marked its pulse.

A systematic study of such gifts of prosperity could offer much to the understanding of the relations of peasants with the lord and, more generally, of peasant society. It is to be hoped that there will be more of this type of research. Already it seems likely that the true Christianization of the country areas was far from being complete in the early eleventh century and that ancestral rituals that had continued to be used despite the teachings of the Church had survived among the majority of the "rustics."

Moving from the peasants to the knighthood and the petty nobility, we seem at first to find ourselves in the same mental world, and the country origins of so many of the *milites castri* is quite clear. Borrowing again from that admirable document, the life of Gerald of Aurillac, we find a portrait of the time of a knight in the saint's escort called Adraldus. This man was, openly and publicly, a magician, and he liked to display his magic powers. Gerald and his escort visiting Marcolés passed by the megalith that still stands there today. Adraldus said he could jump over the stone with the help of his magic. Gerald quietly made the sign of the cross and the magic failed. Not only does a future saint tolerate at the end of the ninth century a magician knight in his escort, but above all he avoids openly opposing, even though he disapproves, such rituals that were obviously enjoyed by his assistants. Adraldus was furthermore famous in the region. The *Miracles* of St. Gerald, at the beginning of the tenth century, recount how he had lit the "fire of the sorcerers" on the night of 1 January; a storm had broken out and two of his servants had been struck by lightning.[22]

More than two centuries later, even when they had exchanged rusticity for chivalry the knights had not forgotten the disquieting practices of their country ancestors. Our informant, once again, is Gervase of Tilbury. At a feast held in Arles attended by Catalan and Provençal knights, they were practicing fighting on horseback. One of them shot like an arrow into the middle of the lists, whereupon another, watching, turned his head and spoke certain words. The horse stopped so abruptly that it fell over and could not get up; then the rider, before the assembled lords and ladies, addressed the knight "whom everyone knew to be the author of this spell" and begged him not to avenge in this way the affronts of an old enmity. Touched, the knight decided to be satisfied with this public revenge. He turned his whole body in another direction and uttered "the contrary words," thus causing the horse to stand up as easily as he had made it fall down.[23] So it comes as no surprise to find in the manuscripts magic invocations intended to protect or heal horses. In Merseburg Wotan was still invoked, in Paris they prayed to Denis, Rusticus, and Eleutherius and the "thousand, thousands and dozens of hundreds of thousand," that is the army of the angels, the celestial hierarchy.[24]

These beliefs and practices were expressed among the petty nobility in stories that differed from those of peasant culture, and in which can be found its hopes and failures. The most striking example is the story of Melusine, the "land-improving and maternal" fairy, who married a petty lord who owed her his fortune and family.[25] As Jacques Le Goff writes, Melusine "comes from a distant time before Christianity": this snake woman who loves the water, who enchants, and who can give wealth is the medieval *guivre* or serpent, the Latin *lamia*, of which Hincmar of Rheims speaks with disgust, who fascinates and weakens men.[26] She is sometimes connected in our texts with the story of the triple fairies. But here again what interests us are the historic inflections of the folk theme. It appears in the written sources at the end of the twelfth century, but the authors who give it reveal at the same time that it had been connected, for several generations at least, with a certain number of families of petty *domini castri*—meaning, at this period, not great castellans but ordinary knights. We are struck both by how widespread the theme is—it is found in Wales, in Normandy, in Langres, in the land around Valence and Provence—and how specifically it is localized, often in precisely named villages.

The motif is reduced to its simplest form. The knight meets in the woods the woman whom he marries, who brings him prosperity and beautiful children. He is forbidden to see her naked. One day he defies her command when she is bathing and he discovers that she is a watersnake woman. As a result of the transgression, she disappears. But she returns in the night, to keep watch over her children. Only the nurses are able to see her. A century later the legend seems to be associated with two great castellan families, the Lusignans in Poitou—and now the fairy is called Melusine—and the Sassenages in the Dauphiné. The accent is on the land clearing carried out by the fairy and the castles she builds. Nicolas Chorier in the seventeenth century was to say that "this story had such an impression on the credulity of the inhabitants of the land of the Sassenage family that they are convinced that their lord is descended from Melusine."[27] So now the motif has passed from the knights to two great families. In Sassenage it is presented as coming from Lusignan, but this should not deceive us; it conceals simply the idea of a relationship, obviously one to be proud of, with a family that had at times risen to the monarchy. In reality we can see time and again on the map how deeply rooted was the cult of Melusine among the peasants. The Sassenage family were also lords of Montélier in the Valentinois where we have one of the first mentions of the snake woman, and the castle of Sassenage is in an area where the cult of St. Agatha, patron saint of nursing mothers, was still very widespread in the nineteenth century.

The women would feast on the saint's day and this meal, from which men were barred, was called having the *gueta*—which in dialect means either the agatha or (female) cat. Special cakes were sometimes made, with the same name. As Arnold Van Gennep has emphasized, the area is quite clearly defined; nowhere else do we find any knowledge of the festival. Similarly in Poitou, the area particularly connected with the cult of Melusine is quite precise and here we find the making of special cakes, "merlusine cakes." There is also a Burgundian area, with mentions occurring in the Yonne, Côte-d'Or and the Jura.[28]

It is tempting to cross over to the third level, properly peasant, but unfortunately it is documented only from the sixteenth century or even later. We find at that time that Melusine is related to crops, the fertility of the fields, and the grape harvest. But at the same time, no doubt under the delayed influence of the Counter-Reformation, she gradually becomes associated with the devil.

Emmanuel Le Roy Ladurie shows in a folk text from the Vendée that reveals the influence of the *Chanson de Geste* a Melusine who has turned witch and who intervenes in the conflicts between legendary castellans—"the one-eyed man of Py-Chabot" and "Thibault the One-armed." At the same time, a large peasant community like that of Les

Jault in the Nivernais, continued to believe in its guardian snake-woman.

It seems that we must presume rather than a progression of the theme in time, a simple progressive discovery with certain inflections which are properly historical of different levels. Let us return to the motif as we find it in the twelfth-century sources. The essence of Melusine at this time is not the building of castles or the clearing of forests nor the corn and grape harvests, but rather the assurance of a posterity. The etymology—*Mater Lucina*—the nurses, the children she watches over, all this clearly refers to maternity. Jacques Le Goff has stressed the fact that the true hero of the story, and an attractive one, is Melusine and not the knight: the snakewoman is a good mother. Unfortunately she is a mother who is dead, and that through the fault of her husband, who did not respect a prohibition deeply concerning her femininity.

It is probable that we have here a properly female folk theme, which is to say one created and transmitted by women. To understand its meaning we need to recall some elements of the question. First is the high rate of female mortality in childbirth; the disappearance of the mother, exhausted by pregnancies, is not then simply a folk motif. Then the situation of women in the peasantry of the time; even if it seems certain that the world of the tenants on the large Carolingian estates was at least quantitatively one where men predominated,[29] we cannot be so sure that this was true among the owners of allods. The high number of peasant women who were simple protegées of the abbeys has already been seen. One might say that it is to be expected that women in a hostile world have more need of protection than men; but these women were protected with their families, of which they were the head. Among the Catalan allodialists—for whom there is rather better documentation—Pierre Bonnassie has also found examples of women heads of household or mistresses of their own property. The survival of a predominantly female cult in some country areas could well correspond to the presence of larger and more dynamic female groups there.

Finally, we need to look at the importance of two special categories of women: nurses and midwives. We know that nurses were the best guardians of the myth of Melusine. But the fairy also ensured a successful delivery, which brings us to the character occasionally glimpsed in the texts, that of the old woman, mistress of births and more generally of sexual relationships; couples who did not get along or who were infertile had recourse to her spells.[30] She could also, when she wanted, limit births, probably with the help of potions inducing abortion. It was no doubt she who "unbewitched" the children who died unbaptized. She was sometimes asked to get rid of a brutal or importunate husband; if things went wrong she might end up being burned at the stake along with her client.[31]

It was an old woman who "broke" the evil spells that separated the mother of Guibert of Nogent from her husband. We learn from the abbot's memoirs that this old woman was the sister of Suger, prior of Saint-Germer-de-Fly, and that she lived an ascetic life near this monastery, esteemed by all. Guibert's mother, when she became a widow, came to join her and lived with her. Both of them were very concerned with the afterlife and one day when they were talking together they promised one another that whichever one of them should die first would come back and tell the other what it was like. Naturally, Guibert is careful to explain that all this was done *per Dei gratiam*. But the old lady was under no illusions: on the point of death she saw in a dream the doors of the church closing before her soul, and at the very moment of her death, she had to drive away, with a terrible conjuration, a demon with enormous eyes that was standing at the foot of her bed. Ask nothing of me, she cried. But it was in vain; Guibert's mother saw her spirit being dragged away by two black figures. Prior Suger too was rather strange.[32] These brief and almost involuntary revelations show that sorcery was an integral part of the life of the knightly families of the Beauvaisis.

Nurses and midwives, witches to a greater or lesser extent, were thus probably and had been for a long time the transmitters of the theme of the ill-used water-snake-woman. But the reemergence of this theme in literature at the end of the twelfth century through the intervention of some knightly families is a timely reminder that demographic prosperity is achieved thanks to women. The theme, with its implicit threat to the husband who ignores what is prohibited and its insistence on the affection of the dead mother for her children, tends to reinforce the place of women, or at least mothers, in the knightly household.

This elevation from "savage" thought thus corresponds to the emergence of a truly knightly culture, of peasant origin, in the written sources. Historians have rightly stressed the suspect Christianity of this culture and at the same time the contamination and pressure exercised by it on properly clerical culture.[33] And it would be wise to remember that the land of the idols with staring eyes, which so struck the master of the cathedral school of Angers, was also a land of long-standing Cluniac influence; that the peace councils of the 1020s, which aimed at disciplining the violence of the knights, were entirely founded on the displaying of relics; that the miracles of the saints at this period could quite as well be ones that caused harm as ones that did good.[34] Beneath the saints of the eleventh century lay the figures of the old heroes or demigods, and it was these that the knights venerated or respected. Later, the clerics born of the Gregorian Reform were able to fight against this tendency, or at the very least to denounce it. Nevertheless, the monks, and Cluniacs foremost among them, had been able to understand it and make use of it. It was after all in the Mâconnais around the great abbey and under its influence that the alliance between *nobilitas* and *militia* had been both early and deep-rooted.[35]

Epic and Chivalry

The knights too participated in the wave of folklore that entered the written culture—a movement of which they were the vanguard. Another current that joined this tide were the epic legends that were to appear at the end of the eleventh and the beginning of the twelfth centuries with the flowering in literature of the *chanson de geste*. This in turn was to be transformed and imbued with the ideas of chivalry.

Experts on the *chanson de geste* seem to be in agreement on one thing at least: the *chanson* first appeared in its written form at the beginning of the twelfth century. It was preceded by a period of development lasting in some cases for a few decades, while for others it went back two or three centuries or even more if one accepts that the *chanson de geste* is merely the expression of a "latent" epic current reaching far into the past.[36] Whatever the value placed on the last decades of the eleventh century—an important stage in a very long development or the sudden appearance as if from nowhere, of an almost unprecedented poetic flowering—it seems to be accepted today that the historical events that gave rise to the legends, far from being "unimportant random facts," had deeply affected people's imaginations.[37] And this is very important. Before the *chanson de geste*, in Bédier's famous words, there was local legend. We are tempted to say, there was nothing but local legend. But is this not more than sufficient? And does not the principal interest of such research lie in the study of the diffusion of these local legends, their confluence, and their eventual emergence in a single culture that was to develop its own themes and its heroes? Increasingly, before the flowering in the twelfth century, we begin to see

> a considerable collection of traditions, more or less complex, fragmentary or dissimilar one from another, which all claimed to be history but none of which was yet more than pseudo-history, where Charlemagne and Charles the Bald were one person, where the Ogiers become so telescoped and interconnected as to be confused, where all sieges and wars lasted for seven years and where all the armies were counted in hundreds of thousands of men.

It is possible to trace different stages in this development. We shall look first at the *Chanson de Roland*. The real existence of a Count Roland, a follower of Charlemagne, who ruled in the west, appears to have survived the most rigorous investigation.[38] And it seems likely that it was precisely this western seat of power that made of Roland the hero of an epic known to the Frankish contingents on the Loire who were traditionally involved whenever there was an expedition to Spain.[39] This road was traveled by as many knights riding to war as pilgrims. At the beginning of the tenth century, a monk of Saint-Denis, forging an important document, associated in the signatures at the bottom the names of Charlemagne and Roland. A century later, Roland is so closely associated with Charlemagne that he appears in the legend woven around the unfortunate exploits of the governor of Vienne, Girart.[40] When the crusades in Spain began in the early eleventh century, Norman adventurers went to seek glory in Catalonia. Thus a whole "Catalan and Navarrese geography" is introduced into the legend. At the end of the century, while they continued to fight in Spain, the Normans were also in Epirus, adding a new layer of place and personal names.[41]

In a *langue d'oïl* version of the *Chanson de Sainte-Foy*, written around 1100 probably at Fleury, we find an interesting list of the tribes of the Saracens, similar to that of the "Baligant" of the *Chanson de Roland*. It seems that there were close links from the early eleventh century between the abbey of Fleury and that of Ripoll in Catalonia, and between the abbey of Sainte-Foy in Conques, Angers, and certain Norman lords. In 1065–1075, a monk of San-Millan in the Rioja, between Navarre and Castille, knew the legend of Roncesvalles.[42]

Thus the legend of Roland appears principally as the justification in the early eleventh century for the expansion of the people of the west and particularly of the Normans. But it encounters other epic traditions and merges with them. We should not forget the other major current of the Spanish crusades, that of the Burgundians. Some of the Cluniac clerics who accompanied Burgundian knights to Spain used the popularity of Charlemagne and Roland in order to support their ambitions in Compostella.[43] Here we meet a second great epic poem, at least as ancient as that of Roland, that of Girart of Vienne or of Roussillon. The epics relating to "Girart of Viane" have been examined in great detail by René Louis, who has demonstrated the extraordinary historical layers that make up the epic poem.[44]

He has shown particularly how the legend of Girard was rooted in the topography of very specific regions; Frankish Burgundy, around the estates of Pothières and Vézelay, where Gerard had founded abbeys and where the legendary battle of Vaubeton explains a funerary site of the second and third centuries, very close to Vézelay; Vienne, where he ruled—and this localization clearly owes nothing to the influence of the monks of Cluny. It is very probable that the Roussillon of the legend is none other than the castle lying a little to the south of Vienne and that the identification with Spain, undeniable in the twelfth century, represents a later interpretation, at a period when the Burgundians had become familiar figures on the roads leading to the Iberian peninsula. The last localization is the most surprising: this associates with the name of Gerard—of Fraite—the memory of the *villa Fretus*—Saint-Rémy-de-Provence, a place-name that disappeared in the tenth century. Very close to the *villa Fretus* is the rock of Gaussier, an ancient natural citadel that guards a pass on the road between Avignon and Arles controlled at the other end by the castle of Les Baux. This place is none other than the Montglane of the epics—taking its name from the small Roman city of *Glanum* that lay at the foot of the rock and of which a triumphal gate and a mausoleum were still visible in the Middle Ages. The influence of the monks of Rheims, who owned this land, in theory at least, has been suggested;[45] but this is to presume that the monks, far removed from Burgundy, had correctly identified the Gerard to whom Hincmar had entrusted his lands in Provence with that same Girart of Vienne who, having been chased from Vienne, had taken refuge in 871 in the *pagus* in Avignon where were founded *Fretus* and the Church of Saint-Rémy. In fact, after the Gregorian Reform, when they succeeded in recovering this church, they had not set foot inside it for two centuries. It is also curious to note how Gerard of Fraite is a "saracenized" character and much less appealing than the rebel who defends Vienne. The further south one goes, the more the legend becomes distorted.[46]

It is certainly from Burgundy in the broad sense of the term that the legend of Girard originates. It is from this legendary core with Oliver, Girard's nephew, as the main character, that the *Geste de Charlemagne* develops. It is significant that one of the first mentions of the pair Oliver-Roland—and not Roland-Oliver—appears in Brioude, which belonged to the same cultural area as Vienne.[47]

It is also tempting, despite appearances, to see a Burgundian origin for the Narbonne cycle. The chief hero is William, count of Toulouse, who fought beside Louis the Pious at the taking of Barcelona and who had himself buried at the Abbey of Gellone, later Saint-Guillem-du-Désert. He was descended from a family of territorial princes who attempted for nearly a century to dominate the Midi, from Clermont in Auvergne to Barcelona. It has long been known that the image created in the legend does not coincide with the real man. The William of the legend is a "kingmaker," who has Louis crowned when still a child but who receives no reward for this. He conquers Orange, a city with no connection with the Carolingian marquisate of Toulouse. However, there is another William, descendant of the Toulouse William and founder of Cluny in 910. This William did indeed support Louis of Provence—son of the usurper Boso and godson of Charles the Fat—at the beginning of his precarious reign. But the clan that was to have the most influence with Louis was that of Hugh of Arles, who soon declared all-out war on the supporters of William in the Midi.[48] Richer of Rheims, on the other hand, has preserved legendary traces of the armed contingents sent by the people of Orange and Nîmes to King Eudes at the time of his wars in Auvergne against this same William in 893.[49] William's nephews died fighting to save their principality. At the same period a line of counts was established in Provence, originating perhaps from Nîmes, which restored the name of William. The most famous member of the family was the Count William (970–993), victor over the Saracens at Le Freinet, who became a monk at Cluny before his death and who endowed that abbey with his priory of Piolenc in the diocese of Orange. It was through a countess of Provence that a little after 1065 the city of Orange was to pass to the family of this name;

this countess's grandson was called William and bore on his shield the "horn," a heroic pun through which he claimed to be the distant heir of the hero Roland.[50] The telescoping process is obvious here, but we should be aware that this is not simply a confusion of memory, a literary device, or the flattery of minstrels. It is more likely due to the idea that all these noble Williams are a continuation of one another because they have in their veins the same noble blood.[51]

A similar approach could shed light on the figure of Aimery of Narbonne. Rita Lejeune has demonstrated the diffusion of this name in Narbonne. It appears at the beginning of the tenth century as the name of an archbishop of that city and of his relative, both in turn abbots of Saint-Paul in Narbonne. In 1050 the name enters the family of the viscounts of the city, whose chief name it becomes. At the same time as taking the name of the Carolingian hero, the viscounts copy his exploits, to the detriment of the Saracens in Spain. The last male member of the family was to die under the walls of Fraga. So it is probable that the revival of the name by the viscounts corresponds to the earlier establishment of the legend of Aimery. He is traditionally presented as having been installed by Charlemagne at the time of the taking of the city. His fate is linked through family connections with that of the Williams. Everything thus hinges on the legendary capture of Narbonne. A martyrology of the abbey of Saint-Paul attributes it— following the legend in this—to Charlemagne and puts the date at 790. We are probably dealing, however, with the capture of the city by Carloman in 880. At that time a Viscount Albericus, vassal of the William family, was installed. His grandson, expelled by the supporters of Hugh of Arles, sought refuge in Mâcon where he proudly bore his surname "of Narbonne." So we can establish the following stages: in 880, a Viscount Albericus, of Burgundian origin, takes Narbonne; around the year 1000 there takes place at the abbey of Saint-Paul a double confusion between Carloman and Charlemagne and between Albericus and Aymericus, the names of two abbots of the monastery, one of whom at least must have been well known, since he was archbishop. Some fifty years later, the viscounts revived the name.[52] Aimery, like William, thus had more connection with Burgundy than with the Midi.

A fourth legendary name allows us to see the extraordinary interweaving of the local epic traditions that the Carolingian epic reveals. This is our friend Bishop Turpin. We have already met Bishop Turpin of Limoges, the pacifier of the Limousin and protector of Odo of Cluny. We must now return to him. It was known at the end of the twelfth century that the famous *Historia Karoli Magni*, then considered to be authentic, had three versions: one at Saint-Denis, probably the most recent, one in Cluny, and a third, seemingly the oldest, at Saint-Martin in Tours. One of the Carolingian forgeries most obviously influenced by the epic tradition was also preserved in the archives of this abbey, but it came in fact from the hand of the canons at Saint-Yrieix, a dependency of Tours in the Limousin.

The document is a forged confirmation by Charlemagne of a hypothetical charter of Pepin. The emperor is portrayed as "leaving for the Spains" in the company of "his princes, lord Turpion, Ogier the Paladin, William with the short nose, Bertram the strong and Roger Cornehaute." The Limousin character of the list is revealed by the presence of this Roger, formerly count of Limoges. The absence of Roland is probably explained by the fact that, conforming with the legend, he is already in Spain. There must surely be a connection between the canons at Saint-Yrieix and the Limousin Gregory Bechada, author of an epic poem about Antioch into which was inserted a passage from *Ronsavals*, the *langue d'oc* version of the *Chanson de Roland*. Gregory was a knight at the castle of Lastours, near Saint-Yrieix. He had written his work at the request of the bishop of Limoges, Eustorge, and of Gaubert the Norman, who may have been the lord of Gourdon, a castle that guarded the road to the south and where Sainte Foy was much venerated. And at Sainte-Foy in Conques were kept the *Gesta* consecrated to Alfonso the Great, emperor of the Spains, by Peire of Andoque, bishop of Pamplona and protector of the priory of Roncesvalles. The attribution of a reworking of this original work to a Bishop Turpin and the localization of this version to Saint-Martin could well be the work of obscure canons of Saint-Yrieix, and this would also explain the passage in it praising the regular canons. When the Cluniacs in Spain produced their version of the text, they had Turpin dying in Vienne; the last comers at Saint-Denis identified him with an archbishop of Rheims who had once been a monk in their community—exemplary adaptations![53]

Thus it is possible at the beginning of the epic to distinguish areas of "local legends." The people of the west have Roland, the Burgundians have Girart, northern Aquitaine has William. In Ponthieu they celebrated Gormont and Isembart, in the Vermandois and Lower Lorraine Raoul of Cambrai and Ibert of Ribemont.[54]

But in the twelfth century it is clear that only the most southern legends were very widespread and that they were beginning to fuse. The pair Oliver-Roland, characteristic of Girart of Viane, can be found in Angers, Béziers, and Béarn, while the Roland influence is apparent in Cologne, where a bishop had a castle named *Rolandseck* built, and in Molesmes in Burgundy where the paired names of Oliver-Roland are reversed.[55] The monks of the abbey of Gellone, reformed in the eleventh century, declared in 1125: "Where are the kingdoms, where the provinces and the nations, where are the towns which do not celebrate and envy the exploits of Duke William. . . ? What assembly of young men, what gathering, above all, of knights and barons, what festive eve does not resound with his glory?"[56] The epic poem has become the common language of chivalry.

It has often been asked who disseminated this body of material: the minstrels or the monks? An interesting debate, but of secondary importance. In either case they were responding to a demand, to a need. The assemblies of young men, the gatherings of barons were only waiting for someone to reflect a certain image of them. It is surely anachronistic to imagine that the only agents of cultural expression were specialists—monks or minstrels—whose professions, literally, it was. "When bad weather confined the 'youth' Arnould of Ardres to the tedium of the domestic hearth, he had stories told to him. His kinsman Walter of Sluys, to amuse the company, would tell not only the stories of Gormont and Isembart, Tristan and Isolde but also the exploits of the former lords of the castle."[57] Thus we see that the lords and the companies of "youths" had their own storytellers; a good soldier can also be a good narrator and a good singer. Minstrels and monks?—certainly—but also, from long before, the soldiers themselves. In these heroic epics—*heroïcae cantilenae*—were blended the great legendary themes and the noble deeds of very real ancestors. Lambert of Wattrelos preserved in this way the memory of the brothers of his ancestor, who had fallen gloriously in battle.[58] When the troubadors refashioned the old heroic epics to the new taste of a chivalrous age, they drew greatly on these names, which as they spread had become for the most part meaningless. Around these names, of people or places, in this pseudo-history, pseudo-genealogy,[59] and even pseudo-geography there crystallized an ancient experience, a lesson. Through these names the legend becomes familiar to the group; it becomes its legend. This explains the extraordinary truths that, despite the reworking and individual poetic creations of the twelfth century, are still to be found in the epic poem: Girart had certainly held the manor of Fraite. And there are deeper truths: despite the reticence of the official annals, Roncesvalles was certainly a disaster—a political disaster—for the Franks; despite Ermold the Black, Duke William was indeed an unfortunate legitimist abandoned by the young King Louis and attacked by a usurper, the Robertian Eudes.[60.]

At a time when the "youths," redundant in knightly households that had grown strong and too dominant, were once again taking the road toward adventures and pillage, it was to their old epics that they looked to overcome their fears and bolster their courage. Normans, Burgundians, and Aquitainians now came to know one another and sometimes exchanged guardian heroes. Could it be that the dominance of the *Chanson de Roland* in the French epic is a reflection of the bravery and ferocity of the Normans? This would explain how so many southern knights gaily sang of deeds in which their own ancestors had come off the worst. In the epics the enemy, the real enemy, is always the Saracen—a historical mistake that contains also its own very ancient truth.[61]

Given these conditions, it is tempting to see the intervention of the clerics, and particularly the monks, as no more than a second phase of the process, a secondary phenomenon. In Potthières, the life of Gerald of Aurillac is a learned reconstruction that borrows from legend; at Saint-Faron of Meaux, the death of a rich donor becomes the pretext for the adoption of Ogier, or rather of the Ogiers. The monks of Saint-Guillem claimed a William who was perhaps not theirs.[62] Was this self-seeking devotion? Certainly, but this was not all. In the early tenth century, Odo of Cluny's idea of an ideal model for the lords was that "of a layman established in the order of warriors, who carries a sword in order to protect those without arms . . . in order also to constrain by the right of arms or by judicial constraint those whom the censure of the church has been unable to subdue."[63] Gerald was a good soldier, but he lacked a legend. The strength of the *vitae* rewritten at the end of the eleventh century is in not trying to create a model but in freeing it from its legendary background. As the more important princely households grew and got organized, the influence of the clerics became more apparent. In the *familia* of Hugh of Avranches the priest Gerald exhorted the young men to mend their ways by preaching on the life of William and the soldier saints. These attempts did not always meet with success: the "youths" whom St. Bernard told to give up arms during Lent returned after drinking to their warlike sports.[64] The patient work of remodeling undertaken by the clerics resulted finally, as we know, in the exaltation of the monarchy.

There is a fundamental conflict underlying the majority of the epic poems[65] between excess and wisdom, revolt and fidelity. On one side stands the hero, on the other the king. The theme of redeemed betrayal can be read in three different ways. First, the efforts confirmed in history of a certain number of the great at the end of the ninth and the beginning of the tenth centuries to set up on their own behalf. Second, the frustration of the warrior "youth" for whom getting established was also an aim, a more modest one perhaps yet even more difficult. Last, the conflict between the restlessness of the knights and the restrictions of the Christian order. In the last analysis, it is this restlessness, this uncontrollable violence, despite the adaptations made by the clerics, that lies at the heart of the epic poem. So many deaths, so many lovingly described blows, so much blood have as their only object the description of a defeat and a failure and the proposal of a remedy. The *heroïca cantilena*, as Lambert of Wattrelos reminds us, speaks above all of the dead. It shows them before the battle, as we read in William of Malmesbury and Wace, when the soldiers are gripped by fear; it fills them with hate and desire for revenge. "On the heights of Roncesvalles—God forgive me—until the end of the World, the loss and injury will be great. And may the Saracens and the pagan people know that vengeance shall be ours again."[66]

"The history of the *Chanson de Roland* begins with the *Chanson de Roland*."[67] It is true that the work that was born at the end of the eleventh century was something different and something more than what had preceded it. But the current of epic had existed for a long time behind the facade of an immobilized church culture, less peasant perhaps than the paganizing current and more suited to the entourage of the great, the warriors par excellence; but like the paganizing current, it forced its way into the culture of the learned as it gradually worked its way into the consciousness of a unified nobility.[68] And its strength became so great that we see the actual identification of certain lords with the heroes of the epics: a real Girart of Roussillon goes to the Crusades, a real Aimery of Narbonne dies in Spain, a real William of Orange defends the high tower of the city.[69] A century after it takes off, the legend has been incarnated, it is more real than reality. The epic ceases to be a myth and becomes a model of society, one of the obligatory elements in a new culture: chivalry.

One of the new ways of approaching the phenomenon of chivalry and of measuring its development and extent in "feudal society" is perhaps to leave aside for the moment its chief characteristic—the creation of a specifically chivalrous literature—in order to study behavior and particularly the question of the fashions of chivalry and the reactions they provoked.

A perceptive writer on the subject, Henri Platelle, in studying the area between the Loire and the Rhine in the period that concerns us, sees two upsurges of contradictory fashions.[70] The first wave begins in 1002 and intensifies around 1017; by 1065 it predominates. The texts that denounce it present it as something foreign; it comes from Aquitaine and more generally from the south. This foreignness of the southerners was not unknown to travelers and well-informed people. Richer, at the end of the tenth century, or Bernard of Angers shortly after 1000, comment on it. The new fashion is not yet at this time the creation of a local social group, but is seen rather as an intrusion from outside. The dislike of change in the order of things in the most ordinary daily life is justified here by a racism whose roots, as we have seen, stretch back a long way.[71] The hair cut high up the back of the neck, the clean-shaven face, the short and slashed clothes are here only the exterior signs of frivolity, vanity, a lack of good faith and respect for the sworn peace, corrupted morals and, all in all, of the indecency of the men from Auvergne and Aquitaine. There follows the usual *deploratio:* the Franks and the Burgundians, formerly most noble of nations, and so forth. Honor, religion, and the nobility of the monarch are compromised. A few years later in a nice reversal of events it is the Lorrainers who are protesting against "the shameful and foolish habits of the French . . . disloyal enemies" and perverted; but our source notes in fairness that "not only are the imitators not corrected, but they even obtain the friendship of the king and the princes, and receive rewards." Thus the court more than tolerates the fashion, it supports and encourages it. The phenomenon becomes particularly clear at the end of the eleventh century when the canons of elegance are reversed: long, trailing clothes, pointed shoes with curled-up ends, elegant beards, hair brushed away from the face and worn long and curling. The authors of these changes—the sources agree—are no longer foreigners but young people of the court—*curialis juventus*—which we could translate as the courtly youth. Those "of the people," meaning the burgesses and even the peasants, began to imitate them. The bishops may have protested, excluding them from churches or processions and holding public head-shearings (by means of scissors concealed in their sleeves), but "those who wished to appear courtly" continued to wear their hair long all through the twelfth century. Chivalry had fought and won its first battle. What did it mean?

We are given an explanation by the zealous bishops and monks who denounced the scandal of it. These young people, by adopting an appearance contrary to what was fixed by custom for the *ordines*, were wrongfully using what had until then been the distinctive mark of outsiders, "contrary" people: actors, penitents and pilgrims, heretical preachers. For all that, the accusation, however important, remains superficial. Another appeared and made itself heard: from the time of the first wave of 1020 we hear the fashion denounced as being indecent, obscene, vicious, frivolous, and an attack on modesty. With the second wave, the criticisms become more specific. "Chivalrous youths wear their hair long like girls . . . they walk with a mincing and lascivious step, swaying from side to side," or again: "The petulant youths adopt a feminine softness." The object of this amorous parading was not necessarily what one would expect.[72] This "lasciviousness" of courtly youth "aims at pleasing the ladies." One bishop declared flatly: "They avoid shaving for fear that their bristles might hurt their mistresses when they kiss them."[73] The important thing in this court is imitation: "Our long-haired youths . . . like to change themselves to take on a feminine appearance," or elsewhere: "Like courtesans they wear their hair long at the back of the head"—like courtesans because an honest woman does not show her hair. The reason for the scandal is now revealed: the probable disturbance at this time of the time-honored equilibrium between the sexes, a disturbance of which we have found traces elsewhere.[74] Not only in poetry, but also in behavior, chivalry, right from the beginning and even in the mouth of its enemies is—or claims to be—a search for woman and sometimes, by default, her evocation. Fashion among the *curiales* was a matter both for the youth of the court—the manifestation of an elite that was beginning its youthful power of diffusion and dominance of cultural schemes—and for the chivalrous knights, for those who wished to please women.

The study of courtly literature revealed long ago the feminine aspect of chivalry. First found among the troubadours of the south, the theme is too well known to need amplification. Suffice it to note the correlation revealed by Henri Platelle already apparent in the first wave between "indecent clothes," "woman's influence"—that of the queen, "the inconstant Constance"—and "actors." Was such an association the product of the monks' attack or should we seek more popular origins for courtly love than its ultimate development might lead us to suspect in a society where the barrier between the knights and the others was less clearly marked than in the north? Certainly the vocabulary of feudal law entered very rapidly into discussions of love: the lady becomes the lord and love becomes service. But such an influence was never to predominate and the troubadours were to use equally both ancient symbols—the ring, for example—and new forms—servile homage, Roman law—without allowing us to derive many conclusions from such usages.[75]

Did the "classicizing romance" also come from the Midi? Pierre Toubert has described the revival in Italy in the eleventh century of the fashion for names borrowed from the ancient heroes. However, it was at just this time that the use of such Graeco-Roman names was disappearing in Provence.[76] More likely would be a connection with the Italian influence, shown in other ways by the diffusion of the legend of Virgil and the knowledge of Justinian's law in the Midi, in Germany at the imperial court, and even as far away as Paris or England. These colorful borrowings from antiquity must also have found a favorable precedent in the legend of the Trojan origins of the Franks.[77] With the romance the theme takes on a new meaning. It had been an aggressive claim by a Frankish aristocracy, unsure of its nobility; it becomes something universal in the time of chivalrous culture. Chrétien de Troyes in his *Cligès* takes from the Carolingian scholars the theory of the *translatio studii* in order to juxtapose onto the traditional "pilgrimage of knowledge"—from Greece to Rome and then to France— the transferred parallel of "chivalry."[78] At the same time affirming the durability of chivalry, the antique romance makes it possible to meet the demands for the supernatural without a lowering of tone. In this respect it is very much a product of the court.

Something similar probably accounts for the success of the Arthurian romance far away from Caerleon and Camelot, or even Broceliande.[79] Here too the supernatural can exist without appearing to be what in fact it is—the sublimated continuation into the world of chivalry of a peasant paganism. The geographical adaptations to the legends connected with the arrival on the continent of a considerable group of English scholars singularly favored the remodelling of the ancient Gaulish heroes.[80] As Jacques Le Goff has said, "between Geoffrey of Monmouth and Robert of Boron, we have scarcely time to glimpse a savage Merlin . . . heir of a *Myrddin* in which form the semi-aristocratic culture of the Celtic bards had allowed a village sorcerer to appear."[81] In the supernatural realm of the courtly romance, as we know, the Lady plays a leading part.

An example of the distortions suffered by very ancient themes is the stag hunt. In Gaul in the late empire much use was made of medallions of horn. They were a sign of strength and fertility and newly married husbands were advised to have one. In addition, the antler, which regrows each year, is a sign and a promise of resurrection, from which probably comes the animal's attribute as the conductor of the souls of the dead. There are examples, admittedly exceptional, of tombs where a stag has been buried with the dead person, its legs folded and its head turned in the attitude of the "backwards-looking monster" commonly found in barbarian ornamentation. Throughout the early Middle Ages, councils repeated the ban on "doing the stag" [cf. Eng. "horn dance"] during the licentious and pagan processions of the Kalends of January. In the Arthurian romance, the stag hunt has become a trial performed in honor of the Lady. The animal is white and has a gold collar, which has been seen as the torque of the ancient Gaulish chiefs also worn by *Cernunnos*. Sometimes the hunter has to cut off its head to win the lady of his choice. The deed of the chivalrous hero, at the same time concealing a past rich with meaning—now little confessed or not confessable—expresses in this way the essence of his quest.[82]

Fashion and courtly literature bring us inevitably to women, and more particularly to the question of the position of the noble woman in chivalrous society. We have already deplored the gaps in our sources when we wish to know more about peasants, heretics, sorcerers, and their world. But perhaps the largest lacuna of all is the one concerning women. The courtly poets may have written of woman: the women, all too frequently, are silent.[83] Too frequently also the types of women described are limited to the classic figures of the old princess with a sometimes brutal energy, or the "mystic" in love with God.[84] Female attitudes may well have been more varied, but the scarcity of documentation available yields portraits that are too brief to be characteristic of our period.

The first path to pursue here is without doubt that of the marriage habits of the knightly class. In the learned game of what is for the noble families a matter of politics,[85] the central piece is the woman, or rather, the woman whom accidents of birth and family have made or will make heiress to a patrimony. This was an inevitable consequence of the patrimonialization of the fief and of banal lordship. These heiresses were not only the prey of old men and fathers, concerned to continue or extend their lines, but they were also coveted by young men, since they represented the only means for men without an inheritance to establish themselves. Georges Duby, having described the seductions, if not quite rapes, carried out by a number of daring younger sons, reminds us that

> the hunt for a rich girl with a rich estate was not always doomed to failure, but the hazards and profits are only explained by the relative abundance of attractive game, that is by the frequent withering of noble lines, which allowed the entire inheritance to come into the hands of a female inheritor. Now this phenomenon itself is closely linked to the adventurous life of the "youth," to the dangers which it ran and which decimated it.[86]

The heiress needed the young men as they did her.

But there is also another path to pursue, the path into the internal and daily equilibrium of the princely households of the time. When there was no heiress for him to marry, a young man of low degree could dream of the favors of a lady whose husband was not too jealous. The misfortunes of so many troubadours of "low extraction" when they tried to add the deed to the words shows that the situation was more imaginary than real.[87] But no matter! The lord of the household took advantage of the dreams of the young men.

> The game consisted for the prince in controlling their amorous impulses without them noticing, using them like a trap for two other people. For his son, who would lead the young knights towards adventure, wounds and bruises, relieving the court of their turbulent presence. And for his wife, allowing the symbolic actions of desire to unfold around her. . . . The stake in this courtly love, this jousting, an alternation of attacks and feints, analogous with the tournament and its displays of virtuosity, was the lady, the master's wife. . . . For the game had to remain unresolved, in order that the suitors should be strictly confined within a network of obligations and services. Through the game of love, just as through his military exercises, the young man was initiated, learning to contain and govern his passions.[88]

We can see from this the formidable pressure exercised by the youth on the ideal schema of the marriage connecting two noble families. They borrowed, as we have seen, the techniques of seduction, through imitative practices that transgressed the barriers of dress in order to approach the woman more closely, as if exalting her power—in reality very limited—as well as her beauty. In response to this pressure from the "bachelors," the "established" men had no option but to take lessons in the school of chivalry in their turn.

There are, however, one or two interesting examples. Two texts from northern France describe the unhappy marriage, in the early eleventh century, of a very young girl to a brutal knight. We get a glimpse of somewhat uncanonical marital relations between the couple: despite the brutality of her husband, the mother of Guibert of Nogent had remained a virgin for three years. When she became a widow, the dreams that she had of him reveal the degree of hate she felt. Godeliève of Ghistelles, in a similar situation, had dared to defy her husband, bringing the matter before the tribunal of the bishop of Tournai. Her husband came to try to win her around, then had her murdered. He then calmly took another wife. This is strikingly differnt from those Norman ladies who at the end of the century warned their husbands, who had left home to seek fiefs and adventures across the Channel and seemed to be in no hurry to return, that they were going to "mark their family line with the indelible stain of shame." Was this not because in the intervening years chivalry had begun to emerge? This would explain why Guibert of Nogent speaks of "the *new* frivolity of women."[89]

At the same time, we can understand the hostility of some of the more austere clerics, also younger sons, toward the youths' womanizing and concern with getting a wife. What these young men could do, the clerics could no longer: the Gregorian reform had closed the path of marriage to them.

Seduction and courtliness, at first the weapons of youth, thus became one of the models of chivalry. It was a model that in some ways coincided with what the clerics had wanted to introduce into the epic poem; but as the secular culture of the nobility developed, the model could not fail to reveal its differences. The courtly romance reproduces the "chivalrous adventure" whose unity and universality it affirms. But as the years passed, another underlying theme began to make itself apparent: the bitterness of the ordinary knights at the decadence of the twelfth century. At that time, the southern knights were still dazzled by the spectacle of their own liberality, intoxicated by their own excesses. We only have to think of the festivals held in the Lower Rhône area at the end of the twelfth century, and in particular that extraordinary court at Beaucaire where Bertrand Raimbaud of Agoult had the town square ploughed up and planted with deniers. Here too William the Fat of Marseilles had the cauldrons at the feast he was giving heated with wax candles, while Raimon of Mévouillon had thirty of his horses burned alive.[91] It is not hard to imagine what a real sacrifice such a holocaust was for the knights. The follies and excesses at Beaucaire, soon admired as far away as the Limousin, marked in dramatic fashion the apogee of chivalry; but one cannot refrain from thinking that people like Simon de Montfort would not have burned their horses, and that the monarchies of the north would instead have strengthened their financial situation.

The vavassours, or under-vassals, must have felt chivalry slipping from their grasp, "that their contribution to the world of chivalry had been taken advantage of by the feudal upper nobility who had their own reasons for favoring the integration at court of very different layers of the knightly class."[92] The princes were beginning to neglect the knights and to surround themselves with new men. This promotion of villeins to the rank of counsellor to the king was a sign of the beginning of the fatal decline of the knighthood, bringing with it the decline of a by-now-debased world. But there can be no end of the world without an antichrist. It is significant that he is depicted as a king hostile to the nobility, who makes knights of simple villeins. To what extent did this introduction of non-nobles into the king's council indicate also a more careful management of the royal coffers? This might explain the decline in "Largesse which was formerly the support of Chivalry." Disillusionment among the vavassours then: *"Je suis, ce vois, uns chevaliers, qui quier ce que trover ne puis. Assez ai quis et rien ne truis"*[93] (I have sought much and I have found nothing). This disenchanted confession from Chrétien de Troyes's Calogrenant finds an echo in the Midi in the bitterly ironic words of Arnaut Daniel: "I am Arnaut who reaps the wind, who hunts the hare with an ox and swims against the current"—disenchantment in the literal sense of the word. Soon the great castellans were able to take advantage of this bitterness among the lower nobility. When St. Louis dared to forbid trial by combat, the rallying cry of the discontented—"Sweet France . . . you are now enslaved"[94]—comes straight out of the courtly romance. The end of the twelfth century saw the coming together in an extraordinary syncretism of the memory of peasant magic, epic memories of the great battles of the ninth century, and the demands of the chivalric ethos. The Englishman Gervase of Tilbury mixes together in his works Roman law and werewolves, Charles's paladins and the tombs of the Alyscamps. He met in Arles the Catalan Guerau of Cabrera, lord and troubadour and a great admirer of the epic poem, who made his magic horse dance before the ladies. Thus there culminates in the collective idea of chivalry a "material" social movement that had led so many peasant allodialists to place themselves at the service of the aristocracy.

Peasant myths, chivalric legends—it now remains to examine a third element of "feudal" attitudes: royalty and the miraculous.

"This King Is a Great Magician"

On our way we have already glimpsed magic in the monarchy and seen how far it was able to serve the interests of the Capetian kings. As with the chivalric tradition, it originated in the great upsurge of legend and folklore at the beginning of the eleventh century. But whereas the former went on to develop an aristocratic exoticism, the latter, perhaps because it was propagated by the knights of the *familia regis*, a group of relatively humble origins, retained a much more popular garb, embedding itself more deeply among the peasants. While the courtly romance gradually "rationalized" itself, moving away from legendary themes, the supernatural element in the monarchy increasingly began to appear as the true heir to the old agrarian cults. Let us look more closely at the popular roots of the mystique and the powers of the "most Christian king."

We should start with the legend of St. Denis, since it was a mainstay of the idea of monarchy. In a first stage we find a Denis who is almost historical, who brought the Gospel to Paris and was martyred in the third century. At this period he appears alone. A second stage is represented by the *passio* of the saint and his two legendary companions and by references in the *vita Genovefe*. A third stage consists of the Carolingian texts written by Abbot Hilduin and Hincmar of Rheims. From this moment, the legend is, in its essentials, fixed.[95]

It is interesting to observe how from the seventh century the meaning of the legendary elements developed and the figure of Denis was remodeled under the pressure of the popular cult. First, there was the element of the three figures. To St. Denis, originally alone, are added two companions of equal importance; in this way he acquires the characteristic epithet of "thrice blessed." The very names of the companions are interesting. Eleutherius—the Free—clearly refers to the liberating function of the saint, and we have seen its importance.[96] Rusticus is no less striking when we realize that the three martyrs were buried by a devout pagan woman in a field ready ploughed for sowing. This brings to mind the name given to the antique god Eustathius—the good ear of corn. The name of the devout pagan woman, by a very strange coincidence, turns out to be *catula*—little she-cat—and it it known that a statue of Isis was still worshipped in the thirteenth century by the women of Saint-Germain-des-Prés. In the ninth century we learn furthermore that St. Denis was Greek—as we would have supposed from his name—that he was beheaded on a *mons mercurii* since named, we are told, the mount of martyrs, Montmartre, and that the headless saint "traveled," carrying his head, to the site of the future basilica.[97]

Hence the question, first raised in the twelfth century, of who had the relics. The Abbey of Saint-Denis claimed to have the whole body of Denis, including the head. The canons of Notre-Dame believed they had the crown of his skull, removed with a first blow. In Rome they had perhaps—the pope was not sure—the genuine relics. The monks of Regensburg made the same claims.[98]

It is clear that the holy bishop had begun to acquire, during the early Middle Ages, an extraordinary resemblance to an associate god of the Good Goddess. In the ninth century we find the connection with the figure of Dagobert. We know that Dagobert, confused with a Merovingian of the same name buried at Stenay in the seventh century, was honored in the province of Rheims where he was venerated as a sower-king, guarantor of miraculous harvests.[99]

Invited to write the miracles of St. Denis, Hincmar of Rheims provides us with a double story, with the key to the still-popular association made between the saint and the king. One day the young Prince Dagobert was out hunting a stag. The animal took refuge in what was then the mausoleum of the martyrs; the dogs stopped, prevented from going forward by a supernatural force. Sometime later, Dagobert rebelled against paternal authority, represented by the twin figures of his father and his tutor.[100] His father orders him to be seized; hunted in his turn, Dagobert takes refuge in the church and the servants pursuing him are in their turn immobilized. Dagobert goes to sleep and sees in a dream his three protectors. Other miracles follow, interesting in that they show us the lowly origin and the exaltation of the devotees of St. Denis. So he is the protector of the humble, and of the young, and particularly of the young future king at this difficult moment in a journey that was to make him one day the equal of his father.[101] And it is extraordinary to see the young Philip-Augustus, three centuries later, literally reliving, shortly before coming to the throne, the same anguish—finding himself alone during a hunt—falling ill and being cured by the intervention of Denis.[102] Once again, what is legend and what reality? When in the twelfth century Denis became the official patron saint of the monarchy, he had behind him a flourishing legendary past.

The parallels with two other royal cults are striking: that of St. James in Galicia and that of the Three Kings in Cologne. In Spain, the first traces of a popular cult of St. James can be seen in the first half of the seventh century, when a Latin translation of a sixth-century Greek manuscript shows him as the bringer of the Gospel to Spain although placing his death in Jerusalem. At the end of the century, Julian of Toledo was still refusing to accept this view, but a little later the Englishman, Aldhelm, knows that "St. James was the first to convert the Spanish." A little later—around 711?—a group of Christians from Merida had to seek refuge in Galicia with the relics of their church, among which were those of St. James. When around 741–745, the Asturian monarchy reestablished its power in Galicia, the cult of the saint was associated with the new monarchy. At the end of the century and perhaps as a reaction against Adoptianism, St. James had become "Head of Spain, powerful defender, special patron, pastor of the king, the clergy and the people." A few years later still we find that it was known in Lyons—from the Spanish entourage of the émigré Agobard?—that the sacred bones of the most holy apostle were in Spain and that they were venerated with an extraordinary devotion. In fact the tomb of the saint had been "discovered" in Spain in the reign of Alfonso II, "restorer of the order of the kingdom of the Goths," and the first of his line to be anointed. A century later we find Alfonso III, a devotee of St. James and anointed in his church, writing to the canons of Tours in order to arrange for the purchase of an imperial crown— Carolingian?—for the tomb of St. James, and it is known that he did at times bear the imperial title. Shortly afterward the first pilgrimages to the Church of St. James at Compostella began.

The cult of the "headless Galician," both popular and royal, emerging from the dark time when a handful of nobles were fighting against their own countrymen to protect a *regnum gothorum*, was to become one of the most important cults in the West.[103] The first areas to take it up outside of Spain were Rouergue, Puy, and Burgundy, around Cluny. It is possible that the practices of the Spanish monarchy may have encouraged, perhaps on two occasions, the French monarchy to look to such cults even though they were of dubious religious orthodoxy.[104] The first occasion would have been through some of the Spanish émigrés, and the second through the Cluniacs, and particularly Vivien, Odilo's right-hand man, who was to restore Saint-Denis.

The veneration of the Three Kings in Cologne, unlike that of St. James, is an example of a much later cult. It begins with the discovery of three embalmed bodies inside a single marble sarcophagus in a church on the outskirts of Milan. The discovery is supposed to have taken place in 1158. The town was taken by Frederick Barbarossa in 1162 and soon, in 1164, the imperial Chancellor and Archbishop of Cologne, Rainald of Dassel, brought the precious relics, believed to be those of the three kings, back to the imperial city where the German emperors were crowned.[105] There is a clear connection with the veritable apotheosis of Charlemagne organized in 1165 by Rainald of Dassel and his friends.[106] We have here an attempt at creating a devotion of the French type, associating with the cult of the great emperor that of saints whose magic character is here openly admitted. On their journey from Milan to Cologne, they left meaningful signs, such as the spring near Dijon with powers to heal scrofula. From this time Epiphany enters the imperial liturgy.[107] Thus the emperor revived to his own advantage the ritual of the kings, the existence of which is known in the eleventh century in places as varied as Rouen, Besançon, Nevers, Limoges, and Freising. And the three crowns offered in 1198 by Otto IV to the three kings—the first kings established by Christ—are a striking demonstration of the alliance thus forged, making the emperor like a fourth king.

On the reliquary of the Three Kings in Cologne, the emperor is shown behind them, also bringing his gift to Christ. The antique cameos decorating the reliquary are equally revealing: one represents Mars standing before Venus and crowned by Victory, the two others are scenes of the apotheoses of emperors—Nero and Ptolemy Philadelphus.

The significance of the royal trio did not escape contemporaries; it was even proclaimed during the "game of the kings" at Epiphany. Each king has his own appropriate gift. Caspar, the Chaldean—the Master of the Treasure—bears gold, "the right of kings"; Melchoir, the Arab—the king of Light—brings incense, "the right of priests," a "celestial" gift; and from Sheba, the black Balthasar—"God protects Life"—bears myrrh, "the sign of Death," but also "the unction" that assures eternal Life.[108]

It seems that Balthasar held an important place in the trio. His funerary character is clear; in a late twelfth-century sermon he is associated, inevitably, with the legendary queen of Sheba. His prestige attracted adherents: the lords of Les Baux in Provence, no doubt to show their connection with the empire, sometime before 1214 took as their emblem the seven-pointed star and as their motto "A l'hazar, Bauthezar" (To hazard, Balthasar).[109]

The end of the eleventh and the twelfth centuries saw the spread of the pseudo-benediction of Bede, where the Three Kings are invoked against epilepsy, the falling sickness. The Dijon spring notwithstanding, the Magi do not in fact heal scrofula but this other royal disease; they are also protectors of travelers and particularly those on their last journey.[110] The new cult of the kings in Cologne seems to have been intended to eclipse that of St. James. In fact, the success of this devotion to the Magi, well-attested in the fourteenth century, was limited to the empire.

A Rhenish preacher claimed to have met in Cologne a Spaniard whose job had been to receive the pilgrims on the road to Compostella.

Wrongly accused of theft, he was saved from the hangman's rope not by the Galician saint, but by the Three Kings of Cologne, and so he had come as a pilgrim to thank them. However unlikely it may sound, the anecdote shows clearly the desire to transfer popular devotion. The author mentions among the other pilgrims "Scots, Bretons, Englishmen, Spaniards, Italians too, Sicilians and the inhabitants of the two Gauls," meaning probably Belgium and France. The study carried out by Catherine Henrion indicates that in fact the pilgrims came chiefly from Flanders, Hainault, and Hungary. The altars and chapels dedicated to the Magi are found particularly eastwards of the Rhine valley but we find pockets around Brussels, in Besançon, in Savoy, and a few scattered traces within the kingdom, as in Vannes, Nevers, and Albi.[111]

It has been asked also how far the kings of England used the Arthurian legends in a similar way to reinforce their power. It is known that in the early twelfth century the monks of Glastonbury in Somerset, perhaps using some analogies—Glass town, Land of Summer—had attempted to localize in their area a number of the Celtic legends and particularly that of the capture of Guinevere, Arthur's wife, by Maelvas-Meleagant, king of the glass island. The writing of the *Historia Regum Britanniae* in 1135 may perhaps mark the beginning of a "policy of legend" of the Norman kings. With the Plantagenets, certainly, this policy is clear. The courts of Poitiers, where Eleanor, wife of Henry II, often stayed and of Troyes, where lived her daughter, Mary, who became countess of Champagne in 1164, both played important roles in the diffusion of the Arthurian legends. The Abbey of Glastonbury, destroyed by fire in 1184, was rebuilt thanks to the generosity of Henry II. In 1187 he had his grandson, destined to reign over Brittany, named Arthur. A little before 1190, Henry encouraged the monks to find the tombs of Arthur and Guinevere. In 1191 his son Richard, now king of England, claimed to be offering Tancred of Sicily the legendary sword Excalibur. It is wiser perhaps to conclude that it was only at the end of the twelfth century that the Anglo-Angevin monarchy thought of using the Arthurian cycle. In any case, how could the Anglo-Normans have done so, when Henry I tried to show his connections with the last Saxon king, Edward the Confessor.[112]

Thus it was in the first decades of the twelfth century that the French and Spanish monarchies deliberately relied on the supernatural and paganizing forms of the cult of the saints. Not until the second half of the century did the German and then English monarchies attempt in their turn to seize the currents of legend.

It seems then that the legendary origins of the four principal European monarchies at the end of the twelfth century were for the most part borrowed from the very widespread Christianized forms of paganism that emerged during the eleventh century. But if one compares their three respective legendary themes, beyond the common elements one begins to see differences emerging. Balthasar, James, and

Denis are clearly, in the popular imagination, funerary saints; the dark skin of the first two, Balthasar's myrrh, and the protection of the burial place of kings by the last show this unambiguously. All three are holy travelers from the East and, in the case of the Magi at least, it is clear that there is an element of the "psychopomp," the guide of souls, for they protect the soul in its dangerous journey toward the next world. Finally, as they travel they carry and they point to something precious: the first, a box containing his gift, the two others, their head. It is difficult to say what this head-carrying represents; one is tempted to make a connection with the gift of gold borne by Caspar, perhaps the crown. However, differences of treatment of the general schema seem very clear, particularly when we examine the triple nature of the Magi and that of Denis. This characteristic of our saints can be compared with many other examples of the "multiplications of intensity" of a single god, such as Hermes Trismegistus. Denis, who protects the young king, is a liberating saint—of serfs but perhaps also of young people who will not be constrained—and a peasant saint. Balthasar, on the other hand, when he appears in his secondary forms, evokes the double figure of priest and king.

Should we associate, in the first case, the emphasis on the future responsibility of the young king with the practice of the precoronation ceremony of the heir of the throne practised by the Capetian monarchy? Should this be contrasted with, in the second case, a monarchy where the accent is on the personal apotheosis of an emperor and also on the relation between king and priest? Although they may appear fanciful, such considerations allow us to grasp better the way in which people at that time understood the scriptures as interpreted for them by the clergy. This would explain how two conceptions of royalty, both inspired by the Bible, could exist side by side for so long without any serious conflict. One wonders whether in Carolingian times the peasants understood the ritual in the same way the educated did. In the twelfth century we are no longer in any doubt, for alongside the scholarly commentaries there appears in the texts the belief in a "magic" monarchy.

To speak of magic and the monarchy and to evoke the healing powers of the king immediately brings to mind Marc Bloch's *Les rois thaumaturges*. This book was a pioneering work, but on rereading it, it seems a singularly cautious one. Would it be presumptuous to think that today we could go further in an interpretation of the evidence assembled by Bloch? To paraphrase Bernard of Chartres, dwarfs see further than giants when they can stand on the giant's shoulders![113]

The first text dealing unambiguously with the healing of scrofula victims with the touch of the king of France is Guibert of Nogent's treatise on the relics of the saints.

What am I saying? Have we not seen our Lord King Louis perform this customary prodigy? I have seen as clearly as I see you how those suffering from scrofula on the neck or elsewhere on the body crowd round to be touched by him and marked with the sign of the cross, and I was there at his side, and I defended him against their importunities. . . . The glory of this miracle had been lost by his father Philip as a result of I know not what fault when before he had performed it with fervor.

As Marc Bloch remarked, the use of the word "customary" is important. Is it possible to fix the date of the ritual of the touching of scrofula victims any earlier than the reign of Philip I? The text itself allows it to be understood: if he mentions Philip, it is not because he was the first to touch, but because he had lost this power. And indeed the biographer of Robert the Pious, Helgaud, writes: "Divine power granted to this perfect man a great grace, that of healing bodies: with his most pious hand, touching the affected in the place of their wound, and making the sign of the cross there, he removed all the pain of the disease." This text too is quite clear; Robert did not inherit his magic powers, they were given to him by God and it is even possible that he cured more than just scrofula.[114]

Marc Bloch looked also for negative evidence. There were no traces of healing powers among the Carolingians. Of the Merovingians we know that Guntram of Burgundy had cured a man with fever and some possessed people, which is to say epilectics or hysterics. Bloch thinks that this was a particular power attributed only to Guntram. This is perhaps too much and too little. Too much, because the text implies that Guntram did not recognize or did not wish to recognize that he possessed this power; the demons expelled from the bodies of the possessed cried out, it was said, the name of the king, proving that he had been invoked but not that he had been present at the scene. One female suppliant who wished to approach him had done it without his knowledge.[115] Guntram did not then exercise a healing power: it was attributed to him, whether he liked it or not. The matter is all the more remarkable because, despite the sympathy that Gregory of Tours may have felt for him, Guntram was far from being a model king.[116]

For all that, the criteria of the popular cult were not the same as those of "official saintliness." This was the case with those Slav or Danish princes whose only mark of sanctity was to have accepted without resistance a sometimes ignominious death; the veneration of the people forced the bishops to accept them.[117]

So it seems certain that neither the Carolingians nor even the Merovingians wished to appear as healing kings. But it is quite possible that a section of the population considered them to be so. Consequently the phenomenon that interests us is not the creation of a belief in the healing powers of the king, but in the recognition of it by the monarchy. Here lies the difference between Guntram and Robert.

We need to look also at the claims of healing powers made by the English monarchy. Around 1125 certain members of the royal entourage claimed that the last Anglo-Saxon king, Edward the Confessor, dead for some sixty years, possessed the power to cure scrofula "not by virtue of his sanctity but by the inheritance of his royal blood." This claim was not without self-interest, because Henry I had married an Anglo-Saxon princess of the same family. William of Malmesbury, our informant, is clearly hostile to this idea. He follows in this respect not only the Gregorian reformers but also the traditions of the Church; saints, whether or not they are kings, can perform miracles, but kings cannot. Some fifty years later, Peter of Blois, in his apologia for the monarchy of Henry II, associates, despite those who doubt, the sacrament of the royal unction and the healing of scrofula, the latter demonstrating, according to him, the efficacy of the former. Does this mean that the royal sacrament was becoming devalued? Perhaps, but it is also a clever justification by a court clerk of the healing power of kings that part of the Church still found hard to accept. It is no longer inheritance that gives this power, but the ritual of coronation, which allows the Church to exercise its control. This theory was not to be fully accepted, however, either in England or in France.[118]

It seems then that Robert the Pious was the first king to touch the sick. A few generations later his descendants considered that he had passed this power on to them. Thus it is interesting to place the "acquisition" by Robert of this power for his family alongside the other beliefs that were to make him at the end of the eleventh century a truly legendary king. Robert's miracles occurred—no man can be a prophet in his own country—during a pilgrimage to the Midi, and particularly in that same Auvergne whose paganizing fervor we have already met. This journey became the pretext for legendary and epic developments from the beginning of the twelfth century. To Robert was attributed the same miracle as Joshua at Jericho: the walls of a city were supposed to have fallen down before him. From before 1072 legend attributed a magical offspring to the dissolved marriage between Robert and Bertha of Blois: a child with a goose's head.

It is not hard to see why Bertha, an excommunicated adulteress, had a bad reputation, especially with clerics. But the birth of a monster child is curious: the goose's head of her son seems to make Bertha one of these half-human half-goose women. And this immediately brings to mind Queen Pédauque, Queen Goose-feet, who was connected in popular belief with the Queen of Sheba. So Robert too seems to have been married to a supernatural woman whose webbed feet, like the tail of the snake-woman Melusine, revealed her aquatic character.[119]

If we accept that the touching of scrofula victims was only the adoption by the Capetians in the eleventh century of a collection of old popular beliefs from a much earlier date and not a new creation deriving from a rather vague idea of the sacred character of the monarchy, then we need to try to find out what were these beliefs and what they might mean. Marc Bloch did this, but it is here that his methodological caution, which today seems related to a rather narrow rationalism, gets in the way of his research.

We will confine ourselves to a few examples. Marc Bloch refers to "those barbarian leaders who, if they had sore feet, would bathe them in a paten." Described in this way, this practice seems ridiculous or amusing. It seems much less so if we compare it with the habit of the Celtic chieftain who, seated on his throne, put his feet on a woman's lap. If these are compared with the tradition of the "stones which cry out" when the legitimate chieftain stood on them, we are confronted not with a prosaic and comical footbath, but with a fundamental ritual of ancient monarchy. A few pages further on Bloch tackles the question of the traditional words uttered by the king when he touched the sick. One chronicler tells us that Philip the Fair secretly taught these words on his deathbed to his successor. The historian comments, "he taught or rather—for they cannot have been very secret—reminded the prince his successor." However, shortly before that he mentions the apologetic words of a biographer of St. Louis, who wrote that the kings when touching "pronounced the *customary* and appropriate words, words that were furthermore perfectly holy and Catholic." If the formula that accompanied the touching—and which should be murmured by the king—was "perfectly holy and Catholic," why, we wonder, was it so secret? Marc Bloch takes the opposite view, thus leaving aside the possibility that there was a magic formula, Christianized to a greater or lesser degree.[120]

Fortunately, the popular belief found expression in a number of "superstitions" that all centered in the north of France around the figure of St. Marcoul (Marculphus). He was a holy abbot who was supposed to have lived in the Cotentin in the sixth century. At the time of the Viking invasions, his relics were, like so many others, protected and transferred beyond the reach of the raiders to Corbeny, an estate in the Laon region and part of the dower of the queen, who later left it to the Church of Saint-Remi in Rheims. The importance of the relics of Marcoul is clear at this time because in 906 Charles the Simple established around them a monastery and decided to keep them. In 1101 the saint performed miracles in the Rheims area, the Laonnais, and in Picardy and he continued of course to be very popular in his birthplace, in Coutances and also in Rouen.[121]

According to Marc Bloch, the life of St. Marcoul "offers nothing more than the most banal of hagiographical fables." Perhaps, but it is not so banal if a saint, while on a retreat on an island, finds himself face to face with a woman from the sea who quotes Virgil and then disappears among the waves like a snake. It is not so common an occurrence for a king to use his healing powers to restore the virility of a "youth" of the royal escort, the victim of an unfortunate riding accident provoked by his irreverence toward the king.[122] At the beginning of the thirteenth century, when the people of Coutances dedicated to their saint a large narrative stained-glass window in the cathedral, it was this miracle they chose to illustrate.

Furthermore, it would be hard to understand, if Marcoul were a saint like any other, why Charles the Simple should have gone to such great lengths to obtain permission from the prelates involved, the bishop of Coutances and the archbishop of Rouen, to keep his relics. "The body of a saint," says Marc Bloch, "was a precious possession." But there were plenty of other relics in circulation at this period in which the kings did not take such an interest. In fact Marc Bloch evades the central question, even though his research is so detailed: in what way can a saint known to restore sexual powers cure scrofula, which is properly speaking tubercular adenitis? The texts themselves provide the answer. The first miracle performed by Edward the Confessor was the healing "of a young woman, married to a man of her own age, who was unable to have a child. . . . The humors had accumulated greatly in her neck. . . . [After the king had touched her] her health returned. . . . within the year she gave birth to twins, thus bearing witness to the sanctity of the king."[123] Thus scrofula has a close link with fertility, because tubercular adenitis is often the exterior sign of genital tuber-culosis, one of the chief causes of sterility. And then there is that other form of adenitis not mentioned by the great historian, which accom-panies venereal diseases. Whatever the cause, scrofula could not fail to be for the people of that time the visible sign of a much more serious disease. To heal one was to heal the other.[124] With the king's touch, as with the dream of the young kings, we are brought back to the theme of royal virility. But is this not "the Capetian miracle"?

The royal miracle is simply the exceptional form of a more general magic, and the legend of St. Marcoul allows us to link the powers of the king with those exercised by a "family" of healers. We find evidence in the sixteenth century of several of these "families," where the healers see themselves as relations of a patron saint. In Spain we find the "relations of St. Catherine," in Italy, the "relations of St. Paul," in France, the "race of St. Martin." All of these are recognizable by the emblems that refer to their magical relations: the whole or broken wheel for those of St. Catherine, the serpent for those of St. Paul.[125] The "family" that interests us here is that of the healers who were born the seventh sons, without the intervention of any girls. They were sometimes called Marcous and this name is given also to a kind of cat whose fur, it was sometimes believed, could cause scrofula.[126] These Marcous also had their emblem—in Spain a cross, in France a lily. They shared this emblem with the king's son, "a cross of a red more brilliant than the rose is in summer."[127] They cured scrofula or sometimes rabies. Lastly, in northern Portugal the seventh sons used to turn each Saturday night into donkeys and be chased by dogs. This putting on of an ass's skin clearly refers to a very rich vein in folklore. The hunting of a quadruped—be it donkey, horse, or stag—by dogs also recalls one of the major folk themes of which the story of Dagobert was a very clear version.[128] Interestingly, the theme of the seventh son does not refer only to the miracle of the healing of scrofula, but to another equally important "Capetian miracle": the fact that the dynasty had always had male heirs to carry on the royal power. The same strength that cured scrofula also made the young princes worthy to succeed their fathers.

So we see the relationship of ideas between the king of France—and by extension the king of England—St. Marcoul, and the seventh sons. In our texts the powers of the king appear first, then those of the saint, and finally those of the seventh sons. What does this chronology tell us? Marc Bloch attributes the concordances to logical comparisons made *a posteriori*: "people's imaginations sought a connection, and since they sought it, they found it." There was "contamination" because of the "constant need of the collective psychology." He attributes to each of the three powers a "very particular psychological origin": for St. Marcoul, the general belief in the miraculous powers of the saints; for the kings, the concept of the sacred monarchy; for the seventh sons, "truly pagan speculations about numbers."[129] This hypothesis seems quite reasonable. But it does not satisfy us because it runs contrary to everything that we find in the general current of the eleventh and twelfth centuries: that nobility and monarchy borrow extensively from a very rich fund of popular beliefs whose coherence certainly existed before that time. Given the present state of documentation, it may seem difficult to believe that the French monarchy drew part of its legitimacy from a mental universe where a king and a seventh son were already, if not the same, then closely related. But it is very hard to believe that a mere belief in the sacred character of the monarchy was able spontaneously to produce the specific power of curing scrofula toward the end of the eleventh century.

Some connections do certainly need to be noted: the miraculous pilgrimage of King Robert, just like the malicious legend of the goose-headed child, brings us back to the influence on royalty in the early eleventh century of a single family, that of the counts of Anjou.[130] The devotion to Melusine, the woman-watersnake, had its chief center of diffusion in Poitou and we know that the count of Anjou was at that time the vassal of the count of Poitiers for a certain number of estates in that county.[131] The cult of Marcoul came from the Cotentin, and the English claimed in the twelfth century that their first royal healer, St. Edward, had first practiced his art in Neustria, that is Normandy.[132] Here are hints of Angevin and Norman influence. Once again we are brought back to the first years of the eleventh century and perhaps more generally to a cultural area of the West that was later, under the Plantagenets, to be the domain where the Arthurian cycle was to spread most vigorously.

But we know also that the 1020s were the years when a shift in royal policy was taking place against the house of Blois-Champagne, the heretics and their sympathizers; the years when Duke Richard of Normandy forced Robert's hand, bringing about the exposure of the scandal of the "Manicheans" of Orleans; the years when Constance of Anjou reigned as mistress over the king's household; the years when

Adalbero of Laon bitterly reproached the king for the influence of Cluny. It was as if, against all those for whom God was only Spirit, a coalition was forming of all those who in different degrees refused to disassociate the sacred from its material manifestations. But we should not go too far with these conjectures. It remains that this important pilgrimage—it is the only one of Robert's journeys mentioned by Helgaud, although there were others—when the king was to begin his healing powers, begins with a visit to Souvigny and an act of reverence at the grave of St. Majolus, the former abbot of Cluny.

Thus, whether we like it or not, for the revival of the cult of St. Denis or the healing of scrofula, we find ourselves once more at Cluny. Cluny, which in 1023 was launching the Peace of God, using as its weapon the relics of the saints; Cluny, which thought up the Truce of God and attempted twenty years later to introduce it all over the kingdom; Cluny, which fostered the Spanish crusades in Burgundy and may have created the story of the four deniers of St. James, prototype of the theory of the relationship between the king and St. Denis. Majolus, Odilon, Hugh—these were the kings of Cluny; kings who, unable to reign themselves, forged mental weapons that were to give the monarchy a popular ascendancy that it would probably never have had otherwise.

Corresponding to the social upheavals that began in the last decades of the tenth century was a prodigious intellectual movement. Prodigious because it involved as well as the schoolmen and the writers of texts all social groups. So it was also for women. Melusine and chivalry bear witness to this; and, as we have shown, so do the groups of women who followed the preachers, whether heretical or still within the limits of Catholicism, and so does the flowering of new religious foundations for women. The significance of the development in the twelfth century of the cult of Mary is more ambiguous the more we examine its specificity in this period: Mary was already venerated in Carolingian times, or perhaps even earlier, in social milieux where the cult of woman seems hardly to have held a place of honor. Nevertheless, the Church came to recognize a more personal religious life for women.[133] But it would be foolish to exaggerate the "feminist" character of the twelfth century; a revival of Roman law by a regime in increasing difficulties quelled the restlessness among women.[134]

So it was also for the peasants. From the twelfth century the myths that formed the framework of their culture began to appear, more or less distorted. But here we meet an apparent paradox: it is at the very moment when the peasants were beleaguered by banal lordship and by the town that the cultural barrier, which for so long had kept peasant ideas in the depths of country society, falls. A barrier, or was it rather ignorance? To deal with the new demands of political life a new power was required with a wider spiritual base. Along with the material attacks on the countryside came the exploitation of the mental structures of peasantry for the benefit of the masters of the land. To ensure that the new relationships of hierarchy and subordination took root in society, force alone was not enough and devotion to one man was insufficient. The secret of the power of monarchy, from the eleventh century onward, was to merge with mental attitudes much older than itself, the better to take hold of them. One wonders how far the development of heresies of the docetic type among some peasants can be explained by their rejection of beliefs they perceived were being placed in the service of their subjugators. The peasants hesitated between the idols of Auvergne and the Spirit that was blowing in Champagne. There appears also the central role in the "movement of ideas" of the eleventh and twelfth centuries of those peasants, allodialists in the south or dependants in the north, who entered the ranks of knights and thus forged links with the nobility. Efficient agents of the lords, they were probably also the ones who provided the inspiration to the clerics, products of their own class, for the ideal constructions that invaded men's consciousnesses and on which power was established.

Notes

1. Le Goff, *Culture cléricale* [634].
2. Duby, *L'an mil* [615], p. 22.
3. Boglioni, *La culture* [608a]; Geary, *La coercition* [621a]; Poulin, *Entre* [648a].
4. Gregory of Tours, *Historia Francorum*, 8:15; Forsyth, *The Throne* [620]. On the sentiment of the continuity between the Virgin and the goddess that preceded her, see Guibert of Nogent, *De vita sua* [46], 2: 1, p. 99ff. Legend and statue of Isis in Paris, Abbo, *Le siège* [21], 1:v.1, p. 12, and Barroux, *Statue* [606].
5. *Miracula Sanctae Fidis* [29], 1:13, pp. 47, 48 and Duby, *L'an mil* [615], p. 93. On the change in mental attitudes with regard to the crucifix, p. 225.
6. *MGH*, Capit. 1, pp. 26, 223; Riché, *La magie* [648].
7. Rabanus Maurus, Sermon, *PL*, 110, col. 78; Riché, *La vie quotidienne* [646], p. 221.
8. Roheim, *Les portes du rêve* (Paris, 1973), p. 498ff.
9. Vogel, *Pratiques* [656]; Guibert, *De vita sua* [46], 1: 18, p. 71. Pierced children, in the Merovingian period, in Roussillon, see Salin, *La civilisation . . .*, 2:354.
10. Vogel, *Pratiques* [656], and Manselli, *Simbolismo* [640]. The hallucinogenic plant recalls the women's nocturnal ride to Diana (the moon) of which the penitentials also speak.
11. Gervase of Tilbury, *Otia* [43], p. 390. On this practice in Merovingian times with traces in the Carolingian period, see Salin, *La civilization mérovingienne*, 2:235, 261 and 271ff.
12. See p. 315 above.
13. Frequent allusions in the sources to *incantationes*; description of a fetish by Hincmar, Riché, *La vie quotidienne* [646], p. 219; Guibert, *De vita sua* [46], 1: 26, p. 97, which describes the sacrifice by a cleric of a cock born from an egg laid on a Thursday in March.

14. "It may be revealing to consider a culture from its obsessions and study the censors affecting it on the level of individual and collective repression," Le Goff, *Les rêves* [636].
15. Cf. pp. 256–57 above.
16. Duby, *L'économie rurale* [300], p. 439.
17. Goffart, *From Roman Taxation* [536]; Perrin, *La seigneurie rurale* [156], p. 682; Duby, *La société* [78], p. 257; Poly, *La Provence* [87], pp. 106 and 135.
18. Dhondt, *Le haut Moyen Age* [475], p. 111; Goffart, *From Roman Taxation* [536]; Bloch, *Les colliberti* [284]; Perrin, *La seigneurie rurale* [156], p. 726. These eggs, sometimes delivered by the hogshead by certain villages in Lorraine, p. 155, were probably hard-boiled!
19. Macrobius, *Saturnalia*, 7:16, p. 418.
20. Bloch, *Les colliberti* [284]; Schneider, *Aspects de la société* [512]; Geoffrey of Vigeois, *Chronica* [40], cap. 69.
21. Compare the cakes offered to the lord at Christmas in Lorraine, Perrin, *La seigneurie rurale* [156] p. 413, those eaten by the peasants of the Dauphiné in honor of St. Agatha on 5 February, and the "merlusin" cakes of the peasants of Poitou, p. 316 above.
22. *Vita Geraldi* [34], 2:31, col. 637 and 4:7, col. 700.
23. Gervase, *Otia* [43], p. 390, no. 83. The Catalan knight Guérau of Cabrera had an enchanted horse, Bonami, who gave good advice and danced when his master played the viol, p. 381, no. 92. On this person, see S. Sobreques-Vidal, *Els barons de Catalunya* (Barcelona, 1970), p. 46. The king of Scotland's birdcatcher caught the birds by uttering some magic words, Gervase, *Otia* [43], p. 390, n. 84.
24. Manselli, *Simbolismo* [640]; Riché, *La magie* [648]; Silvestre, *Deux exorcismes* [651].
25. Le Goff, *Mélusine* [637].
26. Hincmar, *PL*, 125, col. 716.
27. Le Roy Ladurie, *Mélusine* [638].
28. Van Gennep, *Le folklore du Dauphiné* (Paris, 1932), 1:236, and Le Roy Ladurie, *Mélusine* [638].
29. See pp. 256–57 above.
30. The mother of Guibert of Nogent in the Beauvaisis and Godelieve of Ghistelle in Flanders both had recourse to such spells, Huyghebaert, *Les femmes laïques* [628]; Manselli, *Simbolismo* [640], which quotes several spells for love or death.
31. Adhemar de Chabannes, *Chronicon* [24], 3:66, p. 191; and the many legends of husbands poisoned by their wives, as in Chabannes, *Chronicon* [24], 3: 45, p. 167; *Vita Burchardi* [35], p. xvii; Platelle, *La violence* [398].
32. Guibert, *De vita sua* [46], 7:12, 20, and 18, pp. 41, 80, 50, and 72.
33. Le Goff, *Culture cléricale* [634].
34. Thus St. Foy punishes a knight who stole wine, St. Benedict has a thieving *avoué* bitten by a rabid dog, St. Isarn causes fire to come down from heaven on those villages that refused him hospitality, Duby, *L'an mil* [615], pp. 98 and 101; Poly, *La Provence* [87], p. 181.
35. See p. 106 above.
36. For a spirited assessment, see Aebischer, *Le concept d'état latent . . .*, in [659], p. 196. Marc Bloch had said: "Whether we start from the real or

from the imaginary, any attempt at interpretation which fails to take account, equally fully, of each of these elements would be condemned for this same reason," *La société* [70], p. 145.

37. Le Gentil,*La Chanson de Roland* (Paris, 1967), p. 20; Horrent, *La bataille* [667].

38. Horrent, *La bataille* [667].

39. André de Mandach has pointed out that when the name of Roland is introduced into the manuscripts of the *Life of Charlemagne* by Einhard, it is only in those coming from the regions of the Loire and the Marne, *La Geste* [677], p. 13.

40. Lejeune, *La légende . . . et la fausse donation* [675].

41. Defourneaux, *Les Français* [613], pp. 125 and 216. The stories that concern them take on an epic allure, Duby, *L'an mil* [615], p. 215. Place-names, Aebischer, *Deux récits* in [659]. On the Catalan "frontier," see Bonnassie, *La Catalogne* [72], p. 118ff; Grégoire, *La base historique* [669].

42. Robson, *Aux origines* [682]; Ripoll and Fleury, *Vita Gauzlini* [25], app. 3, p. 169; *Miracula Sanctae Fidis* [29], 2:6, 109, and 3:1, p. 129, which deals with Roger of Tosny, founder of Sainte-Foy in Conches in Normandy, and leader of the crusade of 1018 in Catalonia.

43. See 197 above.

44. Louis, *De l'histoire* [676].

45. Poly, *La Provence* [87], p. 85.

46. See pp. 232–33 above.

47. Lejeune, "La naissance du couple littéraire 'Roland et Olivier,' " *Mélanges H. Grégoire* (Brussels, 1950), 2:371. Aebischer, *La Chanson de Roland* [656a]; on Oliver and on the early versions of Girart of Viane, *Bavardages érudits . . . ,* p. 67; *L'etat actuel . . . ,* p. 93; *Deux récits . . . ,* p. 131.

48. 902, R. Poupardin, *Recueil des actes des rois de Provence,* (Paris, 1920), no. 41, p. 77; Poly, *La Provence* [87], p. 21.

49. *Histoire* [66], 1:7, p. 20.

50. Poly, *La Provence* [87], pp. 58 and 356. Is it a coincidence that the first written piece of evidence to mention William and his men is the fragment from The Hague, Aebischer, *Contestation . . . ,* in [659], p. 25; this text must have taken the same route as the will of the countess Tiburge of Orange (d. 1150) which was taken to The Hague by the Orange-Nassau family, Font-Réaulx, "Le testament de Tiburge d'Orange et la cristillisation de la principauté." *Mélanges . . . R. Busquet* (Marseilles, 1957), p. 41.

51. According to this theory, the connection of the legendary William with Saint-Guillem-du-Désert, Lejeune, *L'esprit* [673], would be a relatively recent phenomenon. The continuity from the era of monastic flowering to the eleventh century is in any case more than unlikely; the translation of the body only dates from 1138.

52. Lejeune, *La question* [674]; *HGL,* 5, col. 37; L. Auzias, *L'Aquitaine carolingienne,* p. 403. Saint-Paul is the abbey where the legendary Aimery is supposed to be buried. Archbishop Aimery had given the monastery of Saint-Paul in 958 the ancient *oppidum* of Enserune, which like Vaubeton or Gaussier was a site that caught the imagination. Poly, *La Provence,* p. 21.

53. Text in *GCN*, 2, instr. col. 178; the formula *principibus astantibus* reproduces the royal formulary of the late eleventh and early twelfth centuries, Bournazel, *Le gouvernement* [418], p. 144; Lejeune, *L'esprit de croisade* [673], *Miracula Sanctae Fidis* [29], 4:8, p. 192; Mandach, *La Geste* [677], p. 60ff.

54. All *chansons* that seem to have been firmly based in the battles of the late ninth and early tenth centuries. The magnifying influence of the legend and the epic was already patently obvious in the historical sources of the tenth and early eleventh centuries, see Lauer, *Le règne de Louis IV d'Outre-Mer* (Paris, 1900), p. 267ff.; Bloch, *La société* [70], p. 145. On Ogier "The Dane," see R. Lejeune, *Recherches sur le thème: les Chansons de Geste et l'histoire* (Liège, 1948), and *La base historique* [669]; Aebischer, *Le concept d'état latent*, and *La mesnie Doon de Mayence . . .* , in [659], p. 201.

55. Aebischer, *La Chanson de Roland,*; Lejeune, *La base historique* [669].

56. Lejeune, *L'esprit* [673].

57. Duby, *Les jeunes* [428]. Already in the traditions of the seigneurial families, Bloch, *La société* [70], p. 150.

58. Duby, *Structures* [232].

59. Thus genealogy runs into legend and romance, Duby, *Remarques* [233], *Les jeunes* [428], and chapter 3 above.

60. Siciliano's arguments collapse when, pleading against "neo-traditionalism," he comments ironically on the lack of resemblance between the legendary William and the historical William described by Ermold the Black, *Les Chansons de Geste* [683], p. 225.

61. See p. 232 above. To indicate the enemies of Cluny, see pp. 167–68 above.

62. Louis, *Girart* [676], 2:123; Lejeune, *La base historique* [669].

63. Schneider, *Aspects de la société* [512]. One of the best versions of the life of Gerald is paired, in a Cistercian manuscript, with the life of William.

64. Duby, *Les jeunes* [428].

65. Boutet, *La politique* [661].

66. Gregory Béchade, quoted in Lejeune, *L'esprit* [673].

67. Siciliano, *Les Chansons de Geste* [683], p. 220.

68. Köhler, *L'aventure* [668], p. 35; *contra*, Siciliano, *Les Chansons* [683], p. 224.

69. Aebischer, *Bavardages érudits . . .* ; Lejeune, *La question* [674]. On this process, see Duby, *La vulgarisation* [616a]. In 1097 on the crusade, Robert the Frisian, and Hugh of Vermandois were compared to Roland and Olivier, Mandach, *La Geste* [677], p. 72.

70. Platelle, *Le scandale* [644]. Platelle's work could be paralleled by a corresponding study in the south, starting with Geoffrey of Vigeois, *Chronicon* [40], cap. 73, and with the *Vie d'Etienne d'Obazine*, ed. M. Aubrun (Clermont-Ferrand, 1970), 1:30, p. 89.

71. See pp. 231–32 above.

72. On the depravity of the young men, see Duby, *Les jeunes* [428].

73. We know that during this period the method of shaving left a prickly stubble.

74. See p. 317 above.

75. Pirot, *L'idéologie* [680]; Lejeune, *Formules* [670]; Ourliac, *Troubadours* [678].

76. Toubert, *Le Latium* [89], p. 697; Poly, *La Provence* [87], p. 52.
77. See chapter 7.
78. Köhler, *L'aventure* [668], pp. 48 and 54.
79. On the Arthurian romance, cf. with Köhler, Faral, *La légende arthurienne. Etudes et documents*. 3 vols. (Paris, 1929), and bibliography of Lot's works on the "Matter of Britain," in *Recueil* . . . , 1:188ff.
80. On the role of patronage by women and particularly that of the house of Plantagenet, see R. Lejeune, "La femme dans les littératures française et occitane du XIe au XIIIe siècle," *CCM* (1977): 201.
81. Le Goff, *Culture cléricale* [634].
82. Salin, 4:57, 21, 144; P.-M. Duval, *Les dieux de la Gaule* (Paris, 1967), pp. 37 and 46; H. Hubert, *Les Celtes et la civilisation celtique* (Paris, 1932), p. 255; Markale, *La femme celte* (Paris, 1973), p. 139; Köhler, *L'aventure* [668], p. 106.
83. There are a few exceptions in Lejeune, "La femme," which discusses the popular genres of the weaving song, of the girl's lover, and of the mismatched wife.
84. Huyghbaert, *Les femmes laïques* [628]. The attitude of the theologians even with variations tells us more about them than about women. M.-Th. D'Alverny, "Comment les théologiens et les philosophes voient la femme." *CCM* (1977): 105. The iconography is a little less stereotyped, C. Frugoni, "L'iconographie de la femme au cours des X-XIIe siècles," ibid. p. 177.
85. Duby, *Structures* [232].
86. Duby, *Les jeunes* [428], *Remarques* [233]; Bournazel, *Le gouvernement* [418], p. 103. Example of a man after a dowry, Guibert, *Histoire* [46], 1:13, p. 45.
87. Cf. for example the *faux pas* of Peire Vidal, C. Chabaneau, *Les biographies des troubadours* (Toulouse, 1885), p. 64.
88. Duby, *Les trois ordres* [616], p. 364. At the end of the twelfth century, the treatise "On Love" shows that the art of love is a social strategy, p. 404.
89. Guibert's mother dreamed that she was being pursued by ghostly men; a voice cried out: "Do not touch her!" Guibert, *De vita sua* [46], 1:12, p. 70; Huyghebaert, *Les femmes laïques* [628]; Platelle, *La violence* [398]; Guibert, *De vita sua* [46], 1:12, p. 38.
90. Thus the Cluniac Bernard, who in the early twelfth century criticizes the son who wishes to marry and "fill the paternal house with his offspring," "the little girl who dreams of a husband's kisses," Bultot, *La doctrine* [610] and *Mépris* [611].
91. Geoffrey of Vigeois, *Chronica* [40], cap. 69.
92. Köhler, *L'aventure* [668], p. 35.
93. Ibid., pp. 18, 28, and 96.
94. Bloch, *Les colliberti* [284].
95. Spiegel, *The cult* [467] and *The chronicle* [468], p. 23ff.
96. See pp. 198–99 above.
97. Barroux, *Statue* [606]. In the eighteenth century, a fountain called St. Denis's Fountain existed on the southern slope. According to witnesses, peasants used to come back from it telling of and doing strange things, Bossuat, *Traditions* [609].
98. Spiegel, *The cult* [467]. It is worth noting that the author of *Ruolantes*

liet, Conrad der Pfaffe, appears to have lived in Regensburg; he dedicated his work to the duchess of Bavaria, Matilda, daughter of Eleanor, Mandach, *La Geste* [677], p. 197.
99. Folz, *Tradition* [619]. And for "French" traditions, Theis, *Dagobert* [652].
100. Indeed he cuts his tutor's beard, Spiegel, *The cult* [467].
101. This ordeal, quite common after all, must have been intensified for the young French princes by the custom of the precoronation.
102. Spiegel, *The cult* [467]. Two centuries later, Charles VI, aged twenty-four and having succeeded his father at the age of twelve, gets lost in a forest in Maine where he meets a white stag with a gold medallion around its neck. His madness dates from this time forward. Significant too are the troubled thoughts of the young Philip, wondering whether one day he would be able to emulate Charlemagne, see Mandach, *La Geste* [677], p. 157.
103. Vazquez de Parga, *Las peregrinaciones* [653], and Perez de Urbel, "Los primeros siglos de la reconquista," in *Historia de España*, vol. 6 [Madrid, 1964], p. 53ff., and the introduction to Menendez Pidal, *Historia de España*, pp. xvii and xx; Sigal, *Les marcheurs* [650], p. 112.
104. Poly, *Le diable* [645].
105. Henrion, *Le culte* [626]; Elissagaray, *La légende* [618].
106. Folz, *Le souvenir* [431], p. 203; Kienast, *Deutschland* [450], p. 270ff. The emperor's entourage was also very interested in the Pseudo-Turpin, obtaining a copy around 1180–1189 from Baldwin V of Hainault who had had it compiled from versions originating in Cluny, Tours, and Saint-Denis, Mandach, *La Geste* [677], p. 93.
107. At the end of the eleventh century, the legend of the three Magi took material form in Rheims; a small piece of their gold was melted, it was believed, in one of the cathedral chalices, see Guibert, *De vita sua* [46], 1:11, p. 32. Thus here too the learned construction had been preceded by popular belief.
108. Myrrh is known to have been used by embalmers.
109. Poly, *La Provence* [87], p. 358. The pretensions of the Baux family to identify themselves with the empire date from the 1160s; despite a sharp reaction from the counts of Provence-Barcelona, they were renewed in 1178 and 1184, L. Barthélemy, *Inventaire des chartes de la maison des Baux* (Marseilles, 1882), nos. 57, 62, 63, 71, 72, and 84.
110. Compare the "cramp-rings" of the kings of England, which were also supposed to cure epilepsy, Bloch, *Les rois* [607], pp. 164 and 169. Here we find the question of the magic coins of which the cramp-rings were made.
111. Elissagaray, *La légende* [618], pp. 230 and 240; Henrion, *Le culte* [626], pp. 35 and 80.
112. Köhler, *L'aventure* [668], pp. 68 and 303; Faral, *La légende*, pp. 43ff. and 47.
113. Quoted by D. M. Bell, *L'idéal éthique de la rouyauté en France au Moyen Age* (Geneva-Paris, 1962), p. 34.
114. Bloch, *Les rois* [607], pp. 30 and 36; Helgaud, *Epitoma vitae Roberti* [49], 28, p. 128.
115. Bloch, *Les rois* [607], p. 33.
116. Tessier, *Le baptême de Clovis*, p. 191.
117. Gorski, *Le roi saint* [623].

118. Bloch, *Les rois* [607], p. 221.
119. *Vita Burchardi* [35], introduction, p. xxxi; Pfister, *Etudes sur le règne de Robert le Pieux*, pp. 36 and 58. Reference to a monstrous child in an anonymous chronicle, in 1110, *RHF,* 10:211. A goose's head in Peter Damian, ibid., p. 492.
120. Bloch, *Les rois* [607], p. 78; J. Markale, *La femme celte* (Paris, 1973), pp. 268 and 288; Bloch, *Les rois* [607], pp. 92 and 129, n. 1.
121. Bloch, *Les rois* [607], p. 261ff.
122. *Vita Marculphi* 11 and 19, *Boll. AA SS* 1 (May): 74, 76. In the eleventh-century version of the *Vie,* the accident only harms the victim's intestines. In Bloch, *Les rois* [607], p. 265, the hunter is "punished for his irreverence toward the saint by a severe riding accident then . . . restored to health." Thus the very particular nature of the wound, inflicted and then cured, is repressed and relegated to the unconscious.
123. *PL,* 195, col. 761.
124. We do not reject the connection made by Marc Bloch between *"Marcoul"* and *"mal au cou."* Nevertheless it can only be a popular etymology made *a posteriori* and not the reason for the association between Marcoul, royal saint, and scrofula.
125. Bloch, *Les rois* [607], pp. 170 and 300.
126. Ibid., p. 308. Having made these observations, Bloch makes the nickname derive from the cat "by a sort of onomatopoeia originating in a vague imitation of purring."
127. Ibid., p. 247. The royal procession of the Asturian dynasty on 29 December, the feast of St. James, was in the twelfth century led by the king carrying a sceptre surmonted with the fleur-de-lys, Mandach, *La Geste* [667], p. 47. The shape of a fleur-de-lys or cross can also be considered to be that of a goose's foot.
128. See p. 333 above.
129. Bloch, *Les rois* [607], pp. 293 and 300.
130. Helgaud, *Vie de Robert* [49], 27, p. 124; Poly, *La Provence,* 177.
131. Guillot, *Le comte d'Anjou* [83], p. 5ff.
132. Bloch, *Les rois* [607], p. 47.
133. Huyghebaert, *Les femmes* [628].
134. P. Ourliac and J. de Malafosse, *Histoire du Droit privé* (Paris, 1968), 3:130. In practice, it was not until the Renaissance and the sixteenth century that the principle of the legal incapacity of women was established. On the condition of women, see Robert Fossier, *L'enfance de l'Europe: Aspects économiques et sociaux,* 2 vols. (Paris, 1982). [See Supplementary Bibliography: Recent Publications]

―――

CONCLUSION

Let no one be surprised that these fugitives render unto the monks what is Caesar's, for they have set them up as Caesar to protect themselves, their wives and their children.

—Raimbaud de Liège

What is feudalism? Thirty or forty years—what am I saying, scarcely twenty years ago—historians would have been able to reply without too much hesitation. They talked, of course, about a military aristocracy that exploited the peasants through their seigneurial power. They talked above all of a network of contracts, which to a greater or lesser extent kept this dominant class under control.

They described the rituals: kneeling, bare-headed, unarmed, in an attitude of submission, placing their two hands between the hands of another; then rising, speaking, pronouncing aloud the formula of an oath—a system of gestures and words, gestures of homage, words of fealty, sealing the friendship between two men, the lord and the vassal, ready to defend and help one another, or at the very least to abstain from harming one another. To this system of ritual were, possibly, added on other less specific rituals by which the vassal was invested with a fief, received the enjoyment of a property which entailed a service. Perfected over the years by scholars trained particularly in the field of law, a model was imposed on historians. This was an uncomplicated model of a "classic" feudalism, thought to have been established between the Loire and the Rhine, in the old Frankish and Carolingian kingdom, and from there transplanted and imperfectly spread into the surrounding provinces. . . .

We should no longer speak of "classic" feudalism—this model has had its day. Nor did any such thing as a "perfect" feudalism exist, or rather, all forms were perfect, more or less, in their way. All the evidence points to a single movement, which between the tenth and the thirteenth centuries took with it European society as a whole. "Feudalism," in the sense understood by our masters—the use of the fief and the contract of vassalage—, was never more than the outer trappings of this profound impulse. "Feudalism" was applied to the exterior of the living structures of society, the domestic and familial. Among the knights gathered around the castle, sharing in the profits of seigneury, relations of reverence and devotion were naturally established between old and young, between providers and dependants, within the framework of kinship and conviviality of which the rituals of homage,

351

fealty, and investiture, which certainly varied from region to region, were merely the metaphorical expression or imaginary complement.[1]

The increasing questioning, in the last decade, of the traditional version of medieval history here finds its culmination—not just in a critique of the old model, but in a radical change of viewpoint. Feudal or not, the societies of the tenth to twelfth centuries were neither classic nor perfect; or, rather, they were in their way both these things. Instead of trying to eliminate contradictions through yet further detailed research, by explaining them as exceptions to an ideal schema or as "impurities," we should use them as our starting point. Then the gravitational center of our analysis is shifted; amid the extreme variety of concrete expressions there emerges a single and profound movement.[2]

It is at the end of the tenth century that a very ancient social fabric begins to fall apart; and there was an end in Western Europe, or the beginning of an end, of the dominance of a very ancient mode of production. Neither the slavery of the Roman estates, nor its Carolingian successor, labor service, had succeeded in suppressing the independent peasant communities, except in one or two special cases. The crushing but fragile military domination of Rome or Aachen was in the end powerless to overcome the freedom surviving in the countryside. What was necessary to achieve that end was the proliferation, and at the same time hypertropy, of another very ancient structure, that of the warrior households eventually established in countless, and often anything but paternal, local tyrannies. The castle households prospered, while the allodial communities collapsed. These two aspects of the movement, even if one seems better than the other, are inextricably linked. Mortally wounded this time, country society broke up. The "rustics" who were most affected clustered around the church manors, swelling the ranks of its protégés, only to be overtaken by the nobles. The more courageous went to set up in the forests and mountains; here again the nobles caught up with them, though admittedly with a great degree of compromise. Within two or three generations dependence had become the rule and freedom the exception. Now the lord's *bannum* extended everywhere; the Caesars were legion.

After the storms of the century, the peasants reformed themselves into village communities, but they now could not escape living in the shadow of the castle. The recollection of old times became fixed in the "collective memory," an aching nostalgia born of societies without a state, societies *against* the state. Liberty and equality were one and the same thing—the equality of the first man and first woman, working for themselves and no one else. "When Adam delved and Eve span, who was then the gentleman"?[3] Some academics might find it hard to imagine that the peasants could have dreamed of doing without a master. That itself is not unusual; the clerics of the time were also amazed and indignant at the idea of such folly. And it would be even more difficult for these same scholars to conceive that peasant egalitarianism had taken root in an actual, even if "imperfect," historical situation; thus they would be forced to continue to believe, and to say, that, *mutatis mutandis*, the great seigneurial estate had reigned forever and everywhere, appearing at the dawn of time, and with it had reigned obedience and all the other virtues. There is no need to continue.[4]

Other historians nowadays have seen more clearly the echo—played down by those texts that did not wish to hear it—of the "song of Adam," the hope of peasant revolts long before the Jacqueries of the fourteenth century, at the time of the insurrections of the late twelfth century, and perhaps at the time of the peace movements of the 1020s.[5] What sense can we make of these mutilated and torn tatters and shreds of evidence, so much more precious than many of the treatises on morals and theology of the time? A return to a still remembered past? A "utopian" program? Yes, but also perhaps a lesson and an analysis of the crisis: no liberty without equality; liberty no longer exists because equality has been destroyed.

From the very heart of the "primitive" peasantry came those who allowed its domestication. Here too we can see more clearly today that those not-so-chivalrous knights, whose galloping horses shook the ground and the rocks and mounds where their new masters had entrenched themselves, were not all of noble family, far from it. The vast majority of these henchmen, these "fist men," were born of the decomposition, the "kulakization," of ancient country society.[6] In order to be "higher" than the others, they agreed to serve, thus making possible the final victory of the warrior households over the peasant neighborhoods. Once the fundamental character of this movement was determined, there was little room for chronological fluctuations: by the decades around the year 1000 the Western European world had fundamentally changed.

So where exactly is "feudalism" in this great change: before, after, or nowhere? Marc Bloch, who was aware of this problem, attempted to resolve it by distinguishing between "two successive feudal periods, very different in character," one supposedly beginning at the end of the ninth century, and giving way to the second around the middle of the eleventh century, as a result of an "economic revolution" involving "a veritable transformation of social values."[7] This chronological division is not questioned now, or very little questioned, but its explanation is. For many historians today, one thing seems clear: before the eleventh century, the household, the *familia*, was much more important than the fief or vassalage.[8] Furthermore, in the places where we find the latter, they are neither all the same nor combined in a homogenous structure accepted by all. There were vassalages, fealties, *beneficia*, *feó*; the feudal-vassalic link was not the dominant relationship. In the noble households, more or less juxtaposed and united, life at the side of the master, the *convivium*, was the most important thing; homage, where it existed, was an adjunct that could be dispensed with.

Rather than "feudalism," one could then speak, as Georges Duby does, using the word in its precise meaning, of "conviviality." Bloch's "first period" is not then properly feudal. What is feudal about it is its ending: the time when judicial seigneury was established and when, in correlation with this, the use of what our texts call "fiefs" and "homage" became common among a wide stratum of people with origins in the peasantry. In many regions this happened in the space of a few generations. These crucial decades were indeed clearly feudal, but they do not constitute a period. These years represent the crisis during which the new relationships were crystallized and established, when the structures were formed that were to govern, or claim to govern, society in the following centuries. In this sense there was no first feudal period.

Is this to say that there was no feudalism? We would be close to thinking so if, confining criticism and investigation to the first period, we were to remain prisoners, for the second period, of the traditional analysis. This second period is seen as one of "decadence," or at best as a dismal tidying up of the youthful and enthusiastic first period. If the first period is not feudal, then the second can even less claim to be so. "The governments get organized" and—for this very reason?—"efface in western civilization their most specifically feudal elements." Yet everyone knows that this "organization of governments" in the twelfth and thirteenth centuries was accompanied by a prolonged process of establishing structures that were feudal in the juridical sense of the word. Politically, almost everything had become a fief. An awkward dilemma. Either we can consider that the "subject of fiefs" with its abundant literature is not "specifically feudal"—but then we should have to investigate the correctness of this term—or we can consider it to be a survival, frivolous and essentially superficial; but a survival of what? Of a "historical accident," which had lasted into the eleventh century? In either case there is still a history of society from the tenth to the twelfth century, but there is no longer, *stricto sensu*, any feudalism.

Is it possible that fief, this key word, or at least this word found so frequently in the medieval vocabulary, is basically a historical illusion? This brings us to the introduction to Marc Bloch's great work. We shall simplify a little in order not to be seduced by its charm: fief, feudalism are "palace terms," old-fashioned jargon used by pettyfogging jurists, which an accident of propaganda brought to the fore at the time of the French Revolution. Without Boulainvilliers and Montesquieu, the National Assembly could never have claimed, as it did on 11 August 1789, that it had "totally abolished the feudal regime." And the historian concludes: "How could one henceforth deny the reality of a system which it had cost so much to destroy?"[9]

It takes a man of the caliber of Marc Bloch to risk such an extraordinary paradox. At the time of his writing, it had no doubt the value of a healthy provocation, opening the way to wider studies that paid more attention to everyday and material life. Now that these studies are beginning to appear, we can pose this naive question in another way: why on earth, for so many centuries in the Middle Ages, have kingdoms been considered to be a collection of fiefs? Let us suppose for a moment that the fief is a political and legal idea and belongs only to the vocabulary of the medieval jurists. Is is possible that jurists, in the Middle Ages any more than today, could create a language without profound reference to the social structures of the day? Are we to think that the *Libri feudorum* were nothing but the inconsequential intellectual game of a few Lombard judges? That the territorial princes who, at the beginning of the twelfth century, refused to pay homage to the king were simply rejecting a "palace term"? Or that the petty knights, the bourgeois, and rich peasants who appeared before the tribunal of the bailiff of Clermont in the Beauvaisis needed a jurist to understand Messire Philip of Beaumanoir when he declared, for example: *"Tuit cils qui tiennent de fief en la contée de Clermont ont en leur fiés toutes justices, haute et basse"* (All those holding in fief in the county of Clermont have in their fiefs all justice, high and low), or again: *"Il ne loit pas a nul gentil homme dessous le roi à soufrir de nouvel que bourjois s'accroisse en fief"*? (It is not lawful for any gentleman beneath the king to allow a burgess to newly acquire a fief). However we analyze the subject of the fief, it is impossible to deny its existence. If we accept the evidence of contemporaries and the idea they have of their society, then Marc Bloch's "second period" was certainly a feudal age: it is indeed the only one.

Looked at in this way the crisis of the eleventh century is neither more nor less important than the lengthy evolution that followed. The heroic times of the knights' enthusiasm and violence are not enough to explain the "society of fiefs": although raw beginnings are not always encumbered with ideology, social institutions cannot do without it. The feudal "order" is not the opposite of "anarchy," or should we say, rather, feudal "polyarchy": it is the result of it. It is disorder when established, when instituted. Herein lies the interest of the studies made of the south, which show this much more clearly than does the north.[10] And the "books of fiefs" are clearly a manifestation of this order, mirroring what it claims to be. To use Marc Bloch's words, "the governments get organized" at the same time as "the more specifically feudal characteristics" become more deeply embedded in society's consciousness. Surely there must be a chronological parallelism here?

The "great battles" with lances were not enough to establish authority, even if they helped. The order, whether princely or royal, which established itself after the feudal crisis, created for itself an imaginary structure, the ladder of ranks, the "orders" of society, the social hierarchy in fact, out of the indissoluble joining of homage and fief. The elements of this structure were not in themselves new. The princely entourages drew them from where they could and where they should: from the rituals and customs of the castle household. On this level the rituals of feudo-vassalage were merely a "metaphorical reflection," as Georges Duby puts it, of the domestic structures, and perhaps not the only one. The baron knew how to play on other aspects of his household. Within the framework of kinship and conviviality, the feudal structure was not essential. But not everyone can live under the same roof and eat at the same table; material conviviality has its limits, and very narrow ones at that. More than material structures were required to unite the warrior households in a solid alliance. And since they needed to "think of themselves as a group," the dependent knights imagined the world as one vast household. On the level of the principalities and then of the kingdom, the metaphorical component, adjusting to the needs of a more abstract power, became the principal metaphor, the dominant idea that gave to the dominant social group the cohesion and justification necessary for government.

In a ritual society, the gesture of the valet has become that of an entire class: one nobleman kneels down in public before another, head bent and hands together. A routine, or play-acting? Certainly feudal society did not include only faithful vassals. Should we conclude that the ceremony was of no consequence? But the rituals of politics today are no more significant; and yet we agree that they are important and they are abundantly interpreted for our edification. The age-old gesture of submission by the defeated had not only become general among the nobles, but now that it was attached to the land for which it was owed, it became invariable and inevitable. It is because he kneels that a certain man holds a certain piece of land, that he exists in society. What is a noble without land? The land holds him as much as he holds it. However strong or lucky, he cannot prevent some places from being since time immemorial more venerated, more sacred than others, because they were the "seat" of certain saints who were stronger than others and more profoundly imprinted on human consciousness. What inconstant human society was unable to establish, the celestial hierarchy fixes forever. The fief is not only a "salary"; it is that point in space where the earthly hierarchy is solidly anchored to the unshakable celestial hierarchy. The attachment to land, the "realization" of vassalage, that is, of dependence and service, is not its degradation but the historical *sine qua non* of its stability. Through it, the relations established between their households, great and small, by the princes and knights seem to them fixed for all time beneath the severe gaze of the angelic host. Once attained, their social positions and that of the first among them, the king, no longer really depended on them. "Happy powerlessness!"—the king of France may fail or stumble, he may die with his belly slit open, but his spiritual double, St. Denis, will not die. The jurists who created the state of the ancien régime did no more than add the corollaries to this original principle. The crown was already the state.

Does not the power and the "charm" of feudal power lie precisely in the fact it was for those at the highest level of society only a repetition of something known, something everyday and familiar, something obvious and real, but which is at the same time grander and richer. It has the immediacy and the distance of a kind of waking dream: when they paid homage to the king, the heads of the chief households were allowed to be, for a few days or hours, members of his household, to be part of that archetypal *familia* that the royal household had become or re–become,where their place was already decided for them.Thus there existed, for all those who saw it or had it described to them, a cere-monial "double," somewhere between the real palace of the king and the celestial mansion. And we know who was responsible for this gradual modeling of reality on dream: the royal entourages of the twelfth century and behind them the forces that supported them—the petty knights, living in the cities or perhaps already burgesses, who created the "patron saints of kingdoms," St. Denis, St. James, or the Three Kings, and adapted the legends to make an ideal model. As has been noted long ago, this was not, of course, how things appeared to them, in the *camera obscura* of their consciousness, but rather the other way around. The position of the king was merely the projection of that of the saint, and everything else fitted in with this. Seen from this point of view, the feudo-vassalic bond in its most complete form was nothing more than the image that society, or those who accepted it, had of itself. But what a powerful image!

On this image was founded the royal suzerainty and sovereignty, the incarnation in our lands of an idea that had elsewhere, by other routes, made such progress: power must be unique and supreme, even in relation to freemen: all must submit to it. Royal sovereignty could well become popular sovereignty once mechanisms for political representa-tion, or pseudo-representation, are installed: whatever the basis of its legitimacy, sovereignty remains a total power, being, as Le Bret said in the seventeenth century, "no more divisble than the point is in geome-try." And our modern constitutionalists are quite aware that the rela-tions of the state and its subjects are always based on sovereignty.[11] The state, if it is legitimate, has all the power; but is it in itself legitimate to have all the power? The question might seem ridiculous or even indecent to a modern mind. Our medieval ancestors did not think in the same way. Feudalism, in the strict sense of the word, can perhaps be seen as an essential stage in the development of an ideology of service, of an education in submission. Whatever the case, it is, whether we like it or not, the lasting foundation in Western Europe of a solid and complete political hierarchy. The state, which repudiates intermediary bodies the better to make use of them, can now despise or pretend to despise the submission of one man to another, a ritual fiction of an all-powerful paternity. But can we be so sure that even today it could survive without it. The state versus feudalism? Let us say, rather the state through feudalism.

Notes

1. Duby, "Féodalités méditerranéennes," *Le Monde*, 27 October 1978.
2. The CNRS symposium in Rome 1978, *Structures féodales*. . . , which covered a very wide area, certainly gave this impression, the clearest offering in this respect being that of Reina Pastor, "Sur l'articulation des formations économico-sociales: communautés villageoises et seigneuries au nord da la péninsule Ibérique."
3. There came about in those days among the Gauls a terrible and dangerous movement of insolence, and it began to push the common people to rebellion against their superiors and to the extermination of the powerful. . . . The result was that there was no more fear, no respect towards superiors and power; on the contrary, they dared to demand for themselves the liberty which they said they had received from our first ancestors, at the moment of the creation of Man. . . . The result also was that there was no longer any distinction between the great and the humble. Instead there was confusion, which in a short time would have brought about the ruin of all the institutions that today regulate the government and function of superiors, by the will of God. . . . This epidemic, although it was found to some extent all over Gaul, had begun to be more widespread in the Auxerrois and Berry and within the boundaries of Burgundy, and the disease had reached such a degree of madness that they were ready, when they had gathered together their forces, to rise in arms to claim their forfeited liberty (1181, "Geste des évêques d'Auxerre," *RHF*, 18 : 729; commented on by Georges Duby, *Les trois ordres* . . . , p. 400).

4. Even Marc Bloch felt obliged to distinguish carefully between feudalism and seigneury, which he thought was much older, *La société* [70], p. 605. Indeed, it is still necessary to come to some agreement about the nature and the extent at any given time of this "seigneury."
5. Duby puts much emphasis on this aspect.
6. "Kulak" literally means "man of fist." These were originally wealthier peasants who looked after the business of the landowners.
7. Bloch, *Les rois* [607], p. 99.
8. Cf. the example of Salerno, clearly described in Huguette Taviani, "Le pouvoir à Salerne," *Structures féodales* . . .
9. Bloch, *Les rois* [607], p. 12:
10. We refer once again to the work of Pierre Bonnassie on Catalonia and more generally on the Midi.
11. See, for example, the recent work by M. Gounelle, *Introduction au droit public français* (Paris, 1979), p. 103.

BIBLIOGRAPHY

Note on the English Edition

The bibliography is organized in three major parts: (1) the bibliography of the original French version, with numbers [in brackets] keyed to footnote references; (2) a list of existing English translations of foreign-language works that appear in the original bibliography (p. 393)—an asterisk before an entry in the main bibliography indicates that a translation is listed in this section;* (3) a supplementary bibliography, provided by Professor Richard Landes, of important works published since the appearance of the French edition (p. 394).

Textual Analysis

Before listing the most up-to-date sources, it is necessary to look at the state of research in three areas. The most immediate is lexicography. It is hardly necessary to mention the value of the old Charles Dufresne dictionary (Sieur Du Cange) in the revised edition of Niort, 1883–87, or J.-F. Niermeyer's more recent and manageable *Mediae latinitatis lexicon minus*, Leiden, 1954. These undertakings have recently been overtaken by the vast lexicographical work of the *Novum glossarium mediae latinitatis* (Nouveau Du Cange), which is gradually moving toward at least provisional completion. Lexicography cannot be separated from either the specialist dictionaries (by nation or by discipline) or the indexes compiled for its preparation. The full details can be found in:

[1] Bautier A.-M. *La lexicographie du latin médiéval. Bilan international des trauvaux. Lexicographie* . . . .

and the list of indexes in:

[2] *Archivium Latinitatis Medii Aevi.* 1972, p. 256.

The research specific to each category of sources is set out in the *Typologie des sources du Moyen Age occidental,* published by the Institut d'Etudes Médiévales of the Catholic University of Louvain. The present list [up to 1977] is as follows:

---

*The English edition of the bibliography has been updated under the supervision of Robert Bartlett.

[3] Constable, G. *Letters and Letters-Collections.* Turnhout, 1976.
[4] Despy, G. *Les tarifs de tonlieux.* Turnhout, 1976.
[5] Fransen, G. *Les collections canoniques.* Turnhout, 1973.
[6] Génicot, L. *Les actes publics.* Turnhout, 1972.
[7] ———. *Les généalogies.* Turnhout, 1975.
[8] Huyghebaert, N. *Les documents nécrologiques.* Turnhout, 1972.
[9] McCormick, M. *Les annales du haut Moyen Age.* Turnhout, 1975.
[10] Pastoureau, M. *Les armoiries.* Paris, 1976.
[11] Grierson, P. *Les monnaies.* Turnhout, 1977.
[12] Philippart, G. *Les légendiers et autres manuscrits hagiographiques.* Turnhout, 1977.

There is in addition:

[13] Stiennon, J. *Paléographie du Moyen Age.* Paris, 1973.
[14] Tessier, G. *Diplomatique royale française.* Paris, 1962.

Finally, from 1980 it will be possible to use the episcopal list designed to replace Gams:

[15] Engels, O. et Weinfurter, S. *Series episcoporum ecclesiae catholicae occidentalis, ab initio usque ad annum 1198.* Stuttgart.

The use of computers poses particular problems in the study of documents relevant to the central Middle Ages.[1] Four principal directions seem to be emerging. The first involves the study of charters, particularly original ones, which allows a systematic analysis of the vocabulary then in use.[2] This approach also makes possible the more precise rendering of this vocabulary by capturing its variants in different cultural areas. Second is the analysis of the content of narrative texts, as it has been practiced for some time in the study of more modern texts. A third direction is the more "classic" work on indexes and concordances. Finally, we have the study of onomastics and, beyond that, prosopography, the study bordering on social history that relates and identifies persons and characters, albeit limited to particular contexts.

The department of medieval paleography of the *Centre de Recherches et d'Application linguistique* (CRAL) in Nancy, established by Jean Schneider, records and, with the help of a computer, analyzes original (or presumably original) deeds up to 1120, arranging them according to *département.* The intention is to cover the whole of France in this way. With codification and "lemmatization" (the regrouping of inflections under each corresponding word, as is found in a dictionary), the documents can be exploited both for their vocabulary and for their paleographic formulae. It is possible to discover for each word the chronology of its use (with, if required, concordances that shed light on meaning); the type of document in which it is most employed (according to donor and recipient); and also the geography of its use. It is also sometimes possible to detect a false document where one finds a term not in common use until a much later date. The importance of this research will soon become clear, for it will be able to supply precise chronological and geographical occurrences, taken from original documents. The first trials, applied to a limited number of documents concerned with eastern France, have yielded positive results. The work in process can be consulted by anyone who wishes. (Communication from Michel Parisse, director of the department of medieval diplomatic texts of CRAL).

Thanks to the kindness of Michel Parisse and Michèle Courtois, we have been able to make use of CRAL and carry out a brief sounding on the documentation already processed, which deals with Alsace, Lorraine, and part of Champagne (Châlons) and Burgundy (Langres and Besançon)[3]—382 originals for the periods 750–1120. Admittedly, this is not much, but by using the chronological dictionary set up by the center, different listings (frequent lemmas, encountered in six *départements* at least, and rare lemmas, used less than three times), and the indexes arranged according to *département*, one immediately glimpses a lexicographical picture that may be unclear but is nevertheless promising. Naturally a rigorous investigation would require the setting up of an entire program to study the concordances. Such a program presupposes the closest correlation between computer technology—and the financial means of CRAL—and the most up-to-date and detailed paleography. A computer enables the traditional study of chancelleries (as already carried out by Michel Parisse for that of Langres), their notaries, and their formulae,[4] distinguishing between the different parts of the deed, in order to acquire a better understanding of the language of the clerks who drafted the documents and, in this way, of some aspects of the social life of the time.

We will confine ourselves to a few occurrences whose appearance in time and space are able to tell us something new. We find an example, in the domain explored here, of a group of terms referring to power. *Potestas*, a "classical" but very general Latin form, decreases in use between 800 and 1120. *Bannus* does not appear definitely until 950 and particularly the year 1000; after that date its use is more or less constant. *Mandamentum* is never used. *Justitia* appears from 950 but more clearly after 1050. The absence of *mandamentum* can be explained: it is a term used in the south. The appearance, in charters of c. 950, of *bannus* and *justitia* can perhaps be explained by the growth of a lordship which one could call equally banal or judicial. Let us look also at the relationship of the churches with the important, or less important, laymen. *Advocatus*—any more than the abstract form *advocatia*—does not appear until 950, although we know that there were *advocati* long before. The chronology of these occurrences invites the question: Did advocacy change in meaning and in content? And once again it is no surprise to note the absence of the southern form, *comenda*, which if not analogous was at least "concurrent." *Tensamentum* is similarly absent; *salvamentum* appears only once and, as is to be expected, in the region of Châlons-sur-Marne.

A brief look in the lists of social qualities is no less interesting. *Nobilis* is used quite early, but with a disconcerting lack of regularity. *Ingenuus* and *liber*, used much more frequently than *nobilis*, show a consistent decline between 800 and c. 1000. It will be seen that in these areas *nobilis* and *ingenuus/liber* run the risk of overlapping very similar social realities. If we combine all the lemmas, we come to a series apparently more regular but still showing a decline toward the second half of the tenth century. It would, of course, be necessary to examine closely the co-occurrences and the texts. *Miles*, which is well attested in "literary" use, here only appears in the deeds from 1000–1049; *caballarius* is unknown. Finally, if we look at a group one would think characteristic of feudal institutions—*vassus/vassalus, homi-*

nium, feodum, baro—we see that these terms are rare in these regions and that most of their occurrences are in the western area (Châlons, Langres, Verdun). Their rarity does not allow us to draw any conclusions, but the distribution is nonetheless interesting.[5]

From 1120 the task is taken up by the computer department of the Institut de Recherches et d'Histoire des Textes, under the direction of Lucie Fossier. But the large number of deeds means that the team has had to restrict itself to analyzing content and not the document itself.

The principles of the method chosen are as follows: first, to index the analysis of the deeds, in other words, to represent their content by means of "descriptors" checked off in a thesaurus that is recorded in the memory; second, to provide a hierarchical arrangement of the thesaurus so that, when searching for the presence of a generic "descriptor" in the deed, the computer will give a reference not only to the deeds containing this descriptor, but also to deeds containing descriptors specific to the first; third, to establish syntagmatic relationships between the descriptors of a document and to record them on the computer. In this way it is possible, for each descriptor called up, to receive information on the grammatical role (subject, object, adverbial complement) that it plays in any given document. Lastly, this method seeks to create a descriptive framework that in addition to providing a reference to the deed, its date, the language in which it is couched, an indication of the authors of written and legal deeds and of the recipient (social type), will eventually also include a juridical analysis of the document. This descriptive framework can be consulted on its own, and thus is useful for organizing different classifications of deeds (chronological, linguistic, legal, and so forth); and it can also be consulted at the same time as the descriptors, but without providing the references to the documents where the descriptors figure unless certain conditions, such as time or chancellery, are supplied. Each person appearing in the deed is the object of a vector, whose components (sex, social position, title, function or duty, family relationship) can be consulted globally or individually. Proper nouns of place and person are placed in a third section, correlated with the descriptive framework and the category of descriptors and vectors.

The records of deeds thus treated can be exploited in two ways: by the creation of various tables—chronological, legal, linguistic (using the descriptive framework), and onomastic (using the section on proper nouns); or by occasional and selective consultation, of a Boolian type, on the presence or absence of a descriptor or of given relationships. The work of recording and consulting the deeds is now finished, although the presentation of results still needs some improvement. (Description by courtesy of Lucie Fossier, with our thanks)

A third team, headed by Karl Ferdinand Werner, director of the Institut Historique Allemand in Paris, is working on anthroponomy:

[16] Werner, K. F. "Problèmes de l'exploitation des documents textuels concèrnant les noms et les personnes du Moyen Age latin (IIIe–XIIe s.)," in *L'Informatique . . .*

In Strasbourg, the Centre de Recherche et de Documentation des Institutions Chrétiennes (CEDIC, under the direction of René Metz and Odile Gang-hoffer) is computerizing the Index Verborum of Gratian's Decretals.

[17] Metz, R. et Schlick, J. "L'Index verborum du Décret de Gratien (ca. 1140) en ordinateur," in L'Informatique . . .

All the documentation from the territory of present-day Belgium is dealt with by the Centre de Traitement Électronique des Documents (CETEDOC) at the Catholic University of Louvain, under the direction of Léopold Génicot and Paul Tombeur:

[18] Génicot, L. "Le traitement électronique des textes diplomatiques belges antérieurs à 1200," in L'Informatique . . .

Primary Sources

We have restricted ourselves here to the best-known of the literary sources and to those most recently published. For the others, see the large collections Patrologia latina (PL), Recueil des Historiens de France (RHF), Monumenta Germaniae Historica (MGH), Acta Sanctorum of the Bollandists (Boll.) and to the recent and numerous editions of patristic sources in the Corpus Christianorum. Continuatio mediaevalis published in Turnhout. The review Speculum has a regular section on new publications or those in course of preparation. We are not listing here any paleographic sources. For royal charters see the editions of the Académie des Inscriptions et Belles-Lettres. The latest in date is that of the charters of the French kings Robert I and Raoul.

[19] Dufour, J. Recueil des actes de Robert Ier et de Raoul. Paris, 1978.

For cartularies, the old catalogue of H. Stein, Bibliographie générale des cartulaires français ou relatifs à l'histoire de France (Paris, 1907), will have to suffice. The attempt at a revision appears to have been abandoned. For the cartularies of the province of Rheims, see the list made by Odile Grandmottet for a lexigrapical index, unfortunately interrupted for the moment (in the Institut de Recherche et d'Histoire des Textes).

[20] Abbo of Fleury. Apologeticus. PL, 139, cols. 461–72.
[21] Abbo of Şaint-Germain. Le siège de Paris par les Normands. Edited by H. Waquet. Paris, 1964.
[22] Abelard. Historia calamitatum. Edited by J. Monfrin. Paris, 1967.
[23] Adalbero of Laon. Carmen ad Rotbertum regem. Edited by C. Carozzi. Paris, 1979. The complete works are edited by G. A. Huckel; Les poemes satiriques d' Adalbéron de Laon. Paris, 1901.
[24] Adhemar of Chabannes. Chronicon. Edited by J. Chavanon. Paris, 1897.
[25] Andre of Fleury. Vita sancti Gauzlini. Edited by R. H. Bautier and G. Labory. Paris, 1969.
[26] Actus pontificum cenomanis. Edited by G. Busson and A. Ledru. In Archives Historiques du Maine, 2 (1901).
[27] Andrew of Fleury. Miracula Sancti Benedicti. Edited by E. de Certain. Paris, 1858.

[28] Anselm. *Gesta pontificum leodiensium.* Edited by R. Koepke. *MGH, SS,* 7: 151–234.

[29] Bernard of Angers and continuators. *Miracula Sanctae Fidis.* Edited by A. Bouillet. Paris, 1897.

[30] Bernard of Clairvaux. Opera I to V. Edited by J. Le Clercq and H. M. Rochais. Rome, 1957–1968; *Epistolae. PL,* 182, cols. 67–716.

[31] *Chroniques des comtes d'Anjou et des seigneurs d'Amboise.* Edited by L. Halphen and R. Poupardin. Paris, 1913.

[32] *Conventio Hugonis. RHF* 11: 534. New edition edited by Janet Martin-dale, *English Historical Review* 84 (1969): 528–48.

[33] Dudo of Saint-Quentin. *De moribus et actis primorum Normanniae ducum.* Edited by J. Lair. Caen, 1865.

[34] Odo of Cluny. *Vita Sancti Geraldi comitis Aureliacensis. PL,* 133, cols. 639–704.

[35] Odo of Saint-Maur. *Vita Burchardi.* Edited by Bourel de La Roncière. Paris, 1892.

[36] Flodoard. *Annales.* Edited by P. Lauer. Paris, 1906.

[37] ———. *Historia Ecclesiae Remensis. MGH, SS,* 13: 405–599.

[38] Fulbert. *Letters and Poems.* Edited by F. Behrends. Oxford, 1976.

[39] Galbert of Bruges. *Histoire du meurtre de Charles le Bon, comte de Flandres* (1127/1128). Edited by H. Pirenne. Paris, 1891.

[40] Geoffrey of Vigeois. *Chronica.* Edited by Labbé, *Nova Bibliotheca manuscriptorum,* 2: 279. Edition in course of preparation by Bernadette Barrière.

[41] Gerard of Cambrai. *Acta synodi Atrebatensis. PL,* 142, cols. 1269–1312.

[42] Gerbert. *Letters.* Edited by J. Havet. Paris, 1889.

[43] Gervase of Tilbury. *Otia imperialia.* Edited by W. Arndt. *MGH, SS,* 27: 363–94.

[44] *Gesta episcoporum cameracensium.* Edited by C. Bethmann. *MGH, SS,* 7: 393–489.

[45] Gratian. *Decretum magistri Gratiani.* Edited by E. Friedberg. Graz, repr. 1959.

[46] Guibert of Nogent. *De vita sua.* Edited by G. Bourgin. Paris, 1907.

[47] William of Poitiers. *Gesta Willelmi.* Edited by R. Foreville, Paris, 1952.

[48] Hariulf. *Chronicon Centulense.* Edited by F. Lot. Paris, 1894.

[49] Helgaud. *Epitoma vitae Roberti regis.* Edited by R. H. Bautier and G. Labory. Paris, 1965.

[50] Hugh the Poitevin. *Historia Vizeliacensis Monasterii.* Edited by R. B. C. Huygens. Turnhout, 1976. This includes the annals and cartulary of the abbey and the *Origo et historia brevis Nivernensium Comitum.*

[51] John of Salisbury. *Policraticus.* Edited by C. Webb. London, 1909; reprinted Frankfurt, 1965.

[52] John Scot Eriugena. *Expositiones in Ierarchiam coelestem.* Edited by J. Barbet. Turnhout, 1975.

[53] Lambert of Ardres. *Historia comitum Ghisnensium.* Edited by J. Heller. *MGH, SS,* 24: 550–642.

[54] Lambert of Wattrelos. *Annales Cameracenses.* Edited by C. Bethmann. *MGH, SS,* 16: 509–54.

[55] *Miracles de saint Privat, suivis des opuscules d'Aldebert de Mende.* Edited by C. Bronel. Paris, 1912.

[56] *Miracula sancti Bertini.* Edited by O. Holder-Egger. *MGH, SS,* 15, 1: 507–22.

[57] *Miracula sancti Ursmari in circumlatione per Flandriam. Bollo* (Apr.) 2: 570–578; and O. Holder-Egger, *MGH, SS,* 15 1: 837–42.

[58] Odorannus of Sens. *Opera omnia.* Edited by R. H. Bautier and M. Gilles. Paris, 1972.

[59] Orderic Vitalis. *The Ecclesiastical History.* Edited by M. Chibnall. 6 vols. Oxford, 1969–1980.

[60] Peter the Venerable. *Letters.* Edited by G. Constable. Cambridge, Mass., 1967.

[61] ———. *Contra Petrobrusianos hereticos.* Edited by J. Fearns. Turnhout, 1968.

[62] *Pontifical romano-germanique du Xᵉ siècle.* Edited by C. Vogel, with E. Reinhard. Vols. 1–2. Vatican City, 1963.

[63] Pseudo-Turpin. *Historia Karoli Magni et Rotholandi.* Edited by C. Meredith-Jones. Paris, 1936; and H. M. Smyser. Cambridge, Mass., 1937.

[64] Raoul Glaber. *Historiarum libri quinque.* Edited by M. Prou. Paris, 1886; new edition, John France, Oxford, 1989.

[65] Rather of Verona. *Praeloquia. PL,* 136, cols. 145–344.

[66] Richer. *Histoire de France.* Edited by R. Latouche. Paris, 1967.

[67] Suger. *Vita Ludovici Grossi.* Edited by H. Waquet. Paris, 1964.

[68] Ivo of Chartres. *Epistolae.* Edited by J. Le Clercq. Paris, 1949 (up to 1098 only); for the rest, *PL,* 162, cols. 11–288.

[69] *Vita s. Ysarni abbatis S. Victoris Massiliae. Boll.* (Sept.) 6: 737–49.

Secondary Sources

Still useful is Pacaut, M. *Guide de l'étudiant en histoire médiévale.* Paris, 1968. Still essential reading is the masterly

*[70] Bloch, M. *La société féodale.* Paris (1939), 1968.

Monographs

[71] Beech, G. T. *A Rural Society in Medieval France: The Gâtine of Poitou in the Eleventh and Twelfth Centuries.* Baltimore, 1964.

[72] Bonnassie, P. *La Catalogne du milieu du xᵉ siècle à la fin du xiᵉ siècle; croissance et mutations d'une société.* Toulouse, 1975.

[73] Boussard, J. *Nouvelle histoire de Paris, vi, de la fin du siège du 885–886 à la mort de Philippe-Auguste.* Paris, 1976.

[74] Bur, M. *La formation du comté de Champagne, v. 950–v. 1150.* Nancy, 1977.

[75] Chaume, M. *Les origines du duché de Bourgogne.* Dijon, 1925–1931.

[76] Chédeville, A. *Chartres et ses campagnes (xiᵉ–xiiiᵉ siècle).* Paris, 1973.

[77] Devailly, G. *Le Berry du xᵉ siècle au milieu du xiiiᵉ. Etude politique, religieuse, sociale et économique.* Paris, 1973.

[78] Duby G. *La société aux xiᵉ et xiiᵉ siècles dans la région mâconnaise.* Paris, 1953.

[79] Fossier, R. *La terre et les hommes en Picardie jusqu'à la fin du XIIIᵉ siècle.* Paris, Louvain, 1968.

[80] Fournier, G. *Le peuplement rural en Basse-Auvergne durant de haut Moyen Age.* Paris, 1962.

[81] Garaud, M. *Les châtelains de Poitou et l'avènement du règime féodal, XIᵉ et XIIᵉ siècles.* Poitiers, 1967.

[82] Halphen, L. *Le comté d'Anjou au XIᵉ siècle.* Paris, 1906.

[83] Guillot, O. *Le comte d'Anjou et son entourage au XIᵉ siècle.* Paris, 1972.

[84] Latouche, R. *Histoire du comté du Maine pendant le Xᵉ et le XIᵉ siècle.* Paris, 1910.

[85] Lewis, A. R. *The development of Southern French and Catalan society, 718–1050.* Austin, 1965.

[86] Magnou-Nortier, E. *La société laïque et l'Eglise dans la province ecclésiastique de Narbonne de la fin du VIIIᵉ siècle à la fin du XIIᵉ siècle.* Toulouse, 1974.

[87] Poly, J.-P. *La Provence et la société féodale, 879–1166.* Paris, 1976.

[88] Sanfaçon, R. *Défrichements, peuplement et institutions seigneuriales en Haut-Poitou du Xᵉ au XIIIᵉ siècle.* Quebec, 1967.

[89] Toubert, P. *Les structures du Latium médiéval. Le Latium méridional et la Sabine du IXᵉ à la fin du XIIᵉ siècle.* Paris, Rome, 1973.

Public Institutions and Judicial Lordship

[90] Abadal y de Vinyals, R. d'. *Els primers comtes catalans.* Barcelona, 1958.

[91] Aubenas, R. "Les châteaux forts des Xᵉ et XIᵉ siècles," *RHD* (1938): 548–86.

[92] Bisson, T. N. "La féodalité catalane au XIIᵉ siècle," *Structures féodales . . .*, pp. 173–92.

[93] Bonnassie P. "Du Rhône à la Galice: genèse et modalités du régime féodal." *Structures féodales . . .*

[94] Boussard J. "L'enquête de 1172 sur les services de chevalier en Normandie." *Recueil de travaux . . . Clovis Brunel.* Paris, 1955, pp. 193–208.

[95] ———. "Services féodaux, milices et mercenaires dans les armées en France aux Xᵉ et XIᵉ siècles." *Settimane . . . di Spoleto*, 15 (1968): 131–168.

[96] ———. "Les destinées de la Neustrie du IXᵉ au XIᵉ siècle." *CCM* (1968): 15.

[97] ———. "Le droit de *vicaria* à la lumière de quelques documents angevins et tourangeaux." *Etudes de civilisation médievale (IXᵉ–XIIᵉ siècles). Mélanges offerts à Edmond-René Labande.* Poitiers, 1974, pp. 39–54.

[98] Boutruche, R. *Seigneurie et féodalité.* 2 vols. Paris, 1968–70.

[99] Brühl, C. R. *Fodrum, gistum, servitium regis; studien zu den wirtschaftlichen grundlagen des Königtums.* Cologne-Graz, 1968.

[99a] Bur, M. *Vestiges d'habitat seigneurial fortifié du bas pays argonnais.* Rheims, 1972.

[100] Castaing Sicard, M. *Monnaies féodales et circulation monétaire en Languedoc (Xᵉ–XIIIᵉ s.),* Toulouse, 1961.

[101] Chatelain, A. *Donjons romans des pays d'Ouest.* Paris, 1973.

[102] Cheyette, F. "The Castles of the Trencavels: A Preliminary Aerial Survey." In *Order and Innovation in the Middle Ages: Essays in Honor of Joseph R. Strayer,* ed. William C. Jordan, Bruce McNab, and Teofilo R. Ruiz. Princeton, 1976, pp. 255–72.

[103] De Craecker-Dussart, C. "L'évolution du sauf-conduit dans les principautés de la Basse-Lotharingie du viiie au xive siècle." *MA* (1974): 185–243.

[104] Deprez, R. "La politique castrale dans la principauté épiscopale de Liège du xe au xive." *MA,* ser. 4, 14 (1959): 179–205.

[105] Desportes, P. "Les archevêques de Reims et les droits comtaux aux xe et xie siècles." *Economies et sociétés au Moyen Age. Mélanges offerts à Edouard Perroy.* Etudes 5, Publications de la Sorbonne. Paris, 1973, pp. 79–89.

[106] Devisse, J. "Essai sur l'histoire d'une expression qui a fait fortune: *consilium et auxilium* au xie siècle." *MA,* ser. 4, 23 (1968): 179.

[107] Dhondt, J. "Le titre de marquis à l'époque carolingienne." *Archivium Latinitatis Medii Aevi* 19 (1946): 407–17.

[108] ———. *Etude sur la naissance des principautés territoriales.* Ghent, 1948.

[109] ———. "Note sur les châtelains de Flandre." *Etudes historiques dédiées à la mémoire de M. Roger Rodière.* Commission départmentale des monuments historiques du Pas-du-Calais. Arras, 1947, p. 217.

[110] Didier, N. *La garde des églises au xiiie siècle.* Grenoble, 1927.

[111] Dubled, H. "La notion de ban en Alsace au Moyen Age." *RHD* 39 (1961): 371–81.

*[112] Duby, G. "Recherches sur l'évolution des institutions judiciaires pendant le xe et le xie siècle dans le sud de la Bourgogne" (1946). *Hommes et structures du Moyen Age.* Paris, 1973, pp 7–60.

[113] ———. "Les idées de M. Leo Verriest sur la seigneurie rurale. Discussion et observations." *AB* 20 (1948): 190–94.

[114] ———. "La carte, instrument de recherche: les communes de France. Le point de vue du médiéviste." *AESC* 12 (1958): 463–65.

[115] Dumas, F. *Le trésor de Fécamp et le monnayage en Francie occidentale pendant la seconde moitié du xe siècle.* Paris, 1971.

[116] Duparc, P. "Le sauvement." *BPH* (1961): 389–433.

[117] ———. "La commendise ou commende personnelle." *BEC* 119 (1961): 50–172.

[118] ———. "Le tensement." *RHD* 40 (1962): 43–63.

[119] Dupont A. "L'aprision et le régime aprisionnaire dans le Midi de la France (fin viiie-début xe siècle)." *MA,* ser 4, 15 (1965): 179–213; 375–99.

[120] Feuchère, P. "Une tentative manquée de concentration territoriale entre Somme et Seine: la principauté d'Amiens-Valois au xie siècle." *MA,* ser. 4, 9 (1954): 1–37.

[121] ———. "Un obstacle aux chaînes de subordination: l'alleu dans le Nord de la France." *RN* 37 (1955): 77–78.

[122] Font Rius, J. M. "Les modes de détention de châteaux dans la 'vieille Catalogne' et ses marches extérieures du début du ixe au début du xie siècle." *Les structures sociales . . . de l'Aquitaine,* pp. 63–77.

[123] Fournial, E. "Recherches sur les comtes de Lyon aux ixe et xe siècles." *MA* 58 (1952): 221–52.

[124] ———. "La souveraineté du Lyonnais au xᵉ siècle." *MA* 62 (1956): 413–52.

[125] Fournier, G. *Le château dans la France médiévale.* Paris, 1978.

[126] Ganshof, F. L. "Les *homines de generali placito* de l'abbaye de Saint-Vaast d'Arras." *Etude sur les ministeriales en Flandre et en Lotharique.* Brussels, 1926, pp. 397–414.

[127] ———. *Recherches sur les tribunaux de châtellenies en Flandre avant le milieu du* xiiiᵉ *siècle.* Antwerp, 1932.

[128] ———. La Flandre, in Lot and Fawtier, 1: 367.

[129] ———. "L'immunité dans la monarchie franque." *Receuils de la Société Jean Bodin* 1 (1958): 171–216.

[130] ———. "Charlemagne et les institutions de la monarchie franque." *Karl der Grosse* 1: 349–393.

[131] ———. "L'armée sous les carolingiens," *Settimane . . . di Spoleto* 15 (1968): 109–130.

[132] Garaud, M. "La construction des châteaux et les destinées de la *vicaria* et du *vicarius* carolingien en Poitou." *RHD* 31 (1953): 54–78.

[133] ———. "Les circonscriptions administratives du comté de Poitou et les auxiliaires du comte au xᵉ siècle." *MA* 59 (1953–1954): 11–61.

[134] Génicot, L. "Le premier siècle de la *curia* de Hainaut (1060 env.–1195)" (1947). *Etudes . . .*, pp. 199–216.

[135] ———. "Les premières mentions de droits banaux dans la règion de Liège." *Bull. de l'Acad. royale de Belgique* 54 (1968): 56–65.

[136] ———. "Empereurs et princes en Basse-Lotharingie. Suggestions de recherches (1970)." *Etudes . . .*, pp. 12–38.

[137] ———. "Monastères et principautés en Lotharingie du xᵉ au xiiiᵉ siècle (1965)." *Etudes . . .*, pp. 59–139.

[138] ———. "Princes territoriaux et sang carolingien. La *genealogia comitum Buloniensium.*" *Etudes . . .*, pp. 217–306.

[139] ———. "Noblesse et principautés en Lotharingie du xiᵉ au xiiiᵉ siècle (1961)." *Etudes . . .*, pp. 39–58.

[139a] Gerner, H. *Lyon im Fruhmittelalter: Studien zur Geschichte der Stadt, des Erzbistums und der Grafschaft im 9. und 10. Jahrhundert.* Cologne, 1968.

[140] Gramain, M. "*Castrum,* Structures féodales et peuplement en Biterrois au xiᵉ siècle." *Structures féodales . . .*, pp. 119–34.

[141] Halphen, L. "Prévôts et voyers du xiᵉ siècle (1902)." *A travers . . .*, pp. 203–225.

[142] ———. "La justice en France au xiᵉ siècle (1902)." *A travers . . .*, pp. 175–202.

[143] Héliot, P. "Les châteaux forts en France du xᵉ au xiiᵉ siècle à la lumière de travaux récents." *JS* (1965): 483–514.

[144] Higounet, C. "Structures sociales, *castra* et castelnaux dans le Sud-Ouest aquitain." *Structures féodales . . .*, pp. 109–117.

[145] Koch, A. "L'origine de la haute et de la moyenne justice dans l'Ouest et le Nord de la France." *TVR* 21 (1953): 420–58.

[146] ———. "Continuté ou rupture? De la justice domaniale et abbatiale à la justice urbaine et comtale à Arras." *RN* 40 (1958): 289–296.

[147] Lafaurie, J. "Le trésor du Puy." *Revue numismatique* ser. 45, 14 (1952): 59–169.

[148] Lemarignier, J.-F. "La dislocation du *pagus* et le problème des con-

suetudines." *Mélanges d'histoire du Moyen Age dédiées à la mémoire de Louis Halphen.* Paris, 1951, pp. 401–10.

[149] ———. "Aspects politiques des fondations de collégiales dans le royaume de France au xiᵉ siècle." *Settimana . . . Mendola* (1959): 19–40.

[150] ———. "De l'immunité à la seigneurie ecclésiastique: les 'territoires coutumiers' d'église en Ile-de-France et dans les régions voisines d'après les diplômes des premiers capétiens." *Melanges . . . G. Le Bras.* Paris, 1965, pp. 619–30.

[151] ———. "Autour d'un diplôme de Robert le Pieux pour Saint-Denis (1008)." *CRAIBL* (1971): 329–45.

[152] Lot, F. "La *vicaria* et le *vicarius.*" *Recueil . . .,* 3:165–85.

[153] Musset, L. "Gouvernants et gouvernés dans le monde scandinave et dans le monde normand." *Jean Bodin,* 23 (1968): 438–68.

[154] Navel, H. "L'enquête de 1133 sur les fiefs de l'évêché de Bayeux." *BSAN* 42 (1934): 5–80.

[155] Perret, A. "Les concessions des droits comtaux et régaliens aux églises dans les domaines de la Maison de Savoie." *BPH* (1964): 45–73.

[156] Perrin, C. E. *Recherches sur la seigneurie rurale en Lorraine d'après les plus anciens censiers, ixᵉ-xiiᵉ siècle.* Paris, 1935.

[157] ———. *Essais sur la fortune immobilière de l'abbaye alsacienne de Marmoutier aux xᵉ et xiᵉ siècles.* Strasbourg, 1935.

[158] Platelle, H. *La justice seigneuriale de l'abbaye de Saint-Amand. Son organisation judiciaire, sa procédure et sa compétence du xiᵉ au xviᵉ siècle.* Louvain, 1965.

[159] Richard, J. "Aux origines du Charolais. Vicomté, vigueries et limites du comté en Autunois méridional (xᵉ-xiiiᵉ siècle)." *AB* 35 (1963): 81–114.

[160] ———. *Les ducs de Bourgogne et la formation du duché du xiᵉ au xivᵉ siècle.* Paris, 1954.

[161] ———. "Châteaux, châtelains et vassaux en Bourgogne aux xiᵉ et xiiᵉ siècles." *CCM* 3 (1960): 433–47.

[162] Schneider, J. "L'avouerie de la cité de Toul." *MA* ser. 4, 18 (1963): 631–40.

[163] Semmler, J. "Traditio und Königsschutz. Studien zur Geschichte der königlichen Monasteria." *ZSSKA* 45 (1959): 1–33.

[164] Senn, F. *L'institution des avoueries ecclésiastiques en France.* Paris, 1903.

[165] ———. *L'institution des vidamies en France.* Paris, 1907.

[166] Tabacco, G. "Fief et seigneurie dans l'Italie communale: l'évolution d'un thème historiographique." *MA* ser. 4, 24 (1969): 5–37 and 203–18.

[167] Vercauteren, F. "Etude sur les châtelains comtaux de Flandre du xiᵉ au début du xiiiᵉ siècle." *Etudes d'Histoire dédiées à la mémoire de Henri Pirenne.* Brussels, 1937, pp. 413–23.

[168] ———. "La formation des principautés de Liège, Flandre, Brabant et Hainaut, ixᵉ-xiᵉ siècle." *L'Europe aux IXᵉ-XIᵉ siecles.* Edited by Tadeusz Manteuffel and Aleksander Gieysztor. 1965, pp. 31–41.

[169] ———. "Note critique sur un diplôme du roi de France Charles de Simple du 20 décembre 911." *Miscellanea mediaevalia in memoriam Jan Frederik Niermeyer.* Groningen, 1967, pp. 93–103.

[170] Werner, K. F. "Heeresorganisation und Kriegführung im deutschen Königreich des 10. und 11. Jahrhunderts." *Settimane . . . di Spoleto* 15 (1968): 791–843.

[171] ——. "Quelques observations au sujet des débuts du 'duche' de Normandie." *Droit privé et institutions régionales. Études historiques offertes à Jean Yver.* Rouen-Paris, 1976, pp. 691–701.

[172] Yver, J. "Les châteaux forts en Normandie jusqu'au milieu du xiie siècle." *BSAN* 52 (1955–1956): 28–115, 604–609.

[173] ——. "Contribution à l'étude du développement de la compétence ducale en Normandie." *AN* 8 (1958): 139–83.

[174] ——. "Autour de l'absence d'avouerie en Normandie. Notes sur le double thème du développement du pouvoir ducal et de l'application de la réforme grégorienne en Normandie." *BSAN* 57 (1963–1964): 184–283.

[175] ——. "Les premières institutions du duché de Normandie." *Settimane . . . di Spoleto* 16 (1969): 299–366.

[176] ——. "Le 'très ancien coutumier' de Normandie, miroir de la législation ducale? Contribution à l'étude de l'ordre public normand à la fin du xiie siècle." *TVR* 39 (1971): 333–74.

The Feudal-Vassalic Link

[177] Beech, G. "A Feudal Document of Early Eleventh-Century Poitou." *Mélanges offerts à René Crozet.* Edited by Pierre Gallais and Yves-Jean Riou. Poitiers, 1966, pp. 203–13.

[178] Bloch, M. "Les formes de la rupture de l'hommage dans l'ancien droit féodal." *Mélanges . . .*, 1, pp. 189–209.

[178a] Bonnassie, P. "Les conventions féodales dans la Catalogne du xie siècle." *Structures sociales . . . en Aquitaine,* pp. 187–208.

[179] Chenon, E., "Le rôle juridique de *l'osculum* dans l'ancien droit français." *Mém. de la Soc. nationale des Antiquaires de France* 76 (1919–1923): 124–55.

[180] Dhondt, J. "Quelques aspects du règne d'Henri Ier roi de France." *Mélanges . . . L. Halphen.* Paris, 1951, pp. 199–208.

[181] ——. "Une crise du pouvoir capétien, 1032–1034." *Miscellanea mediaevalia in memoriam Jan Frederik Niermeyer.* Groningen, 1967, pp. 137–48.

[182] Coornaert, E. "Les ghildes médiévales." *RH* 199 (1948): 22 and 208–43.

[183] Duby G. "La féodalité? Une mentalité médiévale." *AESC* 13 (1958): 765–71.

[184] Dumas, A. "Le serment de fidélité et la conception du pouvoir du Ier au IXe siècle." *RHD* 10 (1931): 30–51 and 289–321.

[185] ——. "Le serment de fidélité à l'époque franque." *RBPH* 14 (1935): 405–26.

*[186] Ganshof, F. L. "Charlemagne et le serment," *Mélanges . . . L. Halphen.* Paris, 1951, pp. 259–70.

[187] ——. "L'origine des rapports féodo-vassaliques. Les rapports féodo-vassaliques dans la Monarchie franque au Nord des Alpes à l'époque carolingienne." *Settimane . . . di Spoleto* 1 (1954): 27–67.

[188] ——. "Les relations féodo-vassaliques aux temps postcarolingiens." *Settimane . . . di Spoleto* 2 (1955): 67–114.

[189] ——. *Qu'est-ce que la féodalité?* Brussels, 1957.

[190] Garaud, M. "Un problème d'histoire: à propos d'une lettre de Fulbert de Chartres à Guillaume le Grand, comté de Poitou et duc d'Aquitaine." *Mélanges . . . G. Le Bras,* I. Paris, 1965, pp. 559–62.

[191] Giordanengo, G. "Vocabulaire et formulaire féodaux en Provence et en Dauphiné xiie–xiiie siècle." *Structures féodales. . .*, pp. 85–107.

[192] Grassotti, H. "La durée des concessions bénéficiaires en Léon et Castille: les cessions *ad tempus.*" *Les structures sociales . . . de l'Aquitaine*, pp. 79–102.

[193] Halphen, L. "La royauté française du xie siècle." *A travers. . .*, pp. 226–40.

[193a] ———. "La lettre d'Eudes de Blois au roi Robert." *A travers. . .*, pp. 241–50.

[194] Hollyman, K. J. *Le développement du vocabulaire féodal en France pendant le haut Moyen Age.* Paris, 1957.

[195] Kienast, W. *Untertaneneid und Treuvorbehalt in England und Frankreich.* Weimar, 1952.

*[196] Le Goff, J. "Le rituel symbolique de la vassalité." *Pour un autre Moyen Age.* Paris, 1977, pp. 349–420.

[197] Lemarignier, J.-F. *Recherches sur l'hommage en marche et les frontières féodales.* Lille, 1945.

[198] ———. "Autour de la royauté française du ixe au xiiie siècle." *BEC* 113 (1955): 5–25.

[199] ———. "Les fidèles du roi de France (936–987)." *Recueil . . . C. Brunel.* Paris, 1955, pp. 138–62.

[200] Lewis, A. R. "La féodalité dans le Toulousain et la France méridionale, 850–1050." *AM* 77 (1964): 247–59.

[201] Lot, F. *Fidèles ou vassaux? Essai sur la nature juridique du lien qui unissait les grands vassaux à la royauté depuis le milieu du ixe jusqu'à la fin du xiie siècle.* Paris, 1904.

[202] ———. "Le serment de fidélité à l'époque franque (1933)." *Recueil des travaux historiques*, 2, pp. 343–56.

[203] ———. "Origine et nature du bénéfice (1933)." *Recueil. . .*, 2, pp. 331–41.

[204] Magnou, E. "Note sur le sens du mot *fevum* en Septimanie et dans la Marche d'Espagne à la fin du xe et au début du xie siècle." *AM* 77 (1964): 141–52.

[205] Magnou-Nortier, E. "Fidélité et féodalité méridionales d'après les serments de fidélite (xe–début xiie siècle)." *Structures . . . de l'Aquitaine*, pp. 115–35.

[206] ———. *Foi et fidélite: recherches sur l'évolution des liens personnels chez les Francs du viie au ixe siècle.* Toulouse, 1976.

[207] Ourliac, P. "L'hommage servile dans la région toulousaine." *Mélanges . . . L. Halphen.* Paris, 1951, pp. 551–56.

[208] Painter, S. "Castellans of the Plain of Poitou in the Eleventh and Twelfth Centuries." *Speculum* 31 (1956): 243–57.

[209] ———. "The Lords of Lusignan in the Eleventh and Twelfth Centuries." *Speculum* 32 (1957): 27–47.

[210] Poly, J.-P. "Vocabulaire 'féodo-vassalique' et aires de culture durant le haut Moyen Age." *La lexicographie. . .*, pp. 167–90.

[211] Richardot, H. "Le fief roturier à Toulouse aux xiie et xiiie siècles." *RHD* 14 (1935): 307–59 and 495–569.

[212] ———. "Le problème des fiefs bourguignons sans service." *Mém. de la Soc. pour l'Hist. du Droit et des Instit. des anciens pays bourguignons*, 11 (1946–1947): 171–75.

[213] ———. "Francs fiefs: essai sur l'exemption totale ou partielle des services de fief." *RHD* 27 (1949): 28–63 and 229–73.

[214] ———. "Note sur les roturiers possesseurs de fiefs nobles." *Annales de la Fac. de Droit d'Aix-en-Provence* 33 (1950): 269–81.

[215] ———. "A propos des personnes et des terres féodales." *Etudes d'Histoire du Droit privé offertes a Pierre Petot.* Paris, 1959, pp. 463–71.

[216] Sanchez-Albornoz, C. "El *precarium* en Occidente durante los primeros siglos medievales." *Etudes d'Histoire du Droit privé offertes a Pierre Petot.* Paris, 1959, pp. 481–505.

[217] Vidal, H. "Le *feudum honoratum* dans les cartulaires d'Agde et de Béziers." *Hommage à André Dupont: Etudes médiévales langedociennes.* Montpellier, 1974, pp. 291–99.

The Aristocracy

[218] Amado, C. "Le groupe aristocratique du Narbonnais dans ses relations avec le Razès, le Biterrois et le Minervois au xiᵉ siècle." *Archéologie et histoire: Narbonne au Moyen Age,* 1973, p. 37.

[219] Aubenas, R. "Réflexions sur les fraternités artificielles au Moyen Age." *Etudes historiques à la mémoire de Noël Didier.* Edited by la Faculté de Droit et des Sciences Economiques de Grenoble. Paris, 1960, pp. 1–10.

[220] Baerten, J. "Les Ansfrid au xᵉ siècle." *RBPH* 39 (1961): 1144–1158.

[221] ———. "L'origine de la noblesse alsacienne: à propos d'un article récent." *TVR* 32 (1964): 79–82.

[222] Bastier, J. "Le testament en Catalogne du ixᵉ au xiiᵉ siècle: une survivance wisigothique." *RHD* 51 (1937): 373–417.

[222a] Bernard, C. "Etude sur le domaine ardennais de la famille des Régnier." *MA* (1937): 1.

[223] Boussard, J. "L'origine des familles seigneuriales dans la région de la Loire moyenne." *CCM* 5 (1962): 303–22.

[224] Chenon, E. *Histoire du droit français public et privé des origines à 1815.* Vols. 1 and 2. Paris, 1926, 1929.

[225] Chevailler, L. "Observations sur le droit de bâtardise dans la France coutumière du xiiᵉ au xvᵉ siècle." *RHD* 35 (1957): 376–411.

[226] Chevrier, G. "L'évolution de l'acte à cause de mort en Dauphiné du viiᵉ à la fin du xiᵉ siècle." *Recueil de Mém. et Trav . . . des pays de droit écrit* (1948): 9.

[227] ———. "Les aspects familiaux du parage comtois." *Etudes . . . P. Petot.* Paris, 1959, p. 79–95.

[228] Didier, N. *Le droit des fiefs dans la coutume de Hainaut au Moyen Age.* Paris, 1945.

[229] ———. "Les dispositions du statut de Guillaume II de Forcalquier sur les filles dotées." *MA* (1950): 247.

*[230] Duby, G. "La noblesse dans la France médiévale: une enquête à poursuivre (1961)." *Hommes et structures,* pp. 145–66.

*[231] ———. "Situation de la noblesse en France au début du xiiiᵉ siècle (1963)." *Hommes et structures,* pp. 343–52.

*[232] ———. "Structures de parenté et noblesse dans la France du Nord aux xiᵉ et xiiᵉ siècles (1967)." *Hommes et structures,* pp. 267–85.

*[233] ———. "Remarques sur la littérature généalogique en France aux xiᵉ et xiiᵉ siècles (1967)." *Hommes et structures,* pp. 287–98.

*[234] ———. "Les origines de la chevalerie (1968)." *Hommes et structures,* pp. 325–42.

*[235] ———. "Lignage, noblesse et chevalerie au xiie siècle dans la région Mâconnaise. Une révision (1972)." *Hommes et structures,* pp. 395–422.

[236] ———. "La diffusion du titre chevaleresque sur le versant méditerranéen de la chrétienté latine." *La noblesse. . . ,* pp. 39–70.

[237] ———. "Présentation de l'enquête sur 'Famille et sexualité au Moyen Age'." *Famille. . . ,* pp. 9–11.

[238] Falletti, L. *Le retrait lignager en droit coutumier français.* Paris, 1923.

[239] Flori, J. "La notion de chevalerie dans les *Chansons de Geste* du xiie siècle. Etude historique du vocabulaire." *MA,* ser. 4, 30 (1975): 211–244; 407–445.

[240] ———. "Sémantique et société médiévale: le verbe adouber et son évolution au xiie siècle." *AESC* 31 (1976): 915–40.

[241] ———. "Chevaliers et chevalerie au xie siècle en France et dans l'Empire germanique. A propos d'un ouvrage récent." *MA,* ser. 4, 31 (1976): 125–36.

[242] Fossier, R. "Chevalerie et noblesse en Ponthieu aux xie et xiie siècles." *Etudes de civilisation médiévale (ixe–xiie siècles). Mélanges offert à E. R. Labande.* Poitiers, 1974, pp. 293–306.

[243] Gallet, L. *Les traités de pariage.* Paris, 1935.

[244] Génestal, R. *Le parage normand.* Caen, 1911.

[245] ———. "Le retrait lignager." *Travaux de la semaine de droit normand de Jersey* (1923): 191.

[246] ———. "La formation du droit d'aînesse dans la coutume de Normandie." *Normannia, rev. bibl. et critique d'hist. de Normandie.* (1928): 157.

[247] Génicot, L. *L'économie namuroise au bas Moyen Age,* vol. 2: *Les hommes, la noblesse.* Louvain, 1960.

[248] ———. "La noblesse au Moyen Age dans l'ancienne 'Francie'." *AESC* 17 (1962): 2–22.

[249] ———. "La noblesse dans la société médiévale. A propos des dernières études relatives aux terres d'Empire." *MA,* ser. 4, 20 (1965): 539–60.

[250] ———. "Naissance, fonction et richesse dans l'ordonnance de la société médiévale. Le cas de la noblesse du Nord-Ouest du Continent." *Problèmes de stratification sociale. . . ,* edited by Roland Mousnier. Paris, 1968, pp. 83–92.

[251] Gilissen, J. "Le privilège de masculinité dans le droit coutumier de la Belgique et du Nord de la France." *RN* 43 (1961): 201–16.

[252] Higounet, C. "En Bordelais: *Principes castella tenentes.*" *La noblesse. . . ,* pp. 97–104.

[253] Huyghebaert, N. "Le cas de Mirolfe, un *potens* indigent en Boulonnais." *MA,* ser. 4, 28 (1973): 25–34.

[254] Johrendt, J. *"Milites" und "Militia" im 11. Jahrhundert. Untersuchung zur Frühgeschichte des Rittertums in Frankreich und Deutschland.* Nuremberg, 1971.

[255] Legoherel, H. "Le parage en Touraine-Anjou au Moyen Age." *RHD* 43 (1965): 222–46.

[256] Lot, F. "L'origine de Thibaud le Tricheur (1907)." *Recueil. . . .* 3, pp. 103–23.

[257] Musset, L. "L'aristocratie normande au xie siècle." *La noblesse. . . ,* pp. 71–96.

[258] Newman, W. M. *Le seigneurs de Nesle en Picardie. Leurs chartes et leur histoire.* Paris, 1972.

[259] Olivier-Martin, R. *Histoire de la coutume de la prévôté et vicomté de Paris* (revised). Mayenne, 1972.

[260] Ourliac, P. "Le retrait lignager dans le Sud-Ouest." *RHD* 30 (1952): 328–55.

[261] Parisse, M. *La noblesse lorraine, XIe–XIIIe siècle.* Paris, 1975.

[262] Pastoureau, M. "L'apparition des armoiries en occident. Etat du problème." *BEC* 39 (1976): 281–300.

[263] Richard J. "Chevaliers de mesnie castrale et hobereaux campagnards: les Boujon de Vergy." *Mélanges . . . E. Perroy.* Paris, 1973, pp. 262–72.

*[264] Schmid, K. "Über die Struktur des Adels im früheren Mittelalter." *Jahrbuch für fränkische Landesforschung* 19 (1959): 1–23.

[265] ———. "Welfisches Selbstverstandnis." *Adel und Kirche,* edited by Josef Fleckenstein and Karl Schmid. Freiburg, 1968, pp. 389–46.

[266] ———. "'De regia stirpe Waiblingensium,' remarques sur la conscience de soi des Staufen." *Famille,* pp. 49–56.

[267] Sot, M. "Historiographie épiscopale et modèle familial en Occident au IXe siècle." *AESC* 33 (1978): 433–49.

[268] Störmer, W. *Früher Adel. Studien zur politischen Führungsschicht im fränkisch-deutschen Reich vom 8. bis 11. Jahrhundert.* Stuttgart, 1973.

[269] Tabacco, G. "La connessione fra potere e possesso nel regno franco e nel regno longoboardo." *Settimane . . . di Spoleto* 20 (1973): 133–68.

[270] ———. "Le rapport de parenté comme instrument de domination consortiale: quelques exemples piémontais." *Famille,* pp. 153–58.

[271] Tellenbach, G. "Zur Erforschung des hochmittelalterlichen Adels." *Twelfth International Congress of Historical Sciences.* Vol. 1 of 5 vols. Vienna, 1965, pp. 318–37.

[272] ———. "Der *liber memorialis* vom Remiremont." *Deutsches Archiv* 25 (1969): 64–110.

[273] Van Luyn, P. "Les *milites* dans la France du XIe siècle." *MA,* ser. 4, 26 (1971): 5–51 and 193–238.

[274] Van Winter, J. M. "Uxorem de militari ordine sibi imparem," *Miscellanea . . . J.-F. Niermeyer.* Groningen, 1967, pp. 113–24.

[275] Verriest, L. *Noblesse, chevalerie, lignage.* Brussels, 1959.

[276] Villers, R. "Aperçus sur la formation de la noblesse en Normandie." *RHD* 32 (1954): 148.

[277] Violante, C. "Quelques caractéristiques des structures familiales en Lombardie, Emilie et Toscane aux XIe et XIIe siècles." *Famille,* pp. 87–125.

[278] Werner, K. F. "Untersuchungen zur Frühzeit des französischen Fürstentums (9.–10. Jahrhundert)." *Welt als Geschichte* 18 (1958): 256–89.

[279] ———. "Liens de parenté et noms de personne. Un problème historique et méthodologique." *Famille,* pp. 14–18, 25–34.

[280] Wilsdore, C. "Les Etichonides aux temps carolingiens et ottoniens." *BPH* (1964): 1–38.

[281] Wolff, P. "La noblesse toulousaine. Essai sur son histoire médiévale." *Noblesse. . . ,* pp. 153–74.

[282] Yver, J. *Egalité entre héritiers et exclusion des enfants dotés. Essai de géographie coutumière.* Paris, 1966.

"The Poor," Peasants, and Dependents

[283] Bienvenu, J.-M. "Pauvreté, misère et charité en Anjou aux xıᵉ et xııᵉ siècles," MA, ser. 4, 21 (1966): 389–424; ser. 4, 22 (1967): 5–34 and 189–216.

*[284] Bloch, M. "Les *colliberti,* étude sur la formation de la classe servile (1928)." *Mélanges,* pp. 385–451.

*[285] ———. "Liberté et servitudes personnelles (1933)." *Mélanges,* pp. 286–355.

*[286] ———. "*Collibertus* ou *colibertus* (1926)." *Mélanges,* pp. 379–84.

*[287] ———. "Le procès des serfs de Rosny-sous-bois (1938)." *Mélanges,* pp. 452–61.

*[288] ———. "Un problème d'histoire comparée. La ministérialité en France et en Allemagne (1928)." *Mélanges,* pp. 503–28.

[289] Bosl, K. *Die Reichsministerialitat der Salier und Staufer. Ein Beitrag zur Geschichte des mittelalterlichen deutschen Staates und Reiches.* Hanover, 1950 and 1951.

[290] ———. "Castes, ordres et classes en Allemagne." *Problèmes de stratification sociale. . . .* Paris, 1968, pp. 13–23.

[291] Boussard, J. "Les *colliberti* du cartulaire de Vierzon. A propos d'un article récent." *RHD* 40 (1962): 395–403.

[292] Despy, G. "Serfs ou libres? Sur une notice judiciaire cambrésienne de 941." *RBPH* 39 (1961), p. 1127.

[293] Devailly, G. "Du nouveau sur les *colliberti.* Le témoignage du cartulaire de Vierzon." *MA,* ser. 51, 16 (1961): 425–37.

[294] Devisse, J. "*Pauperes* et *paupertas* dans le monde carolingien: ce qu'en dit Hincmar de Reims." *RN* 48 (1966): 273–87.

[295] Dhondt, J. "Les solidarités médiévales: une société en transition, la Flandre en 1127/1128." *AESC* 12 (1957): 529–60.

[296] Dollinger, P. "Aspects de la noblesse allemande." *Noblesse,* pp. 133–49.

[297] Dubled, H. "Etude sur la condition des personnes en Alsace du vıııᵉ au xᵉ siècle." *BEC* 19 (1961): 21–49.

[298] Duby, G. "Géographie ou chronologie du servage? Note sur les *servi* en Forez et en Mâconnais du xᵉ au xııᵉ siècle." *Eventail de l'histoire Vivante: Hommage à L. Febvre.* Vol. I. Paris, 1953, pp. 147–49.

[299] ———. "Sur les voies ouvertes par Marc Bloch: esclavage et servage au Moyen Age." *AESC* 12 (1957): 123–26.

*[300] ———. *L'économie rurale et la vie des campagnes dans l'Occident médiéval (France, Angleterre, Empire, ıxᵉ–xvᵉ siècles). Essai de synthèse et perspectives de recherches.* Paris, 1962.

[301] ———. "Les pauvres des campagnes dans l'Occident médiéval jusqu'au xıııᵉ siècle." *RHEF* 52 (1966): 25–32.

[302] Dufermont, J.-C. "Les pauvres d'après les sources anglo-saxonnes du vııᵉ au xıᵉ siècle." *RN* 50 (1968): 189–201.

[303] Duparc, P. "La question des 'sainteurs' ou hommes des églises." *JS* (1972): 25–48.

[304] Dupréel, E. "Les *ministeriales* de Cambrai." *Mélanges . . . P. Frédérick.* Brussels, 1904, pp. 203–11.

[305] Fourquin, G. "Le premier Moyen Age." In G. Duby, *Histoire de la France rurale.* Vol. 1. Paris, 1975, pp. 291–371.

[306] Ganshof, F. L. *Etude sur les ministeriales en Flandre et en Lotharingie.* Brussels, 1927.

[307] Guillot, O. "La participation au duel judiciaire de témoins de condition serve dans l'Ile-de-France au xie siècle." *Droit privé et institutions regionales. Etudes historiques, offerts à Jean Yver.* Paris, 1976, pp. 345–60.

[308] Keul, M. "Au Moyen Age: le problème des paysans libres." *AESC* 19 (1964): p. 1208.

[309] Le Jan-Hennebicque, R. "*Pauperes* et *paupertas* aux ixe et xe siècles." *RN* 50 (1968): 69–187.

[310] Mollat, M. *Etudes sur l'histoire de la pauvreté (Moyen Age–XVIe siècle).* Paris, 1974.

*[311] ———. *Les pauvres au Moyen Age.* Paris, 1978.

[312] Ourliac, P. "Le servage à Toulouse aux xiie et xiiie siècles." *Mélanges . . . E. Perroy.* Paris, 1973, pp. 249–61.

[313] Petot, P. "L'évolution du servage dans la France coutumière du xie au xive siècle." *Jean Bodin* 2 (1959): 155–64.

[314] ———. "Serfs d'Eglise habilités à témoigner en justice." *CCM* 3 (1960): 191–94.

[315] ———. "L'origine de la main-morte servile." *RHD* 20 (1941): 275–309.

[316] Rossetti, G. *Società e istituzioni nel contado lombardo durante il medioevo: Cologna Monzese (sec. viiie–x^e).* Milan, 1968.

[317] Schneider, J. "Les gens d'alleu dans le droit messin du Moyen Age." *Etudes . . . J. Yver.* Paris, 1976, pp. 615–22.

[318] Tellenbach, G. "*Servitus* und *libertas* nach den Traditionen der Abtei Remiremont." *Saeculum* 21 (1970): 228–34.

[319] Van de Kieft, C. "Les *colliberti* et l'évolution du servage dans la France centrale et occidentale (x^e–xiie siècles)." *TVR* 32 (1964): 363–95.

[320] Van Winter, J. M. "Note à propos de l'article de M. Leopold Génicot, Noblesse, ministérialité et chevalerie en Gueldre et Zutphen" (summary in French of his thesis: *Ministerialiteit en ridderschap in Geldre en Zutphen,* Groningen, 1962). *MA* (1966): 279.

[321] Verlinden, C. *L'esclavage dans l'Europe médiévale.* Vol. I, *Péninsule Ibérique, France.* Bruges, 1955.

The Church and Society

[322] Abadal, y de Vinyals, R. *L'abat Oliba, bisbe de Vic i la seva epoca.* Barcelona, 1974.

[323] Amann, E. and Dumas, A. *L'Eglise au pouvoir des laïques (888–1057), Histoire de l'Eglise.* 7 vols. Paris, 1948.

[324] Batany, J. "Des 'trois fonctions' aux trois 'états'?" *AESC* 8 (1963): 933–38.

[325] ———. "Abbon de Fleury et les théories des structures sociales vers l'an mil." *Etudes ligériennes d'Hist. et d'Archéol. méd.* Auxerre, 1975, pp. 9–18.

[326] Bates, D. R. "The character and career of Odo bishop of Bayeux." *Speculum* 50 (1975): 1–20.

[327] Becker, A. *Studien zum Investiturproblem in Frankreich, Papsttum, Königtum und Episkopat im Zeitalter der gregorianischen Kirchenreform.* Sarrebrück, 1955.

[328] Becquet, J. "L'érémitisme clérical et laïc dans l'Ouest de la France." *Settimana . . . Mendola.* Vol. 4. Milan, 1962, p. 182.

[329] ———. "Les évêques de Limoges aux xᵉ, xiᵉ et xiiᵉ siècles." *Bull. de la Soc. archéol. et hist. du Limousin* (1977): 63.

[330] Benz, K. J. "Heinrich II und Cluny." *RB* 84 (1974): 313–37.

[331] Bienvenu, J.-M. "Les caractères originaux de la réforme grégorienne dans le diocèse d'Angers." *BPH* (1968): 545–60.

[332] ———. "Aux origines d'un ordre religieux: Robert d'Arbrissel et la fondation de Fontevraud (1101)." *Cahiers d'Histoire* 20 (1975): 227–51.

[333] Bisson, T. N. "The organized peace in Southern France and Catalonia (c. 1140–c. 1233)." *American Historical Review* 82 (1977): 290–311.

[334] Bligny, B. *Histoire religieuse du royaume de Bourgogne, xiᵉ–xiiᵉ siècles.* Grenoble, 1960.

[335] Bonnaud-Delamare, R. "Les institutions de paix dans la province ecclésiastique de Reims au xiᵉ siècle." *BPH* (1955–1956): 143–200.

[336] ———. "La paix d'Amiens et de Corbie au xiᵉ siècle." *RN* 38 (1956): 167–78.

[337] ———. "La paix en Flandre pendant la première Croisade." *RN* 38 (1957): 147–52.

[338] ———. "Les institutions de paix en Aquitaine au xiᵉ siècle." *Jean Bodin* 14 (1962): 415–87.

[339] ———. "La paix de Touraine pendant la première Croisade." *RHE* 70 (1975): 749.

[340] Boüard, M. de. "Sur les origines de la Trêve de Dieu en Normandie." *AN* 9 (1959): 169–89.

[341] ———. "A propos des origines de la Trêve de Dieu en Normandie." *AN* 13 (1963): 329–31.

[342] Boussard, J. "Les évêques en Neustrie avant la réforme grégorienne." *JS* (1970): 161–96.

[343] Bulst, N. *Untersuchungen zu den Klosterreformen Wilhelms von Dijon.* Bonn, 1973.

[344] Chauney, M. "Le recrutement de l'épiscopat bourguignon aux xiᵉ et xiiᵉ siècles." *AB* 47 (1975): 193.

[345] Carozzi, C. "La tripartition sociale et l'idée de Paix au xiᵉ siècle." *Actes du Ciᵉ Congrès des Soc. savantes.* Lille, 1976, pp. 9–22.

[346] "Les fondements de la tripartition sociale chez Adalbéron de Laon." *AESC* 33 (1978): 682–702.

[347] ———. "La vie du roi Robert par Helgaud de Fleury, historiographie et hagiographie." *Congrès de l'Assoc. des Méd. de l'Enseign. sup.* Tours, forthcoming.

[348] Chelini, J. "Les laïcs dans la société ecclésiastique carolingienne. *Settimana . . . Mendola* 5 (1965): 23.

*[349] Chenu, M. D., "Moines, clercs et laïcs au carrefour de la vie évangélique." *RHE* 49 (1954): 59–89.

[350] Congar, Y. "Les laïcs et l'ecclésiologie des *ordines* chez les théologiens des xiᵉ et xiiᵉ siècles." *Settimana . . . Mendola.* Milan, 1965, pp. 83–117.

[351] Cowdrey, H. E. J. *The Cluniacs and the Gregorian Reform.* Oxford, 1970.

[352] David, M. "Les *laboratores* jusqu'au renouveau économique des xiᵉ–xiiᵉ siècles." *Etudes d'histoire du Droit privé offertes à Pierre Petol.*

Paris, 1959, pp. 107–19; "Les *laboratores* du renouveau économique du xiie à la fin du xive siècle. *RHD* 27 (1959): 174–95 and 295–325.

[353] Dereine, C. "Vie commune règle de saint Augustin et chanoines réguliers au xie siècle." *RHE* 41 (1946): 365–406.

[354] ———. "Les origines de Prémontré." *RHE* 42 (1947): 352–78.

[355] ———. "Le premier *ordo* de Prémontré." *RB* 43 (1948): 84–92.

[356] ———. "Les coutumiers de Saint-Quentin de Beauvais et de Springiersbach." *RHE* 43 (1948): 411.

[357] ———. "Odon de Tournai et la crise du cénobitisme au xie siècle." *RMAL* 4 (1948): 137–54.

[358] ———. "Saint-Ruf et ses coutumes aux xie et xiie siècles." *RB* 59 (1949): 161–82.

[359] ———. "L'école canonique liégeoise et la réforme grégorienne." *Annales du Congrès archéol. et hist. de Tournai* (1949): 1.

[360] ———. "Clercs et moines au diocèse de Liège du xe au xiie siècle." *Annales de la Soc. archéol. de Namur* (1951): 183.

[361] Despy, G. "Cîteaux dans les Ardennes: aux origines d'Orval." *Mélanges . . . E. Perroy.* Paris, 1973, pp. 588–600.

*[362] Duby G. "Les laïcs et la Paix de Dieu (1966)." *Hommes et structures,* pp. 227–40.

[363] ———. "Gérard de Cambrai, la paix et les trois fonctions sociales." *CRAIBL* (1976): 136–46.

[364] Fontette, F. de. "Evêques de Limoges et comtes de Poitou au xie siècle." *Mélanges . . . G. Le Bras.* Paris, 1965, pp. 553–58.

[365] Fossier, R. "Les mouvements populaires en Occident." *CRAIBL* (1971): 257–69.

[366] ———. "Remarques sur l'étude des commotions sociales aux xie et xiie siècles." *CCM* 16 (1973): 45–50.

[367] Gaudemet, J. "Les institutions ecclésiastiques en France du milieu du xiie siècle au début du xive." *Lot et Fawtier* 3: 143–335.

[368] Génicot, L. "L'érémitisme du xie siècle dans son contexte économique et social." *Settimana . . . Mendola* 4 (1965): 45–69.

[369] ———. "Haut clergé, princes et nobles dans le diocèse de Liège, du xie au xve siècle (1968)." *Études . . . ,* pp. 140–71.

[370] Graboïs, A. "De la Trêve de Dieu à la paix du roi." *Mélanges René Crozet.* Poitiers, 1966, pp. 585–96.

[371] Guillemain, B. "Les origines des évêques en France aux xie et xiie siècles." *Settimana . . . Mendola* 7 (1974): 374–402.

[372] Guillotel, H. "La pratique du cens épiscopal dans l'évêché de Nantes." *MA,* ser. 4, 29 (1974): 5–49.

[373] Hoffmann, H. *Gottesfriede und treuga Dei.* Stuttgart, 1964.

[374] Hourlier, J. *Saint Odilon, abbé de Cluny.* Louvain, 1964.

[375] Huyghebaert, N. "Moines et clercs italiens en Lotharingie." *Annales du XXXIIIe Congrès de la Féd. archéol. et hist. de Belgique.* Tournai, 1951, p. 95.

[376] Jacobs, H. "Die Cluniazenser und das Papsttum im 10. und 11 Jhdt.: Bemerkungen zum Cluny-Bild eines neuen Buches." *Francia* 2 (1974): 643–63.

[377] Joris, A. "Observations sur la proclamation de la Trêve de Dieu à Liège à la fin du xie siècle." *Jean Bodin* 14 (1962): 503–45.

[378] Le Bras, G. *Institutions ecclésiastiques de la chrétienté médiévale. Préliminaires, première partie.* Paris, 1959–1964.

[379] Le Bras, G., Lefebvre, C., Rambaud, J. *Histoire du droit et des institutions de l'Eglise en Occident.* Vol. 7: *L'âge classique (1140–1378).* Paris, 1965.

[380] Le Clercq, J. "Le poème de Payen Bolotin contre les faux ermites." *RB* 48 (1958): 52–86.

[381] Le Goff, J. "Note sur société tripartite, idéologie monarchique et renouveau économique dans la chrétienté du ixe au xiie siècle (1965)." *Pour un autre Moyen Age.* Paris, 1977, pp. 80–90.

[382] Lemarignier, J.-F. *Etude sur les privilèges d'exemption et de juridiction ecclésiastique des abbayes normandes depuis les origines jusqu'en 1140.* Paris, 1937.

[383] ———. "L'exemption monastique et les origines de la réforme grégorienne." *Congrès scientifique de Cluny.* Mâcon, 1950, p. 288–34.

[384] ———. "Les institutions ecclésiastiques en France de la fin du xe au milieu du xiie siècle." *Lot et Fawtier,* 3:1–139.

[385] ———. "Paix et réforme monastique en Flandre et en Normandie autour de l'année 1023." *Droit privé et institutions regionales. Etudes historiques offertes à Jean Yver.* Paris, 1976, pp. 443–68.

[386] ———. "Le monachisme et l'encadrement religieux dans les campagnes du royaume de France situées au Nord de la Loire, de la fin du xe à la fin du xie siècle." *Settimana . . . Mendola* 8 (1977): 357–94.

[387] Locatelli, R. "L'implantation cistercienne dans le comté de Bourgogne jusqu'au milieu du xiie siècle." *Cahiers d'Histoire* 20 (1975): 167–225.

[388] Magnou, E. "L'introduction de la réforme grégorienne à Toulouse." *Cahiers de l'Assoc. Marc Bloch de Toulouse,* 3 (1958).

[389] Magnou-Nortier E. "La crise de l'Eglise narbonnaise à la fin du xie et au début du xiie siècle." *Narbonne,* pp. 115–19.

[390] Mahn, J.-B. *L'ordre cistercien et son gouvernement des origines au milieu du xiiie siècle.* Paris, 1945.

[391] Moyse, G. "Les origines du monachisme dans le diocèse de Besançon, ve-xe siècle." *BEC* (1973): 21–104 and 369–485.

[392] Newman, W. M. *Le personnel de la cathédrale d'Amiens.* Paris, 1972.

[393] Oexle, O. G. *Forschungen zu monastischen und geistlichen Gemeinschaften im Westfränkischen Bereich.* Munich, 1978.

[394] Pacaut, M. *Les ordres monastiques et religieux au Moyen Age.* Paris, 1970.

[395] ———. "La notion de pauvreté dans la règle de saint Benoît." *Mélanges . . . E. Perroy.* Paris, 1973, pp. 626–33.

[396] ———. "Structures monastiques, société et Eglise en Occident aux xie et xiie siècles." *Cahiers d'Histoire* 10 (1975): 119–36.

[397] Parisse, M. "Les chanoinesses séculières." *Cahiers d'Histoire* 20 (1975): 253–58.

[398] Platelle, H. "La violence et ses remèdes en Flandre au xie siècle." *Sacris eruditi* 20 (1971): 101–73.

[399] Petit, F. "L'ordre de Prémontré de saint Norbert à Anselme de Havelberg." *Settimana . . . Mendola* 1 (1962): 456–79.

[400] Robin, G. "Le problème de la vie commune au chapitre de la cathédrale Saint-Maurice d'Angers du ixe au xiie siècle." *CCM* 13 (1970): 305–22.

[401] Schieffer, T. "Cluny et la querelle des investitures." *RH* 225 (1961): 47–72.

[402] Tellenbach, G. "Einführung zur Erforschung Clunys und der Clun-

iacenser." *Neue Forschungen über Cluny und die Cluniacenser.* Freiburg, 1959, p. 3.

[403] ———. "Zum Wesen der Cluniacenser." *Saeculum* 9 (1958): 370–78.

[404] ———. "Il monachesimo riformato ed i laici nei secoli xi e xii." *Settimana . . . Mendola* 5 (1968): p. 118–42.

[405] Timbal Duclaux de Martin, P. C. *Le droit d'asile.* Paris, 1939.

[406] Vauchez, A. "La pauvreté volontaire au Moyen Age." *AESC* 25 (1970): 1566–73.

[407] ———. *La spiritualité du Moyen Age occidental, viiie-xiie siècles.* Paris, 1975.

[408] Verdon, J. "Les moniales dans la France de l'Ouest aux xie et xiie siècles." *CCM* 19 (1976): 247–64.

[409] Violante, C. "I laici nel movimento Patarino (1965)." *Studi . . .,* pp. 145–246.

[410] ———. *La Pataria milanese e la riforma ecclesiastica, I le premesse.* Rome, 1955.

[411] ———. "Il monachesimo cluniacense di fronte al mondo politico ed ecclesiastico (1960)." *Studi . . .,* pp. 3–67.

[412] Wollasch, J. "Gerard von Brogne im Reformmönchtum seiner Zeit." *RB* 70 (1960): 232–40.

Feudal Hierarchy

[413] Baldwin, J. W. *Masters, Princes and Merchants: The Social Views of Peter the Chanter and his Circle.* Princeton, 1970.

[414] Barroux, R. "L'abbé Suger et la vassalité du Vexin en 1124." *MA* ser. 4, 13 (1958): 1–26.

[415] Benton, J. F. "Philology's search for Abelard in the Metamorphosis Goliae." *Speculum* 50 (1975): 199–217.

*[416] Bloch, M. "L'Empire et l'idée d'Empire sous les Hohenstaufen (1929)." *Mélanges,* pp. 531–59.

[417] Boulet-Sautel, M. "Le rôle juridictionnel de la cour des pairs aux xiiie et xive siècles." *Receuil de Travaux offert à M. Clovis Brunel,* vol. 2. 1955, pp. 517–20.

[418] Bournazel, E. *Le gouvernement capétien au XIIe siècle. Structures sociales et mutations institutionnelles.* Paris, 1975.

[419] Boussard, J. "Les mercenaires au xiie siècle. Henri II Plantegenêt et les origines de l'armée de métier." *BEC* 105 (1945–1946): 189–224.

[420] ———. *Le gouvernement de Henri II Plantegenêt.* Paris, 1956.

[421] Calasso, F. *Medioevo del diritto.* Vol. 1: *Le fonti.* Milan, 1954.

[422] Coino, H. *Handbuch der Quellen und Literatur der neueren europäischen Privatrechtsgeschichte.* Vol. 1: *Mittelalter.* Munich, 1973.

[423] Contamine, P. *L'oriflamme de Saint-Denis aux xive et xve siècles. Etude de symbolique religieuse et royale.* Nancy, 1975.

[424] David, M. *Le serment du sacre du ixe au xve siècle.* Strasbourg, 1951.

[425] ———. *La souveraineté et les limites juridiques du pouvoir monarchique du ixe au xve siècle.* Paris, 1954.

[426] Diament, H. "La légende dionysienne et la juxtaposition des toponymes Montjoie et Saint-Denis dans la formation du cri de guerre." *Romance Notes* 15 (1971): 177–80.

[427] Duby, G. "Le gouvernement royal aux premiers temps capétiens." *MA* 21 (1966): 531–44.

*[428] ———. "Les 'jeunes' dans la société aristocratique de la France du Nord-Ouest au XIIᵉ siècle (1964)." *Hommes et structures*, pp. 213–25.

[429] ———. *Le dimanche de Bouvines (27 juillet 1214)*. Paris, 1973.

[430] Erlande-Brandenbourg, A. *Le roi est mort. Etude sur les funérailles, les sépultures et les tombeaux des rois de France jusqu'à la fin du XIIIᵉ siècle*. Geneva, 1975.

[431] Folz, R. *Le souvenir et la légende de Charlemagne dans l'Empire germanique médiéval*. Paris, 1950.

[432] "Aspects du culte liturgique de saint Charlemagne en France." *Karl der Grosse*, vol. 4, p. 77.

[433] Francastel, P. "Suger et les débuts de l'âge gothique." *AESC* 7 (1952): 237–43.

[434] Gaier, C. "Le rôle militaire des reliques et de l'étendard de saint Lambert dans la principauté de Liège." *MA*, ser. 4, 21 (1966): 235–49.

[435] Gaudemet, J. "La souveraineté au Moyen Age." *TVR* 22 (1954): 460–68.

[436] ———. "Le droit romain dans la pratique et chez les docteurs aux XIᵉ et XIIIᵉ siècles." *CCM* 8 (1965): 365–80.

[437] Gouron, A. "Les étapes de la pénétration du droit romain au XIIᵉ siècle dans l'ancienne Septimanie." *AM* 69 (1957): 103–120.

[438] ———. "Diffusion des consulats méridionaux et expansion du droit romain aux XIIᵉ et XIIIᵉ siècles." BEC (1963): 26–76.

[439] —. "La date et le rédacteur des coutumes de Saint-Gilles." *Annales de l'Univ. de Sciences soc. de Toulouse* 24 (1976): 309–15.

[440] ———. "Autour de Placentin à Montpellier: Maître Gui et Pierre de Cardona." *Studia Gratiana* 19 (1976): 337–54.

[441] ———. "La science juridique française aux XIᵉ et XIIᵉ siècles: diffusion du droit de Justinien et influences canoniques jusqu'à Gratien." *IRMA* I (4). Milan, 1978.

[442] ———. "Le cardinal Raymond des Arènes: Cardinalis, Mélanges . . . J. Gaudemet." *Rev. de Droit can.* 28 (1978): 180–92.

[443] Guenée, B. "Les généalogies entre l'histoire et la politique: la fierté d'être Capétien en France, au Moyen Age." *AESC* 33 (1978): 450–77.

[444] Halphen, L. "La place de la royauté dans le système féodal (1933)." *A travers . . .*, pp. 266–74.

[445] Hibbard-Loomis, L. "L'oriflamme de France et le cri 'Munjoie' au XIIᵉ siècle." *MA* ser. 4, 14 (1959): 469–99.

[446] Horrent, J. "Notes de critique textuelle sur le Pseudo-Turpin." *MA*, ser. 4, 30 (1975): 37–62.

[447] Jacqueline, B. "Saint Bernard et le droit romain." *RHD* 30 (1952): 223–28.

[448] Joris, A. "Notes sur la pénétration du droit savant au pays de Liege." *TVR* (1972): 183–205.

[449] ———. "Wibald de Stavelot et le droit romain." *Mélanges . . . E. Perroy*. Paris, 1973, pp. 601–7.

[450] Kienast, W. *Deutschland und Frankreich in der Kaiserzeit (900–1270)*. Stuttgart, 1974.

[451] Le Bras, G. "L'Eglise médiévale au service du droit romain." *RHD* 44 (1966): 193.

[452] Legendre, P. *La pénétration du droit romain dans le droit canonique classique de Gratien à Innocent IV (1140–1254)*. Paris, 1964.

[453] Le Goff, J. *Les intellectuels au Moyen Age*. Paris, 1957.

[454] Lemarignier, J.-F. "Hiérachie monastique et hiérarchie féodale." *RHD* 31 (1953): 171–74.

[455] ———. *Le gouvernement royal aux premiers temps capétiens (987–1108)*. Paris, 1965.

[455a] ———. "A propos de deux actes sur l'histoire du Droit romain." *BEC* 101 (1940): 157–68.

[456] Lyon, B. D. *From Fief to Indenture. The transition from Feudal to Non-feudal Contract in Western Europe*. Cambridge, Mass., 1957.

[457] Lot, F. "Quelques mots sur l'origine des pairs de France (1894)." *Recueil. . .*, 2, pp. 187–212.

[458] Marchant, D. "Les pairs de Saint-Lambert de Liège." *MA*, ser. 4, 30 (1975): 63–95.

[459] Pacaut, M. *Louis VII et son royaume*. Paris, 1964.

[460] ———. "L'investiture en France au début du xiie siècle." *Mélanges . . . G. Le Bras*, vol. 1. Paris, 1965, pp. 665–72.

[461] Panofsky, E. *Abbot Suger on the Abbey Church of St. Denis and Its Art Treasures*. Princeton, 1946; rev. ed., 1979; *Gothic Architecture and Scholasticism*. Latrobe, Pa., 1961. (*L'abbé Suger de Saint-Denis, Architecture gothique et pensée scolastique*. Paris, 1970.)

[462] Paul, J., *Histoire intellectuelle de l'Occident médiéval*. Paris, 1973.

[463] Poly, J.-P. "Les légistes provençaux." *Mélanges . . . Roger Aubenas*. Montpellier, 1974, pp. 613–35.

[464] ———. "Les Maîtres de Saint-Ruf, pratique et enseignement du droit dans la France méridionale, xiie siècle." *Annales de la Fac. de Droit des Sciences sociales et politiques . . . de Bordeaux* (1978): 183.

[465] Schramm, P. E. *Der König von Frankreich*. Weimar, 1960.

[466] Sczaniecki, M. *Essai sur les fiefs-rentes*. Paris, 1946.

[467] Spiegel, G. M. "The cult of Saint Denis and Capetian Kingship." *Journal of Medieval History* (1975): 43–69.

[468] ———. *The Chronicle Tradition of Saint-Denis: A Survey*. Brookline, Mass. and Leyden, 1978.

[469] Van de Kieft, C. "Deux diplômes faux de Charlemagne pour Saint-Denis, du xiie siècle." *MA*, ser. 4, 13 (1958): 403.

[470] Werner, K. F. "Die Legitimität der Kapetinger und die Entstehung des *reditus ad stirpem Karoli*." *Die Welt als Geschichte* 12 (1952): 203–25.

[471] Wood, C. T. "*Regnum Franciae*, a Problem in Capetian Administrative Usage." *Traditio* 23 (1967): 117–47.

Aristocracies, State, and Feudalism

[472] Abadal y de Vinyals, R. "A propos du legs visigothique en Espagne." *Settimane . . . di Spoleto* 5 (1958): 541–85.

[473] Bloch, M. "La société du haut Moyen Age et ses origines (1926)." *Mélanges*, vol. 1, pp. 61–74.

[474] ———. "Sur les grandes invasions (1945)." *Mélanges*, vol. 1, pp. 90–109.

[474a] Blok, D. P. "Les formules de droit romáin dans les actes privés du haut Moyen Age." *Miscellanea . . . J.-F. Niermeyer*. Groningen, 1967, pp. 17–28.

[475] Dhondt, J. *Le haut Moyen Age. viiie–xie siècle*. Paris, 1976.

*[476] Duby, G. "Les sociétés médiévales: une approche d'ensemble (1972)." *Hommes et structures*, pp. 361–79.

[477] Ewig, E. "L'Aquitaine et les pays rhénans au haut Moyen Age." *CCM* 1 (1958): 37–54.
[478] ———. "Volkstum und Volksbewustsein im Frankreich des 7. Jahrhunderts." *Settimane . . . di Spoleto* 5 (1958): 587–648.
[479] ———. "Les missions dans les pays rhénans." *RHEF* 61 (1976): 37–44.
*[480] Fichtenau, H. *L'Empire carolingien.* Paris, 1958.
[481] Flach, J. "Le droit romain dans les chartes du ixe au xie siècles en France." *Mélanges . . . Fitting.* Montpellier, 1907; rev. ed, Paris, 1969, p. 373.
[482] Ganshof, F. L. "La *gratia* des monarques francs." *Anuario de estudios medievales* 30 (1966): 9–26.
[483] ———. "Contribution à l'étude de l'application du droit romain et des capitulaires dans la Monarchie franque sous les Carolingiens." *Studi . . . E. Volterro,* vol. 3. Milan, 1969, p. 585–603.
[484] ———. "A propos de ducs et de duchés au haut Moyen Age." *JS* (1972): 13–24.
[485] Garaud, M. "Le droit romain dans le chartes poitevines du ixe au xie siècle." *Mélanges de Droit Romain dédiées à Georges Cornil,* vol. 1. Ghent, 1926, p. 399–424.
[486] Gaudemet, J. "Survivances romaines dans le droit de la Monarchie franque du ve au xe siècle." *TVR* 25 (1955): 149–206.
[487] ———. "A propos du droit vulgaire." *Studi B. Biondi,* vol. 1. Milan, 1965, pp. 271–300.
[488] Grassotti, H. "La *ira regia* en León y Castilla." *Cuadernos de historia de Espana* 41–42 (1965): 1–135.
[489] Halphen, L. "L'idée d'Etat sous les Carolingiens (1939)." *A travers. . . ,* pp. 92–104.
*[490] ———. *Charlemagne et l'Empire carolingien* (1947). Revised edition, Paris, 1968.
[491] Hlawitschka, E. *Franken, Alemanen, Bayern und Burgunder in Oberitalien (774–962).* Freiburg, 1960.
[492] ———. "Die vorfahren Karls des Grossen." *Karl der Grosse* 1: 57–82.
[493] Kedar, B. Z. "Noms de saints et mentalité populaire à Gênes au xive siècle." *MA,* ser. 4, 22 (1967): 431–46.
[494] Kienast, W. *Studien über die französischen Volksstämme des Frühmittelalters.* Stuttgart, 1968.
[495] ———. *Der Herzogstitel in Frankreich und Deutschland, 9. bis. 12 Jahrhundert.* Munich, Vienna, 1968.
[496] Labuda, G. "Tendances d'intégration et de désintégration dans le royaume teutonique du xe au xiiie siècle." *L'Europe au ix–xie siècles: Aux origines des etats nationaux,* edited by Tadeusz Manteuffel and Aleksander Gieysztor. Warsaw, 1968, pp. 77–91.
[497] Lemarignier, J.-F. "Quelques remarques sur l'organisation ecclésiastique de la Gaule du viie a la fin du xiiie siecle." *Settimane . . . di Spoleto* (1966): 451–486.
[498] Lewis, A. R. "Count Gerald of Aurillac and Feudalism in South Central France in the Early Tenth Century." *Traditio* 20 (1964): 41–58.
[499] Leyser, K. "The German Aristocracy from the Ninth to the Early Twelfth Century." *Past and Present* 41 (1968): 25–53.
[500] Manteuffel, T. "Problèmes d'integration et de désintégration des états européens aux ixe et xe siècles." *L'Europe aux ixe–xie siècles: Aux*

origenes des états nationaux, edited by Tadeusz Manteuffel and Aleksander Gieysztor. Warsaw, 1968, pp. 21–29.

[501] Morlet, M.-T. *Les noms de personnes sur le territoire de l'ancienne Gaule du vie au xiie siècle.* Vol. 1: *Les noms issus du germanique;* Vol. 2: *Les noms latins ou transmis par le latin.* Paris, 1968–1972.

*[502] Musset, L. *Les Invasions, les vagues germaniques.* Paris, 1965 and *Le second assaut contre l'Europe chrétienne (viie–xie siècle).* Paris, 1966.

[503] Ourliac, P. "La *convenientia.*" *Etudes. . . P. Petot.* Paris, 1959, pp. 413–22.

[504] Perroy, E. *Le monde carolingien.* Paris, 1974.

[505] Poliakov, L. "Des mythes des origines au mythe arien." *AESC* 25 (1970): 408–33.

[506] Poulain, J.-C. *L'idéal de sainteté dans l'Aquitaine carolingienne d'après les sources hagiographiques (750–950).* Quebec, 1975.

[507] Riché, P. "L'enseignement du droit en Gaule du vie au xie siècle." *IRMA* (1965), pars, I, 5 b bb.

*[508] ———. *Education et culture dans l'Occident barbare, vie–viie siècle* (1962). Rev. ed., Paris, 1973.

[509] Rosellini, A. "Les noms de personne du polyptyque de Saint-Remy de Reims." *MA* ser. 4, 17 (1962): 271–91.

[510] Rouche, M. "Les Aquitains ont-ils trahi avant la bataille de Poitiers?" *MA* ser. 4, 23 (1968): 5–26.

[511] ———. *L'Aquitaine des Wisigoths aux Arabes (418–781). Essai sur le phénomène régional.* Lille, 1977.

[512] Schneider, J. "Aspects de la société dans l'Aquitaine carolingienne d'après la *vita Geraldi Auriliacensis.*" *CRAIBL* (1973): 8–20.

[513] Stouff, L. "L'*interpretatio* de la loi romaine des Wisigoths dans les formules et dans les chartes du vie au xie siècle." *Mélanges . . . Fitting,* vol. 2. Montpellier, 1907; rev. ed., Paris, 1969, pp. 165–88.

[514] Stroheker, K. F. *Der senatorische Adel in spätantiken Gallien.* Tübingen, 1948.

[515] Udina Martorell, F. "L'évolution du titre comtal â Barcelone." *CCM* 14 (1971): 149–57, and 17 (1974): 235–45.

[516] Vauchez, A. "*Beata stirps:* sainteté et lignage en Occident aux xiiie et xive siècles." *Famille,* pp. 397–406.

[517] Wemple, S. F. "Claudius of Turin's Organic Metaphor or the Carolingian Doctrine of Corporations." *Speculum* 99 (1974): 222–37.

[518] Werner, K. F. "Bedeutende Adelsfamilien im Reich Karls des Grossen." *Karl der Grosse* 1:42–83.

[519] ———. "Les nations et le sentiment national dans l'Europe médiévale." *RH* 244: (1970): 285–304.

[520] ———. "Les principautés périphériques dans le monde franc du viiie siècle." *Settimane . . . di Spoleto* 20 (1973): 483–514.

[521] ———. "Le rôle de l'aristocratie dans la christianisation du Nord-Est de la Gaule." *RHEF* 62 (1976): 45–73.

[522] Wollasch, J. J. "Königtum, Adel und Kloster im Berry während des 10. Jahrhunderts." *Neue forschungen über Cluny und die Cluniacenser.* Freiburg, 1959, pp. 17–165.

Power and Production

Listed here are only those references strictly necessary for the reading of chapter 8. For a complete bibliography of economic problems, see the work by Robert Fossier, and for the preceding period, that of Renée Doehaerd, *Le haut Moyen Age occidental*, Paris, 1971.

[523] Beyerle, F. "Die beiden süddeutschen Stammesrechte." *ZSSGA* 72 (1956): 84–140.
[524] Bonnassie, P. "La monnaie et les échanges en Auvergne et Rouergue aux xᵉ et xiᵉ siècles." *AM* 90 (1978): 275–88.
[525] Coleman, E. R. "Medieval Marriage Characteristics: A Neglected Factor in the History of Medieval Serfdom." *Journal of Interdisciplinary History* (1971): 205–19.
[526] ———. "L'infanticide dans le haut Moyen Age." *AESC* (1974): 315–35.
[527] Delatouche, R. "Regards sur l'agriculture aux temps carolingiens." *JS* (1977): 73–100.
[528] Dockés, P. *La libération médiévale.* Paris, 1979.
[529] Duby, G. "Un inventaire des profits de la seigneurie clunisienne à la mort de Pierre le Vénérable (1956)." *Hommes et structures. . .* , pp. 87–101.
[530] Duby, G. "Les problèmes des techniques agricoles (1966)." *Hommes et structures*, p. 241.
[531] ———. "Les villes du Sud-Est de la Gaule du viiiᵉ au xiᵉ siècle (1959)." *Hommes et structures*, p. 111.
*[532] ———. *Guerriers et paysans, viiiᵉ–xiiᵉ siècle. Premier essor de l'économie européenne.* Paris, 1973.
[533] Ganshof, F. L. "Quelques àspects principaux de la vie économique dans la monarchie franque au viiᵉ siècle." *Settimane . . . di Spoleto* 15 (1958): 73–101.
[534] Gasnault, P., and Vezin, J. *Documents comptables de Saint-Martin de Tours à l'époque mérovingienne.* Paris, 1975.
[535] Génicot, L. "Sur le domaine de Saint-Bertin à l'époque carolingienne." *RHE* 71 (1976): 69–78.
[536] Goffart, W. "From Roman Taxation to Medieval Seigneurie: Three Notes." *Speculum* 97 (1972): 165–87 and 373–94.
[537] Gurevic, G. "Représentations et attitudes à l'égard de la propriété pendant le haut Moyen Age." *AESC* 27 (1972): 523–47.
*[538] Kula, W. *Théorie économique du système féodal.* Paris, 1970.
[539] Lombard, Jourdan A. "Du problème de la continuite: y a-t-il une protohistoire urbaine en France?" *AESC* 25 (1970): 1121–42.
[540] ———. "Oppidum et banlieue: sur l'origine et les dimensions du territoire urbain." *AESC* 27 (1972): 373–95.
[541] ———. *Paris, genèse de la "Ville": la rive droite de la Seine des origines à 1223.* Paris, 1976.
[542] Lot, F. "Note sur la date du polyptyque de Montierender (1924/1925)." *Recueil . . .,* 2: 721–31.
[543] Lyon, B. D. "Encore le problème de la chronologie des corvées." *MA*, ser. 4, 18 (1963): 615–30.
[544] Ménager, L. R. "Considérations sociologiques sur la démographie des grands domaines ecclésiastiques carolingiens." *Mélanges . . . G. Le Bras*, vol. 2. Paris, 1965, pp. 1317–35.

[545] Mitterauer, M. "La continuité des foires et la naissance des villes." *AESC* 28 (1973): 711–34.

[546] Patlagean, E. " 'Economie paysanne' et 'féodalité byzantine'." *AESC* 30 (1975): 1371–96.

[547] Polge, H. "L'amélioration de l'attelage a-t-elle réellement fait reculer le servage?" *JS* (1967): 5–42.

[548] Poly, J.-P. "Régime domanial et rapports de production 'féodalistes' dans le midi de la France (viiie–xe siècle)." *Structures féodales . . .*, pp. 52–84.

[549] Rizzi, B. *La rovina antica e l'età feudale*, vol. 1. Bussolengo, 1969.

[550] Rouche, M. "La faim à l'époque carolingienne." *RH* 250 (1973): 295–320.

[551] Russell, J. C. "Medieval Cemetery Patterns: Plague and Non-plague." *Mélangès . . . E. Perroy*. Paris, 1973, pp. 525–30.

[552] Sanchez Albornoz, C. "El *tributum quadragesimale*. Supervivencias fiscales romanas en Galicia." *Mélanges . . . L. Halphen*. Paris, 1951, p. 645–58.

[553] Schneider, J. "Aspects de la vie urbaine en France au premier âge féodal."*CRAIBL* (1957): 50–54.

[554] Settia, A. "L'incidenza del popolamento rurale sulla signoria di castello nell' Italia del Nord." *Structures féodales . . .*, pp. 263–84.

[555] Sidorova, N., and Gutnova, E. "Comment l'historiographic soviétique aperçoit et explique le Moyen Age occidental." *AESC* 15 (1960): 330–99.

[556] Slicher Van Bath, B. H. *An Agrarian History of Western Europe from 500 A.D. to 1850 A.D.* London, 1963.

[557] ———. "Le climat et les récoltes au haut Moyen Age." *Settimane . . . di Spoleto* 13 (1966): 399–425.

[558] Toubert, P. "L'Italie rurale aux viiie–ixe siècles: essai de typologie domaniale." *Settimane . . . di Spoleto* 20 (1973): 95–132.

[559] Verhulst, A. "La genèse du régime domanial classique en France au haut Moyen Age." *Settimane . . . di Spoleto* 12 (1965): 135–60.

[560] Werner, E. "De l'esclavage à la féodalité: la périodisation de l'histoire mondiale." *AESC* 17 (1962): 930–39.

[561] White, L., Jr. *Medieval Technology and Social Change*. London, 1964. (*Technologie médiévale et transformations sociales*: Paris, 1969.)

Heresy

An exhaustive bibliography up to 1964 can be found in Grundmann, *Héresies . . .*

[562] Anguelov, D. *Le Bogomilisme en Bulgarie*. Toulouse, 1972.

[563] Bauer, J. B. *Les apocryphes du Nouveau Testament*. Paris, 1973.

[564] Bautier, R. H. "L'hérésie d'Orléans et le mouvement intellectuel au début du xie siècle, documents et hypothèses." *Comité des trav. hist. sect. de philolog. et d'hist.* Paris, 1975, pp. 63–88.

[565] Bonenfant, P. "Un clerc cathare en Lotharingie au milieu du xiie siècle." *MA*, ser. 4, 18 (1963): 271–80.

[566] Bordenave, J. and Vialelle, M. *Aux racines du mouvement cathare: la mentalité religieuse des paysans de l'Albigeois médiéval*. Toulouse, 1973.

[567] Borst, A. *Die Katharer*. Stuttgart, 1953. (*Les Cathares*. Paris, 1974.)

[568] Congar, Y. "*Arriana Haeresis* comme désignation du néo-manichéisme au xiie siècle." *Rev. des Sci. philolog. et théolog.* 43 (1959): 449–61.

[569] Decret, F. *Mani et la tradition manichéenne*. Paris, 1974.

[570] Delaruelle, E. "Dévotion populaire et hérésie au Moyen Age." *Hérésies* . . . , pp. 147–55.

[571] De Smet, J. M. "De monnik Tanchelm en de Utrechtse bisschopszetel in 1112–1114," *Scrinium Lovaniense. Mélanges historiques Etienne Van Cauwenberg*. Gembloux-Louvain, 1961, pp. 207–34.

[572] Dondaine, A. "L'origine de l'hérésie médiévale." *Riv. di Storia della Chiesa in Italia* (1952): 47–78.

[573] Grisart, M. "Les cathares dans le Nord de la France." *RN* 49 (1967): 509–19.

[574] Grundmann, H. "Hérésies savantes et hérésies populaires au Moyen Age." *Hérésies* . . ., pp. 209–18.

[575] Ilarino Da Milano. "Le eresie popolare del secolo xi nell'Europa occidentale." *Studi Gregoriani*, vol. 2. Edited by G. B. Borino. Rome, 1947, pp. 43–89.

[576] Ivanov, J. *Livres et légendes bogomiles. Aux sources du catharisme*. Paris, 1976.

[577] Koch, G. *Frauenfrage und Ketzertum im Mittelalter. Die Frauenbewegung im Rahmen des Katharismus und des Waldensertums und ihre sozialen Wurzeln (12.–14. Jhdt.)*. Berlin, 1962.

[578] Loos, M. *Dualist Heresy in the Middle Ages*. Prague, 1974.

[579] Manselli, R. "Il monaco Enrico." *BISI* 65 (1953): 1–63.

[580] ———. "Per la storia dell'eresia."*BISI* 67 (1955): 189–264.

[581] ———. "Una designazione dell'eresia carata: 'Arriana Heresis'." *BISI* 68 (1956): 233–46.

[582] Manteuffel, T. *Naissance d'une hérésie. Les adeptes de la pauvreté volontaire au Moyen Age*. Paris, 1970.

[583] Montclos, J. de. *Lanfranc et Bérenger, la controverse eucharistique du xie siècle*. Louvain, 1971.

[584] Morghen, R. *Medioevo cristiano* (1951). Rev. ed., Bari, 1958.

[585] ———. "Movimenti religiosi popolari nel periodo della riforma della Chiesa." *Xo Congresso Internaz. di Sci. Storiche*, vol. 3. Florence, 1955, pp. 333–56.

[586] ———. "Problèmes sur l'origine de l'hérésie au Moyen Age." *RH* (1966): 1, or *Hérésies et société* . . ., p. 121; in Italian, "Aspetti ereticali dei movimenti religiosi popolari." *Settimana* . . . *Mendola* 5(1965): 582–96.

[587] Musy, J. "Mouvements populaires et hérésies au xie siècle en France." *RH* 253 (1975): 33–76.

[588] Noiroux, M.-M. "Les deux premiers documents concernant l'hérésie aux Pays-Bas." *RHE* 49 (1954): 842–55.

[589] Puech, H. C. "Catharisme médiéval et bogomilisme." *Convegno di scienze morale storiche et filologiche* (1956). Rome, 1957, pp. 56–84 and 154–61.

[590] Runciman, S. *The Medieval Manichee*. Cambridge, 1947. [*Le Manichéisme médiéval. L'hérésie dualiste dans le christianisme*. Paris, 1972.)

[591] Russell, J. B. "A propos du synode d'Arras de 1025." *RHE* 57 (1962): 66–87.

[592] Shahar, S. "Le catharisme et le début de la Cabale." *AESC* 29 (1974): 1185–1210.

[593] Taviani, H. "Naissance d'une hérésie en Italie du Nord au XIᵉ siècle." *AESC* 29 (1974): 1224–52.

[594] ———. "Le mariage dans l'herésie de l'an mil." *AESC* 32 (1988): 1074–84.

[595] ———. "Du refus au défi: essai sur la psychologie hérétique au début du XIᵉ siècle en Occident." *Actes du CIIᵉ Congrès national des Sociétés savantes*, vol. 2. Limoges, 1977, p. 175.

[596] Thouzellier, C. "Hérésie et croisade au XIIᵉ siècle (1954)." *Hérésie et hérétiques, Vaudois, Cathares, Patarins, Albigeois.* Rome, 1969, pp. 17–37.

[597] ———. *Catharisme et Valdéisme en Languedoc à la fin du XIIᵉ et au début du XIIIᵉ siècle.* Paris, 1966.

[598] ———. "Tradition et résurgence dans l'hérésie médiévale [1968]." *Hérésie et hérétiques, Vaudois, Cathares, Patarins, Albigeois.* Rome, 1969, pp. 1–15.

[599] ———. "Le vocable 'cathare' et la théorie des deux fils." *Mélanges . . . E. Perroy.* Paris, 1973, pp. 650–60.

[600] Violante, C. "La povertá nelle eresie del secolo XI in Occidente [1972]." *Studi sulla christianita medioevale*, pp. 69–107.

[601] ———. "Hérésies urbaines et hérésies rurales en Italie du XIᵉ au XIIIᵉ siècle (1962)." *Hérésies*, pp. 171–98.

[602] Wakefield, W. L. *Heresy, Crusade and Inquisition in Southern France, 1100–1250.* London, 1974.

[603] Werner, E. *Häresie und Gesellschaft im 11. Jahrhundert.* Berlin, 1975.

Ideas

[604] Amargier, P. "Aperçus sur la mentalité monastique en Provence au XIᵉ siècle." *AESC* (1972): 415–26.

*[605] Baroja, P. C. *Les sorcières et leur monde* (1961). Paris, 1972; revised, 1979.

[606] Barroux, R. "Statue et légende d'Isis à Saint-Germain-des-Prés." *MA* (1959): 245–51.

*[607] Blogh, M. *Les rois thaumaturges.* Paris, 1961.

[608] Blumenkranz, B. *Histoire des Fuifs en France.* Toulouse, 1972.

[608a] Boglioni, P. "La culture populaire au Moyen Age." *Culture . . .*, pp. 11–37.

[609] Bossuat, R. "Traditions populaires relatives au martyre et à la sépulture de saint Denis." *MA* ser. 4, 11 (1956): 479–509.

[610] Bultot, R. "La doctrine du mépris du monde chez Bernard le Clunisien." *MA*, ser. 4, 19 (1964): 179–204 and 355–76.

[611] ———. "Mépris du monde et XIᵉ siècle." *AESC* 22 (1967): 219–28.

[612] Chazan, R. *Medieval Jewry in Northern France.* Baltimore, London, 1973.

[613] Defourneaux, M. *Les Français en Espagne aux XIᵉ et XIIᵉ siècles.* Paris, 1949.

[614] Dhondt, J. "Une mentalité du XIIᵉ siècle: Galbert de Bruges." *RN* 39 (1957): 101–109.

[615] Duby, G. *L'an mil.* Paris, 1967.

[616] ———. *Les trois ordres ou l'imaginaire du féodalisme.* Paris, 1978.

*[616a] ———. "La vulgarisation des modèles culturels dans la societé féodale (1966)." *Hommes et structures*, pp. 299–308.

[617] ———. "Histoire sociale et histoire des mentalités: entretien avec Georges Duby." *La nouvelle critique* (1970): 13.

[618] Elissagaray, M. *La légende des rois mages*. Paris, 1965.

[619] Folz, R. "Tradition hagiographique et culte de saint Dagobert, roi des Francs." *MA*, ser. 4, 18 (1963): 17–35.

[620] Forsyth, I. H. *The Throne of Wisdom: Wood Sculptures of the Madonna in Romanesque France*. Princeton, 1972.

[621] Gaudemet, J. "La paroisse au Moyen Age, Etat des questions." *RHEF* 59 (1973): 5–21.

[621a] Geary, P. "L'humiliation des saints." *AESC* 34 (1979): 27–47; "La coercition des saints dans la pratique religieuse médiévale." *Culture. . .*, p. 145.

[622] Gontier, D., and Le Bas, C. "Analyse socio-économique de quelques recueils de miracles dans la Normandie du xiᵉ au xiiiᵉ siècle." *AN* 24 (1974): 3–36.

[623] Gorski, K. "Le roi-saint: un problème d'idéologie féodale." *AESC* 24 (1969): 370–76.

[624] Graboïs, A. "Le souvenir et la légende de Charlemagne dans les textes hébraïques médiévaux." *MA* ser. 4, 21 (1966): 5–41.

[625] ———. "La dynastie des 'rois juifs' de Narbonne, ixᵉ–xiiiᵉ siècles." *Narbonne. . .*, pp. 49–54.

[626] Henrion, C. "Le culte des rois mages en Allemagne au Moyen Age." Thesis (M. Mollat). Paris, 1970.

[627] Herlihy, D. "Land, Family and Women in Continental Europe from 701 to 1200." *Traditio* 18 (1962): 89–120.

[628] Huyghebaert, N. "Les femmes laïques dans la vie religieuse des xiᵉ et xiiᵉ siècles dans la province ecclésiastique de Reims." *Settimana . . . Mendola* 5 (1968): 346–89.

[629] Kapferer, A. D. "Banditisme, roman, féodalité: le Boulonnais d'Eustache le Moine." *Mélanges . . . E. Perroy*. Paris, 1973, 220–40.

[630] Kantorowicz, E. H. *Laudes regiae*. Berkeley, 1958.

[631] Labande, E. R. "Recherches sur les pèlerins dans l'Europe des xiᵉ et xiiᵉ siècles." *CCM* 4 (1958): 159–69 and (1961): 447–511.

[632] La Coste Messelière, R. de. *Pèlerins et chemins de Saint-Jacques en France et en Europe du xᵉ siècle à nos jours*. Paris, 1965.

*[633] Le Goff, J. "Le paysan et le monde rural dans la littérature du haut Moyen Age, vᵉ–viᵉ siècles (1965)." *Pour un autre Moyen Age*. Paris, 1977, pp. 131–44.

*[634] ———. "Culture cléricale et traditions folkloriques dans la civilisation mérovingienne (1967)." *Pour un autre Moyen Age*. Paris, 1977, pp. 223–35.

*[635] ———. "Culture ecclésiastique et culture folklorique au Moyen Age: saint Marcel de Paris et le dragon (1970)." *Pour un autre Moyen Age*. Paris, 1977, pp. 236–79.

*[636] Le Goff, J. "Les rêves dans la culture et la psychologie collective de l'Occident médiéval (1971)." *Pour un autre Moyen Age*. Paris, 1977, pp. 299–306.

*[637] ———. "Mélusine maternelle et défricheuse, I: Le dossier médiéval (1971)." *Pour un autre Moyen Age*. Paris, 1977, pp. 307–31.

[638] Le Roy-Ladurie, E. "Mélusine maternelle et défricheuse, II: Mélusine

ruralisée." *AESC* 26 (1971): 587–621.

[639] Lot, F. "Le baiser à la terre, continuation d'un rite antique (1949)." *Recueil*. . . , 3, pp. 253–59.

[640] Manselli, R. "Simbolismo e magia nell'alto medioevco." *Settimane* . . . *di Spoleto* 23 (1976): 292–329.

[641] ———. "Vie familiale et éthique sexuelle dans les pénitentiels." *Famille*, pp. 363–78.

[642] Ménager, L. R. "Sesso e repressione: quando, perchè? una riposta della storia giuridica." *Quaderni medievali* (1977): 44–68.

[643] *Millénaire monastique du Mont-Saint-Michel.* 3 vols. Paris, 1971.

[644] Platelle, H. "Le problème du scandale: les nouvelles modes masculines aux xie et xiie siècles." *RBPH* 53 (1975): 1071–96.

[645] Poly, J.–P. "Le diable, Jacques l'Intercis et Jean des Portes." *Le Diable au Moyen Age: Doctrine, Problèmes moraux, représentations: Sénéfiance* 53 (1979): 443–60.

[646] Riché, P. *La vie quotidienne dans l'Empire carolingien.* Paris, 1973.

[647] ———. "Recherches sur l'instruction des laïcs du ixe au xiie siècle." *CCM* 3 (1962): 175–82.

[648] ———. "La magie à l'époque carolingienne." *CRAIBL* (1973): 127–38.

[648a] Poulin, J. "Entre magie et religion." *Culture*. . . , p. 121.

[649] Rousset, P. "La description du monde chevaleresque chez Orderic Vital." *MA* (1969): 427–44.

[650] Sigal, P. A. *Les marcheurs de Dieu. Pèlerinages et pèlerins au Moyen Age.* Ligugé, 1974.

[651] Silvestre, H. "Deux exorcismes du haut Moyen Age." *MA*, ser. 4, 16 (1961): 410–11.

[652] Theis, L. "Dagobert, Saint-Denis et la royauté française au Moyen Age." *Le métier d'historien au Moyen Age*, edited by B. Guenée. Paris, 1978, pp. 19–30.

[653] Vazquez de Parga, L., Lacarra, J. M., and Uria-Riu, J. *Las peregrinaciones a Santiago de Compostela.* Madrid, 1948–1949.

[654] Verdon, J. "Les femmes et la politique en France au xe siècle." *Mélanges* . . . *E. Perroy.* Paris, 1973, pp. 108–19.

[655] ———. "Les sources de l'histoire de la femme en Occident aux xe–xiiie siècles." *CCM* 20 (1977): 219–51.

[656] Vogel, C. "Pratiques superstitieuses au début du xie siècle d'après le *Corrector sive medicus* de Burchard, évêque de Worms (965–1025)." *Etudes de civilisation médiévale (ixe–xiiie siecles). Mélanges offerts à E. R. Labande.* Poitiers, 1974, pp. 751–61.

Chansons de geste *and Chivalry*

Useful in this area are the bibliographies regularly published by *CCM*. See also *Recueil* . . . *F. Lot*, vol. 1, p. 184.

[656a] Aebischer, P. "La chanson de Roland dans le 'désert' littéraire du xie siècle." *RBPH* 38 (1962): 718–49.

[657] ———. *Préhistoire et protohistoire du 'Roland' d'Oxford.* Berne, 1972.

[658] ———. *Textes norrois et littérature française du Moyen Age.* Geneva, 1972.

[659] ———. *Des annales carolingiennes à Doon de Mayence: nouveau re-*

cueil d'études sur l'épique française médiévale. Geneva, 1975.

[660] Batany, J. "Chevalerie et religion." *AESC* 19 (1964): 780–81 and 21 (1966): 1343.

[661] Boutet, D. "La politique et l'histoire dans les Chansons de Geste." *AESC* 31 (1976): 1119–29.

[662] Braet, H. "Fonction et importance du songe dans la Chanson de Geste." *MA*, ser. 4, 26 (1971): 405–16.

[663] Duby, G. "Une représentation collective au Moyen Age: le Graal." *AESC* 12 (1957): 672–73.

[664] Frappier, J. "Vues sur les conceptions courtoises dans les littératures d'Oc et d'Oïl au xiie siècle." *CCM* 2 (1959): 135–56.

[665] ———. "Le couronnement Louis." *MA*, ser. 4, 28 (1963): 281–87.

[666] Grisward, J. H. "Individualismé et 'esprit de famille' dans 'Garin le Loherain'." *Famille*, pp. 385–96.

[667] Horrent, J. "La bataille des Pyrénées." *MA*, ser. 4, 27 (1972): 197–227.

[668] Köhler, E. *L'aventure chevaleresque. Idéal et réalité dans le roman courtois. Etude sur la forme des plus anciens poèmes d'Arthur et du Graal* (1970). Paris, 1974.

[669] Lejeune, R. and Grégoire, H. "La base historique de l'épopée médiévale (I and II)." *Europa und der nationalismus.* Baden-Baden, 1950, pp. 15–33.

[670] Lejeune, R. "Formules féodales et style amoureux chez Guillaume ix d'Aquitaine." *viiio Congresso Internazionale di studi romanzi*, vol. 2. Florence, 1956, pp. 227–48.

[671] ———. "Le Poète saxon et les chants épiques francais." *MA*, ser. 4, 16 (1961): 137–47.

[672] Lejeune, R., and Stiennon, J. "Le héros Roland, 'neveu de Charlemagne' dans l'iconographie médiévale." *Karl der Grosse* 4:215–28.

[673] Lejeune, R. "L'esprit de croisade dans l'épopée occitane." *Cahiers de Fanjeaux* 4 (1969): 143–73.

[674] ———. "La question de l'historicitié du héros épique Aimeri de Narbonne." *Mélanges . . . E. Perroy.* Paris, 1973, pp. 50–62.

[675] ———. "La légende de Roland et la fausse donation de Fulrad." *MA*, ser. 4, 30 (1975): 191–210.

[676] Louis, P. *De l'histoire à la légende.* Vol. 1: *Girart comte de Vienne (819–877) et ses fondations monastiques.* Vol. 2: *Girart, comte de Vienne, dans les chansons de geste: Girart de Vienne, Girart de Fraite, Girart de Roussillon.* Auxerre, 1946, 1947.

[677] Mandach, A. de. *La geste de Charlemagne et de Roland.* Geneva, 1961.

[678] Ourliac, P. "Troubadours et juristes." *CCM* 7 (1964): 159–77.

[679] Payen, J.-C. "La chanson de Roland, l'épopée franque et l'épopée chrétienne." *MA*, ser. 4, 17 (1962): 395–405.

[680] Pirot, F. "L' 'idéologie' des troubadours." *MA*, ser. 4, 17 (1968): 301–31.

[681] Raynaud de Lagé, G. "Les romans antiques et la représentation de l'Antiquité." *MA*, ser. 4, 16 (1961): 247–91.

[682] Robson, C. A. "Aux origines de la poésie épique romane: art narratif et mnémotechnie." *MA*, ser. 4, 16 (1961): 41–84.

[683] Siciliano, I. *Les chansons de geste et l'épopée. Mythes, histoire, poèmes.* Turin, 1968.

[684] Wilsdorf, C. "La chanson de Roland, l'épopée française et l'épopée chrétienne." *MA*, ser. 4, 27 (1962): 405–17.

Four important works that appeared after this book was finished were not able to be included in this bibliography:

*Contamine, P. *La guerre au Moyen Age.* Paris, 1980.
Pastor, R. *Resistencias y luchas campesinas in Castilla y León.* Thesis, Madrid, 1979.
Rouche, M. *Des Wisigoths aux Arabes, l'Aquitaine (418–781): naissance d'une région.* Paris, 1979 (see [511]).
Werner, K. F. *Structures politiques du monde franc (vɪeᵉ–xɪɪᵉ siècles).* London, 1979. (See [170], [279], [518 to 521]).

SUPPLEMENTARY

BIBLIOGRAPHY

English Translations

Numbers in brackets refer to listing in main bibliography

Bloch, Marc. *Feudal Society.* Chicago, 1961. [70]
———. *Land and Work in Mediaeval Europe.* London, 1967. [288], [416]
———. *Slavery and Serfdom in the Middle Ages.* Berkeley, 1975. [284]–[287]
———. *The Royal Touch.* London, 1973. [607]
Caro Baroja, Julio. *The World of the Witches.* Chicago, 1964. [605]
Chenu, M. D. "Monks, Canons, and Laymen in Search of the Apostolic Life." In *Nature, Man, and Society in the Twelfth Century,* edited by Jerome Taylor and Lester Little. Chicago, 1968, pp. 202–38. [349]
Contamine, Philippe. *War in the Middle Ages.* Oxford and New York, 1984.
Dockès, P. *Medieval Slavery and Liberation.* Chicago, 1982. [528]
Duby, Georges. *Rural Economy and Country Life in the Medieval West.* London, 1968. [300]
———. *The Chivalrous Society.* London and Berkeley, 1977. [112], [230]–[235], [362], [428], [476]
———. *The Early Growth of the European Economy.* London, 1974. [532]
———. *The Three Orders: Feudal Society Imagined.* Chicago, 1980. [616]
Fichtenau, H. *The Carolingian Empire.* Oxford, 1957. [480]
Ganshof, F. L. *Feudalism.* London, 3rd ed., 1964. [189]
———. "Charlemagne's Use of the Oath." In *The Carolingians and the Frankish Monarchy,* edited by F. L. Ganshof. London, 1971, pp. 111–24. [186]
Halphen, L. *Charlemagne and the Carolingian Empire.* Amsterdam, 1977. [490]
Kula, Witold. *An Economic Theory of the Feudal System.* London, 1976. [538]

Le Goff, Jacques. *Time, Work and Culture in the Middle Ages.* Chicago, 1980. [196], [381], [633]–[637]

Mollat, Michel. *The Poor in the Middle Ages.* New Haven, 1986. [311]

Musset, Lucien. *The Germanic Invasions.* University Park, Penn., 1975. [502]

Riché, Pierre. *Daily Life in the World of Charlemagne.* Philadelphia, 1978. [646]

———. *Education and Culture in the Barbarian West.* Columbia, S.C., 1976. [508]

Schmid, Karl. "The Structure of the Nobility in the Earlier Middle Ages." In *The Medieval Nobility,* edited by Timothy Reuter. Amsterdam, 1978, pp. 37–59. [264]

Recent Publications

Asad, Talal. "Medieval Heresy: An Anthropological View." *Social History* 11 (1986): 345–62.

Aubrun, Michel. *L'Ancien diocese de Limoges des origines au milieu du xi^e siecle.* Institut d'Etudes du Massif Central Fasc. 21. Clermont-Ferrand, 1981.

Babcock, Robert G. "Heriger and the Study of Philosophy at Lobbes in the Tenth Century." *Traditio* 43 (1987): 307–17.

Bachrach, Bernard. "The Pilgrimages of Fulk Nerra, Count of the Angevins, 987–1040." In *Religion, Culture and Society in the Early Middle Ages: Studies in Honor of Richard Sullivan.* Kalamazoo, 1987, pp. 205–17.

Berman, Harold J. *Law and Revolution: The Formation of the Western Legal Tradition.* Cambridge, Mass., 1983.

Blöcker, Monica. "Zur Häresie im 11. Jahrhundert." *Zeitschrift für Schweizerische Kirchengeschichte* 73 (1979): 193–234.

Blumenthal, Uta-Renate. *Die Investiturstreit,* translated by the author, Stuttgart, 1982. In *The Investiture Controversy: Church and Monarchy from the Ninth to the Twelfth Century.* Philadelphia, 1988.

Bouchard, Constance B. *Sword, Miter and Cloister: Nobility and the Church in Burgundy, 980–1198.* Ithaca, 1989.

Carozzi, Claude. "D'Adalbéron de Laon à Humbert de Moyenmoutier: La désacralisation de la royauté." In *La Cristianità dei secoli xie–xiie in Occidente: Coscienza e strutture di una società,* Miscellanea del Centro di Studi Medioevali, vol. 10. Milan, 1983, pp. 67–84.

Chazan, Robert. *European Jewry and the First Crusade.* Los Angeles, 1987.

La Cristianità dei secoli xie–xiie in Occidente: Coscienza e strutture di una società, Miscellanea del Centro di Studi Medioevali, vol. 10. Milan, 1983.

Dasberg, Lea. *Untersuchungen über die Entwertung des Judenstatus im 11. Jahrhundert.* Ecole pratique des hautes études, Sorbonne vi^e section: Etude juives, vol. 11. Paris, 1965.

Debord, André. *La société laïque dans les pays de la Charente: x^e–xiie siecles.* Paris, 1984.

———. "*Castrum* et *castellum* chez Ademar de Chabannes." *Archéologie médiévale* 9 (1979): 97–113.

———. "Château et pouvoirs de commandement." In *Les fortifications de terre en Europe occidentale du xe ay xiie siecles* (Colloque de Caen, 2–5 octobre 1980). *Archéologie médiévale* 11 (1981): 72–122.

Duby, Georges. *The Knight, the Lady and the Priest: The Making of Modern Marriage in Medieval France*. Translated by B. Bray. New York, 1983.

Essays on the Peace of God: The Church and the People in Eleventh Century France, edited by T. Head and R. Landes. *Historical Reflections/Réflexions historiques* 14:3 (1987).

Fenoaltea, Stefano. "The Rise and Fall of a Theoretical Model: The Manorial System." *Journal of Economic History* 35:2 (1975): 386–409.

Fichtenau, H. *Lebensordnungen des 10. Jahrhunderts: Studien über Denkart und Existenz im einstigen Karolingerreich*. Stuttgart, 1984.

Flori, Jean. *L'idéologie du glaive: la préhistoire de la chevalerie*. Droz, Geneva, 1983.

———. *L'Essor de la chevalerie*. Droz, Geneva, 1986.

Fossier, R. *L'enfance de l'Europe: Aspects économiques et sociaux*. Nouvelle Clio 17. 2 vols. Paris, 1982.

Gerberto, Scienza, Storia et Mito. Atti de *Gerberti Symposium* (Bobbio 25–7 iuglio 1983). Archivum Bobiense, studia 2 (Bobbio, 1985).

Goetz, Hans Werner. "Kirchenschutz, Rechtswahrung und Reform: zu den Zielen und zum Wesen der frühen Gottesfriedensbewegung in Frankreich." *Francia* 11 (1983): 193–239.

Guenée, Bernard. *Histoire et culture historique dans l'occident medievale*. Paris, 1981.

Guillot, Olivier. "La conversion des Normands peu apres 911: reflets contemporain a l'historiographie ultérieure (xe–xie siecles)." *Cahiers de civilisation médiévale* (1981).

Gurevich, Aron J. *Categories of Medieval Culture*. Translated by G. L. Campbell. London, 1985.

———. *Medieval Popular Culture: Problems of Belief and Perception*. Translated by J. Bak and P. Hollingsworth. Cambridge and Paris, 1988.

Hallam, Elizabeth. *Capetian France 987–1328*. New York, 1980.

Harouel, Barbey, and Thibaut-Payen Bournazel. *Histoire des institutions de l'epoque franque à la Revolution*. Paris, 1987.

Hlawitschka, Eduard. *Vom Frankenreich zur Formierung der europäischen Staaten- und Völkergemeinschaft, 840–1046*. Darmstadt, 1986.

Iogna-Prat, Dominique. "Continence et virginité dans la conception clunisienne de l'ordre du monde autour de l'an mil." *Comptes rendus de l'Academie des Inscriptions et Belles-lettres* (1985): 127–46.

Jaeger, Stephen C. *The Origins of Courtliness: Civilizing Trends and the Formation of Courtly Ideals, 939–1210*. Philadelphia, 1985.

James, Edward. *The Origins of France: From Clovis to the Capetians (500–1000)*. New York, 1982.

Kaiser, Reinhold. *Bischofsherrsachaft zwischen Königtum und Fürstenmacht: Studien zur bischöflichen Stadtherrschaft im westfränkisch-französichen Reich im frühen und hohen Mittelalter*. Pariser historische Studien, vol. 17. Bonn, 1981.

Landes, Richard. "L'accession des Capétiens: Une reconsidération selon les sources." *Actes du Colloque, Millénaire des Capétiens*. Paris, 1990.

Lauranson-Rosaz, Christian. *L'Auvergne et ses marges (Velay, Gevaudan) du viiie au xie siècle: La fin du Monde Antique!* Le Puy-en-Velay, 1987.

Leyser, Henrietta. *Hermits and the New Monasticism: A Study of Religious Communities in Western Europe, 1000–1150*. London, 1984.

Magnou-Nortier, E. "Les évêques et la paix dans l'espace franc (vie–xie siècles)."

L'évêque dans l'histoire de l'église. Publications du Centre de Recherches d'Histoire Religieuse et d'Histoire des Idées. vol. 7. Angers, 1984.

Moore, Robert I. "Duby's Eleventh Century," *History* 69 (1984): 36–49.

———. "Guibert of Nogent and his World." In *Studies in Medieval History Presented to R. H. C. Davis,* edited by H. Mayr-Harting and R. I. Moore. London, 1985, pp. 107–17.

———. *The Formation of a Persecuting Society: Power and Deviance in Western Europe 950–1250.* Oxford, 1987.

Morris, Colin. *The Papal Monarchy: The Western Church from 1050–1250.* Oxford, 1989.

Mostert, Marco. *The Political Theology of Abbo of Fleury: A Study of the Ideas about Society and Law of the Tenth-century Monastic Reform Movement.* Middeleeuwse Studies en Bronnen, vol. 2. Hilversum, 1987.

Nelson, Janet L. *Politics and Ritual in Early Medieval Europe.* London, 1986.

Nichols, S. G., Jr. *Romanesque Signs: Early Medieval Narrative and Iconography.* New Haven, 1983.

North, Douglass C., and Robert P. Thomas. "The Rise and Fall of the Manorial System: A Theoretical Model." *Journal of Economic History:* 31:4 (1971): 777–803.

Oexle, Otto Gerhard. "Die 'Wirklichkeit' und das 'Wissen': Ein Blick auf das sozialgeschichtliche Oeuvre von Georges Duby." *Historisches Zeitschrift* 232 (1981): 61–91.

Ovitt, George, Jr. *The Restauration of Perfection: Labor and Technology in Medieval Culture.* New Brunswick, 1987.

Pakter, Walter. *Medieval Canon Law and the Jews.* Ebelsbach, 1988.

Philippe, Robert. "L'Eglise et l'énergie pendant le xie siècle dans les pays d'entre Seine et Loire." *Cahiers de Civilisation Médiévale* 27 (1984): 107–17.

Radding, Charles. *A World Made by Men: Cognition and Society, 400–1200.* Chapel Hill, 1985.

Renaissance and Renewal in the Twelfth Century, edited by R. Benson and G. Constable. Cambridge, 1982.

Reynolds, Roger E. "Odilo and the *Treuga Dei* in Southern Italy: A Beneventan Manuscript Fragment." *Medieval Studies* 46 (1984): 450–62.

Reynolds, Susan. *Kingdoms and Communities in Western Europe, 900–1300.* Oxford, 1984.

Riley-Smith, Jonathan. *The First Crusade and the Idea of Crusading.* Philadelphia, 1986.

Rosenwein, Barbara. *Rhinoceros Bound: Cluny in the Tenth Century.* Philadelphia, 1982.

———. *To Be the Neighbor of Saint Peter: The Social Meaning of Cluny's Property, 909–1049.* Ithaca, 1989.

Schmugge, Ludwig. " 'Pilgerfahrt macht frei'—Eine These zur Bedeutung des mittelalterlichen Pilgerwesens." *Römische Quartalschrift* 74:1–2 (1979): 16–31.

Searle, Eleanor. *Predatory Kinship and the Creation of Norman Power, 840–1066.* Berkeley, 1988.

Sigal, Pierre-André. *L'homme et le miracle dans la France médiévale (xie–xiie siècles).* Paris, 1985.

Spufford, Peter. *Money and Its Use in Medieval Europe.* Cambridge, Eng.: 1988.

Stock, Brian. *The Implications of Literacy: Written Language and Models of Interpretation in the 11th and 12th Centuries* (Princeton, 1983).

Tabuteau, Emily Z. *Transfers of Property in Eleventh-century Norman Law.* Chapel Hill, 1988.

The Use and Abuse of Eschatology in the Middle Ages. W. Verbeke, D. Verhelst, and A. Welkenhuysen, editors. Leuven, 1988.

Ward, Benedicta. *Miracles and the Medieval Mind: Theory, Record and Event, 1000–1215.* Philadelphia, 1982.

White, Stephen. *Custom, Kinship and Gifts to Saints: The Laudatio Parentum in Western France, 1050–1150.* Chapel Hill, 1988.

Notes

1. See Lucie Fossier, "Les langues documentaires," in *L'informatique* . . . ; also "Ordinateur et diplomatique médiévale," in *Annali della scuola speciale per archivisti* . . . *dell'Universita di Roma*, 1972, p. 98, and "Informatique et documents médiévaux," in *AESC* (1976), 1131. Compare also Michel Parisse, "Traitement des documents diplomatiques: exploitation de l'Index verborum," in *L'informatique* . . . .

2. On the relationship between traditional lexicography and computers [informatique], see Olga Weijers, "Le systeme traditionnel da la lexicographie appliqué au latin médiéval," in *La lexicographie* . . . .

3. The *départements* of Bas-Rhin, Haut-Rhin, Moselle, Meurthe-et-Moselle, Meuse, Vosges, Haute-Marne, Marne and Doubs.

4. M. Parisse, "A propos du traitement automatique des textes diplomatiques médiévaux; la chronologie du vocabulaire et le repérage des actes suspects," in *L'informatique* . . . .

5. On these various lexical assemblages, see pp. 32–33 and 97–98 above. It is interesting to compare this approach with the conclusions of the investigation of the same region carried out by Michel Parisse, *La Lorraine* [261].

INDEX

Aachen: capitulary, 59; palace at, 9–10
Abbey contingents, system of, 21
Abbeys, suburban, 265–66
Abbo of Fleury, 175; on fealty owed to king, 16–17; ternary social system of, 146–47; will of, 221–22
Abduction, 30
Adalbero of Laon, 87; on custom changes, 141; genealogy of, 92; on King Robert, 149; on nobility, 97; opposition of to peace, 166–67; on power and production, 246; on tripartite system, 149–50
Adhemar of Chabannes, 285
Adjutorium, 40n
Adraldus: magic of, 314–15
Advocacy, feudal, 34–39
Agricola, eulogy of, 245n
Agriculture: productivity, 253–54; technical innovations in, 254–56
Aimery of Narbonne, 322; death of, 326
Albigensians, 284
Alfred the Great, 144
Allodial communities, break-up of, 176
Allodialists, 126; of eleventh century, 132; precarious situation of, 126–27; in tenth century, 131
Allodial peasants, universality of, 259–60
Allods: curial, 84n; disappearance of, 31–32; transformation of into fiefs, 65–66
Amboise, lord of, 67
Andrew of Fleury, on heresy, 285
Angevin genealogies, 92–93
Apocrypha, 300
Apostolic life, 170–80
Aprisio system, 24
Aquitainian disloyalty, 235
Archambaud of Fleury, reform of, 165
Aristocracy, new, 136
Arles, archbishop of, household of, 111
Armed forces: horsemen in, 21–23; Norman pirates in, 23
Arnulf of Flanders (the Great), 13; genealogy of, 92; nobility of, 90
Arnulf of Orleans, 164
Arras missionaries, 287–88
Arson, 30
Attitudes, 309–50
Auxerre list, 219, 220

Banalités, 31; disparity of, 261
Banal lordship: creation of, 25–39; development of, 263; effects of powers of, 137; and fate of poor, 178; origin of, 30–31, 45n; peasants under, 132
Banal seigneury: emergence of, 176
Bannum, 28–29, 352; exercise of power of, 264; land rent and, 262; redirection of, 38; sacred, 37; strengthening of, 260–61
Barbarossa, Frederick, 47
Baron, 199–200, 356
Bautier, Robert-Henri: on accusations against heretics, 281
Benedictine monks, 174
Benefice, and fief, 61–62
Beneficium, 55–57, 59, 61
Berengar of Puiserguier, 208
Bernard, St.: on abbey of Saint-Denis, 195; on Count Thibaud, 204–205
Bernard of Angers, 309–10
Bernard of La Marche, 70
Bishops: conflict of with monks, 163–70, 184n; nominations of by princes, 16; power in hands of, 37–38; on spiritual vs. temporal realms, 180
Bloch, Marc, 1; on *colliberti*, 130–31; on *coloni*, 123; on continuity of nobility, 87–88; on delay in use of *fevum*, 62; on feudalism vs. seigneury, 358n; on feudal periods, 353, 354–55; on fief-gift, 60; on healing power of king, 338; on magic of king, 339–41; on servitude, 129
Boni homines, 18, 19, 110
Bonnassie, Pierre: *casamenta* system described by, 64; on inheritance, 66; on knights and nobles, 99
Boso, 10; appointing self king, 12
Boutruche, Robert: on communal life, 45n; on concept of feudalism, 4
Burchard of Worms, 311–12
Burgundian campaign, 235
Burgundian peace, 154, 165
Burgundy: Frankish culture in, 228; nobility of, 96

Caballerias, 64
Canonical order, 184n
Capet, Hugh, 16, 23; fortresses of, 27
Capetian(s): miracle, 341–42; monarchy, 186; replacement of Carolingian dynasty by, 10
Carcassonne, countess of, lands of, 60–61
Carissima, 223; genealogy of, 241–42n

397